To my husband, James M. Hill,
Love, Barbara

To Sarah Price, Kyle Neu, Matthew Price,
and Andrew Price with much love,
Grandma Barbara

To my husband, Jim Corwin, with love,
Linda

Children's Literature

DISCOVERY FOR A LIFETIME

SECOND EDITION

BARBARA D. STOODT-HILL
UNIVERSITY OF CINCINNATI

LINDA B. AMSPAUGH-CORSON
UNIVERSITY OF CINCINNATI

Merrill
Prentice Hall

Upper Saddle River, New Jersey
Columbus, Ohio

Library of Congress Cataloging-in-Publication Data
Stoodt-Hill, Barbara D.
  Children's literature : discovery for a lifetime / Barbara Stoodt-Hill, Linda
Amspaugh-Corson.—2nd ed.
    p. cm.
  Includes bibliographical references and index.
  ISBN 0-13-087729-8
    1. Children's literature—Study and teaching (Elementary) 2. Children—Books and
reading. I. Amspaugh, Linda B. II. Title

LB1575 .S86 2001
372.64′044—dc21   00-032422

Vice President and Publisher: Jeffery W. Johnston
Editor: Linda Ashe Montgomery
Production Editor: Mary M. Irvin
Project Coordination: Betsy Keefer Production Services
Design Coordinator: Diane C. Lorenzo
Cover Design: Ceri Fitzgerald
Cover Art: SuperStock
Text Design: Carlisle Publishing Services
Production Manager: Pamela D. Bennett
Director of Marketing: Kevin Flanagan
Marketing Manager: Amy June
Marketing Services Manager: Krista Groshong

This book was set in Times Roman by Carlisle Communications, Ltd. and
was printed and bound by Courier Kendalville, Inc.
The cover was printed by Phoenix Color Corp.

Earlier edition © 1996 by Gorsuch Scarisbrick, Publishers.

Photo Credits: Anthony Magnacca/Merrill: 211. All other photos by Barbara Stoodt-Hill
Art Credits: See p. 409

Merrill
Prentice Hall

10 9 8 7 6 5 4 3 2
ISBN 0-13-087729-8

Preface

Television extols the virtues of reading to children. Children's librarians are busier than ever before. Bookstores featuring children's books are flourishing. The authors and illustrators who create exquisite children's books are popular. Although the profusion of books and the widespread interest in children's literature are welcome, they create an even greater need to educate parents, teachers, and librarians about books and literary experiences. Because the dull, the difficult, and the obscure can stymie children's pleasure in literature, adults must optimize children's interactions with literature. Moreover, the subjects and the textbooks used in elementary classrooms cry out for the richness of literature.

This book is the product of many experiences as teachers, professors, parents, and grandparents. Our goal is to help adults infuse literature into children's lives very early and to promote a continuing interest in books throughout their lives. Our theme is *literature for a lifetime*. We hope to prepare the adults in children's lives to:

- know which books children will respond to
- share literature with children in authentic ways that stimulate their responses
- infuse literature into elementary classrooms and homes
- identify books that portray children with special needs so their classmates will understand these needs
- use computer programs and the Internet to enhance literary experiences
- use multimedia in creating literary experience
- choose literature that will develop children's cultural consciousness

Chapters 1 through 5 develop a basis for understanding children's literature, including evaluating and selecting literature and encouraging children's response. Chapters 6 through 11 explore the content of children's literature in picture books, poetry, traditional literature, modern fantasy, realistic fiction, historical fiction, and nonfiction. We have continued our emphasis on authors and illustrators in this edition by including profiles of them throughout the book. In these profiles, we hope to acquaint students with authors and illustrators and their works, as well as offer models for classroom study. Chapters 12 through 15 prepare adults to nurture children's response to literature by showing how creating a community of readers as well as providing oral and silent reading experiences enhance literary experiences. Moreover, adults need to select literature that develops students' sensitivity to other cultures as well as the life challenges faced by people in our world. Finally, Chapter 15 synthesizes and presents sample guides and units that teachers have used in developing literature-based classroom experiences.

Each chapter opens with a list of key terms, guiding questions, and an overview that previews the content of the chapter. Vignettes are included in each chapter, which give examples of teachers and children involved with literature—examples that will serve as models for others. Throughout the book experiences are presented that develop deeper cognitive and affective understandings as well as aesthetic awareness.

Each chapter includes thought questions and research and application experiences. Annotated bibliographies of cited books and recommended books include genre identifications and suggested grade levels. Where appropriate, asterisks (*) indicate books that will appeal to reluctant readers.

NEW TO THIS EDITION

Users of the first edition of *Children's Literature: Discovery for a Lifetime* will find several important changes in the second edition.

- All bibliographies and references have been thoroughly updated to reflect the latest children's books.
- Author and illustrator profiles have been placed throughout the text.

- Historical fiction and realistic fiction are now treated in two separate chapters, giving greater attention to each genre.
- A new chapter, "Culturally Conscious Literature," explores multicultural and international children's literature while focusing on broad-based units of study that transcend individual cultures.
- Books that are especially appropriate for struggling readers are indicated in the bibliographies.

SUPPLEMENTS

Supporting this second edition are three supplements that we hope you and your students will find valuable.

- The updated **Instructor's Manual** contains chapter outlines, teaching tips, suggested test items, and model syllabi. Instructors may contact their local Merrill/Prentice Hall representatives to obtain this supplement.
- Extensive bibliographies have been placed on a dual-platform, searchable **CD database** packaged free with every copy. Instructors and students can easily use this software to search for children's books by author, title, illustrator, genre, subject, reading, interest level, publisher, copyright year, and combinations thereof. Furthermore, readers can save comments on existing entries and enter bibliographic information for other titles of their choosing. This software will be an indispensable professional resource for years to come.
- A free **Companion Website** allows on-line posting of syllabi and has an interactive study guide, links to web-based resources, a message board, and numerous other features. Instructors and students may access the Companion Website at

http://www.prenhall.com/stoodt-hill

We hope that our enthusiasm will stimulate you to read to children, talk about books with them, and acquaint them with the joy of literature that will last them a lifetime.

We wish to express our sincere appreciation for the support and encouragement of Brad Potthoff and Mary Evangelista.

We would also like to thank the following reviewers: Susan Knell, Pittsburgh State University; Barbara N. Kupetz, Indiana University of Pennsylvania; Deborah Overstreet, University of Southwestern Louisiana; Robert F. Smith, Towson University; Pat T. Sharp, Baylor University; and Barbara Stein, University of North Texas.

Discover the Companion Website Accompanying This Book

Technology is a constantly growing and changing aspect of our field that is creating a need for content and resources. To address this emerging need, Prentice Hall has developed an online learning environment for students and professors alike—Companion Websites—to support our textbooks.

In creating a Companion Website, our goal is to build on and enhance what the textbook already offers. For this reason, the content for each user-friendly website is organized by chapter and provides the professor and student with a variety of meaningful resources. Common features of a Companion Website include:

FOR THE PROFESSOR

Every Companion Website integrates **Syllabus Manager™,** an online syllabus creation and management utility.

- **Syllabus Manager™** provides you, the instructor, with an easy, step-by-step process to create and revise syllabi, with direct links into Companion Website and other online content without having to learn HTML.
- Students may logon to your syllabus during any study session. All they need to know is the web address for the Companion Website and the password you've assigned to your syllabus.
- After you have created a syllabus using **Syllabus Manager™,** students may enter the syllabus for their course section from any point in the Companion Website.

- Clicking on a date, the student is shown the list of activities for the assignment. The activities for each assignment are linked directly to actual content, saving time for students.
- Adding assignments consists of clicking on the desired due date, then filling in the details of the assignment—name of the assignment, instructions, and whether or not it is a one-time or repeating assignment.
- In addition, links to other activities can be created easily. If the activity is online, a URL can be entered in the space provided, and it will be linked automatically in the final syllabus.
- Your completed syllabus is hosted on our servers, allowing convenient updates from any computer on the Internet. Changes you make to your syllabus are immediately available to your students at their next logon.

FOR THE STUDENT

- **Chapter Objectives**—outline key concepts from the text.
- **Interactive Self-quizzes**—complete with hints and automatic grading that provide immediate feedback for students.

After students submit their answers for the interactive self-quizzes, the Companion Website **Results Reporter** computes a percentage grade, provides a graphic representation of how many questions were answered correctly and incorrectly, and gives a question by question analysis of the quiz. Students are given the option to send their quiz to up to four email addresses (professor, teaching assistant, study partner, etc.).

- **Message Board**—serves as a virtual bulletin board to post—or respond to—questions or comments to/from a national audience.
- **Chat**—real-time chat with anyone who is using the text anywhere in the country—ideal for discussion and study groups, class projects, etc.
- **Web Destinations**—links to WWW sites that relate to chapter content.

- **Additional Resources**—access to chapter-specific or general content that enhances material found in the text.

To take advantage of these and other resources, please visit the *Children's Literature: Discovery for a Lifetime* Companion Website at

www.prenhall.com/stoodt-hill

Brief Contents

ONE   Introduction to Children's Literature   2

TWO   Understanding Literature   22

THREE   Connecting Children and Literature: Evaluating and Selecting Books   48

FOUR   Encouraging Children's Response to Literature   72

FIVE   Literature for the Youngest   100

SIX   Picture Books   118

SEVEN   Poetry for Every Child   144

EIGHT   Make-Believe: Traditional Literature and Modern Fantasy   168

NINE   People Now: Contemporary Realistic Fiction   200

TEN   People Then: Historical Fiction   222

ELEVEN   Truth is Stranger than Fiction: Biography and Nonfiction   246

TWELVE   Oral and Silent Literature   274

THIRTEEN   Literature for Children with Real-Life Challenges   302

FOURTEEN   Unit Studies: Literature, Response, and Learning   320

FIFTEEN   Culturally Conscious Literature   346

               Appendix: Book Awards   368

               Glossary   373

               Subject Index   378

               Index of Children's Book Titles, Authors, and Illustrators   385

               Credits   409

Contents

ONE   *INTRODUCTION TO CHILDREN'S LITERATURE*   2

KEY TERMS • GUIDING QUESTIONS • OVERVIEW • INTRODUCTION • VIGNETTE

WHAT IS LITERATURE?   4
     What Is Children's Literature?   4
     Response to Literature   5

THE POWER OF LITERATURE   6
     Providing Enjoyment   6
     Appreciating Aesthetics   7
     Enhancing Understanding   7
     Developing Imagination   8
     Increasing Information and Knowledge   8
     Stimulating Cognition   9
     Providing a Language Model   9

LITERATURE AND THE CURRICULUM   10
     Balanced Reading Instruction   10
     Literature and Language Arts   11
     Literature and Writing   11
     Integrated Instruction   11
     Literature and Other Content Areas   11

EXPERIENCING LITERATURE   13
     Creating Effective Literary Experiences   13

SUMMARY   16
THOUGHT QUESTIONS   17
RESEARCH AND APPLICATION EXPERIENCES   17
CHILDREN'S LITERATURE REFERENCES AND RECOMMENDED BOOKS   17
REFERENCES AND BOOKS FOR FURTHER READING   20

TWO   *UNDERSTANDING LITERATURE*   22

KEY TERMS • GUIDING QUESTIONS • OVERVIEW • INTRODUCTION • VIGNETTE

GENRE IN CHILDREN'S LITERATURE   24
     Genre Classifications in Children's Literature   24
     Genre as a Teaching Tool   25

THREE

LITERARY ELEMENTS   27
    Plot   27
    Characters   30
    Setting   33
    Theme   34
    Style   35

LITERARY EXPERIENCES THAT ENHANCE UNDERSTANDING   37
    Discussion as Literary Experience   38
    Genre   38
    Story Grammar   38
    Literary Experiences   39

CLASSROOM ACTIVITIES   40

SUMMARY   41

THOUGHT QUESTIONS   42

RESEARCH AND APPLICATION EXPERIENCES   42

CHILDREN'S LITERATURE REFERENCES AND RECOMMENDED BOOKS   43

REFERENCES AND BOOKS FOR FURTHER READING   46

THREE   *CONNECTING CHILDREN AND LITERATURE: EVALUATING AND SELECTING BOOKS*   48

KEY TERMS • GUIDING QUESTIONS • OVERVIEW •
INTRODUCTION • VIGNETTE

EVALUATING CHILDREN'S LITERATURE   50

LITERARY QUALITY AS A SELECTION STANDARD   50
    Award Books and Recommended Reading Lists   50
    Selection Aids   51
    Criticism of Award Books and Reading Lists   53

ISSUES-CENTERED CRITICISM OF CHILDREN'S LITERATURE: CENSORSHIP   53
    Racial and Ethnic Issues   55
    Gender Stereotyping Issues   56
    Addressing Censorship   56

CHILD-CENTERED CRITICISM: WHAT DO CHILDREN LIKE TO READ?   57
    What Attracts Children to Certain Books?   58
    Reading Interest Research   58
    Developmentally Appropriate Literature   60
    Identifying Reading Interests   63
    Guidelines for Literature Selection   63

MEDIA-BASED LITERATURE   65
    Evaluating Media-Based Literature   66
    Using Media-Based Literature   66

SUMMARY   66

THOUGHT QUESTIONS   66

RESEARCH AND APPLICATION EXPERIENCES   67

CHILDREN'S LITERATURE REFERENCES AND RECOMMENDED BOOKS   67

MULTIMEDIA REFERENCES   69
RECORDED BOOKS   69
COMPUTER SOFTWARE   69
REFERENCES AND BOOKS FOR FURTHER READING   69

FOUR   ENCOURAGING CHILDREN'S RESPONSE TO LITERATURE   72

KEY TERMS • GUIDING QUESTIONS • OVERVIEW •
INTRODUCTION • VIGNETTE

LITERARY THINKING   74
   Literature as a Means of Knowing   74
   Envisionment: Individual Meaning   75
   Intertextuality: Individual Connections   76

REASONS FOR READING   76

UNDERSTANDING RESPONSE   77

DIMENSIONS OF RESPONSE   77
   Sound   77
   Event   78
   World   78
   Author Style   78

GUIDING RESPONSE   78
   Community of Response   79
   Warm, Literate Environment   80
   Engaging with Literature   80

NURTURING RESPONSE   80
   Introducing Books   82
   Experiencing Books   83

ENHANCING READERS' ENGAGEMENT AND RESPONSE   83
   Discussion   84
   Writing   85
   Oral Language   86
   Maps and Charts   86
   Author and Illustrator Studies   89

CLASSROOM ACTIVITIES   93

SUMMARY   92
JOURNALING EXPERIENCES   95
THOUGHT QUESTIONS   95
RESEARCH AND APPLICATION EXPERIENCES   95
CHILDREN'S REFERENCES AND RECOMMENDED BOOKS   96
REFERENCES AND BOOKS FOR FURTHER READING   98

FIVE   LITERATURE FOR THE YOUNGEST   100

KEY TERMS • GUIDING QUESTIONS • OVERVIEW •
INTRODUCTION • VIGNETTE

THE VALUE OF EARLY LITERARY EXPERIENCE   102
Success in School   103
Cognitive Development   103

EFFECT OF ENVIRONMENT ON EMERGENT LITERACY   104
The Family Environment   106
The Preschool, Day-Care, and School Environment   107
The External Environment   108
Libraries and Media Centers   108

SELECTING AND EVALUATING LITERATURE FOR YOUNG CHILDREN   109
Authors and Illustrators for Younger Children   109

ENHANCING LITERARY EXPERIENCE WITH ACTIVITIES   110
Oral Reading   110
Big Books   111
Media   111

UNIT SUGGESTIONS   112

SUMMARY   112
THOUGHT QUESTIONS   113
RESEARCH AND APPLICATION EXERCISES   113
CHILDREN'S LITERATURE REFERENCES AND RECOMMENDED BOOKS   113
SOURCES OF INFORMATION ABOUT CHILDREN'S BOOKS   116
REFERENCES AND BOOKS FOR FURTHER READING   116

SIX   PICTURE BOOKS   118

KEY TERMS • GUIDING QUESTIONS • OVERVIEW •
INTRODUCTION • VIGNETTE

THE NATURE OF PICTURE BOOKS   120
The History of Picture Books   120
Contemporary Picture Books   121

ILLUSTRATORS   121

AUTHORS AND ILLUSTRATORS   122

ILLUSTRATIONS   122
Style   124
Medium   124
Technique   125
Color   125
Line   126
Design   126

TYPES OF PICTURE BOOKS   126
Picture Books for Older Students   127

VISUAL LITERACY   127

SELECTING AND EVALUATING PICTURE BOOKS   128

CLASSROOM ACTIVITIES   129

SUMMARY 137

THOUGHT QUESTIONS 137

RESEARCH AND APPLICATION EXPERIENCES 138

CHILDREN'S LITERATURE REFERENCES AND RECOMMENDED BOOKS 138

REFERENCES AND BOOKS FOR FURTHER READING 142

SEVEN   POETRY FOR EVERY CHILD 144

KEY TERMS • GUIDING QUESTIONS • OVERVIEW •
INTRODUCTION • VIGNETTE

THE NATURE OF POETRY 146
    Emotional Intensity 146
    Expressing Feelings 146

ELEMENTS OF POETRY 147
    Poetic Language 147
    Sound Patterns 148
    Rhythm 149
    Word Play 149
    Figures of Speech 149

TYPES OF POETRY 149
    Narrative Poems 150
    Dramatic Poetry 150
    Lyric Poetry 150
    Haiku 150
    Free Verse 150
    Concrete Peotry 150
    Nonsense Poetry 151

CONTENT OF POETRY 151

CHILDREN'S RESPONSE TO POETRY 152

POETS AND THEIR POETRY 152

SELECTING AND EVALUATING POETRY 153
    Locating Poetry 154
    Children's Preferences 154
    Finding Winners 154

ENRICHING POETIC EXPERIENCES 156
    Rhythm 156
    Movement 157
    Riddle-Poems 158
    Themes and Topics 159
    Writing 160
    Discussion 160

CLASSROOM ACTIVITIES 161

SUMMARY 162

THOUGHT QUESTIONS 162

RESEARCH AND APPLICATION EXPERIENCES 163

CHILDREN'S LITERATURE REFERENCES AND RECOMMENDED BOOKS 163

REFERENCES AND BOOKS FOR FURTHER READING 167

EIGHT   MAKE-BELIEVE: TRADITIONAL LITERATURE AND MODERN FANTASY 168

KEY TERMS • GUIDING QUESTIONS • OVERVIEW • INTRODUCTION • VIGNETTE

UNDERSTANDING REAL AND MAKE-BELIEVE 170

TRADITIONAL LITERATURE 170
The Contemporary Values of Traditional Literature 171
Elements of Traditional Literature 171
Types of Traditional Literature 175
Selecting and Evaluating Traditional Literature 177

MODERN FANTASY 178
The Historical Roots of Fantasy 178
Children and Fantasy 179
The Nature of Fantasy 180
Elements of Fantasy 180
Types of Fantasy 182
Selecting Fantasy 183

CLASSROOM ACTIVITIES 183

SUMMARY 191

THOUGHT QUESTIONS 191

RESEARCH AND APPLICATION EXPERIENCES 192

CHILDREN'S LITERATURE REFERENCES AND RECOMMENDED BOOKS 192

REFERENCES AND BOOKS FOR FURTHER READING 197

NINE   PEOPLE NOW: CONTEMPORARY REALISTIC FICTION 200

KEY TERMS • GUIDING QUESTIONS • OVERVIEW • INTRODUCTION • VIGNETTE

CONTEMPORARY REALISTIC FICTION 202
Similarities and Differences in Contemporary and Historical Realistic Fiction 202

ISSUES IN REALISTIC FICTION 203
Didacticism 203
The Value of Realism 203
Violence 203

TYPES OF REALISTIC FICTION 204
Families 204
Challenges from Outside the Family 209
Survival 210

SPECIAL INTERESTS AND SERIES BOOKS 212
Sports 212
Mysteries 213

Animal Stories 213
Other Series Books 214

UNIT SUGGESTIONS 214

SUMMARY 215
THOUGHT QUESTIONS 215
ENRICHMENT ACTIVITIES 216
CHILDREN'S LITERATURE REFERENCES AND RECOMMENDED BOOKS 216
REFERENCES AND BOOKS FOR FURTHER READING 221

TEN PEOPLE THEN: HISTORICAL FICTION 222

KEY TERMS • GUIDING QUESTIONS • OVERVIEW •
INTRODUCTION • VIGNETTE

HISTORICAL FICTION 224
An Issue 225
When does the Present Become the Past? 225

ORGANIZING THE CATEGORIES OF HISTORICAL FICTION 225
Families and Friends 226
Survival and Growing Up 227

HISTORICAL PERIODS 228
Pre-Colonial Era 228
Colonial Era 228
Revolutionary War Era 229
Building and Expansion 229
Civil War Era 230
Industrialization 231
Immigration 231
The Twentieth-Century: Wars, Issues, and Events 232

REALISTIC FICTION IN THE CLASSROOM 234
Suggested Audio Books 235
Resource Guides for Using Trade Books in Classrooms 235
Guides That Provide Multiple Approaches to Integrating Literature in
Classrooms 235

CLASSROOM ACTIVITIES 236

SUMMARY 237
THOUGHT QUESTIONS 237
CHILDREN'S LITERATURE REFERENCES AND RECOMMENDED BOOKS 238
REFERENCES AND BOOKS FOR FURTHER READING 245

ELEVEN TRUTH IS STRANGER THAN FICTION: BIOGRAPHY AND
NONFICTION 246

KEY TERMS • GUIDING QUESTIONS • OVERVIEW •
INTRODUCTION • VIGNETTE

THE CHANGING PERSPECTIVE ON NONFICTION   248
    Trends in Current Nonfiction   248

THE VALUE OF NONFICTION   248

BIOGRAPHY   249
    Writing Biography   250
    Types of Biography   250
    Selecting and Evaluating Biography   251
    Subject   251

INFORMATIONAL BOOKS   253
    Types of Informational Books   253
    Innovative Informational Books   255
    Selecting and Evaluating Informational Books   255

CLASSROOM ACTIVITIES FOR ENHANCING NONFICTION EXPERIENCE   258
    Trade Books and Science   259
    Trade Books and Social Studies   260
    Trade Books and the Arts   260
    Teaching Strategies for Nonfiction   261

UNIT SUGGESTIONS   262

SUMMARY   265
THOUGHT QUESTIONS   265
RESEARCH AND APPLICATION EXPERIENCES   265
CHILDREN'S LITERATURE REFERENCES AND RECOMMENDED BOOKS   266
REFERENCES AND BOOKS FOR FURTHER READING   271

TWELVE   ORAL AND SILENT LITERATURE   274

KEY TERMS • GUIDING QUESTIONS • OVERVIEW •
INTRODUCTION • VIGNETTE

READING ALOUD TO CHILDREN   276
    Reading Aloud in the Classroom   276
    Selecting Material for Reading Aloud   276
    Planning a Read-Aloud Session   278

READER'S THEATER   278
    Selecting Material   278
    Planning a Reader's Theater Performance   279

STORYTELLING   280
    The Roots of Storytelling   280
    Storytelling in the Classroom   281
    Selecting Material   282
    Planning Storytelling   282
    Storytelling Variations   283

CHORAL READING   285
    Selecting Material   285
    Planning a Choral Reading   285

CREATIVE DRAMA 286
  Selecting Material 287
  Planning Creative Drama 287
  Pantomime 287
  Puppets 288

BOOKTALKS 288

EVALUATING ORAL STORY EXPERIENCES 289

SILENT READING 289
  Literature Circles 289
  Uninterrupted Sustained Silent Reading (USSR–DEAR–SSR) 290
  Fostering Silent Reading 291

UNIT SUGGESTIONS 292

SUMMARY 294
THOUGHT QUESTIONS 295
RESEARCH AND APPLICATION EXPERIENCES 295
CHILDREN'S LITERATURE REFERENCES AND RECOMMENDED BOOKS 295
REFERENCES AND BOOKS FOR FURTHER READING 299

THIRTEEN   LITERATURE FOR CHILDREN WITH REAL-LIFE CHALLENGES 302

KEY TERMS • GUIDING QUESTIONS • OVERVIEW •
INTRODUCTION • VIGNETTE

THE VALUE OF REAL-LIFE LITERATURE 304

SELECTING AND EVALUATING REAL-LIFE LITERATURE 304
  Hearing Challenges 306
  Vision Challenges 307
  Mobility Challenges 307
  Health Challenges 308
  Emotional Challenges 309
  Learning Challenges 309
  Abused Children 310
  Substance Abuse 311
  Lifestyle Challenges 311
  Homeless Children 312

CLASSROOM ACTIVITIES 312

SUMMARY 313
THOUGHT QUESTIONS 314
RESEARCH AND APPLICATION EXPERIENCES 314
CHILDREN'S LITERATURE REFERENCES AND RECOMMENDED BOOKS 314
REFERENCES AND BOOKS FOR FURTHER READING 319

FOURTEEN   UNIT STUDIES: LITERATURE, RESPONSE, AND LEARNING 320

KEY TERMS • GUIDING QUESTIONS • OVERVIEW •
INTRODUCTION • VIGNETTE

UNITS OF STUDY   322
    Literature in the Curriculum   322
    Making Connections Through Inquiry   323

DEVELOPING THEMES AND UNITS   324
    Shared Book Experiences   325
    Planning Units   325
    Assessing Unit Experiences   330

UNIT SUGGESTIONS   331

SUMMARY   340
THOUGHT QUESTIONS   340
RESEARCH AND APPLICATION EXPERIENCES   340
CHILDREN'S LITERATURE REFERENCES AND RECOMMENDED BOOKS   340
REFERENCES AND BOOKS FOR FURTHER READING   344

FIFTEEN   CULTURALLY CONSCIOUS LITERATURE   346

KEY TERMS • GUIDING QUESTIONS • OVERVIEW •
INTRODUCTION • VIGNETTE

CULTURAL STUDIES   348

LITERATURE AND CULTURAL STUDIES   349

SELECTING CULTURALLY CONSCIOUS LITERATURE   350

FAMILY BONDS   350
    Friends and Neighbors   352

ADMIRABLE PEOPLE   353

RACISM AND PREJUDICE   354

THE ARTS   355

TRADITIONAL LITERATURE   356
    Authors of Culturally Conscious Literature   356

UNIT SUGGESTIONS   357

SUMMARY   360
THOUGHT QUESTIONS   360
RESEARCH AND APPLICATION EXPERIENCES   360
CHILDREN'S LITERATURE REFERENCES AND RECOMMENDED BOOKS   360
REFERENCES AND BOOKS FOR FURTHER READING   367

APPENDIX: BOOK AWARDS   368

GLOSSARY   373

SUBJECT INDEX   378

INDEX OF CHILDREN'S BOOK TITLES, AUTHORS, AND ILLUSTRATORS   385

CREDITS   409

Children's Literature

DISCOVERY FOR A LIFETIME

Introduction to Children's Literature

KEY TERMS

authentic literary
   experiences
character
community of readers
literature
plot

reader response
setting
story grammar
theme
touchstone
trade books

GUIDING QUESTIONS

Think about a book that you enjoyed as a child. Can you remember the title or the main character's name? What did you like about this book? What children's books have you read in the last year?

Have you ever read a book to an elementary school child? Think about the following questions as you read this chapter.

1. What is children's literature?

2. What value does children's literature have in children's lives?

3. What do teachers need to know about children's literature?

OVERVIEW

Do you remember favorite books from childhood? If so, you were a fortunate child whose early experiences with books led you to a lifelong love of reading. Stories are a powerful presence in our lives; they influence us in untold ways. Daniel Boorstin (1998), a Pulitzer Prize–winning historian, the former Librarian of Congress, and a best-selling author, says that we are a nation of readers whose freedom to read and enthusiasm for reading keep our nation alive and thriving. Moreover, he believes that "an unrelenting quest for knowledge and learning and a passion for books and reading are the root of the American character" (p. 10). This philosophy, as well as contemporary educational thought, recognizes the importance of literature in constructing knowledge, creating a context for literary experiences that will develop children's meaning-making processes that are central to their learning. Children who have a rich variety of literary experiences become literate, caring, cultured, humanized, and informed people (Livingston, 1988).

Over the years, children's books have grown increasingly more plentiful, giving teachers, librarians, and parents a broad array of books from which to choose. Such abundance makes it important for the adults to learn about the body of children's literature, as well as the authors and illustrators who create fine children's literature. In this chapter, we create a foundation for those concerned with fostering children's literary experiences, exploring the nature of children's literature and its value in children's lives as well as identifying the literary experiences that facilitate the meaning-making process.

INTRODUCTION

In the opening vignette, Susan Stanley, a kindergarten teacher, selects a trade book, which is a book written to spark an audience's general interest, in contrast with a textbook, which is written for specific instructional purposes. Ms. Stanley selects *The Napping House* because it has repetitive, rhythmic language and interesting illustrations. She recognizes that young children love the sounds of words and anticipates that first graders will respond to the poetic cadence of language in this story. Ms. Stanley consistently encourages her pupils to talk about the language and illustrations in books, making it a point to acquaint students with the idea that writers and illustrators communicate through their books.

Ms. Stanley relates *The Napping House* to the children's experiences, establishing a connection that enriches both their understanding and their response. After listening to the story, the children discuss their thoughts and feelings in response to the book, after which the teacher rereads the story so they can build deeper appreciation for it.

Bringing children and books together in meaningful ways is one way this teacher builds children's interests. In addition, her own enthusiasm for literature sparks her students' interest. She tells them about her favorite books, authors, and illustrators so they realize how important literature is in her life.

Stimulating literary experiences motivate readers to share their thoughts with others and to create communities of readers, informal groups of readers who stimulate, encourage, motivate, and sustain one another's reading activities. These reading communities give students opportunities to explore exciting literature, to find connections among books, and to relate books with their own lives.

VIGNETTE

Susan Stanley watched as her kindergarten students settled on the story rug, then she held up *The Napping House* and said, "Audrey and Don Wood wrote this funny story and illustrated it with beautiful pictures. What do you think the book is about?"

Marissa, Kyle, and Catherine chorused, "It's about taking a nap."

Ms. Stanley said, "What is a napping house?"

Will answered, "It's a house where you take a nap."

Mary Ann offered, "It's a special house for taking a nap." Several children nodded in agreement.

"What do you think is special about a napping house?" Ms. Stanley asked.

The children volunteered ideas, such as it has soft beds, quiet rooms, soft music, bedtime stories, stuffed toys, and dark rooms with night lights.

Ms. Stanley said, "Close your eyes and think about the place where you nap and imagine how it looks. Do your pets take naps when you do? Do you have special toys in your bed?" She paused for a moment, then continued, "Open your eyes and look at the first illustration. As you listen to the story, think about the way you imagined it and the way Don Wood drew it."

She then began to read, "There is a house, a napping house, where everyone is sleeping. . . ." As she read, the children joined her on the repetitive lines.

When she finished, she asked, "What surprise was in this story, boys and girls?"

Matt laughed and said, "When the flea bit the mouse and everyone waked up."

"I think it was when the rainbow came out," Jenny said.

(continued)

"I think it was when the bed broke," Christy laughed.

"Those are thoughtful answers," Ms. Stanley responded. "Many times we have different ideas about stories because each person has different thoughts." Then she asked, "What special things did you notice in this story?"

"The parts where they said the things that happened over and over," said Jeremy.

"Why do you think the writer repeated those parts?"

Jimmy said, "Because she wanted us to remember those parts."

"Because the words go together kind of like a song," Mary said.

After more discussion, Ms. Stanley asked the children to find the words in the story that told about napping. The children identified *snoozing, dozing, dreaming, snoring,* and *sleeping.*

WHAT IS LITERATURE?

The Napping House is children's literature, but why is it classified as literature? *Literature* is thought, experience, and imagination shaped into oral or written language that may include visual images. Literature takes a variety of forms such as stories, ballads, family narratives, jokes, jump-rope jingles, street rhymes, videos, paintings, drawings, film, recorded books, and computer programs. Does *The Napping House* fit this description?

Literature entertains listeners and readers, at the same time giving them access to the accumulated experience and wisdom of the ages. "Offering stories to children is the way our print-dominated society carries on a habit even older than writing and as common as bread—telling stories and listening to them" (Meek, 1977, p. 36). Literature contributes to readers' growing experiences—extending and enriching their knowledge while stimulating reflection.

Stories are a natural part of life. Constructing stories in the mind is a fundamental way of making meaning (Wells, 1986). Through literature and language, humans record, explain, understand, and control their experience. Authors reflect about experiences and events, organizing the significant episodes into a coherent sequence. The order and form thus created show life's unity and meaning (Lukens, 1986). Reading what oth-

ers have written gives us insight about ourselves and helps put our own experiences in perspective. Clarissa Estes (1992) claims, "Stories are medicine. I have been taken with stories since I heard my first. They have such power; they do not require that we do, be, act anything—we need only listen" (p. 5).

Stories are behind the nightly news, the comics, and the 11 o'clock sports report. When you ask a friend about her experiences in a hurricane, she creates a narrative to tell what happened, helping both of you understand her experience. Through telling, retelling, believing, and disbelieving stories about one another's pasts, futures, and identities, we come to know one another.

What Is Children's Literature?

Children's literature explores, orders, evaluates, and illuminates the human experience—its heights and depths, its pains and pleasures. Like adults, children learn about the breadth and depth of life from literature. Memorable children's authors skillfully engage readers with information, language, unique plots, and many-faceted characters. Katherine Paterson (1981), a noted children's author, shared a writer's perspective when she wrote, "By allowing our readers into the soul of a character we are letting them know more than life will ever divulge about another human being" (p. 35).

A visual journey reveals America's beauty.

Children's literature is literature to which children respond; it relates to their experiences and is told in language they understand. The major contrast between children's literature and adult literature takes into account the more limited life experience of the audience, because readers use their experiences to understand text. Paterson (1981) illustrates this distinction through comparing adult literature to a symphony orchestra with themes, characters, plots, and subplots creating harmonies such as those found in a great orchestra. On the other hand, fine children's literature has the qualities of the clear, true notes of a flute solo: its beauty and truth are not complicated by experiences that go beyond the readers' ability to understand and respond.

Response to Literature

Readers make books come alive. They relate the text they read to life as they know it in order to construct meaning within the text, using the author's words as meaning cues and constructing meaning for the words based on their personal knowledge, associations, and feelings. In this way, readers construct and confer meaning on the text rather than extracting a single given meaning from it (Rosenblatt, 1978; Smith, 1998). Because each reader brings a different set of experiences to the text, different readers may create different meanings for the same text (Rosenblatt, 1978). In addition, because the meaning of a text depends on the reader's experience, the same reader may construct different meanings for the same text in separate readings of that text. "Each time we talk about a book we discover our sense of it, our ideas about it, our understanding of what it is and means, even the details we remember have changed and shifted and come to us in different arrangements, different patterns" (Chambers, 1983, p. 167).

Responses to literature fall on a broad continuum ranging from total absorption in the experience to a total lack of interest. Total absorption occurs when a reader enjoys the sense of becoming a character who is engaged in the story events. In this instance, the reader feels that she is a part of the story and does not want it to end (Chambers, 1983). A story may be so delightful that it prompts the reader to search for another book the author has written. The reader may want to compare responses with a friend who has read the book. Literature can be so moving that a reader cries, laughs aloud, or hurls the book across the room. At the other end of the continuum, the reader may simply close the book with satisfied feelings, or at times close it even before finishing it. Figure 1.1 illustrates the literary response continuum.

Because understanding the nature of reader response is significant to guiding children's literary experiences, this text is anchored in a response-centered philosophy. Throughout the book we focus on learner-centered literary experiences with quality children's books. The literature suggested in this text establishes benchmarks, standards of quality to which you can compare the books you read. These benchmarks will help you select literature that inspires children's responses. Readers' personal responses to literature become the basis for literature explorations. The general characteristics of reader response are:

1. Response implies active involvement of the reader.
2. Response includes both immediate reactions and later effects.
3. Readers' responses are cultivated through giving them occasions to read, discuss, discover, consider, represent, and reread—to make their own meanings.

The literature suggested in this text establishes benchmarks that will help adults select books that inspire children's responses. Literary experiences such as those suggested throughout this book will help you foster children's response to literature, a topic explored in detail in chapter 4.

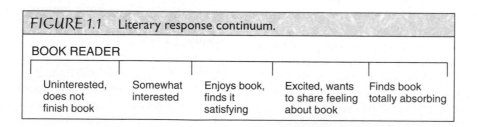

FIGURE 1.1 Literary response continuum.

BOOK READER

| Uninterested, does not finish book | Somewhat interested | Enjoys book, finds it satisfying | Excited, wants to share feeling about book | Finds book totally absorbing |

THE POWER OF LITERATURE

Books enrich, broaden, and bring joy to children's lives. However, isolating and identifying the values of children's literature is a daunting task because literature affects our lives so deeply. Literature motivates readers to think, enhances language and cognitive development, and stimulates thinking. It takes them beyond everyday experiences, broadening their background, developing their imagination and sense of humor, enabling them to grow in humanity and understanding (Viguers, 1964). Literature entertains, enriches knowledge, and provides for aesthetic responses. It expands knowledge and experience, helps readers solve problems, and plays a significant role in children's developmental journey. Literature permits readers to walk in another's shoes for a time, thus giving them a better understanding of someone else's feelings. From this beginning, we can distinguish some of the major values of children's literature—enjoyment, aesthetics, understanding, imagination, information and knowledge, cognition, and language—that are examined in this section.

Providing Enjoyment

Some readers immerse themselves so completely in an enjoyable book that they seem removed from their environment; they laugh or cry with the mood of the story. Some readers experience enjoyment from the new, fascinating information acquired from nonfiction. A well-written informational book piques interest in new topics and whets the appetite for more knowledge. For instance, the book *Gentle Giant Octopus* by Karen Wallace captures the grace and mystery of a marvelous creature. Readers learn that 150 kinds of octopuses exist that can move quickly by sucking in seawater to jet backward. The author uses picturesque language as she compares a giant octopus with glowing eyes and long tentacles to a spaceship.

Children respond emotionally to a good book. They will laugh heartily at the imaginative and comic fantasy in Nickle's *The Ant Bully*. In this book, Lucas is reduced in size and forced to work in an ant colony to learn a lesson about bullying ants; however, in the end, he triumphs and returns home a wiser child. David Wisniewski taps our sense of humor with *The Secret Knowledge of Grown-Ups*. After enjoying this hilarious book, you will discover that children who are offered milk giggle and sagely reply, "Yes, save the Atomic Cow."

It's always fun to plan gifts for those you love.

Leon's Story by Leon Walter Tillage packs an emotional wallop of an entirely different nature. The unvarnished truth of a black child growing up in the United States shocks and horrifies some readers. Moreover, Leon Tillage tells his truth without judgment in a voice that says, "that was just the way it was," moving readers to ask, "Did this actually happen?" to which Leon answers "Yes." Readers can share Leon's triumph over adversity in his own words.

Poetry gives children enjoyment too. Many readers appreciate poets' efforts to capture the essence of their experiences and ideas in succinct language. In *Sports! Sports! Sports!: A Poetry Collection,* Lee Bennett Hopkins has selected poems that explore the pleasures of sports from baseball to skating with immediate images and rhyme.

Readers who experience pleasure in literature read more and more. The best literature is so enjoyable that they are oblivious to any value other than enjoyment. Books that obviously preach or teach are usually too didactic to invite enjoyment. Unless children can relate to the ideas and experiences expressed, they will not listen to the voice of a work, and often they will not finish reading it. Superb writers first and foremost share their stories with readers, who find these stories fascinating and come back for more.

Appreciating Aesthetics

Aesthetics pertain to the beauty readers perceive in a literary work. Literature is verbal art that helps readers appreciate the beauty of language. It adds aesthetic dimensions to readers' lives, leading them to view their personal experiences in different ways. Fiction, nonfiction, and poetry are artistic interpretations of experiences, events, and people. Picture books add the dimension of visual art, which interacts with language to tell a story, create a poem, or impart information.

Readers have personal concepts of beauty that evolve from individual experiences and therefore exhibit considerable variation in literary appreciation. A book that transforms one person may not affect someone else. Of literature he considered second-rate, author W. H. Auden (1956) said, "That's just the way I always felt." But his response to first-rate literature was quite different: "Until now, I never knew how I felt. Thanks to this experience, I shall never feel the same way again." Books that project beauty and truth to many people become classics. In the United States, E. B. White's *Charlotte's Web* and Madeleine L'Engle's *A Wrinkle in Time,* as well as the books of Margaret Wise Brown, are among the books considered classics because they have given so much pleasure to so many people over the years.

Enhancing Understanding

Understanding self and others

Books stimulate readers' emotional responses. They chuckle over the outlandish capers of teachers in *Hooray for Diffendoofer Day!* by Dr. Seuss, Jack Prelutsky, and Lane Smith and identify with Alexander's feelings in *Alexander and the Terrible, Horrible, No Good, Very Bad Day* by Judith Viorst. Readers gain insights about the life of a youngster with attention deficit disorder in *Joey Pigza Swallowed the Key,* which is narrated by Joey himself who explains:

> Usually I wake up with springs popping inside my head, like I'm in the middle of a pinball game where I'm the ball, and I shoot out of bed and directly to the kitchen where I ricochet around after food. (Gantos, 1998)

Conly touches readers' emotions in the book *While No One Was Watching.* Reading this book will lead intermediate-grade students to encounter a tough and compelling survival story of three motherless children living in a working-class setting.

Children can acquire compassion for others and insight into their own behavior and feelings from reading. As they read, children begin to realize that others have basically the same feelings as they do and that people around the world share their hopes, dreams, and fears. Through stories children learn about happiness, sadness, fears, warm family relationships, death, and loneliness. Indeed, they learn that many life experiences are universal. In *Swimming Lessons* by Betsy Jay, children learn that fear of swimming lessons is something that others face too. And many intermediate-grade children empathize with Eileen in *Changing Tunes* by Donna Jo Napoli as she tries to accept her parents' separation and pending divorce. Chapter 10 introduces realistic fiction.

Reading about story characters' feelings and actions develops children's ability to understand and appreciate other's feelings (Aaron, 1987). Moreover, identifying with characters gives readers a deeper involvement with a story, making reading a meaningful experience. In the book *Rock River,* Maynard portrays Luke's overprotective mother who fears he will drown like his reckless older brother, but his father recognizes the difference between fortitude and foolishness. The hero of *Charlsie's Chuckle* by Clara Widess Berkus has Down syndrome. His infectious laugh brings harmony to his hometown. Charlsie shows that children of all abilities have the power to make a significant contribution, and that laughter is very important. Chapter 14 explores this literature in greater depth.

Today's authors discuss death, birth, anger, mental illness, alcoholism, and brutality more explicitly than was acceptable in earlier times. Adults who have not read recently published children's books may find the realism shocking; nevertheless, contemporary realism contributes to children's self-understanding. Sharon Creech writes about Dinnie, who lives in a haphazard and disordered family that is strained to the breaking point by her older sister's new baby in *Bloomability.* After Dinnie is sent to live with her uncle, who is headmaster at a U.S. school, her experiences enable Dinnie to accept herself and her individuality.

Understanding cultures

Through identifying with children in other cultures, readers learn about the ties that unite people everywhere.

Children who come to understand and appreciate various cultures are more likely to realize that people around the world share the same emotions, experiences, and problems. Understanding the shared aspects of life fosters children's appreciation of the cultures that comprise the United States and the world at large.

Traditional literature, which includes *folktales,* acculturates children to the values of their own and others' cultures. Such tales help children learn the taboos of cultures, identifying the behavior, attitudes, values, and beliefs that are acceptable and unacceptable. They teach that good is rewarded and evil is punished. Many of the plots and characters appearing in folktales are similar from culture to culture, and reading traditional stories from other cultures helps children realize the similarity of human qualities that exists in all cultures. (Chapter 15 explores culturally conscious literature in greater depth.)

Developing Imagination

Imagination is a creative, constructive power that is intimately related to higher order thinking skills. Every aspect of daily life involves imagination. People imagine as they talk and interact with others, make choices and decisions, analyze news reports, or assess advertising and entertainment. Critical and creative thinkers

Audrey and Don Wood have written and illustrated many books. Readers return again and again to Little Penguin's Tale, only to discover that some of us can just hear a story—and others have to experience it.

strive to develop or invent novel, aesthetic, constructive ideas (Beyer, 1995; Wilks, 1995).

Literature is essential to educating the imagination because it illustrates the unlimited range of the human imagination and extends readers' personal visions of possibilities (Frye, 1964). Literature nourishes readers' creative processes by stirring and stretching the imagination, providing new information, ideas, and perspectives so that readers can imagine possibilities and elaborate on original ideas. In this way, it expands readers' ability to express imagination in words and images.

Many children's books inspire creative thought. The imaginary worlds that writers create help readers understand the real world. For instance, in *Just Another Ordinary Day,* Rod Clement writes about Amanda who lives an ordinary life except she wakes up to the blaring clash of a gong instead of an alarm clock. She rides to school with a neighbor—a Tyrannosaurus. One of her classmates is an alien and her cat Fluffy is not an ordinary pet. Books such as this one connect real and make-believe worlds, making clear to children that imagining is a valuable activity. Fantasy is presented in chapter 8.

Children in the intermediate grades love both ghost stories and the Wild West. Vande Velde combined these elements to create an absorbing story of revenge, justice, and love in *Ghost of a Hanged Man.* The colorful characters and their dialogue focus upon the spooky events. In the climax, the protagonists defeat the murderous outlaw with the assistance of their deceased mother.

In Richard Peck's *A Long Way from Chicago: A Novel in Stories,* two children visit Grandma Dowdel, who is both amazing and intimidating. Joey, the narrator, tells an incident from each summer visit between 1929 and 1935. Grandma is a deadpan wit who gets even with pranksters, conspires with a ghost to aid eloping lovers, and refers to Abraham Lincoln to protect a neighbor from foreclosure.

Increasing Information and Knowledge

Children find the real world and real events fascinating, and through reading they can participate in experiences that go far beyond mere facts. Trade books can give readers a sense of people, times, and places that textbooks do not because they draw from all types of subjects to expand children's background experiences.

For example, Anita Lobel's Holocaust memoir *No Pretty Pictures: A Child of War* is superb nonfiction. The author's tightly styled writing is true to her childhood perceptions. She writes about horrific details in a clean, straightforward style that gives voice to these experiences. Moreover, she is clear about the aftereffects of her disrupted childhood, recognizing its lingering effects on her life today.

Intermediate-grade and middle school students can learn the details of life in a Japanese American Internment Camp through an interned third-grade teacher's daily diary and photographs. In *The Children of Topaz,* Tunnell and Chilcoat place the diary in a historical context, expanding readers' understanding of daily life in a war relocation camp.

Fine nonfiction writers not only increase their readers' store of knowledge, they also stimulate readers to think about the many dimensions of the concepts explored in their books, encouraging questioning and critical thinking. Often their readers discover new interests as well as continuing to explore a topic that has been opened to them. The author–illustrator of *Walter Wick's Optical Tricks* cleverly designed photographic arrangements employing angles and concepts to arouse interest in optical illusion. He created optical teasers to entice readers' fascination.

Nonfiction and informational books can also give children an awareness of things they have not yet experienced for themselves. In *Planting a Rainbow,* Lois Ehlert shares a young child's experiences planting flowers and the brilliant rainbow colors of summer flowers. The illustrator's clear, simple pictures expand readers' awareness of nature. Many nonfiction books are introduced in Chapter 11.

Stimulating Cognition

Literature is a way of thinking. It serves as a source of knowledge and a sounding board for children's reasoning. It plays a role in developing a sharp and critical mind (Langer, 1992). All literature, stories, and poems, as well as nonfiction, stimulate thinking by giving readers substance for reflection. Literature can provoke readers to analyze, synthesize, connect, and to respond thoughtfully, which facilitates cognitive development. Gordon Wells (1986) points out that humans construct stories to make sense of perceptual information and that stories are the means by which we enter into a shared world, which is broadened and enriched by the stories

we exchange with others. For instance, in the fictional *Alexander and the Terrible, Horrible, No Good, Very Bad Day,* Judith Viorst recounts the events in a day when everything went wrong for Alexander. Children identify with the ups and downs of Alexander's life, connecting his day to their own "terrible, horrible, no good, very bad" days. On the other hand, the nonfiction *Dinosaur Ghosts* by J. Lynett Gillette introduces facts about the study of Coelophysis fossils at the Ghost Ranch in New Mexico. Then the author explores the scenarios scientists have suggested to explain the remarkable find at Ghost Ranch. Readers have the opportunity to unravel the mystery of one of the most puzzling dinosaur discoveries of all time.

Literature is a forum that offers readers diverse perspectives on familiar topics by giving readers a safe medium for trying different roles, imagining new settings, and puzzling out unique solutions to problems. Many books model thinking processes such as problem solving, inferencing, evaluative thinking, relational thinking, and imagining. Readers of *Math Curse* by Jon Scieszka will be stimulated to discover the many times they confront mathematical reasoning in their lives.

Providing a Language Model

Language and thinking are so closely interrelated that "the ability to think for one's self depends upon one's mastery of the language" (Didion, 1968, p. 14). Exposure to language as an interactive process is a critical factor in acquiring higher order thinking (Healy, 1991). Literature assumes greater importance when considered as a model of language and the interactive language processes.

Children acquire language through social activities such as conversations, hearing and telling stories, and discussions. Literature, however, often furnishes a richer model for language than conversation, because authors frequently use elaborate sentences and sumptuous words, whereas speakers tend to employ the same few words again and again in conversation. Children learn language from literature when the stories are associated with their experiences so they can relate the text to their lives and thus build meaning. Children appreciate authors' artistry with language in books and will repeat phrases and sentences they like again and again.

In *Swimmy,* Leo Lionni provides a rich language base, with a lobster that walks like a "water-moving machine" and an "eel with a tail that is too long to re-member." Katherine Paterson demonstrates her way with language in *The Great Gilly Hopkins* when she introduces the phrases "trailing clouds of glory" and "a flower child gone to seed." Such literature expands children's range of experience and enriches their language; from this store of language they develop a greater facility in thinking, imagining, reading, and writing. Thus literature has a major impact on language and thought because children incorporate literary language and use it to express their ideas. Teachers, parents, and librarians often hear children use language acquired from their favorite stories.

Literary experiences are significant throughout the life span, but they are most important in the early years when children are establishing foundations for future development. Furthermore, researchers tell us that "the single most important activity for building the knowledge required for eventual success in reading is reading aloud to children" (Anderson, Hiebert, Scott, & Wilkinson, 1985, p. 23). In a joint position statement from the International Reading Association and the National Association for the Education of Young Children (1998), the associations state "failing to give children literacy experiences until they are school age can severely limit the reading and writing levels they ultimately attain" (p. 4). Chapter 5 explores these concepts in depth.

LITERATURE AND THE CURRICULUM

Literature gives students access to the accumulated experience, knowledge, and wisdom of the past. Integrating literature in the curriculum can enhance learning in all subject areas regardless of the prevailing philosophy of learning. Contemporary teaching philosophies such as literature-based instruction, integrated instruction, and readers' workshop usually are based on literature, although teachers vary widely in their implementation of these approaches (Hoffman, 1998; Pahl & Monson, 1992). Contemporary views of literacy are based on the philosophy that children learn best through interacting with text that has meaningful content. This is the basis for most reading programs, although the specific development of these programs differs. Moreover, we find a growing realization that literacy develops best in classrooms in which the guiding philosophy provides for integration across the instructional areas—which means that language arts, social studies, science, and math are

connected rather than separated in teaching and learning. Integration may involve connecting all of these subjects or only some of them, depending on the topic and instructional goals. This section explores the use of literature throughout the curriculum, beginning with reading instruction.

Balanced Reading Instruction

Many schools are shifting to a balanced approach to reading instruction that combines language and literature-rich activities that enhance meaning, understanding, and love of literature with explicit teaching of skills as needed to develop proficient readers (Adams, 1990; Sensenbaugh, 1997). Balanced reading instruction focuses on both words and comprehension with meaningful reading, writing, and discussion about what is read and written (Bear & Templeton, 1998; International Reading Association & National Association for the Education of Young Children, 1998; Weaver, 1998). In balanced reading instruction, teachers may use basal readers, literature, graded reading materials, or any combination thereof. Selecting reading materials that will engage readers in balanced reading programs makes literature central to meaningful literacy activities that encompass the language arts.

Whole language

Whole language is a philosophy and a set of beliefs about reading. As in any approach to reading instruction, teachers vary widely in their individual interpretations of this philosophy (Weaver, 1994). Most whole language programs concentrate on helping children learn to read through immersion in a print-rich environment that encourages them to read and respond to literature; however, many educators believe that some children need direct instruction to become successful readers.

Literature-based instruction

Many educators recognize that children's literature is an important aspect of developing literacy. They implement quality literature programs so students can apply their reading skills in context, using "real" books. Canavan and Sanborn (1992) identify children's literature that can be used with a traditional basal program effectively. They also identify the particular skills that the books emphasize, focusing on these skills:

1. letter recognition
2. letter–sound association
3. decoding skills—context clues, syntax clues, word structure clues
4. sight vocabulary

Literature and Language Arts

The language arts encompass speaking, listening, reading, and writing. Children's literature is essential to teaching and learning the language arts. Much of the content for teaching speaking, listening, reading, and writing is derived from children's books. Reading to children builds their sense of story and enhances their understanding of the ways authors structure and organize text (Meyer & Rice, 1984); for example, children who hear and read many stories learn about language and literature through finger rhymes such as "John Brown's Baby Had a Cold Upon Its Chest" and other interactive rhymes in Marc Brown's *Finger Rhymes*. They also enjoy chanting the repeated phrases and rhythmic language found in some books. They savor the language in books, such as Margaret Wise Brown's *Goodnight Moon* and *Elbert's Bad Word* by Audrey and Don Wood. After reading these books, parents and teachers often hear children repeating words, phrases, and sounds they have learned.

Literature and Writing

Most writers are also avid readers (Stotsky, 1984). When prominent authors were asked to advise young writers about ways to improve their writing, they consistently stated that reading was indispensable for learning to write (Gallo, 1977). Literature provides young writers with a source of ideas and inspiration as well as structural models for organizing ideas in text. Surrounding children with literature prepares children for writing.

Reading cultivates writing abilities because it enlarges children's sensitivity to and understanding of language, thus enabling them to choose the words and create the syntax that best express their thoughts. Fiction, exposition, and poetry help children remember what they have read, promote their sense of the ways in which discourse may be structured, and give them

patterns for structuring their own writing. Research reveals that the stories children write reflect the characteristics of their reading materials (Bissex, 1980; Deford, 1981; Eckhoff, 1983). Children whose reading reflects a wide range of writing structures, complex sentence patterns, and rich vocabulary exhibit these characteristics in their own writing, whereas those who read simple, repetitive stories write in a simple, repetitive style. Reading and discussing a wide variety of stories seem to help students discover the ways authors create meaning in written language, as these children are more sensitive to plot, character, setting, and writing style than their less well-read peers (Calkins, 1986; Graves, 1983).

Integrated Instruction

Integrated instruction enables students to see the connectedness of separate subjects. An integrated curriculum is one in which teachers plan for students to learn language at the same time they are learning something else, which may be science, social studies, math, or art, or even a project such as planning a program for an assembly. New knowledge more often than not is created interdisciplinarily (Harste, 1993). For example, new scientific knowledge is generally interrelated with social and cultural aspects of life. In the same way, language learning does not occur in a vacuum but is always context bound (Wilson, Malmgren, Ramage, & Schulz, 1993). These contexts anchor students' language learning so that it is meaningful to them rather than arbitrary instruction.

Integrated instruction enables learners to make connections and find patterns throughout their lives, carrying ideas from one subject to another. Learning is a process of making connections and finding patterns when students connect their old knowledge with new experiences (Short, 1993; Vygotsky, 1978). This is why integrated instruction, thematic units, and literature-based instruction support optimal learning.

Literature and the Other Content Areas

Literature supports learning in other content areas as well; it can make a topic memorable and understandable by widening the reader's world beyond the immediate time and place. Reading is an instrument for accessing ideas and information. Moreover, it gives students opportunities to interact with one another and to understand the ways that others think and respond. For example, students who read Kurusa's true story *The Streets Are Free* for a social studies unit learn that Venezuelan children became community activists to get a playground. They learn that children in Venezuela have some of the same concerns as children in the United States.

Literature also enables students to generate hypotheses and cultivate multiple perspectives, ways of thinking that are used in all subject areas (Bruner, 1986). For instance, scientists generate hypotheses and test these hypotheses through experiments. Social scientists examine various cultures using multiple perspectives to help them understand the differences within and among cultures. Reading literature gives students the content to generate hypotheses and to understand different perspectives.

Literature is an excellent vehicle for interrelating and integrating science and social science. Consider the book *Water Sky,* which portrays cultural change through an Inuit youngster's search for his cultural heritage. Jean Craighead George carefully researched cultural change and scientific information to create an accurate portrayal that goes beyond mere facts and descriptions. For example, the scientific information revealed how sled dogs were trained and managed, as well as how to drive them on different types of snow. Moreover, the author expressed the feelings and sensory experiences of a driver who communes with the dogs as they fly over the snow. Readers can identify with the main character and experience the story through his eyes, giving them a greater understanding of another culture. Students who read and write about science thoughtfully get a picture of how scientists think and communicate (Shanahan, 1992).

The role of literature in science and social science is clear, but literature as a means of enriching mathematics understandings and concepts may appear less useful. Nevertheless, literature can indeed contribute to the subject of mathematics. In *The Librarian Who Measured the Earth* by Kathryn Lasky, children learn mathematics concepts. Both novels and informational books can be used to develop logic, problem solving, and mathematics concepts. In *The King's Chessboard,* based on a folktale from ancient India, David Birch demonstrates the squaring of numbers.

Literature enhances understandings across the curriculum at all grade levels. Preschool students acquire concepts about street signs from books such as Tana Hoban's *I Read Signs,* and elementary children acquire concepts of biology in *A Drop of Water: A Book of Science and Wonder,* which Walter Wick illustrated with photographs of the various forms of water. History and social studies concepts emerge from *Passage to Freedom: The Sugihara Story* by Ken Mochizuki, which tells how a Japanese diplomat helped Jewish refugees during World War II. These and other informational books enhance children's subject matter knowledge.

Literature and fine arts

Writers are verbal artists who use language as their medium; other artists search for truth in visual art, music, and drama. Literature is an excellent medium for cultivating children's appreciation of the fine arts. They can learn about music from books such as *I see the rhythm* by Toyomi Igus, which illustrates the rhythms of work songs, jazz, and swing. Vincent van Gogh is the

Sarah painted this picture after reading Camille and the Sunflowers.

subject of *Camille and the Sunflowers* by Laurence Anholt. The author introduces elementary-grade children to some of van Gogh's masterpieces. Children respond to and extend the books they read, as shown in the picture painted by a child who read *Camille and the Sunflowers*. One child may create a mural to express appreciation of a book. Another may paint or draw a picture to illustrate feelings about a story or poem. Still others may use music to re-create the mood of a story or poem.

EXPERIENCING LITERATURE

Reading is a demanding activity that requires a significant expenditure of energy. Interesting literature increases students' willingness to put forth this energy and cultivates their desire to read. For instance, discovering humorous stories motivates many children to read, and reading such stories aloud is a good means of initially engaging children's interest. *The True Story of the 3 Little Pigs* and *The Stinky Cheese Man and Other Fairly Stupid Tales*, both by Jon Scieszka, are guaranteed to tickle everyone's sense of humor and motivate them to read more.

Clearly, literature is a major asset in creating within students the desire to read, an unquestionably crucial skill in education. Children need a host of reading experiences with all types of literature to build interest and motivation. As students read more and more books, they establish a basis for comparison that in time will lead them to recognize the qualities of fine writing. Moreover, offering children extensive opportunities to discuss books encourages students to weigh their own responses against those of others in their community of readers. This section explores ways of offering children opportunities to explore literature as well as ways of structuring and nurturing these experiences.

Creating Effective Literary Experiences

Four major approaches are commonly used to create effective literary experiences. They are the story approach, the great books or classics approach, the author approach, and the unit approach.

The story approach

The story approach focuses on literary genres and the elements of literature. The genres of literature commonly included in children's literature are picture books, traditional literature, fantasy, poetry, contemporary realistic fiction, historical fiction, biography, and informational books. Literary genres and the elements of literature as aspects of children's literature are discussed in chapters 6, 7, 8, 9, 10, and 11.

The great books or classics approach

The great books approach to literature focuses on works of established literary value, which become models of quality for readers and writers. Many lists, reviews, and evaluations of children's books exist that teachers and librarians can consult for information and guidance in choosing great books. Chapter 3 examines great books, sources of information about them, and their relation to children's reading interests.

The author approach

The author approach focuses on in-depth studies of authors and their bodies of works. In studying an author, students often read all or many of the author's books. As readers explore an author's various writings, they scrutinize writing styles, techniques, and subjects and research the author's background and experiences. Relating authors' lives to their bodies of work develops children's understanding of the relation between reading and writing. More and more books and biographies of children's writers are being published, most of which provide photographs, interviews, and authors' discussion of their work. Videos featuring current children's authors also enrich these studies. The Internet provides several children's author sites that are delightful and informative; many publishers of children's books also include sites for authors. Visiting *The Children's Literature Web Guide* on the World Wide Web at *www.underground.org/children.htm* will enable you to identify authors' and illustrators' Web sites. We identify and discuss authors and illustrators throughout this book.

The unit approach

In developing literature units, teachers may choose a diverse collection of literary and artistic styles to build students' in-depth understandings of a concept. For instance, a thematic unit focusing on courage amplifies children's understanding of ideas such as moral courage, physical courage, integrity, and responsibility. The theme of courage could be developed through poetry, fiction, nonfiction, and fine arts.

Themes are important ideas or universal understandings that evolve from reading a work or works of literature. One of several themes emerging from Maurice Sendak's *Where the Wild Things Are* is children's anger with parents when they are punished, although they continue to need the reassurance of parental love. Thematic understanding emerges gradually from reading a variety of related materials; therefore, thematic units are organized around all types of literature, including fiction, nonfiction, and poetry.

Subject-matter units address topics, such as farm life, problem solving, or the circus, rather than themes. In developing these units, teachers select a variety of materials that enrich students' understanding of the focus topic. Chapter 14 explores various kinds of units.

The teacher and children's literature

Enthusiastic teachers create classrooms where children read books, talk about them, experience them, and learn to love them. Teachers who share their favorite books and who read aloud to children create warm, literate environments and a community of readers within their classrooms. This section identifies and discusses the knowledge, skills, and attitudes that enable teachers, librarians, and other concerned adults to create exciting literary experiences for children.

Teachers need to know a wide variety of books written for children. This is a formidable task: More than 6,000 children's books are published each year. Obviously, teachers cannot read every available book. They can, however, use reviews of children's books to identify a sampling from different genres as a basis for selecting books to read aloud and for developing units of study. Knowledgeable teachers can help children find appealing books and suggest ones related to their interests. They use the resources offered by librarians and media specialists.

In the early stages of learning about children's books, teachers and students read widely, voraciously, and indiscriminately. They read entertaining books that engage their attention. This reading style enables them to compare books and authors and eventually identify touchstone books that represent standards of literary quality against which they can compare subsequent reading. According to Holman and Harmon (1986) a *touchstone* is a hard black stone used to test the quality of gold or silver. Matthew Arnold used the term *touchstone* as a metaphor for literary work that meets a critical standard:

"lines and expressions of the great masters" that the critic should hold always in mind when reading (Holman & Harmon, 1986, p. 112). In this book, the term denotes literature of recognized quality against which to compare other works. For instance, E. B. White's *Charlotte's Web* is one touchstone in fantasy with which we compare other fantasies.

Touchstone books help adults learn about literary quality in children's books. Their knowledge of literary quality helps them select children's books. Children identify their own touchstone books through reading widely and use these books as measures of quality in later reading. Touchstone books are identified throughout this book.

Teachers and prospective teachers often keep card files for future reference of the books they read. The first step in creating a file is choosing an organizational structure, such as genre, author, theme, or grade level. Whatever the organizational structure, the file cards should contain basic information such as author's name, title, publisher, year of publication, and appropriate grade levels on one side of the card. The reverse should contain a brief synopsis and identify the outstanding elements in the book (i.e., plot, characterization, setting, theme, style). Figure 1.2 shows what a file card might look like.

Teachers need to read widely in order to be able to select appropriate books. Book knowledge enables teachers and other concerned adults to make informed choices about books for children. In addition to reading widely, they supplement this knowledge by using book selection reference tools such as *The Elementary School Library Collection, Bookfinder,* and *Media Yearbook,* which are published on regular cycles. They combine book knowledge with understanding of children's development, interests, and reading abilities. Teachers who create a literature-based reading program or a literature-based curriculum choose books that enhance the classroom program. For instance, they identify books that relate to specific themes or topics to generate teaching units. Chapter 3 and the appendix will help teachers learn more about these guides.

Teachers need to know about children's authors. As children (and adults) learn about an author, they come to feel the person is a friend and a member of their community of readers and writers, so teachers should be prepared to help children find information about authors. Students become very excited when given op-

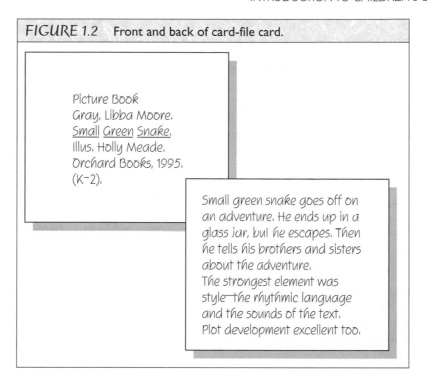

FIGURE 1.2 Front and back of card-file card.

Picture Book
Gray, Libba Moore.
<u>Small Green Snake.</u>
Illus. Holly Meade.
Orchard Books, 1995.
(K-2).

Small green snake goes off on
an adventure. He ends up in a
glass jar, but he escapes. Then
he tells his brothers and sisters
about the adventure.
The strongest element was
style—the rhythmic language
and the sounds of the text.
Plot development excellent too.

portunities to actually meet authors, including children as young as 5 and 6. Teachers and children can learn about authors through reading their works and through profiles published in professional journals, biographies, interviews, profiles on the Internet, Web sites, and personal appearances.

Teachers need to create a warm, literate environment where children have time to read each day. Many children in our hectic modern world have limited opportunities to read outside school because they attend after-school programs or are involved in a variety of activities. Thus schools play a pivotal role in providing books and creating time to read. A warm, literate environment should include an inviting physical setting in addition to a teacher's positive attitudes toward literacy. The physical environment may feature an attractive book-browsing center, book displays, and bulletin boards for authors' pictures and book jackets. Children are more likely to read when surrounded by inviting reading materials, which teachers can provide through school materials or long-term book loans from public libraries. Many teachers purchase secondhand books and paperbacks for their classroom book collections. All of these materials should be displayed in ways that invite children to pick them up.

Teachers need to encourage children's response to literature. Teachers who understand response theory are better able to provide experiences that build children's response to literature and nurture their growth. As discussed, response to literature varies widely, as does readers' expression of their responses. However, realizing that each reader comprehends and responds to literature in individual ways recognizes the importance of motivating readers to respond in unique ways. Perhaps the most important stimulus of all is a teacher who respects each varying response.

Teachers need to understand the genres and elements of literature and story structures. One way of organizing literature experiences is through the structures that characterize the various genres of children's literature. These include picture books, traditional literature, fantasy, poetry, realistic fiction, historical fiction, biography, and nonfiction. (Chapters 6, 7, 8, 9, 10, and 11 explore these genres in detail.)

Studying story elements is another approach to understanding literature. *Story elements* include plot, character, setting, theme, and style. *Plot* is the sequence of events in a story. The *characters* are the people or personified animals or objects that are responsible for the action in the story. Characters and story events occur in a *setting,* the place and time of the story. As the story unfolds, a central meaning or theme emerges; this central meaning is usually a universal idea or truth. For example, one of the lasting truths expressed in *Charlotte's Web* is the concept of loyalty in friendship; like many books, this one has several layers of meaning so that readers may identify other themes that are meaningful to them. (The elements of literature are explained in chapter 2.)

A story's elements can also be studied through *story grammars,* literary structures organized around setting, story problem, attempts to solve the problem, and problem resolution. Figure 1.3 illustrates a story grammar.

Teachers need to know storytelling and read-aloud techniques.   Storytelling is a natural activity for children, and oral stories are often children's first encounter with literature. Stories are so important in children's lives, they should hear stories every day. Reading and telling stories builds teachers' confidence in their ability to entertain and motivate their students. Children also enjoy telling stories and should have occasions to do so. Chapter 12 explores storytelling and other oral strategies for presenting literature.

FIGURE 1.3   Story grammar.

Title:
Author:

Setting (who, where, when):

  time

  character

  place

Problem:

Efforts to solve the problem (also called events):

  1.

  2.

  3.

  4. (number of events vary)

The resolution:

Teachers need to know strategies for guiding children's literature experiences.   Teachers and other adults concerned about children's response to literature should prepare to introduce books to children. Sharing their own favorite books and authors, guiding discussions, and creating a community of readers and writers in their classrooms are all ways of providing literature experiences. Teachers should give children many opportunities to respond to literature through speaking, listening, reading, writing, and the fine arts.

Teachers need to develop authentic literary experiences. *Authentic literary experiences* are those that preserve the integrity of the literature, that grow out of children's responses to the books they read. In some instances, their responses will be expressed in thoughts and feelings rather than a concrete project or product. Authentic experiences are those that are founded on the reader's response to the entirety of the piece, to the overall theme, plot, characters, setting, and author style. Fragmenting literature to examine it word by word, line by line, or chapter by chapter reduces the impact of the author's work and can evolve into requiring that children learn the teacher's interpretation and response to a piece rather than encouraging them to construct their own understanding. Authentic literature-based approaches are child centered and focus on a seamless literary experience.

Teachers need to incorporate children's literature throughout the curriculum.   Literature can easily be used to build children's interest in a particular subject area, as discussed earlier in this chapter. Trade books can also be used to provide more current sources of information than textbooks, which may become dated. As more parents, teachers, and school administrators learn the value of literature in the curriculum, teachers have been encouraged to enrich instruction with related literature. Some schools encourage teachers to use literature throughout the curriculum.

SUMMARY

This chapter introduced various concepts of children's literature—literature that children understand and enjoy—and established its importance in the elementary classroom as a means of exploring and seeking meaning in human experience. Successful teachers involve their students with literature daily by reading aloud and providing time for students to read on their own.

Children's literature includes all types of books that entertain and inform children, including picture books, traditional literature, realistic fiction, historical fiction, biography, fantasy, poetry, and nonfiction, among other media such as narratives, videos, verbal stories, and the fine arts. The content of children's literature is limited only by the experience and understanding of the reader. Teachers should remember that many children's books were intended for children to hear rather than for them to read independently.

Literature has many personal values for children. Foremost among these are entertainment, aesthetics, thinking, and imagination. Learning is an important value of literature in elementary classrooms. Fine books can contribute to learning in language arts, social sciences, science, mathematics, and fine arts.

A knowledge of literature will enable teachers and other adults to select appropriate literature and to guide literature experiences. These experiences can be organized around stories (genres), great books, authors, and units. Many programs use all of these approaches.

Thought Questions

1. Write your own definition of *children's literature*.
2. How does literature develop children's imagination?
3. Which values of literature are most important, in your opinion?
4. How is a good children's book like a good adult book? How is it different from an adult book?
5. What do you think you need to learn in order to teach children's literature?
6. Could the same criteria be used to evaluate both adult and children's literature? Why or why not?
7. Do you think computers and software will replace literature?

Research and Application Experiences

1. Interview three of your friends to determine their favorite books from childhood, and then interview three children. Compare their responses. What do the responses tell you about children's reading interests?

2. Read three new children's books (published within the last 5 years). How are they like the ones you read as a child? How are they different? Make file cards for each of these books to start your children's literature file.

3. Interview three teachers. Ask them how often they read aloud and what books they choose to read aloud.

4. Read several books by the same author to help you become acquainted with a children's author. What did you learn about the author from his or her writing? Look up the author on the Internet and add that information to what you have already learned. Add these books to your children's literature file.

5. If you are participating in an internship experience accompanying this course, observe the following in your classroom:
   a. How often does the teacher read aloud?
   b. What does the teacher read aloud?
   c. How often do the children independently read trade books?

6. Read one of the children's books mentioned in this chapter and compare your response to the book with the author's comments about it.

7. If you are participating in an internship experience related to this course, ask the students to identify their favorite authors.

Children's Literature References and Recommended Books

Note: Books designated with an asterisk (*) are recommended for reluctant readers.

Anholt, L. (1994). *Camille and the sunflowers*. New York: Barron's. (2–4). HISTORICAL FICTION.

Based on an actual encounter, this picture book tells how Camille made friends with Vincent van Gogh, who was lonely and unknown.

Berkus, C. W. (1992). *Charlsie's chuckle* (M. Dodd, Photog.). Rockville, MD: Woodbine House. (2–4). CONTEMPORARY REALISTIC FICTION.

Charlsie has Down syndrome, but he brings harmony to his hometown.

Birch, D. (1988). *The king's chessboard* (D. Grebu, Illus.). New York: Dial. (2–4). MODERN FANTASY.

The wise man asks for an unusual reward, a grain of rice for the first square on his chessboard, and double the second, and so on.

Brown, M. (1980). *Finger rhymes*. New York: Dutton. (PreK). PICTURE BOOK.

A collection of traditional rhymes for young children.

Brown, M. W. (1947). *Goodnight moon* (C. Hurd, Illus.). New York: Harper & Row. (PreK–1). PICTURE BOOK.

A child says goodnight to each of the things in his room.

Clement, R. (1997). *Just another ordinary day*. New York: HarperCollins. (2–4). MODERN FANTASY.

Amanda lives an ordinary life except that she has unusual neighbors, school, and so forth.

Conly, J. L. (1998). *While no one was watching*. New York: Holt. (4–8). CONTEMPORARY REALISTIC FICTION.*

This tough and compelling survival story depicts children growing up in a poor urban culture. The happy ending offsets the feeling that the children are neglected and out of control.

Creech, S. (1998). *Bloomability*. New York: HarperCollins. (4–8). CONTEMPORARY REALISTIC FICTION.

Dinnie lives in a strained family situation, which her sister's new baby makes even more difficult. Living with an aunt and uncle and attending a private school give her a new outlook.

Ehlert, L. (1988). *Planting a rainbow*. New York: Harcourt Brace. (K–2). INFORMATIONAL BOOK.

The author discusses planting a garden in simple language.

Gantos, J. (1998). *Joey Pigza swallowed the key*. New York: Farrar. (4–8). CONTEMPORARY REALISTIC FICTION.*

The protagonist, a child with attention deficit disorder, narrates this story in a style that gives readers great insight into his problem.

George, J. C. (1987). *Water sky*. New York: Harper & Row. (4–8). CONTEMPORARY REALISTIC FICTION.

A boy learns about the importance of whaling in his Eskimo culture.

Gillette, J. L. (1997). *Dinosaur ghosts* (D. Henderson, Illus.). New York: Dial. (3–7). INFORMATIONAL BOOK.

The author explores the various theories developed to explain the large number of Coelophysis fossils that have been unearthed at the Ghost Ranch in New Mexico.

Hoban, T. (1983). *I read signs*. New York: Greenwillow. (PreK–1). PICTURE BOOK.

A picture book based on signs in the everyday environment.

Hopkins, L. B. (1999). *Sports! Sports! Sports!: A poetry collection* (B. Floca, Illus.). New York: HarperCollins. (3–6). POETRY.*

Twenty poems in various forms explore baseball, track, soccer, swimming, and football. Easy-to-read short poems made appealing by rhyme and concrete images.

Igus, T. (1998). *I see the rhythm* (M. Wood, Illus.). San Francisco: Children's Book Press. (3–8). INFORMATIONAL BOOK.*

Using paintings and poetry, the author and illustrator teach readers about the rhythms of hip-hop, work songs, jazz, swing, and gospel music.

Jay, B. (1998). *Swimming lessons* (L. Osiecki, Illus.). Flagstaff, AZ: Rising Moon. (1–3). CONTEMPORARY REALISTIC FICTION.

Kids will recognize themselves in this story about a youngster who is afraid of swim lessons. She does take the plunge and becomes a swimmer.

Kurusa (1995). *The streets are free* (K. Englander, Trans; M. Doppert, Illus.). Toronto: Annick Press. (3–6). INFORMATIONAL BOOK.

A group of children seek to have a playground in this true story set in Caracas, Venezuela.

Lasky, K. (1994). *The librarian who measured the earth* (K. Hawkes, Illus.). Boston: Joy Street. (2–4). BIOGRAPHY.

Eratosthenes discovered many exciting theories, facts, and ideas long ago. Among his most exciting ideas were those about measurement.

L'Engle, M. (1962). *A wrinkle in time*. New York: Farrar, Straus & Giroux. (5–8). MODERN FANTASY.

Meg and her brother, Charles Wallace, set out to find their missing father. Their search leads to interesting adventures.

Lionni, L. (1963). *Swimmy*. New York: Pantheon. (K–2). MODERN FANTASY.

After a fierce tuna eats his family, Swimmy sets out to see the world and escape the big fish.

Lobel, A. (1998). *No pretty pictures: A child of war*. New York: Greenwillow. (4–Adult). BIOGRAPHY.

Lobel documents the Holocaust through her childhood experiences. This beautifully written book tells the story through a child's eyes.

Maynard, B. (1998). *Rock river.* New York: Putnam. (4–8). CONTEMPORARY REALISTIC FICTION.*

Luke suffers with an overprotective mother who fears that he will die the same way his reckless older brother did. With his father's support he develops self-understanding.

Mochizuki, K. (1997). *Passage to freedom: The Sugihara story* (D. Lee, Illus.). New York: Lee & Low. (3–6). BIOGRAPHY.

A little-known true story is the subject of this book, which is told from a child's perspective. It is the story of how a Japanese diplomat helped Jewish refugees during World War II.

Napoli, D. J. (1998). *Changing tunes.* New York: Dutton. (4–8). CONTEMPORARY REALISTIC FICTION.*

Ten-year-old Eileen struggles to understand her parents' separation and pending divorce. Then she has another blow: her father took the piano. Her eventual adjustment is well delineated.

Nickle, J. (1999). *The ant bully.* New York: Scholastic. (PreK–2). MODERN FANTASY.

A child who bullies ants is reduced to the size of one and learns about bullying so that he can return home a better person.

Paterson, K. (1978). *The great Gilly Hopkins.* New York: Crowell. (4–6). CONTEMPORARY REALISTIC FICTION.

Gilly is a foster child who resents her placement with a foster mother and dreams about her mother.

Peck, R. (1998). *A long way from Chicago: A novel in stories.* New York: Dial. (4–8). CONTEMPORARY REALISTIC FICTION.

The story of two children who spend summers with their unusual grandmother.

Scieszka, J. (1989). *The true story of the 3 little pigs* by A. Wolf (L. Smith, Illus.). New York: Viking. (K–6). MODERN FANTASY.*

Mr. A. Wolf gives his version of what happened to the three little pigs. Of course, he was grossly misjudged in the original story.

Scieszka, J. (1992). *The stinky cheese man and other fairly stupid tales* (L. Smith, Illus.). New York: Viking. (K–6). MODERN FANTASY.*

This is a collection of fractured fairy tales that delight all ages.

Scieszka, J. (1995). *Math curse* (L. Smith, Illus.). New York: Viking. (All ages). CONTEMPORARY REALISTIC FICTION.

This book tells of the problems of living in a world where math is so important.

Sendak, M. (1963). *Where the wild things are.* New York: Harper & Row. (K–2). MODERN FANTASY.

Max is wild, so his mother sends him to bed without dinner. He escapes, but returns to where he is loved.

Seuss, Dr., with Prelutsky, J., & Smith, L. (1998). *Hooray for Diffendoofer day!* New York: Knopf. (K–6). MODERN FANTASY.*

A parody of school, but the teachers teach children to think. The book also demonstrates the writing process.

Tillage, L. W. (1997). *Leon's story* (S. Roth, Illus.). New York: Farrar, Straus & Giroux. (4–9). BIOGRAPHY.*

This moving true story chronicles the growing up years of a black man, Leon Tillage, based on his talks to schoolchildren.

Tunnell, M. O., & Chilcoat, G. W. (1996). *The children of Topaz.* New York: Holiday House. (4–9). INFORMATIONAL BOOK.

A diary and photographs document the story of a Japanese American internment camp in this book. The details of everyday life in a camp give children authentic information about this time.

Vande Velde, V. (1998). *Ghost of a hanged man.* Tarrytown, NY: Cavendish. (4–8). MODERN FANTASY.*

The best qualities of ghost stories and the Wild West are combined in this delightful story. Two children overcome the villain with the assistance of their deceased mother. (Also good for challenged readers.)

Viorst, J. (1972). *Alexander and the terrible, horrible, no good, very bad day.* New York: Atheneum. (K–4). CONTEMPORARY REALISTIC FICTION.

Alexander has one of those days when everything goes wrong.

Wallace, K. (1998). *Gentle giant octopus* (M. Bostock, Illus.). Cambridge, MA: Candlewick. (1–4). INFORMATIONAL BOOK.

In beautiful language, this informational book provides fascinating facts and understandings about the giant octopus.

White, E. B. (1952). *Charlotte's web* (G. Williams, Illus.). New York: Harper & Row. (3–6). MODERN FANTASY.

Charlotte the spider saves Wilbur the pig's life with a unique solution.

Wick, W. (1997). *A drop of water: A book of science and wonder.* New York: Scholastic. (1–4). INFORMATIONAL BOOK.

Beautiful photographs illustrate the various forms of water and the water cycle.

Wick, W. (1998). *Walter Wick's optical tricks.* New York: Cartwheel/Scholastic. (3–6). INFORMATIONAL BOOK.*

As the title suggests, this book illustrates fascinating optical tricks with photographs.

Wisniewski, D. (1998). *The secret knowledge of grown-ups* (D. Wisniewski, Illus.). New York: Lothrop, Lee & Shepard. (K–4). MODERN FANTASY.*

Based on the things that parents say to children such as, "Drink your milk." The author reveals the real reason for these admonitions.

Wood, A. (1984). *The napping house* (D. Wood, Illus.). New York: Harcourt Brace Jovanovich. (K–2). MODERN FANTASY.

When a child and a series of animals fall asleep on Granny's bed, they nap until a flea breaks up the nap.

Wood, A. (1988). *Elbert's bad word* (A. Wood & D. Wood, Illus.). New York: Harcourt Brace. (K–3). MODERN FANTASY.

Elbert catches a bad word, but learns to control it with the help of a friendly wizard.

Woolf, F. (1990). *Picture this: A first introduction to paintings.* New York: Doubleday. (4–8). INFORMATIONAL BOOK.

This book surveys Western art between 1400 and 1950 through 24 paintings selected to show artistic styles and how art has changed.

References and Books for Further Reading

Aaron, I. (1987). Enriching the basal reading program with literature. In I. Aaron (Ed.), *Children's literature in the reading program* (pp. 126–137). Newark, DE: International Reading Association.

Adams, M. J. (1990). *Beginning to read: Thinking and learning about print.* Cambridge, MA: MIT Press.

Anderson, G., Higgins, D., & Wurster, S. R. (1985). Differences in the free-reading books selected by high, average, and low achievers. *The Reading Teacher, 39,* 326–330.

Anderson, R. C., Hiebert, E. H., Scott, J. A., & Wilkinson, I. A. (1985). *Becoming a nation of readers: The report of the commission on reading.* Urbana, IL: The Center for the Study of Reading.

Auden, W. H. (1956). As quoted by R. B. Heilman in Literature and growing up. *English Journal, 45,* 307.

Bear, D. R., & Templeton, S. (1998). Explorations in developmental spelling: Foundations for learning and teaching phonics, spelling, and vocabulary. *The Reading Teacher, 52,* 222–242.

Beyer, B. (1995). *Critical thinking.* Bloomington, IN: Phi Delta Kappa.

Bissex, G. (1980). *Gnys at wrk: A child learns to read and write.* Cambridge, MA: Harvard University Press.

Boorstin, D. (July, 1998). Why books are important. *Parade Magazine,* 10–12.

Bruner, J. (1986). *Actual minds, possible worlds.* Cambridge, MA: Harvard University Press.

Calkins, L. (1986). *The art of teaching writing.* Portsmouth, NH: Heinemann.

Canavan, D., & Sanborn, L. (1992). *Using children's books in reading/language arts programs.* New York: Neal-Schuman.

Chambers, A. (1983). *Introducing books to children.* Boston: Horn Book.

Deford, D. (1981). Literacy: Reading, writing and other essentials. *Language Arts, 58,* 652–658.

Didion, J. (1968). *Slouching toward Bethlehem.* New York: Delta-Dell.

Eckhoff, B. (1983). How reading affects children's writing. *Language Arts, 60,* 607–616.

Estes, C. P. (1992). *Women who run with wolves.* New York: Ballantine.

Frye, N. (1964). *The educated imagination.* Bloomington: Indiana University Press.

Gallo, D. (1977). Teaching writing: Advice from the professionals. *Connecticut English Journal, 8,* 45–50.

Graves, D. (1983). *Writing teachers and children at work.* Portsmouth, NH: Heinemann.

Harste, J. (1993, April). Inquiry-based instructions. *Primary Voices K–6,* 2–5.

Healy, J. M. (1991). *Endangered minds.* New York: Simon & Schuster.

Hoffman, J. V. (1998). When bad things happen to good ideas in literacy education: Professional dilemmas, personal decisions, and political traps. *The Reading Teacher, 52,* 102–113.

Holman, C. H., & Harmon, W. (1986). *A handbook to literature* (4th ed.). New York: Macmillan.

Hubbard, R. S. (1996). Invitations to reflect on our practice: A conversation with Gordon Wells. In B. M. Power & R. S. Hubbard, *Language development: A reader for teachers.* Upper Saddle River, NJ: Merrill/Prentice Hall.

International Reading Association and the National Association for the Education of Young Children. (1998). *Learning to read and write: Developmentally appropriate practices for young children.* Newark, DE: International Reading Association.

Langer, J. A. (1992). A new look at literature instruction. *ERIC Digest.* Bloomington: Indiana University Clearinghouse on Reading and Communications Skills.

Livingston, M. C. (1988). Children's literature today: Perils and prospects. *New Advocate, 1,* 18–28.

Lukens, R. (1986). *A critical handbook of children's literature* (3rd ed.). Glenview, IL: Scott Foresman.

Meek, M. (1977). Introduction. In M. Meek, A. Warlow, & G. Barton (Eds.), *The cool Web: The pattern of children's reading.* London: Bodley Head.

Meyer, B., & Rice, G. (1984). The structure of text. In P. D. Pearson (Ed.), *Handbook of reading research* (pp. 319–352). New York: Longman.

Pahl, M., & Monson, R. C. (1992). In search of whole language: Transforming curriculum and instruction. *Journal of Reading, 35,* 518–524.

Paterson, K. (1981). *The gates of excellence: On reading and writing books for children.* New York: Dutton.

Rosenblatt, L. M. (1978). *The reader, the text, the poem: The transactional theory of the literary work.* Edwardsville: Southern Illinois University.

Sensenbaugh, R. (1997). Phonemic awareness: An important early step in learning to read. *ERIC clearinghouse on reading, english, and communication digest,* 119.

Shanahan, T. (1992). Nine good reasons for using children's literature across the curriculum. In R. Shanahan (Ed.), *Distant shores: Teachers resource package, level N* (pp. 19–22). New York: McGraw Hill School Division.

Short, K. (1993). Making connections across literature and life. In K. Holland, R. Hungerford, & S. Ernst (Eds.), *Journeying: Children responding to literature* (pp. 284–301). Portsmouth, NH: Heinemann.

Smith, F. (1998). *Reading without nonsense* (3rd ed.). New York: Teachers College Press.

Stotsky, S. (1984). Research on reading/writing relationships: A synthesis and suggested directions. In J. Jensen (Ed.), *Composing and comprehending* (pp. 7–22). Urbana, IL: ERIC Clearinghouse on Reading and Communications Skills and National Conference on Research in English.

Viguers, R. H. (1964). *Part of the pattern.* Boston: Little Brown.

Vygotsky, L. (1978). *Mind in society.* Cambridge, MA: Harvard University Press.

Weaver, C. (1994). *Reading process and practice.* Portsmouth, NH: Heinemann.

Weaver, C. (1998). *Reconsidering a balanced approach to reading instruction.* Urbana, IL: National Council of Teachers of English.

Wells, G. (1986). *The meaning makers: Children learning language and using language to learn.* Portsmouth, NH: Heinemann.

Wilks, S. (1995). *Critical and creative thinking.* Portsmouth, NH: Heinemann.

Wilson, L., Malmgren, D., Ramage, S., & Schulz, L. (1993). *An integrated approach to learning.* Portsmouth, NH: Heinemann.

Understanding Literature 2

KEY TERMS

antagonist	plot
climax	poetry
conflict	problem resolution
denouement	protagonist
elements of literature	realistic fiction
episode	schemata
fantasy	setting
foreshadowing	story grammar
historical fiction	style
literary convention	theme
literary genre	traditional literature
nonfiction	

GUIDING QUESTIONS

Think about the types of books that were your favorites as a child; what genres did they belong to? Do you continue to enjoy the same genres that you enjoyed as a child? How has your taste changed? Understanding how your own literary tastes have developed and changed will help you to understand how children's literary tastes also develop and change. Keep in mind these guiding questions as you read the chapter:

1. Think about the plot and characters in the last book you read. How would you describe the plot? Who was the principal character? How was the character revealed?

2. How do the plots and characters in adult books differ from those in children's books?

3. Why do teachers and librarians need to understand the elements of literature?

OVERVIEW

Authors tell their stories through literary elements and story structures. Children learn these recurring patterns and structures through hearing and reading stories (Applebee, 1978). As they read, thoughtful readers learn how authors select, arrange, and structure language to tell stories and poems and give information (Alexander, 1981). Readers who can anticipate the genre patterns in literature can understand and respond more fully to it.

Genres are literary classifications or patterns of fiction, according to Van Vliet (1992); however, we also include nonfiction genre patterns. Books classified as belonging to a specific genre share certain characteristics, which follow the rules of that genre for the plot, characters, settings, tone, mood, and theme (Van Vliet, 1992). For example, the fantasy genre includes literature that has an element of make-believe: perhaps a place where magical things happen, a futuristic time setting, or any other fantastic element the author chooses to invent.

Understanding the patterns authors use to create stories enhances readers' understanding and response. This understanding comes about as a result of extensive reading—both being read to and reading independently. Reading enables readers to focus on the ways authors design stories, poems, and information. Readers build implicit understandings about the structural elements of story—plot, character setting, theme, and style—which they use to construct meaning (Holman & Harmon, 1986). This knowledge of literary elements and story structures is used in conjunction with prior experience to understand books.

Genre classifications, literary elements, and story structures (also called *story grammars*) commonly found in children's books are explored in this chapter. As you read, refer to the touchstone books mentioned throughout the chapter as models of excellent literature. Reading exemplary books and learning about their authors helps you develop insights into children's literature.

INTRODUCTION

"What is it about?" is the first question children usually ask about a book. Even before they understand the concept of genre, children want to have some notions about a book they are going to read or hear. The children in the opening vignette listen to a story and discuss their concepts of *real* and *make-believe*, concepts that further contribute to their understanding of fantasy. After experiencing a certain type of genre, readers construct understandings that can be used when reading other books. The vignette illustrates how teachers can develop genre understanding—in this case, fantasy—with primary-grade children.

VIGNETTE

Christopher wiggled with anticipation as Kathy Lee finished reading Jerdine Nolen's *Raising Dragons*.

"Is it real?" he asked.

"Do you mean, did the story really happen?" Ms. Lee asked.

"Yes."

Shannon said, "I know it didn't really happen. Dragons are not real. I've never seen one even in a zoo."

Then several other first graders chimed in, "We never saw a dragon!"

"How can we tell whether a story really happened?" Ms. Lee asked.

"When there are things in the story that are not real," Sarah answered.

"When characters do things that we know couldn't really happen," Wong Sun answered.

Tyler said, "We could go on the World Wide Web and find out if dragons are real and we could ask what they can do."

Andrew said, "Could dragons have another name like monsters or dinosaurs?"

"We could go on the Internet and ask questions about dragons, monsters, and dinosaurs. What questions would you like to ask?" Ms. Lee said.

The children identified these questions to research:

- Are there real dragons?
- Are they born from eggs?
- Do they breathe fire?
- Do they like to eat fish, frogs, eels, and insects?
- Do they like to hear bedtime stories?
- Can they fly?
- Could a person ride on a dragon's back?

(continued)

23

- Can a dragon fan the heat away from tomatoes?
- Could a dragon pop corn with his fire-eating breath?

The children compared the dragon in *Raising Dragons* with the monster in Snow's *The Monster Book of ABC Sounds* and with the unusual animals in the poetry book *The Originals: Animals That Time Forgot,* by Jane Yolen. After completing their research, the children decided there were some real dragons, but Hank was not a real one. They also thought they would like to find a dragon egg and have imaginary adventures with their own dragons, so they wrote stories about the things they would do with a dragon.

The following chart is another class comparison activity.

What Can Mice Do?

MAKE-BELIEVE MICE	REAL MICE
wear clothes	chew things up
bake cookies	run around the house
buy food at a grocery	get into food and eat it
talk to cats	do not have furniture
wear sneakers	do not wear clothes

After completing the chalkboard comparisons, Kathy read the poem "I Think Mice Are Rather Nice" by Rose Fyleman, which describes real mice. The children compared the poem to their chart. This experience helped them understand some of the characteristics of the fantasy genre.

GENRE IN CHILDREN'S LITERATURE

Genre is a French word that means kind or type. *Literary genres* are classifications of literature based on literary form and theme, works that share common characteristics or conventions. A *literary convention* is an element of form, style, or content that is universal throughout the genre (Morner & Rausch, 1991). Each genre of literature has such conventions or universals associated with its literary form. For instance, a convention reflected in picture books is the interaction between illustrations and text. These universal characteristics permit readers and reviewers to analyze and identify individual books as belonging to a particular genre, a basic step in critically analyzing a book (Frye, 1964). Once readers know that James and Deborah Howe's *Bunnicula* is classified as modern fantasy, they expect to find the literary conventions for a fantasy within the plot, theme, characterization, setting, and style.

Genre Classifications in Children's Literature

The fundamental patterns, conventions, or universals of literature occur repeatedly in all literature, including children's literature. Children's literature is usually classified into one of these genres: picture book, contemporary realistic fiction, historical fiction, modern fantasy, traditional literature, poetry, biography, and informational book. Table 2.1 summarizes the basic distinguishing characteristics of each genre.

The characters in *contemporary realistic fiction* could be real, the settings could exist, and the plots could happen, although they are products of an author's imagination rather than actual history or fact (Morner & Rausch, 1991). Phyllis Reynolds Naylor's *Shiloh* is realistic fiction about Marty, who likes to practice shooting his rifle in the West Virginia hills. Then he encounters a dog that appears to have been abused and discovers that he would do almost anything to save the dog. Most readers recognize this story could actually happen. Chapter 9 examines contemporary realistic fiction in detail.

In *historical fiction* the author tells a story associated with historical events, characters, incidents, or time periods. But historical setting alone is not enough to make the book worthwhile; it has to be a good story as well. Sally Walker tells a story set during the American Revolution in *The 18 Penny Goose.* The authentic historical setting creates a backdrop for this rich story about Letty and her family who flee from British soldiers. She leaves a note begging the soldiers not to hurt her gander, Solomon. When the family returns, Solomon is waddling about wearing a sack of coins as payment for the geese the soldiers did eat. Historical fiction is discussed in chapter 10.

Authors of well-written *modern fantasy* convince readers to suspend disbelief so they can believe in the unbelievable for the duration of a story. Fantasy is characterized by one or more imaginary elements,

TABLE 2.1
Distinguishing characteristics of various genres.

Genre	Distinguishing Characteristics
Picture Books	combine pictures and language or depend entirely on pictures
Contemporary Realistic Fiction	could happen in the contemporary world
Historical Fiction	set in the past
Modern Fantasy	could not happen in the real world; science fiction is fantasy set in the future
Traditional Literature	based on the oral tradition, the stories are spread through word of mouth rather than print
Poetry	intense, imaginative writing in rhythmic language structured in shorter lines and verses
Biography	based on the life of a person who has made a significant contribution to a culture
Informational Books	present information, explain

such as a make-believe world, characters who have magic powers, or imaginary events. In *Fog Magic* by Julia Saver, a young girl discovers a village she can only visit when there is a heavy fog. The characters are engaging. Both visuals and language mesh to tell this story for third and fourth graders.

Science fiction also belongs to the fantasy genre. Writers of science fiction often employ principles of science and physics as yet undiscovered (Morner & Rausch, 1991). In the book *Eva,* author Peter Dickinson describes a time when scientists learned to implant a human brain in the body of an animal. Modern fantasy is examined in chapter 8.

Traditional literature is based on oral tradition: stories such as *Cinderella* have been passed from one generation to the next by word of mouth and were not written down until scholars collected them (Morner & Rausch, 1991). Among the oral conventions traditional stories share are formulaic beginnings and endings: "once upon a time" and "they lived happily ever after." The settings are created in a sentence or two and the characters are stereotypes. Traditional literature is covered in chapter 8.

Intense and imaginative literature describes the *poetry* genre. Poets strive to capture the essence of an experience in imaginative language, as Christopher Myers captures the essence of a black street cat's life as it prowls city thoroughfares in his book *Black Cat.* His focused and vivid free verse expresses the gritty reality of urban life, creating a greater concentration of meaning than is found in prose (Morner & Rausch, 1991). Poetry differs visually from other types of literature in that it generally has short lines and is in verse form, often rhyming. Chapter 7 discusses poetry in detail.

Informational books are organized and structured around main ideas and supporting details that present information and explain in several styles, such as description, cause and effect, sequential order, comparison, and enumeration. Authors of informational books identify key ideas and themes to grab readers' attention and motivate them to learn more. Because informational books focus on actual events, places, people, and facts, authors and illustrators often use photographs and realistic drawings to illustrate these matcrials. Diane Hoyt-Goldsmith used photographs to inform readers in *Lacrosse: The National Game of the Iroquois.* Chapter 11 explores informational books in depth.

Genre as a Teaching Tool

Although books within a genre share common characteristics, each piece of literature represents a unique experience. Readers return again and again to books that are unique. For example, both *Little Red Riding Hood* and *Goldilocks and the Three Bears* are traditional literature, but each story has distinct qualities. Literally hundreds of versions of these tales exist, and each version has distinctive characteristics. Usually the variants reflect the culture in which the story originated.

The genre approach to literature is a valid, time-honored approach to structuring children's experiences and is commonly used in literature textbooks and children's literature programs (Norton, 1995; Stewig, 1988; Van Vliet, 1992). In the genre approach to teaching literature, students learn to understand form and content in books through hearing and reading from the various genre. Gradually, they learn to expect different forms in the various genre: a story that actually happened will differ from a fantasy. In time, readers learn to recognize the strategies authors use to give credibility to their particular book, identifying the way in which E. B. White grounds the beginning of *Charlotte's Web* in reality to prepare readers for the fantastic elements introduced later in the story.

As they learn to recognize authors' strategies through their many experiences with literature, readers develop a frame of reference or schema for literature that they integrate with the author's cues to construct meanings appropriate to the reader's specific context of memories based on experience. Schemata are clusters of experience and knowledge about a given topic (Pearson & Johnson, 1977). These cognitive structures encompass readers' concepts, beliefs, expectations, and processes; virtually everything from a reader's experience goes into constructing meaning.

The vignette in the box shows Jeremy, a fifth-grade student, demonstrating how his knowledge of literary elements functions when reading a novel. Jeremy is an active reader whose understanding of the language of narrative and narrative structure gave him this confidence (Tierney, 1990). He anticipated the story elements that appeared in the book because he had read and heard many other stories (Dias, 1987). From his many experiences with books, he had developed a frame of reference for literature. Like other experienced readers, he anticipated that the story and the story conflict would make sense and he expected the author to say something of consequence, which focused his comprehension (Adams & Collins, 1986).

Teachers use their explicit understanding of literary elements to guide students' experiences with literature as they explore the elements of fiction and nonfiction. The teacher in the vignette encouraged Jeremy to compare *Black Whiteness: Admiral Byrd Alone in the Antarctic* with a book of recognized quality to enlarge his understanding. Comparing and contrasting

how ideas are expressed in various literary forms and the characters, plots, settings, styles, and themes in a variety of books cultivate students' understanding of the elements of literature and enhance their appreciation of how the literary experience operates (Sebesta & Iverson, 1975). Jeremy's teacher could have suggested that he compare this with fiction, nonfiction, biographies, or poetry on the same topic to enrich his understanding.

VIGNETTE

Jeremy Hamilton closed his copy of Robert Burleigh's *Black Whiteness* and thrust his hand in the air. His fifth-grade teacher, Robert Morse, asked, "What is it, Jeremy?"

"This book has just one character, but it has more than one conflict."

"Why do you think this?" asked Mr. Morse.

"Well he fought the environment in the Antarctic, but he also battled loneliness, and he was so sick that he almost died, so he fought illness."

"Do you think *Black Whiteness* has more conflicts than other books you have read?" Mr. Morse responded.

Well, I just read *The Great Gilly Hopkins,*" Jeremy said. "I guess it had several conflicts too, but there were more characters in it."

"What were the conflicts in that book?" Mr. Morse asked.

"Well Gilly had conflicts with Mrs. Trotter, Agnes, her teacher, and the social worker. Her mother and grandmother had conflicts. Oh! I just remembered. Gilly had conflicts within herself, too," he answered.

"But, Richard Byrd's conflicts were not with people, they were with things that weren't obvious."

Mr. Morse asked, "Do Richard Byrd's conflicts seem less important than Gilly's?"

"No, if anything they seem more important because they almost took his life and the conflicts were more difficult to battle than more concrete conflicts," Jeremy responded.

"How do you think the conflicts changed Richard Byrd?"

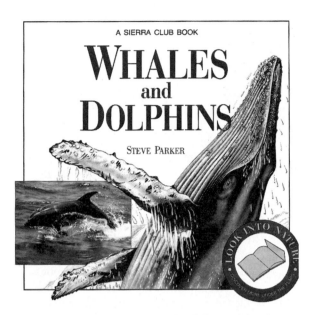

A SIERRA CLUB BOOK

WHALES and DOLPHINS

STEVE PARKER

Special fold-out pages in this book feature the drama of a Baleen whale swallowing hundreds of krill in one gulp and an Irrawaddy dolphin giving birth.

LITERARY ELEMENTS

Joseph Conrad (1922) tells us that the novelist's aim is "to make you hear, to make you feel—it is, before all, to make you see." Narrative style is a way of organizing human experience that authors employ to help readers see their stories (Hardy, 1977). In much the same way that readers use their own lives as a basis for understanding literature, writers create plot, character, setting, and theme out of their own experiences.

Authors build events into coherent sequences highlighting dramatic events to tell an exciting story. Even when telling true or nonfiction stories, writers organize the events, which would otherwise be too chaotic to form a coherent story. In the process, authors take liberties with reality, just as memories do when we reflect on experiences. We remember the high points in life—the dramatic events.

Plot

A *plot* is a chain of interacting events, just as life is. Each of us is involved in many plots as our lives unfold. Children need books where the story is the center of the writer's attention, where the plot actually matters (Wadham, 1999). These various plots are the raw material for stories. Each story leads to another because life happens that way. Some people believe plot is the most important element of a story (Wadham, 1999).

The plot holds the story together, making it a critical element in literature. Plot is the plan of action, the events in the story that are linked by cause and effect. Wyndham and Madison (1988) describe plot as "a plan of action devised to achieve a definite and much desired end—through cause and effect" (p. 81). Their definition is similar to Giblin's (1990), who calls plot the blueprint of the story, or the path it will follow from beginning to end. In developing plot, the author weaves a logical series of events explaining why events occur. In *Where the Wild Things Are,* Maurice Sendak tells readers that Max was sent to bed without his supper because he acted like a "wild thing," which initiates the cause-and-effect chain in this adroitly woven plot. "A well-crafted plot, like some remarkable clockwork, can fascinate us by its sheer ingenuity" (Alexander, 1981, p. 5).

Credible plots unfold gradually, building a logical cause-and-effect sequence for story incidents. Story events inserted without adequate preparation make a contrived and uninteresting plot. Story characters act out the causes and effects of story incidents. *Cause* establishes the main character's line of action to solve a problem, get out of a situation, or reach a certain goal; *effect* is what happens to the character as a result of the action taken.

Storytellers can make all sorts of imaginary events credible by laying the groundwork for them (Alexander, 1981). *Foreshadowing* is the groundwork that prepares for future story events, the planted clues in situations, events, characters, and conflicts. In Ken Kesey's *Little Tricker the Squirrel Meets Big Double the Bear* we find two instances of foreshadowing in the book's title. First, the squirrel is named "Little Tricker," and he is tricky in this story. Second, the mention of Big Double the Bear identifies the antagonist.

Interesting plots usually have unique characteristics because children enjoy stories that grab their attention. *Where the Wild Things Are* begins with a common incident, a child who misbehaves and consequently must go to bed without supper. The uniqueness of the story is introduced when Max escapes this punishment through his imagination. He goes to where the wild things are, where he can be as wild as he likes. He has fun for a while, but discovers he prefers to be "where

A Civil War soldier writes the sights, sounds, and feelings of war in his diary.

Conflict

Story conflicts create tensions that arouse readers' suspense (Giblin, 1990). The characters in stories with interesting plots have difficulties to overcome, problems to solve, and goals to achieve. Believable conflicts and problems provide the shape, drama, tension, and movement in a story (Bond, 1984). *Conflict* is "the struggle that grows out of the interplay of two opposing forces in a plot" (Holman & Harmon, 1986, p. 107). One of these opposing forces is usually the main character in the story, who struggles to get what he or she wants and is opposed vigorously, either by someone who wants the same thing or by circumstances that stand in the way of the goal (Wyndham & Madison, 1988).

A conflict implies struggle, but it also implies that a motivation exists behind the conflict or a goal that will be achieved through the conflict. The central problem or conflict must remain out of the main character's reach until near the end of the story. Nevertheless, readers are aware that a fateful decision is at hand that will precipitate a crisis in the principal character's affairs, but the outcome of this struggle is never certain.

Chris Van Allsburg creates an unusual and suspenseful conflict in *Jumanji.* Tension is introduced early in the story through a note warning the principal characters that once they begin playing a jungle-adventure board game they cannot stop until the game is completed. Heedless of the warning, the children begin playing the game, which rapidly gets out of hand as a python appears on the mantle and a rhinoceros crashes through the living room. They desperately need to stop the game—their parents are returning and the house is in chaos!

Types of conflict.   Writers commonly involve characters in four major types of conflict:

1. a struggle against nature;
2. a struggle against another person, usually the antagonist;
3. a struggle against society; and
4. a struggle for mastery by two elements within the person (Holman & Harmon, 1986).

Although the four types of conflict are distinct in literature, most stories have more than one type of conflict. In *Hatchet* Gary Paulsen tells the story of a boy fighting to obtain food and shelter to survive (struggle with

someone loves him best." The illustrations give a unique quality to the story: as Max sails off in an imaginary boat, his surroundings grow larger and larger, and when he leaves the wild things to return to his own bedroom, they grow smaller again to show that he is leaving the land of the wild things.

Some enjoyable books begin more slowly. In *The Secret Garden* by Frances Hodgson Burnett the protagonist waits until nearly halfway through the book to enter the garden. Nevertheless, the book is so popular that it became a very successful Broadway play and a motion picture. Although children's likes and dislikes are not entirely predictable, interesting, well-structured plots are important to fine literature. The elements that comprise interesting plots include conflict, climax, and denouement.

Foster's most important war is within himself.

nature) after he is involved in a plane crash that killed the pilot. His struggle is one of trial and error because he lacks the knowledge that would help him, but his perseverance enables him to survive. This character also has internal conflicts because he has just learned that his parents plan to divorce.

As shown in these examples, story characters often have conflicts within themselves, which may or may not be the only or the most obvious conflict. In *Foster's War* by Carolyn Reeder, 11-year-old Foster is caught up in the effects of the World War II. Foster struggles with the inner battle he wages against his stern, demanding father. He also struggles with himself when he asks, "Which are you more afraid of [he asks himself], an air raid or your father?" (p. 82). Moreover, Foster is conflicted with society because his best friend is confined to a Japanese internment camp. In *The View from Saturday* by E. L. Konigsburg, a sixth-grade team competes in an academic bowl contest that leads to conflicts with other students and among the team members. The protagonist in *Out of the Dust* by Karen

Hesse is in conflict with both herself and her father regarding her mother's death.

Climax

The main character's most intense struggle occurs at the climax, which is the highest point of interest in the story, the point at which readers learn how the conflict is resolved. A strong conflict keeps readers turning pages until the climax because they want to know whether the protagonist makes the right decision.

The Village by the Sea by Paula Fox contains an excellent example of conflict and climax. When sending Emma to spend two weeks with an aunt and uncle whom she barely knows, Emma's father warns her that her Aunt Bea "can be a terror" and "make your life a misery" (p. 5), thus preparing readers for her conflict with Aunt Bea. Emma overhears Aunt Bea and Uncle Crispin quarreling and encounters Aunt Bea's acerbic tongue, which heightens the conflict. Eventually, Emma escapes to the nearby seashore to alleviate her tension and finds a friend. Together they build a village from shells and bits of things that have washed up. When Aunt Bea destroys the village, Emma experiences internal conflicts. However, the conflicts lead to a climax when Emma reads Aunt Bea's diary and discovers that Aunt Bea realizes that she was wrong.

Denouement

Denouement is the falling action that occurs during the unwinding of the story problem after the climax. This part of the story ties up the various threads of the plot into a satisfying, logical ending, but not necessarily a "happily ever after" ending. In *The Village by the Sea,* Aunt Bea was an unhappy person throughout her life and an alcoholic for many years. Serious problems such as alcoholism are not solved in two weeks, the time frame of this story. Emma grew and developed through her experiences and achieved closure regarding Aunt Bea's actions, thus creating a satisfying ending. The conflict resolution is revealed when her lump of hate dissolves and she is able to tell her parents about building the village by the sea.

Types of plot

Dramatic and episodic plots are the most common types of plot structure, but several others appear in children's books, such as parallel plot and cumulative plot, which appear often in traditional literature and picture books.

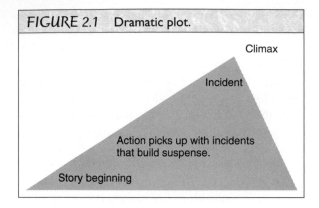

FIGURE 2.1 Dramatic plot.

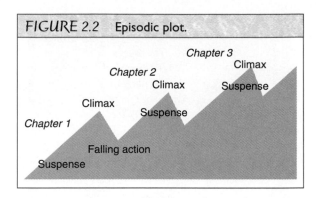

FIGURE 2.2 Episodic plot.

Dramatic plot. *Dramatic plots* establish setting, characters, and conflicts with fast-moving action that grabs children's attention and creates enough tension to hold their interest until the exciting climax. (Figure 2.1 illustrates a dramatic plot line.) Vivien Alcock creates a good dramatic plot in the mystery *Stranger at the Window.* She quickly establishes tension when 11-year-old Lesley sees a strange child peering at her from the attic next door. The tension in this book grows when three neighbor children accuse Lesley of hallucinating. However, their secret is revealed—they are hiding a frightened illegal immigrant.

Episodic plot. *Episodic plots* are quite similar to dramatic plots. The major difference is that in an episodic plot each chapter or part has its own "mini-plot," or a story within the main story. Each episode or incident is at least loosely linked to the same main character or characters, has a problem relating to the total book, and is unified by the common theme of the main story. (Figure 2.2 illustrates an episodic plot.) In Dick King-Smith's *The School Mouse,* Flora, a misunderstood mouse, learns to read, but no one can see the use for her ability. So Flora has to convince them that reading is important. She does so after finding a bag labeled "poison." Each chapter is an episode in Flora's efforts to become a scholar and her efforts to prove the value of her skill. The overall theme of this book is a misunderstood student and the importance of being able to read.

Parallel plot. In *parallel plots,* which appear only rarely in children's literature, two plots unfold side by side and are intertwined into a single story. In *Holes,* Louis Sachar's story line moves back and forth between Stanley's life in a juvenile facility and his grandfather's story of bad luck.

Cumulative plot. *Cumulative plots* unfold through a pattern of repetition in which characters or events are added to each other with each new character or event paralleling a previous character or event, building toward a climax that solves the problem. Cumulative plot stories, which usually appear in traditional literature or picture books, often contain repeated refrains. *King Bidgood's in the Bathtub,* a picture book written and illustrated by Audrey Wood, tells about a fun-loving king who refuses to get out of his bathtub to rule his kingdom despite the pleas of his court. This problem makes sense to children, who often feel the same way. Each character tries to lure the king out of the bathtub with a different ploy but all are met with the same refrain: the king will deal with that problem "in the tub." When the knight announces that it is time to battle, the king counters with "today we battle in the tub." Finally, after the king rejects the efforts of all of the adults to get him out of the bathtub, a pageboy pulls the plug and solves the problem. The plot conclusion is satisfying because children enjoy solving problems that baffle adults.

Characters

Good authors have the ability to create believable, memorable characters (Holman & Harmon, 1986). These characters must seem real, even though they are imaginary and different from real people, so that people will want to know them very well (Silvey, 1988). Readers care about believable characters with whom they can identify and feel truly involved. Authors use a variety of strategies to make characters live and breathe in readers' minds. One is telling the details of a character's thoughts, feelings, motivations, and attitudes. Another is depicting characters in ways consistent with their social background, educational level, and age.

Portraying the human qualities, emotions, desires, hopes, dreams, and motivations that distinguish characters as individuals creates memorable characters.

Characters are essential to stories because they propel the plot. They are the driving force behind the story that makes things happen (Stewig, 1988) and the actors who direct and act out the plot. In *Shades of Gray* by Carolyn Reeder, Will's family is lost in the Civil War and he is forced to live with his Uncle Jed, a pacifist. Readers learn how Will thinks and feels about being thrust into a situation that challenges his basic beliefs; they become acquainted with Uncle Jed through Will's thoughts and Uncle Jed's actions. The drama is drawn from the series of conflicts between a man who believes in peace and a boy who believes that fighting solves disagreements.

Developing characters

Like many chapter books, *What Jamie Saw,* by Carolyn Coman, includes several characters, but the protagonist is the principal or central character idea or concept that is the focus of the plot. The central character is presented in greater detail than other characters. The antagonist is a character who is in conflict with the protagonist. The antagonist is sometimes a villain and sometimes a foil character, one whose traits provide a complete contrast to those of the protagonist. An antagonist lends excitement and suspense to a story but is developed with less detail than a protagonist.

The detailed information given about the protagonist usually leads readers to identify with and follow this character throughout the story. Many readers can relate to Jamie's fear of Van in *What Jamie Saw* after he wakens Jamie by throwing his baby sister. Jamie's fears about safety, school, lack of money, and a car that will not start could overwhelm him. However, Jamie practices his magic tricks and excites his teacher's interest, so life is good until Van turns up!

Jamie is a well-developed protagonist with three-dimensional or round characteristics. Well-rounded characters have complex, multifaceted personalities that readers come to know as they learn about their individual traits, revealed through the trouble in their lives, which never run smoothly. If there were no trouble, there would be no story (Wyndham & Madison, 1988). Well-rounded characters make readers care and want to know how the characters will resolve their predicaments. Readers come to know Jamie so well

that they can anticipate his thoughts and actions. They know when he will practice magic tricks, how he will react to his teacher, and when he will protect his mother and sister.

Supporting characters

Not all the characters are developed with the same depth as the protagonist. Supporting characters are flat or less round because they lack the depth and complexity of a real person. These characters are built around a single dominant trait or quality representing a personality type (Morner & Rausch, 1991). Flat characters are needed as part of the interactive background; their primary function is to advance the protagonist's development. Fully portraying these characters would make the story too complex for children. Supporting characters often include the protagonist's best friend, a teacher, or parents. In *What Jamie Saw,* his mother, teacher, baby sister, and Earl are flat characters.

Some flat characters are stereotypes who lack individualizing characteristics and instead represent traits generally attributed to a social group as a whole (Morner & Rausch, 1991). They exhibit a few traits representative of conventional mothers, fathers, friends, or teachers and are developed quickly with brief bits of information so that drawing their characters does not interrupt the story flow. In traditional literature, all characters are stereotypes representing traits such as good, evil, innocence, and wisdom.

Dynamic and static characters

Dynamic characters.   **Dynamic or developed characters** change significantly during the course of a story as incidents cause their personalities to emerge and expand. In *What Jamie Saw,* seeing Van throw his baby sister forever changes Jamie, and his continuing nightmares about the experience show its dramatic force. But Jamie comes to know himself better and to see Van more realistically when he does show up.

Katherine Paterson's Gilly is a well-developed dynamic character in *The Great Gilly Hopkins.* Gilly begins as a rebellious, unmanageable foster child who gradually comes to understand her foster mother, Mrs. Trotter. Later Gilly meets and comes to know her grandmother. Readers see Gilly develop into a sensitive girl who is able to tell Mrs. Trotter she loves her. Although some readers do not like Gilly at the outset, they come to view her more sympathetically as she develops.

Static characters. *Static or delineated story characters* are the opposite of developed characters. They seem impervious to experience and remain essentially the same throughout the story. These are the "Peter Pan" characters who never grow up. The principal character in Astrid Lindgren's *Pippi Longstocking* is static. Pippi, a 9-year-old Swedish girl, is well-rounded and fully described. She lives alone with a monkey and a horse and has many unusual adventures. Although her adventures are novel, she does not change; she is always irrepressible. Not all static characters are juvenile Peter Pan types, however. Charlotte in *Charlotte's Web* solves Wilbur's problem and is helpful to animals in the barnyard, but her character remains the same throughout the story.

Character interaction

Authors use any number of characterizations that work together to create vivid and interesting stories. For instance, the fantasy *The Music of Dolphins* by Karen Hesse has a variety of characters: Mila, the girl who was raised by dolphins; Doctor Beck, the researcher who teaches Mila language and music; Sandy, a helper who feeds and watches her; Shay, a little girl who also is different; and Justin, the beautiful human boy. Mila is the most developed character in this story. The other characters are developed as they interact with Mila and the other story characters. Although these characters are introduced in less detail than Mila, the author uses each one to teach her about locked doors and broken promises, disappointment, and betrayal. Each character, even those who are not drawn with the same in-depth detail as Mila, contributes to her education about what it means to be human and causes her to long for her dolphin family. Readers understand that the characters are trying to help Mila adjust to her new environment, but her life with the dolphins did not teach her what it means to be human. Mila's dolphin family consists of one-dimensional characters. Her longing for the comfort of her dolphin family and her safe ocean home foreshadows her decision to return to them.

Revealing characters through narration

Readers come to know characters the way they come to know an acquaintance—from the way the character talks and acts. Character traits are revealed through a number of narration techniques. First-person narration, in which the main character is usually the narrator, allows readers to infer traits from what the main character says and how others react. Similarly, a limited narrator may tell the story from the main character's point of view. An omniscient narrator, on the other hand, may tell all about the main character and also tell about others from their points of view.

Walter Dean Myers uses a first-person narrator in *Me, Mop, and the Moondance Kid* to reveal the main character, Tommy, and his brother, Moondance:

> Most of the kids at the Academy are young. Mop and me were just about the oldest. When kids get to be eleven or twelve, they're usually sent out to another home. I would have been sent out to Tiverhead except for Moondance. They like to keep brothers together. (p. 2)

Authors often use conversations to help readers know characters; manner of speaking and subject matter are revealing, especially when combined with the characters' actions, and build the readers' understanding of the characters. The following interchange occurs between Tommy and his brother Moondance after Moondance drops his teddy bear, Dinky, in the toilet and stops it up. Tommy rescues the bear and unstops the toilet.

> "The toilet's still stopped up, isn't it?"
>
> "I don't think so," I said.
>
> Mom gave me one of those is-something-strange-going on looks and went into the bathroom. She flushed the toilet and it worked fine.
>
> That night just before I went to sleep, . . . Moondance came to my bed and shook me.
>
> "What's the matter?" I asked.
>
> "Thanks a lot for saving Dinky," he said.
>
> "We had to save Dinky," I said. "He's your best friend."
>
> "No," he said. "You're my best friend. Dinky's my second-best friend." (p. 49)

Authors sometimes reveal aspects of characters' personalities through their thoughts. Tommy's thoughts reveal some of his character in this quotation:

> I didn't get any hits because I was nervous on account of Rocky. He was hanging around watching the game. I was standing near the fence talking to Mop when he came up on the other side of the fence. (p. 35)

A character's traits may be revealed through the eyes of another character. Sheila Klass uses this technique in *Kool Ada*:

> Since I cut school fairly regular, I didn't spend much time with Ms. Walker. But I already understood her

better'n any other teacher I ever had. It wasn't hard. Ms. Walker said what she meant and she meant whatever she said. Every time. She was famous all over the school for that. If she gave her word—promise or punishment—you could count on it. No use pouting, or whining, or apologizing. (p. 8)

Character traits, descriptions, and actions are usually developed through illustrations in picture books. In these books, the words and the pictures are integrated to reveal character. In *Marven of the Great North Woods,* written by Kathryn Lasky, we see Marven going off alone on a train headed for a logging camp, not knowing if he will ever see his family again. The illustrations make his loneliness among the enormous woodsmen and the endless snow apparent.

Setting

Setting is the time and place of a story. Vivid settings give a story reality; they give readers a sense of being there. The importance of setting varies from story to story. In some it creates the stage for the characters' actions, whereas in others it is indefinite, a universal setting that is secondary to the story. The story itself dictates the importance of setting.

When creating setting, authors choose a location (an urban, rural, or small town and a country) and time (past, present, or future). Contemporary settings take place in the here and now, whereas historical settings occur in the past—for example, *Marven of the Great North Woods* is set in Duluth, Minnesota, in 1918. Marven's family sends him away to keep him safe from the influenza epidemic that struck that city.

Once the general location and time are identified, authors decide on details of a specific time and place: perhaps a very specific designation such as a certain district in London, England, in the summer of 1993, or a more universal setting requiring fewer details and a more indefinite time and place. Time and location dictate many of the rest of the details of the story: the type of home and furniture, the scenery, and the flora and fauna of the surrounding countryside. The social environment, foods, newspapers, magazines, and games are all aspects of the setting. Authors depict setting through sensory imagery, using visual, auditory, tactile, and olfactory images.

In fantasy, the time and place of a story may be a make-believe setting that no one has ever seen. Writers of fantasy create imaginary worlds, people, and events.

For instance, Philippa Pearce creates a clock that strikes 13, signaling the appearance of a garden that does not exist at other times, in *Tom's Midnight Garden.* This fantasy garden is a playground for Tom and his friend, who is an old woman during the day and a young girl at night. On the other hand, setting in fantasy may be as ordinary as everyday life, as it is in E. B. White's *Charlotte's Web.*

Setting is especially significant in historical fiction; these stories depend on setting perhaps more than any other genre. Authors must carefully research such common things as food, clothing, housing, social attitudes, and language to ascertain the appropriate details for the historical period. Authentic historical settings permit readers to move into other times and places to develop greater understandings about them. For example, Bruchac re-creates a little-known incident in U.S. history when Native Americans and the Quakers cooperated in *The Arrow Over the Door.*

Developing setting

Illustrations develop setting in some books, whereas others portray it through words. Some stories are closely tied to the setting, whereas others are not. Kate Banks's book *And if the Moon Could Talk* is a book closely related to setting and Georg Hallensleben's paintings combine with the language to convey the mood of nightfall.

Settings for fantasy are a special challenge: authors must not only imagine places and times that do not exist, they must make readers see them, as Donn Kushner does in the following excerpt from *A Book Dragon:*

> Nonesuch was—and still is, for that matter—the last of a family of dragons that lived over five hundred years ago in a limestone hill, honeycombed with caverns. . . . The dark mouth of the family's cavern opened towards an ugly tangled scrub forest that ended, at the lap of the hill, in an evil bog. (p. 2)

Creating mood

The mood or tone of a story is created through the setting. The author uses words and the artist uses illustrations to create the feelings readers should experience. Consider the following excerpt from Ruth White's *Sweet Creek Holler:*

> The holler was skinny between the mountains. The road was chiseled out of the side of one mountain base. . . . Houses were stuck on the sides of the hills,

Counting is fun way out in the desert.

many with stilts underneath to prop them up level. Some were made of cinder blocks, a few were whiteboard, or brick, but most of them were tar-paper shacks. (p. 6)

The words and phrases used here—such as *skinny, chiseled, stuck, sides of the hills,* and *tar-paper shacks*—create a feeling for the hard life in a depressed area of the United States. These words and phrases express the author's interpretation of the significance of the place and time. Moreover, the author's language reflects the tone and theme of the story (Sebesta & Iverson, 1975).

Theme

The word *theme* identifies a statement about the story that steps back from the literal interpretation (Lehr, 1991). Theme is the important idea, the meaning, the significance behind a story. It is a central or dominating idea in a work. In nonfiction prose it may be thought of as the general topic of discussion, the sub-

ject of the discourse, or the thesis. In poetry, fiction, and drama it is the abstract concept that is made concrete through its representation in person, action, and image in the work. No proper theme is simply a subject or an activity. The theme of a story has both a subject and a predicate; for example, vice cannot be used as a theme without some proposition about vice posited by the author. For instance, the statement "vice seems more interesting than virtue but turns out to be destructive" (Holman & Harman, 1986) is an adequate theme because it has both a subject (vice) and a position on the subject.

Theme is the melody, the motive, or the dominant idea developed in the story (Wyndham & Madison, 1988). Fine writers weave theme subtly into their stories. Children, like adults, prefer authors who trust their readers to infer theme from story events, characters, and setting rather than preaching or explicitly stating the theme. In *Charlotte's Web,* the theme emerges through the animals' actions and the cycle of life and death, and the continuity of life is paralleled in the cycle of the seasons. Readers experience the dominant idea that death is as necessary as birth; both are part of the life cycle. Every event and every character in the story resonates with this theme.

Multiple themes

Stories may have multiple themes that intertwine as elements of a story. In the book *When Mama Comes Home Tonight* by Eileen Spinelli, multiple themes emerge. A young child is lonely for Mama to come home and feels like she will never get home. Then Mama comes home and they celebrate their time together before bedtime, which is a soothing theme for any child who has a working mother.

The most common themes in children's books are associated with fundamental human needs, including:

1. the need to love and be loved;
2. the need to belong;
3. the need to achieve;
4. the need for security—material, emotional, spiritual; and
5. the need to know (Wyndham & Madison, 1988).

These universal themes are expressed through the ideas, characters, plots, and settings developed in fiction, nonfiction, and poetry.

Children's response to theme

Building meaning is a complex developmental process. A 3-year-old understands a story differently than an 8-year-old; younger children can, however, identify theme. In kindergarten, children are "able to identify thematically matched books 80% of the time for realistic fiction and 35% for folktales, thus indicating that thematic identification is a fairly early developmental strategy," but older children are better able to talk about the themes in stories (Lehr, 1991, p. 67). Developmentally, children move from responding at a concrete level to a more abstract response. Children who have more exposure to literature are better able to talk about meaning in books.

Themes are subject to readers' interpretation, so different individuals may identify different themes in the same book; the dominant idea or theme, however, should be apparent to readers. Individuals respond differently to the same story because their response is based on their individual experience, which they use to interpret and understand the material. Individuals remember what is important to them and see what they expect to see or are capable of seeing. Readers who have experiences with their fathers' girlfriends may interpret *Totally Uncool* by Janice Levy in different ways: those who have had positive experiences with the new people in their parents' lives would respond differently from those who have had negative experiences. The varying responses of students are explored in greater depth in chapter 4.

Many stories offer readers opportunities to respond at different levels of understanding. Readers can take as much or as little from literature as their developmental level and experiential background permit. *Charlotte's Web* offers many layers of meaning to readers. Younger children are apt to understand this book as an animal fantasy. Older children are ready to apprehend the cycle of life and death, and adults will recognize the irony in a situation that gives one character credit for the creativity of another. This is why we recommend using *Charlotte's Web* in the third or fourth grade when children are ready to understand its major theme.

Some adults mistake sentimental books that reflect on the "cuteness" of childhood, such as Joan Walsh Anglund's *Morning Is a Little Child,* as books for children. These books, however, are about children rather than for them. Nostalgia rarely appeals to children, who are usually future oriented. Such books are more appropriate as gifts for adults who enjoy childhood memories.

Style

Authors express their style through the language they use to shape their stories: the words they choose, the sentences they craft, the dialogue they create, and the amount and nature of the descriptive passages. Authors arrange words in ways that express their individuality. "Style is a combination of the two elements: the idea to be expressed and the individuality of the author" (Holman & Harmon, 1986, p. 487). No two styles are exactly alike. Ultimately, the author's use of language determines the lasting quality of a book (Saxby & Winch, 1987).

Language devices

Author style is most apparent in the language devices used to achieve special effects or meanings, stimulating their readers through use of figurative language, imagery, allusion, hyperbole, understatement, and symbolism. Readers then use these devices to infer and connote individual interpretations based upon their experiential background. *Connotation* refers to an association or emotional response a reader attaches to a particular word that goes beyond the dictionary definition or *denotation*; it is a meaning drawn from personal experience. For example, many people associate warm, loving feelings with the word *mother* that go far beyond the literal denotation of a female parent.

Figurative language.   Figurative language is connotative, sensory language that incorporates one or more of the various figures of speech such as simile, metaphor, repetition, and personification (Holman & Harmon, 1986). Figurative language is used to develop character, show mood, and create setting. Katherine Paterson uses figurative language to great effect in *The Great Gilly Hopkins.* Gilly moves to Mrs. Trotter's home, the latest in a long line of foster homes. There she meets William Ernest, another foster child living in the same home: "He was rattling the tray so hard that the milk glass was threatening to jump the edge" (p. 47). Paterson's figurative language vividly shows that William Ernest is a scared, nervous, timid person.

Her figurative language also creates mood when she describes Gilly's new foster home: "Inside, it was dark and crammed with junk. Everything seemed to need dusting" (p. 4). The words *dark, junk,* and *dust* have connotative meanings for most people that conjure visions of a dank, uninviting place. This clearly gives the reader a sense of Gilly's negative feelings about her new foster home without explicitly stating "Gilly had negative feelings about her new home," which is a drab and uninteresting way of conveying meaning.

Imagery.   Sensory language widens the mind's eye and helps the reader build images that go beyond the ordinary to new and exciting experiences. These experiences can be the sensory kind in which one sees or hears new things; they can be an intellectual kind in which one thinks new things (Saxby & Winch, 1987). Dr. Seuss's book *Hooray for Diffendoofer Day!* illustrates the role of imagery. In this noisy book the pages are full of movement and unusual, dramatic characters such as the teacher who teaches yelling and the one who teaches smelling!

Allusion.   *Allusion* is a figure of speech that makes indirect reference to a historical or literary figure, event, or object (Holman & Harmon, 1986). In an amusing passage, Gilly alludes to godfathers and the Mafia in reference to William Ernest, but it is the direct contrast to William Ernest's timid personality that makes the idea even funnier. "An inspiration came to [Gilly]. . . . It was William Ernest. She laughed out loud at the pleasure of it. Baby-Face Teague, the frog-eyed filcher. Wild-eyed William, the goose-brained godfather. . . . The midget of the Mafia" (p. 48). Paterson also uses allusion to describe Mrs. Trotter: "Trotter smiled impatiently and closed the door quickly. When she turned back toward Gilly, her face was like Mount Rushmore stone" (p. 97), thereby demonstrating that Trotter is impassive to Gilly's efforts to antagonize her.

Hyperbole.   *Hyperbole* is exaggeration used to make a point, as shown in this passage: "Gilly gave her the 300-watt smile that she had designed for melting the hearts of foster parents. 'Never better!' She spoke the words with just the right musical lilt" (p. 48). In this instance, the size and impact of Gilly's smile and the sound of her voice are exaggerated to make the point that she is trying to be congenial with her foster parent.

Understatement.   *Understatement* is almost the opposite of hyperbole. It plays down a situation or person and is often used for comic effect. Gilly deliberately wrecks her own hair with chewing gum to antagonize Trotter, who ignores it. Gilly then shakes her head dramatically to draw attention, to which Trotter calmly says, "You got a tic or something, honey?" (p. 18). Trotter's understatement creates a comical situation—she appears not to notice Gilly's dreadful hair—which is embellished as Gilly tries to remove the chewing gum, further ruining her hair.

Symbolism.   *Symbols* are persons, objects, situations, actions, or words that operate on two levels of meaning. A symbol has both a literal meaning—a denotation—and an inferential meaning, one that is implied. Gilly's mother is described as a "flower child," which literally refers to someone who lived a free-spirited lifestyle in the 1960s, but Paterson uses the phrase as a symbol in two separate instances: (1) "Miss Ellis suddenly looked tired. 'God help the children of the flower children,' she said" (p. 119); and (2) "Her hair was long, but it was dull and stringy—a dark version of Agnes Stokes's, which had always needed washing. A flower child gone to seed" (p. 145). In the first instance, Paterson implies that the children of flower children need help that will not be forthcoming from these free spirits. The second suggests that Gilly's mother is stuck in an adolescent stage of development and continues to live as she did in her younger days, in spite of the fact that she is growing older.

Point of view

Point of view is the perspective or stance from which the author tells a story. It is the eye and mind through which the action is perceived (Morner & Rausch, 1991). The point of view determines the vocabulary, sentences, and attitudes expressed. Essentially, authors can use two general narrative points of view, first person and third person. A first-person narrator actually appears within the story and tells the tale using the pronoun "I." The first-person point of view has some advantages; one is its conversational nature, which makes readers feel they know the narrator. First-person narrators tell the reader what they are thinking and feeling, giving readers an intimate feeling. Plot, setting, and character are more likely to be unified when the main character says, "This is what happened to me, this is where it happened, this is how I felt" (Sebesta & Iverson, 1975, p. 78).

Vivien Alcock chose first-person narration for the main character in *The Monster Garden,* Frankie Stein.

Frankie tells the readers about the problems she faces in feeding and caring for a monster she has grown and must keep secret from the hostile world. Frankie, the protagonist, graphically describes the monster, bringing it to life for readers. She says:

> There was no safe place for Monnie anywhere on land. It was too large and alien and gentle to live among us. It stood up, a huge royal figure with its shining crest. Perhaps it would make its own kingdom under the sea, a kinder, friendlier place than we have made on earth. (p. 134)

A third-person narrator, unlike a first-person narrator, stands outside the story and tells the tale using pronouns such as *he, she,* and *they.* Third-person narration has two commonly used variations: omniscient perspective and limited omniscient perspective. Children's literature most frequently uses omniscient perspective to tell stories.

With omniscient perspective, the narrator sees all, knows all, and reveals all to the reader. This narrator has access to and reveals the thoughts and motives of all the characters, knows the present, past, and future, and also comments on or interprets the actions of all of the characters. A major advantage of this style lies in the unlimited scope and relative freedom a narrator has in unfolding the story. With omniscient perspective, authors can speak to readers directly, telling whatever they choose to tell or speaking over the heads of the characters in an aside to help readers understand the significance of an event or a character (Sebesta & Iverson, 1975). Dianne Snyder uses this point of view in her picture book *The Boy of the Three-Year Nap*:

> All day long the widow sewed silk kimonos for the rich ladies in town. As she worked, her head bobbed up and down, up and down, like the heads of the birds hunting for fish. . . . Her only son, Taro, was, oh, such a clever lad and as healthy as a mother could wish. But, alas! He was as lazy as a rich man's cat. All he did was eat and sleep, sleep and eat. (p. 7)

Throughout the story, the narrator makes asides to the reader that reveal her feelings. The author's style is just right for this tale.

Narrators with limited omniscience, on the other hand, focus on the thoughts of a single character and present the other characters externally (Morner & Rausch, 1991). In this approach, the author typically follows one character throughout the story, the reader knows only what this one character knows and sees only those incidents in which that character is involved. Judy Cox uses this style in the *Third Grade Pet.* Rosemary, the main character, is revolted when the class chooses a rat as a pet, but it gets worse. She is chosen to be "Rat keeper, for a whole week. It was like a nightmare come true" (p. 41). Rosemary changes her mind about the rat as she cares for it. The author's style in this book is just right for the story.

LITERARY EXPERIENCES THAT ENHANCE UNDERSTANDING

Literary experiences can motivate children to read, as well as enhance their understanding. Getting to know authors, their experiences, writing techniques, and interests are among the most powerful. Authors make their stories come alive with details, stylistic devices, genre, and the elements of literature. What writers create comes from hearsay, incidents, people, places, and truths they have experienced. Betsy Byars (1993) says, "I always put something of myself into my books, something that happened to me. Once . . . a wanderer came by the house and showed me how to brush my teeth with a cherry twig. That went in *The House of Wings.*"

Many writers describe themselves as storytellers. Paula Fox (1991) says:

> I am a storyteller and I have been one for more than 30 years. When I finish one story, I watch the drift in my head, and very soon am thinking about another story. All one's experience shapes one's stories. However, readers expect authors to take them "there" to help them recreate the writer's reality; what matters is what they make of it—what they do with it.

Simply reporting incidents and characters as they took place is not enough to draw in readers; the author must create illusions with the facts. Illusion—what writers make of their experiences—must convince readers that it is reality by resonating with their emotions and moving them to new feelings and insights (Alexander, 1981). The following vignette illustrates how getting acquainted with authors enhances the literary experience.

VIGNETTE

MY FIRST AUTHOR VISIT

Watching children in a local bookstore waiting to meet an author brought to mind my own first meeting with an author, Elizabeth Yates, at Ohio State University in the summer of 1963. She told about discovering the tombstone in a church cemetery that piqued her curiosity and her research that led her to write *Amos Fortune: Free Man.* I listened spellbound, as did everyone in the large audience.

Later someone asked where she got the ideas for her other books, and she shifted to telling about a forthcoming book, *Carolina's Courage,* and a buffalo-hide doll belonging to a little girl she knew. The doll, a family heirloom, was handed down from generation to generation along with the story of its origins. This doll and the family story became the impetus for *Carolina's Courage.* Later she told the story of another book that was based on a short newspaper clipping.

Of course, I eagerly read every book that Elizabeth Yates wrote. I thought about the ways she found ideas for her stories and the research she did to validate these stories. But, most of all, the beauty of her language and voice telling the stories made me want to help children experience the same excitement I felt that day. . . .

Discussion as Literary Experience

Although reading seems like a solitary activity, its social aspects become apparent when readers discuss their literary experiences. When a group of seven or eight students discusses a book they have all read, they stimulate one another to think about the story, enhancing the understanding and response of each person in the group. Moreover, each time a different group of children discusses a story, they bring up ideas that no one has mentioned. The elements of fiction and story grammar are useful concepts for guiding children's discussions of literature and writing experiences.

Teachers, librarians, parents, and other concerned adults serve as children's guides to literary experiences. They cannot teach literature; they can only increase children's awareness of the inner world of ideas and feelings through literary experiences, which en-

courage children to build their own understanding of genre and to express their own response to the story. When planning activities, consider the following guidelines, which are adapted from Routman (1991).

- What is the purpose for using this activity or strategy?
- Does this activity relate to the true nature of the book?
- How does this activity fit with my philosophy of literature?
- How will this activity enhance the children's knowledge and response to the literature?

The best literature-based activities are those that grow naturally out of the literature and relate to the plot, theme, setting, characters, or style of the book. Activities that grow out of the literature encourage students to think critically and enable readers to demonstrate or share their response to the book. Later chapters discuss experiencing literature in much greater detail.

Genre

When working on developing understanding of genre, select titles that are clear examples of the genre being studied. Picture books are useful for developing genre activities because they are appealing as well as clear and direct examples for teaching genre. They are also useful for developing understanding of plot, theme, style, characterization, setting, and style.

Story Grammar

Stories can be analyzed not only through the structural elements of literature (plot, theme, etc.), but also with story grammar, a set of rules that describes the possible structures of well-formed stories (Rumelhart, 1975; Stein & Glenn, 1979). Although researchers describe story grammars in various ways, many of the differences are merely semantic. Most researchers agree that story grammars include character, setting, a problem or conflict, and a series of one or more episodes (Black & Wilensky, 1979).

Story grammars give readers a way of describing and discussing what they read, which helps refine their comprehension and gives them a means of organizing their recollections. Readers who understand story structure expect to encounter characters, setting, prob-

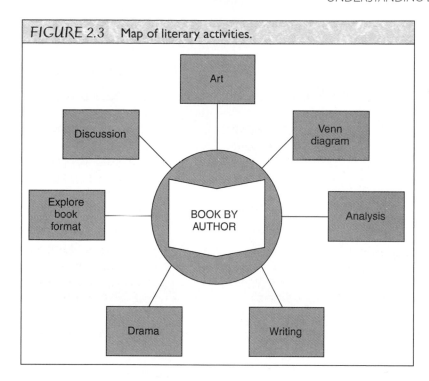

FIGURE 2.3   Map of literary activities.

lems, and efforts to solve problems in books; these anticipations enrich their comprehension.

Writers also use story grammars to generate stories (Meyer & Rice, 1984), to plan the elements, and to organize the tale. The story grammar in Figure 2.4 is based on *The Red Racer* by Audrey Wood. In this book, Nona has an old, worn-out bicycle; the neighborhood kids call it a junker. She wants a new Deluxe Red Racer, but her parents think she does not need a new bicycle. Nona decides that her parents will have to buy the Red Racer if her old bike disappears. She makes several unsuccessful attempts to make her bike disappear. But the surprise resolution makes everyone happy.

Literary Experiences

The suggested activities are suitable for individuals, pairs, small groups, or whole classes. We have not included extensive directions because in most instances the best way to introduce an activity is through demonstration and example. When planning literary experiences, think of ways to enhance appreciation of the literature; for instance, ask a few appropriate discussion questions to enhance understanding. You are, after all, guiding children to respond to a book; you are not conducting an inquisition. Questions for each chapter are undesirable.

The map in Figure 2.3 shows some of the many appropriate literary activities. Do not do all of these activities with a single work of literature, however, but choose the most appropriate activity or activities in a specific instance.

FIGURE 2.4	Story grammar.
Book:	*The Red Racer* by Audrey Wood
Setting:	Any small town in the United States; contemporary.
Characters:	Nona, her parents, neighborhood kids, adult neighbors.
Problem:	Nona needs a new bicycle, but her parents won't buy one.
Efforts to solve the problem (also called events):	1. Nona put the bike in the town dump.
	2. Nona pushed the bike off the pier.
	3. Nona put the bike on the railroad tracks.
Resolution:	Nona's bike is not crushed by the train. Her parents fix up her bicycle to make it look new like a Red Racer.

Classroom Activities

ACTIVITY 2.1 LITERARY ELEMENTS

This activity deals with analyzing the literary elements of a piece of realistic fiction. Although all of the elements are mentioned here, in an actual classroom you would probably choose to discuss only one of the elements, such as plot or characterization or setting.

Book: *Marvin Redpost: Class President* by Louis Sachar

1. Introduce the book, asking questions to help students predict the elements of the story.

   a. What might the title indicate about the story?

   b. What can the dust jacket help you predict about it?

   c. Where do you think the story takes place? Who is the main character? How old is the main character?

2. Students read the story silently.

3. Discuss the story with the students, stimulating them to think about the story.

   a. Describe Marvin at the beginning of the story. How does he change in the story? What events caused him to change?

   b. What is the theme of this story? What makes you think this is the theme?

   c. What is hole day? Why does this make the president's visit more difficult?

   d. What are the comical events in this story?

   e. Do you know anyone like Marvin's teacher? What characteristics does that person share with his teacher? Do you think the president will visit? Why or why not?

   f. Now that you have read the story, what do you think the significance of the title is?

   g. Why did Mrs. North tell the children how to behave when the president visited after she said, "Now, I know I don't have to tell everybody how to behave when the president gets here."?

   h. Did you anticipate the ending of this story?

4. Use extension activities to allow students to respond to the story.

   a. Make a time line for this story that shows the preparation for the president's visit, his visit, and after the visit.

   b. Write a note to the president thanking him for the visit.

   c. Write a review for this book that will cause another person to want to read it.

   d. Read another book by Louis Sachar. Discuss similarities between the two books.

ACTIVITY 2.2 EXPLORING A BOOK WITH YOUNG CHILDREN

Book: *Together* by George Ella Lyon and pictures by Vera Rosenberry

1. Introduce the book to the children, focusing on the words *author, illustrator,* and *title,* and on the book's theme.

   a. Hold up the book, identify the author and illustrator, and explain that the illustrator used her daughter and her daughter's best friend as models for the pictures.

   b. Ask the children what the title means to them. Discuss togetherness and how it makes them feel.

   c. Ask what things they like to do together with their best friends. Have them tell about or draw a picture of their favorite things to do together.

2. Read the book aloud.

3. Discuss the story with the students, stimulating them to think about the story.

   a. What did the author and illustrator say to you through this story?
   b. What was your favorite part of the story?
   c. What is your favorite thing to do with a friend?
   d. Can friends dream the same dreams?
   e. What are some dreams that you and your friends have?

4. Use extension activities to allow students to respond to the story.

   a. Sing or chant the story to a familiar tune. (This story is easily adaptable to music. Ask the music teacher for assistance if necessary.)
   b. Act out a favorite scene.
   c. Think of new scenes and act them out.
   d. Paint a mural about things to do together or about their dreams.
   e. Draw or write about their dreams.

ACTIVITY 2.3 SUGGESTED INDIVIDUAL LITERARY EXPERIENCES

Teachers can suggest these activities for students to perform individually or in groups of two or three.

1. Prepare discussion questions for the book. (Students may need to be given models of open-ended questions until they become adept at creating such questions.)
2. Prepare a Venn diagram that compares and contrasts this book with another.
3. Prepare a diorama of an important scene or setting from the book.
4. Act out a scene from the book.
5. Prepare a poster or commercial for the book.
6. Keep a reading journal summarizing each day's reading and responding to the reading experience.
7. Prepare a story grammar or story map. (See the model in this chapter.)
8. Draw a plot line for the story. (See the models in this chapter.)

SUMMARY

Genres are classifications of literature with each member of a classification exhibiting common characteristics. Genre classifications give teachers, librarians, and students the language to discuss and analyze books. The genres of children's literature include picture books, traditional literature, modern fantasy, contemporary realistic fiction, historical fiction, biography, poetry, and informational literature; all these categories of genres have the same characteristics as adult literature.

Initially, readers like or dislike the books they read for indefinable reasons; readers respond emotionally to literature. Through many experiences with stories, they gradually discover the elements that comprise literature: story, plot, characters, setting, theme, and style. As their experience with literature grows, they develop schemata, cognitive structures that enable them to make sense of what they read and to anticipate what the author will say, thus enriching their understanding. Children's understanding of literature exceeds their ability to verbalize story knowledge, but concerned adults can help them expand their appreciation and understanding. As one of those concerned adults, your understanding of the elements and organizational patterns of fiction discussed in this chapter will assist you in choosing books and planning literary experiences. The box *Elements of Fiction* reviews the elements of fiction and suggests some questions to ask yourself when reviewing a piece of literature.

Elements of Fiction

PLOT

1. Does the plot grab the reader's attention and move quickly?
2. Are the story events sequenced logically, so that cause and effect are clear?
3. Is the reader prepared for story events?
4. What is the conflict in this story (e.g., character with another character, character and society, character and a group, within the character)?
5. Is there a climax?
6. Is the denouement satisfying?

CHARACTER

1. Does the main character seem like a real person?
2. Is the main character well rounded with character strengths and weaknesses revealed? (In a shorter story fewer traits are exhibited.)
3. How are character traits revealed (e.g., conversation, thoughts, author tells reader, actions)? Does the author rely too much on a single strategy?
4. Does the character grow and change?
5. Is the character a delineated character?
6. Are the character's conversations and behavior consistent with age and background?

SETTING

1. Where does this story take place?
2. When does this story take place?
3. How are time and place related to the plot, characters, and theme?
4. Is this a universal setting?

THEME

1. What is the theme?
2. Is the theme developed naturally through the actions and reactions of story characters?
3. Does the author avoid stating the theme in words (except in traditional literature)?
4. Is the abstract theme made concrete by the story?

STYLE

1. What stylistic devices characterize the author's writing (e.g., connotation, imagery, figurative language, hyperbole, understatement, allusion, symbol)?
2. What is the mood of the writing (e.g., gloomy, happy, evil, mysterious)?
3. What point of view is used?
4. Is the point of view appropriate to the story?

Thought Questions

1. How can teachers use the elements of literature?
2. What is *author style*? Identify the components of style that you would expect to find in a novel.
3. Compare a picture book character with a character in a novel. How do they differ in development and the amount of detail included?
4. What themes have you discovered in the children's books you have read thus far?
5. Why do you think teachers choose to read fiction aloud more often than nonfiction?

Research and Application Experiences

1. Choose a fiction book to read and identify each of the elements of literature in that book. Then map the story grammar of the book.
2. Choose a nonfiction book and identify the patterns of organizing information in it.
3. Compare characters in two different fiction books.
4. Compare a poem, a story, and an informational book that are about the same topic.
5. Read a book of fiction, nonfiction, and poetry to a group of children. Ask them to identify the aspects of each type of literature that they enjoy.

6. Survey an elementary school class. Ask the students to identify the structures in various types of literature. Which type of literature do they seem to know the most about? Why do you think this is true?

7. Identify any weaknesses revealed, keeping in mind that fewer traits are exhibited in a shorter story.

Children's Literature References and Recommended Books

Note: Books designated with an asterisk (*) are recommended for reluctant readers.

Alcock, V. (1988). *The monster garden.* New York: Delacorte. (4–6). MODERN FANTASY.

Frankie accidentally grows a baby monster and learns the responsibility involved in caring for a living thing. She also learns the fears humans harbor for anyone who is different.

Alcock, V. (1998). *Stranger at the window.* Boston: Houghton Mifflin. (4–6). CONTEMPORARY REALISTIC FICTION.

Lesley is drawn into a mystery after seeing a strange child in the attic window of the house next door. The tension and mystery mount as the neighbors accuse her of hallucinating.

Banks, K. (1999). *And if the moon could talk* (G. Hallensleben, Illus.). New York: Farrar, Straus & Giroux. (PreK–2). CONTEMPORARY REALISTIC FICTION.

The illustrations and the text capture the world outside a child's room at bedtime. The paintings that illustrate the text show the darkening sky as dusk falls.

Bruchac, J. (1998). *The arrow over the door* (J. Watling, Illus.). New York: Dial. (4–7). HISTORICAL FICTION.*

The story of a little-known historical meeting between Quakers and Native Americans during the American Revolution.

Burleigh, R. (1998). *Black whiteness: Admiral Byrd alone in the Antarctic* (W. L. Krudop, Illus.). New York: Atheneum. (4–8). BIOGRAPHY.*

This exquisite book tells about the 6 months that Admiral Richard Byrd stayed alone in an underground house in Antarctica.

Burnett, F. H. (1962). *The secret garden.* Philadelphia: Lippincott. (4–6). MODERN FANTASY.

A spoiled girl and a pampered invalid find themselves in an old garden. They learn compassion as they solve their problems.

Byars, B. (1993). *The house of wings* (D. Schwartz, Illus.). New York: Viking. (4–6). CONTEMPORARY REALISTIC FICTION.

Protagonist is abandoned and lives with grandfather. Grandfather has hobby of taking care of wounded birds. The two learn about each other while learning to take care of the birds.

Coman, C. (1995). *What Jamie saw.* Arden, NY: Front Street. (4–7). CONTEMPORARY REALISTIC FICTION.*

After Van throws his baby sister, Jamie and his mom move to a place where he feels isolated, but he practices his magic tricks and learns how to take care of his mom and sister.

Cox, J. (1998). *Third grade pet* (C. Fisher, Illus.). New York: Holiday House. (K–4). CONTEMPORARY REALISTIC FICTION.*

Rosemary is shocked when her class chooses a rat for a class pet, but things get worse when she is chosen to take care of the rat.

Dickinson, P. (1988). *Eva.* New York: Delacorte. (5–9). MODERN FANTASY.

The protagonist's body dies in an accident. Her brain is transplanted to a chimp's body.

Fox, P. (1988). *The village by the sea.* New York: Orchard. (4–7). CONTEMPORARY REALISTIC FICTION.

Emma must stay with an aunt and uncle during her father's surgery. She learns the family secret and matures in the process.

Fyleman, R. (1932). "I think mice are rather nice." In *Fifty-one new nursery rhymes* (D. Burroughes, Illus.). New York: Doubleday. (PreK–3). POETRY.

This is a poem about mice and their activities.

Hesse, K. (1996). *The music of dolphins.* New York: Scholastic. (4–8). MODERN FANTASY.*

Mila is rescued from an unpopulated island off the coast of Florida, where she has been raised by dolphins since age 4. She discovers that being human includes rules, expectations, disappointment, and betrayal, making her yearn for her dolphin family and ocean home.

Hesse, K. (1997). *Out of the dust.* New York: Scholastic Press. (4–8). HISTORICAL FICTION.

In this story set during the Great Depression Billie Jo's father caused the accident that killed her mother. Billie Jo must find a way to forgive herself and her father.

Howe, D., & Howe, J. (1979). *Bunnicula: A rabbit tale of mystery* (A. Daniel, Illus.). New York: Atheneum. (K–5). MODERN FANTASY.

This is the tale of three pets—Harold, a dog; Chester, a cat; and Bunnicula, who may be a vampire rabbit.

Hoyt-Goldsmith, D. (1998). *Lacrosse: The national game of the Iroquois* (L. Migdale, Photog.). New York: Holiday House. (3–6). INFORMATIONAL BOOK.*

Thirteen-year-old Monte Lyons, an American Indian citizen of the Onondaga Nation, tells about his family as a springboard for an in-depth look into the origins of the game of lacrosse.

Kesey, K. (1990). *Little Tricker the squirrel meets Big Double the bear* (B. Moser, Illus.). New York: Viking. (K–4). MODERN FANTASY.

The author retells a story that his grandmother told him about a grizzly bear that is outwitted by a squirrel.

King-Smith, D. (1995). *The school mouse* (C. Fisher, Illus.). New York: Hyperion Paperbacks. (2–4). MODERN FANTASY.

The story of Flora the mouse who learns to read. Her family is unimpressed until Flora is able to read the word "poison."

Klass, S. (1991). *Kool Ada.* New York: Scholastic. (4–6). CONTEMPORARY REALISTIC FICTION.*

Ada never speaks, causing teachers to believe she is slow.

Konigsburg, E. L. (1996). *The view from Saturday.* New York: Atheneum. (3–6). CONTEMPORARY REALISTIC FICTION.

Mrs. Olinski's sixth-grade academic bowl team had four members who worked together so well that they surprised everyone. The members resolved conflicts within themselves to achieve team cooperation.

Kushner, D. (1987). *A book dragon* (N. R. Jackson, Illus.). New York: Holt Rinehart Winston. (4–6). MODERN FANTASY.

Nonesuch, the dragon, has adventures in a cathedral, London, and a bookshop.

Lasky, K. (1997). *Marven of the Great North Woods* (K. Hawkes, Illus.). New York: Harcourt Brace. (2–4). HISTORICAL FICTION.

A true story of how one family protected a child from the influenza epidemic that struck the United States in 1918.

Levy, J. (1999). *Totally uncool* (C. Monroe, Illus.). Minneapolis, MN: Carolrhoda. (3–6). CONTEMPORARY REALISTIC FICTION.*

Dad's new girlfriend is "totally uncool." She has some downright alarming traits such as a kitchen floor that is too shiny. But she does have some redeeming qualities, such as clapping the loudest.

Lindgren, A. (1950). *Pippi Longstocking* (F. Lamborn, Trans., L. S. Glanzman, Illus.). New York: Viking. (2–4). MODERN FANTASY.

In this translation from Swedish, Pippi lives alone with a monkey and a horse. While doing what she pleases, she has many unusual adventures.

Lyon, G. E. (1989). *Together* (V. Rosenberry, Illus.). New York: Orchard Books. (K–2). PICTURE BOOK.

Two girls who are best friends enjoy many adventures together.

Myers, C. (1999). *Black cat.* New York: Scholastic. (All ages). POETRY.*

This poem about a slinky black cat and its urban lifestyle captures the visual and sound imagery of life on the street.

Myers, W. D. (1988). *Me, Mop, and the Moondance Kid* (R. Pate, Illus.). New York: Delacorte. (3–5). CONTEMPORARY REALISTIC FICTION.

Tommy and Moondance are adopted, but their friend Mop remains without a family.

Naylor, P. R. (1991). *Shiloh.* New York: Harper & Row. (5–7). CONTEMPORARY REALISTIC FICTION.

A boy tries to prevent abuse of the dog that he befriends.

Nolen, J. (1998). *Raising dragons* (E. Primavera, Illus.). San Diego: Silver Whistle. (1–3). MODERN FANTASY.

While taking a walk a little girl finds a pulsing egg that hatches a baby dragon that becomes her friend.

Paterson, K. (1978). *The great Gilly Hopkins.* New York: Crowell. (4–6). CONTEMPORARY REALISTIC FICTION.

Gilly, a foster child, moves to a new foster home and attempts to outdo her foster mother, but Mame Trotter wisely wins her over. Gilly begins to mature through her disappointments.

Paulsen, G. (1987). *Hatchet.* New York: Viking Penguin (5–7). CONTEMPORARY REALISTIC FICTION.*

Brian survives an airplane crash and spends the next 54 days trying to survive with only the hatchet his mother gave him.

Pearce, P. (1958). *Tom's midnight garden.* Philadelphia: Lippincott. (4–7). MODERN FANTASY.

A time fantasy wherein a girl and boy play when the clock strikes 13.

Reeder, C. (1989). *Shades of gray.* New York: Macmillan. (5–7). HISTORICAL FICTION.

The protagonist is forced to live with his pacifist uncle after his family succumbs to the Civil War.

Reeder, C. (1998). *Foster's war.* New York: Scholastic. (4–8). HISTORICAL FICTION.

Foster's War is the story of 11-year-old Foster who has conflicts about his father, his best friend, and his older brother who is in the air corps.

Sachar, L. (1998). *Holes.* New York: Farrar, Straus & Giroux. (4–8). CONTEMPORARY REALISTIC FICTION.*

The protagonist is sentenced to a juvenile facility for a crime he did not commit. In this unusual situation, he must dig holes all day, every day.

Sachar, L. (1999). *Marvin Redpost: Class president* (A. Wummer, Illus.). New York: Random House. (2–4). CONTEMPORARY REALISTIC FICTION.*

Marvin's class is visited by the president of the United States in this comic story about a classroom thrust into the limelight.

San Souci, R. D. (1998). *A weave of words: An Armenian tale* (R. Colón, Illus.). New York: Orchard. (1–4). TRADITIONAL LITERATURE.

This folktale reverses the usual pattern by having the queen rescue the king.

Sauer, J. L. (1943). *Fog magic* (L. Ward, Illus.). New York: Viking. (3–6). MODERN FANTASY.

Ten-year-old Greta discovers the Village of Blue Cove, only to realize that it only exists in the fog.

Sendak, M. (1963). *Where the wild things are.* New York: Harper & Row. (K–2). MODERN FANTASY.

Max is wild, so he is sent to bed without supper. He escapes in his imagination, but discovers that he wants to return.

Seuss, Dr., with Prelutsky, J., & Smith, L. (1998). *Hooray for Diffendoofer day!* New York: Knopf. (K–6). MODERN FANTASY.*

The story of a zany school where teachers view education differently.

Snow, A. (1991). *The monster book of ABC sounds.* New York: Dial. (PreK–2). INFORMATIONAL BOOK.

Monsters play hide and seek in this book that introduces sounds and words for each letter.

Snyder, D. (1988). *The boy of the three-year nap* (A. Say, Illus.). Boston: Houghton Mifflin. (2–4). TRADITIONAL LITERATURE.

This Japanese tale features a lazy character who uses his wits to acquire a rich wife.

Spinelli, E. (1998). *When mama comes home tonight* (J. Dyer, Illus.). New York: Simon & Schuster. (K–2). PICTURE BOOK, CONTEMPORARY REALISTIC FICTION.

A child waits for Mama to come home in this story. When she does arrive, they have a lovely time together before bedtime.

Van Allsburg, C. (1981). *Jumanji.* Boston: Houghton Mifflin. (2–4). MODERN FANTASY.

Children play a board game that they cannot stop playing.

Walker, S. M. (1998). *The 18 penny goose* (E. Beier, Illus.). New York: HarperCollins. (K–2). HISTORICAL FICTION.*

When the family flees approaching soldiers, they fear their geese will be eaten. The little girl pleads for her gander's life and it is saved.

White, E. B. (1952). *Charlotte's web* (G. Williams, Illus.). New York: Harper & Row. (3–6). MODERN FANTASY.

Charlotte the spider saves Wilbur the pig's life with a unique solution.

White, R. (1988). *Sweet Creek Holler.* New York: Farrar, Straus & Giroux. (4–8). HISTORICAL FICTION.

Portrays life in a 1948 Appalachian town. Focuses on Ginny and her best friend.

Wood, A. (1988). *King Bidgood's in the bathtub* (D. Wood, Illus.). New York: Harcourt. (K–2). PICTURE BOOK.

The king refuses to leave the bathtub until a page pulls the plug.

Wood, A. (1996). *The Red Racer.* New York: Simon & Schuster. (1–3). CONTEMPORARY REALISTIC FICTION.

A dream of owning a shiny, new bicycle leads this character to take extreme measures, but it all ends well.

Yolen, J. (1998). *The originals* (T. Lewin, Illus.). New York: Philomel. (1–4). POETRY.

This book celebrates animals across the world in poetry. Included are a red jungle fowl and a churro sheep.

References and Books for Further Reading

Adams, S. M., & Collins, A. (1986). A schema-theoretic view of reading. In H. Singer & R. Ruddell (Eds.), *Theoretical models and processes of reading* (pp. 404–425). Newark, DE: International Reading Association.

Alexander, L. (1981). The grammar of story. In B. Hearne and M. Kaye (Eds.), *Celebrating children's books* (pp. 3–13). New York: Lothrop, Lee & Shepard.

Anglund, J. W. (1963). *Morning is a little child.* New York: Hallmark.

Applebee, A. (1978). *The child's concept of story.* Chicago: University of Chicago Press.

Black, J. B., & Wilensky, R. (1979). An evaluation of story grammars. *Cognitive Science, 3,* 213–230.

Bond, N. (1984, June). Conflict in children's fiction. *The Horn Book, 49,* 297–306.

Byars, B. (1993). Writing for children. *Speech.* Durham, NC: Southeastern Children's Writers Association.

Conrad, J. (1922). Preface to a career. In *The nigger of the Narcissus* (p. x). New York: Doubleday.

Dias, P. (1987). *Making sense of poetry.* Ottawa, Ontario: Canadian Council of Teachers of English.

Fox, P. (1991, September). Writing *The village by the sea. Book Links, 1,* 48–50.

Frye, N. (1964). *The educated imagination.* Bloomington: Indiana University Press.

Giblin, J. (1990). *Writing books for young people.* Boston: The Writer.

Hardy, B. (1977). Narrative as a primary act of mine. In M. Meek, A. Warlow, & G. Barton (Eds.), *The cool Web: The pattern of children's reading* (pp. 12–23). London: Bodley Head.

Holman, C. H., & Harmon, W. (1986). *A handbook to literature* (4th ed.). New York: Macmillan.

Lehr, S. (1991). *The child's developing sense of theme.* New York: Teachers College Press.

Meyer, B., & Rice, G. E. (1984). The structure of text. In P. D. Pearson (Ed.), *Handbook of reading research* (pp. 319–352). New York: Longman.

Morner, K., & Rausch, R. (1991). *NTC's dictionary of literary terms.* Lincolnwood, IL: National Textbook.

Norton, D. (1995). *Through the eyes of a child.* Upper Saddle River, NJ: Merrill/Prentice Hall.

Pearson, P. D., & Johnson, J. (1977). *Teaching reading comprehension.* New York: Holt Rinehart Winston.

Routman, R. (1991). *Invitations: Changing as teachers and learners.* Portsmouth, NH: Heinemann.

Rumelhart, D. E. (1975). Notes on a schema for stories. In D. G. Bobrow & A. M. Collins (Ed.), *Representation and understanding* (pp. 573–603). New York: Academic Press.

Saxby, M., & Winch, G. (1987). *Give them wings: The experience of children's literature.* South Melbourne, Australia: Macmillan.

Sebesta, S., & Iverson, W. J. (1975). *Literature for Thursday's child.* Chicago: Science Research Associates.

Silvey, A. (1988). The goats. *The Horn Book, 54,* 23.

Stein, N. L., & Glenn, C. G. (1979). An analysis of story comprehension in elementary school children. In R. O. Freedle (Ed.), *New directions in discourse processing* (pp. 53–101). Norwood, NJ: Ablex.

Stewig, J. (1988). *Children and literature* (2d ed.). Boston: Houghton Mifflin.

Tierney, R. (1990, March). Redefining reading comprehension. *Educational Leadership, 47,* 37–42.

Van Vliet, L. (1992). *Approaches to literature through genre.* Phoenix, AZ: Oryx.

Wadham, T. (1999). Plot does matter. *The Horn Book, LXXV,* 445–450.

Wyndham, L., & Madison, A. (1988). *Writing for children and teenagers.* Cincinnati, OH: Writer's Digest Books.

Connecting Children and Literature

3

EVALUATING AND SELECTING BOOKS

KEY TERMS

bibliotherapy   Children's Choices
BIR   literary criticism
Caldecott Medal   Newbery Award
catharsis   videos
censorship   Young Adult Choices

GUIDING QUESTIONS

How do you choose books to read? Do you read different types of books on vacation than for class? Do you read best-sellers? Who are your favorite authors? Examining your personal criteria for book selection will help you better understand how to choose books for others, especially children. How would you feel if you were denied the right to read a book that you really wanted to read? As you read this chapter keep in mind these questions:

1. What are some appropriate criteria adults can use when selecting books for children?

2. How do children's interests influence the books they choose and the ones adults choose for them?

3. Why is censorship such an important issue for adults choosing children's books?

4. What factors influence children's reading interests?

OVERVIEW

We believe that stories are what we grow on. Our future is shaped by our childhood, and the books of our childhood are an important part of our journey. Your sense of children and their needs and their responses to books will serve you well as you foster their love of books. This chapter will help you formulate a basis for selecting quality literature. You will explore the kinds of literature appropriate for children—whether classics, award winners, or books with popular appeal—and develop a framework for evaluating them. Bear in mind that literature is more than books: computer software, cassette tapes, films, videos, and newspapers and magazines are different forms of literature, but they too are literature.

INTRODUCTION

As you will see in the opening vignette, finding the connections that spark children's interest in literature is a complex process. Moreover, the large number of children's books currently in print and the thousands of new ones published each year complicate the search for quality literature. As children's books have become more popular, censors have grown ever more critical of books they perceive to be harmful.

Children's reading interests are a powerful influence on their overall literacy development. They learn to read by reading, and the more they read, the better they read; thus, cultivating children's reading interests is beneficial to their reading growth. The books children read, the videos they watch, the audiotapes they hear, the computer programs they use, and the Internet become a part of their experiential background. All forms of media play a larger role in classrooms than ever before.

Children's books and the way they are used in the classroom have changed. The most striking change is the integration of children's literature and multimedia throughout the curriculum.

Teachers, librarians, and parents hope to stimulate children to read more books. To this end, teachers and librarians select a variety of books that includes both great books and popular books. To entertain students we might elect to read *Monster Soup and Other Spooky Poems* by Evans for its humor and imaginative illustrations. To motivate further reading we could select Dick King-Smith's *The Water Horse*. After hearing this story, many third-grade children will seek other King-Smith books featuring his unusual characters.

If our goal is to develop students' appreciation for the author's craft, a teacher might choose to read *Out of the Dust* by Karen Hesse for its exemplary literary quality and timeless appeal. Fifth graders could compare this book about a young girl's experiences during the Great Depression with those of an Australian boy in Disher's book, *The Bamboo Flute*.

Literature selection criteria are dynamic and change with the goals and purposes of the individual making the choices. Exposing children to a wide variety of reading materials helps them develop a sense of literary quality. In addition, providing children with many opportunities to select books they would like to read encourages them to choose reading as a leisure-time activity.

VIGNETTE

When he was planning his lesson, Jim Smith glanced at his calendar and noticed that it was November 1, and he realized that at least half of his class read no better than they did the first week of school. Their reading skills were still below grade level. Mr. Smith knew their best hope for acquiring reading fluency lay in reading extensively in books they enjoyed.

At the beginning of the school year, he had given the class an interest inventory, but they had joked around rather than completing it. He considered engaging them in a group discussion, but thought they might not discuss their interests any more seriously than they did previously. Instead, he decided to identify books that appealed to this age group, then read some books aloud to the class to see what sparked their interests. After consulting *Great Books for Boys* (Odean, 1998), *The Read-Aloud Handbook* (Trelease, 1995), *Once Upon a Heroine* (Cooper-Mullin and Coye, 1998), *Children's Reference Plus* (Bowker, 1991), and *The Bulletin* from the University of Illinois, he identified three books to read aloud: *Slake's Limbo* by Felice Holman, *Hatchet* by Gary Paulsen, and *Scorpions* by Walter Dean Myers. He started the read-aloud sessions with *Slake's Limbo*. When his students pleaded "keep on reading, please," he knew he was on the right track. They were interested! He searched for other books with the same appeal. After obtaining copies from the public and school libraries, Mr. Smith prepared brief synopses of each book and created a display so the students could choose the ones they wanted to read.

He continued reading aloud and watching the students' responses, gathering ideas for other displays. The students read more and more and with increasing fluency as the school year progressed.

EVALUATING CHILDREN'S LITERATURE

Literary quality is a primary consideration in evaluating any literature. However, book selection based on literary quality should never preclude consideration of whether children will want to read the book. Both literary quality and popularity are important in choosing and evaluating literature for children (Bauer & Sanborn, 1981).

Current literary criticism reflects the growing interest in children's books and book selection. In general, literary criticism falls into three categories: work-centered criticism (focused on the quality of the work), child-centered criticism (focused on children's response to the work), and issues-centered criticism (focused on the appropriate presentation of various social issues in the work). All three components of criticism are important when choosing literature for children: A book may present social issues accurately while failing to achieve excellence in storytelling; a book of excellent literary quality may not appeal to children's interests. A comprehensive approach emphasizes the importance of finding a good fit between reader and story.

LITERARY QUALITY AS A SELECTION STANDARD

One of the first criteria applied by most adults in selecting children's literature is that of quality.

> We should put in their hands only the books worthy of them: the books of honesty, integrity, and vision—the books on which they can grow. Books of high quality are those that have stood the test of time and that continue to attract readers generation after generation. (Hill, 1986)

These books possess high literary quality as well as transmitting the significant values of the culture. Despite children's changing tastes and interests, great books continue to attract a wide audience and sell large numbers. According to *U.S. News and World Report,* "Sales of old favorites remain the backbone of the [children's book market]" (Rachlin, 1988, p. 50). Walk into any bookstore and you will see displays of older books that are being sold at a rapid rate.

What is the appeal of a truly great children's book? Why do so many children return to these books year after year? First of all, some of them are magnificent stories. Today's children find Mark Twain's *Adventures of Tom Sawyer* and Daniel Defoe's *Robinson Crusoe* as intriguing as did earlier generations, so they continue to be reissued. Second, the characters are memorable and well drawn, they live on in our adult minds—consider Peter Pan and Captain Hook. Included in this number are books of lasting appeal such as *The Secret Garden* by Frances Hodgson Burnett and *The Borrowers* by Mary Norton. Third, many great books combine memorable text with vivid illustrations. Books such as Beatrix Potter's *The Tale of Peter Rabbit* and Maurice Sendak's *Where the Wild Things Are* illustrate this union of text and illustration. The true classics of literature are books that remain popular because children want to read them.

Award Books and Recommended Reading Lists

Some adults believe the best way to choose books for children is to focus on award winners. The majority of children's literature awards, such as the Newbery Award, are given by adults who tend to choose books based on authors and titles they have heard of previously and favorites from their own childhood (Stoodt-Hill, 1999), and professional adults (teachers, librarians, and professors) who tend to select books that reflect high literary standards.

Newbery award

Newbery Awards are given to books that have outstanding literary quality. Each year this award goes to the author of a book published in the United States that represents the most outstanding contribution to the field of children's literature. This prestigious award is named after John Newbery, the first British publisher of books intended expressly for children. It is a sought-after award because it represents artistic achievement and carries significant media attention.

A 15-member committee of the Association for Library Service to Children of the American Library Association determines the winners. Although the award is given to only one book, others are identified as honor books. (See the Appendix for a list of winners and some honor books.) Criteria for the award are shown in the box on page 52. Newbery Award books are fine examples of literature; as noted, however, adults rather than children select them. Research indicates that many Newbery titles are beyond the reading ability of

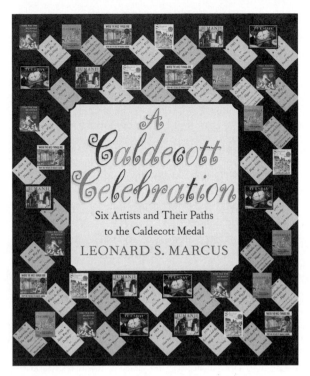

A celebration of illustrators and artists.

Other awards

Although the Newbery Award and the Caldecott Medal are the best known of all children's book awards, a number of additional awards are presented each year to exemplary children's books. (See the Appendix for a list.) The following list identifies a few of these.

- The Hans Christian Andersen International Medal is awarded to living authors and artists by the International Board on Books for Young People.
- The International Reading Association presents the Children's Book Award to authors with unusual promise.
- The Laura Ingalls Wilder Award is given to authors or illustrators who have made lasting contributions to children's literature.
- The Boston Globe/Horn Book Award is presented to authors of fiction and nonfiction and to illustrators.
- The Coretta Scott King Award is given to the best books for children about the Black experience.
- Pura Belpré Award is given to the best books for children about the Latino experience.
- The Consortium of Latin American Studies Programs (CLASP) gives the Americas Award in recognition of books that authentically and engagingly portray Latin America, the Caribbean, or Latinos in the United States.

Selection Aids

A number of educational organizations offer lists of recommended books that include great books, good books, and classics. For instance, the American Library Association compiles lists of notable books. The Teachers' Choices project, administered by the International Reading Association, identifies outstanding trade books for children and adolescents that effectively enhance the curriculum. The books listed are identified by regional teams of teachers who field test between 200 and 300 books annually and compile a list of 30 books categorized as primary (grades K–2), intermediate (grades 3–5), and advanced (grades 6–8). Books are selected on the basis of literary quality and presentation.

The Child Study Children's Book Committee of Bank Street College compiles an annual list, as does the California State Department of Education. Each year the

elementary children. In fact, Shafer (1976) found the readability of almost one third of the Newbery titles to be fifth grade or higher; therefore, they are best presented as read-alouds to interested children.

Caldecott medal

The Caldecott Medal, named for the great British illustrator Randolph Caldecott, is awarded annually to the illustrator of the most distinguished picture book published in the United States. (See the Appendix for the list.) The criteria require that the award be given not only for excellence in artwork, but also for the effective interaction of text and illustrations (see the box on page 52). Books featuring a wide range of media have won the Caldecott Medal; watercolor, pen and ink, and collage have all been represented. Caldecott Medal winners are typically suitable for younger children, but some, such as Chris Van Allsburg's *The Polar Express,* appeal to all age groups. Caldecott names honor books as well.

Criteria for the Newbery Award

1. In identifying distinguished writing in a book for children, committee members must:

   a. consider:

   - interpretation of the theme or concept
   - presentation of information, including accuracy, clarity, and organization
   - development of plot
   - delineation of characters
   - delineation of setting
   - appropriateness of style

   NOTE: Because the literary qualities to be considered will vary depending on content, the committee need not expect to find excellence in each of the named elements. The book should, however, have distinguished qualities in all the elements pertinent to it.

   b. consider excellence of presentation for a child audience

2. Each book is to be considered as a contribution to literature. The committee is to make its decision primarily on the text. Other aspects of a book are to be considered only if they distract from the text. Such other aspects might include illustrations or overall design of the book.

   NOTE: The committee should keep in mind that the award is for literary quality and quality of presentation for children. The award is not for didactic intent or for popularity.

From: Peterson, L. K., & Solt, M. L. (1982). *Newbery and Caldecott Medal and Honor Books*, p. 399. New Providence, NJ: Bowker.

Criteria for the Caldecott Medal

1. In identifying a distinguished picture book for children, committee members must:

   a. consider the excellence of:

   - execution in the artistic technique employed
   - pictorial interpretation of story, theme, or concept
   - appropriateness of style of illustration to the story, theme, or concept
   - delineation of plot, theme, characters, setting, mood, or information through the pictures

   b. consider the excellence of presentation in recognition of a child audience

2. The only limitation to graphic form is that the form must be one that may be used in a picture book (film photography is not considered, but still photography is).

3. Each book is to be considered as a picture book. The committee is to make its decision primarily on the illustrations, but other components of a book are to be considered, especially when they make a book less effective as a children's picture book. Other components might include elements such as the written text or the overall design of the book.

   NOTE: The committee should keep in mind that the award is for distinguished illustrations in a picture book and for excellence of pictorial presentation for children. The award is not for didactic intent or for popularity.

From: Peterson, L. K., & Solt, M. L. (1982). *Newbery and Caldecott Medal and Honor Books*, p. 400. New Providence, NJ: Bowker.

Children's Book Council works with the National Science Teachers Association and the National Council for the Social Studies, respectively, to compile "Outstanding Science Trade Books for Children" and "Notable Children's Trade Books in the Field of Social Studies," which are annotated bibliographies published in the periodicals *Social Education* and *Science and Children*.

School Library Journal is a periodical that publishes lists and book reviews: for instance, "Reference Book Roundup" appears in the May issue each year. In addition to these lists, children's books are regularly reviewed and recommended in periodicals such as *The*

Horn Book, The Horn Book Guide to Children's and Young Adult Books, The Bulletin of the Center for Children's Books, The Reading Teacher, Journal of Reading, Language Arts, Perspectives, and *The New Advocate.*

The Internet is a superb source of information about children's books, videos, recordings, and computer programs. *The Children's Literature Web Guide* (see Appendix) is an invaluable resource for identifying good books. *The Bulletin of the Center for Children's Books,* The American Library Association, *Smithsonian Magazine,* and Cooperative Children's Book Center (School of Education, University of Wisconsin-Madison) all maintain Web sites.

Adults will find a number of reference books to consult when choosing books for children. The following list identifies some of the best of these guides.

- Bowker, R. R. (Ed.). (1991). *Subject guide to children's books in print.* New York: Bowker.
- Dreyer, S. S. (Ed.). (1990). *The bookfinder: A guide to children's literature about the needs and problems of youth aged 2–15.* Chicago: American Guidance Service.
- Hearne, B. (1990). *Choosing books for children.* New York: Delacorte Press.
- Isaacson, R., Hellas, F., & Yaakov, J. (annual). *Children's catalog.* New York: Wilson.
- Liggett, T. C., & Benfield, C. M. (1995). *Reading rainbow guide to children's books.* Chicago: Citadel Press.
- Lima, C. W., & Lima, J. A. (1990). *A to zoo: Access to children's picture books.* New York: Bowker.
- Miller-Lachmann, L. (1993). *Our family our friends our world.* New York: Bowker.
- Sutton, W. K., et al. (Eds.) *Adventuring with books: A booklist for preK through grade 6.* Urbana, IL: National Council of Teachers of English.
- Thomas, J. L. (1990). *Play, learn & grow.* New York: Bowker. (Books for young children.)
- Winkel, L. (Ed.) (Biannually). *The elementary school library collection: A guide to books and other media.* Philadelphia: Brodart Foundation.

Criticism of Award Books and Reading Lists

Children's book awards and recommended lists have been criticized on several counts. First, such awards are often given to books appealing to only a small segment of the population, selected not on the basis of popularity with children but only on the basis of their quality. This can create the problem of elitism.

Second, many children's favorites are outstanding works that did not receive Newbery Awards. For example, the Little House books by Laura Ingalls Wilder and *Charlotte's Web* by E. B. White were not recipients.

Third, the vast majority of awards and lists reflect the standards and taste of adults; they should be viewed as resources rather than prescriptions for children's reading. Ohanian (1990) points out the dangers of such lists:

> Rather than including children in some sort of common cultural foundation, they exclude [children] from the rich possibilities of language and literature. . . . Lists . . . end up driving the curriculum, making us forget the needs of individuals. (p. 176)

Bauer and Sanborn (1981) believe that both children's preferences and adult preferences should be considered in giving awards. One example of a children-selected award is Children's Choices by the International Reading Association. The winners are published annually in *The Reading Teacher.*

Betsy Hearne (1990) also stresses the importance of personal appeal and involvement in selecting children's books. She suggests that adults choose books that meet their standards but that also appeal to children. She maintains that children's responses to books are as important as experts' recommendations. The power of personal attraction to a book cannot be underestimated. During their school years, children will read many types of literature, and the appeal of some books will not be apparent to adults.

The goal in connecting children and literature is to attract them to reading (Smith, 1988). Great books, award-winning books, and recommended books are a good beginning, but when used to the exclusion of other guidelines, these books may expose children to an extremely limited view of the world and the people who inhabit it. When adults censor the books that children read, they are limiting readers' access to books. Censorship limits children's reading to books that are considered acceptable, thereby limiting their interests.

ISSUES-CENTERED CRITICISM OF CHILDREN'S LITERATURE: CENSORSHIP

Teachers and parents have become aware of how important children's literature can be to children's learning and development. A natural result is that literature is used more and more frequently in classrooms today. When all students in a class are assigned the same book, that book becomes a part of the curriculum. Moreover, when literature is used as part of the curriculum, it can be a catalyst for intense reactions. After all, the things we read make us who we are by presenting our image of ourselves as girls and women, as boys and men. Children's literature is perhaps the most influential genre. The stereotypes and worldview embedded in these stories become accepted knowledge.

As we have come to recognize the importance of literature in children's lives, the literature itself has changed. Today's books use realistic language, including nonstandard English and expletives. Formerly taboo topics such as drugs, sex, homosexuality, fights, death, and divorce are found in children's books (McClure, 1995). Coincidentally, our culture is becoming more conservative in the face of national concern for values and morals, which stimulates censors to believe that they must protect children from influences they consider evil or harmful.

Until they are faced with it, many teachers and librarians tend to believe that censorship happens in other places. Many adults believe children's literature comprises simple stories populated with charming magic toys and animals. But the nature of objectionable content often depends on the reader's perceptions. For example, a lovely Halloween book that featured kittens playing at night was so frightening to a grandmother that she wrote to a major newspaper decrying its use with young children. Consider an editor who re-

fused to list these books for recommended reading in a teacher's guide: Kellogg's *Best Friends* because the girls wore cone shaped hats that might be considered satanic; and a book about two playful elephants who sprayed water on one another because this was not a good model of child behavior. These are just a few of the many books that have been subjected to censorship. Listed in Figure 3.1 are additional examples of censored books.

Censorship is usually based on removing a book from circulation because of sexual references, profanity, sexism, racism, ageism, nudity, drugs, or violence. Censors focus on books they consider harmful or evil, and they seek to protect children from these books McClure (1995). However, the harmful or evil influences are identified from the censors' own biases, which may well differ from the biases of other censors. For example, liberals want books that avoid racist or sexist stereotypes; conservatives fear books that permit characters to question God, parents, or teachers. At the same time, proponents of intellectual freedom believe that children should have free access to ideas and the right to examine and challenge ideas (McClure, 1995). Where do we draw the line? Should no book be challenged? On the other hand, if every book is challenged, whose values will be the basis for challenging books in libraries and schools? Certainly, parents have the right to question reading material assigned to their children. But should they determine what other children read? Does anyone have the right to determine what others will or will not read? These

---

FIGURE 3.1   Examples of censored books.

Book	Author	Alleged Reason for Censorship
Scary Stories to Tell in the Dark	Alvin Schwartz	Witchcraft/occult/satanic
Missing May	Cynthia Rylant	References to spirits, ghosts
Bridge to Terabithia	Katherine Paterson	Use of words *Lord* and *hell*
The Great Gilly Hopkins	Katherine Paterson	Remarks about God and religion
Starring Sally J. Freedman as Herself	Judy Blume	Questions adults
Daddy's Roommate	Michael Wilhoite	Concerns gay parents
Heather Has Two Mommies	Leslea Newman	Concerns lesbian parents
My Puppy Is Born	Joanna Cole Word	Uses word *mating*
Noah's Ark	Peter Spier	Piles of manure on ark
Stonewords	Pam Conrad	Concerns New Age philosophy
My Special Best Words	John Steptoe	Has child on toilet

Hank, the dragon, hatches from an egg and saves the day for his farm family.

are not easy questions to answer; nevertheless, they must be addressed. We recommend that adults seek out and read books that are worthy of children's attention and offer them as alternatives to unacceptable books. The following sections examine some of the specific issues related to censorship.

Racial and Ethnic Issues

The Council on Interracial Books for Children (1976), as an example, states that books should promote human values "that lead to greater human liberation" (p. 4), and this is the primary criterion whereby this group evaluates children's books. They evaluate children's literature for the presence of racism, sexism, ageism, classism, materialism, and elitism based on their understanding of human liberation. This section addresses some aspects of evaluating children's books to ensure appropriate portrayal of the diversity in our culture. (These issues are examined further in chapters 4 and 15.)

Children's books are powerful allies in socialization, so they should present positive and accurate portrayals of minority cultures. In addition to evaluating books for literary quality, adults need to consider whether they (a) provide diversity and range of representation, (b) avoid stereotyping, (c) use appropriate language, and (d) have appropriate cultural perspectives.

In order to address diversity and range of representation, children's books should portray minorities in a wide variety of economic circumstances, lifestyles, and occupations. Consistent portrayal of Asian Americans as studious scientists or engineers stereotypes them in a way that is just as inaccurate and damaging as portraying all Latinos as poor migrant workers. Members of particular cultural groups must be regarded as unique individuals with their own values, beliefs, and opinions, not merely as representatives of those groups.

African Americans reflected this attitude when they reported having specific criteria in mind to choose children's books. These adults explained that they were concerned with accurate portrayal of their culture, lives, and concepts of beauty, and illustrations that looked like their children (Costello, 1992). Violet Harris (1994) considers the portrayal of the African American experience in this country when identifying culturally conscious books.

In order to avoid stereotyping, authors should refrain from using certain items that traditionally have been associated with particular ethnic groups, such as *sombreros*. Customs and values of each group should be accurately portrayed. Illustrations should capture the distinctive characteristics of a particular group and should portray scenes containing members of many cultures. Illustrations of characters of color should be readily recognizable as members of a particular racial or cultural group.

Excellent multicultural literature tells the story from the perspective of a member of the cultural group told about in the story rather than from the perspective of the White majority. It depicts characters as capable of making their own decisions and meeting their own needs without the intervention of White benefactors. Non-White characters are represented as being equal to White characters, not subservient or inferior.

Gender Stereotyping Issues

Evaluation of children's books includes attention to gender stereotyping. Many children's books have traditionally depicted women only in traditional roles such as housewives, reflecting the culture that existed at the time they were written. Traditional literature sometimes portrays helpless, vulnerable female characters waiting for strong, capable men to rescue them, as in the Grimm Brothers' *Snow White* and *Cinderella.*

Although we often point to such works as examples of female stereotyping, they also stereotype men as perpetually strong, capable, and competent. Although criticizing such works for reflecting the needs, values, and mores of people long ago is unfair, it is important, especially in selecting contemporary literature, to offer students a wide variety of all types of literature, ensuring that they have access to plenty of books that carefully avoid gender stereotypes.

Appropriate portrayal of females includes presenting them in a variety of occupations, accurately portraying their contributions to society, showing them deriving satisfaction from their achievements, and describing them as intelligent, independent, and strong. Modern folktales are reversing the stereotyping found

Georgia O'Keeffe created a unique artistic style.

in the aforementioned examples from this genre. Robert Munsch provides a view of a contemporary princess who takes charge of her own life in *The Paper Bag Princess;* other stories, such as Betsy Hearne's *Seven Brave Women* and Jeanette Winter's *My Name Is Georgia,* portray women as strong and capable.

Additional examples of books that avoid stereotyped portrayals of women include *The Hero and the Crown* by Robin McKinley and *Sarah, Plain and Tall* by Patricia MacLachlan. The heroine of *The Hero and the Crown* is a strong, capable female who slays dragons and overcomes an evil magician. Although the setting of this epic is common to traditional literature, the heroine is not depicted in a stereotypical manner. Sarah, of *Sarah, Plain and Tall,* describes herself as "not mild mannered" in a letter to her prospective husband. Although Sarah is a "mail order bride," we find no sense that she is desperate for marriage, only that she welcomes the opportunity for adventure provided by her trip west.

Literature that avoids stereotyping men and boys portrays them as sensitive human beings with a wide range of emotions. In addition, males as well as females should be portrayed in a variety of occupations, including those traditionally reserved for women. Books such as Gary Paulsen's *Hatchet* show an adolescent boy learning to survive in the wilderness while coping with his parents' divorce. Although he lacks the skills and knowledge needed, he uses trial and error strategies to survive. In *On My Honor,* Marion Dane Bauer describes a young man's emotional struggle to deal with his friend's death. These characters exemplify nonstereotyped character development.

Addressing Censorship

It is vitally important that children learn about the ways in which literature may convey prejudice. It is not possible, and it may not be desirable, to insulate children from reading books that do not display a proper appreciation of the dignity of every person (Pinsent, 1997). Teachers, librarians, and parents need to recognize prejudice in literature and to use it when it exists to teach children how to identify it.

The American Library Association sponsors Banned Books Week and provides a *Resource Guide* for schools. They also offer Library Advocacy Training and sponsor the Freedom to Read Foundation. Its Web site is helpful for learning more about censorship and ways of addressing it. The National Coalition Against Censorship maintains a Web site that offers information and resources for people who must navigate the shoals of censorship.

Teachers and librarians may find censors challenging books that have significant literary value so they should be sensitive to community feelings regarding literature. To avoid challenges, they can introduce the literature to parents and offer them opportunities to preview books by including parents in meetings and committees. The National Council of Teachers of English offers a CD–ROM resource entitled *Challenged Books,* which provides rationales for more than 200 literary works that have been frequently challenged and removed from classroom and library shelves. Materials for grades K–12 are included; however, the work emphasizes middle school and high school levels. M. Jerry Weiss (1989) and the International Reading Association's Intellectual Freedom Committee offer the following professional strategies for addressing censorship issues.

1. Communicate with parents regarding their concerns about certain books. This might include forming a book discussion group for parents so that they can read and discuss children's books.
2. Provide a variety of books for children so that if parents prefer their child not to read a specific book, plenty of others are available from which to choose. A well-balanced library collection will contain many books about a given subject.
3. Clearly state and write down the school's adoption and purchasing policy for classroom and library books. The school may create an advisory board to assist in decisions about purchasing books and include parents on the board. Provide forms for parents to complete when they have concerns about a book with room to detail specific objections.
4. A school review committee should consider objections to books by using the questionnaire in Figure 3.2, or a similar one, to guide deliberations regarding objections.

CHILD-CENTERED CRITICISM: WHAT DO CHILDREN LIKE TO READ?

Many teachers advocate children's free choice of literature as an important element for promoting reading in classrooms. Some suggest that children themselves should be the ultimate critics of their literature, that children's preferences for certain kinds of books not only should be honored, but also should form a basis for evaluating books. Children's reading selections frequently include series books such as R. L. Stine's Goosebumps series, American Girl series, and Babysitter's Club series, as well as books based on television

---

FIGURE 3.2 Questionnaire for concerned parents.

1. Have you read the entire book?
2. What is the teacher's purpose for using this material?
3. Identify the specific passages that you find objectionable.
4. In your view, what problems would reading this material cause?
5. What action do you think should be taken?
6. Can you suggest an acceptable substitute?

Jack uses his golden lasso and the help of a buffalo to escape the beanstalk giant.

shows and movies. Thousands of teachers and librarians compiled bibliographies of what their children read, revealing that "the respondents became momentarily addicted to both the series and comic books. . . . These materials seem to be as much a part of one's literary maturation as are the children's classics" (Carlsen & Sherrill, 1988, p. 16).

How do we explain the popularity of such books? First, they possess predictable language, action, and characters. This predictability, coupled with following the same characters' adventures through several books, creates a familiarity that many children enjoy. Second, children identify readily with the characters in these books. Although the characters are often one dimensional, they do possess the larger-than-life characteristics of mythological heroes that are important in traditional literature (Purves & Monson, 1984). The characters in many of these books have characteristics that we admire and find agreeable. Although they are clichés, they sustain children in the same ways that *Cinderella* and *Little Red Riding Hood* do (Purves & Monson, 1984).

Outstanding authors wrote some of the more recent series, such as the Aunt America series, Orphan Train series, Harry Potter series, and Brian Jacques's Redwall series. These books attract many children to reading, developing both motivation and fluency along with other values.

Series books do have value for young readers. "The experience of making patterns, putting stories together, extrapolating and confirming may be providing a crucial step toward more substantial reading" (Mackey, 1990, p. 44). Series books also help children see connections between books from a variety of genres. Teachers can help children discern similarities between series book characters and those found in myths, legends, and other traditional literature. Moreover, such books simply add to "the reservoir of experiences and ideas created from the sum total of all their reading"; the richer this reservoir of experience and ideas, the more effective children's transactions with literature will become over time (Purves & Monson, 1984).

What Attracts Children to Certain Books?

Content is typically regarded as the most important criterion children use in selecting books. Studies over a period of years yield surprisingly consistent results about the topics that appeal to children (Wolfson, Manning, & Manning, 1984). The general interests of children of all

ages include animals, humor, action, suspense, and surprise. Research indicates that reading ability affects reading interests (Swanton, 1984). Lehman (1991) studied nine award-winning books that appeared on the Children's Choices list (published annually by the International Reading Association in *The Reading Teacher*). After analyzing and categorizing the theme, style, and structure of each, she generalized the following:

1. Substantial differences do exist among award-winning books children do and do not prefer.
2. Children prefer predictable qualities, optimistic tone, and a lively pace.
3. Children prefer action-oriented structures and complete plot resolutions.
4. Children do not choose books with unresolved endings, tragic tones, or slow-paced, introspective plots.

Authors and illustrators attract readers

Many children are attracted to books by an author or artist whose work they have enjoyed previously. Readers of all ages from preschool through college seek out known and enjoyed authors and illustrators, and, correspondingly, they may avoid others due to negative experiences (Stoodt-Hill, 1999). For example, the Harry Potter series by J. K. Rowling, published in the United States by Levine, could be termed a phenomenon with middle-grade children who wait for the publication of each new book in the series. Young children look for Steven Kellogg's books because they love his zany illustrations.

Understanding the attraction of known authors suggests that teachers and librarians should be aware of current authors and illustrators so they can make them available to children. Author and illustrator visits attract children to their works. Getting acquainted with artists and illustrators through in-depth studies is also highly motivating for children.

Reading Interest Research

The majority of research into children's reading interests is dated, but the most pertinent is summarized here to help concerned adults think about the reading interests of children (Greenlaw & Wielan, 1979). These studies suggest that the physical characteristics and story elements have significant impact on readers' interests.

Physical characteristics

The physical appearance of books is important to children. Type size, style, illustrations, and cover design influence their choice of books. Children in grades 3 through 8 select books on the basis of appearance, author, recommendation, or some combination of these factors. Older children base their decisions on peer recommendations and the information on the book jacket (Burgess, 1985). Elementary children prefer paperback to hardcover when selecting books (Campbell, 1990).

Illustrations are important to children's choices at all grade levels. Young children generally prefer color illustrations (Stewig, 1972). Even middle school students prefer books with illustrations to those without (Robbins, 1982).

Story elements

Children express preferences based on story structures and elements. Abramson (1980) analyzed the plot structure of 50 picture books on the Children's Choices list. He found that children most frequently chose picture books with one of three plot structures:

1. a main character who confronts a problem and attempts to solve it,
2. a story that unfolds incident by incident, and
3. characters who have opposing viewpoints or who experience the same thing in different ways.

Sebesta's (1979) analysis of the Children's Choices list indicated that children's favorites had fast-paced plots, detailed information and descriptions, and a variety of plot structures. Books with a strong theme and with characters who had warm relationships appeared frequently on the list.

Children's characteristics that influence reading interests

Many factors influence children's reading interests, including age, home environment, developmental appropriateness, gender, race, and reading ability. Children's reading interests are an important aspect of their response to literature, and adults have a better chance of creating pleasurable reading experiences for children when they understand children's reading interests. Students who enjoy books spend more time reading.

Age. Age is clearly related to reading interests. Children's book preferences gradually change as they mature. Younger children exhibit narrow reading interests that gradually broaden as they move from the primary to the elementary grades and then to middle school. Younger children generally have narrower reading interests because they have had fewer life experiences and thus have not developed a range of interests. Research indicates that younger children enjoy fairy tales, animals, make believe, and stories about children. First and second graders in 10 countries preferred fairy tales and fantasy to other types of stories (Feeley, 1981). Research also suggests that children enjoy humorous books and poetry (Sebesta, 1979), particularly poetry with rhyme (Fisher & Natarella, 1982).

Children in grades 4 through 6 consistently exhibit a wider range of interest than their younger counterparts. As children mature they become more interested in realistic literature (Purves & Beach, 1972). Elementary students enjoy adventure stories, fantasies, social studies and history, mysteries, animals, and humor (Pieronek, 1980). Table 3.1 summarizes the research regarding elementary and middle school students' preferences. Students between the ages of 10 and 13 generally are more interested in recreational reading and develop a broader range of interests because they dip into many genres that reflect their range of experiences. In fact, students at this age probably indulge in more recreational reading than they will at any time during their educational lives. As students progress through school, the academic and social demands of their lives leave less and less time for recreational reading.

TABLE 3.1
Elementary and middle school reading preferences.

Topic	Title	Author
Adventure	*Bandit's Moon*	Sid Fleischman
Animal stories	*Not My Dog*	Colby Rodowsky
Fantasy	*Cougar*	Helen V. Griffith
History	*Foster's War*	Carolyn Reeder
Humor	*Granville Jones, Commando*	Natalie Honeycutt
Mystery	*Sammy Keyes and the Skeleton Man*	Wendelin Van Draanen
Social Issues	*Nowhere to Call Home*	Cynthia DeFelice

Developmentally Appropriate Literature

It is important that adults selecting books for children have a sound knowledge of child development. Such knowledge can help them select books appropriate to children's individual needs and abilities and can help promote their progress toward greater literary appreciation. A child who is not developmentally ready for a particular book will derive less meaning and will respond differently to it. Although all children pass through all developmental levels, they do so at their own rate. Even though different age groups are associated with particular developmental levels, these levels are approximate and all children have individual preferences.

Authorities in the field have postulated several child development models. For example, Piaget's (1969) levels of cognitive development provide one means of evaluating how children change and grow. Current theory suggests that children are in the process of becoming literate from birth and are capable of learning to understand written language before attending school (Adams, 1990).

Schlager (1978) examines the relation between child development and children's literature, analyzing the relation between the characteristics of middle childhood (ages 7 through 12) and the children's book choices. She found a clear correlation between the books that were most read and the developmental characteristics of middle childhood; the children's interest was aroused by the developmental characteristics displayed by the main characters in the story rather than the literary quality of the books.

Table 3.2 summarizes children's stages of development and the developmental characteristics for each stage, and it includes books appropriate to each level.

Gender. Although the role of gender in reading interests is unclear because of the individual nature of children's reading interests, research indicates that these differences become more prominent at about age 9 (Haynes, 1988) with the greatest number of differences appearing between ages 10 and 13. The impact of gender on reading interests has been observed in many different countries (Fisher, 1988). Sex stereotypes in reading preferences have been observed in preschool children as well as school-age students (Kropp & Halverson, 1983). Boys prefer the main characters to be male and girls prefer them to be female. However, determining whether these are actual differences or merely a reflection of culturally transmitted behavior is difficult.

The Stetson hat helped win the West.

In general, elementary girls prefer fiction about home, family, and animals (Haynes, 1988). Elementary girls enjoy fantasy, whereas boys in these grades exhibit a growing interest in nonfiction. Boys like action and adventure stories and sports stories (Haynes, 1988). Table 3.3 summarizes the gender differences in children's reading interests.

Environment. The home, school, teacher, and community are all powerful influences on children's interests, motivations, and development. Morrow (1983) finds that young children who express interest in literature come from homes with environments supportive of literacy: books are available and parents read for themselves and to their children and use the public library. According to Morrow, "Before the child gets to school many background characteristics that have been linked to high and low interest in literature have been established" (p. 229).

The school, classroom, and teacher also have substantial impact on children's reading interests. An increasing number of studies point to the positive effects of teachers' influence on children's reading interests.

TABLE 3.2 Appropriate literature for each developmental stage.

Age and Stage	Characteristics	Book Types	Sample Books
0–6 prereading	acquire language rapidly understand simple concepts, environmental print, signs, brand names	concept	*Planting a Rainbow*, Lois Ehlert *Airport*, Donald Crews
	recognize letters, numbers, their own names	alphabet	*A. B. See*, Tana Hoban *One Day Two Dragons*, Lynne Bertrand
	enjoy listening to stories	simple, predictable	*Goodnight Moon*, Margaret Wise Brown *Brown Bear, Brown Bear*, Bill Martin, Jr.
	engage in pretend reading	wordless books	*The Snowman*, Raymond Briggs *Deep in the Forest*, Brinton Turkle
6–7 initial reading	learn letters and associate them with words	easy to read	*Mine's the Best*, Crosby Consall *A Dark, Dark Tale*, Ruth Brown
	develop concepts of print	animal books	*Go Dog Go*, P. D. Eastman *Little Bear*, Else Minarick
	bring meaning to print	predictable	*Hop on Pop*, Dr. Seuss
7–8 confirmation fluency	read to increase fluency	high frequency words	*Frog and Toad*, Arnold Lobel *Henry and Mudge*, Cynthia Rylant *Babar's Little Circus Star*, Laurent de Brunhoff
		nonfiction	*Going on a Whale Watch*, Bruce McMillan
9–12	read for knowledge, information, ideas, and experiences	more complex and sophisticated fiction	*Lon Po*, Ed Young *Bunnicula*, Deborah & James Howe *Tuck Everlasting*, Natalie Babbitt
	word meanings and prior experiences are important	nonfiction	*Honest Abe*, Malcah Zeldis *The Hospital Book*, James Howe *Whales and Dolphins*, Steve Parker *A Medieval Feast*, Aliki *A Walk on the Great Barrier Reef*, Caroline Arnold *The Great Little Madison*, Jean Fritz
	longer, more complex sentences		

TABLE 3.3
Gender differences in children's reading interests.

Boys' Interests	Girls' Interests
Male characters	*Female characters*
Nonfiction topics	*Fiction topics*
■ science	■ families
■ animals	■ home
■ history	■ romance
■ biography	■ historical fiction
■ geography	■ mystery/adventure
■ sports	■ fantasy
■ cars	■ multiethnic
■ war	*Nonfiction topics*
■ machines	■ sports
■ applied science	■ arts
■ adventure	■ multiethnic

Blatt and Cunningham's (1981) longitudinal study of classroom environments in which children learned to read finds that teachers are most successful in fostering reading interests when they give children time to read, use literature to teach reading, or read aloud regularly to students. Fielding, Wilson, and Anderson (1986) find that avid readers belong to communities of readers that begin at home but expand to include peers and teachers. In fact, Zimet (1966) finds that peers have the greatest influence on children's reading.

Hiebert, Mervar, and Person (1990) find that second graders whose classrooms contain many trade books and commonly used literature give more detailed reasons for their book selections and have specific reasons for their book selections and have specific reasons in mind when they visit the library. Morrow (1983) finds that kindergartners from classrooms with literature programs that rate as good or excellent show higher interest in books than children who do not come from such classrooms.

Family and school have a stronger influence on children's interest in reading than some other factors. Studies of the reading interests of urban and suburban children, however, show that other factors are at work as well. Feeley (1981) reports that suburban boys prefer sports and historical fiction more than urban boys. Suburban females prefer social empathy and animal stories, whereas urban females show higher preference for books related to the arts.

Race and ethnic origins. The research results regarding the racial and ethnic differences in children's reading interests are dated and inconclusive. The availability of literature with minority characters as protagonists was so limited in the past that children had little opportunity to exhibit differences in reading interests. We do know, however, that children enjoy reading about people who are like themselves, so with exposure to multicultural literature, researchers find a good chance that minority children will prefer it.

Reading ability. The influence of reading ability on reading interest is unclear. Several studies indicate that reading interests of students at different achievement levels do not differ (Hawkins, 1984; Stanchfield & Fraim, 1979). Swanton (1984), however, finds that gifted readers prefer mysteries, fiction, science fiction, and fantasy, whereas average readers prefer mysteries, comedy/humor, realistic fiction, and adventure. She also finds that children in different groups choose different favorite authors. Style may contribute to these differences; for example, some authors write in abstract language, which appeals to some children, whereas other children prefer authors who use concrete language. Readers with higher ability select longer books than those with less reading ability (Anderson, Higgins, & Wurster, 1985).

Readability. Books with too many unknown words daunt even the most determined readers. Some books are meant to be read aloud to children and others to be read independently. Although children with a strong interest in a topic can compensate for difficult readability, expecting too much of readers is unwise.

Readability refers to the reading level of a book, and this level should be considered not only by teachers, parents, and librarians when selecting books for children to read, but also by children themselves as they select books to read on their own. Readability formulas provide a rough measure of the range of difficulty of a book based on the number of difficult words and the average sentence length. Teachers can apply several readability formulas to determine book levels, but children can use a simple one to check the difficulty of a particular book themselves. The "five-finger test" simply involves selecting a page in a book and counting on the fingers of one hand the number of unknown words. If a child finds five or more unknown words on the page, the book may be too difficult.

Some children's books include information regarding the readability level on the dust jacket or cover. The designation "RL 4.0" means that the book is written at a fourth-grade reading level. This does not mean the book is appropriate for every fourth grader, however, because reading abilities in a fourth-grade classroom may range from first to seventh grade. Moreover, children must be able to pronounce 98 to 100 percent of the words and answer 90 to 100 percent of the questions asked about the book if they are to read with understanding. Therefore, if the book is to be read independently, it might well be appropriate for an average reader in fifth grade.

Identifying Reading Interests

Teachers can identify individual children's reading interests through three techniques:

1. Observe children as they engage in classroom activities, noting and recording interests exhibited during class assignments, oral discussions, group projects, and so forth.
2. Conduct informal discussions with the children themselves, their parents, peers, and others, which will reveal some interests.
3. Conduct interest inventories, which take a variety of forms, asking children directly about their reading interests. Children can list favorite book titles, respond to questions through a multiple-choice format, or complete sentence starters (illustrated in Figure 3.3).

Guidelines for Literature Selection

Remember to consider not only literary quality when selecting children's books, but also children's reading interests and issues as well. This will help create a well-balanced literary experience for the children.

Bibliotherapy literally means "helping with books." A book that presents a story or information about a problem that is troubling a child is often helpful to the child in working through the trouble. Historically, doctors, therapists, and other health-care professionals have used bibliotherapy. According to Bernstein (1989), bibliotherapy involves the "self examination and insights gained from reading" (p. 159). Such experiences may result from planned and unplanned encounters with print. They

FIGURE 3.3   Interest inventory.

1. I like to read _____.
2. I go to the library every _____.
3. I like to read when _____.
4. I like to read more than I like to _____.
5. I like to watch television every _____.
6. I like television shows about _____.
7. Books about sports are _____.
8. I think horse stories are _____.
9. I think mysteries are _____.
10. My favorite author is _____.
11. Books bore me when _____.
12. I read funny stories about _____.
13. When I have spare time, I _____.
14. I like to read in _____.
15. Good books make me feel _____.
16. The best books are about _____.
17. I own _____

_____

_____

_____

_____ books.

18. My favorite video is _____.
19. The best taped book I have heard is _____.
20. I read _____ because my friend told me about it.

Scoring: Score one point for each positive answer. Positive answers are answers that indicate the student enjoys reading and has identifiable reading, listening, and viewing interests.

13–17 = child has positive attitude toward reading.
9–12 = child has average interest in reading.
1–8 = child needs guidance in developing greater interest in reading.

Guidelines for Literature Selection

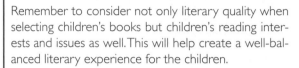

Remember to consider not only literary quality when selecting children's books but children's reading interests and issues as well. This will help create a well-balanced literary experience for the children.

1. Is the book of high literary quality?

   a. Fiction

   - Is the plot well developed?
   - Are characters well drawn and memorable?
   - Does the setting accurately reflect the time and place?
   - Is the theme significant?
   - Is the book carefully crafted and well written?

   b. Nonfiction

   - Is the author qualified to write this book?
   - Is the information clearly organized and presented?

   - Is the information accurate?
   - Is this book appropriate to a child audience?

2. Does the book appeal to children's reading interests?
3. Does the book avoid stereotyping on the basis of race, sex, age, and other discriminatory factors?
4. Is the book's readability level appropriate to the audience that is expected to read it?
5. Is the book's physical format appealing to children?
6. Will this book enhance the child's personal growth and development?
7. Will this book contribute to the child's development as a reader?
8. Will this book help foster a love of reading in this child?
9. Am I creating an environment that will help promote love of literature?

---

may occur when an individual seeks out a book relating to a particular problem or when a teacher or librarian directs a student to a specific book.

Bibliotherapy can help meet children's most basic human needs. Children's needs for love, belonging, esteem, and self-actualization can be met through the three fundamental responses associated with bibliotherapy: identification, catharsis, and insight. Through *identification,* readers associate themselves with story characters, recognizing similarities to their own lives. Sometimes talking about the problems that book characters encounter enables children to reveal their own difficulties. *Catharsis* is the emotional release that occurs when readers identify with a character. Some readers express their response orally, an important part of the therapeutic process; others find writing about their experience, which can lead to and facilitate discussion, easier. *Insight* is a form of self-discovery whereby attitudinal and behavioral changes occur; it is therefore often regarded as the crucial factor in bibliotherapy (Stephens, 1981). When children respond to their reading, they may grow and change as a result of the experience of reading.

For the child experiencing the fear, loneliness, and confusion created by the loss of a parent, a book such as *How It Feels When a Parent Dies* by Jill Krementz may be helpful. This book is a collection of interviews with children who describe their feelings about this traumatic event. A child who has recently experienced this loss may identify with all of the children in the book or with the feelings of one particular child. Identification may help the child feel less alone with the grief and may ultimately result in catharsis and insight. Moreover, this process can enhance children's sense of self, thereby contributing to their self-esteem.

Children's response to books is central to the concept of bibliotherapy, but we cannot accurately predict the response of a particular individual to a particular book. Teachers often find that a book that appealed to a previous class holds no interest for this year's class. Often a book that one individual does not enjoy is of particular interest to another person to whom the book speaks. For instance, one student commented to a teacher that she had enjoyed a certain book more than any other she had ever read. The teacher was puzzled because in her opinion the book had no redeeming qualities. The student explained, however, that she had blamed herself for her mother's suicide until she read this book, in which the same tragic event had happened. The student developed insight about her own life through reading this book. Unfortunately, such responses are not predictable, so, although teachers can make suggestions, children should choose books that appeal to them and seem to meet their needs.

Bernstein (1989) suggests guidelines for selecting books to use therapeutically in the classroom:

1. Allow children to select their own books.
2. Discuss books with the students, and the adults should listen with empathy rather than sympathy.
3. Use group discussions to help children generate new solutions to problems. Group discussions should focus on expressing and clarifying feelings. Children who are uncomfortable with discussing feelings should not be forced into revelations.

MEDIA-BASED LITERATURE

Audio books, computerized books, television, and movies and videos are legitimate forms of literature that are here to stay. High-quality media actively involve children with the literature they are experiencing—an advantage for many children that they may carry into other literary experiences. *Reading Rainbow,* which is aired on local PBS stations, is a superb television show for children.

The availability of media-based literature is growing rapidly: Listening Library now offers more than 200 unabridged children's recordings. Although these media do not replace books, they do offer a different dimension, and narrators and actors can make stories come alive for children. Many children will go on to read books they have been exposed to through various media; others will not because the media offer an alternative route to literature they could not access otherwise. Videos such as *The Very Hungry Caterpillar* (Disney) offer animation and music to enhance this well-loved story. The various genres of children's literature are represented in videos. The *James Marshall Library* (Children's Circle/Scholastic) includes popular fairy tales that primary-grade children will enjoy. Videos include feature-length films such as *Beethoven Lives Upstairs.* The *Children's Literature Web Guide* on the Internet can direct you to multimedia materials that have

been evaluated by parents' groups and the American Library Association.

The growth of literature available on the computer has surged since CD–ROM drives have been added to computers. *Living Books,* featuring children's authors such as Mercer Mayer, are very popular (Random House/Broderbund). *Busy Town* by Richard Scarry has received the Parents Award for Quality (Paramount International). Microsoft published some of the *Magic School Bus* titles on CD–ROM and children find them fascinating. The interactive, involving nature of computerized books adds to their popularity and their value for children.

Media-based literature should not be based on offering alternative editions of existing books; it should offer additional dimensions. Some writers create original literature for CD–ROM rather than converting existing literature to a media format. Shelley Duvall writes computer-based adventure stories centered on Digby, a little dog with a big bark (Sanctuary Woods). *Where in the World Is Carmen Sandiego?* (Broderbund) is an interactive detective story that also provides geography lessons to participants. *Freddi Fish and the Case of the Missing Kelp Seeds* (Humongous Entertainment) is another entertaining and original computer story.

Some exceptional audiotapes for upper elementary students are *Anapao* by Jamake Highwater (Recorded Books), Gary Paulsen's *Canyons* (Bantam Doubleday Dell Audio), and Scott O'Dell's *Island of the Blue Dolphins* (Recorded Books). Peter Coyote narrates *Canyons,* a parallel story of two boys, one contemporary and one an Apache who lived a century earlier. Audio recording is the perfect medium for *Anapao,* which was intended to be read aloud, and this recording captures the distinctive style of Native American storytelling. Listening to the recording of *Island of the Blue Dolphins* brings the story alive even for those who have read it many times before.

Some of these media stories will become classics for future generations. Certainly the movie *Fantasia* is a Disney classic and Disney's *Jungle Book* has led to a resurgence of interest in the original writing of this wonderful story, popularizing Rudyard Kipling's book for a new generation. Raffi, a singer and storyteller, is a superstar to many in the younger set, who flock to his concerts, listen to his audiotapes, and watch his videos.

Evaluating Media-Based Literature

The standards for literature identified earlier in this chapter are applicable to media presentations of literature. Some children's bookstores and companies that distribute media to schools will allow teachers to try out or preview their materials, an advantage because catalog descriptions and advertising materials cannot predict how the children will respond. In addition to trying before buying, the following guidelines should be helpful in selecting media-based literature.

1. The literature must tell a good story or a wonderful poem or give accurate, interesting information (check the guidelines established in the genre chapters).
2. The literature must actively involve viewers or listeners.
3. The literature should convey the essence of the literature so that plot, theme, characterization, and setting are authentic, although style may differ according to the medium.
4. The literature should meet all of the standards set for written literature; for instance, informational literature should meet nonfiction standards and the difference between theory and fact should be apparent.
5. The literature should have all illustrations in scale and accurately identified.
6. The literature should not be simplified so that it loses literary quality; literature prepared for film, computer, video, and so forth may require changes but these can be achieved without loss of quality.
7. The literature should not trivialize the story, for instance, by making the presentation too "cute."

Using Media-Based Literature

Media-based literature is easy to present: it can be done by turning a switch. It should always, however, be a part of a planned literary experience. Parents, teachers, or librarians presenting the literature should share the experience with the children. First, creating a context for the experience by introducing the piece and helping the children see connections to themselves will help ensure their active involvement and response; afterward, adults can discuss the experience with the children and share their responses. Discussion and opportunities to respond are just as important for media

as for books. The suggestions in chapter 4 will be helpful in planning responses to media-based literature.

SUMMARY

Choosing well-written, interesting books for classrooms and libraries is basic to creating successful literature programs. Such a large number of children's books are published each year, and these books vary so widely in quality, that book selection is too important to be left to chance. Carefully selected literature engages readers' minds and interests and feelings. Considerations in selection include interests, age, grade, and developmental stage. Books should be evaluated from a variety of perspectives, including references and Web sites. Censorship denies children free access to books, which does not prepare them to make responsible choices or to promote their intellectual growth.

A broad collection of excellent literature drawn from all genres is the cornerstone of literary experience. Books selected should appeal to both readers and listeners. In selecting books, consider the elements that make a story, a poem, or an informational book excellent literature. Children's reading interests are important considerations in choosing literature.

When stocking a library or media center, remember that literature is not confined to print. Media such as films, videos, audiotapes, filmstrips, recordings, puppets, reader's theater, dramatizations, and storytelling are forms of literary experience. Experiencing literature through various media expands background knowledge, deepens students' response, and strengthens their understanding.

Thought Questions

1. What factors should you consider when selecting children's books?
2. Summarize the research related to children's reading interests in your own words.
3. What books did you enjoy as a child? How old were you when you enjoyed these books? How do you think these books related to your development?
4. Why is avoiding books that have gender or racial stereotyping important?
5. Describe some ways that teachers, parents, and librarians can promote children's reading interests.

Research and Application Experiences

1. Select several books for a child with whom you are well acquainted. Consider the criteria listed on page 52. Which of these criteria did you apply when choosing these books? Which were least important?

2. Read three Newbery and three Caldecott books. Evaluate each one according to the award criteria, then rank the books according to your own evaluation.

3. Interview children who have read Newbery or Caldecott winners. Find out which were their favorites and why.

4. Imagine that a parent has challenged you for using a particular children's book. Role-play the meeting you would have with him or her.

Children's Literature References and Recommended Books

Note: Books designated with an asterisk (*) are recommended for reluctant readers.

Alcott, L. M. (1924). *Little women.* Boston: Little, Brown. (5–8). CONTEMPORARY REALISTIC FICTION.

A classic tale of a warm, loving family.

Arnosky, J. (1983). *Secrets of a wildlife watcher.* New York: Lothrop, Lee & Shepard. (2–5). INFORMATIONAL BOOK.

A children's manual for observing wildlife, animals' tracks, and so forth.

Bauer, M. D. (1986). *On my honor.* New York: Clarion. (4–7). CONTEMPORARY REALISTIC FICTION.

A boy must cope with guilt and self-blame when his friend drowns.

Burnett, F. H. (1962). *The secret garden.* Philadelphia: Lippincott. (4–6). MODERN FANTASY.

A spoiled girl and a pampered invalid find themselves in an old garden. They learn compassion as they solve their problems.

DeFelice, C. (1999). *Nowhere to call home.* New York: Farrar. (3–6). CONTEMPORARY REALISTIC FICTION.

After Elizabeth Barrow's father commits suicide, she decides to hop a freight train, and this is the story of her adventures.

Defoe, D. (1999). *Robinson Crusoe.* New York: Dover. CONTEMPORARY REALISTIC FICTION.

Shipwrecked man makes a life on an isolated island with the assistance of a native that he names "Friday."

Disher, G. (1993). *The bamboo flute.* New York: Ticknor & Fields. (4–8). HISTORICAL FICTION.*

Paul lives in Australia during hard times, the legacy of World War I. Beautifully written and includes authentic Australian life, as well as adolescent self-discovery.

Evans, D. (1995). *Monster soup and other spooky poems* (J. Rogers, Illus.). New York: Scholastic. (1–4). POETRY.

The humorous side of spooky creatures appears in these poems.

Fleischman, S. (1998). *Bandit's moon* (J. A. Smith, Illus.). New York: Greenwillow. (4–6). HISTORICAL FICTION.*

An adventure story in which Annyrose escapes a horse thief only to fall into the clutches of the Robin Hood of the California Gold Rush.

George, J. C. (1972). *Julie of the wolves.* New York: Harper & Row. (5–7). CONTEMPORARY REALISTIC FICTION.

This is a survival story set in the Alaskan wilderness.

Griffith, H. V. (1999). *Cougar.* New York: Greenwillow (4–7). MODERN FANTASY.*

In this unusual fantasy, a boy meets a ghost horse in a mysterious, but believable, situation.

Grimm, J., & Grimm, W. (1972). *Snow-White and the seven dwarfs* (N. E. Burkert, Illus.). New York: Farrar, Straus & Giroux. (2–4). TRADITIONAL LITERATURE.

A classic version of this tale.

Grimm, J., & Grimm, W. (1987). *Cinderella.* New York: Holiday. (1–3). TRADITIONAL LITERATURE.

An older version of the well-known folktale.

Hearne, B. (1997). *Seven brave women* (B. Andersen, Illus.). New York: Greenwillow. (2–6). INFORMATIONAL BOOK.*

This is the history of seven women who expressed their bravery in many ways.

Hesse, K. (1997). *Out of the dust.* New York: Scholastic. (4–8). HISTORICAL FICTION.

In this story set during the Great Depression, Billie Jo's father caused the accident that killed her mother. Billie Jo must find a way to forgive herself and her father.

Holman, F. (1986). *Slake's limbo*. New York: Aladdin. (5–7). CONTEMPORARY REALISTIC FICTION.*

Slake goes underground in the subway system when life overwhelms him above ground.

Honeycutt, N. (1998). *Granville Jones, Commando*. New York: Farrar. (2–4). CONTEMPORARY REALISTIC FICTION.

Granville Jones stalks through the neighborhood in combat boots and fatigues. He has problems—his parents are having a baby.

Kellogg, S. (1986). *Best friends*. New York: Dial. (K–3). PICTURE BOOK.

Kathy is lonely when her best friend goes away for the summer.

King-Smith, D. (1998). *The water horse* (D. Parkins, Illus.). New York: Crown. (3–5). MODERN FANTASY.*

When Kirstie discovers a giant egg on their beach in Scotland, she puts it in the bathtub and it hatches into a kelpie, or water horse. It grows from 15 inches to 15 feet and more.

Krementz, J. (1981). *How it feels when a parent dies*. New York: Knopf. (3–6). INFORMATIONAL BOOK.

This book tells a child's feelings about a parent's death.

Lewis, C. S. (1950). *The lion, the witch and the wardrobe* (P. Baynes, Illus.). New York: Macmillan. (5 and up). MODERN FANTASY.

This allegorical fantasy explores the experiences of four children who enter the kingdom of Narnia.

MacLachlan, P. (1985). *Sarah, plain and tall*. New York: Harper & Row. (3–6). HISTORICAL FICTION.

Sarah, a mail-order bride, comes to live with a man and his two children.

McKinley, R. (1985). *The hero and the crown*. New York: Greenwillow. (3–5). MODERN FANTASY.

Aerin, the daughter of the Damarian king and a witchwoman of the North, wins her birthright.

Munsch, R. N. (1980). *The paper bag princess*. Toronto: Annick Press. (1–4). MODERN FANTASY.

A modern princess discovers her prince is not husband material.

Myers, W. D. (1988). *Scorpions*. New York: Harper & Row. (5–7). CONTEMPORARY REALISTIC FICTION.

Jamal is forced by family tragedies to grow up quickly.

Norton, M. (1953). *The borrowers*. New York: Harcourt Brace Jovanovich. (2–4). MODERN FANTASY.

A family of tiny people live by borrowing from the "human beans."

O'Dell, S. (1960). *Island of the blue dolphins*. Boston: Houghton Mifflin. (4–6). HISTORICAL FICTION.

A true story of a girl who survived alone on a Pacific island.

Paterson, K. (1978). *The great Gilly Hopkins*. New York: Crowell. (4–6). CONTEMPORARY REALISTIC FICTION.

Gilly, a foster child, moves to a new foster home and attempts to outdo her foster mother, but Mame Trotter wisely wins her over. Gilly begins to mature through her disappointments.

Paulsen, G. (1987). *Hatchet*. New York: Viking Penguin. (5–7). CONTEMPORARY REALISTIC FICTION.*

Brian survives an airplane crash and spends the next 54 days trying to survive with only the hatchet his mother gave him.

Potter, B. (1934). *The tale of Peter Rabbit*. New York: Frederick Warne. (PreK–2). PICTURE BOOK, MODERN FANTASY.

A classic tale of a naughty rabbit.

Reeder, C. (1998). *Foster's war*. New York: Scholastic. (4–8). HISTORICAL FICTION.

This is the story of 11-year-old Foster who has conflicts about his father, his best friend, and his older brother who is in the air corps.

Rodowsky, C. (1999). *Not my dog* (T. Yezerski, Illus.). New York: Farrar, Straus & Giroux. (4–7). CONTEMPORARY REALISTIC FICTION.*

Ellie always wanted a dog, but not the one she got.

Rowling, J. K. (1999). *Harry Potter and the chamber of secrets* (M. GrandPré, Illus.). New York: Levine. (4–6). MODERN FANTASY.

Harry Potter is an orphaned wizard who attends the Hogwarts School for Witchcraft and Wizardry.

Sendak, M. (1963). *Where the wild things are*. New York: Harper & Row. (PreK–2). PICTURE BOOK, MODERN FANTASY.

A classic favorite in which a boy visits the land of wild things.

Speare, E. G. (1983). *The sign of the beaver*. Boston: Houghton Mifflin. (4–6). HISTORICAL FICTION.

A boy left alone in the wilderness survives with the assistance of a Native American boy.

Tolkien, J. R. R. (1938). *The hobbit.* Boston: Houghton Mifflin. (6–Adult). MODERN FANTASY.

A hobbit and 13 dwarves seek to overcome the evil dragon.

Twain, M. (1999). *The adventures of Tom Sawyer.* New York: Random House. (7–Adult). HISTORICAL FICTION.

The story of a boy growing up on the Mississippi River.

Van Allsburg, C. (1985). *The polar express.* Boston: Houghton Mifflin. (K–4). MODERN FANTASY.

This story of a train to the North Pole could almost be considered a classic.

Van Draanen, W. (1998). *Sammy Keyes and the skeleton man.* New York: Knopf. (4–6). CONTEMPORARY REALISTIC FICTION.*

In this mystery, Sammy goes trick-or-treating at the creepy home of Chauncy LeBard.

White, E. B. (1952). *Charlotte's web* (G. Williams, Illus.). New York: Harper. (3–6). MODERN FANTASY.

This classic book describes the friendship between Charlotte and Wilbur, a spider and a pig.

Winter, J. (1998). *My name is Georgia.* San Diego: Silver Whistle/Harcourt Brace. (1–4). BIOGRAPHY.

This is the story of Georgia O'Keeffe, the artist, who saw the world in her own way.

Multimedia References

Children's circle. Scholastic offers a variety of titles for primary grades.

Reading rainbow. Public Broadcasting System. Individual videos of programs can be ordered and teachers can videotape to use in their own classes.

The very hungry caterpillar. Disney (Based on the picture book by E. Carle). (PreK–2). MODERN FANTASY.

Recorded Books

Highwater, J. *Anapao.* Recorded books. (4–6). CONTEMPORARY REALISTIC FICTION.

Paulsen, G. *Canyons.* Bantam Doubleday Dell Audio. (3–6). CONTEMPORARY REALISTIC FICTION.

Listening Library has a large variety of titles available.

Computer Software

Duvall, S. *Digby* (several titles). Sanctuary Woods. (PreK–2). MODERN FANTASY.

Freddi Fish and the case of the missing kelp seeds. Humongous Entertainment. (K–2). MODERN FANTASY.

Mayer, M. Various titles. Random House/Broderbund. (PreK–2). MODERN FANTASY.

Magic school bus. Various titles. Scholastic. (K–4). MODERN FANTASY, INFORMATIONAL.

Scarry, R. *Busy town.* Paramount International. (PreK–1).

Activities about neighborhoods and building.

Where in the world is Carmen Sandiego? Broderbund. (1–3). INFORMATIONAL.

References and Books for Further Reading

Abramson, R. (1980). An analysis of children's favorite picture storybooks. *The Reading Teacher, 34,* 167–170.

Adams, J. J. (1990). *Thinking and learning about print.* Cambridge, MA: MIT Press.

Anderson, G., Higgins, D., & Wurster, S. R. (1985). Differences in the free-reading books selected by high, average, and low achievers. *The Reading Teacher, 39,* 326–330.

Bauer, C. J., & Sanborn, L. (1981). The best of both worlds: Children's books acclaimed by adults and young readers. *Top of the News, 38,* 53–56.

Bernstein, J. E. (1989). Bibliotherapy: How books can help young children cope. In *Books to help children cope with separation and loss* (2nd ed., pp. 166–178). New York: Bowker.

Blatt, G., & Cunningham, J. (1981). *It's your move: Expressive movement activities in the classroom.* New York: Teachers College Press.

Bowker, R. R. (Ed.). (1991). *Children's reference plus.* New York: Bowker.

Burgess, S. A. (1985). Reading but not literature: The ChildRead survey. *School Library Journal, 31,* 27–30.

Campbell, R. (1990). *Reading together.* London: Open University.

Carlsen, G. R., & Sherrill, A. (1988). *Voices of readers: How we came to love books.* Urbana, IL: National Council of Teachers of English.

Carlson, A. D. (1991). *The preschooler and the library.* Metuchen, NJ: Scarecrow.

Cooper-Mullin, A., & Coye, J. M. (1998). *Once upon a heroine.* Chicago: Contemporary Books.

Costello, J. H. (1992). *An inquiry into the attitudes of a selected group of African Americans towards the portrayal of African Americans in contemporary children's literature.* Unpublished doctoral dissertation, University of North Carolina at Greensboro.

Council on Interracial Books for Children. (1976). *Human (and anti-human) values in books for children.* New York: Racism and Sexism Resource Center for Educators.

Feeley, J. T. (1981). What do our children like to read? *New Jersey Education Association Review, 54,* 26–27.

Fielding, L. G., Wilson, P., & Anderson, R. (1986). A new focus on free reading: The role of trade books in reading instruction. In T. Raphael (Ed.), *The contexts of school-based literacy* (pp. 149–169). New York: Random House.

Fisher, C., & Natarella, M. (1982). Young children's preferences in poetry: A national survey of first, second, and third graders. *Research in the Teaching of English, 16,* 339–354.

Fisher, E. (1988). The artist at work: Creating nonfiction. *The Horn Book, 64,* 315–323.

Greenlaw, M. J., & Wielan, O. P. (1979). Reading interests revisited. *Language Arts, 56,* 432–434.

Harris, V. J. (1994). No invitations required to share multicultural literature. *Journal of Children's Literature, 20,* 9–15.

Hawkins, S. (1984). Reading interests of gifted children. *Reading Horizons, 24,* 18–22.

Haynes, C. (1988). Explanatory power of content for identifying children's literature preferences. *Dissertation Abstracts International, 49–12A,* 3617. University Microfilms, No. DEW8900468.

Hearne, B. (1990). *Choosing books for children: A commonsense approach.* **New York: Delacorte.**

Hiebert, E. H., Mervar, K., & Person, D. (1990). Children's selection of trade books in libraries and classrooms. *Language Arts, 67,* 758–763.

Hill, S. (1986). What are children reading? *Australian Journal of Reading, 7,* 196–198.

Hopkins, L. B. (1986). Profile in memoriam: E. B. White. *Language Arts, 63,* 491–494.

Kropp, J. J., & Halverson, C. (1983). Preschool children's preferences and recall for stereotyped versus non-stereotyped stories. *Sex Roles, 9,* 261–272.

Lehman, B. A. (1991). Children's choice and critical acclaim: A united perspective for children's literature. *Reading Research and Instruction, 30,* 1–20.

Mackey, M. (1990). Filling the gaps: The baby-sitters club, the series book, and the learning reader. *Language Arts, 67,* 484–489.

McClure, A. (1995). Censorship in children's books. In S. Lehr (Ed.), *Battling dragons: Issues and controversies in children's literature.* Portsmouth, NH: Heinemann.

Morrow, L. (1983). Home and school correlates of early interest in literature. *Journal of Educational Research, 75,* 339–344.

Odean, K. (1998). *Great books for boys.* New York: Ballantine.

Ohanian, S. (1990). How to create a generation of aliterates. In K. Goodman, L. Bird, & Y. Goodman (Eds.), *Whole language catalog* (p. 76). New York: American School.

Peterson, L. K., & Solt, M. L. (1982). *Newbery and Caldecott Medal and honor books.* New Providence, NJ: Bowker.

Piaget, J. (1969). *Judgement and reasoning in the child* (M. Warden, Trans.). Totawa, NJ: Littlefield Adams.

Pieronek, F. T. (1980). Do basal readers reflect the interests of intermediate students? *The Reading Teacher, 33,* 408–412.

Pinsent, P. (1997). *Children's literature and the politics of equality.* New York: Teachers College Press.

Purves, A., & Beach, R. (1972). *Literature and the reader: Research in response to literature, reading interests, and the teaching of literature.* Urbana, IL: National Council of Teachers of English.

Purves, A., & Monson, D. (1984). *Experiencing children's literature.* Glenview, IL: Scott Foresman.

Rachlin, J. (1988, August 1). Timeless tales + big sales. *U.S. News & World Report,* 50–51.

Robbins, P. (Ed.). (1982, November 22). *National geographic books for world explorers.* Presentation to Children's Literature Association, Washington, DC.

Schlager, N. (1978). Predicting children's choices in literature: A developmental approach. *Children's Literature in Education, 9,* 136–142.

Sebesta, S. (1979). What do young people think about the literature they read? *Reading Newsletter, 8,* 3.

Shafer, P. J. (1976, May). The readability of Newbery Award and Caldecott Medal books. *Language Arts, 53,* 557–559.

Smith, F. (1988). *Joining the literary club: Further essays into education.* Portsmouth, NH: Heinemann.

Stanchfield, J., & Fraim, S. (1979). A follow-up study on the reading interests of boys. *The Reading Teacher, 39,* 326.

Stephens, J. W. (1981). *A practical guide in the use and implementation of bibliotherapy.* Great Neck, NY: Todd & Honeywell.

Stewig, J. (1972). Children's preferences in picture book illustration. *Educational Leadership, 30,* 276–277.

Stoodt-Hill, B. (1999). How children choose their books. Unpublished research paper.

Swanton, S. (1984). Minds alive! What and why gifted students read for pleasure. *School Library Journal, 30,* 99–102.

Trelease, J. (1995). *The read-aloud handbook.* New York: Penguin Books.

Weiss, M. J. (1989). International Reading Association stands out against censorship. *Reading Today, 6,* 6.

Wolfson, B., Manning, G., & Manning, M. (1984). Revisiting what children say their reading interests are. *The Reading World, 14,* 81–82.

Zimet, S. (1966). Children's interests and story preferences. *Elementary School Journal, 67,* 123–130.

Encouraging Children's Response to Literature

KEY TERMS

aesthetic reading
character map
community
  of response
efferent reading
engaging with
  literature
envisionment

inferencing
intertextuality
knowledge charts
plot
prediction
stance
story map
story pyramid

GUIDING QUESTIONS

Think about your responses to the different kinds of literature you read. What aspect of that literature arouses the strongest response? As you read this chapter, think about the following questions and answer them after you complete the chapter.

1. Why is response to literature important?

2. How do literary experiences change over time?

3. How can teachers nurture children's response to literature?

4. How do readers construct meaning?

5. Describe the response process in your own words.

OVERVIEW

Children's response to literature is a relatively young area of study. Prior to 1979, researchers studied only the literary responses of adults and adolescents because they did not view children's books as "real" literature. Moreover, they assumed that children did not have a sufficient store of experience to respond to literature (Holland, Hungerford, & Ernst, 1993). Since that time children's literature has gained stature, and we recognize that children do respond to literature.

Readers construct meaning by interacting with text. They use not only what is in the text—words and their meanings—but also what they bring to the text to make meaning (Short, 1995; Thacker, 1995; Musthafa, 1996). Readers respond to the meaning they create, and they continue to respond as they rethink and reread the book or parts of the book, or even read another book that is somehow related. *Response* refers to the reader's reactions and feelings about a book or books. This view of reading is the impetus for a response-centered literature program. In this chapter we explore ways of creating meaningful literary experiences and nurturing children's response to literature.

INTRODUCTION

Children will respond to poetry, fiction, and nonfiction. Their choices of reading material are as diverse as their background experiences; and giving them opportunities to respond will enhance their literacy experiences. Both comprehension and response increase through offering children opportunities to reflect on their literacy experiences. Moreover, relating their understanding of books with other literacy experiences increases their appreciation of literature and motivates them to read more extensively. Children's ways of responding to literature are as diverse as their individual experiences.

In the vignette, you will discover that children have wide-ranging reading interests that reflect their previous experiences. Readers make intertextual connections among the books they enjoy, and their life experiences. Furthermore, their literacy experiences and opportunities for response motivate them to read additional books.

VIGNETTE

It is language arts time in Jane Morrison's third-grade classroom. Christopher finishes his book, Jerdine Nolen's *Raising Dragons,* and holds it up. "This book is really good! The dragon is a good guy. He helped the family solve their problems, and he had a bunch of adventures. I wish I could find a dragon egg."

"What would you like to read next?" Ms. Morrison asks.

"I want to read about another good guy dragon; could I ask the librarian?"

"Yes, she is in the media center now."

In another part of the classroom Annie is engrossed in *Birdie's Lighthouse* by Deborah Hopkinson. She looks up and a friend asks, "Is that a good book?"

"Oh, yes!" she answers. "Birdie is so smart! I really like the way she keeps her head and struggles so hard to keep the lighthouse burning when her father is sick. I saw a lighthouse last summer. I want to read *The Light at Tern Rock* next."

Jimmy and Patsy are on the floor doing something with paper. The teacher assistant observes them for a time, then asks, "What are you making, kids?"

"We just finished reading Gail Gibbons's book, *Catch the Wind!* And it has directions for making a cool kite, so we're making it. Then we're going to read a book about Japanese kites."

"Do you enjoy flying kites?"

"Oh, yeah! We fly kites at the beach."

LITERARY THINKING

Meaning in literature is expressed in several unique ways (Langer, 1992): through written language, the conventions of language, and literary structures such as characters, setting, plot, theme, and so forth. Developing literary thinking is a natural and necessary part of the well-developed intellect. Langer maintains that readers use distinct patterns of thinking to understand literature. These patterns of thinking entail relating prior knowledge, experiences, and the text to understand genre, content, structure, and language (Langer, 1992).

Literature as a Means of Knowing

Literary thinking encourages five kinds of knowing (Probst, 1992): knowing about self, knowing about others, knowing about books, knowing about contexts, and knowing based on what kind of thinker an individual is—concrete or abstract.

Self. First, the reader learns about self through literature. This occurs when the reader recalls experiences related to the text and integrates them with the text, thus expanding self-understanding. For instance, after reading *Family Pictures* by Carmen Lomas Garza, 9-year-old Julia recalled her family's activities and thought how much her family was like the Mexican family in the book.

Others. Children also begin to realize that each reader has different experiences. For instance, Julia's classmate Josh said the family portrayed in *Family Pictures* was not real because he could not relate to their activities. Both Julia and Josh discovered new ideas about one another from this experience and deepened their understanding of the book.

Books. Literary thinking helps readers understand books and literary devices used by authors to stimulate readers' thinking. In *Who Came Down That Road?* George Ella Lyon uses the image of a road to stir readers to imagine all the different people and animals that came down an old, old road—all the way back to before the Native Americans when mastodons roamed the earth. These images invite students to respond by thinking about roads they have encountered, to look at the text more carefully, and to think about related historical images.

Contexts. Literature helps learners know about contexts. A 5-year-old reader has a different perspective

The poet and artist create images of dinosaurs dancing to the beat of a hard rock band.

than a 15-year-old reader. The younger child reading *Who Came Down That Road?* might think of Native Americans or cowboys, whereas the older one might think of settlers in covered wagons. Each of these readers brings a different context or background to the book depending on the extent of their personal experiences. Discussion helps readers clarify and activate their contexts.

Ways of thinking. Each reader thinks about text in a unique way. Some students are highly analytical, concrete thinkers, whereas others are subjective and abstract. Some readers race through the text, whereas others proceed slowly, reflecting as they read. In time, children come to understand that each individual thinks differently about text, which leads to different understandings of the same text. One child reading *Family Pictures* will reflect on happy family outings; another may think of family gatherings made sad by anger and disputes.

Envisionment: Individual Meaning

Understanding of literature depends on the author's words and sentences that stimulate a reader's memories, associations, thoughts, and questions (Probst, 1992). A single text yields varying meanings to individuals because they use personal backgrounds to construct and shape meaning in their minds (Barksdale-Ladd & Nedeff, 1997). This means that individuals with dissimilar background experiences construct different meanings for the same text. Approaching literature with this understanding is essentially different from approaching literature through literary criticism, which is based on an authority determining the meaning of a text and passing the meaning on to teachers, who then convey the meaning to their students.

Langer uses the word *envisionment* to refer to this reader-derived meaning. In her theory, an envisionment is created as the child reads and understands the text (Langer, 1992). The box Envisioning "The New Kid on the Block" describes how one reader creates an envisionment from Jack Prelutsky's poem. Another reader might emphasize different words and fill in gaps in meaning from a dissimilar set of world experiences, creating an entirely different envisionment of the poem. This reader might not know any bullies or might not know what the word *bully* means. A reader well acquainted with Jack Prelutsky's poetry will have different expectations of the poem than one

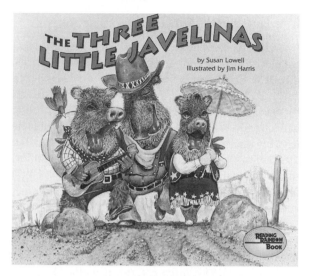

Javelinas are cousins to pigs and they have to fend off coyotes instead of wolves.

who does not and will expect a funny poem with a surprise near the end.

Involved readers actively pursue meaning from the first instant of reading, thinking about the book and predicting its meaning. As they make sense of the written language, they confirm or cancel their predictions of meaning. Active, involved readers constantly build and synthesize meaning, paying attention to the words and attending to the images and emotions within the text.

When readers think, rethink, reread, and discuss books, they discover what a book means to them and how they feel about it. They select aspects of the text to remember based on their understanding and response; they fill in gaps in meaning from their world knowledge. They infer, interpret, and think critically as they revise and sharpen their understanding of the text. They discover their sense of the text, their ideas about it, their understanding of what it is and what it means. Even the details they remember change and shift and come to them in different arrangements. This is why communities of readers, discussed later in this chapter, are important. Although response is individual, community discussions encourage individuals to share their unique verbal, artistic, dramatic, and written interpretations of and responses to literature (Jewell & Pratt, 1999).

Envisioning "The New Kid on the Block"

In Jack Prelutsky's poem "The New Kid on the Block," I first read that the new kid is *real tough.* These words create an image of a muscular bully in my mind. The next few lines tell how the new kid *punches hard, pulls hair,* and *likes to fight,* which elaborates on my envisionment of a neighborhood bully. Then the poet describes the bully's behavior with the words *swiped* and *bad,* so my interaction with the text adds the fact that the bully is also unpleasant to my envisionment. But the surprise in the last line of the poem makes me reconsider my earlier envisionments: "I don't care for *her* at all."

Intertextuality: Individual Connections

Literature is woven with quotations, references, and echoes of prior literary experiences that give it virtually unlimited meaning (Barthes, 1975). Meaning in each new book one reads is enriched in some measure by the shadows of texts read previously. This process, called *intertextuality*, is the process of interpreting one text by means of another (Hartman, 1992; Lundin, 1998). Two or more texts, written or oral, are involved in the intertextuality process (Bloome & Bailey, 1992) and may include films, videos, class lectures, Internet sites, conversations, and books (Hartman, 1992).

Intertextuality plays a strong role in understanding San Souci's *The Talking Eggs.* Readers of this story usually recognize the plot and character are similar to *Cinderella.* In *The Talking Eggs,* a widow, her bad-tempered daughter Rose, and her sweet and kind daughter Blanche are the main characters. The story is set in the rural South rather than a palace, and the magic character is an old woman who blesses Blanche. In the end, the widow and her bad-tempered daughter run into the woods, chased by whip snakes, toads, frogs, yellow jackets, and a big gray wolf. Movies, television, and books have developed the intertextual links that facilitate readers' response.

In discussing *Birdie's Lighthouse,* the reader in the opening vignette revealed that her response was based on intertextuality. She compared her experiences sailing with her father and their reliance on lighthouses and other signals to Birdie's need to keep the lights burning. She admired Birdie's determination and loyalty.

In an intertextuality study, researchers found incredible diversity in the links that are made and they concluded the following (Cairney, 1990):

1. All children poach from stories they have read previously, and almost all children are aware that this intertextuality influences their writing.
2. Among children of different achievement levels, we find only minor differences in awareness of intertextuality.
3. The most common intertextual links include genre, character, plot ideas, and combining several narratives.
4. The majority of intertextuality links students use are related to ideas and plot.

Like creating meaning, readers apply intertextuality differently from one individual to the next. Intextuality is not a linear process; even when reading exactly the same stories, readers identify different links to use in making meaning. We have no way of predicting which links will occur to a specific reader. Each one creates a highly personal mosaic of intersecting texts with intertextual relations that may not be apparent to others reading the same texts. Although intertextuality is highly individual, teachers, librarians, parents, and other involved adults can encourage readers to use ideas from previous experiences to build meaning.

REASONS FOR READING

All readers have a purpose for reading, or stance (Holland et al., 1993). *Stance* is an active process that indicates what the reader is paying attention to in the reading process, and stance influences the reader's re-

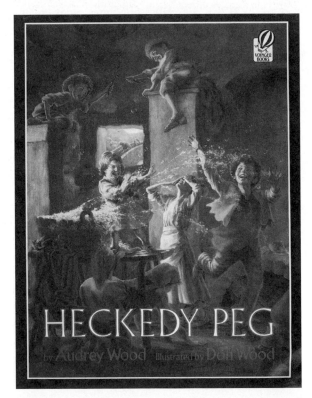

Heckedy Peg, inspired by a sixteenth-century game still played by children today, is about seven children, a wicked witch's intrusion into their lives, and a spell that only their mother can break.

| FIGURE 4.1 | Reading stance continuum. |

Mostly aesthetic — Half efferent, half aesthetic — Mostly efferent

sponse. Response gives form to these literary experiences and a mode for expressing them. Response shows us what has caught the reader's attention (Many, 1996). We find two major stances in literature, aesthetic and efferent.

Aesthetic reading. The purpose of aesthetic reading is to have a pleasurable, interesting experience for its own sake. Aesthetic readers center on the sound and rhythm of the words and the personal feelings, ideas, and attitudes created during reading (Rosenblatt, 1982). Focusing on seeing, feeling, and thinking, they create new experiences as they live through the literature: participating in the story, identifying with the characters, sharing their conflicts and their feelings. As a byproduct of the aesthetic reading stance, readers may acquire values, information, or related benefits, but these are not the purpose of the reading.

Efferent reading. The efferent reading stance focuses on the meanings and ideas in the text (Rosenblatt, 1982). Efferent reading has a narrow focus because the readers are seeking information, directions, solutions, and conclusions and attempting to build these into memory to use in another situation. Rosenblatt points out, however, that any reading event may fall anywhere on a continuum between the aesthetic and the efferent poles, so a stance cannot be only aesthetic or only efferent because most reading experiences have elements of both (see Figure 4.1).

UNDERSTANDING RESPONSE

In the opening vignette, Jimmy and Patsy chose to read a book about kites because they had enjoyable experiences with kites. Their previous reading and knowledge created intertextual links that helped them construct meaning. They acquired some new knowledge after reading *Catch the Wind!*, built kites, and planned to read more books about kites. Both of these responses to literature extended their efferent experience.

Response to literature is many things: what readers make of a text as they read; how it comes alive and becomes personal; what happens during reading; how they feel about what they have read. Response is also the pleasure and satisfaction readers feel and the way they display these feelings (Blake, 1995; Langer, 1995). "It is this combination of personal, social, and cultural contexts which has tremendous influence on the reader's interpretation" (Largent, 1986, p. 17).

Literature affects readers in all sorts of ways. We really cannot read without responding in some way: with excitement or pleasure or boredom. We may go to sleep or become so fascinated that we read all night long. Young children are responding to literature when they plead, "read it again, read it again."

Literary experience does not stop when the last page is read, however (Martinez & Nash, 1991). The reader's feelings remain and continue to evolve after completing the book, sometimes long after the book is read (Rosenblatt, 1978). After hearing William Steig's *Pete's a Pizza,* Andrew likes to pretend that he is Pete and his father made him into a pizza. He frequently returns to this character and thinks of another food he could become, such as a chocolate chip cookie.

DIMENSIONS OF RESPONSE

Children's response to literature is developmental, meaning that it changes with age and stage of development. Preschool children, for instance, enjoy the rhythms and sounds of nursery rhymes—Mother Goose is developmentally appropriate for children in this age group. The various facets of response include sound, event, world, and author style, which are explored in this section.

Sound

Children who are sensitive to sound respond to the words and rhythms of language in a book. They hear the text in their head as they read, listening to the dialogue as they would conversation. This is why "reading aloud to children of all ages is vital . . . because this is the way we learn how to turn cold print into a dramatic enactment in the theater of our imagination" (Chambers, 1983, p. 163). The dialogue in Edith Thacher Hurd's *I Dance in My Red Pajamas* is so realistic that many children reading the story identify with the conversations between grandchild and grandparents.

Event

Readers who respond to event are sensitive to the form of story, poem, or nonfiction. They can anticipate events, characters, and setting when they read. They expect stories to have characters, setting, problems or conflicts, and efforts to solve problems. Experienced readers have learned that events increase suspense in a story, that characters usually have conflicts as they try to solve problems. Their expectations are based on genre, story elements, story grammar, poetic form, and expository grammars, which are discussed in chapter 3.

Children identify with story characters, which is why they enjoy reading about people near their own age or a bit older. Children who enjoy dramatic play will enjoy being Pete in *Pete's a Pizza,* and they may reshape and revise this story to fit their own reality and personal experiences. For example, a child who remembered that Dad said "Pizzas are not supposed to laugh," commented, "I'll be a cake instead of a pie then."

World

The world response occurs when readers incorporate aspects of all dimensions of response. When reading the poem "If I Were in Charge of the World" by Judith Viorst, children connect it with their own lives and with other literature that stimulates a similar response. They respond to sounds in the poem, such as the alliterative phrases "healthy hamsters" and "basketball baskets." Children who have allergies identify with the author's desire to "cancel" allergy shots, and both children and adults identify with the poet's desire to eliminate "Monday mornings." Anyone who has had pet hamsters can relate to the author's desire for "healthier hamsters." Viorst consistently enters the children's world with her poems and stories.

Author Style

"To enter and hold the mind of a child or a young person is one of the hardest of all writers' tasks" (Zinsser, 1990, p. 1). The ability of outstanding children's writers to communicate with children on their own level—to respect their experience and understanding—is the key to their success, to their ability to make the stories come to life for children. They seem to be able to remember what it feels like to be a child and how the world looks when the main character is 3 feet tall.

These writers are able to create images, language, characters, plots, themes, and settings that ring true to children, that relate to and respect their experiences (Thacker, 1996).

Although children have not lived as long as adults have, their experiences permit them to respond to their books. Moreover, children have enough experience to recognize a writer who does not respect their experience or intelligence. They identify and reject shallow books or didactic, preachy books.

Truth is a critical quality in children's books even when the story is not literally true. E. B. White (1970) said of his own writing:

> I have two or three strong beliefs about the business of writing for children. I feel I must never kid them about anything. I feel I must be on solid ground myself. I also feel that a writer has an obligation to transmit, as best as he can, his love of life, his appreciation for the world. I am not averse to departing from reality, but I am against departing from the truth. (p. 544)

Fine writers express truth as they understand it, through fiction, poetry, or nonfiction. Truth in literature is also expressed in the integrity of the transaction between the writer and the reader (Zinsser, 1990). When the writer's truth resonates with the child's truth, the reader responds to the author's storytelling skill.

Truth is the foundation of the picture book *Amazing Grace* by Mary Hoffman, in which one classmate tells Grace that she cannot be Peter Pan in the school play because she is a girl, and a second classmate says that she cannot be Peter Pan because she is black. The truth of a book must be an integral feature; to omit the truth or to tiptoe around it is dishonest. Children respond to honest characters such as Grace and the authors who create them.

GUIDING RESPONSE

This text emphasizes the individual nature of literary meaning, a theory that implies respect for individual, unique understandings and an attitude that welcomes individual response. The ways adults guide literary experiences can encourage students actively to make meaning of the texts they read, awakening their reading interests by planning literary encounters inviting their response. Literary experiences have much to offer the growing mind (Langer, 1992). The major reason for providing children with literary experiences is to help them read with more pleasure and understanding. "Helping children to read for themselves, widely, voraciously, and indiscriminately" is something every adult can do (Chambers, 1983, p. 48). Although they cannot directly teach literature to children, they can set the stage for them to experience literature so that the children can actively construct their own knowledge and beliefs.

Well-read teachers create literary experience through the literature they select and present. They create a literate environment that encourages children to engage with books and gives them opportunities to express their responses to literature. (Figure 4.2 presents the dimensions of creating literary experience.) To develop literary experiences, teachers, librarians, and parents encourage children to make meaning of the texts they read, choosing books that will facilitate this process (McClure & Kristo, 1996). Focusing the way readers feel about a book and providing ways of expressing their responses is a part of guiding the literary experience. Books that support literary experiences will:

- invite dialogue,
- awaken memories,
- raise questions,
- stimulate connections with other literature and with life, and
- encourage problem solving.

Guiding children's literary experiences involves encouraging them to think about and respond to literature: literary thinking is not linear, nor is it predictable (Langer, 1995). Children's literary experiences are guided by helping them connect with books and build the background needed for understanding. Leading discussions and encouraging readers to lead discussions clarify their understandings and assist them in learning from one another. Students build their own understanding of literature and raise their own questions rather than focusing on content questions created by someone with different experiences and knowledge. Enhance children's experiences through selecting and introducing books for children to hear, read aloud, or read silently, and through stimulating their thinking beyond the book after reading.

Community of Response

Although each reader creates a unique understanding of text, each relies on common understandings and language for discussions and sharing responses. These shared understandings emerge from a mutual focus that Sebesta and Iverson (1975) call a community of response. Readers externalize their response best when their discussion focuses on the literary work itself (Chambers, 1983). For instance, a community of readers can agree that stories include plot and character, and they can agree about the identity of the principal character, but they may disagree agree about character motivation.

FIGURE 4.2 Dimensions of creating literary experience.

Processes for enhancing literary experience	Ways of Organizing Literature Study				
	Genre studies	Studies of outstanding books	Studies of the elements of literature	Illustrator studies	Author studies
Read aloud Reader's Theater	x	x	x		x
Read silently	x	x	x	x	x
Drama		x	x		x
Writing	x	x	x	x	x
Art		x	x	x	
Music		x	x	x	x
Discussion	x	x	x	x	x
Movement		x		x	

As children share their individual understandings with one another, they learn that a story can have many interpretations. One person's interpretation of an incident or a character might not occur to another individual without the opportunity for discussion. Sharing individual perceptions of literature with one another in discussion or conversation enhances understanding and response to literature. Giving students such occasions to share their personal understandings and responses will inspire their response.

Story structures such as plot, setting, characterization, theme, and author style are common understandings that readers share, just as main ideas and supporting details are common understandings they share about nonfiction. Genre characteristics are another source of agreement. Identifying a book as historical fiction, poetry, or nonfiction is a relatively concrete task. Such knowledge influences the way readers engage with a book as well as the way they respond to it.

Without shared understandings "there would never be the sort of agreement that makes a book well-loved or well-hated. Children as well as adults seem to seek this commonality" (Sebesta & Iverson, 1975, p. 412). They talk over their thoughts and reactions to a best-selling book, a television show, or a play; they may even argue the finer points of the piece. Chambers (1983) says the need to re-create the story in our own words is so strong that "when two friends discover they have both read and enjoyed the same book their talk often consists simply of sharing retellings: 'I especially liked that part where. . . .'" These discussions clarify understanding and response; therefore, the community of response is an important issue for those who work with children. These adults nurture students' response when they give them opportunities to form a community of readers. They can also give them time to share thoughts about their reading.

Warm, Literate Environment

A warm, literate environment sets the stage for children's engagement with and response to literature. In this setting, students are surrounded with many appealing, interesting books that set the stage for pleasurable experiences. Both centralized school libraries and classroom library centers are essential to literacy experiences. The classroom reading center gives children immediate access to literature. Parents and caregivers create warm, literate environments when they have books and magazines in the home or center.

Pleasing arrangements of books, displays, posters, and bulletin boards in the library center invite children to explore books. Books displayed open at eye level encourage more reading than book shelves lined so that only the spines show.

Engaging with Literature

Children must engage with literature in order to respond to it. Engaging with literature makes the characters and events come alive for readers. Engagement activities focus on what the story, poem, or nonfiction is really about so that readers can understand and respond to it. The following are some typical engagement activities:

- discussion of genre,
- writing or discussing story grammar,
- creating a story map,
- predicting story events,
- comparing/contrasting characters, settings, and so forth (Venn diagram),
- problem solving related to a book,
- creating plot maps,
- creating a story summary,
- creating a story pyramid,
- creating character maps,
- answering student-generated questions,
- reading author studies, and
- identifying new facts gleaned from reading.

NURTURING RESPONSE

Nurturing children's response to literature means creating pleasurable experiences with books in a warm, accepting setting. Chambers (1983) sums up the literary experience as one in which adults and children share what they read and discover together what is "entertaining and revealing, recreative, re-enactive, and engaging" (p. 40). The focus of a literary experience is discovering the meaning, thinking about it, and discovering the reader's feelings about the experience. Literature is an experience "to be entered into, to be shared and contemplated" (p. 39).

Appropriate literary experiences are essential to children's development and thinking. These experiences are not an effort to teach children the content of a book, but rather they are intended to develop understanding and appreciation. As Rosen (1986) states, "receiving a story is an exploration . . . , not a set of responses to someone else's questions in right/wrong format" (p. 229). We are concerned with *why* children remember a story, not simply *what* they remember. C. S. Lewis (1961) makes a distinction between "using" and "receiving" literature:

> A work of [whatever] art can be either "received" or "used." When we "receive" it we exert our senses and imagination and various other powers according to a pattern invented by the artist. When we "use" it we treat it as assistance for our own activities. (p. 44)

When readers open a book, they accept an invitation to collaborate with the author or the illustrator, to explore existing meanings, and to forge new meanings. No matter how good the writing may be, a book is never complete until someone reads it (Paterson, 1981). All of the experiences authors have influence their writing. Paula Fox explains: "It is my view that all the moments and years of one's life are part of any story that one writes" (Elleman, 1991, p. 48). Studying authors and illustrators yields many benefits. Readers who know something about the person who wrote or illustrated a literary work have a better understanding of it. Finding connections between books and their creators challenges children to think in new ways. Because an author's experiences influence writing so heavily, knowing about the author greatly enhances the response process.

Response activities sustain the reader–text interaction and nurture literary development (Martinez & Nash, 1991). Morrow (1989) finds that in a literature-based after-school program including response activities such as storytelling, puppets, drama, writing, and art, primary-grade students develop deeper understandings, greater interest in reading, and read more books than their peers not in the program; they are also more interested in literature when they can interact with and share their responses with adults.

Response may be written or oral, formal or informal, and may make use of a variety of media. Teachers and other concerned adults can create opportunities for varied responses to literature through activities before reading, during reading, and after reading. We explain strategies and activities for introducing books, experiencing books, and encouraging response to literature in later sections.

Literature loses its appeal when it is misused. Chambers (1983) offers an example of such abuse

Jamie saw such a frightful sight that he and his family fled.

when he tells of an English teacher who taught 12-year-olds to parse with a paragraph from J. M. Falkner's novel *Moonfleet*. No doubt this activity taught many students to dislike literature. Misuse of literature involves deliberately reading and questioning a piece of literature in order to teach specific information or skills. Creating comprehension exercises from literary passages, phonics drills that focus on the sounds of words in a fine book, and spelling lists from great books are the stuff of which literary abuse is made. They focus on inappropriate aspects of the book or poem. Questions and activities such as, What color was the main character's dress, why did the dog run away, and pretend you are the main character and write a letter to . . . do not contribute to literary experience; these activities treat literature as content. On the other hand, a child writing a letter to a friend to tell why she

A First-Grade Literature Experience

INTRODUCTION

Ms. Osaka showed her first-grade students a picture of a mouse to introduce them to the poem "Mice" by Rose Fyleman. After reading the first line of the poem, she asked them what reasons they thought the poet would give for saying that mice were nice, and she listed their reasons on the chalkboard. She then read the entire poem aloud.

DISCUSSION AND UNDERSTANDING

After reading the poem through a second time when the children asked to hear it again, Ms. Osaka asked them what the poet said she liked about mice. She listed their responses next to the earlier list on the board. Several children said their families did not like

mice, so Ms. Osaka let the class discuss the reasons for this.

Afterward, she asked them what kind of words the poet used to help listeners see mice in their mind. Some of the children recognized "scurrying" words in the poem.

RESPONSE ACTIVITIES

Ms. Osaka asked the children to think about the things they could do to show another person how they felt about this poem. Many of the children chose to draw pictures. Some of them selected mouse puppets and acted out the poem. Some others remembered the book *Whose Mouse Are You?* by Robert Kraus and asked the teacher to read it again.

---

liked a book or an author is a response. The literary experience is not a quest for a predetermined right answer. The process of making meaning is not one of learning a correct interpretation prescribed by an authority in the field (Langer, 1995).

Introducing Books

Introductions may be elaborate or very simple. They may consist of a question, discussion, or picture; a comparison to another book, a film, or a piece of music; reading the opening paragraph or paragraphs; or presentation of an object that symbolizes some aspect of the book. Introductions arouse children's interest in the text and give them background that enriches their comprehension. The teacher, parent, or librarian acquaints children with the genre, content, structure, and language of the text (Langer, 1995). Children will usually meet the main character and identify the setting during the introduction.

The first step in planning a book introduction is considering what readers need to know to understand the book. To understand a fantasy such as Marjorie Priceman's *My Nine Lives by Clio* readers have to

imagine places and people outside of their experience. Following the story when it switches from century to century can be a challenge. A good introduction could include a discussion of the superstition that cats have nine lives. Skilled writers of fantasy make us believe that such things could happen and that a cat could write a book. Readers form different expectations for a book introduced as a fantasy, such as *My Nine Lives by Clio,* rather than for a book introduced as realistic fiction or poetry.

Creating a relation between a piece of literature and previous reading develops intertextuality and facilitates response. Use *Snow* by Uri Shulevitz to introduce Jacqueline Martin's *Snowflake Bentley.* This will prepare children for the intensity of Snowflake Bentley's study of snowflakes. Literary experience is not based on a single book, but the ideas, experiences, and understandings that come from reading many books.

Children learn to preview books themselves from the techniques used to introduce books to them. By the time students reach the middle grades, they are ready to explore independently a book before reading and know that the dust jacket usually provides background information.

Marven escaped the deadly flu by going to a lumber camp.

Experiencing Books

After the introduction, the children read or listen to the book or poem. They link their prior knowledge with the new information presented, building comprehension and creating a new understanding. Readers who immerse themselves in the literature gradually build an understanding of the piece, identifying and coming to understand the main character's personality. As the story unwinds, readers recognize the escalating tension in the plot, the cause and effect, and the problem or conflict that builds suspense. Readers who ask themselves "why" and "who" can relate literature to their own experiences and will increase their comprehension.

Through the personal interpretation of both narrative and informational text, learners come to better understand themselves, others, and the world in which we live, and through the comprehension of both narrative and informational text, learners build a knowledge base about our world (Gambrell & Almasi, 1996). Understanding is related to inferencing or interpretation of literature, which is concerned with meanings that are not directly stated in the text. The author suggests and hints at ideas rather than stating them directly, and the reader must interpret the author's words to under-

stand the intended meaning. Authors cannot tell readers everything: the stories would be too long and the detail would make them too boring. Authors must rely on their audience to fill in the empty spaces. In *Holes,* Mr. Sir tells Stanley, "This isn't a Girl Scout Camp" (p. 14). Louis Sachar, the author, is telling the reader that Camp Green Lake is a bad place. Mr. Sir also tells Stanley that he is going to be thirsty for the next 18 months. The reader can interpret these statements to mean that this is a really hard place.

Critical thinkers make judgments about the quality, value, and validity of text. They evaluate the accuracy of the material, synthesize information, make comparisons and inferences, and suspend judgment until they have all the information they need. Critical readers recognize the author's purpose, point of view, and use of language. They distinguish fact from opinion and test the author's assertions against their own observations, information, and logic. For instance, a critical reader would probably conclude that Stanley was in a much worse place than he realized.

ENHANCING READERS' ENGAGEMENT AND RESPONSE

Students who are members of a community of readers who discuss, dramatize, and share books with one another engage and respond with literature more fully (Hancock & Hill, 1988). Engagement and response activities focus on readers' responses rather than detailed analysis.

> Students will not be dissecting the text, nor will they inspect it; rather they will be focused on such literary elements as the main characters, the setting, the problem to be resolved, the major events, the problem solution and what the story is really about. . . . The purpose of engagement activities is to get students immersed, engrossed, absorbed, and totally involved in literature. (Macon, Bewell, & Vogt, 1991, p. 3)

Response to literature grows from literary experience and is expanded through engagement activities.

The understanding and responses generated through the activities in this section will increase students' comprehension as well as create a springboard for discussion and writing.

> Students must understand that they should complete the assigned reading *prior* to tackling the assigned activity rather than interrupting the flow of the story to record

their data. Preserve the integrity of the text, then work on the activities. (Macon et al., 1991)

Unless readers read the entire story, article, poem, or informational piece *before* exploring it in discussion or response activities, they lack full understanding of the piece. Understanding grows as readers follow the unfolding of character, the story problem and its resolution, or the full development of the theme. This is the way they learn how the story works or the way the informative pieces fit together.

The activities described in this section may be conducted as individual activities, small-group activities, or whole-class activities. Pencil-and-paper activities help students organize and remember their thoughts for discussion. Activities for engagement and response should not be overused because overdoing even the most interesting ones can discourage reading. Students who are required to do something with everything they read will lose interest in literature—the main purpose of reading should be simply to read.

Discussion

Response requires social interactions centered around text (Gambrell & Almasi, 1996). Moreover, a Vygotskian (Vygotsky, 1978) framework views social interaction as effectively driving cognitive development. Therefore, engaging in discussions about text can help students become part of the active conversation that is reading, the conversation between the reader and text, between text and community and among readers (Bloem & Manna, 1999; Borders & Naylor, 1993; Musthafa, 1996). Therefore, discussion is an integral part of developing understanding and engagement with literature. The questions raised with others in the discussion process and the teacher's thoughtful questions increase comprehension (Macon et al., 1991). Thoughtful discourse gives students many occasions to raise questions and make comments about the literature they read (Jewell & Pratt, 1998–99). Friendly debate regarding various reactions fosters readers' response to literature (Larrick, 1991). The teacher's role is to facilitate discussion, keep it going, encourage full participation, and inspire children to talk about literature. Plan thoughtful questions based on listening to the voice of the book rather than analyzing it. The most useful questions are broad and open-ended because these questions help students develop a sense of the

entire story, poem, or informational piece. Thoughtful questions avoid the trivial and obvious and focus on a few significant ideas that stimulate higher levels of understanding and response, which involve inferential thinking, critical thinking, and creative thinking. Lower levels concentrate on "right" answers.

Developing discussion

A few thoughtful questions, especially those that the students ask, will stimulate a good discussion. The inquisition approach of asking many, many questions is guaranteed to destroy children's response to literature. The teacher who comments, "I feel like I have wrung the life out of this book and neither the students nor I ever want to see it again," has assuredly overanalyzed the book and ensured that her students will never enjoy that book, even though it may be a favorite of many children who have not been subjected to overteaching or overanalysis.

Discussions that focus on the characters suggest that readers wonder what kind of person the main character will turn out to be (Hansen, 1991). The well-developed characters in Katherine Paterson's books invite this kind of response. When focusing on character, develop questions to guide students' thinking, such as:

- What kind of character is the main character?
- What words describe the character?
- What character have you read about that is like the main character in this book? How are they alike?
- Do you know anyone who is like the main character? How so?

Some books are plot driven, so students read for the story events or the adventures. Many of these stories are action packed and have story events that build suspense. Guiding children's response to these stories could involve questions such as:

- What events create suspense?
- What is the main problem or conflict in this story?
- What is the climax of this story?
- How is the problem or conflict solved?

Prompts, such as the ones listed in the Discussion Prompts box, can elicit children's oral and written responses to literature. Using these prompts for a full year in a third-grade class shows that the students are more actively involved in learning and more enthusiastic about literature than their peers, with an observable difference in fluency and increased reflection of emotional involvement as the students use the process (Kelly, 1990). Adapting the prompts to statements shows that they are effective for discussion and that the more the prompts are used, the more effective they are. Children as young as age three respond to the prompts; moreover, the children involved in the latter study used the prompts on the teachers and asked what they noticed in the story (Borders & Naylor, 1993).

Writing

Discussion and writing are valuable literary response activities (Hancock, 1991). Students who read well usually write well because literature stimulates background knowledge, thinking, and writing. Reading gives students models for organizing writing and language to express their thoughts. The response journal is one of many appropriate writing response activities.

DISCUSSION PROMPTS

Kelly's (1990) prompts:

1. What did you notice about the story?
2. How did the story make you feel?
3. What does the story remind you of in your own life?

Borders and Naylor's (1993) prompts:

1. Talk about what you notice in the story, which may include any aspect of the book such as text, format, illustrations, characters, and so forth. Children will notice things that teachers never noticed.
2. Talk about how the story makes you feel. When members of a group share feelings and thoughts they bond, and the group is a safer place to explore issues.
3. Talk about what the story reminds you of in your own life. Our own experiences help us understand a book and the book helps us understand our experience.

Response journals

Literature response journals, also called reading journals, reading logs, and dialogue journals, are a form of response activity that leads students to engage with literature because the journals consist of students writing down their thoughts about their reading. Flitterman-King (1988) defines the *response journal* as:

> sourcebook, a repository of wanderings and wonderings, speculations, questionings . . . a place to explore thoughts, discover reactions, let the mind ramble—in effect, a place to make room for the unexpected. (p. 5)

Response journals are an effective means of linking writing and thinking with the active reading process (Barone, 1990; Kelly, 1990; Raphael & McMahon, 1994). Some students find it difficult to get started writing in their journal, or they may say the same things again and again, so plan ways to encourage their responses when they seem to have difficulty thinking of something to write.

Hancock (1991) reports an analysis of a sixth-grade girl's literature response journal. The journal reveals the student's personal meaning-making process as well as insights into her personal feelings, which the teacher had rarely seen. This student was encouraged to record all of the thoughts going on in her head as she read the book and not concern herself with correct spelling or the mechanics of writing because the objective was to capture her thoughts. Her entries were classified in these ways: (a) character interaction, (b) character empathy, (c) prediction and validation, (d) personal experiences, and (e) philosophical reflections. When writing about character interaction, the student wrote comments directly to the character she was reading about. The researcher notes her responses were of the quality of reading and writing that teachers hope to inspire. After the student wrote entries, the researcher made encouraging, nonevaluative responses to her entries. Students are motivated by teachers' comments. They try to repeat the kind of writing to which teachers respond.

Literature response journals can have several formats. A few are suggested here, but teachers can try anything that fits the situation. Langer (1992) suggests a two-part journal with a student entry on one side and the teacher's response (or the response of another student) on the other side. (See the sample entry in Figure 4.3.) Another format, which Langer suggests and which

---

FIGURE 4.3   Two-part literature response journal.

Book: <u>Owl Eyes</u> by Frieda Gates, illustrated by Yoshi Miyake

Notes	Comments
Mohawk legend Funny story because the owl is always complaining. The story explains why the owl looks like it does and why it sleeps at night.	The art is beautiful! I guess the Master of All Spirits and Everything Maker is like God. Raweno made the owl sleep at night so that he wouldn't bother him.

FIGURE 4.4   A sample story map for *Bloomability* by Sharon Creech.

Main characters: The main characters are Dinnie, her Aunt Sandy and Uncle Max, and her school friends, Lila and Guthrie.

Setting: Most of the story takes place in Switzerland and at a Swiss Boarding School.

Story Problem: Dinnie's father constantly moves the family, so she has few possessions and no friends. She does not want to move to Switzerland.

Story event 1:   Dinnie's aunt and uncle take her to Switzerland to attend boarding school.

Story event 2:   She makes friends.

Story event 3:   She discovers the beauty of nature.

Problem solution: She makes friends who help her find her place in the world and the possibilities (bloomabilities) of her life. She discovers the beauty of Switzerland.

Theme: The value of friendship and the possibilities of life.

Stoodt and Amspaugh (1994) researched, shows that children's responses change over time as they relate new information, feelings, and ideas to previous knowledge. Immediate response is more detailed, whereas longer reflection permits children to relate these data to a larger context. In this journal format, the students make entries under three headings: immediate reaction, later reaction, and reading and writing. A third approach is for students to make comments in the journal and then pass it to another student who has read the book to respond to the comments.

In research into book clubs, Raphael and McMahon (1994) identified reading log entry possibilities that can be useful for journaling. These possibilities include character maps, wonderful words, pictures, special story parts, sequences of events, book/chapter critique, relating the book to myself, and author's writing techniques and language use.

After reading nonfiction books, some students become so interested in the information that they want to learn all they can about the subject, which could lead to writing an article about it. Students may decide to develop their own original information and create a nonfiction book to share with classmates. Writing response activities are unlimited. Students will think of their own when they have the opportunity.

Oral Language

Dramatic activities are important response activities for children. These activities are explored in Chapter 12. They give children opportunities to act out their interpretations of characters and events. They can see how the action evolved.

Maps and Charts

Literature may be mapped or charted (sometimes called *diagrams*) as a means of summarizing and organizing thoughts and responses to the text. Many kinds of maps and charts are available.

Story maps

The sample story map in Figure 4.4 is based on *Bloomability* by Sharon Creech. A story map is a diagram of a story grammar. Readers complete the vari-

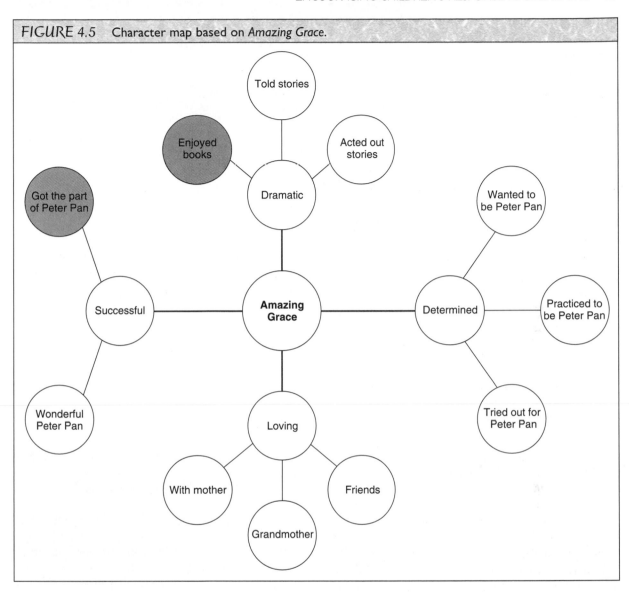

FIGURE 4.5　Character map based on *Amazing Grace*.

ous parts of the map based on the story structure (grammar) of the book they have read.

Character maps

Character maps focus on the main character in a story. They assist children in developing a more thorough understanding of characters in a story and their actions, thereby helping readers identify character traits (Toth, 1990). They also serve to summarize the story.

This exercise may be conducted as an individual activity, a cooperative group activity, or a paired activity. Students write or cut and paste the character's name on the map. Then they write in the qualities (e.g., honesty, loyalty, bravery) that character exhibits. Finally, they identify the actions that support the qualities identified.

This activity can be varied by having students draw pictures or locate magazine photographs that illustrate a character's behavior. Figure 4.5 shows a sample character map based on *Amazing Grace* by Mary Hoffman.

Language charts

Language charts, originally developed as part of the Language to Literacy Program designed for at-risk students in kindergarten through fifth grade, are a means of

---

FIGURE 4.6   Native American language chart.

Meanings and origins of state names from your reading:

Alaska	"great land"	Aleut
Arizona	little spring place	Pima
Connecticut	long river place	Algonquin and Mohican
Idaho	Comanche	Kiowa Apache
Illinois	men or soldiers	Algonquin
Indiana	land of the Indians	English
Iowa	beautiful land	Sioux
Michigan	great water	Chippewa
Minnesota	sky-tinted water	Sioux
Mississippi	great river	Chippewa
Missouri	muddy water	Algonquin
Ohio	good river	Iroquois
Tennessee	tanasi	Cherokee Village
Utah	upper	Navajo

Illustrate these Native American words:

canoe	squash
hickory	toboggan
moccasin	totem
moose	wigwam
skunk	woodchuck

---

introducing discussion and writing to children in a literature response program (Hoffman, 1992; Roser, Hoffman, Labbo, & Farest, 1991). The program focuses on literature units with clusters of books that have some common element (e.g., theme, genre, author). Each unit includes 10 children's books read over a 2-week period, and the unit guide includes background information and suggestions for sharing and discussing books as well as response activities. The organization of the units provides a framework for the children's discoveries of the connections among the literature selections.

The language charts help children and teachers explore many aspects of literature and response to literature. At the close of story-time talk, children's responses to the stories are gathered and written on a language chart that the students may use to recall other stories in the unit and to find similarities and differences among stories. (See Figure 4.6 for a sample language chart.) The charts have several functions:

- show the importance of sharing and studying literature,
- make a record of classroom literacy experiences,
- show oral to written language connections,

- stimulate children to express personal responses to literature,
- connect the individual books to the unit theme or topic,
- encourage students to reflect on a literary experience,
- create a bridge between trade books and content area study,
- serve as a springboard for other responses to literature, and
- encourage students to use higher order thinking skills.

Plot relationships charts

This plot relationships chart, similar to one developed by Barbara Schmitt and Marilyn Buckley (1991), categorizes story information under four headings: somebody, wanted, but, and so. The chart guides children as they identify the major elements of a selection they have heard or read and helps them understand relationships between characters, problems, and solutions. Figure 4.7 shows a sample plot relation chart for the book *When Agnes Caws* by Candace Fleming.

FIGURE 4.7 A sample plot relation chart for *When Agnes Caws*.			
When Agnes Caws			
Somebody	Wanted	But	So
Agnes	to spot the pink-headed duck	Evil Professor tried to foil Agnes	Agnes used bird-calling skills to outwit him

FIGURE 4.8   A sample story pyramid for *Journey*.

1	Journey
2	young boy
3	farm fields barn
4	wants to see mother
5	mother sends money no words
6	Journey adopts cat named Bloom
7	Journey discovers torn photographs of his family
8	grandfather finds negatives, Journey becomes photographer, replaces photographs

Adapted from Waldo, 1991.

Story pyramids

A story pyramid (Waldo, 1991) gives students a convenient way to summarize a story. Each line of the pyramid gives specific information about the story in a specific number of words: the first line has one word, the second line has two words, and so forth. See Figure 4.8 for a sample pyramid based on *Journey* by Patricia MacLachlan. The lines of the pyramid force the student to encapsulate the plot. The lines of the pyramid should describe the following:

1. the main character's name,
2. the main character,
3. the setting,
4. the problem,
5. one main event,
6. a second main event,
7. a third main event, and
8. a solution to the problem.

Prediction charts

Prediction charts guide children to predict what will happen next as they move through a story. Prediction charts guide readers to activate prior knowledge and establish purposes for reading (Hammond, 1991). When using a prediction chart, the teacher introduces the book to stu-

dents. Students predict orally or in writing what will happen next in the story. They also summarize what actually did happen and compare the results to their predictions.

This activity can be done individually or in a group. Younger children who are not able to write can dictate their predictions. For longer books, predictions can be broken into smaller parts (Part I, Part II, Part III) or into the book's chapters. Figure 4.9 shows a sample prediction chart based on *Three Names* by Patricia MacLachlan.

Knowledge charts

Knowledge charts are quite useful with nonfiction, but they also apply to fictional materials. The purpose of knowledge charts is to engage and focus students' reading, as well as to help them access the knowledge they already have regarding the topic. If students do not have previous knowledge regarding a particular topic, then as part of this study teachers need to help them acquire background knowledge. Figure 4.10 shows a sample knowledge chart based on *Dinosaur Ghosts* by J. Lynett Gillette.

Author and Illustrator Studies

Author studies can be motivating for students as well as stimulate their response to a favorite author's work. Author and illustrator studies also motivate children to read and to continue reading (Jenkins, 1999).

FIGURE 4.9   A sample story prediction chart for *Three Names.*

	WHAT DO YOU REALLY THINK WILL HAPPEN?	WHAT DID HAPPEN?
Part I		The reason for the Three Names is that three people call the dog three different names.
Part II		Three Names goes to school with the children in the family.
Part III		Three Names misses school when it closes for vacation.

FIGURE 4.10   A sample knowledge chart based on *Dinosaur Ghosts* by J. Lynett Gillette

Prior Knowledge about Dinosaurs	New Knowledge about Dinosaurs
1. Dinosaurs lived long ago.	1. Coelophysis lived in New Mexico.
2. Some dinosaurs ate plants.	2. They lived 225 million years ago.
3. Some dinosaurs ate meat.	3. Coelophysis lived in large herds.
4. Dinosaurs were big and little.	4. Something killed many of these dinosaurs at the same time.
5. They hatched from eggs.	5. Scientists did detective work to unravel the mystery.
6. Their fossils were discovered at Ghost Ranch.	6. The best theory they came up with is a drought and a flood killed them.

Reading a body of work

The body of an author's work differs from a single work. Studying the body of an author's work reveals how his or her writing has changed over time. Students can discuss how a reader's view of an author can develop through comparing factors such as genre, subject, characters, plot, theme, and style in examining all of the author's books. This will help them understand the body and significance of a single author's work. For instance, James Howe's work was humorous fantasy, such as *Bunnicula,* until his first wife's death, when his writing took a more serious turn and he wrote *The Hospital Book.*

Reading all of an author's books in the order of publication will help readers understand the ways in which the author's work has changed over time. They can compare one or all of these factors in examining the body and significance of a single author's work: plot, character, setting, theme, and style. They may also consider whether the body of work is diverse or seems to follow a single thread. Figure 4.11 compares some of the writings of Katherine Paterson.

Studying influences on illustrators

Other artists influence illustrators. For example, Maurice Sendak (1988) identifies Randolph Caldecott, George Cruikshank, and Boutet de Monvel among others. Students can study an illustrator by (a) studying the illustrator's books, (b) identifying some of the major influences on the illustrator's work, and (c) comparing the work of the illustrator to the work of the influence. Consider concepts such as color choice and use, style, medium, size, and shape. (We discuss these concepts in chapter 6.)

Becoming an author expert

A student can become expert on favorite authors or illustrators by reading their works and finding articles, interviews, book reviews, and other sources of information about them. After becoming expert on a particular author, the student may write magazine or newspaper articles about the author or write and design a new dust jacket for a favorite book. In the persona of the author or illustrator, the student may participate in

---

FIGURE 4.11 Examining an author's body of work.

Book:	*The Master Puppeteer* by Katherine Paterson (historical novel with a few black line drawings)
Plot:	Jiro joins puppet theater during time of famine. He discovers a mysterious bandit is robbing the rich to help the poor.
Character:	The main character is a 13-year-old boy.
Setting:	Osaka, Japan. Time is nonspecific but not contemporary.
Theme:	Friendship between two boys; caring for others.
Style:	Japanese words, concepts, and symbols. The language and character interactions reflect the setting and characters.
	Characters demonstrate their growing sensitivity and concern for others in a different social system.
Book:	*Lyddie* by Katherine Paterson (historical fiction)
Plot:	Lyddie and her brother are left alone on the farm to fend for themselves. Finally she goes to Lowell, Massachusetts, to become a factory girl.
Character:	The main character is a 13-year-old girl.
Setting:	Vermont and later Lowell, Massachusetts, in 1843.

Theme:	Lyddie grows in understanding and spirit through this story of social change.
Style:	The setting, conversation, and descriptions are carefully researched and authentic. Lyddie's problems in the story are based on research of factory girls' lives. Well-drawn characters, and conversation supports their development.
	Characters demonstrate their growing sensitivity and concern for others in a different social system.
Book:	*The Tale of the Mandarin Ducks* by Katherine Paterson (a picture book)
Plot:	A greedy lord imprisons a beautiful duck. The duck pines for his mate and a servant releases him and is sentenced to death. The drake and his mate save him.
Character:	The main character is the drake.
Setting:	Eighth-century Japan.
Theme:	Sharing happiness and trouble.
Style:	This story is told in a folktale style.

---

interviews, round-table discussions, or television talk shows staged by the class. Let students take turns conducting the interviews or directing the discussion and film the interviews or talk shows if possible.

Studying how book illustration has changed

Study the illustrations in the book *75 Years of Children's Book Week Posters* by the Children's Book Council (1994). Compare the posters with book illustrations by the same artist, considering how the posters and slogans have changed over the years. Students can design book week posters and slogans.

Learning about authors

Divide the class into three groups. Group 1 will read books written by the author; Group 2 will read articles or reference materials about the author; and Group 3 will read reviews of books written by the author. After the reading is completed, the students will share their information in discussion as a means of developing their understanding and appreciation of the author's work.

Studying author–illustrator collaboration

Study the art of your students' favorite illustrators in this activity. Have them choose a picture book to study and answer the following questions.

1. Why did the artist chose the particular color, size, style, and other design elements for this book?
2. How do these design elements affect the reading of the text? Do they enhance or detract from understanding the author's meaning?
3. How do the illustrations relate to the text?
4. Do the illustrations add anything that is not stated in the text?
5. What is the mood of the illustrations? Would you feel this mood if you had only read the text without seeing the illustrations?
6. Can you think of another way to interpret the text in art?

Studying author technique

Gaining a deeper understanding of an author's technique not only helps students understand the author

A Biographical Profile: James Cross Giblin

James Cross Giblin served as editor and publisher at Clarion Books for more than 20 years and has published books with several publishers. Many of his books are nonfiction, and he points out that organizing and shaping facts into readable, interesting prose require all the skills of a storyteller (Giblin, 1990). Many of his books deal with unusual aspects of history or information, but he always blends his research with wit and drama.

He explains how he gets his writing ideas in *Writing Books for Young People* (1990). He came up with the idea for *Chimney Sweeps* after meeting a chimney sweep on an airplane. In fact, he asked his new acquaintance to read the book manuscript for accuracy. Another book, *The Truth About Santa Claus,* resulted from seeing a picture of a contemporary Santa Claus juxtaposed next to his tall, thin ancestor, St. Nicholas.

He points out that an idea not only should be interesting to the writer, but it must also be an idea to which the writer is willing to devote a year or more. Six months of research and six months or more of writing and rewriting represent a major commitment of time and energy.

When researching a topic, Giblin looks for dramatic or amusing anecdotes that will bring the subject to life for young readers. His readers will attest to his successful use of this technique. For example, in *From Hand to Mouth* he tells how Cardinal Richelieu had his knives ground down so the points could not be used for picking teeth. When researching *The Riddle of the Rosetta Stone,* he found previously unpublished photographs to use in the book. These unusual angles on topics are a hallmark of his writing.

---

but is beneficial in developing their own writing skills. Students investigate an author's technique in several ways, including:

1. Use a single book to study a specific technique; for instance, explore the techniques Louis Sachar used to create Stanley in *Holes.*
2. Compare a specific technique in several books by the same author; for instance, study setting in Pamela Service's books, such as *Stinker from Space,* and the techniques she uses to develop it.
3. Compare how different authors achieve the same goal; for instance, study dialogue in books by two

authors to see how each author develops character through conversation.

Profiling an author

Learning about authors and their interests helps readers understand how they get story ideas. After studying an author or illustrator through one of the methods described in previous activities, students can write biographical profiles to summarize their research. The profile of James Cross Giblin (see accompanying box) describes some of his strategies for selecting and developing ideas.

Classroom Activities

ACTIVITY 4.1   SAMPLE BOOK INTRODUCTION FOR HISTORICAL FICTION

Book: *Lyddie* by Katherine Paterson
Synopsis (for teachers): This historical fiction relates the struggles of Lyddie, the oldest child of impoverished parents. Her father has disappeared and her mother seems very confused, so Lyddie and her brother must

look after their mother and two little sisters. Lyddie is sent to work in a local tavern. Later she leaves this job to become a factory girl in a mill where workers weave fabric. The focus of this literary experience is to analyze character growth and historical setting and to understand the relationship between them. The following topics will aid in the discussion and help children apply new insights gained to their own lives.

1. The life of girls and women during this historical period. (This focus is both setting- and theme-related.)

2. The central character and character growth (the causes and effects of character growth, as well as the relationship of setting to character development).

3. How have children's work and women's work changed? Why do you think these changes occurred?

These steps provide organization for introducing a book.

1. Introduce *Lyddie*.

   a. Ask students if they know any children who have jobs. Discuss the age at which children can legally work today.

   b. Explain that *Lyddie* is about a girl who had to go to work at age 13. She is paid only 50 cents a week and her employer pays the money she earns to her mother.

   c. Read the first few pages of the book that tell about the bear incident. This incident portrays Lyddie as a courageous girl who, with the help of her brother, protects her mother and little sisters from a marauding bear.

   d. Read or write on an overhead the note on page 9 that Lyddie's mother wrote after taking the younger children to live with her sister and brother-in-law, leaving Lyddie and her brother to fend for themselves.

   e. Introduce the language in the book. Explain that it is characterized by expressions that are uncommon today. For example, Lyddie uses the expression "ey" at the end of many sentences.

   f. Explain that Lyddie uses sentences that today we consider incorrect, such as, "It were only a black bear." Discuss Lyddie's dialect and the reasons for it (e.g., age, story setting, lack of education, and historical period). Readers will notice Lyddie's language changes near the end of the book. In addition to Lyddie's dialect, the author uses Quaker expressions, and during Lyddie's factory work, she en-counters Irish immigrants whose language reflects this heritage.

2. If students read the story silently, discussion will prepare them to read with greater understanding. Focus their silent reading by reading Lyddie's statement that she is no better than a slave and ask the students to think about it as they read the story. The meaning of this statement evolves as the story unfolds, thus focusing silent reading.

3. Discuss the story with the students, stimulating them to think about the story. Follow-up discussion takes place after the students have read the entire story, focusing on the following:

   a. What did Lyddie mean when she said that she was no better than a slave?

   b. Describe Lyddie's personality. How does she change during the story?

   c. How did the setting influence Lyddie and the changes she displays?

4. Use extension activities to allow students to respond to the story. One class did the following after reading *Lyddie*:

   a. The class discussed whether this story could happen today. Students researched the child labor laws, unions, legal work days, overtime, and related topics. They interviewed some legally employed 16-year-olds and discovered that some local businesses violated the law by making the students work more hours than the law permitted. The students were afraid to complain because they believed they would lose their jobs. The sixth graders were incensed at some of the violations they discovered, and several of them wrote reports and others wrote stories about modern-day Lyddies.

   b. Compare *Lyddie* to other stories such as *Homecoming* by Cynthia Voigt and *The Mill Girls: Lucy Larcon, Harriet Hanson Robinson, Sarah G. Bagley* by Bernice Selden. Some students had seen the movie *Norma Rae*, recognized the connection, and asked if they could compare the movie to *Lyddie*. Some of the parents arranged to rent the video and the students watched it as an out-of-school activity and reported on it in class.

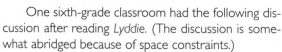
Class Discussion Script

One sixth-grade classroom had the following discussion after reading *Lyddie*. (The discussion is somewhat abridged because of space constraints.)

Mrs. Daniels: How would you describe Lyddie?

Sally: She seemed very brave at the beginning and at the end, but it was hard to understand why Lyddie did what her mother told her even when she knew her mother was wrong.

Jeremy: You have to remember she was only 13 years old and didn't have any education. She couldn't do anything else.

Christopher: The people working in that factory didn't have any rights. They can't treat people like that today, can they?

Mrs. Daniels: What do you think? Can they? Do you know anyone who has a job at 13? Do you know anyone who works for fifty cents a week?

Children: We don't know.

Mrs. Daniels: Would you like to find out?

Children: Yes!

Mrs. Daniels: After our discussion, we'll go to the library and find out about child labor laws. You may want to interview some people about this subject too. Let's go back to Lyddie's character now.

Sally: You know—I thought she was getting her dream when she got the factory job. But then things got worse and I was sorry that she was afraid to sign the petition.

Christopher: But the factory owners and bosses had too much power; she couldn't do anything else. Would you have been as brave as she was?

Sally: I don't know, but I want to be.

Sarah: But she really got a lot of self-confidence and education in this story and she did finally sign the petition. That really took a lot of courage. I think she was brave and a good friend.

Mrs. Daniels: Why did she say that she was no better than a slave?

Richard: Because she was the same as a slave when she worked at the tavern and the factory job wasn't much better—she still didn't have any freedom.

ACTIVITY 4.2   SAMPLE BOOK INTRODUCTION FOR AN INFORMATIONAL BOOK

Book: *Sea Otter Rescue* by Roland Smith

Synopsis (for teachers): This book is based on an oil spill in Prince William Sound, Alaska. The author headed a team of people who worked at the Otter Rescue Center in Valdez, Alaska, which gave him first-hand information and opportunities to photograph the otters.

1. Introduce *Sea Otter Rescue*.

   a. The photographs, the author's note, and the dust jacket give background information that establishes the author's credentials and experiences.

   b. The irresistible photographs in this book are the best introduction. Let students browse through the pictures and discuss the problem of preventing the deaths of "oiled" otters.

   c. Give background information and statistics concerning the oil spill, the otters, and ways the otters were located and taken to the rescue center.

2. Have students read the story silently and look at the photographs again and again as they read the book and see different things each time.

3. Discuss the story with the students, stimulating them to think about the story.

   a. Ask students to think about and discuss the relation between the oil spill and ecology and between the otters' deaths and ecology.

   b. Ask students to raise questions about the book.

4. Use extension activities to allow students to respond to the story.

SUMMARY

This chapter examines children's understanding of and response to literature. The ultimate response, of course, is pleasure in reading. Teachers, librarians, parents, and other concerned adults can guide children's literary experiences and inspire their response to literature by selecting good literature and creating a warm, literate environment. They can introduce literature, provide activities to develop understanding, and encourage follow-up activities to enhance response, including discussion, writing, drama, and further reading. We discuss response activities in subsequent chapters.

Literary experiences may involve children reading or listening to stories or experiencing media. Focusing on text meaning to address their reading purpose enhances their response to literature. This is influenced by the child's stance or purpose for reading. Readers have individual understanding of and response to literature based upon their experiences and interactions with text, but they must also have the knowledge that enables them to share their understanding and discuss their response with a community.

Journaling Experiences

1. Discuss the response process that you observe in a classroom.
2. Identify the response activities that you would like to use in your own classroom.

Thought Questions

1. What is response to literature?
2. Why is response to literature important?
3. What is the teacher's role in creating literary experiences?
4. Why is discussion central to literary experience and response?
5. How are author studies related to response?
6. What is the librarian's role in creating literary experiences?

Research and Application Experiences

1. Read a book to a group of children and observe their responses to the book. Note facial expressions, attentiveness, and comments. Write a paper that describes their responses. Tape-record your reading if possible. Identify the responses that are characteristic to the grade level of the children in the experience.
2. Read a book to a small group of children. Have each child retell the story individually and tape-record them if you can. How are their understandings alike? How are they different?
3. Create a discussion plan that fosters children's questions and comments about a book rather than a teacher-directed discussion. Conduct this discussion with a group of children and tape it for further analysis.
4. With one student or a small group of students, conduct a teacher-directed discussion. Using the same book and a different student or group, hold a student-focused discussion. Tape both discussions and compare them.
   a. Which discussion involved the most students?
   b. Which discussion revealed the greatest depth of understanding?
   c. Which students appeared to be the most interested in the book?
   d. How were the discussions similar?
   e. How were the discussions different?
5. Use one of the maps or charts presented in this chapter as an introduction or a follow-up to a book with a group of children. Bring the maps or graphics that the students developed to class and discuss them.
6. Make plans for introducing three books to a group of children, using a different technique for each. Identify the introduction needed for each book (e.g., character introduction, plot introduction, setting introduction, or story problem or conflict introduction).
7. Plan questions that could be used to guide the discussion of a book. If possible conduct the discussion with a group of children and tape it for further analysis.
8. Select three books that are related that could be used together in the classroom.
9. Select five books that would stimulate language development.

Children's Literature References and Recommended Books

Note: Books designated with an asterisk (*) are recommended for reluctant readers.

Creech, S. (1998). *Bloomability.* New York: Harper Collins. (4–8). CONTEMPORARY REALISTIC FICTION.

Dinnie's aunt and uncle whisk her off to a private school in Switzerland where she discovers her place in the world and the value of friendship.

Fleming, C. (1995). *Women of the lights* (J. Watling, Illus.). Chicago: Albert Whitman. (3–6). INFORMATIONAL BOOK.

The history of women as American lighthouse keepers is the theme of this book.

Fleming, C. (1999). *When Agnes caws* (G. Potter, Illus.). New York: Atheneum. (K–3). MODERN FANTASY.

Agnes, an accomplished bird caller, travels to the Himalayan Mountains to spot the elusive pink-headed duck. But she encounters a villain.

Fyleman, R. (1931). Mice. In *Fifty-one new nursery rhymes.* New York: Doubleday. (1–3). POETRY.

This is a poem about mice and their activities in homes.

Gibbons, G. (1989). *Catch the wind!* New York: Little, Brown. (K–3). INFORMATIONAL BOOK.

When visiting a kite shop these children learn all about kites.

Giblin, J. C. (1982). *Chimney sweeps* (M. Tomes, Illus.). New York: Crowell. (3–6). INFORMATIONAL BOOK.*

A nonfiction book packed with little-known information about chimney sweeps.

Giblin, J. C. (1985). *The truth about Santa Claus.* New York: Crowell. (3–6). INFORMATIONAL BOOK.

Santa Claus myths and traditions are the focus of this book.

Giblin, J. C. (1987). *From hand to mouth.* New York: Crowell. (3–6). INFORMATIONAL BOOK.

A historical study of eating implements.

Giblin, J. C. (1990). *The riddle of the Rosetta Stone.* New York: Crowell. (3–6). INFORMATIONAL BOOK.

A history of the Rosetta Stone illustrated with pictures.

Gillette, J. L. (1997). *Dinosaur ghosts* (D. Henderson, Illus.). New York: Dial. (3–7). INFORMATIONAL BOOK.

This informational book tells about a speedy little dinosaur called Coelophysis and how his bones are found.

Hoffman, M. (1991). *Amazing Grace* (C. Binch, Illus.). New York: Dial. (1–3). CONTEMPORARY REALISTIC FICTION.

Grace loves to pretend and hopes to be Peter Pan in the school play, but she first has to overcome prejudice.

Hopkinson, D. (1997). *Birdie's lighthouse* (K. B. Root, Illus.). New York: Atheneum. (K–3). HISTORICAL FICTION.

Birdie keeps the lighthouse lamps burning when her father falls ill during a storm.

Howe, D., & Howe, J. (1979). *Bunnicula: A rabbit tale of mystery* (A. Daniel, Illus.). New York: Atheneum. (K–5). MODERN FANTASY.

The hilarious story of three pets: Harold, a dog; Chester, a cat; and Bunnicula, a suspicious bunny.

Howe, J. (1994). *The hospital book* (M. Warshaw, Photog.). New York: Morrow. (3–7). INFORMATIONAL BOOK.

This book introduces all aspects of the hospital experience to children.

Hurd, E. T. (1982). *I dance in my red pajamas* (E. A. McCully, Illus.). New York: Harper & Row. (1–3). CONTEMPORARY REALISTIC FICTION.

Jenny visits her grandparents, who prepare her favorite foods and play games with her.

Kraus, R. (1970). *Whose mouse are you?* (J. Aruego, Illus.). New York: Macmillan. (K–1). MODERN FANTASY.

The hero of this picture book is a mouse who lost his family, but he is unable to reclaim them.

Lomas Garza, C. (1990). *Family pictures.* San Francisco: Children's Book Press. (K–4). INFORMATIONAL BOOK.

This picture book is illustrated with paintings that capture the artist's family involved in family dinners, picking oranges, and so forth.

Lyon, G. E. (1992). *Who came down that road?* (P. Catalanotto, Illus.). New York: Orchard Books. (1–4). PICTURE BOOK.

A mother tells her son about an old, old road, and they think about the people who might have traveled that road.

MacLachlan, P. (1991a). *Journey.* New York: Delacorte. (2–5). CONTEMPORARY REALISTIC FICTION.

Journey and his sister, Cat, live with their grandparents because their mother has gone away. Journey has difficulty adjusting when his mother sends money but no words.

MacLachlan, P. (1991b). *Three Names* (A. Pertzoff, Illus.). New York: HarperCollins. (2–4). CONTEMPORARY REALISTIC FICTION.*

Three Names is a dog who has three names because different people in the family have different names for him.

Martin, J. B. (1998). *Snowflake Bentley* (M. Azarian, Illus.). Boston: Houghton Mifflin. (1–3). BIOGRAPHY.

Wilson Bentley researches snowflakes through photography.

Miller, C. G., & Berry, L. A. (1989). *Coastal rescue.* New York: Atheneum. (4–6). INFORMATIONAL BOOK.

This informational book addresses the coastal crises of erosion and coastal resources in the United States.

Nolen, J. (1998). *Raising dragons* (E. Primavera, Illus.). New York: Silver Whistle/Harcourt Brace. (K–2). MODERN FANTASY, PICTURE BOOK.

A little girl finds an egg that hatches a dragon that becomes her friend.

Paterson, K. (1975). *The master puppeteer* (H. Wells, Illus.). New York: Crowell. (4–7). HISTORICAL FICTION.

The child of a poor Japanese family uses his talent to succeed.

Paterson, K. (1990). *The tale of the Mandarin ducks* (L. Dillon & D. Dillon, Illus.). New York: Lodestar. (1–3). TRADITIONAL LITERATURE.

A pair of Mandarin ducks is separated by a cruel lord, but a compassionate husband and wife risk their lives to aid the ducks.

Paterson, K. (1991). *Lyddie.* New York: Lodestar. (4–7). HISTORICAL FICTION.

This story portrays the life of a New England factory girl who labors under conditions similar to slavery.

Prelutsky, J. (1984). *The new kid on the block.* New York: Greenwillow. (1–6). POETRY.

This collection of poems introduces unusual things such as jellyfish stew, a bounding mouse, a ridiculous dog, and a boneless chick to name a few.

Priceman, M. (1998). *My nine lives by Clio.* New York: Atheneum. (1–3). MODERN FANTASY.

A cat's journal about her nine extraordinary lives in nine historical periods.

Sachar, L. (1998). *Holes.* New York: Farrar, Straus & Giroux. (4–7). CONTEMPORARY REALISTIC FICTION.

This Newbery Award and National Book Award book tells the story of Stanley Yelnats and his bad-luck family.

San Souci, R. (1989). *The talking eggs* (J. Pinkney, Illus.). New York: Dial. (1–4). TRADITIONAL LITERATURE.

This is a colorful version of the Cinderella story.

Sauer, J. (1994). *The light at Tern Rock.* New York: Puffin. (3–6). HISTORICAL FICTION.

Ronnie and his aunt tend the Tern Rock lighthouse while the keeper takes a vacation. But the keeper does not return.

Selden, B. (1983). *The mill girls: Lucy Larcon, Harriet Hanson Robinson, Sarah G. Bagley.* New York: Atheneum. (4–8). HISTORICAL FICTION.

The books tells the story of the lives of three mill girls.

Service, P. (1989). *Stinker from space.* New York: Scribner. (3–6). MODERN FANTASY.

When space warrior Tsynq Yr crashes his space vehicle, he must find a body to use and a power source for his return trip.

Shulevitz, U. (1998). *Snow.* New York: Farrar, Straus & Giroux. (K–2). PICTURE BOOK, CONTEMPORARY REALISTIC FICTION.

An exquisite picture book that shows a child's optimism in the face of adults' view of snow.

Smith, R. (1990). *Sea otter rescue.* New York: Cobblehill. (3–6). INFORMATIONAL BOOK.

This photographic account of rescuing animals after an oil spill graphically illustrates the process in a step-by-step sequence.

Steig, W. (1998). *Pete's a pizza.* New York: HarperCollins. (K–2). CONTEMPORARY REALISTIC FICTION.

A family story about imaginative play between father and son.

Taylor, M. D. (1987). *The friendship* (M. Ginsburg, Illus.). New York: Dial. (4–7). HISTORICAL FICTION.

Taylor writes about the rude treatment of an elderly black man as seen through the eyes of some black children who know that the rude man owes his life to the old black man.

Viorst, J. (1981). *If I were in charge of the world and other worries* (L. Cherry, Illus.). New York: Atheneum. (1–6). POETRY.

Poems about everyday children's everyday problems. The compilation includes topics such as goodbye, wicked thoughts, thanks and no thanks, facts of life, and night.

Voigt, C. (1981). *Homecoming.* New York: Atheneum. (4–6). CONTEMPORARY REALISTIC FICTION.

When 13-year-old Dicey, her brothers, and her sister are abandoned by their mother, Dicey takes her siblings to her grandmother.

References and Books for Further Reading

Barksdale-Ladd, M. A., & Nedeff, A. R. (1997). The worlds of a reader's mind: Students as authors. *Reading Teacher, 50,* 564–573.

Barone, D. (1990). The written responses of young children: Beyond comprehension to story understanding. *New Advocate, 3,* 49–56.

Barthes, R. (1975). *The pleasure of the text.* London: Jonathan Cape.

Blake, R. W. (1995). *From literature-based reading to reader response in the elementary classroom.* Paper presented at the Annual Meeting of the National Council of Teachers of English, San Diego, CA.

Bloem, P. L., & Manna, A. (1999). A chorus of questions: Readers respond to Patricia Polacco. *Reading Teacher, 52,* 802–809.

Bloome, D., & Bailey, F. M. (1992). Studying language and literature through events, particularity, and intertextuality. In R. Beach (Ed.), *Multidisciplinary perspectives on literacy research* (pp. 181–210). Urbana, IL: National Conference on Research in English.

Borders, S., & Naylor, A. (1993). *Children talking about books.* Phoenix, AZ: Oryx.

Cairney, T. (1990). Intertextuality: Infectious echoes from the past. *The Reading Teacher, 43,* 478–484.

Chambers, A. (1983). *Introducing books to children.* Boston: Horn Book.

Children's Book Council. (1994). *75 years of children's book week posters.* New York: Knopf.

Elleman, B. (1991). Paula Fox's *The Village by the Sea. Book Links, 1,* 48–50.

Flitterman-King, S. (1988). The role of the response journal in active reading. *Quarterly of the National Writing Project and the Center for the Study of Writing, 10,* 4–11.

Gambrell, L., & Almasi, J. (Eds.). (1996). *Lively discussions! Fostering engaged reading.* Newark, DE: International Reading Association.

Giblin, J. C. (1990). *Writing books for young people.* Boston: The Writer.

Hammond, D. (1991). Prediction chart. In. J. Macon, D. Bewell, & M. Vogt (Eds.), *Responses to literature* (p. 3). Newark, DE: International Reading Association.

Hancock, J. (1991). *Teaching with picture books.* Portsmouth, NH: Heinemann.

Hancock, J., & Hill, S. (1988). *Literature-based reading programs at work.* Portsmouth, NH: Heinemann.

Hansen, J. (1991, Spring). I wonder what kind of person he'll be. *The New Advocate,* pp. 89–100.

Hartman, D. K. (1992). Eight readers reading: The intertextual links of able readers using multiple passages. *Reading Research Quarterly, 27,* 122–133.

Hoffman, J. (1992). Critical reading/thinking across the curriculum: Using I-charts to support learning. *Language Arts, 69,* 121–127.

Holland, K., Hungerford, R., & Ernst, S. (1993). *Journeying: Children responding to literature.* Portsmouth, NH: Heinemann.

Jenkins, C. B. (1999). *The allure of authors: Author studies in the elementary classroom.* Portsmouth, NH: Heinemann.

Jewell, T., & Pratt, D. (1998–99). Literature discussions in the primary grades: Children's thoughtful discourse about books and what teachers can do to make it happen. *Reading Teacher, 52,* 842–855.

Kelly, P. R. (1990). Guiding young students' responses to literature. *Reading Teacher's Journal, 43,* 464–470.

Langer, J. (1992). Rethinking literature instruction. In J. Langer (Ed.), *Literature instruction: A focus on student response* (pp. 35–53). Urbana, IL: National Council of Teachers of English.

Langer, J. (1995). *Envisioning literature: Literary understanding and literature instruction.* New York: Teachers College Press.

Largent, M. (1986). Response to literature: Moving towards an aesthetic transaction. Unpublished manuscript. Berkeley: University of California.

Larrick, N. (1991). Give us books! . . . But also . . . Give us wings! *The New Advocate, 2,* 77–84.

Lewis, C. S. (1961). *An experiment in criticism.* Cambridge, England: Cambridge University Press.

Lundin, A. (1998). Intertextuality in children's literature. *Journal of Education for Library and Information Science, 39,* 210–213.

Macon, J. M., Bewell, D., & Vogt, M. E. (1991). *Responses to literature.* Newark, DE: International Reading Association.

Many, J. (1996). Exploring the influences of literature approaches on children's stance when responding and their response complexity. *Reading Psychology, 17,* 1–41.

Martinez, M., & Nash, M. F. (1991). Bookalogues: Talking about children's books. *Language Arts, 68,* 140–147.

McClure, A. A., & Kristo, J. V. (Eds.). (1996). *Books that invite talk, wonder, and play.* Urbana, IL: National Council of Teachers of English.

McMahon, S., & Raphael, T. (1994). The book club program: theoretical and research foundations. In S. McMahon, T. Raphael, V. Goatley, & L. Pardo (Eds.), *The book club connection.* New York: Teachers College Press.

Morrow, L. M. (1989, November). *Research report.* Paper presented at the Annual Meeting of the National Council of Teachers of English, Baltimore, MD.

Musthafa, B. (1996). *Nurturing children's response to literature in the classroom context.* ERIC NO: ED398577.

Paterson, K. (1981). *The gates of excellence: On reading and writing books for children.* New York: Dutton.

Probst, R. (1992). Five kinds of literary knowing. In J. Langer (Ed.), *Literature instruction: A focus on student response* (pp. 54–77). Urbana, IL: National Council of Teachers of English.

Raphael, T., & McMahon, S. (1994). Book club: An alternative framework for reading instruction. *Reading Teacher, 48,* 102–116.

Rosen, B. (1986). *And none of it was nonsense: The power of storytelling in school.* Portsmouth, NH: Heinemann.

Rosenblatt, L. M. (1978). *The reader, the text, the poem: The transactional theory of the literary work.* Edwardsville: Southern Illinois University.

Rosenblatt, L. M. (1982). The literary transaction: Evocation and response. *Theory into Practice, XXI,* 268–277.

Roser, N., Hoffman, J., Labbo, L., & Farest, C. (1991). Language charts: A record of story time talk. *Language Arts, 69,* 44–52.

Schmitt, B., & Buckley, M. (1991). Plot relationships chart. In J. Macon, D. Bewell, & M. Vogt (Eds.), *Responses to literature.* Newark, DE: International Reading Association.

Sebesta, S., & Iverson, W. J. (1975). *Literature for Thursday's child.* Chicago: Science Research Associates.

Sendak, M. (1988). *Caldecott and co.: Notes on books and pictures.* New York: Farrar, Straus & Giroux.

Stoodt, B., & Amspaugh, L. (1994, May). *Children's response to nonfiction.* Paper presented to the Annual Meeting of the International Reading Association, Toronto, Canada.

Thacker, D. (1996). The child's voice in children's literature. In *Sustaining the vision: Selected papers from the annual conference of the International Association of School Librarianship,* Worcester, England, July 1995.

Toth, M. (1990). Character map. In J. Macon, D. Bewell, & M. Vogt (Eds.), *Responses to literature K–8.* Newark, DE: International Reading Association.

Vygotsky, L. (1978). *Mind in society.* Cambridge, MA: Harvard University Press.

Waldo, B. (1991). Story pyramid. In J. Macon, D. Bewell, & M. Vogt (Eds.), *Responses to literature.* Newark, DE: International Reading Association.

White, E. B. (1970). Laura Ingalls Wilder Award Acceptance Speech. *Horn Book, 56,* 540–547.

Wollman-Bonilla, J., & Werchadlo, B. (1995). Literature response journals in a first-grade classroom. *Language Arts, 72,* 562–570.

Wollman-Bonilla, J., & Werchadlo, B. (1999). Teacher and peer roles in scaffolding first graders' responses to literature. *Reading Teacher, 52,* 598–608.

Zinsser, W. (Ed.). (1990). Introduction. In *The art and craft of writing for children* (pp. 1–21). Boston: Houghton Mifflin.

Literature for the Youngest

5

KEY TERMS

developmentally appropriate
emergent literacy

GUIDING QUESTIONS

As you read this chapter, think about the following questions and answer them after you complete the chapter.

1. Why is literature important in the lives of young children?

2. What kinds of books should children experience during their preschool years?

3. What is the primary caregiver's responsibility in children's literary experiences?

OVERVIEW

The sensory data from sight, sound, and sensation spark young children's learning processes and determine in large measure the sort of people they will become. Children's experiences during early childhood not only influence their later functioning in school but also can have effects throughout life (National Association for the Education of Young Children [NAEYC], 1997). From birth, brain development and cognition are impacted by environment and experience (Caine & Caine, 1991; Kuhl, 1994). Studies show that "from infancy through about age 10, brain cells not only form most of the connections they will maintain throughout life but during this time they retain their greatest malleability" (Dana Alliance for Brain Initiatives, 1996, p. 7). Moreover, the preschool years are the optimum time for development of fundamental motor skills (Gallahue, 1993), for language development (Dyson & Genishi, 1993), and for other key aspects of development that have lifelong implications (NAEYC, 1997).

Mounting evidence shows that children who have developmentally appropriate experiences in preschool and kindergarten have greater success in the early grades (Charlesworth, Hart, Burts, & DeWolf, 1993; Frede & Barnett, 1992; Marcon, 1992). They are dependent on others, however, to create their literary environment and offer experiences that introduce them to the pleasures of literature. Parents are children's first and most significant teachers. In contemporary life, many mothers and fathers are employed outside the home; therefore, primary caregivers, librarians, and grandparents also play critical roles in children's literary lives (Heath, 1982, 1983; Kulleseid & Strickland, 1989; Teale & Sulzby, 1989). Parents and primary caregivers can initiate read-alouds and conversations that develop emergent literacy skills, "the reading and writing behaviors of young children that precede and develop into conventional literacy" (Sulzby, 1991, p. 273).

INTRODUCTION

The preschool years are a remarkably active period for learning about written language. Educators believe the knowledge of why and how people use literacy, knowledge of story structure, attempts to make meaning of written messages, and attempts to produce meaning through writing are central to emergent literacy. These understandings emerge from extensive experiences with literature at an early age.

Recent research in cognitive and developmental psychology has produced different and broader conceptualizations of early literacy development than in the past. The psychologist Vygotsky (1985) believed that children's language developed in a social context and that children's use of language stimulated their cognitive development. In the early stages children talk to themselves to think things through and achieve their goals. According to current theory, human beings acquire literacy in much the same way they acquire language; that is, they learn in context through interaction with a caring adult (Hiebert, 1988). The acquisition of literacy is now viewed as a social process; consequently, the role of parents and primary caregivers has assumed greater importance (Greene, 1991). The NAEYC's (1997) Position Statement on Early Literacy acknowledges the importance of enabling children to learn about their environment through a variety of themes and subjects that bolsters confidence and augments literacy development. For example, Zimmerman and Clemesha's *Trashy Town* tells about Mr. Gilly whose job it is to pick up trash all over Trashy Town. He drives all over town in a big truck dumping and smashing trash. The refrain "Is the trash truck full yet? NO!" invites children to join in, especially the children who love big trucks.

In the following vignette, you will learn how one young child began to grow into literacy during her early years.

VIGNETTE

At her first birthday party, Sarah received two books, *Where's Spot?* by Eric Hill and *The Very Hungry Caterpillar* by Eric Carle. She opened the books, looked at the pictures, and asked her mother to read them. As the day progressed, she enjoyed "reading" her birthday cards again and again. She asked her father to read them several times. Then she pretended to read the cards to her guests. These activities culminated a single year of growth and development.

From birth to 3 months, Sarah enjoyed nursery rhymes. Her parents, grandparents, and babysitter recited them from memory. She listened to her favorites, *Goodnight Moon* by Margaret Wise Brown and *The Wheels on the Bus* by Paul Zelinsky, and she insisted on doing the hand motions with this traditional rhyme. Early on, she appeared to recognize the rhythm of language in her favorites and laughed when anyone started chanting familiar rhymes. She owned many books and accompanied her mother and father, who are avid readers, to the library.

Between 4 and 9 months, Sarah began to handle books herself, and her parents gave her board books. She enjoyed other books as well. Her favorite was *Fish Eyes* by Ehlert, which went where she went and was read again and again. Her other favorites included *I Went Walking* by Sue Williams, and *Max's Breakfast* by Rosemary Wells. When family members read to her, they pointed to the pictures and identified them. Her parents and primary caregiver often gave Sarah books to read when she was riding in her car seat.

(continued)

At 11 months, Sarah began "reading" her books to other people. Her idea of reading was to turn the pages and babble. Sarah saw her parents, her grandparents, and her caregiver reading. Her playmate, Adam, who was 9 months older, enjoyed books too. Both of them saw books, newspapers, and magazines in their homes. In many situations she observed her parents reading books, magazines, and newspapers for a variety of purposes. The adults around her called attention to her name written on birthday cards and Christmas cards. She had seen her mother and father write notes and letters and had gone to the mailbox and the post office. Sarah started scribbling with crayons, magic markers, and pencils as soon as she learned not to eat them. By age 1, Sarah had a joyful concept of literacy.

At age 2, Andrew loves his books.

The opening vignette profiles a child who had many opportunities to interact with caring adults. Her parents were readers who modeled reading behavior, read to her, and complimented her efforts to read. Printed materials abounded in her environment. Each of these elements is significant. The presence of printed materials is as important as listening to stories; research demonstrates that the language and illustrations in books contribute to the development of children's cognitive and language abilities (Purcell-Gates, 1988, 1991). The Harvard Preschool Project clearly demonstrated the importance of children's first 3 years in their intellectual, emotional, and social development (White, 1988). Young children are born with the innate drive to seek solutions actively to the puzzles the world presents. "From birth the human brain is programmed to seek for meaning and to organize sensations into coherent mental structures" (Kulleseid & Strickland, 1989).

THE VALUE OF EARLY LITERARY EXPERIENCE

During the early months of life, for the child who is read to, literature provides a rich source of language from which the brain takes in a lasting repertoire of sounds and nuances of the native language (Healy, 1991). The growth and development of children's thinking and language skills are enhanced through ap-

propriate, informal experiences (DeVries & Kohlberg, 1990; Kamii & Ewing, 1996; Piaget, 1952). Early experiences with literature develop children's ability to apprehend meaning. For example, Voss (1988) observed her young son's experiences with literature and noticed they led him to understand that letters and words hold messages and the messages should make sense. By age 3, he realized that a printed label held a message.

Research shows that language experiences are a factor in young children's story retellings. In retelling these stories, they did not merely memorize words, but used their own words, which deviated from the original text, showing that they were not merely mimicking what they had heard but were deriving meaning from the story and internalizing it (Sulzby, 1985).

Language experiences enable children to sort the words, sounds, and patterns of language. They learn valuable language skills—the patterns and rhythms of language—from listening to and chanting nursery rhymes (Dickinson & Smith, 1994; Healy, 1991). Listening to many books teaches story patterns, which are very important in all aspects of learning and thinking (Healy, 1991). In the book *Little Fish Lost* by Nancy Van Laan, the language pattern is rhythmic:

> *Little Fish lost his mother, where was she,*
> *where was she?*
> *Little Fish lost his mother, yes, he did.*

In this book the refrain, "but his mother, no, no, no, was not there," gives the story structure. After searching for his mother, he finds her and completes the circle story structure. In Laura Numeroff's *If You Give a*

Moose a Muffin readers encounter a circle story, one that ends at the same place that it began, and a cause-and-effect pattern. Listening to stories helps young children internalize common story patterns.

Literature helps young children solve language and cognitive puzzles to communicate meaning. Immersing children in a steady stream of language augments their language proficiency. Telling and reading stories to them and expanding on characters, events, and ideas they encounter immerse children in language, thus enriching their language and cognitive repertoire. Listening to stories, telling stories, and talking all help children learn that language should make sense, as well as help them learn the words and sentences that express their thoughts. Between the ages of 3 and 6, children recognize the difference between formal and informal language; when asked to "read" a familiar storybook, they produce formal speech rather than conversational speech (Dickinson & Smith, 1994).

Children who learn to read early consistently exhibit certain characteristics (Clark, 1976; Durkin, 1966; Kulleseid & Strickland, 1989):

- They hear stories from an early age.
- They live in homes that provide exposure to all kinds of reading materials and pictures.
- They see parents or caretakers reading regularly, giving them examples of reading and pleasure in reading.
- They have opportunities to talk about books, reading, and pictures with adults.
- They can choose books they want to hear and look at.

Success in School

Library activities afford children the interactions with speaking, listening, reading, and writing that are catalysts to language and cognitive development. Sustained experiences with books develop children's vocabulary and sense of story structure, both of which are significant factors in emergent literacy. Specific experiences with literature closely related to reading appear to have the greatest impact on emergent literacy. Parents who read to children develop their comprehension processes through discussing books and encouraging children to ask questions about books. Many preschoolers ask their parents questions after hearing stories, ranging from story meaning and word meaning (the most frequent

questions) to characters, events, story line, motives, printed word forms, letters, authors, book titles, and the act of reading (Yaden, Smolkin, & Conlon, 1989). Thus early experiences with language have profound, long-term effects on school achievement.

Wells (1986) reports that the experiences children have with books by age 5 are directly related to reading comprehension at age 7 and age 11. Children who hear stories regularly from an early age and whose homes are filled with reading material are ready for the literacy tasks of the school (Cullinan, Greene, & Jaggar, 1990). Morrow (1988) finds that 4-year-old children who are read to for 10 weeks become better and more frequent question askers, give more interpretive responses to the stories they read, and respond more often to print and the story structure. Children who have occasions to listen and look while someone reads stories learn that a relation exists between printed words and spoken words. Furthermore, children from book-oriented homes have greater interest in print because their experiences with stories have demonstrated the enjoyment they can derive from books.

The impact of early literary experiences continues into the early years of school. The most significant factor in school success is hearing stories read aloud at home before school entry age (Wells, 1986). In addition, teachers who increase the amount of storybook reading in low-socioeconomic kindergartens develop students who have greater story comprehension, attend to picture clues more frequently, infer causal relations better, and tell more connected stories (Feitelson, Kita, & Goldstein, 1986).

Cognitive Development

Experiences directly affect neurological development of the brain with important and lasting implications for children's capacity to learn (Dana Alliance, 1996). Hearing stories is an aspect of experience. Immersing children in literature can begin early in life. Even though their ability to listen attentively is limited, children who are read to during the early months of life develop attentiveness to stories, rhymes, and songs sooner than those who have not been read to (Strickland & Morrow, 1990). These early experiences with print and language are the beginning of a lifelong process of developing literacy (Dickinson & Smith, 1994; Neuman, 1996).

During the first months of life, children are adapting to their new environment and bonding with the primary caregiver. They spend much of their time sleeping, crying, and babbling. At this stage, infants should have soft books, soft alphabet blocks, and caregivers who read or chant rhymes and stories to them. Librarians can help parents and caregivers by making available both books on parenting and children's literature to share with infants—Mother Goose rhymes, books that show patterns, lullabies, and books that feature pictures of objects. Infants are also interested in the sounds of words, which expands into an interest in the meaning of words between 7 and 14 months. At this age, their vocabulary is limited, but they understand more words than they can produce. Parents of young children who read to them daily, who tell stories, who are receptive to their children's questions, who respond to children's pretend "reading," and who are readers themselves create a warm, literate environment that enhances their understanding.

Print awareness develops as young children see their parents reading labels, cereal boxes, telephone books, magazines, and so forth. Through these experiences, they realize reading and writing are important activities that are used and valued in their homes. Exploring books enables them to discover the relation between the print in books and the visual symbols they see around them (Smith, 1997). Young children learn to expect written language to make sense and to have predictable structure from their experiences. When an adult shares a book with a child and asks, "What do you think will happen?", the adult is demonstrating the cognitive process—encouraging prediction, responding, wondering, and looking for more information (Greene, 1991).

Children who are age 15 to 24 months are interested in taking things apart, in action toys, and in reading pictures in books. They often engage in reading-like behavior by pretending to read stories from their books and enjoy listening to music and moving to rhythm (Greene, 1991). Popular books for this age are *Bouncing on the Bed* by Jackie French Koller, *What Can You Do in the Rain?* by Anna Grossnickle Hines, and *Mockingbird* by Allan Ahlberg.

At approximately age 2, children progress to Piaget's preoperational stage of development and enjoy books with rhythmic chants and action that invite their participation, such as Judy Hindley's *Eyes, Nose, Fingers, and Toes* and Joan Blos's *Hello Shoes*. The pre-operational stage extends to age 7, subdivided into two stages, the preconceptual stage and the intuitive stage. In the preconceptual stage (2 to 4 years), children possess a subjective logic, classifying things on the basis of a single attribute. For instance, they associate movement with life, so they believe that moving things are alive. Children in the preconceptual stage of cognitive development can follow simple plot lines such as those in simple picture books and folktales. Denise Fleming's *In the Tall, Tall Grass* invites children to view the world from the perspective of a caterpillar crawling in tall grass.

According to Piaget, children enter the second half of the preoperational stage of development, the intuitive stage, around age 4 and continue in this stage until approximately age 7. During the intuitive stage, they acquire a full language system, although it will be further refined during the elementary school years. In this stage, youngsters are aware of the world around them and are less egocentric than in earlier stages. During this stage as well, children begin to explore and discover their lifelong interests. This is the ideal time to expose them to a wide range of literature types and subjects. *Corduroy* by Don Freeman is an old favorite about a stuffed toy bear. *Mud* by Mary Lyn Ray introduces the joys and sounds of mud, which introduces the sensory world. *Good Knight* by Linda Rymill is the story of a boy's efforts to avoid a bath and getting ready for bed. All of these books are appropriate for this developmental stage.

Table 5.1 summarizes the general characteristics of children's development from birth through age 5 and developmentally appropriate literature for these ages.

EFFECT OF ENVIRONMENT ON EMERGENT LITERACY

Three major environments affect children's development: the home; the day care, preschool, or school the child attends; and the external environment, which includes the parent's work, the neighborhood, and the church (Bronfenbrenner, 1986). Each of these environments may enhance or detract from emergent literacy. For instance, children who live in a neighborhood with a public library may have greater access to books and library programs. Children whose environments offer many opportunities to learn about written language enter school with much knowledge about literacy incidentally derived from their environment (Sulzby, 1991).

TABLE 5.1
Child development characteristics and appropriate literature.

Age	Characteristics	Appropriate Literature
Birth to 6 months	<ul><li>cries, coos, and gurgles</li><li>human voice comforts</li><li>attends to musical toys and mobiles</li></ul>	<ul><li>rhythmic language</li><li>rhymes, songs, and chants</li><li>Mother Goose</li></ul>
6 months to 9 months	<ul><li>laughs</li><li>repeats syllables (da da, ma ma)</li><li>grasps books</li></ul>	<ul><li>rhythmic language</li><li>rhymes, songs, and chants</li><li>simple board books</li><li>repetitive books with one object per page</li><li>Mother Goose, traditional songs</li></ul>
9 months to 18 months	<ul><li>responds to words</li><li>uses holophrases (one word that represents larger unit) such as "juice" for "I want some juice."</li><li>plays peek-a-boo</li><li>points to objects</li><li>waves bye-bye</li></ul>	<ul><li>simple stories that include family and pets</li><li>stories that relate to daily life</li><li>cumulative tales</li><li>books with objects child can point to</li></ul>
18 months to 24 months	<ul><li>vocabulary of 50–400 words</li><li>uses 2- and 3-word phrases</li></ul>	<ul><li>all of the stories mentioned</li><li>predictable stories</li></ul>
24 months to 36 months	<ul><li>more language is comprehended than is used</li><li>uses some pronouns</li><li>uses 3- and 4-word phrases</li></ul>	<ul><li>all of the stories mentioned</li><li>counting and alphabet books</li><li>somewhat longer stories</li><li>same story repeated</li><li>several stories at once</li></ul>
36 months to 48 months	<ul><li>understands about 1,000 words</li><li>forms sentences and questions</li><li>language system complete</li></ul>	<ul><li>all of the stories mentioned</li><li>dramatizing</li><li>puppets</li><li>retelling stories to others</li></ul>
48 months to 60 months	<ul><li>understands about 1,500 to 1,800 words</li><li>names objects, colors, number, and letters</li><li>aware of sounds and letters</li></ul>	<ul><li>all of the stories mentioned</li><li>"reading" to self</li><li>dramatizing</li><li>recognizes hero and villain</li><li>compares self to characters</li></ul>

The Benefits of Literature for Young Children

Choosing appropriate literature and sharing it effectively with children gives them the benefits of literature. They learn that reading and writing are prominent parts of their world and that these abilities will help them accomplish many things. Meaningful experiences with literature help children learn many things:

1. To enjoy, appreciate, and respond to fine literature. *And If the Moon Could Talk* by Kate Banks and *Mama Cat Has Three Kittens* by Denise Fleming are superb early literary experiences.

2. To develop understanding of story structure by parts such as beginnings, middles, and endings. Introduce books such as *Max's Dragon Shirt* by Rosemary Wells and *Piggies* by Don and Audrey Wood.

3. To interpret literature and understand what the author is saying to readers. Introduce *I Lost My Bear* by Jules Feiffer and *Gramma's Walk* by Anna Grossnickle Hines, which are books that young children can interpret.

4. To communicate more effectively. Using Kevin Henkes's *Chrysanthemum* shows the importance of sounds, vocabulary, and language for children, and *Little Penguin's Tale* by Audrey Wood includes language play.

5. To broaden their understanding of cultural consciousness and individual differences. Read *More, More, More, Said the Baby* by Vera Williams and *Abuela* by Arthur Dorros.

6. To build interests and encourage children to think. Read *What Can You Do in the Sun?* by Anna Grossnickle Hines.

7. To recognize sequence. Introduce Ellen Walsh's *Mouse Count,* which demonstrates counting and uncounting, and *Arlene Alda's 1 2 3* illustrating number shapes in photos.

8. To understand and appreciate different forms of literature (fiction and nonfiction). Introduce an informational book such as *Water* by Frank Asch, poetry such as *Dancin' in the Kitchen* by Wendy Gelsanliter and Frank Christian, nursery rhymes, and fiction such as *Cat Up a Tree* by John and Ann Hassett.

9. To enhance their development in all areas, social, emotional, linguistic, cognitive, and physical. Read Kathy Henderson's *The Baby Dances,* a book young children will enjoy. Children who have looked for their mothers will relate to *Little Fish Lost* by Nancy Van Laan.

10. To introduce a wide variety of experiences and specific facts about the world. *Way Out in the Desert* by T. J. Marsh and Jennifer Ward introduces desert animals in a rhyming counting book.

11. To develop children's cultural literacy. Nursery rhymes such as *Michael Foreman's Mother Goose* introduce children to well-known literary figures such as Mother Goose and Little Boy Blue.

12. To create a bond with parents and caregivers. Any book read with a child develops bonds, but books such as Sue Heap's *Cowboy Baby* are especially good because they show a warm relationship between father and son.

The Family Environment

For children in a literate society the foundations for learning to read and write are established in the home. When parents hold a little one on their laps to share a nursery rhyme, a story, or a poem, they create a pleasurable social event. These special moments of closeness will remain with them both for a lifetime. Parents who talk and read to their infants and look at books with them create a literate home environment. Parents are indispensable in this process because they are the ones who go to the library, purchase books, and read them aloud. Parents of early readers tend to be habitual readers themselves (Strickland & Morrow, 1990). Their children respond to books, chant familiar words and phrases, and retell familiar stories without assistance.

Researchers investigating home storybook reading have identified several interactive behaviors between adults and young children that lead to positive effects from family reading. Adults who question, praise, offer information, discuss, share responses, and relate concepts to life experiences are encouraging cognitive and language development in children (Strickland & Morrow, 1990). Most of all, reading to and with young children gives parents and children opportunities to have fun together—to interact—thereby building their interest in reading.

Children who grow up in literate homes or attend preschool programs that value literacy have definite advantages over children who lack these experiences. The fortunate ones have heard many stories, looked at books, listened to audiotapes, watched videos, socialized with other children, explored their environment, conversed with adults and children; in short, they have developed the language, thinking, and physical abilities, the knowledge and experience, and the interests and motivation that prepare them for entering kindergarten.

Writing

Writing is an aspect of family literacy. Families who read to their children also provide the materials and motivation for children to experiment with writing (Teale & Sulzby, 1989). Children who see their parents writing letters and notes become aware of the importance of writing in their lives and are prepared to view writing as a tool when they enter school. Moreover, children who have been read to extensively before entering school use language that has features of written language when composing stories to accompany wordless picture books (Purcell-Gates, 1988). "In these and other ways, young children are ushered into the world of literacy, viewing reading and writing as aspects of a much larger system for accomplishing goals" (Teale & Sulzby, 1989, p. 3). Both reading and writing are processes that develop through continued use. Children learn about writing through experimenting with various writing implements. They enjoy scribbling and creating pictures with crayons. Writing (scribbling) messages and reading them to others extend their interest in literacy.

Love of literature

Young children need to see books displayed, as well as see adults and other children enjoying books. Children acquire literacy concepts and skills when given the opportunity to see adults using literacy for work and pleasure (Adams, Treiman, & Pressley, 1998). Books, magazines, newspapers, and writing materials should therefore be a prominent part of children's surroundings, and the setting should foster enjoyment of these materials.

Many parents who themselves love literature do not realize its importance to infants and toddlers. They realize that books will become influential in their children's lives when they are older, but do not understand that literacy begins at birth. "It's amazing that children's learning to read is considered important, but children's books often are not. Plastic toys sell better than books. Yet if children's minds are important, so are their books" (Hearne, 1990, p. 7). Parents and grandparents emphasize the expense of books for children, although they do not hesitate to spend three times as much for a toy that may be cast aside in a few days. But children return again and again to fine literature when they have the chance.

The Preschool, Day Care, and School Environment

Young children who are taken out of their homes in the early months of life and entrusted to outside caretakers depend on these significant people for experiences their parents would otherwise provide. In the best situations, parents and caretakers work together to create a secure environment for these little ones. Books they enjoy can bridge the home environment to day care. Ideally, day-care centers and preschool classrooms become communities in which home experiences are valued and used as building blocks for language and literacy development (NAEYC, 1997). Early childhood teachers and primary caregivers who provide many opportunities for children to enjoy books are planting the seeds that can develop into a lifelong fondness and appreciation for literature.

As arrangements for care outside the home for young children have become more prevalent due to parental employment, the programs of these various facilities have been scrutinized more carefully, raising awareness of the consequence of young children's environment and activities both at home and outside the home. The adults who care for children during the early years of life are responsible for their most important years—the years when they acquire language competence, cognitive abilities, social skills, emotional development, and physical skills. This growing recognition of the importance of the early years in children's lifelong learning means that all agencies and people concerned must become knowledgeable about young children, their literature, and appropriate literary experiences. Experts generally agree that quality of life and emergent literacy are enhanced when parents, caregivers, and preschool teachers provide young children with books and a wide variety of activities with books (Cullinan et al., 1990). When literature and literary activities are available, children have incentives for language experimentation, dramatic play, singing, and chanting.

> The ideal environment for children to become engaged with books includes an inviting library or book center with soft cushions to sit on, stuffed animals to hold or lean on, a book shelf with a variety of choices changed frequently, a rocking chair or teacher's lap for cuddling in, and finally, a well-prepared, enthusiastic teacher who thoroughly enjoys books and reading. (Ford, 1991)

The setting should also encourage children to explore books individually and with friends in a quiet uninterrupted place in the classroom. Choosing the books to place in these settings is an important task, discussed later in this chapter in the section Selecting and Evaluating Literature for Young Children, and in chapter 3.

Early childhood programs

Due to the growing recognition of emergent literacy and child development as crucial stages in a child's life, 28 states currently fund or have committed funds to prekindergarten programs (O'Neil, 1988). Teachers and caretakers of young children are teaching children and guiding them in ways that once were the province of the parents. The increasingly important role of these adults in the lives of little children is accompanied by greater responsibilities as well. Increasingly, parents are relying on them to both select literature for their children to read in the classroom and to suggest literature that parents should have at home.

Early childhood education differs widely among programs because the programs and personnel preparation lack uniformity. The National Academy of Early Childhood Programs, sponsored by NAEYC, is attempting to alleviate this situation by accrediting programs. To obtain accreditation, the program must promote children's learning by encouraging the use of age-appropriate literature and language arts experiences in the classroom daily (Ford, 1991). The accreditation standards require that caregivers provide a broad cross-section of children's books that includes

multicultural, nonstereotypical picture books to assist children in learning about the cultural diversity of society as well as the traditional books found in child-care centers.

The External Environment

Children's experiences are also related to the neighborhood environment, their parents' work situation, and their church. Neighborhoods with public libraries offer children opportunities to borrow books and many of them offer story hours and other programs for young children. Bookstores sometimes sponsor visits by children's authors and story reading programs. Natural science museums, art museums, and similar institutions offer stimulating activities and exhibits for children of all ages. Parents and caregivers can use current events as incentives for reading. When the circus comes to town, children are motivated to listen to and read circus stories. Local newspapers and magazines such as *Parents* magazine often include book lists and book reviews to guide parents and teachers in selecting good books. *The Children's Literature Web Guide* on the Internet (www.underdown.org/children), provides excellent information for parents, teachers, and librarians as does the American Library Association's Web site (www.ala.org). Some employers bring speakers into the workplace to help parents realize the importance of literature and reading to children. Ministers in some churches and Sunday school teachers often include storytelling and children's literature in their presentations.

Libraries and Media Centers

Librarians play a major role in creating a literate environment for young children. They serve as resources for children, their parents, and their caregivers by sharing enjoyable books with them. They offer programs for parents and children that introduce them to fine literature and ways of appreciating that literature. Moreover, they educate adults about child rearing and literature on that topic.

Many quarters of society today recognize the importance of educating the adults who care for young children. One of the libraries addressing this need is the New York Public Library, whose Children's Services created the Early Childhood Resource and Information Center (ECRIC) for children from birth to

7 years and their caregivers (Cullinan et al., 1990). As a part of this program, participants had opportunities to discuss young children and their books. The library also developed criteria for selecting print and nonprint materials and explored ways of working with children and caregivers from diverse populations.

SELECTING AND EVALUATING LITERATURE FOR YOUNG CHILDREN

When confronted with rows of shelves containing books, how can parents, teachers, and librarians choose the right book, the one that will be a hit with a 3-year-old child? Many people select books they enjoyed as children and are dismayed when children today do not enjoy them. Although certain books such as *Where the Wild Things Are* and *Goodnight Moon* are favorites of every generation, children will also like many of the newer books. "Evaluating children's books is a matter of practice as well as taste. The best way to start is with a few touchstone titles, surefire suggestions that rarely miss" (Hearne, 1990, p. 26). The following guidelines are helpful in selecting and evaluating literature for young children:

1. Choose developmentally appropriate literature.
   a. For infants: Cloth or board books that focus on single objects or simple rhymes and chants are appropriate for beginning literary experiences.
   b. For toddlers: "Point and say" books and books with clear pictures of familiar objects are books that will be enjoyed.
   c. For preschoolers: Books with characters, plots, and situations with which children can identify are appropriate.
2. Find books with a multicultural attitude toward society, which will cultivate appreciation for the individual worth of every person because children develop attitudes about other cultures based on their perception of the views of their parents, teachers, or caregivers. (A good resource to check is *Anti-Bias Curriculum: Tools for Empowering Young Children* by L. Derman-Sparks and the ABC Task Force and the Web site for the Cooperative Children's Book Center sponsored by the School of Education, University of Wisconsin–Madison; http://www.soemadison.wisc.edu/ccbc/jensen2.htm).
3. Consider the children's experiences to determine whether the situations and characters are familiar to them. For example, Mercer Mayer's *There's Something in My Attic* is a story about being afraid of nightmares and noises, a situation with which many children will identify.
4. Consider the story and setting from a young child's perspective. Is the story interesting to children? Some books *about* children are not developmentally appropriate *for* children; these books are sentimental favorites more suited to adults.
5. Locate simple stories with plots, characters, climax, and a satisfying conclusion that help children understand the ways stories work. For example, *Come Along, Daisy!* by Jane Simmons has a simple plot that will speak to little children. In this story, a little duck gets separated from her mother, but they get together in the end. This book could be compared to *Little Fish Lost* by Nancy Van Laan. To supplement your appreciation of these books, read a variety of selections and identify your favorite authors for this age group.

Authors and Illustrators for Younger Children

Authors and illustrators often find a niche in the world of children's books that they enjoy, but the majority write and illustrate for diverse audiences, including adults. Many of these talented people get their ideas from their children or those they have observed. Unfortunately, we do not have the space to list all of the talented authors and illustrators, but a few of our favorites follow:

Bryon Barton has illustrated books for various audiences. For younger children he has created books that focus on technology such as trains, trucks, and astronauts.

Marc Brown created the popular Arthur books and several other series. We particularly like his finger play books for younger children.

Denise Fleming uses wonderful colors in creating books with simple plots for little ones about mice, ponds, kittens, and so on.

Anna Grossnickle Hines creates concept books and other books devoted to the interests and experiences of young children. A profile of her follows.

Tana Hoban uses brilliant photography in her beautiful concept books that help young children see their familiar environment with fresh eyes.

Rosemary Wells created the well-known toddler rabbit, Max. A profile of her follows.

Profiles of select authors and illustrators

Anna Grossnickle Hines.　　Ms. Hines enjoyed drawing from an early age. She enjoyed a Little Golden picture book edition of *Heidi* as a child and decided very early that she wanted to make books for boys and girls. In college she checked out stacks of books from the library and read them to the preschoolers in the day-care center where she worked. She started writing poetry and then picture books. She left school to study on her own, married, and divorced, which left her with two children to support. She taught school, remarried, and had another child. During this time, she collected rejection letters from various publishers. Finally in 1981 she published *Taste the Raindrops* with Greenwillow.

She continues to write and illustrate books for young children because she is fascinated by children, by how they think and what they accomplish daily, by learning about their bodies, language, the world around them, relationships with others . . . sorting it all out and making sense of it. This fascination is demonstrated in her book titles: *What Can You Do in the Rain?, What Can You Do in the Wind?, What Can You Do in the Snow?,* and *What Can You Do in the Sun?* Greenwillow published all of these books as board books in 1999. Other books to review include *My Own Big Bed,* published by Greenwillow in 1998, and *Bean, Bean's Games,* and *Bean's Night* from Harcourt Brace, 1998. (Oh, yes, Bean is a cat.)

Ms. Hines has a wonderful Web site that has interesting things for children, teachers, librarians, and parents. The address is: www.aghines.com/annabook

Rosemary Wells.　　Ms. Wells has created unforgettable characters in her books. Max, a toddler bunny, and his bossy older sister, Ruby, are popular with the preschool set. Ruby, in true big sister style, tries to control Max, who often outwits her. Ms. Wells has two daughters who provided her with incidents and themes to develop for Max and Ruby. She likes to create animal characters and humorous books. She re-creates child and adolescent behavior in her books. Ms. Wells also writes for young adults (Knoth, 1995).

Of her illustrations she says, "My drawings look as if they are done quickly. They are not. First they are sketched in light pencil, then nearly rubbed out, then drawn again in heavier pencil" (Silvey, 1995, p. 674). She creates a series of layers of tiny ink lines intensifying all day until they are ready for color.

Ms. Wells's books for young children, all published by Dial, include *Max's First Word* (1979), *Shy Charles* (1988), *Max's Dragon Shirt* (1991), and *Moss Pillows: Voyage to the Bunny Planet* (1992).

ENHANCING LITERARY EXPERIENCE WITH ACTIVITIES

Initially, children are attracted to storytelling and story reading because these are social activities that they enjoy with their parents. They respond to the parent's voice and may find it calming. Toddlers are interested in the illustrations and like to point at pictured objects and animals, as well as repeat words and phrases from the story (Yaden et al., 1989). Such interactive behavior leads children to respond with questions and comments that become increasingly complex over time and demonstrate more sophisticated thinking about printed text. Eventually, children remark on story content, time, setting, characters, and story events (Morrow, 1988; Roser & Martinez, 1985). Activities with literature can build on these responses.

Oral Reading

Because young children cannot read for themselves, hearing stories read is their primary avenue for accessing literature; therefore read-aloud activities are central to literary experience both at home and in the preschool. Some guidelines for reading aloud to children include the following:

1. Choose a book that can be read at a single sitting of not longer than 10 to 15 minutes.
2. Ensure that all of the children in the group are able to see and enjoy the pictures while you read.
3. Choose a book that has interesting words with distinctive sounds and repetition to captivate the listener.
4. Know that young children frequently ask to have their favorite books read again and again. This is a valuable experience for them. Some children will ask to hear a favorite book 30 or 40 times (not all at once, though!).
5. Introduce each book in the same way that you would a new toy or game. Connect story content to what children already know and have experienced.

After reading Raising Dragons, Kyle and his friends dramatized the story.

6. Encourage children to ask questions and discuss the book. Respond to their questions. Compare the books to their own experiences and to other books they have read.

7. Provide children with browsing time. They should have constant, free access to books. Place books where children can easily pick them up and look at them.

8. Encourage dramatic play. Provide a chest of dress-up clothing, puppets, and art materials for dramatization purposes.

9. Encourage children to retell stories or to read them to others or to their toys or pets.

10. Encourage children to make up their own stories and tell them.

Refer to chapter 12 for ideas regarding oral literature experiences.

Big Books

At the emergent literacy stage, literature is often integrated through shared book experiences based on big books. These are enlarged books that are placed so the children can see the print as the teacher models reading, pointing to each word while reading aloud. When children become familiar with the story, they can join in by predicting the upcoming words and phrases. The teacher may ask students to point out specific words or phrases. Soon, the children "read" the big books from memory (Slaughter, 1993).

The big books for emergent reading should have simple, highly predictable language. Cumulative tales and stories with repeated phrases, words, and refrains are especially useful in the early stages of literacy. These books give children the foundation for language—related activities that help them grow into literacy. Students who have several opportunities to read a big book can tell their own versions of the story and their stories can be written on charts for more big book reading. Big book activities lead naturally into choral reading, dramatization, role-playing, music, and art.

Big books can be purchased from publishers or made by the class: The teacher prints the text from the children's own stories or favorite books, and the children illustrate it. Big books can be created from predictable books, rhymes, riddles, camp songs, finger plays, jump-rope rhymes, or anything else imaginable. Laminate the big books to preserve them for the classroom literature collection.

Media

Technology is growing so rapidly that many sources of stories are now available to young children. The Internet accesses stories and guides adults to books, videos, CD–ROM, audiotapes, and computer software. Although viewing or listening to electronic media is no substitute for a personal read-aloud, it can expand children's literary repertoire. Media should meet the same standards of quality as books. In addition, toys, puzzles, games, puppets, dramatic play props, chalkboards, paper bags, boxes, and paints are useful materials to encourage children's response to literature. Most public libraries can provide up-to-date information about the latest technology available and have such materials available for borrowing.

Media offer an added dimension to enhance literary experiences. For example, the video *Critter Hunt* from SVE shows young children exploring a springtime pond, which would enhance the book *In the Small, Small Pond* by Denise Fleming. The video *Dr. Seuss's Alphabet* is an excellent accompaniment to any alphabet book. We have found that children who were uninterested in the alphabet became interested through this video.

Some sources for selecting literature-related media are identified at the end of this chapter.

Unit Suggestions

ACTIVITY 5.1   THE FIVE SENSES

Week One: Seeing

1. Introduce the senses with questions such as these:
   a. How do you know the color of flowers?
   b. How do you know how loud music is?
   c. When a lemon is sour, how do you know it?
2. Read *What Joe Saw* by Anna Grossnickle Hines aloud. Discuss the reason Joe saw things that no one else saw and identify the things he saw on his walk. Discuss the children's favorite colors, animals, and objects. Then take the children for a seeing walk. Explain that they will look for things that Joe saw as well as their own favorite things. When they return have each one draw a picture of the best thing he or she saw on the walk.
3. Read books such as the *I Spy* series, which is a series of picture riddles that features Walter Wick's photos and Jean Marzollo's riddles, and have children identify the various objects.
4. The children can create their own *I Spy* books using magazine pictures or by drawing their own. Scholastic Publishing has an online demonstration of *I Spy* as well as suggestions for children to make their own picture riddles.
5. Read *Gramma's Walk* by Anna Grossnickle Hines to the children. Then discuss the senses that Gramma and Donnie use on their walk. Have the children draw or tell about their best sense to culminate the unit.

Week Two: Taste

1. Introduce taste by reading Eric Carle's *The Very Hungry Caterpillar* aloud, and then have a fruit-tasting party. Each child can bring a fruit to taste. After tasting the individual fruits, mix them to make a fruit salad.
2. Discuss the children's favorite foods and have a tasting party with items such as pickles, lemons, pretzels, potato chips, marshmallows, and chocolate kisses. Have the children tell about or draw their favorite tastes.
3. Read Lois Ehlert's *Growing Vegetable Soup* and have a vegetable-tasting party. After tasting the vegetables, mix them together and make vegetable soup. (This book includes a recipe.)
4. Have the children tell a story about making vegetable soup. The teacher can write it on posters as they tell the story.
5. Make posters of the children's favorite vegetables to exhibit. You can use magazine pictures or seed catalog pictures.

SUMMARY

Literacy is very important in life. Infants and young children should have many opportunities for experiences to develop the knowledge and abilities that will enable them to read and to write later. Most young children cannot read or write in their early years, but they should have considerable exposure to print so that their literacy will enable them to develop these proficiencies later. Parents and caretakers should read to children and let children see them using their reading ability in a variety of situations. The environment should include many books that children can handle. Providing children with writing materials encourages them to scribble and eventually to convey their thoughts in writing.

Literary quality is just as important for young children's first literary experiences as for adults, but available books should be appropriately geared to their stage of development. Simple plots and satisfying conclusions are important to children in developing emergent literacy.

Thought Questions

1. What factors should you consider when selecting books for young children?
2. Describe an imaginary book that would be just right for a toddler.
3. Identify each of the three environments that affect children's development and suggest ways that the contribution of each could be improved to enhance children's development.
4. How do you think multimedia should be used with preschool children?
5. Describe a preschool program that would enhance emergent literacy and fit with beginning reading instruction.

Research and Application Experiences

1. Visit a preschool or Head Start Program center and observe the availability of books and writing materials.
2. Interview one or more preschool teachers. Ask them how often they read aloud to children and how they select the books they read.
3. Create a literature unit for preschool children.
4. Create a file of books for infants, toddlers, and preschoolers.
5. Arrange to read stories to an infant, a toddler, and a preschooler. How did the books they preferred differ?
6. Create a display or bulletin board related to children's books for use in a preschool.

Children's Literature References and Recommended Books

Ahlberg, A. (1998). *Mockingbird* (P. Howard, Illus.). New York: Candlewick. (PreK). POETRY, PICTURE BOOK.

This beautiful picture book is based on the folk song "Hush, Little Baby."

Alda, A. (1998). *Arlene Alda's 1 2 3*. Berkeley, CA: Tricycle Press. (PreK–2). PICTURE BOOK.

This counting book uses color photographs to reveal number shapes.

Asch, F. (1995). *Water*. New York: Harcourt Brace. (PreK–2). INFORMATIONAL BOOK.

Colorful illustrations tell about the forms of water, as well as tears, floods, and rivers.

Bang, M. (1991). *Yellow ball*. New York: Morrow. (PreK). CONTEMPORARY REALISTIC FICTION.

A yellow ball travels until it bounces into the ocean.

Banks, K. (1998). *And if the moon could talk* (G. Hallensleben, Illus.). New York: Farrar, Straus & Giroux. (PreK–1). CONTEMPORARY REALISTIC FICTION.

Beautiful paintings in this book show the scenes outside a child's room at bedtime.

Blos, J. W. (1998). *Bedtime!* (S. Lambert, Illus.). New York: Simon. (PreK–K). CONTEMPORARY REALISTIC FICTION.

Grandma says it's bedtime, but a little boy says he is not sleepy. However, his animals are tired. Grandma tucks them in and reads a story.

Blos, J. (1999). *Hello shoes* (A. Boyajian, Illus.). New York: Simon & Schuster. (Infant–PreK). PICTURE BOOK.

A toddler and grandfather hunt for a pair of missing shoes.

Brown, M. W. (1947). *Goodnight moon* (C. Hurd, Illus.). New York: Harper & Row. (PreK–K). PICTURE BOOK.

A child says goodnight to each object in the bedroom.

Carle, E. (1979). *The very hungry caterpillar*. New York: Philomel. (PreK–1). PICTURE BOOK.

A tiny egg hatches into a tiny caterpillar who eats its way through all sorts of food.

Carlstrom, N. W. (1986). *Jesse bear, what will you wear?* (B. Degen, Illus.). New York: Macmillan. (K–2). POETRY.

These verses make getting dressed and undressed fun.

Chorao, K. (1998). *Little farm by the sea.* New York: Holt. (PreK–1). CONTEMPORARY REALISTIC FICTION.

This simple story introduces children to farm life.

Dorros, A. (1991). *Abuela.* New York: Dutton. (K–3). MODERN FANTASY.

A little girl and her grandmother have an imaginary flight over New York.

Ehlert, L. (1987). *Growing vegetable soup.* San Diego: Harcourt Brace Jovanovich. (PreK–1). PICTURE BOOK, INFORMATIONAL BOOK.

A child plants vegetables that grow and are made into vegetable soup.

Ehlert, L. (1990). *Fish eyes.* New York: Harcourt Brace Jovanovich. (PreK–1). PICTURE BOOK.

Readers count brightly colored fish and add the number of fish to the reader to make one more.

Feiffer, J. (1998). *I lost my bear.* New York: Morrow. (PreK–1). PICTURE BOOK.

A little girl faces a terrible crisis in this humorous book.

Fleming, D. (1991). *In the tall, tall grass.* New York: Holt. (PreK–1). PICTURE BOOK.

This picture book is of a caterpillar's view of the world as he crawls through the grass.

Fleming, D. (1992). *Lunch.* New York: Holt. (K–2). MODERN FANTASY.

A young mouse has lunch and gets different colored juice all over his clothing.

Fleming, D. (1993). *In the small, small pond.* New York: Holt. (PreK–1). PICTURE BOOK.

Pond life and pond inhabitants are the topic of this book.

Fleming, D. (1998). *Mama Cat has three kittens.* New York: Henry Holt. (PreK–1). MODERN FANTASY.

Fluffy and Skinny always do everything their mother does, but Boris sleeps. The author uses rhythm, repetition, and predictability to hold the reader's attention.

Foreman, M. (1991). *Michael Foreman's Mother Goose.* New York: Harcourt Brace Jovanovich. (PreK–1). PICTURE BOOK.

Foreman's illustrations of the traditional Mother Goose rhymes decorate this book.

Freeman, D. (1968). *Corduroy.* New York: Viking. (PreK–K). MODERN FANTASY.

This well-known story is about a stuffed bear who searches for his lost button and finds a friend.

Gelsanliter, W., & Christian, F. (1998). *Dancin' in the kitchen.* New York: Putnam. (PreK–2). POETRY.

Rhymed text tells the story of a family cooking and dancing in the kitchen.

Hassett, J., & Hassett, A. (1998). *Cat up a tree.* Boston: Houghton Mifflin. (PreK–1). MODERN FANTASY.

Nana Quimby calls the police to rescue a cat up a tree in this hilarious story.

Heap, S. (1999). *Cowboy baby.* New York: Candlewick. (PreK–K). CONTEMPORARY REALISTIC FICTION.

Sheriff Pa says it is bedtime, but his "deputy" must round up his "gang."

Henderson, K. (1999). *The baby dances* (T. Kerins, Illus.). New York: Candlewick. (PreK–K). INFORMATIONAL BOOK.

This book shows a baby's development through the first year of life. Children can look back at their own development.

Henkes, K. (1991). *Chrysanthemum.* New York: Greenwillow. (K–2). MODERN FANTASY.

A young mouse is disturbed by her long name when she goes to school, but she learns to appreciate it.

Hill, E. (1980). *Where's Spot?* New York: Putnam. (PreK). PICTURE BOOK.

Spot the dog is lost. The reader lifts flaps to hunt for him.

Hindley, J. (1999). *Eyes, nose, fingers, and toes.* (B. Granstrom, Illus.). New York: Candlewick. (Infant–PreK). PICTURE BOOK.

The book invites the readers to join in finding eyes, ears, and so forth.

Hines, A. G. (1983). *Taste the raindrops.* New York: Greenwillow. (PreK–1). PICTURE BOOK.

Readers experience the sensory impressions of raindrops.

Hines, A. G. (1993). *Gramma's walk.* New York: Greenwillow. (PreK–1). PICTURE BOOK.

Gramma takes a walk and enjoys the sights.

Hines, A. G. (1994). *What Joe saw.* New York: Greenwillow. (PreK–1). PICTURE BOOK.

Joe is a slowpoke because he stops to look at everything.

Hines, A. G. (1998). *My own big bed* (M. Watson, Illus.). New York: Greenwillow. (PreK–1). PICTURE BOOK.

A child graduates from crib to a big bed.

Hines, A. G. (1999a). *What can you do in the rain?* (T. Kiros, Illus.). New York: Greenwillow. (PreK). INFORMATIONAL BOOK.

The book explores rainy day activities such as making a mud pie.

Hines, A. G. (1999b). *What can you do in the snow?* New York: Greenwillow. (PreK). INFORMATIONAL BOOK.

Hines, A. G. (1999c). *What can you do in the sun?* (T. Kiros, Illus.). New York: Greenwillow. (PreK). INFORMATIONAL BOOK.

The book explores the sun through the five senses.

Hines, A. G. (1999d). *What can you do in the wind?* New York: Greenwillow. (PreK). INFORMATIONAL BOOK.

Hines-Stephens, S. (1998a, 1998b, 1998c). *Bean; Bean's Games; Bean's Night* (A. G. Hines, Illus.). New York: Harcourt Brace. (PreK–1). PICTURE BOOK.

These books portray the antics and life of Bean, a cat.

Koller, J. F. (1999). *Bouncing on the bed.* (A. G. Hines, Illus.). New York: Orchard. (PreK–K). CONTEMPORARY REALISTIC FICTION.

Most children love to jump on the bed just like these in this story.

Marsh, T. J., & Ward, J. (1998). *Way out in the desert* (K. J. Spengler, Illus.). Flagstaff, AZ: Rising Moon. (PreK–2). PICTURE BOOK.

Desert creatures populate the beautiful illustrations and rhythmic text.

Mayer, M. (1988). *There's something in my attic.* New York: Dial. (PreK–2). MODERN FANTASY.

A big, noisy nightmare lives in the attic so the heroine saves her toys.

Numeroff, L. (1991). *If you give a moose a muffin.* (F. Bond, Illus.). New York: HarperCollins. (PreK–2). MODERN FANTASY.

A circle story composed of cause-and-effect situations that arise after offering a moose a muffin.

Ray, M. L. (1996). *Mud.* (L. Stringer, Illus.). New York: Harcourt Brace Jovanovich. (PreK–1). INFORMATIONAL BOOK.

This book offers a rhythmic description of the sights and sounds of mud.

Rymill, L. R. (1998). *Good knight.* New York: Henry Holt. (PreK–K). CONTEMPORARY REALISTIC FICTION.

A boy resists his bath time and bedtime.

Sendak, M. (1963). *Where the wild things are.* New York: Harper & Row. (PreK–2). PICTURE BOOK, MODERN FANTASY.

A classic favorite in which a boy visits the land of wild things.

Simmons, J. (1998). *Come along, Daisy!* Boston: Little, Brown. (PreK–1). PICTURE BOOK.

Daisy searches for her mother.

Van Laan, N. (1998). *Little fish lost.* New York: Atheneum. (PreK–1). MODERN FANTASY.

Little Fish searches the ocean for his mother in this rhythmic story.

Walsh, E. S. (1991). *Mouse count.* New York: Harcourt Brace Jovanovich. (K–1). PICTURE BOOK.

Introduces counting sequences with mice.

Wells, R. (1979). *Max's first word.* New York: Dial. (PreK). PICTURE BOOK.

Wells, R. (1985). *Max's breakfast.* New York: Dial. (PreK–3). PICTURE BOOK.

Max and his sister, Ruby, are rabbits. Their activities are so amusing because they are just like little children.

Wells, R. (1991). *Max's dragon shirt.* New York: Dial. (PreK–K). MODERN FANTASY.

Max goes shopping with his big sister Ruby.

Wells, R. (1992a). *Moss pillows: Voyage to the bunny planet.* New York: Puffin. (PreK). MODERN FANTASY.

Wells, R. (1992b). *Shy Charles.* New York: Puffin. (PreK).

Wells, R. (1993). *Waiting for the evening star.* (S. Jeffers, Illus.). New York: Dial. (K–3). PICTURE BOOK, HISTORICAL FICTION.

Family life before World War II is portrayed through the lives of two brothers.

Wick, W., & Marzollo, J. (1995). *I spy school days.* New York: Scholastic. (PreK–2). PICTURE BOOK.

The author and illustrator have created riddles for young children.

Williams, V. B. (1990). *More, more, more, said the baby: 3 love stories.* New York: Greenwillow. (PreK). PICTURE BOOK.

Wood, A. (1989). *Little Penguin's tale.* San Diego: Harcourt Brace Jovanovich. (K–2).

Granny Penguin tells a story to all the little ones about a penguin who danced with the gooney birds and participated in other dangerous activities. The illustrations show Little Penguin is a joyful, carefree character.

Wood, D., & Wood, A. (1989). *Piggies.* New York: Harcourt Brace Jovanovich. (PreK–1). RHYME.

An old rhyme about the little piggies is applied to fingers.

Zelinsky, P. O. (Adapter). (1990). *The wheels on the bus.* New York: Dutton. (PreK–2). TRADITIONAL RHYME.

This book of the rhyming song includes text, music, and hand movements.

Zimmerman, A., & Clemensha, D. (1999). *Trashy town.* (D. Yaccarino, Illus.). New York: HarperCollins. (PreK–2). CONTEMPORARY REALISTIC FICTION.

With a big smile, Mr. Gilly picks up trash all over Trashy Town.

Sources of Information about Children's Literature

American Library Association, 50 E. Huron St., Chicago, IL 60611

Children's Video Report, P. O. Box 3228, Princeton, NJ 08543

KIDSNET: A computerized clearinghouse for children's television and radio; Suite 208, 6856 Eastern Ave., NW, Washington, DC 20012

Parents Choice Guide to Videocassettes for Children, Parents Choice Foundation, P.O. Box 185, Newton, MA 02168

Reading Rainbow: A Guide for Teachers, P.O. Box 80669, Lincoln, NE 68501

Video Source Book Annual, Gale Research Company, Detroit, MI

References and Books for Further Reading

Adams, M. J., Treiman, R., & Pressley, M. (1998). Reading, writing and literacy. In I. E. Sigel & K. A. Renninger (Eds.), *Handbook of child psychology (*Vol. 4). New York: Wiley.

Bronfenbrenner, U. (1986). Ecology of the family as a context for human development. *Developmental Psychology, 22,* 723–742.

Caine, R., & Caine, G. (1991). *Making connections: Teaching and the human brain.* New York: Addison-Wesley.

Carlson, A. D. (1991). *The preschooler and the library.* Metuchen, NJ: Scarecrow.

Children's books annotated guide to the best books and recordings for your preschool child. (1991). New York: Holt.

Charlesworth, R., Hart, Burts, D. C., & DeWolf, M. (1993). The LSU studies: Building a research base for developmentally appropriate practice. In S. Reifel (Ed.), *Perspectives on developmentally appropriate practice* (pp. 3–28). Greenwich, CT: JAI Press.

Clark, M. (1976). *Young fluent readers.* London: Heinemann Educational Books.

Cullinan, B., Greene, E., & Jaggar, A. (1990). Books, babies, and libraries: The librarian's role in literacy development. *Language Arts, 67,* 750–755.

Dana Alliance for Brain Initiatives. (1996). *Delivering results: A progress report on brain research.* Washington, DC: Author.

Derman-Sparks, L., & ABC Task Force. (1989). *Anti-Bias curriculum: Tools for empowering young children.* Washington, DC: National Association for the Education of Young Children.

DeVries, R., & Kohlberg, W. (1990). *Constructivist early education: Overview and comparison with other programs.* Washington, DC: National Association for the Education of Young Children.

Dickinson, D., & Smith, M. (1994). Long term effects of preschool teacher's book readings on low-income children's vocabulary and story comprehension. *Reading Research Quarterly, 29,* 104–122.

Durkin, D. (1996). *Children who read early.* New York: Teachers College Press.

Dyson, A. H., & Genishi, C. (1993). Visions of children as language users: Language and language education in early childhood. In B. Spodek (Ed.), *Handbook of research on the education of young children* (pp. 122–136). New York: Macmillan.

Feitelson, D., Kita, B., & Goldstein, Z. (1986). Effects of listening to series stories on first graders' comprehension and use of language. *Research in the Teaching of English, 20,* 339–356.

Ford, E. A. (1991, January-June). *CBC Features.* New York: Children's Book Council.

Frede, E., & Barnett, W. S. (1992). Developmentally appropriate public school preschool: A study of implementation of the high/scope curriculum and its effects on disadvantaged children's skills at first grade. *Early Childhood Research Quarterly, 7,* 483–499.

Gallahue, D. (1993). Motor development and movement skill acquisition in early childhood education. In B. Spodek (Ed.), *Handbook of research on the education of young children* (pp. 24–41). New York: Macmillan.

Greene, E. (1991). *Books, babies, and libraries.* Chicago: American Library Association.

Healy, J. M. (1991). *Endangered minds.* New York: Simon & Schuster.

Hearne, B. (1990). *Choosing books for children: A commonsense approach.* New York: Delacorte.

Heath, S. B. (1982). What no bedtime story means: Narrative skills at home and school. *Language in Society, 11,* 49–76.

Heath, S. B. (1983). *Ways with words: Language, life and work in communities and classrooms.* Cambridge, England: Cambridge University Press.

Hiebert, R. (1988). The role of literacy experiences in early childhood programs. *Elementary School Journal, 89,* 161–171.

Kamii, C., & Ewing, J. K. (1996). Basing teaching on Piaget's constructivism. *Childhood Education, 72,* 260–264.

Knoth, M. V. (1995). Rosemary Wells. In A. Silvey (Ed.), *Children's books and their creators* (pp. 673–675). Boston: Houghton Mifflin.

Kuhl, P. (1994). Learning and representation in speech and language. *Current Opinion in Neurobiology, 4,* 812–822.

Kulleseid, E. R., & Strickland, D. (1989). *Literature, literacy and learning: Classroom teachers, library media specialists, and the literature-based curriculum.* Chicago: American Library Association.

Marcon, R. (1992). Differential effects of three preschool models on inner-city 4-year-olds. *Early Childhood Research Quarterly, 7,* 517–530.

Morrow, L. (1988). Young children's responses to one-to-one story readings in school settings. *Reading Research Quarterly, 23,* 89–107.

National Association for the Education of Young Children. (1997). *Developmentally appropriate practice in early childhood programs serving children from birth through age 8.* Washington, DC: Author.

Neuman, S. (1996). *Evaluation of the books aloud project: An executive summary.* Report to the William Penn Foundation from Books Aloud, Temple University, Philadelphia.

O'Neil, J. M. (1988). *Early childhood education: Advocates square off over goals.* Alexandria, VA: Association for Supervision and Curriculum Development.

Piaget, J. (1952). *Judgment and reasoning in the child.* Totowa, NJ: Littlefield, Adams.

Purcell-Gates, V. (1988). Lexical syntactic knowledge of written narrative held by well-read-to kindergartners and second graders. *Research in Teaching English, 22,* 128–160.

Purcell-Gates, V. (1991). Ability of well-read-to kindergartners to decontextualize/recontextualize experience into a written-narrative register. *Language and Education, 5,* 177–188.

Roser, N., & Martinez, M. (1985). Roles adults play in preschool responses to literature. *Language Arts, 62,* 485–490.

Silvey, A. (Ed.). (1995). *Children's books and their creators.* Boston: Houghton Mifflin.

Slaughter, J. P. (1993). *Beyond storybooks: Young children and the shared book experience.* Newark, DE: International Reading Association.

Smith, C. B. (1988). Emergent literacy—An environmental concept. *The Reading Teacher, 42,* 528.

Smith, F. (1997). *Reading without nonsense.* New York: Teachers College Press.

Strickland, D., & Morrow, L. (1990). Family literacy: Sharing good books. *Reading Teacher, 43,* 518–519.

Sulzby, E. (1985). Children's emergent reading of favorite storybooks: A developmental study. *Reading Research Quarterly, 20,* 458–481.

Sulzby, E. (1991). The development of the young child and the emergence of literacy. In J. Flood et al. (Eds.), *Handbook of research on teaching the English language arts.* New York: Macmillan.

Teale, W., & Sulzby, E. (1989). Emergent literacy: New perspectives. In D. Strickland and L. Morrow (Eds.), *Emerging literacy: Young children learn to read and write.* Newark, DE: International Reading Association.

Voss, M. (1988). Make way for applesauce: The literate world of a three-year-old. *Language Arts, 65,* 272–278.

Vygotsky, L. (1985). *Mind in society.* Cambridge, MA: Harvard University Press.

Wells, G. (1986). *The meaning makers: Children learning language and using language to learn.* Portsmouth, NH: Heinemann.

White, B. (1988). *Educating the infant and toddler.* Lexington, MA: Lexington Books.

Yaden, D., Smolkin, L., & Conlon, A. (1989). Preschoolers' questions about pictures, print conventions, and story text during reading aloud at home. *Reading Research Quarterly, 24,* 188–214.

Picture Books

6

KEY TERMS

benchmark
compositions
illustrated book
medium
picture book
visual literacy
wordless picture book

GUIDING QUESTIONS

1. What was your favorite picture book when you were a child? Why did you like this book?

2. Why are picture books unique works of art?

3. How do picture books differ from other genres?

4. What challenges do authors and illustrators face when creating picture books?

5. Who is your favorite picture book illustrator?

OVERVIEW

Picture books bring images and ideas together in a unique and exciting art form that adults and children can explore at many levels (Kiefer, 1995). "The picture book is a book in two media—words and paint or whatever media the artist uses" (Smith, 1991, p. 106). Read a picture book to young children and you will discover they grasp meaning and respond to illustrations even before they learn to read words. Illustrations evoke both cognitive and aesthetic understanding as well as response, and children as young as 14 months of age express preferences for specific types of illustrations (Stoodt, 1995). Art stimulates children to participate in literary experiences, cultivates their aesthetic responses, exercises their imagination, and expands their experience. Today the picture book is a part of growing up, an entertainment medium, a memory to treasure, and a teaching tool (Lima & Lima, 1993). Fine picture books give children a window on the wider world, enabling them to know and learn things outside their own limited experience. In picture books, authors may tell stories, share poems, or convey information.

Books with pictures have three main forms: some have written language and illustrations that work together to tell the story; others are wordless picture books in which the pictures take the place of any text; still others are illustrated books whose pictures illustrate parts of the text but are neither integral to it, nor do they add to or elaborate on the text. In what are generally thought of as picture books, illustrations are an integral part of the story, poem, or information. Writers use a few hundred words to tell their story, and artists work with the basic elements of line, shape, color, texture, and value, envisioning the text they are interpreting. They organize these elements into compositions that involve eye movement, balance, rhythm, and pattern (Ocvirk, Bone, Stinson, Wigg, & Wigg, 1991). *Owen* by Kevin Henkes shows this blend of story and art: Owen, a young mouse, has difficulty giving up his security blanket until his mother finds a unique solution. This delightful character and his problem are expressed through Owen's facial expressions, his body language, and his blanket.

This chapter includes examples of excellent picture books to enrich your understanding of picture books and their value in the classroom. The exemplary books discussed in this chapter represent benchmarks or standards of quality to which you can compare the books you read. Your ability to distinguish between outstanding picture books and those of lesser quality will increase with experience.

INTRODUCTION

Picture books have unique attributes that enhance literary experiences. Picture book art invites children to engage with literature and anchors their attention. Children's attention can drift with nothing but a lattice of language to hang it on (Perkins, 1994). By engaging children with books, we enable them to empathize with different experiences and points of view.

Pictures and language become instruments for building children's minds as they reflect, remember, relate, and respond to literature. Picture books are resources for music, art, science, social studies, math, and drama, to name a few subjects. In the following vignette, you will learn about some of the ways children may respond to picture books.

VIGNETTE

As Pam Myers's second graders entered their classroom, they heard the music of *Appalachian Spring* by Aaron Copeland

playing. Ms. Myers told them to sit in a circle and listen. Then she asked, "How many of you know what a mole is?" Mark's hand went up first. "Mark, would you describe a mole?" she asked.

Mark described a mole and drew one on the chalkboard. Several of the children had seen moles.

They talked about where moles lived. Some of the children asked why the music was playing.

Ms. Myers continued, "You'll understand about the music later, but now I'm going to read a story about a mole who was tired of the same old routine of work—dinner, television, and bedtime—so he changed his life. As you listen to *Mole Music* by David McPhail, think about his problem and his solution."

After hearing the story, the children talked about the mole's problem. Then Ms. Myers asked them how the illustrations helped tell the story.

Stacy volunteered that the colors of blue and brown showed the peace and happiness that his music brought to the world. Several of the children agreed. They also pointed out that the colors of the world were brighter than those of Mole's underground home.

Jerome said, "I like the way the tree roots drooped and curled up when he played bad."

"Yeah," several of the children agreed.

"But the roots really looked good and they grew big when he played better," said Anna.

Ms. Myers asked, "Does anyone have an idea of why I played the tape of *Appalachian Spring* before reading this story?"

Christopher responded, "Because the music is pretty and peaceful like the music Mole played."

Taylor added, "Because Mole's music was soothing, and you thought that music would soothe us."

THE NATURE OF PICTURE BOOKS

Illustrations contribute greatly to the meaning derived from picture books. Children know that illustrations can tell stories, and they use them to construct meaning, which is the foundation for responding to literature. In the opening vignette, children perceived the meanings and feelings expressed in the illustrations and related them to their own responses. They appreciated the artist's ability to express the effects of Mole's music. The readers responded to the illustrations, which extended the text.

Caldecott medalist Ed Young (1990) believes that "there are things that words do that pictures never can, and likewise, there are images that words can never describe." He cites the Chinese philosophy of painting as the inspiration for his work as an artist and writer, explaining, "A Chinese painting is often accompanied by words. They are complementary" (Young, 1990).

Illustrators and authors are actually coauthors working together to create picture books. The illustrations in picture books are an integral part of each page, adding dimension to the text. Although the text itself is brief, the interaction of text and illustrations makes picture books a complex genre.

In the Haunted House by Eve Bunting is an example of the blending of text and art that occurs in this genre. Only 280 words were used in telling this story; the entire book takes only 10 minutes to read. Susan Meddaugh's art amplifies the rhythmic language and creates visual and auditory images. The book opens with the text: "This is the house where the scary ones hide. Open the door and step softly inside." Readers see two pairs of sneakers, one large and one small, step through the door, and this action builds suspense and moves the plot along.

The language increases the suspense: "An organ is playing a funeral air. It's playing and playing, but nobody's there." The picture shows an organ, a spider, an arrow, and sneaker-clad feet. The author and illustrator establish a dramatic situation through implied questions: What is this house? Who is wearing the sneakers? Readers next see ghosts, witches, and bats. Sneakers appear in each illustration; the author and illustrator communicate the spooky feeling of the story and the wary feelings of the person wearing the large sneakers and the confidence of the person wearing the small sneakers. Contrasting the characters through illustrations develops humor in the story.

In a true picture book like this one, the illustrations tell as much about the story as do the words.

The text goes on: "faces that don't look like faces at all," accompanied by running feet; the tension mounts. A mummy appears, but readers see only the characters' shadows. The shadow of a werewolf gargles in the bathroom, and the sneakers run downstairs and outside. The climax occurs when the characters wearing the sneakers step "into the day that's asparkle with sun," and the text concludes, "Halloween Houses are so much fun!"

Readers see a father and daughter in the illustrations—the father pauses and wipes his brow (see Figure 6.1). The little girl looks back at the house, while her father heads down the sidewalk. The falling action shows a little girl stepping through the front door of the haunted house, followed by a large sneaker. In true picture book style, readers encounter an interesting twist at the end.

The History of Picture Books

Three great nineteenth-century British illustrators, Walter Crane, Randolph Caldecott, and Kate Greenaway, are the predecessors of the artists of modern picture books (Townsend, 1990). Walter Crane designed and illustrated many books, but his books of nursery rhymes paved the way for modern picture books. Caldecott, for whom the

Halloween Houses are so much fun!

American picture book award is named, illustrated traditional nursery rhymes with pictures that communicate a feeling of action and great fun. The Caldecott Medal is engraved with one of his illustrations. Kate Greenaway's illustrations portray gentle, old-fashioned children in formal British gardens, dressed in soft, pastel-colored clothing. The Kate Greenaway Medal is the British equivalent to the U.S. Caldecott Medal.

Beatrix Potter, whose *The Tale of Peter Rabbit* is one of the most popular children's books of all time, was influenced by these early artists. Peter Rabbit originated in Beatrix Potter's letters to her former governess's child (Townsend, 1990). Potter, a skillful wordsmith, wrote with elegant rhythmic language. Her watercolors enriched the text of these small books that fit so well in little children's hands.

Like Max in Maurice Sendak's contemporary picture book *Where the Wild Things Are,* Peter is anxious to escape parental authority. Both are curious about forbidden places, and both return home to the warmth of food. The publication of *Where the Wild Things Are* signaled a change in picture books and children's literature in general. With the publication of this book, writing about and illustrating children's conflicts, internal struggles, and feelings of frustration became acceptable (Scott-Mitchell, 1987). Max's struggle for au-

tonomy is illustrated when he tames the wild things he creates. Although the theme of *Peter Rabbit* was similar, adults found a rebellious bunny more acceptable than a rebellious child (Scott-Mitchell, 1987). Adults' values are significant because they purchase books or borrow them from the library for young children.

Contemporary Picture Books

The short text of picture books (usually 2,000 words or fewer with 60 words per page and only 32 pages per book) allows the author to give only the bare bones of a story (Ardizzone, 1980). These textual constraints mean that writers must be downright stingy with their words, yet they have to create enough suspense to make readers turn the pages. The excitement of an outstanding picture book is created through the constant tension between the moments isolated by the pictures and the flow of words joining those moments together (Lukens, 1986).

Pictures stimulate dramatic, active responses in children that compare with their responses to theater or film. Researchers have found that illustrations are important to readers' understanding, as well as contributing to intellectual and emotional development (Kiefer, 1995). Don and Audrey Wood (1986) suggest that picture books exist in a literary twilight zone as "the spectacular child of the marriage of images and text. As such, it is probably as close to drama or a thirty-two page movie, as it is to either literature or art" (p. 556). For this reason the picture book makes unique demands on its creators, who must carefully choose the parts of a story to tell through art (Cummings, 1998). They explore various media to identify the best way to interpret the story, poem, or information (Dillon and Dillon, 1992a) and make careful selection of color, technique, and style for their illustrations, considering the nature of the subject at hand.

ILLUSTRATORS

Illustrators are artists who create visuals that tell or interpret stories. The key to "telling stories with pictures" is creating a flow of graphic images that is readable, coherent, and obviously related to the text (Shulevitz, 1985). The sequential flow of art is an important aspect of illustrating picture books (Egielski, 1992). Artists strive to evoke the essence of a work rather than to simply "make pictures." For instance, Thomas Locker used lush oil paintings to capture a sense of each place portrayed in *Home: A Journey Through America.* Christopher Myers chose photographs of Harlem and Brooklyn as backgrounds for bold collage art in *Black Cat.* The art and rhythmic poetry will stimulate readers to explore their own feelings about identity, beauty, and home.

Artists do not "make pictures" for books; they show parts of the story that writers cannot put into words. Artists embellish—and often even establish—story elements such as plot, character, setting, mood, and style. Picture book illustrators are artists who find that this medium offers them another form of creative expression (Schwarcz & Schwarcz, 1991). In the children's book *What Do Illustrators Do?* Eileen Christelow (1999) demonstrates the uniqueness of each artist's interpretation of a story by following two illustrators as they make dramatically different creative choices to illustrate *Jack and the Beanstalk.*

Although artists can choose from the entire world of art when illustrating a picture book, many artists develop new techniques, media, and style to express their ideas. In an unusual artistic effort, Audrey Wood illustrated *The Red Racer* with a digital pen on a digital palette. She mixed the colors on her digital palette, created digital pens, and designed a textured background for this dramatic story. Color is significant in expressing Nona's (the protagonist) emotions.

Artistic styles create the "feel" of a book. In illustrating Gloria Houston's historical picture book, *The Year of the Perfect Christmas Tree,* Barbara Cooney chose soft colors to illuminate the Appalachian setting and the traditions of an old-time Christmas celebration. Peter Parnall creates a desert feeling for Byrd Baylor's poem in *The Other Way to Listen* with clean pen-and-ink drawings and spare use of color. Janell Cannon used liquitex acrylics and Prismacolor pencils on bristol board to create a lovable and loving character in *Stellaluna.* The little fruit bat's facial expressions and her language breathe life into her character as she learns to live in a bird nest and eat with the birds.

AUTHORS AND ILLUSTRATORS

Illustrators and authors meld written text with images to clarify and explain the facts presented (Thomas, 1983). Dress and countenance reveal more than a name does. Both the author and the illustrator work to make the reader care about a character and what happens to that character. The setting is depicted in illustrations

The Shaman saved Kamanya's life and he dreamed of becoming a Shaman too.

and language that establish the time and place as well as the mood and atmosphere of the story.

The Napping House, written by Audrey Wood and illustrated by Don Wood, shows how an illustrator and author work together to tell a story. Figure 6.2 depicts a rainy day from the exterior of a house. The picture in Figure 6.3 has more yellow in it, showing that the sun is emerging. Figure 6.4 shows the last page of the story: an exterior view of the napping house with a rainbow in the background. The author did not describe in words the setting change from outside the house to inside the bedroom to outside again, nor does she identify the child as a boy or girl. Furthermore, the cumulative language in the story does not mention rain, sun, or rainbow, but the mood gradually changes as the sun comes out, and the rainbow on the last page conveys an entirely different feeling.

ILLUSTRATIONS

Fine illustrators use their talents to create original, interesting pictures that speak to children. They arrange

FIGURE 6.2   A rainy day in *The Napping House.*

FIGURE 6.3   The sun comes out in *The Napping House.*

FIGURE 6.4   A rainbow in *The Napping House.*

the art and text to create meaningful compositions, well-planned designs that help readers understand and visualize the text, which encourages them to create their own interpretation of literature. The art enlarges the personal experience of its viewers, heightens their awareness of the world around them, and helps them understand their own experiences.

Artists express their thoughts, feelings, and interpretations through illustrations. In much the same way that authors choose words to create a story, artists choose style, medium, technique, and color to create their own interpretation of a particular piece of literature. An illustrator creates a sequence of images to accompany text rather than a single image for one picture.

In the picture book *Snow,* Uri Shulevitz used the elements of art and of narrative to show how snow transforms a town and its residents. The book begins with gray skies and gray buildings styled with vertical, pointed lines. On the following pages, the people are dressed in muted colors, but one snowflake falls and the colors brighten a bit. As the snow begins to fall, the white snow softens the vertical, pointed lines of the houses. Gradually, the buildings become less forbidding as the roofs lighten and small splashes of color enliven the illustrations, and finally the town is all white. His use of dark and light create the mood to accompany the spare text. For example, after three snowflakes fall, the television said "no snow," and the radio said "no snow." "But snowflakes don't watch television. Snowflakes don't listen to radio." The author uses the words *circling, swirling, spinning,* and *twirling, dancing, playing,* and *floating* to describe the mood of the season's first snowfall.

Style

"*Style* in its simplest sense is a manner of expressing" (Kiefer, 1988, p. 261). Artists combine visual elements and artistic media to create styles that express their thoughts, feelings, and interpretations. In much the same way that authors choose words and sentences to create a certain story, artists choose style, medium, technique, and color to interpret a particular piece of literature. Illustrators may choose among an array of styles—from impressionism that suggests and implies ideas, to literal representation that is very detailed and specific—to fit the mood of the story. For example, Gary Bennett's brilliantly colored, detailed illustrations fit the mood of a Powwow in Linda Raczek's *Rainy's Powwow*. Table 6.1 summarizes artistic styles commonly used in picture books.

Jerry enjoys reading to his children.

Medium

Medium refers to the material used in creating the illustrations for a story, including pen and ink, watercolor, pastels, woodcut, fabrics, and many other materials; artists may select a single medium or a combination of media from an almost unlimited range to enable them to interpret an idea. In *Tar Beach,* Faith Ringgold uses acrylic on canvas paper, similar to the canvas fabric she used to create the original quilt paintings on which the story is based, and the page borders

TABLE 6.1
Artistic styles commonly used in picture books.

Style	Example
Cartoon The artist uses a cartoon style based on line drawings.	*Meanwhile* — by Jules Feiffer
Expressionism The artist expresses strong emotions with vivid colors.	*Red Racer* by Audrey Wood
Folk or primitive art The artist uses bold lines and colors.	*A Gift for Abuelita* by Nancy Luenn, illustrated by Robert Chapman
Impressionism The artist suggests or gives an impression.	*Between Earth & Sky* by Joseph Bruchac, illustrated by Thomas Locker
Realistic The artist depicts subjects as they actually appear.	*Home Run* by Robert Burleigh, illustrated by Mike Wimmer

are reproduced from her original story quilt. Her bright colors and primitive style communicate the spirit of her childhood. Table 6.2 lists some of the more popular media for children's picture books, and it also cites examples of books illustrated in each medium.

Identifying the particular medium an artist has used in illustrating a picture book is often difficult and at times impossible. However, consulting the dust jacket, the book's introductory material, reviews, and author–illustrator interviews may help. (See chapter 3 for additional information regarding illustrations in Caldecott Award and Caldecott honor books.)

Technique

Technique refers to the way a medium is used (Kiefer, 1995). Denise Fleming creates the illustrations for her books by pouring colored cotton pulp through hand-cut stencils. This technique results in images set in handmade paper, which creates a feeling of texture. She has used this technique in *Mama Cat Has Three Kittens*. Mike Wimmer used oil on canvas to create the exquisite, detailed illustrations for *Home Run*. The text and illustrations in this book are supplemented with vintage-style baseball cards detailing the career of George Herman Ruth, Jr. After seeing this beautiful art, thinking of a better way to illustrate it is impossible.

Some artists consistently use the same technique, which becomes their trademark. However, other illustrators vary their technique with the particular story they are interpreting. For example, Leo and Diane Dillon used a style inspired by ukiyo-e, a Japanese art form based on woodcuts, to tell the traditional story *The Tale of the Mandarin Ducks,* by Katherine Paterson. However, they chose an airbrush technique to illustrate Verna Aardema's African folktale, *Why Mosquitoes Buzz in People's Ears,* because it creates the mood they desired for the story.

Color

Color is an expressive element of illustration, conveying temperature, personality, and emotion. Color has a sensuous and emotive appeal (Ocvirk et al., 1991). Artists generally use the warm colors—red, yellow, and orange—to create feelings of excitement, energy, friendship, and anger, whereas the cool colors—blue and green, the colors of sky and water—create peaceful, quiet moods and sometimes sad or depressed moods. Artists use color to express mood, character, setting, and theme. For example, Barbara Cooney used light, warm green, and light blue with touches of white and warm brown to portray spring in the mountains and warm family feelings in *The Year of the Perfect*

TABLE 6.2	
Popular media for illustrations in children's picture books.	
Medium	**Example***
Pastels	*The Polar Express* by Chris Van Allsburg
Watercolors	*The Shaman's Apprentice* by Lynne Cherry and Mark Plotkin, illustrated by Lynne Cherry
Handmade paper and stencils	*Mama Cat Has Three Kittens* by Denise Fleming
Watercolor and color pencils	*Pigs* by Gail Gibbons
Cut paper collage	*Top Cat* by Lois Ehlert
Oil	*Home: A Journey Through America* by Thomas Locker and Candace Christiansen, illustrated by Thomas Locker
Oil on wood	*The Pilgrims of Plimoth* by Marcia Sewall
Gouache**	*Arrow to the Sun* by Gerald McDermott
Digital painting	*Swimming Lessons* by Betsy Jay, illustrated by Lori Osiecki
Photographs and cut paper	*Black Cat* by Christoper Myers

*When one name is listed as author, the author both wrote and illustrated the book.
**Gouache is an opaque watercolor created by using a white base with tempera.

Christmas Tree. She portrayed winter using white touched with warm brown and blue gray.

Intensity

Intensity, which refers to the brightness or dullness of color, affects the meaning and mood of illustrations. Bert Kitchen used intense, rich browns to illustrate Sally Tagholm's *The Barn Owl.* The night sky is created with rich, deep shades of blue, which contributes to our understanding that the barn owl is nocturnal. Contrasting bright colors illustrate the adventures of Joseph Anthony's *The Dandelion Seed* as it moves through the stages of its life. Soft white clouds move in a bright blue sky as it moves around the world. Shades of pink mix with the blue sky to illustrate beauty, but when the dandelion seed moves into the dark city, the mood becomes lonely and the colors of the illustrations grow dark. Soft white snow creates a quiet mood.

Contrast

Contrast is an aspect of color value and is developed through the use of opposite colors. This also affects the final illustration and the reader's perception of it. Rachel Isadora used high contrast black and white art deco illustrations to give readers a 1930s feeling in the historical fiction *Ben's Trumpet.* In Eloise Greenfield's book of poetry *Honey, I Love, and Other Love Poems,* the poetry and the contrast of brown illustrations on a soft white background convey the beauty of the principal character's face and focus on its energy.

Line

Line is the most common artistic element (Kiefer, 1995). Lines are expressive: they communicate meaning, mood, and movement. Thin lines speak of fragility and thick lines convey weight and strength. Curves and circles suggest warmth and softness. In Ruth Krauss's *The Happy Day,* Marc Simont creates circles on every page to suggest the warmth of animals sleeping contentedly, drowsy awakening from sleep, and the joy of laughing and dancing. Vertical lines convey stability, whereas sharp, diagonal lines establish excitement and movement. Horizontal lines are calm and peaceful, which is why Barbara Cooney used them to create peaceful feelings for spring and winter pictures in *The Year of the Perfect Christmas Tree.*

Design

In *design* or composition the artist combines the elements of color, line, and texture into a balanced, satisfying pattern between pictures and text. The layout and size of pictures are chosen to create a rhythm that expresses the meaning of the book. Artists use design to create both unity and variety, as well as to focus on certain characters, develop main ideas, and show details and setting. In *The Red Racer,* Audrey Wood used a deep green background with lighter green to show the wicked thought that led Nona to get rid of her bicycle.

Size

Size communicates a variety of ideas in children's books. Readers see the largest things first. Maurice Sendak used size to show that Max was dreaming in *Where the Wild Things Are:* The illustrations grow larger as Max moves into his imagination until they fill two pages with the wild rumpus; when Max begins to return to reality, the pictures gradually grow smaller and calmer.

Placement and perspective

Cris Arbo used perspective effectively in *The Dandelion Seed.* Readers see the dandelion seed looking down on houses and buildings, then it is silhouetted in the headlights of a car, and finally it lands softly in snow where "peace covered it like a blanket." The dandelion seed is not visible again until it sprouts and its placement focuses readers' attention on it.

Through placement and perspective of Mother Bear in Wargin's *The Legend of Sleeping Bear,* illustrated by Van Frankenhuyzen, readers realize her sorrow at losing her cubs and her determination to wait for them. In each picture, Mother Bear's placement, shape, and perspective change with the mood of the story and her long wait for her cubs.

TYPES OF PICTURE BOOKS

Realistic fiction, modern fantasy, traditional literature, biography, historical fiction, poetry, and informational books—all genres of children's literature are represented by picture books, and artists clarify concepts and ideas in all of them. Up to this point we have discussed the integration of picture and language in picture books; however, some picture books are wordless.

Wordless picture books or visual stories are told entirely through pictures. This format is very appealing for today's children, whose experiences with television and film orient them to visual communication. Teachers find wordless picture books invaluable for developing vocabulary, comprehension, and critical reading (Cianciolo, 1990). These books are like other picture books: they delight all age groups, address all subjects, and belong to all genres.

Illustrators of wordless picture books use their artistic talents to create character, setting, plot, theme, and style without using any words at all. Each frame or page leads readers to the next. David Wiesner tells a visual story in the wordless picture book *Sector 7,* which recounts the story of a boy who visits the Empire State Building on a school field trip. On the observation deck, the boy makes friends with a cumulus cloud. Wiesner created a vast cloud station that is magnificently constructed (Hearn, 1999). Other artists who create wonderful wordless picture books include Raymond Briggs, John Goodall, Pat Hutchins, Peter Spier, and Paula Winter.

Peter Spier explores many dimensions of *Rain* in his book by the same name. It opens with raindrops on the title page and goes on to portray rain in many ways: from splashing raindrops to the glistening drops caught in a spider's web to children's delight in playing in the rain. Spier captures a rainy-day mood that makes the reader think of cozily enjoying cookies and cocoa while warm and dry inside—and he never writes a single word.

Picture Books for Older Students

Several appealing picture books are available for all ages. One should remember, however, that "the best children's writers say things to a five-year-old that a fifty-year-old can also respect" (Hearne, 1990, p. 9). Both a 5-year-old and a 50-year-old can enjoy picture books, although they probably appreciate them in different ways. The sheer beauty of the oil paintings of various places in the United States found in *Home: A Journey through America* gives it ageless appeal. Although the comedy of *The Secret Knowledge of Grown-Ups* by David Wisniewski appeals to all ages, preschoolers will probably miss the humor. An entirely different approach appears in Jules Feiffer's *Meanwhile—,* which is illustrated with cartoons. Raymond, the main character, learns to use the word *meanwhile* to escape difficult situations. This wonderful book is just right for intermediate-grade children. *Purple Mountain Majesties* (Younger, 1998), a nonfiction picture book that tells the story of Katharine Lee Bates and "America the Beautiful," is a superb choice for children

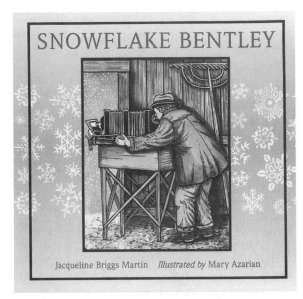

Snowflake Bentley devoted his life to studying snowflakes.

in Grades 3 through 5. Picture books have great value for both younger and older readers in our increasingly visual culture.

VISUAL LITERACY

Visual literacy is the ability to comprehend and evaluate illustrations and the visual elements of media and artistic style the artist uses (Camp and Tompkins, 1990). Visual texts are not simple; they are complex, multilayered texts that communicate meaning (Moline, 1995). Illustrations convey meaning to readers and viewers because they are the artist's rendering of plot, theme, setting, mood, and character.

We know that children can respond to visual texts to construct actively both cognitive and affective meaning (Kiefer, 1995). Children who have many opportunities to describe, compare, interpret, and value illustrations in picture books learn to interact with visual information (Stewig, 1992). For instance, focusing on an illustration and describing it clearly and completely is a good beginning. The *I Spy* books by Walter Wick and Jean Marzollo are excellent beginning books for kindergarten children; children enjoy examining these puzzles and later creating their own. They also enjoy *Look-Alikes Jr.* by Joan Steiner.

Encouraging children to compare two versions of the same story such as *Cinderella, Stone Soup,* or *Goldilocks* builds their visual literacy. Provide children opportunities to focus on illustrations, describe them, and compare them. As children explore the work of various artists, they will develop preferences for illustrators and styles of art.

SELECTING AND EVALUATING PICTURE BOOKS

What makes a picture book an outstanding example of the genre? This question is at once simple and complex, just as are fine picture books. Young children, of course, enjoy picture books, leading many adults to think they are only for young children.

Excellence in narrative is difficult to achieve in picture books because they must be short and simple and yet interesting enough to retain freshness and quality even through many readings (Lobel, 1981). Certainly, quality picture books have well-drawn characters, suspenseful plots, authentic settings, and all of the factors that contribute to literary excellence in all categories of literature. The art is integrated with the narrative and is appropriate to the mood and subject matter. Arnold Lobel established the most important standard: "A good picture book should be true. That is to say, it should rise out of the lives and passions of its creators" (p. 74).

The Internet can be invaluable in helping media specialists (librarians) and teachers in locating and evaluating books. The National Center for Children's Illustrated Literature, located in Abilene, Texas, sponsors exhibits and educational programs, as well as maintaining a Web site. The site currently located at *www.nccil.org/children* has illustrations, biographies, and teaching activities. The *Children's Literature Web Guide* is a rich source of information; most publishers of children's picture books such as Houghton Mifflin, Random House, and Simon and Schuster maintain Web sites that include book information, author information, and teaching ideas. Web locations and addresses often change, so we suggest that you include key words into your search engine, which will pull up a list of Web sites for you to explore.

In choosing picture books to read, consider the visual components of color, line, shape, space, texture, and perspective (Lacey, 1986), as well as the standards suggested for that particular genre, because picture books encompass all genres. The best indicators for picture books that children will enjoy, however, are these qualities:

1. The book is appropriate for the age and stage of development of the potential readers or listeners.

Do you think birds know when it's going to snow?

Fine picture books are works of art appropriate for a broad range of students.

2. Children can identify with the main character. Consider whether the main character is developed as a rounded character or a stereotype. (Stereotypes are appropriate characters in traditional literature, of course.)
3. Children can understand the plot, which has an identifiable climax and an identifiable ending.
4. The theme grows out of characters and plot and is appropriate for children.
5. The story is told in interesting, expressive language with simple narrative, and the author avoids long descriptions—it is a "page turner."
6. The illustrations enrich the text, are integrated with the text, and are appropriate to the mood and subject matter.

Classroom Activities

Picture books are written to be read aloud while the listeners look at the pictures—an integral part of the literary picture-book experience. (Chapter 10 gives information regarding oral presentations of literature.) Children often cluster in a group to listen so that they can better see the illustrations, frequently asking the teacher to read it again; they do benefit from multiple hearings. They like to pick up the books they have heard read and pore over the pictures at their own pace.

This section presents strategies and activities to engage students with picture books, encourage response, and develop visual literacy. Many of the suggestions focus on the illustrations and careful observations of them. Although these activities are based on picture books, they are applicable to other literature.

Classroom Activities

ACTIVITY 6.1 READING A PICTURE BOOK TO CHILDREN

1. Introduce the book. An introduction can motivate listeners and anticipate the ideas in the book. Show them the cover and title, and tell them the author's and illustrator's names.
2. Read the story aloud to give students the opportunity for appreciative listening. Make sure that all the children have the chance to view the pictures as you read.
3. Discuss the story with the children, stimulating them to think about the story. Discussion following appreciative listening enhances understanding. Ask them what things they noticed in the book.

Encourage children to compare themselves and their experiences to the picture book and its illustrations. Does the main character look like them? act like them? Would they do the same things the character did? Would they like to have the character as a friend?

4. Use extension activities to allow students to respond to the story and enrich their understanding. Exploring how the author and artist express meaning in text and illustrations is useful. Comparing and contrasting experiences are very helpful to learning.

ACTIVITY 6.2 COMPARING FOLKTALE VARIATIONS

Studying various versions of the same story facilitates children's understanding and response. Traditional literature is especially appropriate for this experience because many children know these tales that have been told, retold, and illustrated in many ways. Figure 6.5 shows one way that an artist interpreted the traditional tale *Little Red Riding Hood*. Compare the interpretations of the wolf illustrator with that of other illustrators. Of course, the other characters and the setting can be compared as well. Examine the art in each version, including the line, shape, texture, color, value, and layout used in each version. Find other versions of this story for children to compare. A good example comparing various interpretations of the *Little Red Riding Hood* tale follows.

Trina Schart Hyman drew on her childhood love of the Little Red Riding Hood story when creating her Caldecott honor book. Her elegantly detailed illustrations are rich in color. She framed the text and illustrations with elaborate designs of flowers, hearts, and plaids. The characters are soft and rounded. The wolf is soft and fuzzy looking.

FIGURE 6.5 Hyman's Little Red Riding Hood.

In Beatrice Schenk de Regnier's version, Edward Gorey used a more primitive style: his long, sharp lines for drawing Red Riding Hood, the mother, the wolf, and the grandmother contrast with Hyman's softer characters. Gorey's spare, simple settings create a vastly different mood than the lushness of Hyman's illustrations. In this version, the wolf looks lean and mean.

Lon Po Po: A Red-riding Hood Story from China, a Caldecott Medal winner translated by Ed Young, is a Chinese version of the Red Riding Hood story although it does not have a Red Riding Hood character. In this version, three little children stay at home while their mother goes to visit their grandmother Po Po. The wolf plans to eat the children while their mother is away, but they outwit him. Young renders a more realistic treatment of the wolf than either Hyman or de Regniers; his wolf is more dangerous looking than the others.

1. Older students can do the previous activity as a writing activity.

2. Students can create their own versions of *Red Riding Hood* (or another favorite).

3. Students can compare the written text of various versions of *Red Riding Hood.*

4. Additional aesthetic experiences can involve making puppets, drawing or painting pictures, painting friezes, designing bulletin boards, creating posters, and doing craft projects.

5. Retelling stories through creative drama and storytelling gives children opportunities to respond to the language of picture books. Encourage students to relate prior knowledge to picture clues to construct understanding.

6. Writing stories, poems, or informative pieces based on picture books gives children additional literary experiences. They could even develop their own illustrations to accompany their written response.

7. Choosing music that fits the mood of a book extends the aesthetic experience.

ACTIVITY 6.3   DEVELOPING A UNIT OF STUDY ON THE TOPIC OF DOGS

Select several appropriate books for a teaching unit on dogs, which could extend over a week or more. A partial list of good picture books about dogs appears at the end of this activity. Although this unit focuses on dogs, the topic could be virtually anything–trees, giants, boys, girls, teachers, mothers, fathers.

1. Introduce the book you have selected to the children and encourage them to make predictions from the title and the cover of the book or from the opening sentences.

2. Read the story aloud to give them the opportunity for appreciative listening. Ask them to think about the pictures of the dog in the book and what the text says about the dog. Ask them to think about how this dog is similar to dogs they know or have seen.

3. Discuss the story with the children and encourage them to think about the story. Ask appropriate questions to start discussion such as:

   a. Do the pictures look like real dogs or make-believe dogs?

   b. How is this dog special (unique)?

   c. What things did the dog do in the story?

   d. What is special about the things the dog did?

   e. Does this dog remind you of any dog that you know?

   f. How is the dog different from dogs that you know?

   g. If you could talk to the author or illustrator, what questions would you like to ask?

4. Use extension activities to allow students to respond to the story.

   a. After reading several books to the children and letting them enjoy the illustrations, have them think of ways to compare and contrast dogs. They may suggest things such as size, color, personality (some dogs are gentle, some are not), whether they are real or make-believe, and so forth.

   b. Have students draw pictures of their favorite dog and tell or write why this is their favorite.

   c. Have students tell or write about the dog they would like to have as a pet and explain why.

   d. Ask older students to compare the dog characters by creating grids such as the one in Figure 6.6.

FIGURE 6.6	Grid for comparing characters, in this case dogs.			
Title	Dog's Looks	Dog's Personality	Dog's Actions	Dog's Likable Characteristics

e. Ask students to write about the things that make dogs good pets or ways of caring for pet dogs.

f. Suggest that children make up stories about dogs that they can tell aloud, dictate to the teacher, or write on their own.

The following are suggested picture books to use in a unit on dogs.

- *The First Dog* by Jan Brett.
- *Dogs in Space* by Nancy Coffelt.
- *A Dog Like Jack* by DyAnne DiSalvo-Ryan.

- *Nobody's Dog* by Charlotte Graeber.
- *Dogs Don't Wear Sneakers* by Laura Numeroff.
- *Martha Calling* by Susan Meddaugh.
- *A Home for Spooky* by Gloria Rand.
- *SPEAK!: Children's Illustrators Brag About Their Dogs* by Michael J. Rosen, Ed.
- *Guard the House, Sam!* by Charnan Simon.
- *It's Hard to Read a Map with a Beagle on Your Lap* by Marilyn Singer.
- *The Sweetest Fig* by Chris Van Allsburg.

ACTIVITY 6.4   EXPLORING A SINGLE BOOK IN DEPTH

Book: *What! Cried Granny: An Almost Bedtime Story* by Kate Lum, illustrated by Adrian Johnson.

Story Synopsis: Patrick is sleeping over at Granny's. He comes up with many reasons to delay going to bed. He says he cannot go to bed because he does not have a bed, or a blanket, or a teddy bear. So Granny solves the problems. She chops down a tree to build a bed, shears a sheep and weaves a blanket, and stitches up an enormous bear. Her efforts take all night, but they give Patrick a new excuse because "it's morning."

The illustrations are collage-like figures, and the background is in vibrant color. The illustrator included whimsical details, such as a dog and the colors Granny paints with.

1. Introduce the book.

a. Hold the book up, read the title, and ask the children if they have ever slept over with their grandparents.

b. Ask what they think will happen in this story about Patrick's sleep over at Granny's.

2. Read about half of the story aloud. Ask the children what they think will happen next. They should be able to explain why they predict as they do, using details from the story for support.

3. Complete the story and compare the outcome with their predictions both before and halfway through.

4. Discuss the story with the children, encouraging them to think about the story.

   a. Which picture in the book do you like the best? Why?

   b. What was the funniest thing that Granny did?

   c. Why did Granny make things for Patrick?

   d. Did this story really happen? Why or why not?

   e. How did Granny feel when Patrick could not go to sleep because it was morning?

   f. How did Patrick feel when he found out it was morning?

   g. What was your favorite part of the story?

5. Discuss the illustrations in this book. Prepare to discuss the illustrations by holding up the book and looking at each page to examine the illustrations.

   a. Ask the children to identify their favorite illustrations.

   b. Have them identify their favorite details in the pictures.

   c. Ask them what color they like best in the illustrations.

   d. Ask if they can think of another book that has illustrations similar to these. (Lois Ehlert and others use collages.)

6. Use extension activities to allow students to respond to the story.

   a. Introduce the word *exaggerate* to first or second graders, and discuss the ways that exaggeration is related to this story. Ask the children if they have ever used exaggeration.

   b. Compare this story with *Just Another Ordinary Day* by Rod Clement. Ask how these stories are alike and how they are different. Ask students how exaggeration is related to this story. Ask students why they think Amanda exaggerated in her imagination. You can compare both of these books to Steve Kellogg's *Paul Bunyan*.

   c. Have the children tell about or draw pictures of the funniest thing that ever happened with a grandparent.

ACTIVITY 6.5   INTRODUCING ART CONCEPTS

To introduce the art concepts of media, technique, line, color, and perspective, you may wish to first refer to *Words About Pictures: The Narrative Art of Children's Picture Books* (Nodelman, 1988), *Art Fundamentals* (Ocvirk et al., 1991), or *The Potential of Picturebooks* (Kiefer, 1995).

Use examples from picture books (any mentioned throughout the chapter or those listed at the end of this activity) to illustrate these various concepts for children. Discuss the concepts with the students, using stimulating questions such as the ones in the following list. They may complete a grid like the one in Figure 6.6 to compare the illustrations in books. This will give students a basis for comparing illustrations and choosing ways of illustrating their own work. Once they understand the various concepts, have them experiment in creating illustrations for their compositions.

Example Questions

1. How do artists portray setting in pictures?

2. How do pictures of night settings differ from daytime settings?

3. How can pictures contribute to the plot?

4. How do artists create characters in pictures?

5. How are the illustrations similar to you and things you have done?

6. What artistic style did the illustrator use?

7. What medium was used?

8. Can you identify the author's favorite colors?

FIGURE 6.7 **Elements of Art: Picture Book Examples**

Element—Line
- Arnosky, J. (1986). *Deer at the brook.* New York: Lothrop, Lee & Shepard.
- Brown, M. (1954). *Cinderella.* New York: Scribner's.
- Carle, E. (1977). *The grouchy ladybug.* New York: T. H. Crowell.
- Fleming, D. (1991). *In the tall, tall grass.* New York: Henry Holt.
- Yenawme, P. (1991). *Lines.* New York: Delacort.

Element—Color
- Ehlert, L. (1990). *Color farm.* New York: HarperCollins.
- Serfozo, M. (1988). *Who said red?* New York: McElderry.
- Walsh, E. (1989). *Mouse paint.* New York: Harcourt Brace Jovanovich.
- Wood, A. (1984). *The napping house.* San Diego: Harcourt Brace Jovanovich.

Element—Texture
- Ehlert, L. (1991). *Red leaf, yellow leaf.* San Diego: Harcourt Brace Jovanovich.
- Hoban, T. (1984). *Is it rough? Is it smooth? Is it shiny?* New York: Greenwillow.
- Steptoe, J. (1987). *Mufaro's beautiful daughters.* New York: Lothrop, Lee & Shepard.

Element—Shape
- Baker, K. (1991). *Hide and snake.* San Diego: Harcourt Brace Jovanovich.
- Bang, M. (1980). *The grey lady and the strawberry snatcher.* New York: Four Winds.
- Baylor, B., & Parnall, P. (1979). *Your own best secret place.* New York: Scribner's.
- Hoban, T. (1986). *Shapes, shapes, shapes.* New York: Greenwillow.

ACTIVITY 6.6   VISUAL LITERACY

1. Have children tell stories using wordless picture books such as Briggs's *The Snowman* and others suggested in this chapter.

2. Have children find hidden objects in illustrations. The *I Spy* books by Walter Wick and Jean Marzollo are good for this experience.

3. Have children look at part of something to identify the whole. *I Went Walking* by Sue Williams shows a little boy who sees part of an animal and identifies the animal.

4. Have children create their own pictures for storytelling or puzzles for the *I Spy* books by Walter Wick and Jean Marzollo or *Look Alikes Jr.* by Joan Steiner.

5. Have children study individual illustrators, their body of works, or both.

The following suggestions for picture books are for use in a study of particular artistic concepts and visual literacy.

Illustrated Books for Children
- *Errata: A Book of Historical Errors* illustrated by Hemesh Alles.
- *The Snowman* by Raymond Briggs.
- *Draw Me a Star* by Eric Carle.
- *Hattie and the Wild Waves* by Barbara Cooney.
- *The Art Lesson* by Tomie dePaola.
- *Look Around: A Book About Shapes* by Leonard Everett Fisher.
- *I Can Paint!* by Kate Hart.
- *I Spy* by Jean Marzollo.
- *Where's Waldo?* by Martin Handford.
- *I Spy: An Alphabet in Art* by Lucy Micklethwait.
- *A Child's Book of Art* by Lucy Micklethwait.
- *I Went Walking* by Sue Williams.
- *Who's Hiding Here?* by Yoshi.

ACTIVITY 6.7   ARTIST/ILLUSTRATOR PROFILES

Studying illustrators yields many benefits to young readers. Readers who know something about the person who illustrated a picture book have a better understanding of it. Finding connections between books and their creators challenges children to think in new ways, which widens their life experiences. Artists often project their own experiences into their work. The accompanying profile of Paul Zelinsky demonstrates this.

A Biographical Profile: Paul O. Zelinsky

Paul O. Zelinsky is a versatile artist who has won three Caldecott Honor medals and a Caldecott Medal in 1997.

Zelinsky's artistic talent emerged early in life, although he considered becoming an astronomer, a ventriloquist, a scientist, and another Frank Lloyd Wright rather than an illustrator. However, after completing his master's degree, Zelinsky realized he was destined to illustrate children's books.

He once used art to create identity and stability during his many moves as his father relocated from one college to another. Now he adjusts his style to give each book a distinctive character. He says, "I don't like to do the same thing over and over." Variety in medium and technique keeps his work interesting and fresh (National Center for Children's Illustrated Literature n. d.). Moreover, Zelinsky is a meticulous artist who researches subject matter carefully so he can authentically depict the era of the book he is illustrating.

In discussing his work, Zelinsky shares a story about his great-grandmother who started oil painting and painted a picture of the witch's house from the story *Hansel and Gretel* for his sister. He has this picture and cherishes its character and air of mystery. He realized early in his illustrating career that he wanted to create that feeling in a whole book of *Hansel and Gretel*. Of course, his illustrations for *Hansel and Gretel*, which was retold by Rika Lesser, culminated in a Caldecott Honor book in 1985. In 1987 his work for Grimm's *Rumpelstiltskin* was honored with another Caldecott Honor book designation. His third Caldecott honor book was *Swamp Angel* by Anne Isaacs in 1995. Grimm's *Rapunzel*, which was published in 1997, brought him the Caldecott Medal. However, *The Wheels on the Bus* is the personal favorite of this author, just as it is the favorite of many young children.

———

This biographic profile drew on information from the dust jackets of Paul Zelinsky's books and from the National Center for Children's Illustrated Literature Web site.

ACTIVITY 6.8   EXPERIMENTING WITH MEDIA

Students can experiment with the media that artists use and make their own picture books. You may choose to involve the art teacher in this experience and explore media such as paint, collage, chalk, photographs, pencil, lithograph, water color, fabric, or quilt paintings. Students could create a picture book or photographic essay using photographs they have taken. They can create a composition based on the photographs, write the text, make a cover, and bind the book.

ACTIVITY 6.9   ILLUSTRATING A TEXT

Read a picture book to the class without showing them the pictures, then ask them to create appropriate illustrations to accompany the story. Compare their illustrations with those in the book.

ACTIVITY 6.10   IDENTIFYING ILLUSTRATION TECHNIQUES

Show the children wordless picture books and ask them to identify which details change from picture to picture to show progression in the story and to illustrate character, setting, and plot. Have students create their own wordless picture books, making certain to include details that will help to tell the story.

ACTIVITY 6.11   CREATING A STORY MAP

Create a story map using a format similar to the one shown in Figure 6.8 for a picture book or a wordless picture book. Both the illustrations and the narrative will contribute to the story map. (See chapter 15 for more information on story maps.)

FIGURE 6.8   Blank story map.

Setting: (time, place, character)

Problem:

Efforts to Solve the Problem:

1.

2.

3.

Resolution:

ACTIVITY 6.12   RECITING IN UNISON

After students have listened to a picture book of a traditional story, have them read the refrain in unison from a chart you have prepared. Paul Galdone's picture book versions of traditional stories such as *The Little Red Hen*, *Henny Penny*, and *The Three Little Pigs* are good choices for this activity because he includes refrains in the story narrative. Many of the children will then join in to read the entire story.

ACTIVITY 6.13 CREATING A FINISHED PICTURE BOOK

Older students may choose a Grimm folktale, another traditional story, or a poem and create their own illustrations for it. They should be prepared to explain their choices of media, technique, colors, and lines. They should include the text of the story or poem with their illustrations, so this would be a good opportunity for them to work on penmanship or even calligraphy. This is also a good opportunity to teach book binding so they can produce a finished-looking book. They may read their picture books to younger children.

ACTIVITY 6.14 (K–2) TEDDY BEAR AND DOLL WEEK

Plan a week for bears or dolls. Have students bring their favorite teddy bear or doll to school. Students can help prepare bulletin boards announcing the activity to the rest of the school and write invitations to other classes to visit the classroom during the week. Children may read about toys and read to their own toys. They may write stories about their toy's adventures. Younger children may draw their stories or dictate them to a teacher or teacher assistant. Older children may study the histories of teddy bears and dolls.

The following are some suggestions for picture books to use in a teddy bear and doll theme week.

- *I'll Protect You From the Jungle Beasts* by Martha Alexander.
- *Paddington* (series) by Michael Bond.
- *Jessie Bear, What Will You Wear?* by Nancy White Carlstrom.
- *Corduroy* by Don Freeman.
- *Winnie-the-Pooh* by A. A. Milne.
- *Peabody* by Rosemary Wells.
- *The Velveteen Rabbit* by Margery Williams.
- *William's Doll* by Charlotte Zolotow.

ACTIVITY 6.15 (K–4) STIMULATING INTEREST IN THE ARTS

Picture books are works of art and therefore are particularly useful vehicles for generating interest in the arts. Picture books give visual images to music. Young children love to sing, hum, and chant, so books based on music are highly motivating for them. Many picture books build aesthetic appreciation.

The following are some suggestions for picture books you can use to stimulate interest in the arts.

- *Go Tell Aunt Rhody* by Aliki.
- *When the Sky Is Like Lace* by Elinor Horwitz.
- *Max* by Rachel Isadora.
- *My Ballet Class* by Rachel Isadora.
- *Peter and the Wolf* by Sergei Prokofiev.
- *The Magic Flute* by Stephen Spender.
- *The Moon Jumpers* by Janice May Udry.
- *Music, Music for Everyone* by Vera Williams.
- *Something Special for Me* by Vera Williams.
- *Mommy, Buy Me a China Doll* by Harve Zemach.

ACTIVITY 6.16   USING ILLUSTRATIONS TO LEARN MORE ABOUT STORIES

Students can examine the illustrations in a book to glean information that is not presented in the story. Answering questions like the following will guide their studies (Stewig, 1992). These questions and their answers are based on an illustration from *Chicken Little* by Steven Kellogg.

1. What can we tell from the characters' clothing? (The animals are wearing clothing, which suggests that the story is make believe. They are not wearing cold-weather clothing, so it is probably not winter.)

2. Where do you think Chicken Little is going? Why? (She is carrying a lunch box and pencil, which suggest that she is going to school.)

3. How did the fox happen to see Chicken Little? (He is using binoculars.)

4. Why does the fox have a book in the car? (It is a poultry recipe book: He is planning to cook Chicken Little.)

5. What can we infer about the time of year? (It is probably fall, because school is in session, but it is not cold yet, because the leaves are green and acorns are on the tree.)

6. How does the fox plan to kill Chicken Little? How do you know? (With a hatchet, because the picture of his imagination shows one.)

7. What do we learn about the fox? (He likes to eat chickens.)

ACTIVITY 6.17   EXPLORING THE USE OF COLOR IN PICTURE BOOKS

Explore the ways that artists use color throughout an entire book (Marantz, 1978). Look, for example, at the shades of tan and brown found throughout the pictures in Molly Bang's *The Paper Crane. King Bidgood's in the Bathtub* by Audrey Wood uses tones of purple to give the book visual unity (Stewig, 1992). Children can analyze how colors are used to create unity, to establish mood and changes of mood, and to extend the story.

Teachers can refer to Marantz for additional information about exploring color. They can also choose a group of colorful picture books and have children work in cooperative groups to identify colors that are important in the pictures and the ways the artists have used art to give the stories meaning. Also the children can create their own writing with pictures to illustrate the ways color gives meaning to their stories and reports.

SUMMARY

The picture book genre includes books in which the illustrations and the text interact to tell a story or in which there are no words, only pictures. Picture books usually have fewer than 2,000 words and no more than 32 pages. These constraints force authors to choose their words carefully and make the illustrations very important in developing the story, information, or poetry in the book. Picture books are complex art forms. Many artists experiment with a variety of styles, me-

dia, and colors to achieve the interpretation they feel is appropriate for the text. Their interpretations of literature are very important because picture books are usually children's first experience with literature.

Thought Questions

1. Which picture book illustrations are your favorites? Why?

2. How did the work of Beatrix Potter influence today's picture books?

3. What is a picture book?

4. Do you think picture books are intended only for preschool children? Why or why not?

5. How can you use picture books to extend children's aesthetic experience?

6. How do language and illustrations interact in picture books?

7. Why do artists choose to illustrate children's books?

Research and Application Experiences

1. Create a bibliography of picture books that children could use to compare and refine their understanding of art. You may wish to categorize the books by color, line, style, and so forth.

2. Read three picture books to a group of children. Ask them to choose their favorites and explain why they are their favorites.

3. Read *Talking with Artists* (vol. 2), compiled and edited by Pat Cummings (1998), or *A Caldecott Celebration* by Leonard S. Marcus (1998), and identify ways you could use it in the classroom.

4. Interview the parents of preschoolers to identify which books they read to their children and which of these books are their children's favorites.

5. Visit a children's bookstore and study the picture books. Which genre had the most selections? Can you identify any trends in the artwork?

6. Create a picture book of your favorite traditional story.

7. Write a book and have a friend illustrate it, then discuss why your friend chose a particular style for this story.

8. Develop a picture book teaching unit based on suggestions from the Activities section beginning on page 129.

9. Create a list of picture books that parents could read to their children.

Children's Literature References and Recommended Books

Note: Books designated with an asterisk (*) are recommended for reluctant readers.

Aardema, V. (Reteller). (1975). *Why mosquitoes buzz in people's ears: A West African Tale* (L. Dillon & D. Dillon, Illus.). New York: Dial. (1–3). PICTURE BOOK, TRADITIONAL LITERATURE.

A pourquoi that explains the why of mosquitoes' buzz.

Alexander, M. G. (1973). *I'll protect you from the jungle beasts.* New York: Dial. (PreK). PICTURE BOOK.

Aliki. (1974). *Go tell Aunt Rhody.* New York: Macmillan. (PreK–2). PICTURE BOOK.

Illustrates a traditional ballad. The patchwork quilt end papers contribute to the mood of this book.

Anthony, J. (1997). *The dandelion seed* (C. Arbo, Illus.). Culver City, CA: Dawn Publications. (1–3). PICTURE BOOK.

A dandelion seed sees the world as it blows from place to place.

Bang, M. (1987). *The paper crane.* New York: Mulberry Books. (3–5). MODERN FANTASY.

This Japanese tale is about kindness and its rewards. The author shows the importance of cranes in Japanese culture.

Baylor, B. (1978). *The other way to listen* (P. Parnall, Illus.). New York: Scribner's. (3–7). PICTURE BOOK, POETRY.

A boy learns to listen from an elderly man.

Bond, M. (1958, 1994). *Paddington* (series). Boston: Houghton Mifflin. (K–2). PICTURE BOOK.

Brett, J. (1989). *The first dog.* New York: Harcourt Brace. (K–2). PICTURE BOOK.

Briggs, R. (1986). *The snowman.* New York: Putnam. (1–3). PICTURE BOOK.

A snowman is built and melts.

Bruchac, J. (1996). *Between earth & sky* (T. Locker, Illus.). New York: Harcourt. (2–5). TRADITIONAL LITERATURE.

This collection of Native American legends is illuminated with beautiful paintings.

Bunting, E. (1990). *In the haunted house* (S. Meddaugh, Illus.). New York: Clarion. (K–3). PICTURE BOOK, CONTEMPORARY REALISTIC FICTION.

Father and daughter visit a haunted house.

Burleigh, R. (1998). *Home run* (M. Wimmer, Illus.). San Diego: Silver Whistle. (3–4). PICTURE BOOK, BIOGRAPHY, POETRY.*

This book tells about the career of Babe Ruth.

Cannon, J. (1994). *Stellaluna.* New York: Harcourt. (1–3). PICTURE BOOK, MODERN FANTASY.

A small fruit bat loses her mother and has to learn to live in a bird's nest.

Carle, Eric. (1992). *Draw me a star.* New York: Philomel. (K–2). PICTURE BOOK.

Carlstrom, N. W. (1980). *Jessie Bear, what will you wear?* (B. Degen, Illus.). New York: Macmillan. (PreK). PICTURE BOOK, POETRY.

Cherry, L., & Plotkin, M. J. (1998). *The shaman's apprentice.* San Diego: Harcourt Brace. (2–5). PICTURE BOOK.

In this story set in the Amazon rain forest, a boy, Kamanya, dreams of becoming a shaman, but he must first learn the healing secrets of the forest plants to realize his dream.

Christelow, E. (1999). *What do illustrators do?* New York: Clarion Books. (1–4). PICTURE BOOK, INFORMATIONAL BOOK.

Eileen Christelow shows how two author–illustrators interpret the same story in words and pictures.

Clement, R. (1998). *Just another ordinary day.* New York: HarperCollins. (1–3). PICTURE BOOK.

A young girl goes through an ordinary day with extraordinary flair.

Coffelt, N. (1993). *Dogs in space.* New York: Harcourt Brace. (K–2). MODERN FANTASY.

Cooney, B. (1990). *Hattie and the wild waves.* New York: Viking Penguin. (1–3). PICTURE BOOK.

dePaola, T. (1989). *The art lesson.* New York: Putnam. (1–3). PICTURE BOOK.

de Regniers, B. S. (1972). *Red Riding Hood* (E. Gorey, Illus.). New York: Atheneum. (1–3). PICTURE BOOK, TRADITIONAL LITERATURE.

This version of the traditional tale is told in verse.

DiSalvo-Ryan, D. (1999). *A dog like Jack.* New York: Holiday. (K–2). CONTEMPORARY REALISTIC FICTION.

Elhert, L. (1998). *Top cat.* New York: Harcourt Brace. (K–2). PICTURE BOOK.

Top cat shows readers his world.

Feiffer, J. (1997). *Meanwhile —* New York: HarperCollins. (2–6). PICTURE BOOK.

Raymond discovers that *meanwhile . . .* can take him somewhere else, so he finds it a useful device in the comedic adventure.

Fisher, L. E. (1987). *Look around: A book about shapes.* New York: Viking Penguin. (1–3). PICTURE BOOK.

Fleming, D. (1998). *Mama Cat has three kittens.* New York: Holt. (PreK–1). PICTURE BOOK.

Two of Mama Cat's kittens do exactly what Mama Cat does, but Boris naps until the others nap, and then he wakes up.

Freeman, D. (1968). *Corduroy.* New York: Viking. (PreK). MODERN FANTASY.

Galdone, P. (1979). *The three little pigs.* Boston: Houghton Mifflin. (PreK–1). PICTURE BOOK.

All three pigs want their fortune, but only one is successful.

Galdone, P. (1984). *Henny Penny.* Boston: Houghton Mifflin. (PreK–1). PICTURE BOOK.*

Henny Penny thinks the sky is falling when she is hit by an acorn.

Galdone, P. (1985). *The little red hen.* Boston: Houghton Mifflin. (PreK–1). PICTURE BOOK.

The little red hen is busy planting and harvesting, but without help from her lazy friends, the dog, cat, and mouse.

Gibbons, G. (1999). *Pigs.* New York: Holiday House. (1–4). INFORMATIONAL BOOK.

Pigs are the smartest of all farm animals. This is just one of the interesting facts that the author includes in this book.

Graeber, C. (1998). *Nobody's dog* (B. Root, Illus.). New York: Hyperion. (K–4). CONTEMPORARY REALISTIC FICTION.

Greenfield, E. (1978). *Honey, I love, and other love poems* (D. Dillon & L. Dillon, Illus.). New York: Crowell. (K–2). POETRY.*

The poetry in this book demonstrates an African-American child's love of life.

Handford, M. (1987). *Where's Waldo?* Boston: Little Brown. (1–4). PICTURE BOOK.

Hart, K. (1994). *I can paint!* Portsmouth, NH: Heinemann. (K–4). INFORMATIONAL BOOK.

Henkes, K. (1993). *Owen.* New York: Greenwillow. (P–2). PICTURE BOOK, MODERN FANTASY.

Owen has a difficult time giving up his blanket, but Mother solves his problem.

Horwitz, E. L. (1975). *When the sky is like lace* (B. Cooney, Illus.). Philadelphia: J. B. Lippincott. (K–4). POETRY.

Describes night.

Houston, G. (1988). *The year of the perfect Christmas tree* (B. Cooney, Illus.). New York: Dial. (K–4). PICTURE BOOK, HISTORICAL FICTION.

A family celebrates Christmas while the father, a soldier, fights in World War I.

Hyman, T. S. (Reteller). (1983). *Little Red Riding Hood.* New York: Holiday House. (1–3). PICTURE BOOK, TRADITIONAL LITERATURE.

This version of Red Riding Hood is a traditional version.

Isaacs, A. (1994). *Swamp angel* (P. O. Zelinsky, Illus.). New York: Dutton. (1–4). MODERN FANTASY.

This is a tall tale about a larger-than-life woman who performs amazing feats.

Isadora, R. (1976). *Max.* New York: Macmillan. (K–2). CONTEMPORARY REALISTIC FICTION.

Max (a boy) discovers that he enjoys ballet and baseball.

Isadora, R. (1979). *Ben's trumpet.* New York: Greenwillow. (K–3). PICTURE BOOK, HISTORICAL FICTION.

A child dreams of becoming a trumpet player and eventually realizes he can do it.

Isadora, R. (1980). *My Ballet Class.* New York: Greenwillow. (3–4). CONTEMPORARY REALISTIC FICTION.

Introduces the world of ballet.

Jay, B. (1998). *Swimming lessons* (L. Osiecki, Illus.). Flagstaff, AZ: Rising Moon. (1–3). PICTURE BOOK, CONTEMPORARY REALISTIC FICTION.

Jane's Momma signs her up for swimming lessons, but Jane tells her that she does not want to learn how to swim.

Kellogg, S. (Reteller). (1985). *Chicken Little.* New York: William Morrow. (PreK–1). PICTURE BOOK.

This is Steve Kellogg's version of the cumulative folktale, wherein the sky is falling because a helicopter goes awry.

Kellogg, S. (Reteller). (2000). *Paul Bunyan.* New York: William Morrow. (PreK–3). PICTURE BOOK.

Krauss, R. (1949). *The happy day* (M. Simont, Illus.). New York: Harper. (PreK–2). PICTURE BOOK, CONTEMPORARY REALISTIC FICTION.

Animals discover a flower blooming in the snow, a sign that spring is coming.

Lesser, R. (Reteller). (1984). *Hansel and Gretel* (P. O. Zelinsky, Illus.). New York: Dutton. (K–3). PICTURE BOOK.

The stepmother sends Hansel and Gretel to the forest.

Locker, T., & Christiansen, C. (1998). *Home: A journey through America* (T. Locker, Illus.). San Diego: Harcourt Brace. (3–5). PICTURE BOOK.

Thirteen authors describe in prose and poetry the landscape in different parts of the country. Locker's lush oil paintings capture the sense of each place.

Luenn, N. (1998). *A gift for Abuelita* (R. Chapman, Illus.). Flagstaff, AZ: Rising Moon. (1–4). PICTURE BOOK, CONTEMPORARY REALISTIC FICTION.

This family story focuses on the Day of the Dead's memorial day celebrated in many Mexican-American communities.

Lum, K. (1999). *What! Cried Granny: An almost bedtime story* (A. Johnson, Illus.). New York: Dial. (PreK–3). PICTURE BOOK.

Patrick goes for a sleepover at his granny's and discovers that granny can do some truly amazing acts.

Marzollo, J. (1992). *I spy* (W. Wick, Photog.). New York: Scholastic. (1–6). PICTURE BOOK.

McDermott, G. (1974). *Arrow to the sun.* New York: Viking Penguin. (3–5). PICTURE BOOK.

This is a popular Native American folktale.

McPhail, D. (1999). *Mole music.* New York: Holt. (PreK–2). PICTURE BOOK.

Mole lives a solitary life, but after hearing a violinist he decides to play the violin. After years of practice, he learns to play well, and Mole changes those around him with his music.

Meddaugh, S. (1994). *Martha calling.* Boston: Houghton Mifflin. (K–2). MODERN FANTASY.

Micklethwait, L. (1992). *I spy: An alphabet in art.* New York: Greenwillow. (2–4). PICTURE BOOK.

Micklethwait, L. (1993). *A child's book of art.* New York: Dorling Kindersley. (1–3). PICTURE BOOK.

Milne, A. A. (1926). *Winnie-the-Pooh* (E. H. Shepard, Illus.). New York: Dutton. (K–2). MODERN FANTASY.

Myers, C. (1999). *Black cat.* New York: Scholastic. (1–3). PICTURE BOOK.*

The story of a cat living on the streets of New York told in a rap.

Numeroff, L. (1993). *Dogs don't wear sneakers* (J. Mathieu, Illus.). New York: Simon & Schuster. (PreK–2). MODERN FANTASY.

Paterson, K. (1990). *The tale of the Mandarin ducks* (L. Dillon & D. Dillon, Illus.). New York: Lodestar. (1–3). PICTURE BOOK, TRADITIONAL LITERATURE.

A cruel lord separates a pair of Mandarin ducks.

Potter, B. (1902). *The tale of Peter Rabbit* (F. Warne, Illus.). London: Frederick Warne. (K–2). PICTURE BOOK, MODERN FANTASY.

Peter gets into trouble in Mr. MacGregor's garden.

Prokofiev, S. (1986). *Peter and the wolf* (C. Mikolaycak, Illus.). New York: Viking. (3–6). MODERN FANTASY.

This Russian tale tells about a boy named Peter who goes into the forest and the wolf who hopes to catch him. The birds and forest animals try to warn Peter.

Raczek, L. T. (1999). *Rainy's powwow* (G. Bennett, Illus.). Flagstaff, AZ: Rising Moon. (2–4). PICTURE BOOK, CONTEMPORARY REALISTIC FICTION.

Rainy is planning to dance at the Thunderbird Powwow, but she has a problem. In this story Rainy learns to listen to and follow her own heart.

Rand, G. (1998). *A home for Spooky.* New York: Holt. (K–3). CONTEMPORARY REALISTIC FICTION.

Ringgold, F. (1991). *Tar beach.* New York: Crown. (1–4). PICTURE BOOK, BIOGRAPHY.

The author tells about her childhood life and dreams.

Rosen, M. J. (Ed.). (1993). *SPEAK!: Children's illustrators brag about their dogs.* New York: Harcourt Brace Jovanovich. (K–4). INFORMATIONAL BOOK, PICTURE BOOK.

Sendak, M. (1963). *Where the wild things are.* New York: Harper. (All ages). PICTURE BOOK, MODERN FANTASY.

Max is sent to bed without his dinner because he had been a "wild thing," but he escapes in his imagination.

Sewall, M. (1986). *The Pilgrims of Plimoth.* New York: Atheneum. (1–4). PICTURE BOOK, HISTORICAL FICTION.

This book portrays the story of the Pilgrims.

Shulevitz, U. (1998). *Snow.* New York: Farrar, Straus & Giroux. (K–2). PICTURE BOOK.

In this book, snow transforms a town, and a boy and his dog celebrate the first snowfall.

Simon, C. (1998). *Guard the house, Sam!* Chicago: Children's Book Press. (K–2). CONTEMPORARY REALISTIC FICTION.

Singer, M. (1993). *It's hard to read a map with a beagle on your lap* (C. Oubrerie, Illus.). New York: Holt. (K–2). POETRY.

Spender, S. (Reteller). (1966). *The magic flute.* New York: G.P. Putnam's Sons. (5–7). HISTORICAL FICTION.

Illustrates Mozart's life.

Spier, P. (1982). *Peter Spier's rain.* New York: Doubleday. (PreK–3). PICTURE BOOK.

The artist explores rain from many perspectives.

Steiner, J. (1999). *Look-alikes, jr.* (T. Lindley, Photog.). Boston: Little, Brown. (PreK–2). PICTURE BOOK.

Everyday places are constructed from a variety of objects, such as pencils and crackers. Children can identify over 700 objects.

Tagholm, S. (1999). *The barn owl* (B. Kitchen, Illus.). New York: Kingfisher. (1–4). PICTURE BOOK, INFORMATIONAL BOOK.

An informational book about barn owls.

Tullet, H. (1999). *Night/day: A book of eye-catching opposites.* Boston: Little, Brown. (PreK–3). PICTURE BOOK.

Udry, J. M. (1959). *The moon jumpers* (M. Sendak, Illus.). New York: Harper & Row. (K–2). PICTURE BOOK.

Gives readers the feeling of movement and dance.

Van Allsburg, C. (1985). *The polar express.* Boston: Houghton Mifflin. (K–4). PICTURE BOOK.

A boy discovers the spirit of Christmas after traveling to the North Pole on the Polar Express and meeting Santa Claus.

Van Allsburg, C. (1993). *The sweetest fig.* Boston: Houghton Mifflin. (K–4). MODERN FANTASY.

Wargin, K. (1998). *The legend of Sleeping Bear* (G. Van Frankenhuyzen, Illus.). Chelsea, MI: Sleeping Bear Press. (K–2). TRADITIONAL LITERATURE.

An ancient tale that tells of a bear and her cubs swimming Lake Michigan to escape a forest fire.

Wells, R. (1979). *Max's first word.* New York: Dial. (PreK). PICTURE BOOK.

Max the white bunny learns his first word.

Wells, R. (1983). *Peabody.* New York: Dial. (PreK). PICTURE BOOK.

Wells, R. (1988). *Shy Charles.* New York: Dial. (PreK). PICTURE BOOK.

Charles is a bunny, but he is very shy.

Wells, R. (1991). *Max's dragon shirt.* New York: Dial. (PreK–K). PICTURE BOOK.

Max and his sister, Ruby, shop for a new shirt.

Wells, R. (1992). *The island light.* New York: Dial. (PreK–K). PICTURE BOOK.

A young bunny explores space travel in this Voyage to the Bunny Planet book.

Wick, W. (1998). *Walter Wick's optical tricks.* New York: Cartwheel/Scholastic. (3–6). INFORMATIONAL BOOK.*

A wonderful collection of optical illusions.

Wick, W., & Marzollo, J. (1999). *I spy treasure hunt: A book of picture riddles.* (K–3). PICTURE BOOK.

Children enjoy solving these riddles. The series has several titles, including a *Gold Challenger* for really serious riddlers.

Wiesner, D. (1999). *Sector 7.* New York: Clarion. (1–3). PICTURE BOOK.

This wordless book tells the story of a boy who visits the Empire State Building on a school field trip. On the observation deck of the building, the boy makes friends with a cumulus cloud.

Williams, M. (1983). *The velveteen rabbit* (M. Hague, Illus.). New York: Henry Holt. (K–2). PICTURE BOOK.

Williams, S. (1990). *I went walking* (J. Vivas, Illus.). San Diego: Harcourt Brace Jovanovich. (PreK–1). PICTURE BOOK.

A child goes walking and identifies animals.

Williams, V. (1983). *Something special for me.* New York: Greenwillow. (K–2). PICTURE BOOK.

The specialness of a birthday is the subject of this book.

Williams, V. (1984). *Music, music for everyone.* New York: Greenwillow. (K–2). INFORMATIONAL BOOK.

Addresses the importance of music in our lives.

Wisniewski, D. (1998). *The secret knowledge of grown-ups.* New York: Lothrop, Lee & Shepard. (K–4). PICTURE BOOK, MODERN FANTASY.

Secret files that grown-ups have hidden from children for thousands of years are opened to reveal knowledge to children such as why they say, "Eat your vegetables."

Wood, A. (1984). *The napping house* (D. Wood, Illus.). New York: Harcourt Brace. (K–2). PICTURE BOOK, MODERN FANTASY.

A child and some animals fall asleep on Granny's bed; they nap until a flea bites a mouse, and then they break the bed.

Wood, A. (1985). *King Bidgood's in the bathtub* (D. Wood, Illus.). New York: Harcourt Brace Jovanovich. (K–3). PICTURE BOOK.

The King will not leave his bathtub for any reason, but a young page solves the problem by pulling the plug.

Wood, A. (1996). *The red racer.* New York: Simon & Schuster. (1–3). PICTURE BOOK.

Nona has an old bicycle, but she wants a new Red Racer. When her parents say no because it costs too much, Nona sets out to solve her problem.

Wood, A. J. (1992). *Errata: A book of historical errors.* New York: Green Tiger. (3–6). PICTURE BOOK.

Yoshi. (1987). *Who's hiding here?* Saxonville, MA: Picture Book Studio. (1–3). PICTURE BOOK.

Young, E. (Trans.). (1989). *Lon Po Po: A Red-Riding Hood story from China.* New York: Philomel. (1–3). PICTURE BOOK.

This version of Little Red Riding Hood received the Caldecott Award. In this variation, the mother leaves her three daughters home and goes to visit the grandmother, and the wolf comes to the girls.

Younger, B. (1998). *Purple mountain majesties* (S. Schuett, Illus.). New York: Dutton. (2–5). PICTURE BOOK, HISTORICAL FICTION.

The story of the song "America the Beautiful."

Zelinsky, P. O. (Adapter). (1990). *The wheels on the bus.* New York: Dutton. (PreK–2). PICTURE BOOK.

The illustrator has created new illustrations and formatting for this traditional song.

Zelinsky, P. O. (Reteller). (1986). *Rumpelstiltskin* (P. O. Zelinsky, Illus.). New York: Dutton. (1–4). TRADITIONAL LITERATURE.

The Grimm version of Rumpelstiltskin with beautiful illustrations.

Zemach, H. (1966). *Mommy, buy me a China doll* (M. Zemach, Illus.). Chicago: Follett. (PreK–2). PICTURE BOOK.

Illustrates a traditional ballad.

Zolotow, C. (1972). *William's doll* (W. P. Du Bois, Illus.). New York: Harper & Row. (K–2). PICTURE BOOK.

References and Books for Further Reading

Ardizzone, E. (1980). Creation of a picture book. In S. Egoff, G. Stubbs, & L. Ashley (Eds.), *Only connect: Readings on children's literature.* (pp. 289–298). New York: Oxford University Press.

Camp, D. J., & Tompkins, G. E. (1990). Show-and-tell in middle school? *Middle School Journal, 21,* 18–20.

Christelow, E. (1999). *What do illustrators do?* New York: Clarion.

Cianciolo, P. (1990). *Picture books for children* (3rd ed.). Chicago: American Library Association.

Cummings, P. (1998). *Talking with artists* (Vol. 3). New York: Bradbury.

Dillon, L., & Dillon, D. (1992a). Diane's story. In P. Cummings (Ed.), *Talking with artists* (pp. 24–25). New York: Bradbury.

Dillon, L., & Dillon, D. (1992b). Leo's story. In P. Cummings (Ed.), *Talking with artists* (pp. 22–23). New York: Bradbury.

Egielski, R. (1992). Richard's story. In P. Cummings (Ed.), *Talking with artists* (pp. 30–35). New York: Bradbury.

Hearn, M. P. (1999). *David Wiesner: Master of incongruity.* Abilene, TX: National Center for Children's Illustrated Literature.

Hearne, B. (1990). *Choosing books for children: A commonsense approach.* New York: Delacorte.

Kiefer, B. (1988). Picture books as contexts for literacy, aesthetic, and real-world understandings. *Language Arts, 65,* 272–278.

Kiefer, B. (1995). *The potential of picturebooks.* Englewood Cliffs, NJ: Merrill/Prentice Hall.

Lacey, L. E. (1986). *Art and design in children's picture books.* Chicago: American Library Association.

Lima, C., & Lima, J. (1993). *A to zoo: Subject access to children's picture books.* New Providence, NJ: Bowker.

Lobel, A. (1981). A good picture book should. . . . In B. Hearne & M. Kaye (Eds.), *Celebrating children's books* (pp. 73–80). New York: Lothrop, Lee & Shepard.

Lukens, R. (1986). *A critical handbook of children's literature* (3rd ed.). Glenview, IL: Scott Foresman.

Marcus, L. S. (1998). *A Caldecott celebration.* Walker.

Moline, S. (1995). *I see what you mean.* York, ME: Stenhouse.

National Center for Children's Illustrated Literature (n. d.). *The NCCIL presents Paul O. Zelinsky* [Online]. Available: http://www.NCCIL.org/exhibit/zelinsky.html [2000, March 23].

Nodelman, P. (1984). Some presumptuous generalizations about fantasy. In P. Dooley (Comp.), *The first steps: Best of the Early CHLA Quarterly* (pp. 115–116). West Lafayette, IN: Purdue University, Children's Literature Association.

Nodelman, P. (1988). *Words about pictures: The narrative art of children's picture books.* Athens: University of Georgia.

Ocvirk, O., Bone, C., Stinson, O., Wigg, R., & Wigg, P. (1991). *Art fundamentals: Theory and practice* (6th ed.). Dubuque, IA: Brown & Benchmark.

Perkins, D. (1994). *Learning to think by looking at art.* Santa Monica, CA: The Getty Center for Education in the Arts.

Schwarcz, J. H., & Schwarcz, C. (1991). *The picture book comes of age: Looking at childhood through the art of illustration.* Chicago: American Library Association.

Scott-Mitchell, C. (1987). Further flight: The picture book. In M. Saxby & G. Winch (Eds.), *Give them wings: The experience of children's literature* (pp. 61–75). South Melbourne, Australia: Macmillan.

Shulevitz, U. (1985). *Writing with pictures: How to write and illustrate children's books.* New York: Watson-Guptill.

Smith, L. H. (1991). *The unreluctant years.* New York: Viking.

Stewig, J. (1992). Reading pictures, reading text. *New Advocate, 5,* 11–22.

Stoodt, B. D. (1995). Preschool children's preferences for picturebook illustrators. Unpublished research. Northern Kentucky University, Highland Heights, KY.

Thomas, J. A. (1983). Nonfiction illustration: Some considerations. In J. May (Ed.), *Children and their literature: A readings book* (pp. 47–53). West Lafayette, IN: Purdue University, Children's Literature Association.

Townsend, J. R. (1990). *Written for children.* New York: HarperTrophy.

Wood, D., & Wood, A. (1986). The artist at work: Where ideas come from. *Horn Book, 60,* 556–565.

Young, E. (1990). Caldecott acceptance speech. *Horn Book, 66,* 452–456.

Poetry for Every Child

KEY TERMS

alliteration	metaphor
assonance	meter
concrete poetry	narrative poem
connotative meaning	nonsense poetry
epics	onomatopoeia
figurative language	personification
free verse	rhyme
haiku	rhythm
imagery	simile

GUIDING QUESTIONS

Think about your early experiences with poetry—did you enjoy it? Barbara Abercrombie (1977) admits that she did not like poetry at all when she was young. She says, "Either I couldn't understand it, or the poems were about things I didn't care about" (p. 1). She later discovered poets who wrote about things she did care about. Did you discover poems about the things you liked as a child?

What types of poems did you like? Do you think your early experiences affected whether you like or dislike poetry now? What was the last poem you read? Reflect on your own experiences while reading this chapter. Thinking about your response to poetry will help you understand your students' responses. Keep these questions in mind as you read:

1. What are at least three ways of describing poetry?

2. What are some common misconceptions about poetry?

3. Who are some of the popular contemporary children's poets?

OVERVIEW

Poems are tiny, well-crafted pieces of language; they contain multiple layers of meaning. "Their words reflect subtle shadows, images, and symbols that lead children to see beyond the literal and surface-level meanings" (Cullinan, Scala, & Schroder, 1995, p. 3). When children were asked, "What do you think poetry is?" they responded, "A poem is something that rhymes," and "Poems are about nature and love and stuff like that" (Abercrombie, 1977). Of course, not all poetry has to rhyme. Nor is all poetry about nature and love and stuff like that. Today we have poetry about "real life" experiences such as baseball, vegetable soup, and skating.

Poetry helps us envision a world we cannot see; it helps us imagine a world that is better than the one we live in. Poetry cultivates the imagination. A poem can start us thinking and talking about feelings and subjects. A poem can express feelings that we cannot put into words ourselves.

After selecting poetry that appeals to children, the most important thing to know is that it should be read aloud. Reading aloud gives children occasions to explore the different things a poem can do, the feelings a poem can generate, and the imaginative, melodic language that poets use. Reading poetry aloud and talking about it with others helps us realize that others have the same worries and joys and fears and dreams as we do (Lenz, 1992).

INTRODUCTION

Children's poetry holds an important place in children's literature. Contemporary poetry is very appealing to children because it addresses topics and themes that are relevant for today's children. They will discover baseball, dinosaurs, insects, and humor in poetry. Moreover, due to its nature, poetry can be relatively short, easy-to-read poems as well as longer poems that appeal to more sophisticated readers.

The opening vignette demonstrates the infusion of poetry into a classroom. The children demonstrate their appreciation for poetry when they ask to hear it again. They respond to the poetry by relating it to a story they read earlier. You will notice that the teacher encourages the class to relate poetry to their lives and their experiences, which engages their interest and stimulates their response.

VIGNETTE

Teachers choose poetry related to children's lives and experiences to engage their interest. They introduce children to the various poetic forms. This opening vignette demonstrates the infusion of poetry into a classroom. The children's requests to hear it again show how much they like this poetry. They respond to the content and the illustrations, comparing the poem with a story they had read earlier.

Because her first graders responded enthusiastically to the book *Whose Mouse Are You?* by Robert Kraus, Gayle Andrews decided to surprise them with *Mice Are Nice*, a book of poems about mice compiled by Nancy Larrick.

When the children returned to their classroom after lunch, Gayle directed them to the story rug. "I'm going to read a poem called 'Mice,' which Rose Fyleman wrote."

As she read, the room was quiet except for the rustling of wiggling children and an occasional cough. When she had finished, Mark asked, "Did you read that poem because we heard *Whose Mouse Are You?* this morning?"

"What do you think?" she asked in return.

"Yes, yes," the children chimed in.

"Are the mice in the poem the same as the mouse in the story?" the teacher asked.

"No," Richard said.

"Why do you say that?" Ms. Andrews asked.

"The mice in the poem are like real mice; they ran around the house and got into all kinds of stuff," he answered.

"But the mice in the story did all kinds of things that mice can't really do," Shirley mentioned. "In the story, the mice were talking."

Sarah added, "In the poem, it was like someone was talking about the mice."

"The pictures of the mice in the poem are different from those in the story," Andrea said.

"How are they different?" Ms. Andrews asked.

"The ones in the story were like newspaper drawings and they were gray, but the pictures in the poetry book were like mouse fur," Serena said.

THE NATURE OF POETRY

Young children have a natural affinity for poetic language. Language play is a natural activity for them. They relish inventing words and rolling them over their tongues. They are intrigued with the unusual combinations of words and respond to their musical, rhythmic qualities. Poets use language in ways that not only re-create the rhythms of oral language, but also extend it to include novel and unusual applications. Childhood songs and nursery rhymes are natural springboards into poetry. These initial experiences are followed later with jump rope rhymes and nonsense verse. As children mature, they enjoy chanting simple, rhythmic conversational poems as they go about daily activities.

Children's poetry has experienced a renaissance in recent years. Contemporary children's poets such as Jack Prelutsky, Paul Fleischman, Paul Janeczko, and Eloise Greenfield are very popular (Crisp, 1991). "More than ever before, poetry for children has climbed to its proper station" (Hopkins, 1987, p. 4). Teachers, librarians, and parents have the opportunity to choose from a wide variety of poems and poetry books to nurture children's interests.

Many people consider poetry to be the highest form of literature. Certainly, it is literature in its most intense, imaginative, and rhythmic form, expressing and interpreting the essence of experience through language (Morner & Rausch, 1991; Perrine, 1969). The major difference between poetry and prose is its compactness. One word in a poem says much more than a single word in prose. The rich imagery of poetry permits a far greater concentration of meaning than is found in prose (Morner & Rausch, 1991).

Poetry's economy of expression is comparable to the terseness of a conversation between longtime friends—it relies on the ring of familiarity in voice inflections, and images to create meaning. In *Stories I Ain't Told Nobody Yet,* Jo Carson's poems are conversations like those most of us hear daily. Paul Janeczko relies on these same qualities in *The Music of What Happens.*

Poetry's rhythm, sound patterns, figurative language, compactness, and emotional intensity set it apart from prose and contribute to the compactness of poetic expression (Lukens, 1986). In turn, this compactness contributes to poetry's emotional intensity. "You can't say anything much more briefly than a poem or folktale says it, nor catch a fact or feeling much more expressively" (Hearne, 1991, p. 107). Imagery enables poets to create dense meaning with a few words. They use words economically, choosing and polishing each one like a gem to create associations in readers' minds. This characteristic is illustrated in the lyrical text of *The Jazz of Our Street* by Shaik, which pulses with the rhythms and spirit of a jazz melody. The rhythm draws children to the jazz parade and they join in shimmying, shaking, and swaying in joyful movements. The children telling this poetic story say that the band's beat has the. . .

> *stamping and hauling*
> *we hear on our block every day.*

Emotional Intensity

"The best poetry is a union of beauty and truth. . . . The best poets speak to us with beauty that we can appreciate and in truths we can understand" (Russell, 1991, p. 77). Poetry, rooted in the world of emotions as well as in the mind, is emotionally intense. Poets capture universal feelings, writing about experiences that have affected them in such a way that the experiences will affect readers as well. The experiences may be everyday happenings that have been commemorated with an emotional intensity that meets the needs and interests of listeners and readers. For instance, Charlotte Zolotow expresses emotional intensity when she demands *Say It!* in the book by that title. In this joyful book, a little girl and her mother celebrate the pleasure of walking on a beautiful autumn day . . .

> *"Say it," shrieked the little girl. "Say it say it say it!"*
> *"I love you," said her mother. "I love you I love you*
> *I love you!"*

Expressing Feelings

Poetic language may be unpretentious and the number of words limited, but the emotional intensity of poetry makes it a natural form for expressing feelings. *Honey, I Love, and Other Love Poems* by Eloise Greenfield shares an African-American child's love for members of her family and her enthusiasm for life. Leo and Diane Dillon help us visualize these emotions with their illustrations. Paul Janeczko expresses the feelings of both baseball players and fans in *That Sweet Diamond: Baseball Poems.* The poem "The Pitcher" is from this collection.

The Pitcher

Standing
alone
above the rest
in the center of the diamond
his art is foolery,
casting a spell,
never showing the batter
more than he needs to know
for the moment
it takes a slider, change, or
tantalizing curve
to break the heart
of the plate.

Shel Silverstein addresses the fears and joys of childhood in his enormously popular book *Where the Sidewalk Ends: The Poems & Drawings of Shel Silverstein.* His humor and zany illustrations help us examine our feelings with a light heart. "Sick," a popular poem in this collection, tells about a character who is gravely ill—until she realizes that it is Saturday. The feelings of young children are explored in books such as *The Candlewick Book of First Rhymes* and Lee Bennett Hopkins's *Still as a Star: A Book of Nighttime Poems.*

Cynthia Rylant explores growing up in her book *Waiting to Waltz: A Childhood.* She tells of the crises of a girl growing up in a small mountain town, who loses a spelling bee and is punished for swearing. Rylant shares her personal experiences, her joys, and her sorrows in this book, which is related to her autobiography *But I'll Be Back Again.*

Poetry can be categorized according to various criteria: poetic form, content, theme, and audience appeal. Teachers and librarians who develop a broad acquaintance with children's poetry will be able to nurture children's appreciation. They can also experiment with various ways of sharing poetry to build children's responses.

ELEMENTS OF POETRY

Poets use words in melodious combinations to create singing, lyric qualities. Sound patterns and figurative language connote sensory images appealing to sight, sound, touch, and smell. These images build on children's experiences and relate to their lives, as shown in "Poem to Mud" by Zilpha Keatley Snyder, which is about the tactile sensations of playing in mud.

This collection of poems and lullabies perfectly captures the dreamy nighttime mood when a child leans out of her window to gaze at the moon, and a boy dreams of giants up in the mountains.

Poetic Language

The words in a poem are carefully chosen to imply a range of ideas, images, and feelings. Each word implies and suggests more than it says. Poets create rich metaphors that summon hundreds of associations to stimulate readers' thoughts and emotions. Readers' individual connotative understandings are based on their emotional responses to words or concepts. For instance, readers who grew up in the Blue Ridge Mountains will have many and more varied responses to poetry about mountains than those who have never seen mountains. In the book *From the Bellybutton of the Moon and Other Summer Poems* by Alarcón, the poet's vivid images are built on his memories of summer vacations in Mexico. He compares the "Summer Sun" with

luminous orange
hanging from the tree

TABLE 7.1
Examples of sensory language.

Sense	Imagery
Vision	Fire-engine red, gigantic, elongated
Touch	Soft, hard, rough
Sound	Crunch, rumble, squeak
Smell	Rotting leaves, wet dog, bread baking
Movement	Hop, skip, trudge
Taste	Sweet, salty, bitter

Sensory language stimulates these associations in readers. This language arouses readers' senses and reminds them of concrete experiences. Poets continually search for fresh imagery to arouse the senses, a sample of which is shown in Table 7.1.

Sound Patterns

Children learn the sound patterns of language before they learn words; in fact, sound patterns appear to be instrumental in children's acquisition of language. The sounds of poetry attract young children, who realize early on that words have sounds as well as meanings. "They love to rhyme words, to read alliterative tongue twisters, to laugh at funny-sounding names" (Fleischman, 1986, p. 553). Sound patterns are a delight to the ear of everyone, young and old. Rhyme, alliteration, onomatopoeia, and assonance are several devices commonly used by poets to achieve these sound patterns, and are often combined to give sound effects to a poem.

The delightful sound patterns of nursery rhymes, combined with their brevity and simplicity, invite children to roll them over their tongues."Hickory Dickory Dock" is a good example. Repeat it aloud to yourself or read it to a young child. Think about your own or the child's response to its patterns of sound. How many devices can you identify in this verse?

> Hickory, dickory, dock,
> The mouse ran up the clock.
> The clock struck one,
> and down he run.
> Hickory, dickory, dock.

Rhyme. Rhyme is one of the most recognizable elements in poetry, although poetry does not have to rhyme. Rhyme is based on the similarity of sound between two words such as *sold* and *mold* or *chrome* and *foam.* "When the sounds of their accented syllables and all succeeding sounds are identical, words rhyme" (Morner & Rausch, 1991). A good rhyme, a repetition of sounds, pleases readers. It gives order to thoughts and pleasure to the ears (Livingston, 1991). Rhyme gives poetry an appealing musical quality.

The most common form of rhyme in poetry is *end rhyme,* so named because it comes at the end of the line of poetry (Morner & Rausch, 1991). End rhyme is illustrated in Rhoda Bacmeister's poem "Galoshes." *Internal rhyme* occurs within a line of poetry and is illustrated in the poem "Hughbert and the Glue" by Karla Kuskin in Arbuthnot's *Time for Poetry.* Rhyming patterns in poetry are grouped in stanzas. A common end rhyming pattern is to rhyme the last word in every other line. An example of this appears in the book *Advice for a Frog* by Alice Schertle. In this book, "A Traveler's Tale" illustrates the end rhyme.

> *At length we found a land of mud and flowers.*
> ....
> *And slipped into the New World that was ours*

The stanzas thus formed have special names depending on the number of lines in the rhyming pattern:

> two lines: couplet
> three lines: tercet
> four lines: quatrain
> five lines: quintet
> six lines: sextet
> seven lines: septet
> eight lines: octave

Alliteration. *Alliteration* is achieved through repetition of consonant sounds at the beginning of words or within words. It is one of the most ancient devices used in English poetry to give unity, emphasis, and musical effect. This technique is also shown in the poem "Galoshes."

Onomatopoeia. Onomatopoeia gives poetry a sensuous feeling. *Onomatopoeia* refers to words that sound like what they mean. For example, the word *bang* sounds very much like the loud noise to which it refers. In *Stories to Begin On,* Rhonda Bacmeister uses the words *splishes, sploshes, slooshes,* and *sloshes* in the poem "Galoshes" to create the sounds of walking in slush.

Assonance.   *Assonance* is the close repetition of middle vowel sounds between different consonant sounds such as the long /a/ sound in *fade* and *pale*. Assonance creates near rhymes rather than true rhymes commonly found in improvised folk ballads (Morner & Rausch, 1991). Assonance gives unity and rhythmic effect to a line of poetry.

Rhythm

Rhythm is the patterned flow of sound in poetry created through combinations of words that convey a beat. Rhythm can set the sense of a story to a beat, but it can also emphasize what a writer is saying or even convey sense on its own, as in a speaker's gestures (Fleischman, 1986). In traditional English poetry, rhythm is based on meter, the combination of accent and numbers of syllables (Morner & Rausch, 1991). Patterns of accented and unaccented syllables and of long and short vowels work together to create meter and rhythm (Lukens, 1986). Karla Kuskin demonstrates this meter in her poem "Thistles," which appears in *Dogs & Dragons, Trees & Dreams: A Collection of Poems.*

Rhythm is natural to children. In the first months of life they wave their arms and legs to the rhythm of nursery rhymes. By 18 months, they enjoy marching in circles to "ring around the rosie . . . all fall down." In school, primary-grade children use rulers and pencils to tap out the rhythm of David McCord's "Song of the Train" which appears in *Far and Few.*

Word Play

Word play is an inviting characteristic of children's poetry. The patterns of sound in poetry create the playful language patterns that are a source of pleasure for children. They roll interesting words over their tongues and repeat them to savor their flavor. Douglas Florian's *Laugh-eteria* and his *Bing Bang Boing* are collections of humorous short verse. Many of his poems are based on word play. These lines from *Laugh-eteria* illustrate word play.

> *Hello, my name is Dracula*
> *My clothing is all blackula.*

Figures of Speech

Writers use *figures of speech,* also called *figurative language,* to express feelings and create mental pictures (images). Figures of speech offer writers many possibilities for expressing themselves. One of the major challenges in creating poetry is to choose figures of speech that offer fresh images and that uniquely express the writer. In fact, a poet's facility in using figures of speech is what makes the major difference between pleasant verse and fine poetry (Livingston, 1991). The best-known figures of speech are *simile, metaphor,* and *personification.*

Simile.   A *simile* is a figure of speech using *like* or *as* to compare one thing to another. Most of you will recognize that "white as snow" is a simile, but it is so timeworn that it has become a cliché. Poets must be acute observers, seeing and hearing in new ways to offer fresh figures of speech. Look for similes used by Valerie Worth in "Frog," a poem from her book *Small Poems.* Think about the observations that enabled the poet to create these comparisons.

Metaphor.   *Metaphor,* like simile, is a figure of speech comparing two items, but instead of saying something is *like* something else, metaphor says that something *is* something else. Langston Hughes uses metaphor to arouse the reader's feelings and imagination in his poem "Dreams," calling life a "broken-winged bird" and a "barren field! Frozen with snow." These metaphors create images that clarify our thoughts about dreams. The reader recognizes, of course, that life is not actually a bird or field (Livingston, 1991), but these comparisons communicate vivid and unique images. In the following example, the poet gives spring the attributes of a baseball player, using the words: *swings, pitches, throws, catches, slides, bunts,* and *tags.*

> *Spring brings out her baseball bat, swings it*
>   *through the air,*
> *Pitches bulbs and apple blossoms, throws them*
>   *where it's bare,*
> *Catches dogtooth violets, slides to meadow sweet,*
> *Bunts a breeze and tags the trees with green buds*
>   *everywhere.*

TYPES OF POETRY

Free verse has become the popular form for contemporary children's poetry, whereas older poetry follows traditional forms. Authorities divide poetry into three categories (i.e., narrative, lyric, and dramatic), although these elements are often combined in a single poem (Bagert, 1992). Poets choose and combine poetic forms to create a form that best tells their ideas and feelings. This means that attempts to categorize poems by type are usually impossible. This section examines poetic form and introduces examples to clarify understanding.

Narrative Poems

Narrative poems tell stories. The story elements—plot, character, setting, and theme—make narrative poems especially appealing because everyone enjoys a good story. Narrative poems that tell about the adventures of characters who are children or who are childlike make compelling reading for children. Anne Isaacs's book *Cat Up a Tree* tells a humorous story in a narrative poem. U.S. history is the story narrated in Lee Bennett Hopkins's collection of poems in the book *Hand in Hand.*

Narrative poems may be short or long. Book-length narrative poems are called *epics.* Byrd Baylor and her illustrator Peter Parnall share their love of the desert with readers in their illustrated epic *The Other Way to Listen.* J. Patrick Lewis tells a thrilling and spooky epic tale in *The House of Boo.*

Personification. Personification attributes human characteristics to something that does not actually have these qualities. Poets have a talent for endowing inanimate objects with life, as Myra Cohn Livingston does in the poems in her book *A Circle of Seasons:* "Spring brings out her baseball bat, swings it through the air."

Dramatic Poetry

Dramatic poetry often appears in the form of a monologue in which a single character tells about a dramatic situation (Morner & Rausch, 1991). The poet sometimes pretends to be something or someone else in a dramatic poem (Livingston, 1991). Poets have pretended to be the wind, bugs, and seashells among other things. Many examples of dramatic form are found in traditional ballads, as well as in the work of Carl Sandburg, T. S. Eliot, and Robert Frost. Dramatic poetry often appears in anthologies of children's poetry.

Lyric Poetry

Lyric poems are short, personal poems expressing the poet's emotions and feelings. They speak of personal experience and comment on how the writer sees the world. Originally such poems were written to be sung to the music of a lyre, so it is not surprising that lyric poetry has a feeling of melody and song (Livingston, 1991). Lyric poetry is the most common form for children's poetry. It can be identified through the use of the personal pronouns *I, me, my, we, our,* and *us* or related words (Livingston, 1991). The distinguishing characteristics of these poems are emotion, subjectivity, melodiousness, imagination, and description (Morner & Rausch, 1991). Angela Johnson's poems, *The Other Side: Shorter Poems,* tell about the razing of her hometown. She uses the first-person voice to draw a picture of growing up in Shorter, Alabama; her poems are personalized with photographs of the writer as a child.

Haiku

Authentic *haiku,* a poetic form that originated in Japan, describes nature and the seasons. Haiku are patterned poems based on syllables, words, and lines. The first line contains 5 syllables, the second contains 7, and the third contains 5 for a total of 17 syllables in 3 lines. The book *Cool Melons—Turn to Frogs!: The Life and Poems of Issa* by Matthew Gollub introduces haiku and the life of Issa, who is considered Japan's premier haiku poet.

Free Verse

Free verse differs from traditional forms of poetry in that it is "free" of a regular beat or meter (Morner & Rausch, 1991). Free verse usually does not rhyme, does not follow a predetermined pattern, and has a fragmentary syntax. Free verse incorporates many of the same poetic devices that writers of structured poetry employ, but writers of free verse are more concerned with natural speech rhythms, imagery, and meaning than with rhyme and meter.

Concrete Poetry

The form of concrete poetry is inseparable from the content. *Concrete poetry* merges visual, verbal, and auditory elements, arranging the words and letters to suggest something about the subject of the poem. For example, a poem about a rock might be written in the shape of a rock, or a poem about a cloud is written in the shape of a cloud. Or several carefully selected words may be suspended on a mobile so that as the air moves the mobile, the words move and a poem evolves, but each person sees a different poem. As with all poetry, each reader brings his or her own ideas, feelings, and experiences to the poem. *Doodle Dandies: Poems That Take Shape* by J. Patrick Lewis is a marvelous collection of shape poems. *Splish Splash,* by Joan Bransfield Graham, is another superb book of concrete poetry.

Nonsense Poetry

Nonsense poetry ordinarily is composed in lyric or narrative form, but it does not conform to the expected order of things. It defies reason. It is playful poetry in which meaning is subordinate to sound (Morner & Rausch, 1991). "Nonsense is a literary genre whose purpose is to rebel against not only reason but the physical laws of nature. It rejects established tenets and institutions, pokes fun at rational behavior, and touts destruction. It champions aberrations" (Livingston, 1981, p. 123). Writers of nonsense poetry create unusual worlds in which objects and characters are recognizable but do absurd things and become involved in absurd situations. They do not behave in a sensible, reasonable manner. Nothing is impossible in nonsense poetry; perhaps this is the very reason it is so popular with children. They know cows cannot jump over the moon, but they like the fun of such implausible antics as those in the following lines.

> Hey diddle diddle,
> The cat played the fiddle,
> The cow jumped over the moon.

Edward Lear, the master of nonsense, wrote poems that appealed to all ages. Although his *Complete Nonsense Book* was published in 1948, it remains popular today. J. Patrick Lewis shows that he is an outstanding student of Lear in his book *Boshblobberbosh: Runcible Poems for Edward Lear.* Some of these poems are about Lear and some are pure nonsense. Calef Brown created the funky nonsense in *Polkabats and Octopus Slacks: 14 Stories,* and it will appeal to all ages.

Nonsense writers use a variety of strategies in their craft. They invent words, as Laura Richards does in "Eletelephony." Lear frequently uses alliteration, a common technique, in his "Pelican Chorus." Personification lends itself well to nonsense verse, as animals, objects, and even pieces of furniture take on human characteristics. Exaggeration is a useful device to writers of nonsense, as Shel Silverstein shows in "Sarah Cynthia Sylvia Stout Would Not Take the Garbage Out," one of many nonsense poems in his book *Where the Sidewalk Ends.*

CONTENT OF POETRY

The subject matter of poetry is unlimited. Poetry embodies life and reveals its complexity; it is a part of the fabric of life. Poets look at ordinary things and events more closely than the rest of us and see things that we overlook. Constance Levy fosters new ways of seeing the everyday world in her poems, which are presented in *A Crack in the Clouds and Other Poems.* She uses simple language and varied cadences to tell about cricket songs, icicles, weeds, and comets.

A plethora of poems on subjects ranging from garbage to fairy tales and from side-splittingly funny to serious are readily available. Teachers can find poems to fit every mood, interest, and topic, available in any form: narrative, free verse, limericks, ballads, or whatever is desired. Content is more important than form when selecting poetry for children.

Although the range of content in poetry is far too broad to catalog here, we will highlight humor as one of the most popular subjects in children's poetry. Jack Prelutsky is a poet well known for his zany poems. He uses splendid words such as *disputatious* and *alacrity,* and his poems have unexpected twists that delight his readers. Perhaps most important, all children (including boys, who are sometimes hard to interest in poetry) love his poems. His book *Something Big Has Been Here* has many ridiculous images to delight readers. In "The Turkey Shot Out of the Oven," a turkey shoots out of an oven because it is stuffed with unpopped popcorn. Then there is the character in "Denson Dumm" who planted light bulbs in his hair so that he would be forever bright. Like all of Prelutsky's books, however, this one offers a diverse range of topics, including serious poems such as "Don't Yell at Me."

Again, space constrains us from cataloging the variety of ways of treating subjects in poetry, but we briefly discuss three poems on a topic elementary children love: dinosaurs. Each poet chose different stylistic devices to portray dinosaurs: the first two poems could be categorized as realistic fiction or even informational compositions because they communicate the essence of actual dinosaurs, whereas the third poem is delightful fantasy.

The first poem, "When Dinosaurs Ruled the Earth" by Patricia Hubbell, uses repeated words to create rhythm and to tie the verses together. The phrases "teeth were made for tearing flesh, his teeth were made to gnash" creates auditory images, whereas later phrases establish visual images. This poet dramatizes the dinosaurs' sizes by comparing them with buildings and trees. Continuing on, the poet says that the dinosaurs have "pygmy brains."

In "Brachiosaurus," Jack Prelutsky, in his book *Tyrannasaurus was a Beast*, describes the dinosaur as a "perpetual eating machine," and as "clumsy and slow." These phrases give us visual images. Prelutsky also points out that the dinosaur did not need "to be clever and wise." These phrases reiterate the idea of "pygmy brain" found in the first poem. But Prelutsky uses fewer words and rhymes every other line in his poem, distinguishing it from Hubbell's "When Dinosaurs Ruled the Earth."

The third poem, "Dinosaur Dances," is bound to be a hit with children. In this poem, Jane Yolen writes about make-believe dinosaurs in costumes, dancing everything from a ballet to a hula. She creates a rhythmic beat with words and rhymes in the title poem, telling readers that "anything goes" at a prehistoric party with "lights low, couples doing Twist and Shout" and "hopping all about." Bruce Degen's illustrations create unusual images—clumsy dinosaurs dancing a refined minuet. Each of the poems in this book has a different dance beat, which makes it unique and delightful. The best of these poems makes toes tap and leads to movement.

CHILDREN'S RESPONSE TO POETRY

Poetry speaks to the emotions and the intellect. It is pleasurable and comfortable, amusing and relaxing. Poetry can be an important part of children's literary life, clarifying and illuminating experience and enriching daily life. The rhythms of poetic language stick in memory and children repeat the words again and again, savoring the feel of them on their tongues. Poetry lifts their spirits and stimulates their imaginations, stirring them to communicate in interesting ways (Peck, 1979). Poetry can be enjoyed at any grade, any age. It addresses the interests and abilities of anyone,

anywhere, whether gifted or reluctant reader. Poetry appreciation is personalized—even more so than response to other literary forms. A single poem may arouse different responses in each reader based on the highly individual images evoked by the carefully selected imagery packed into the poem.

Children need many and varied opportunities to respond to poetry that makes sense to them. Positive attitudes toward poetry are built when interesting poetry is presented in meaningful ways. Poetry appreciation begins with the premise that it merits a prominent place in children's lives. "Poetry must flow freely in our children's lives; it should come to them as naturally as breathing, for nothing—nothing—can ring and rage through hearts and minds as does poetry" (Hopkins, 1987, p. 4). Unfortunately, some teachers and parents believe poetry is dreary and uninteresting because their experiences were concerned with memorizing, dissecting, and analyzing works such as *Romeo and Juliet*. These experiences generated the belief that poetry was obscure, meaningless, and irrelevant. Their beliefs then become a self-fulfilling prophecy.

However, teachers, librarians, and parents who wish to engage children's interest in poetry will be pleased to learn that extensive technical knowledge is unnecessary. Although sometimes helpful, expertise regarding poetic form is not as important as having many experiences with interesting poetry. Response to poetry is largely a matter of experience. Presenting a variety of poems gives children opportunities to identify their favorites, and with experience, teachers, librarians, and parents can acquire a discriminating sense for the poetry, and they may even discover an unrealized passion for poetry.

POETS AND THEIR POETRY

Learning about the people who create poetry will motivate children to read more. When choosing a poet to study, the teacher may do read-alouds that focus on a single poet's works with younger children. On the other hand, middle-grade children can immerse themselves in the work of a single poet. They should focus on a poet they like very much, but children who lack experience with poetry may have to experience more poetry to find a favorite.

We chose Jack Prelutsky for a poet's profile because he is a favorite of children all over the United States with his keen sensitivity to children's fears,

Jack Prelutsky

Jack Prelutsky says that he was a challenge to parents and teachers probably because schools and parents were not prepared for individuals with great creativity. His multifaceted talents are demonstrated by his various occupations, including musician, photographer, truck driver, entertainer, and sculptor.

When a publisher expressed an interest in his poems when he was really trying to sell his photographs, he was shocked. He did not like poetry due to his experiences in school. In fact, he thought poets were very strange people. Moreover, he grew up in a tough Bronx neighborhood where poets were generally considered boring, sissies, or dead.

Prelutsky's goal is to write fresh, contemporary poems with humor as a basic ingredient. He believes that life does not have to be so serious, so his poems are almost always humorous, and he throws in a good bit of nonsense. Prelutsky is recognized for his irreverent style, technical versatility, and awareness of what children like.

Prelutsky loves what he is doing, writing poems and traveling around the United States meeting and talking with children. He likes writing, travel, and people, and he likes to see how children are growing through his books. Among his more than 30 volumes are:

Rolling Harvey Down the Hill
The New Kid on the Block
The Baby Uggs Are Hatching
The Dragons are Singing Tonight
Something Big Has Been Here

pleasures, and funny bones (Behr, 1995). This poet's profile was prepared with materials from the *Highlights' Teacher Net, www.teachingk-8.com* and *Children's Books and Their Creators* (Silvey, 1995).

SELECTING AND EVALUATING POETRY

Some teachers and parents may believe they are ill equipped to select poetry. Fortunately, poets and others who are well versed in poetry have come to their rescue, writing books that expand teachers' knowledge of poetry and suggesting ways of integrating it into their classrooms. Many of these volumes offer exemplary poetry and suggestions for classroom activities: *Let's Do a Poem!* by Nancy Larrick and *Pass the Poetry, Please!* by Lee Bennett Hopkins are only two. Other writers focus on writing poetry: how they got started, sources of ideas, and the processes they use to create fresh ideas. *The Place My Words Are Looking For* by Paul Janeczko and *Near the Window Tree* by Karla Kuskin are two good examples. Myra Cohn Livingston (1991) gives poetry a more formal treatment in *Poem-Making: Ways to Begin Writing Poetry*. However, she introduces a game of poetry in *I Am Writing a Poem About. . . .* Books such as these will help you develop more confidence in selecting poetry for children.

One of the very best ways to cultivate confidence is through reading many poems and deciding which poems and poets you like the best. Once you have discovered a poem or a poet who speaks to you, look for more poems by the same poet. Through this process your own taste will evolve, and interesting children in something that you really enjoy is always easier. Develop your own wide collection of poems, both for your own use and to stimulate children's interests.

Identify appealing kinds of poetry and offer a variety of poems in read-aloud sessions. A particular poem or book, however, may not be for everyone. It is for the person who relates to the feelings and ideas expressed. In the introduction to *A Tune Beyond Us,* Myra Cohn Livingston (1968) cautions readers: "Every poem in this collection will not speak for you. But perhaps one, or two, will. And that will be enough (p. iv)."

The brevity of poems can be motivating. Readers find them less demanding than other genres of literature. Despite their brevity, however, poems should be read at a leisurely pace to allow readers to savor the words and ideas (Hearne, 1991). Children relish poetry in classrooms and other settings where it is cultivated as a natural happening, a part of daily life.

Spontaneous experiences with poetry cultivate opportunities to read and listen. Because poets carefully choose each word for its sound and meaning, poems should be read as complete entities rather than fragments subjected to analysis (Dias, 1987).

Locating Poetry

Poetry appears in several types of books: anthologies, specialized collections, and book-length poems. Poetry anthologies are collections of poetry that include many types of poems on many subjects. One of the most comprehensive is *The Random House Book of Poetry for Children* (Prelutsky, 1983), edited by Jack Prelutsky and illustrated by Arnold Lobel, which includes poems arranged in broad categories. Specialized collections are books of poems that focus on a specific theme or topic. All of the poems in Jane Yolen's *Dinosaur Dances,* illustrated by Bruce Degen, relate to dinosaurs—more specifically, dancing dinosaurs. A lengthy single poem may be published as an entire book, usually a picture book, as is Byrd Baylor's *The Other Way to Listen.*

Evaluating poetry anthologies can be especially difficult because the poems represent such a broad range of subject matter and style, but reviewing the table of contents and examining the literary quality of a few poems in different sections can identify the range of topics. An anthology can provide appropriate poetry at a moment's notice for everyday reading needs—holidays, weather, daily incidents. Of course, one or two good anthologies cannot fulfill all the poetry needs of children, and poetry should be a part of planned experiences as well as incidental experiences. Table 7.2 presents several examples each of good anthologies, specialized collections, and book-length poems.

Children's Preferences

Children's appreciation of poetry is motivated by careful choice of poems on the part of the teacher, librarian, or parent. This entails considering children's poetry preferences, which in turn emerge from their experiences and interests. Of course, asking children what they like has obvious value. Research also offers information about children's poetry preferences. Children seem to appreciate poems that are generously spaced and tastefully illustrated, suggesting that visual appeal is a factor to consider (Sebesta, 1983). Fisher and Natarella (1982) report that primary-grade children's poetry preferences include narrative poems and limericks, poems about strange and fantastic events, traditional poems, and those that use alliteration, onomatopoeia, and rhyming. Intermediate-grade students like poems related to their experiences and interests, humorous poems, and those with rhythm and rhyme (Bridge, 1966). They respond better to contemporary poems than to traditional ones and also prefer poems that address familiar and enjoyable experiences, funny poems, and those telling a story (Terry, 1974). Narrative poems and limericks are the most popular form with fourth, fifth, and sixth graders, whereas haiku and free verse are among the least popular (Terry, 1974).

Later studies of children's poetry preferences are consistent with the earlier studies (Ingham, 1980; Simmons, 1980), although their conclusions are limited to the geographic area used in the study. Both report that children prefer humorous poetry and poetry that addresses familiar experiences. Poems by Shel Silverstein and Dennis Lee are preferred to traditional poetry (Ingham, 1980). The weight of research therefore indicates that humorous poetry—that of Shel Silverstein, Jack Prelutsky, and Dennis Lee, for instance—should be included in a poetry collection because it attracts children to poetry, and that collections should be up-to-date because children find contemporary poetry more appealing than traditional poetry. This is not to suggest that only research-validated poetry be used, but the research does provide an obvious beginning point for building children's appreciation of and pleasure in poetry. In the final analysis, good poetry speaks to children. It communicates, inspires, informs, and tells of things that are, were, may be, and will never be (Peck, 1979).

Finding Winners

After reviewing teachers' reports, Crisp (1991) found that the top ten books of poetry in the 1980s were:

1. *Joyful Noise: Poems for Two Voices* by Paul Fleischman
2. *Under the Sunday Tree* by Eloise Greenfield
3. *Brickyard Summer: Poems* by Paul Janeczko
4. *Did Adam Name the Vinegarroon?* by X. J. Kennedy
5. *Knock at a Star: A Child's Introduction to Poetry* by X. J. and Dorothy M. Kennedy, editors
6. *American Sports Poems* by R. R. Knudson and May Swenson, compilers

	TABLE 7.2	
	Examples of books of poetry.	
Author	Title	Grade Level
	Anthologies	
Beatrice de Regniers	Sing a Song of Popcorn	K–8
Tomie dePaola	Tomie dePaola's Book of Poems	1–6
Jack Prelutsky	The Random House Book of Poetry for Children	1–8
Ann McGovern	Arrow Book of Poetry	3–7
Nancy Larrick	Piping Down the Valleys Wild	3–7
	Specialized Collections	
Zena Sutherland	The Orchard Book of Nursery Rhymes	Preschool–1
Valerie Worth	Small Poems	K–2
Mary Ann Hoberman	Yellow Butter Purple Jelly Red Jam Black Bread	K–3
Nancy Larrick	Mice Are Nice	K–3
Edward Lear	Of Pelicans and Pussycats: Poems and Limericks	K–4
Jack Prelutsky	Something Big Has Been Here	K–4
Aileen Fisher	When It Comes to Bugs	K–6
Karama Fufula	My Daddy Is a Cool Dude	1–5
Robert Froman	Seeing Things: A Book of Poems	1–6
Nancy Larrick	On City Streets	1–6
David McCord	One at a Time	1–6
Jack Prelutsky	Rolling Harvey Down the Hill	1–6
Paul Fleischman	Joyful Noise: Poems for Two Voices	2–6
Arnold Adoff	Sports Pages	4–7
Cynthia Rylant	Waiting to Waltz: A Childhood	4–8
	Single-Book Poems	
Nadine Bernard Westcott	Peanut Butter and Jelly: A Play Rhyme	K–2
Myra Cohn Livingston	Up in the Air	K–4
Robert Frost	Stopping by Woods on a Snowy Evening	1–6
Arnold Adoff	All the Colors of the Race	3–8
Byrd Baylor	The Desert Is Theirs	3–8
Byrd Baylor	The Other Way to Listen	3–8
George Ella Lyon	Together	K–6

7. *Poems for Jewish Holidays* by Myra Cohn Livingston, editor

8. *Fresh Paint: New Poems* by Eve Merriam

9. *Tyrannosaurus Was a Beast: Dinosaur Poems* by Jack Prelutsky

10. *A Visit to William Blake's Inn: Poems for Innocent and Experienced Travelers* by Nancy Willard

Honorable mentions on her list included:

- *Tomie dePaola's Book of Poems* by Tomie dePaola, compiler and illustrator
- *The Music of What Happens: Poems That Tell Stories* by Paul Janeczko, compiler
- *Dogs & Dragons, Trees & Dreams: A Collection of Poems* by Karla Kuskin

- *Overheard in a Bubble Chamber and Other Science Poems* by Lillian Morrison
- *Waiting to Waltz: A Childhood* by Cynthia Rylant
- *Small Poems Again* by Valerie Worth

Books of poetry such as these can serve as a beginning point for exploring poetry, but remember that students should be given many experiences with all kinds of poetry because appreciation for poetry develops slowly. Use the following questions to help you in selecting poetry:

1. Can children understand it?

2. Does the poem stir emotions such as humor, sadness, empathy, and joy?

3. Does the poem create sensory images such as taste, touch, smell, or sight?

4. Does the poem play with the sounds of language? Does the sound echo the senses (Cullinan et al., 1995; Lenz, 1992)?

5. Does the rhythm enhance the meaning? Does the poem bring the subject to life? (Literary critics agree that fine poets bring an experience or emotion to life, making it live for others.)

6. Will this poem motivate children to read other poetry?

7. Does the poem evoke a response in the listener/reader?

Using such guidelines, however, is no substitute for old-fashioned observation: Children's eyes light up over a splendid poem that speaks directly to them; they grimace over ones they do not like. The clearest signal that you have read a winner is, of course, a request to read it again.

ENRICHING POETIC EXPERIENCES

Children's responses to poetry are closely linked to the ways in which they customarily explore the world: observing and manipulating. As they explore the nature and parameters of language, poetry can give them access to specific characteristics or elements not found in their everyday experience (Parsons, 1992).

Surround children with poetry: Display poems, posters, and books related to classroom activities and studies. Place poem posters (that you or the children make and laminate) around the classroom. Recite or read poems whenever opportunities arise. Celebrate poets and poetry books that the children especially enjoy. Play tapes of poets reading their own work. Make up poems on the spur of the moment that fit classroom events and studies.

Experiencing poetry begins with oral experience. It comes to life when read or said out loud. Young children enjoy repeating and intensifying the magic of poetry; they like to hear it again and again and will often object to changes in delivery or any attempt to leave out verses (Parsons, 1992). Children love to chime in with the reader, clap with the rhythm, mime facial expressions, act out events, or just repeat the words. Such oral experiences intensify their appreciation of the rhythm, rhyme, figurative language, and imagery of poetry.

The poet's use of unfamiliar words and combinations of words, definite rhythms, vocal stress on words and syllables, and even the ideas, however, can complicate reading poetry aloud. Stumbling over words or rhythm can interfere with children's experiences of the poem, so prepare for reading poems aloud by being thoroughly familiar with the language of the poem so that you can read fluently, well, and at a comfortable rate. A tape recorder can be helpful in practicing oral reading.

Children need to hear poetry daily. Particularly appealing poems should be read again and again to enable children to develop an ear for the rhythm and sound of poetry. Daily readings of poetry should be both incidental and planned. Incidental poetry reading occurs when an event is taking place: someone is celebrating a birthday or the birth of a new baby. Holidays and events such as the first day of spring and the first day of winter are good reasons to read a poem. Rain, sunshine, snow, and the first robin of the spring are all events to be marked with poetry. Planned poetry reading occurs when the teacher chooses poetry that fits the curriculum or develops thematic units with poetry; the diversity of subject matter and form in poetry makes such planning easy. A few unit suggestions are included at the end of this chapter.

Rhythm

Sound effects.   Students can express the rhythms of poetry through sound effects. Organize a team to create background sound effects as a poem is read aloud (Larrick, 1991); for instance, for "The Merry-Go-Round Song," a sound effects team could re-create the up-and-down rhythm of a carousel by repeating the sounds OOM-pa-pa, OOM-pa-pa in the rhythm of the song.

Encourage the children to vary the sound effects and work at identifying the most effective ones for poems they enjoy. Groaning, snapping fingers, stomping feet, and rubbing hands together may be appropriate sound effects for some poems. For other poems, students might make crying sounds, or laugh, moo, or cluck; or they may even invent sounds.

Repetition.   Young children enjoy repeating sounds, words, and phrases they hear. Joining in on the repeated lines in nursery rhymes, ballads, camp songs, spirituals, and traditional play rhymes is a fine way to involve them with poetry. Invite them to join in on the repeated parts during reading or singing such songs and rhymes as "The Muffin Man," "John Brown's Baby Had a Cold Upon His Chest," "The Wheels of the Bus Go Round and Round," or "He's Got the Whole World in His Hands."

Echo.   Echoing lines and words are another way of inviting children into poetry. Repeated words or phrases can be treated like an echo or a series of echoes (Larrick, 1991), as shown in the traditional folk song "Miss Mary Mack" (see accompanying box). The echo can be developed in a number of ways: one individual can read or recite the poem with another individual echoing the repeated words; or groups can do the parts instead of individuals. Another variation is to emphasize the beat on the repeated words by clapping with the chant on those words.

Miss Mary Mack

Miss Mary Mack, Mack, Mack
All dressed in black, black, black
With silver buttons, buttons, buttons
All down her back, back, back.
She asked her mother, mother, mother
For fifteen cents, cents, cents,
To see the elephant, elephant, elephant
Jump the fence, fence, fence.
He jumped so high, high, high
That he touched the sky, sky, sky
And never came back, back, back
Till the Fourth of July, July, July.

Hubbell, 1991

Choral reading.   Activities such as repetition and echoing prepare children for choral reading of poetry. Many poems lend themselves to choral reading. "The Poor Old Lady Who Swallowed a Fly," shown in the box on page 158, can be a choral reading involving two or three groups of students. Assign the various stanzas to different groups and have the repeated words chanted in unison by the entire group. You can find literally hundreds of poems for this and similar activities; the examples here are provided to give you an idea of what to look for. If you try a poem and it does not work out, try others until you find some that you and the students enjoy. Material for choral reading should be meaningful, have strong rhythm, have an easily discernible structure, and perhaps rhyme (McCracken & McCracken, 1983). Some good ones are:

- "The Pickety Fence" by David McCord, in *Far and Few, Rhymes of the Never Was and Always Is.*
- "The Umbrella Brigade" by Laura Richards in *Time for Poetry* by Karla Kuskin.
- "Godfrey, Gordon, Gustavus Gore" by William B. Rand in *Time for Poetry* by Karla Kuskin.
- "Yak" by William Jay Smith in *Oh, That's Ridiculous* by Jane Yolen.

Movement

The rhythm of poetry gives it a feeling of movement, making it difficult for children to be still when listening to it. "Poetry is not irregular lines in a book, but something very close to dance and song, something to walk down the street keeping in time to" (Frye, 1964). "Or jog down the trail keeping time to. Or do the dishes by. Or jump rope on the playground with" (Hearne, 1991). Being involved with poetry makes it more appealing. "Doing" creates opportunities for children to respond to, to participate in, to be involved with the poetry. "Doing" can involve chanting, singing, dancing, tapping, and swinging to the rhythms of poetry (Larrick, 1991). Children appreciate the rhythmic aspect of poetry and rhymes. Tapping, clapping, and swinging arms with poetry sensitizes participants to the rhythms and involves them with poetry. They need opportunities to hop, skip, jump, and march to poetry. They enjoy trying out various assignments such as: "Walk with confidence. Tiptoe stealthily. Walk flatfoot like a clown. Walk like

The Poor Old Lady Who Swallowed a Fly

There was an old lady
who swallowed a fly.
I don't know why she swallowed a fly.
Perhaps she'll die.
There was an old lady who swallowed a spider,
that wriggled and jiggled and tickled inside her.
She swallowed the spider to catch the fly.
I don't know why she swallowed a fly.
Perhaps she'll die.
There was an old lady who swallowed a bird.
How absurd, to swallow a bird!
She swallowed the bird to catch the spider.
She swallowed the spider to catch the fly.
I don't know why she swallowed the fly.
Perhaps she'll die.
There was an old lady who swallowed a cat.
Think of that, she swallowed a cat!
She swallowed the cat to catch the bird.
She swallowed the bird to catch the spider.
She swallowed the spider to catch the fly.
I don't know why she swallowed the fly.
Perhaps she'll die.
There was an old lady who swallowed a dog.
She went the whole hog and swallowed a dog.
She swallowed the dog to catch the cat.
She swallowed the cat to catch the bird.
She swallowed the bird to catch the spider.
She swallowed the spider to catch the fly.
I don't know why she swallowed the fly.
Perhaps she'll die.
There was an old lady who swallowed a cow.
I don't know how she swallowed a cow!
She swallowed the cow to catch the dog.
She swallowed the dog to catch the cat.
She swallowed the cat to catch the bird.
She swallowed the bird to catch the spider.
She swallowed the spider to catch the fly.
I don't know why she swallowed the fly.
Perhaps she'll die.
There was an old lady who swallowed a horse.
She died of course.

Unknown

a sad old man. Imagine you are picking up a heavy sack of apples and carry it on your shoulder. . . . Swim like a fish. Fly like a bird" (Larrick, 1991).

Movement is a natural introduction to poetry. Some traditional singing games such as "If You're Happy and You Know It, Clap Your Hands" and "The Wheels on the Bus Go Round and Round" are excellent vehicles for making students more aware of rhythm. Movement is an important element in Lillian Morrison's *Rhythm Road: Poems to Move To.* This fresh, inventive collection of nearly 100 poems is an excellent introduction to the genre and to motion for all ages. Morrison has arranged the poems in sections that include dancing, riding, watching water, and hearing music; other sections include the topics of living things, active entertainments, sports, work, television, technology, and the mind. When using this book in the classroom, read the poems aloud and encourage listeners to move with the sounds.

Lillian Morrison has accommodated the need for movement in much of the poetry she has written. *The Break Dance Kids* is just one of her books that stimulate poetic movement. *A Rocket in My Pocket,* compiled by Carl Withers, is a collection of rhythmic chants, songs, and verses that are part of the folklore of the United States; all of the works in this volume can be used in developing movement activities in classrooms. Nancy Larrick (1991) recommends the poem "Bedtime," by Patricia Hubbell for encouraging children to experiment with movement.

Riddle-Poems

Riddle-poems delight young children and their brevity invites young readers. The reader must identify items using hints in the verses and sometimes in illustrations. Such poems introduce a sense of fun and wordplay. In *Riddle-Lightful: Oodles of Little Riddle-Poems,* J. Patrick Lewis has indirectly described common objects such as a fire truck, a raisin, and a kite. Both children and adults enjoy solving the riddles in Brian Swann's *The House with No Door: African Riddle-Poems.* Ashley Bryan's illustrations evoke the African landscape. Brian Swann presents poetic riddles in *Touching the Distance: Native American Riddle-Poems.*

Themes and Topics

One way of organizing poetry experiences and activities is through themes and topics (Parsons, 1992). By identifying a topic and using that focus to integrate classroom experiences, teachers encourage, support, and reinforce children's learning. Theme or topic exploration may include activities such as field trips, art, dramatic play, music, and further reading. Themes and topics for poetry explorations can focus on any number of topics, including colors, animals (wild animals, imaginary animals, zoos), myself, out-of-doors, or any other content area that is of interest. Even houses can be a theme for poetry as Mary Ann Hoberman demonstrates in her picture book *A House Is a House for Me.* She explores the concept of houses with interesting ideas such as a glove (a house for a hand) and a hand (a house for money).

Quiet is Peter Parnall's theme in his book of the same name. In this book-length poem a boy sprinkles apple cores and seeds on his chest while lying in the grass so that he can observe the life around him. A chipmunk, a mouse, a bumblebee, and a chickadee see the treats from different perspectives, shown in the charcoal-and-colored-pencil illustrations. After reading this poem, children may want to lie in the grass themselves, observing what happens and writing their own poems or stories about the experience. They could also examine the meaning of some other word in the same way that Parnall did in *Quiet.*

Another book-length poem, *Train Song* by Diane Siebert, contrasts with Parnall's *Quiet.* The rhythm and rhyme of the rolling wheels of a train create the movement, sights, and sounds of a train. Richly colored paintings illustrate this picture book. *Train Song* could be the beginning of a transportation unit along with *Truck Song,* also by Diane Siebert, or of a train unit with George Ella Lyon's picture book *A Regular Rolling Noah* and Robert Welber's *The Train.*

Two thematic units that are highly popular with children and that offer plenty of material for study are animals, birds, and bees and holidays. (For other specific unit suggestions, see the Activities section beginning on page 161.)

Animals, birds, and bees

Animals, birds, and insects are frequent subjects for poets and often favorite subjects of children, and we have no shortage of books from which to build a thematic unit on this topic. William Jay Smith's *Birds and Beasts* is both a poetry collection and an art book. Smith's poems and the graphic images created by Jacques Hnizdovsky's woodcuts combine to create a funny, lighthearted tone. Myra Cohn Livingston's *If the Owl Calls Again: A Collection of Owl Poems* views owls from many perspectives. Many readers will be surprised at the number of great poets from various cultures who have written about owls.

Insects are the theme of Paul Fleischman's Newbery Award book, *Joyful Noise: Poems for Two Voices.* These poems are wonderful fun in the classroom because two or more individuals must read them, and they can be the basis for creating choral readings. In these poems, sounds create the images, movements, and appearance of many insects. Douglas Florian writes about bugs that creep, crawl, and fly in *Insect-lopedia.*

Holidays

Poetry is a natural part of holiday celebrations, and holidays are a good time for integrating poetry in classrooms. Almost every holiday or season has more than enough poetry written about it to serve as the basis for a unit study at the appropriate time of year. Several poets and compilers have created holiday poems and collections, a few examples of which are in the following list.

- *New Year's Poems* by Myra Cohn Livingston
- *Valentine Poems* by Myra Cohn Livingston
- *Easter Poems* by Myra Cohn Livingston
- *Merrily Comes Our Harvest In* by Lee Bennett Hopkins
- *Best Witches: Poems for Halloween* by Jane Yolen
- *Halloween A B C* by Eve Merriam
- *Halloween Poems* by Myra Cohn Livingston
- *Hey-How for Halloween* by Lee Bennett Hopkins
- *Thanksgiving Poems* by Myra Cohn Livingston, ed.
- *Christmas Poems* by Myra Cohn Livingston, ed.
- *An American Christmas* by Diane Goode
- *Sing Hey for Christmas Day* by Lee Bennett Hopkins
- *A Visit from St. Nicholas and Santa Mouse, Too!* by Clement C. Mouse
- *Celebrations* by Myra Cohn Livingston

Writing

Children are natural poets because poetic language comes naturally to them. Those who are immersed in poetry often express their own ideas in the same patterns as their favorite poems. Writing models encourage children to run with their imaginations—to take off with a concept and see where it goes. They may write or dictate concept poems to be bound into a class book to share with visitors to the classroom.

Myra Cohn Livingston (1976) suggests another method for encouraging children to write and respond to poetry, an approach that expedites children's discovery of their own poetic voice. First, share with them many imaginative poems, then give them observation sheets for recording their responses to questions similar to these: what I saw, and what I thought about what I saw.

Writing requires keen observation, and Livingston's method builds students' ability to scrutinize their environment. For instance, she recommends prompting them to consider sounds, smells, and tastes in their surroundings by bringing in potato chips and other noisy foods. In Livingston's plan, children keep a daily observation journal in which they record feelings and observations that can be used in writing poetry.

Students can learn about the differences between poetry and prose by comparing the treatment of a subject in a poetry selection, a prose selection, and an informational selection. Ideas and information are imparted in different ways in each form of literature. Students can write sentences that tell about the similarities and differences in various literary forms on the same subject or create a list such as that in Figure 7.1 to demonstrate the comparisons. This figure compares three picture books on the topic of flying.

FIGURE 7.1   Comparing three literary forms.

- *First Flight* by David McPhail. This picture book fantasy features a naughty teddy bear that is taking a first flight with his very well-behaved owner. The teddy bear breaks all the rules for flying.
- *Up in the Air* by Myra Cohn Livingston. This picture book, illustrated by Leonard Everett Fisher, features illustrations that are from the perspective of a person looking down toward the earth from an airplane.
- *Flying* by Donald Crews. This informational picture book follows an airplane flight from the passengers boarding the plane to their arrival at a destination.

Discussion

Many people are unsure about discussing or asking questions about poetry. Poetry is art and many of us agree that it should not be overanalyzed, but does that mean it cannot be discussed or examined at all? Discussions of poetry should avoid overanalysis as well as overgeneralization. The best guide for poetry discussion comes from Perrine (1969):

1. Consider the speaker and the occasion. Discuss who wrote the poem, whether the speaker or character is the same person as the poet, and the point of view the poet uses.
2. Consider the central purpose of the poem. Discuss why the poet wrote it and what type of poem it is: a circus poem, a wildlife poem that celebrates nature, and so on.
3. Consider the means by which that purpose is achieved: rhythm, rhyme, imagery, or repeated words, phrases, or lines, and so on.

As children become fluent readers, they can prepare poems to read aloud either as individuals or as groups, implementing some of the suggestions in the activity section that follows. One way of generating student participation in poetry is to write a poem on a chart, then cut it apart and give each student the part they are to read. The parts can be numbered to assist the students. Playing music as a background when reading poetry dramatizes it. Puppets, pantomime, and creative drama are appropriate activities for many poems because they tell stories. Nursery rhymes such as "Jack and Jill" or "Humpty Dumpty" are appropriate to these activities, as are many other poems. "The Poor Old Lady Who Swallowed a Fly" works well for puppets or drama. Children may experiment and explore with the sounds of poetry through their voices, create their own poetry, examine various themes, and relate poetry to the arts.

Classroom Activities

ACTIVITY 7.1 HUMOR

Suggested Book List
- *Faint Frogs Feeling Feverish* by Lillian Obligado
- *If I Were in Charge of the World* by Judith Viorst
- *The New Kid on the Block* by Jack Prelutsky
- *Rolling Harvey Down the Hill* by Jack Prelutsky
- *The Complete Nonsense Book* by Edward Lear
- *Where the Sidewalk Ends* by Shel Silverstein
- *You Read to Me, I'll Read to You* by John Ciardi

Guiding Questions
1. What makes you laugh? Think about television shows, books, poems, and real-life events. Some people laugh at exaggeration, word play, jokes on other people, or unexpected events.
2. Can you think of other things that make people laugh? Make a list with your classmates.
3. Listen to the poems that your teacher reads. Which ones did you think were the funniest? Which ones were not funny?
4. How did the poet make you laugh? What techniques, elements, forms, and so forth did he or she use?
5. Why did the poet write this poem?
6. What poems made your classmates laugh? Why did they laugh?
7. Vote for the funniest poem or poems of those your teacher reads. Find out why these were the funniest.
8. Make a bulletin board display to tell the school about funny poems and the ways authors make them funny.
9. Find more funny poems and make a class book. Read funny poems to your family and friends to find out what poems make them laugh.

ACTIVITY 7.2 WEATHER

Suggested Book List
- *A Circle of Seasons* by Myra Cohn Livingston
- *Go with the Poem* by Lilian Moore
- *I Like Weather* by Aileen Fisher
- *Rain Talk* by Mary Serfozo
- *Rainbows Are Made: Poems* by Carl Sandburg, Lee Bennett Hopkins, and Fritz Eichenberg
- *Season Songs* by Ted Hughes
- *Sky Songs* by Myra Cohn Livingston

Guiding Questions
1. What is your favorite kind of weather? Why?
2. What is your least favorite kind of weather? Why?
3. In the poem you have selected for study, what is the poet's favorite weather? How do you know?
4. How does weather in the poem make you feel?
5. Why did the poet write this poem?
6. How did the poet help you experience a particular kind of weather?
7. Compose a poem of your own that is parallel to one of those studied in this unit.

ACTIVITY 7.3 ANIMALS

Suggested Book List

- *Animals, Animals* by Eric Carle
- *A Gopher in the Garden and Other Animal Poems* by Jack Prelutsky
- *Birds and Beasts* by William Jay Smith
- *Cat Poems* by Myra Cohn Livingston
- *Circus! Circus!* by Lee Bennett Hopkins
- *Dinosaurs* by Lee Bennett Hopkins
- *My Mane Catches the Wind: Poems About Horses* by Lee Bennett Hopkins
- *Turtle in July* by Marilyn Singer
- *Tyrannosaurus Was a Beast* by Jack Prelutsky
- *Welcome to the Ice House* by Jane Yolen

Guiding Questions

1. What kinds of animals are good pets? Why?
2. Do you have a pet? What is it?
3. How does the poet feel about animals? How do you know?
4. What did the poet tell you about animals?
5. How did the poet tell you about animals?
6. Why did the poet write this poem?
7. What did you learn about animals from the poems your teacher read?
8. Which animal poem did you like best? Why?
9. Do you have different ideas about animals after hearing poems about them? How did your ideas change?
10. How are animals in poems similar to those in stories? How are they different?
11. Write a poem about your favorite animal.

SUMMARY

Poetry is compressed language and thought that implies more than it says. Poetry is literature in verse form. The good news about children's poetry is its plentiful supply. Current poetry addresses contemporary themes and experiences that children can appreciate. Children see poetic language as natural unless they have had negative experiences that turn off their interest in this form. Unfortunately, many adults view poetry with a mixture of awe and insecurity because they believe they must have academic knowledge in order to do justice to it in the home or classrooms. However, teachers, librarians, and parents can read poetry with and to children as an organic part of their daily experiences and celebrations. Oral read-aloud experiences are the best way to introduce poetry to children.

Adults must carefully choose poetry for students. They need a wide acquaintance with all forms and types of poetry so they can discover that which will entice children to read. Children enjoy the rhyme, humor, rhythm, and movement of poetry; however, response to poetry is more personal than to other literary genres, so

a wide-ranging collection of poetry enhances children's opportunities to respond to it. Emphasizing meaning, response, and enjoyment is important in incorporating poetry into children's lives.

Thought Questions

1. How is poetry different from prose?
2. What are the major characteristics of poetry?
3. Why does poetry appeal to children?
4. How can you as a teacher prevent children from disliking poetry?
5. Do you think poetry is natural for children? Why or why not?
6. How should poetry be presented in classrooms? Why?
7. Identify three strategies for presenting poetry that you plan to use as a classroom teacher. Why do you like these strategies?

Research and Application Experiences

1. Start a poetry file or collection for use in your classroom. This collection should relate to everyday events, holidays, and the curriculum.

2. Start a thematic collection of poetry. The themes you identify will depend upon the ages of the children with whom you will be working.

3. Compare the treatment of a single subject in poetry, prose, and informational writing.

4. Survey the teachers in an elementary school. Ask them how often they use poetry in their classrooms and what the children's favorite poems are. What conclusions can you reach based on your research?

5. Survey students at one grade level. Ask them to identify their favorite poems. Create a graph that shows the titles, poets, and types of poems they enjoy most.

6. Practice reading three poems aloud. Tape yourself, so that you can realize your progress in the oral interpretation of poetry.

7. Examine three or more anthologies of poetry. Which one would you find most useful in the classroom? Why?

Children's Literature References and Recommended Books

Note: Books designated with an asterisk (*) are recommended for reluctant readers.

Alarcón, F. X. (1998*). From the bellybutton of the moon and other summer poems/Del ombligo de la luna y otros poemas de verano.* Chicago: Children's Press. (K–3). POETRY.

The poems in this collection, presented in Spanish and English, focus on summer vacations in Mexico.

Arbuthnot, M. (Ed.). (1951). *Time for poetry.* Chicago: Scott, Foresman. (K–8). POETRY.

Bacmeister, R. W. (1940). *Stories to begin on* (T. Maley, Illus.). New York: Dutton. (1–3). POETRY.

This is a collection of poems for young children. "Galoshes" is included in the collection.

Baylor, B. (1978). *The other way to listen* (P. Parnall, Illus.). New York: Scribner's. (2–8). POETRY.

This is a book-length poem that explores ways of knowing. The theme is respect for all.

Brown, C. (1998). *Polkabats and octopus slacks: 14 stories.* Boston: Houghton Mifflin. (PreK–3). POETRY.*

Many adults have purchased this book for themselves. It is an exuberant, unforgettable collection of poems.

Candlewick Press. (1996). *The Candlewick book of first rhymes.* Cambridge, MA: Candlewick Press. (PreK–2). POETRY.

A superb collection of poems for younger children. These poems are probably unfamiliar to most children.

Carson, J. (1989). *Stories I ain't told nobody yet.* New York: Orchard Books. (5–9). POETRY.*

The poems in this book are really conversations that the poet eavesdropped on in grocery store lines, beauty parlors, and emergency rooms.

dePaola, T. (1988). *Tomie dePaola's book of poems.* New York: Putnam. (K–3). POETRY.

Fleischman, P. (1988). *Joyful noise: Poems for two voices* (E. Beddows, Illus.). New York: Harper. (3–6). POETRY.

These are poems about insects to be read by two people.

Florian, D. (1994). *Bing bang boing.* New York: Harcourt. (3–6). POETRY.*

This is a popular collection of humorous short verse. Children like the word play they discover in these poems.

Florian, D. (1998). *Insectlopedia.* New York: Harcourt Brace. (K–3). POETRY.*

Bugs that creep, crawl, and fly are the subjects of this poetry book.

Florian, D. (1999). *Laugh-eteria.* New York: Harcourt. (3–6). POETRY.*

This collection of humorous short verse is decorated with line drawings. The poems are about subjects that children know and love.

Gollub, M. (1998). *Cool melons—turn to frogs!: The life and poems of Issa* (K. G. Stone and K. Smith, Illus.). New York: Lee & Low. (3–6). POETRY.

This book is an introduction to an eighteenth-century Japanese writer of haiku.

Graham, J. B. (1994). *Splish splash* (S. Scott, Illus.). New York: Ticknor & Fields. (K–3). POETRY.*

This is a collection of concrete poetry.

Greenfield, E. (1978). *Honey, I love, and other love poems* (D. Dillon & L. Dillon, Illus.). New York: Crowell. (1–4). POETRY.

This book of poems shares an African-American child's enthusiasm for love and family life.

Greenfield, E. (1988). *Under the Sunday tree* (A. Ferguson, Illus.). New York: Harper & Row. (1–5). POETRY.

This collection of poems focuses on family and the Caribbean Islands.

Hoberman, M. A. (1982). *A house is a house for me* (B. Fraser, Illus.). New York: Penguin. (PreK–2). POETRY.*

Rhyming verses tell about many kinds of houses.

Hopkins, L. B. (1989). *Still as a star: A book of nighttime poems* (K. Milone, Illus.). Boston: Little, Brown. (K–3). POETRY.

A collection of bedtime poems.

Hopkins, L. B. (1994). *Hand in hand* (P. M. Fiore, Illus.). New York: Simon & Schuster. (3–7). POETRY.*

U.S. history is developed through poetry.

Hopkins, L. B. (1999). *Sports! Sports! Sports! A poetry collection* (B. Floca, Illus.). New York: HarperCollins. (3–6). POETRY.*

Twenty poems explore the pleasures of sports, from baseball to basketball, track, soccer, swimming, and football.

Hubbell, P. (1987). When dinosaurs ruled the earth (M. Tinkleman, Illus.). In L. B. Hopkins (Ed.), *Dinosaurs: Poems.* New York: Harcourt Brace Jovanovich. (3–6). POETRY.

A collection of dinosaur poems.

Hubbell, P. (1991). Bedtime and Miss Mary Mack. In N. Larrick (Ed.), *Let's do a poem!* New York: Delacorte. (K–3). POETRY.

A bedtime poem in a collection of poems to fit most occasions.

Hughes, L. (1932). Dreams. In *The dream keeper and other poems.* New York: Knopf. (3–7). POETRY.

This wonderful poem is ageless.

Isaacs, A. (1998). *Cat up a tree: A story in poems.* New York: Dutton. (K–3). POETRY.*

This book is a series of narrative poems that expresses how all of the participants feel about catching the cat.

Janeczko, P. B. (1988). *The music of what happens: Poems that tell stories.* New York: Orchard. (4–8). POETRY.

The poems in this book tell true stories about the lives of unknown people. Their lives create the music of what happens.

Janeczko, P. B. (1989). *Brickyard summer.* New York: Orchard. (5–7). POETRY.

Janeczko, P. B. (1990). *The place my words are looking for: What poets say about and through their work.* New York: Bradbury. (4–8). POETRY.

An anthology of contemporary poets with comments by the poets.

Janeczko, P. B. (1998). *That sweet diamond: Baseball poems* (C. Katchen, Illus.). New York: Atheneum. (3–7). POETRY.

The poet has captured the tension of baseball players, the fans—everyone in the stadium for a big game.

Johnson, A. (1998). *The other side: Shorter pieces.* New York: Orchard. (4–6). POETRY.

The poet writes about the razing of her hometown in the first person voice and illustrates it with photographs.

Kennedy, X. J. (1982). *Did Adam name the vinegarroon?* (H. J. Selig, Illus.). Boston: David Godine. (1–3). POETRY.

Poems about unusual animals.

Kennedy, X. J., & Kennedy, D. M. (Eds.). (1982). *Knock at a star: A child's introduction to poetry* (K. A. Weinhaus, Illus.). Boston: Little, Brown. (K–2). POETRY.

A collection of bedtime poems.

Knudson, R. R., & Swenson, M. (Eds.). (1988). *American sports poems.* New York: Orchard POETRY. (4–6).

Athletes and sports fans will enjoy these poems.

Kraus, R. (1970). *Whose mouse are you?* (J. Aruego, Illus.). New York: Macmillan. (PreK–2). POETRY, MODERN FANTASY.

A poem about a mouse whose family is gone, but he rescues them.

Kuskin, K. (1975). *Near the window tree.* New York: Harper. (4–6). POETRY.

Kuskin addresses childhood concerns and explains why she wrote each poem.

Kuskin, K. (1980). *Dogs & dragons, trees & dreams: A collection of poems.* New York: HarperCollins. (1–3). POETRY.*

Kuskin's introductions to the poems are an added asset.

Kuskin, K. (1992). *Soap soup and other verses.* New York: HarperCollins. (K–2). POETRY.*

Appealing poems about exploring the world.

Larrick, N. (1990). *Mice are nice* (E. Young, Illus.). New York: Philomel. (K–3). POETRY.

These verses describe mice, their habits, and their houses.

Lear, E. (1948). *The complete nonsense book.* New York: Dodd, Mead. (K–6). POETRY.

This is classic nonsense poetry.

Levy, C. (1998). *A crack in the clouds and other poems* (R. B. Corfield, Illus.). New York: McElderry. (4–6). POETRY.*

The poet uses simple language and varied cadences to tell about everyday things.

Lewis, J. P. (1998a). *Boshblobberbosh: Runcible poems for Edward Lear* (G. Kelley, Illus.). New York: Creative Editions. (4–6). POETRY.

The poet is a student of Lear's work, and he demonstrates his skill in creating nonsense in this book.

Lewis, J. P. (1998b). *Doodle dandies: Poems that take shape* (L. Desimini, Illus.). New York: Atheneum. (K–5). POETRY.

A collection of concrete poems.

Lewis, J. P. (1998c). *Riddle-lightful: Oodles of little riddle-poems* (D. Tilley, Illus.). New York: Knopf. (K–3). POETRY.*

A collection of short riddle-poems.

Lewis, J. P. (1998d). *The house of boo* (K. Krénina, Illus.). New York: Atheneum. (K–3). POETRY.

This is a spooky poem that is just right for Halloween.

Livingston, M. C. (1982). *A circle of seasons* (L. E. Fisher, Illus.). New York: Holiday House. (2–5). POETRY.

A collection of seasonal poetry.

Livingston, M. C. (1986). *Poems for Jewish holidays* (L. Bloom, Illus.). New York: Holiday House. (PreK–3). POETRY.

A collection of poems celebrating Jewish holidays.

Livingston, M. C. (1990). *If the owl calls again: A collection of owl poems* (A. Frasconi, Illus.). New York: McElderry. (3–6). POETRY.

All kinds of owl poems.

Livingston, M. C. (1991). *Poem-making: Ways to begin writing poetry.* New York: Harper. (5–8). POETRY.

This is a guide to creating poetry and includes excellent examples.

Livingston, M. C. (1997). *I am writing a poem about— A game of poetry.* New York: McElderry (3–6). POETRY.

Lyon, G. E. (1986). *A regular rolling Noah* (S. Gammell, Illus.). New York: Bradbury. (1–3). POETRY, PICTURE BOOK.

The story of moving farm animals in a train, which compares the boxcar to Noah's ark.

McCord, D. (1952). *Far and few, rhymes of the never was and always is* (H. B. Kane, Illus.). New York: Little, Brown. (K–4). POETRY.

This collection includes many of McCord's best rhythmic poems, including "Song of the Train."

Merriam, E. (1986). *Fresh paint: New poems.* New York: Macmillan. (1–4). POETRY.

This collection has 45 poems whose subjects range from squat mushrooms to the new moon.

Morrison, L. (1981). *Overheard in a bubble chamber and other science poems* (E. de Lanux, Illus.). New York: Lothrop, Lee, & Shepard. (3–6). POETRY.

Morrison, L. (1985). *The break dance kids.* New York: Lothrop. (3–6). POETRY.*

Morrison's poems have strong rhythms that invite people to move.

Morrison, L. (Selector). (1988). *Rhythm road: Poems to move to.* New York: Lothrop. (K–2). POETRY.*

Poems to move to. The topics include dancing, riding, watching water, hearing music, sports, work, and so on.

Parnall, P. (1989). *Quiet.* New York: Morrow Junior Books. (3–6). POETRY.

This book-length poem explores the meaning of quiet.

Prelutsky, J. (Comp.). (1983). *The Random House book of poetry for children* (A. Lobel, Illus.). New York: Random House. (K–6). POETRY.

A large collection of poetry arranged thematically.

Prelutsky, J. (1988). *Tyrannosaurus was a beast: Dinosaur poems.* (A. Lobel, Illus.). New York: Greenwillow. (K–4). POETRY.

Humorous poems about dinosaurs.

Prelutsky, J. (1990). *Something big has been here* (J. Stevenson, Illus.). New York: Greenwillow. (K–4). POETRY.*

This collection ranges from the boy who planted light bulbs in his hair to the more serious "Don't Yell at Me!"

Richards, L. (1983). Eletelephony. In J. Prelutsky (Ed.), A. Lobel (Illus.). *The Random House book of poetry for children.* New York: Random House. (K–6). POETRY.

A funny, nonsense poem.

Rylant, C. (1984). *Waiting to waltz: A childhood* (S. Gammell, Illus.). New York: Bradbury. (3–6). POETRY.

Autobiographical poems about the small and large crises in a child's life.

Rylant, C. (1989). *But I'll be back again: An album.* New York: Orchard. (4–8). POETRY.

This work is autobiographical of Rylant's childhood experiences.

Schertle, A. (1995). *Advice for a frog and other poems* (N. Green, Illus.). New York: Lothrop. (K–4). POETRY.

This collection of poems pays tribute to some of nature's most remarkable animals.

Shaik, F. (1997). *The jazz of our street* (E. B. Lewis, Illus.). New York: Dial. (1–5). POETRY.

This poetic story is set in New Orleans where jazz parades are common. The rhythmic language creates the feel of jazz music.

Siebert, D. (1984). *Truck song* (B. Barton, Illus.). New York: Crowell. (1–5). PICTURE BOOK, POETRY.

The rhythm of wheels on the road is expressed in this poem.

Siebert, D. (1990). *Train song* (M. Wimmer, Illus.). New York: Crowell. (1–5). POETRY, PICTURE BOOK.

A book-length poem with the rhythm of train wheels. Movement, sights, and sounds of trains are expressed through rhyme and rhythm.

Silverstein, S. (1974). *Where the sidewalk ends: The poems & drawings of Shel Silverstein.* New York: Harper (5–12). POETRY.*

Humorous poetry exploring the joys and fears of childhood.

Smith, W. J. (1990). *Birds and beasts* (J. Hnizdovsky, Illus.). Boston: Godine. (3–6). POETRY.

Creative verses illustrated with woodcuts that enhance the humor.

Snyder, Z. K. (1969). Poem to Mud (J. Arms, Illus.). In *Today is Saturday.* New York: Atheneum. (1–4). POETRY.

Poems about life outside of school.

Swann, B. (1998a). *The house with no door: African riddle-poems* (A. Bryan, Illus.). New York: Browndeer Press/Harcourt Brace. (1–4). POETRY.*

A collection of riddles from Africa.

Swann, B. (1998b). *Touching the distance: Native American riddle-poems.* New York: Browndeer Press/Harcourt Brace. (1–4). POETRY.*

A book of riddle-poems from Native American cultures.

Viorst, J. (1981). *If I were in charge of the world and other worries: Poems for children and their parents* (L. Cherry, Illus.). New York: Atheneum. (1–4). POETRY.

Poetry about children's lives and worries.

Welber, R. (1972). *The train* (D. Ray, Illus.). New York: Pantheon. (K–2). POETRY.

Explores everyday things that frighten children such as trains and unexplained noises.

Willard, N. (1981). *A visit to William Blake's Inn: Poems for innocent and experienced travelers* (A. and M. Provensen, Illus.). San Diego: Harcourt Brace Jovanovich. (2–4). POETRY.

Withers, C. (Comp.). (1988). *A rocket in my pocket: The rhymes and chants of young Americans.* (S. Suba, Illus.). New York: Henry Holt. (K–4). POETRY.

A collection of rhythmic chants, songs, and verses.

Worth, V. (1972). *Small poems* (N. Babbitt, Illus.). New York: Farrar, Straus & Giroux. (PreK–3). POETRY.

Small poems for young children, including "Frog."

Worth, V. (1978). *Small poems again* (N. Babbitt, Illus.). New York: Farrar, Straus & Giroux. (PreK–3). POETRY.

This is another volume of small poems.

Yolen, J. (1990). *Dinosaur dances* (B. Degen, Illus.). New York: Putnam. (1–4). POETRY.

This work includes poems about all kinds of dinosaurs who dance everything from ballet to chorus line.

Zolotow, C. (1980). *Say it!* (J. Stevenson, Illus.). New York: Greenwillow. (PreK–3). POETRY.

Mother and child play a language game as they walk through the autumn air.

References and Books for Further Reading

Abercrombie, B. (Ed.). (1977). The other side of a poem (H. Bertschamann, Illus.). New York: Harper.

Bagert, B. (1992). Act it out: Making poetry come alive. In B. Cullinan (Ed.), *Invitation to read: More children's literature in the reading program.* Newark, DE: International Reading Association.

Behr, C. C. (1995). Jack Prelutsky. In A. Silvey (Ed.), *Children's books and their creators.* Boston: Houghton Mifflin.

Bridge, E. (1966). *Using children's choices and reactions to poetry as determinants in enriching literary experience in the middle grades* (University microfilm no. 67-6246). Philadelphia: Temple University.

Crisp, S. (1991). Children's poetry in the United States: The best of the 1980's. *Children's Literature in Education, 22,* 143–160.

Cullinan, B., Scala, M., & Schroder, V. (1995). *Three voices: An invitation to poetry across the curriculum.* York, ME: Stenhouse Publishers.

Dias, P. (1987). *Making sense of poetry.* Ottawa, ONT: Canadian Council of Teachers of English.

Fisher, C., & Natarella, M. (1982). Young children's preferences in poetry: A national survey of first, second, and third graders. *Research in the Teaching of English, 16,* 339–354.

Fleischman, P. (1986). Sound and sense. *The Horn Book, 62,* 551–555.

Frye, N. (1964). *The educated imaginations.* Bloomington: Indiana University Press.

Hearne, B. (1991). *Choosing books for children: A commonsense approach.* New York: Delacorte.

Hopkins, L. B. (1998). *Pass the poetry, please!* New York: Harper.

Ingham, R. (1980). *The poetry preferences of fourth- and fifth-grade students in a suburban setting in 1980.* Unpublished doctoral dissertation, University of Houston, Texas.

Larrick, N. (1991). *Let's do a poem!* New York: Delacorte.

Lenz, L. (1992). Crossroads of literacy and orality: Reading poetry aloud. *Language Arts, 69,* 597–603.

Livingston, M. C. (Ed.). (1968). Editor's note. In *A tune beyond us.* New York: Harcourt.

Livingston, M. C. (1976). But is it poetry? *The Horn Book, 52,* 24–31.

Livingston, M. C. (1981). Nonsense verse: The complete escape. In B. Hearne and M. Kaye (Eds.). *Celebrating children's books* (pp. 122–142). New York: Lothrop, Lee, & Shepard.

Livingston, M. C. (1991). *Poem-making: Ways to begin writing poetry.* New York: HarperCollins.

Lukens, R. (1986). *A critical handbook of children's literature* (4th ed.). Glenview, IL: Scott Foresman.

McCracken, R., & McCracken, M. (1983). Chants, charts and 'chievement. In J. Cowen (Ed.), *Teaching through the arts* (pp. 44–50). Newark, DE: International Reading Association.

Morner, K., & Rausch, R. (1991). *NTC's dictionary of literary terms.* Lincolnwood, IL: National Textbook Company.

Parsons, L. (1992). *Poetry themes and activities.* Portsmouth, NH: Heinemann.

Peck, P. (1979). Poetry: A turn-on to reading. In J. Shapiro (Ed.), *Using literature and poetry affectively* (pp. 92–105). Newark, DE: International Reading Association.

Perrine, L. (1969). *Sound and sense: An introduction to poetry* (3rd ed.). New York: Harcourt.

Russell, D. L. (1991). *Literature for children: A short introduction.* New York: Longman.

Sebesta, S. (1983). Choosing poetry. In N. Roser & M. Frith (Eds.), *Children's choices: Teaching with books children like* (pp. 56–70). Newark, DE: International Reading Association.

Silvey, A. (1995). *Children's books and their creators.* Boston: Houghton Mifflin.

Simmons, M. (1980). *Intermediate-grade children's preferences in poetry.* Unpublished doctoral dissertation, University of Alabama, Birmingham.

Terry, A. (1974). *Children's poetry preferences: A national survey of upper elementary grades.* Urbana, IL: National Council of Teachers of English.

Make-Believe: Traditional Literature and Modern Fantasy

KEY TERMS

ballad	legend
fable	modern fantasy
fantastic elements	myth
folktale	pourquoi tales
high fantasy	science fiction

GUIDING QUESTIONS

Consider the folktales you heard as a child. What were your favorites: *Goldilocks, Tom Thumb, Jack and the Beanstalk,* or *Cinderella*? Do you still like these stories? Do you think children still enjoy these stories? Thinking about the stories you enjoyed as a child will help you understand what children today enjoy. As you read, keep the following questions in mind:

1. Why is traditional literature so popular?

2. How are traditional literature and modern fantasy alike?

3. How are the *Star Wars* movies related to modern fantasy?

4. Why is fantasy an important type of literature for children?

OVERVIEW

Traditional literature or folklore is ancient make-believe that combines myth, legend, folktales, anecdotes, sayings, and songs that have been passed down from one generation to the next, and oral storytelling. These tales reflect a people's concept of themselves—"their beliefs,

hopes and fears, courage and humor, sense of delight in the odd, fascination with the supernatural" (Miller, 1995, p. 22). In fact, Frye (1964) claims that all literature is rooted in these ancient tales. As you read folktales, you will discover current stories that have similar themes and plot structures. For example, the *Jack and the Beanstalk* story is a hero tale wherein a young boy overcomes a larger, dangerous character to prove himself. A similar pattern is found in all genre of literature including realistic fiction, such as *Shiloh* (Naylor, 1991).

Similar characters apppear in traditional literature and fantasy. Among the most obvious common characters are dragons. *The Dragon's Robe* by Lattimore is a traditional Chinese tale set in the Sung dynasty. In this tale, a weaver saves her people from disaster brought on by dishonest characters who refuse to honor the dragon shrine. Children who read the foreword notes will discover how carefully Lattimore researched the enchanting illustrations. Margaret Shannon gives readers quite a different take on dragons in *Elvira* who enjoys dressing up and playing with daisy chains rather than eating princesses. In this fantasy, Elvira runs away to join a group of princesses after she is teased. Stories like these offer many opportunities for reader responses, and they motivate further reading to learn about the many varieties of dragons.

INTRODUCTION

Traditional literature and modern fantasy are treated together in this chapter because they are closely related genres. Similar patterns, themes, and characters appear in these make-believe stories. Traditional tales were make-believe stories spun by storytellers, and these stories continue in contemporary cultures as well.

Fantasy is contemporary make-believe that usually focuses on philosophical questions such as the conflict between good and evil in the universe. Writers of fantasy have a formidable task: they must convince readers to believe in magic, at least for a little while. "The more fantastic a piece of fiction is, the harder the writer must work to make it believable" (Hearne, 1990, p. 84). In creating fantasy, authors must adhere to strict rules; they cannot wave a wand to solve all of the dilemmas confronting the protagonist. Fantasy stimulates the imagination and should be an important part of children's lives so that they continue to dream and imagine. Reading workshops such as the one described in the following vignette enhance children's explorations of traditional literature and fantasy.

VIGNETTE

Jim Summers took advantage of his second graders' physical education class to check out the *Children's Literature Web Guide.* He found 7 pages of material related to Cinderella stories, including versions of the story, references, other Internet resources, and teaching ideas. This made his planning much easier. After the students returned, he directed them to their reading workshop groups.

The children eagerly joined their workshop groups.

Mr. Summers said, "Last week, I read *Stone Soup* and *Nail Soup,* and quite a few of you asked to read more folktales like these. I couldn't locate more versions of *Stone Soup* at the library, so I collected 'Cinderella' stories. You'll find several of these stories at each workstation. Scan the books and decide on one for your group to read and study." The workshop groups chose from the following books:

- *The Girl Who Wanted to Hunt* by Emery Bernhard and Durga Bernhard.
- *Cinderella* by Charles Perrault, illustrated by Marcia Brown.
- *The Korean Cinderella* by Shirley Climo.
- *Tattercoats* by Joseph Jacobs.
- *The Way Meat Loves Salt* by Nina Jaffe.

- *Yeh-Shen: A Cinderella Story From China* by Ai-Ling Louie.
- *The Rough-Face Girl* by Rafe Martin.
- *The Turkey Girl: A Zuni Cinderella Story* by Penny Pollock.
- *Cendrillon: A Caribbean Cinderella* by Robert San Souci.

After reading and discussion, each group settled on a book to read.

"Why are these books called 'Cinderella' books?" Matt queried. "They don't even have 'Cinderella' in the title. This one is called *The Rough-Face Girl.*"

Mr. Summers answered, "That is a Native American Cinderella. Each of these books is from a different country or culture."

"Oh! This one is from Siberia. Where is Siberia?" Shannon asked.

"And this one is from China," Melissa said.

"How do you think we should study these Cinderella stories?" Mr. Summers asked.

Cory suggested, "We need to figure out what countries our stories are from first."

"Good idea," Mr. Summers said. "What other questions should we ask?"

Each group discussed the questions they should ask and compiled this list:

1. What country or culture did this story come from?
2. What is the main character's (i.e., Cinderella) name?
3. Does the story have a fairy godmother?
4. Does every story have a magic slipper?
5. Does every story have a prince?
6. How are the stories different?
7. How are the stories alike?
8. What does the story tell us?
9. How do you think the story is different because of the country it comes from?
10. How does each story begin and end?

UNDERSTANDING REAL AND MAKE-BELIEVE

Children's understanding of the difference between real and make-believe is vital to their appreciation of both folk literature and fantasy and also to their ability to discriminate fact from fiction (Applebee, 1978). Children eventually learn that underlying patterns exist in both fiction and fact. Pitcher and Prelinger (1963) studied children's stories to identify formal openings or titles, formal closings, and consistent use of past tense. They discovered that even 2-year-olds understood some story structures and used introductions such as "once upon a time" and closings such as "they lived happily ever after," showing the early influence of folktales. Children need fantasy in their lives: Even very young children who are protected from fairy tales and exposed only to informative literature invent their own fantasies, which include many of the same characteristics as traditional folktales (Chukovsky, 1963).

Ability to understand make-believe is linked to development, and children exhibit a wide range of individual differences in acquiring this ability. Five-year-olds generally are still developing concepts of fantasy and realism, while 7- and 9-year-olds ordinarily have acquired these concepts (Harms, 1972). Some children are still confused about fantasy and reality as late as age 6: Many 6-year-olds recognize that Cinderella is not real, although they tend to think that she once lived, and some 73% in one study were uncertain whether story characters and events were real (Applebee, 1978). The same study, however, reports that children recognize nonsense at quite an early age.

TRADITIONAL LITERATURE

Traditional literature includes folktales from all the cultures in the world. It differs from other literature in that it was transmitted orally from generation to generation. Although folk literature now exists in both written and oral forms, it survived for centuries only in the memory of storytellers who shared their personal versions of the same stories with different audiences, perpetuating them in much the same way a pebble sends ripples out in a pool. The Cinderella story alone has nearly 1,000 variants (Thompson, 1951). Folktales were transferred from oral language to written by collectors such as the Brothers Grimm and Charles Perrault.

Both traditional literature and modern fantasy originate in humanity itself in stories of the "folk" that mirror the culture of origin, as well as the mores and values of that culture. The make-believe in traditional literature and fantasy entertain as well as disseminate cultural beliefs and mores to other generations and cultures. They provided children with cautionary tales to guide their behavior. Folktales have to do with accomplishing impossible feats, escaping from powerful enemies, outwitting wicked people, earning a living, securing food, and protecting the weak. For example, *Little Plum,* a modern picture-book version of the Tom Thumb story by Ed Young, teaches that size has very little to do with success and ability.

Traditional literature is a chain of communication through the centuries—a long folk memory stretching from ancient times to the present (Hunter, 1975). "Before writing there was story. Before story there was language" (Saxby & Winch, 1987). Folk literature represents the accumulated wisdom and art of humankind springing from the many cultures in the world. Primitive humans shared, celebrated, and remembered experiences through story, art, and dance. Stories in these early days were transmitted by word of mouth—in fact, the word *tale* means "oral" in the original Anglo-Saxon language. Storytellers entertained and instructed with timeless tales of greed, jealousy, love, and need for security as they relaxed around nightly campfires. Storytellers, bards, minstrels, poets, and rhymers of old were venerated; they were welcomed into palaces and huts alike and accorded places of honor.

The tales we enjoy today have been polished and edited by storytellers throughout history as they shared stories from their own cultures using their own idioms, perspectives, and values. Every time a storyteller tells a tale, the story changes, giving rise to thousands of variations of a single tale, which grows or shrinks over time as portions are expanded or omitted by different tellers. A folktale is a living thing that outlives its creator. The names of the people who first told these tales are lost in the mists of time. Today's written versions are derived from those ancient stories; for this reason folktale creators are called *retellers, collectors,* and *illustrators.*

The form and content of folktales, although grounded in vastly different cultures, are often remarkably similar. People throughout the world share common human concerns. The details and modifications that appear in folktale variations reflect the society or culture that produced them, giving anthropologists a window into culture. Folklore tells about the times in which its creators lived (Schwartz, 1977).

The Contemporary Values of Traditional Literature

Traditional literature enjoys continued popularity; it entertains modern children just as it once delighted children and adults around the campfires of long ago. Over the years, many of the Caldecott Medal books have belonged to this genre, including Marcia Brown's *Cinderella* and Paul Zelinsky's *Rapunzel*. Moreover, authors continue to create many delightful books in this genre. For example, Jeanne Steig's *A Handful of Beans: Six Fairy Tales* is a recent collection of fairy tale retellings that is an excellent read-aloud. Another popular tale is *Ouch!*, which is Natalie Babbitt's retelling of a Grimm tale. In this story, Marco, who was born into an unremarkable family, becomes king by using his wits. Even though characters' feats are imaginary, we enjoy imagining they could happen.

In traditional stories, characters can do things not permitted in real life (Dundes, 1965). Storytellers can comfort children or frighten them depending upon the teller's purpose. They can express anger and frustration without fear of reprisal. When folktale heroes celebrate overcoming monsters, giants, dragons, and other disreputable forces, they give us heroes, wise men, wizards, and magicians.

> Nothing in the entire range of children's literature—with rare exceptions—can be as enriching and satisfying to child and adult alike as the folk fairy tale. . . . A child can learn more about the inner problems of man and about solutions to his own (and our) predicaments in any society, than he can from any other type of story within his comprehension. (Bettelheim, 1975, p. 76)

Traditional literature is a rich source of content for multicultural studies and global education that can be used to develop children's cultural consciousness. Leigh Casler's Native American tale *The Boy Who Dreamed of an Acorn* teaches that all children are searching for their place in the world and that all children have dreams. *The Lion's Whiskers: An Ethiopian Folktale* by Nancy Raines Day develops both cultural and personal understanding. Ann Grifalconi portrayed the lifestyle of the Amhara people when she created the original illustrations for this book. Alison Lurie

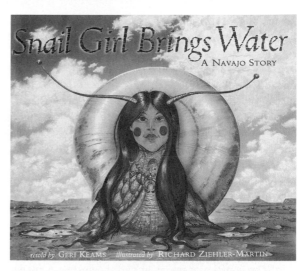

This Navajo tale tells how the snail brought water and why snails carry a water bottle on their backs.

featured a well-known folktale figure in the Russian tale *The Black Geese: A Baba Yaga Story from Russia*. The Baba Yaga is the house that walks on chicken-like legs and feet.

Folktales have been and continue to be controversial. Early in the nineteenth century they were controversial because they did not provide direct, specific moral instruction (Saxby & Winch, 1987). More recently, parents and teachers have expressed concern about the violence in folktales; some versions of traditional stories have been rewritten to "launder" or "sanitize" them (Rothman, 1990). In some instances, the vocabulary of traditional tales is changed; in others the plot is altered. For example, a puppet show of *Little Red Riding Hood* punished the wolf by sending him to the zoo. Fortunately, traditional tales seem to be resilient and indestructible; they have withstood all assaults.

Elements of Traditional Literature

Traditional stories have the elements of plot, setting, characters, theme, and style; however, they are developed in different ways than in other forms of fiction. Characters are usually stereotypes and few in number, plots and settings lack subtle nuances and development, and description is minimal. Storytellers include just enough events to make the story interesting. Plot and setting can be sketched quickly and the stereotyped characters dropped into place. The story becomes boring when too many attempts are made to solve a problem or conflict; therefore, storytellers quickly introduce the conflict.

In the European tradition, three is the magic number, so we find three attempts to climb the glass mountain, three riddles to answer, three brothers to seek their fortune, or three wishes. In Asian folktales, the magic number is usually four. Three or four attempts or incidents seem to be just the right number to make most stories interesting without dragging them out too long. Figure 8.1 illustrates the components of traditional tales and models a comparison of these tales which you may use in the classroom.

Plot

A well-structured plot has conflict, suspense, and action. The conflict or problem and the suspense appear early in the story. The suspense builds as the hero or heroine makes a series of attempts to resolve the conflict or problem. Plot development is logical within the framework of the story: Each incident builds on the preceding action. The mounting suspense surrounding the problem solution or conflict resolution holds attention. After the climax, story action ends with the falling action of the denouement.

Plots in traditional literature are always extremely brief and highly predictable. The characters are usually symbolic of good and evil. After a quick start, the plot moves forward rapidly and the principal character moves the plot along to a quick climax. Although magic may be used to move the plot forward, it must be logical within the framework of the story. The listener expects good to reign supreme, and it always does, and so we find few surprises regarding story outcomes.

Typical story structures in traditional tales are sequential (beginning, middle, end), circular (ends up about where it began), and cumulative (additions and repetitions build the story). Figure 8.2, *Goldilocks and the Three Bears,* illustrates the sequential building of events to a quick resolution, and Figure 8.3 shows the circular structure of *The Little Red Hen.*

Setting

Brevity is a hallmark of story introductions in traditional literature. Descriptions of times and places are unnecessary to the fast-moving plot. Time is developed with stock phrases such as "once upon a time" and "long ago and far away." This brevity sets a stage for the story that would be difficult to improve upon. The setting may be a castle, a peasant's hut, or a forest, but again brevity is the key word. In telling the Molly Whuppie story, a teller changed the setting from a peasant's hut to the forest, then to the giant's castle, and finally to the king's castle with no more description than that the king's castle was grander than the giant's castle, which was simply described as being huge. The most important aspect of place in traditional literature is creating a backdrop for characters' actions.

Characters

Only a few characters are needed to tell most folktales. These flat, stereotyped characters are clearly recognizable as symbols of good or evil who spring into action at the outset of the story to solve a problem or end a conflict without much in the way of character development. The good characters are totally good and the bad ones are altogether bad. Listeners learn almost nothing about Cinderella other than her stereotypically "good" traits; therefore, she is a flat rather than a round character because the finer nuances of her character are not re-

FIGURE 8.1	Chart comparing *Molly Whuppie* to other traditional tales.				
Title	Characters	Setting	Villain	Hero/Heroine	Conclusion
Molly Whuppie	Three girls	Woods/giant's castle/king's castle	Giant	Molly	Molly saves herself and her sisters
Jack and the Beanstalk	Jack, his mother, the giant's wife, the giant	Giant's house	Giant	Jack	Jack saves himself and gets the means to support his mother
Hansel and Gretel	Hansel and Gretel, stepmother, father, and witch	Woods, witch's hut	Wicked stepmother and witch	Hansel and Gretel	Hansel and Gretel escape and get to eat all the food they want

vealed. The flat characters are one reason children enjoy folktales. Good characters are rewarded and bad characters are punished, such as when the wolf villain in *Red Riding Hood* is killed to rescue the grandma he ate. These moralistic stories appeal to children, who tend to see people as completely good or completely bad. They love to cheer when the "bad guys" get what they deserve and when dreams come true for good characters. Small, weak characters win and are rewarded, whereas evil characters lose and are punished.

Theme

Traditional stories have significant themes illustrating cultural values and mores. Characters exhibit traits of humility, courage, honesty, patience, and dreams come true for good characters. Small, hard-working characters are honored with riches, magical powers, palaces, and delicious banquets. Traditional literature teaches lessons such as the importance of the inner qualities of love and kindness. Seemingly weak characters have

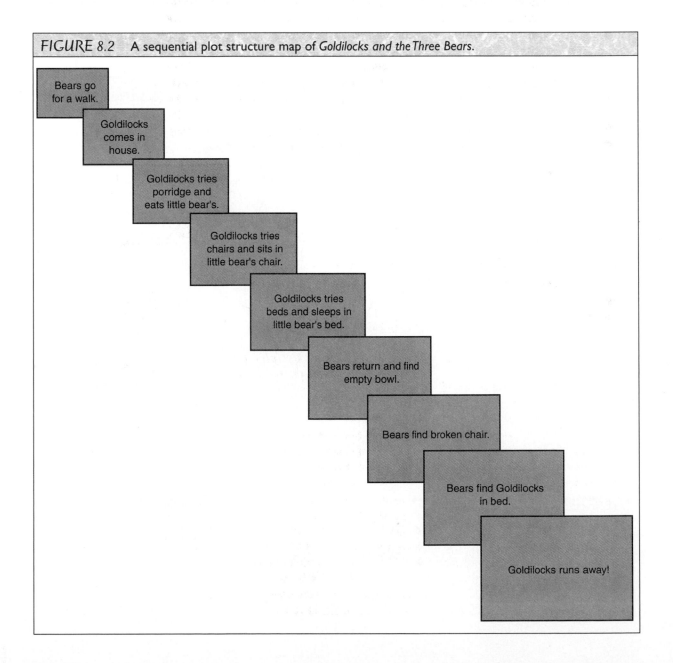

FIGURE 8.2   A sequential plot structure map of *Goldilocks and the Three Bears*.

Bears go for a walk.

Goldilocks comes in house.

Goldilocks tries porridge and eats little bear's.

Goldilocks tries chairs and sits in little bear's chair.

Goldilocks tries beds and sleeps in little bear's bed.

Bears return and find empty bowl.

Bears find broken chair.

Bears find Goldilocks in bed.

Goldilocks runs away!

virtues that enable them to achieve success in the face of violence and cruelty.

Style

One of the hallmarks of folktale styles is the formulaic beginnings used to establish setting and characters and invite listeners: "long ago and far away" or "once there was and was not." Folktales also have formulaic endings such as "they lived happily ever after" or the ending of *Three Billy Goats Gruff,* "snip, snap, snout; this tale's told out."

The language style is succinct and direct. These stories are compact; they retain a sense of their oral language beginnings although they may be read. Some folktales include stylistic devices such as rhymes, verses, or repetition. *The Three Little Pigs* is built around these devices with a repeated rhyming verse appearing several times:

Wolf: "Little pig, little pig, let me come in!"

Pig: "Not by the hair of my chinny chin chin."

Wolf: "Then I'll huff, and I'll puff, and I'll blow your house in."

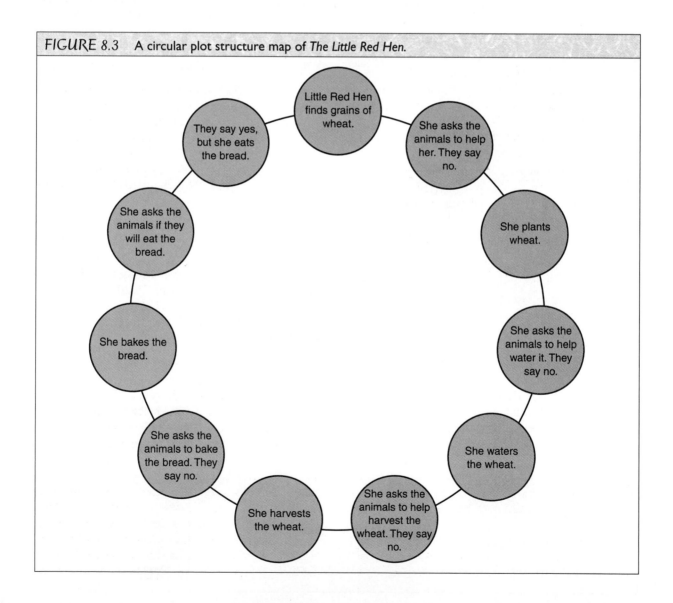

FIGURE 8.3   A circular plot structure map of *The Little Red Hen.*

Types of Traditional Literature

The term *folk* can refer to any group of people whatsoever who share at least one common factor (Dundes, 1965). Folklore exists where people share an identity, when they recognize themselves as members of a group united by race, nationality, occupation, class, geography, or age (Opie & Opie, 1974). Consequently, the category of folklore embraces the lore of groups such as lumberjacks, railroad workers, African Americans, Jews, Armenians, and schoolteachers because each of these groups shares common factors and has its own stories.

According to Dundes (1965), folklore includes myths, legends, folktales, jokes, proverbs, riddles, chants, charms, blessings, curses, oaths, insults, retorts, taunts, teases, toasts, tongue-twisters, greeting and leave-taking formulas, folk costumes, folk dance, folk drama, folk art, folk superstition, folk medicine, folk instrumental music, folk songs, folk speech (slang), folk similes (e.g., blind as a bat), folk metaphors (e.g., paint the town red), and names (e.g., nicknames). Many of these types of folklore are found in *Granny, Will Your Dog Bite, and Other Mountain Rhymes*. To experience the folklore in this volume, Gerald Milnes, the reteller, collected the rhymes, songs, riddles, and so forth in West Virginia from a man who greeted him with, "Just throw your hat on the bed, spit on the fire, sit down on your fist, lean back against your thumb, and make yourself at home."

Folk poetry ranges from oral epics to autograph-book verse, epitaphs, latrinalia (i.e., writings on the walls of public bathrooms), limericks, ball-bouncing rhymes, jump-rope jingles, finger and toe rhymes, dandling rhymes (to bounce children on the knee), counting-out rhymes (to determine who will be "it" in games), and nursery rhymes.

Folk literature is published in two forms, picture books of single tales and collections of folktales, also usually illustrated. Both collections and single tales generally identify retellers rather than authors because these are retellings or reinterpretations of existing stories rather than original tales. In some instances, an illustrator is creating new pictures for a well-known folktale, which may also constitute a new interpretation of a story.

Traditional literature is classified in various ways and authorities differ in the terminology they use. However, folktales (also called *wonder tales* and *household tales*) consist of all kinds of narrative originating in the oral tradition (Thompson, 1951). In this sense, the category of folktales encompasses all traditional literature. Fairy tales, animal tales, myths, legends, tall tales, and ballads are all folktales. The forms of folktales, discussed in this section and summarized in Table 8.1, represent the majority of traditional literature in print for children today.

"New folktales"

Authors who create alternate versions of classic folktales are creating "new folktales"; in fact, some people call these "fractured fairy tales." These stories are not true folktales, but they are fun. Both children and adults find these stories stimulating and they are particularly good for stimulating writing experiences. Following are a few examples of these excellent stories.

- *Jim and the Beanstalk* by Raymond Briggs.
- *The Frog Prince, Continued* by Jon Scieszka, illustrated by Steve Johnson.
- *The True Story of the 3 Little Pigs* by Jon Scieszka, illustrated by Lane Smith.
- *The Stinky Cheese Man and Other Fairly Stupid Tales* by Jon Scieszka, illustrated by Lane Smith.

Fairy tales

Fairy tales are unbelievable stories featuring magic and the supernatural. Fairies, giants, witches, dwarves, good people, and bad people in fairy tales live in supernatural worlds with enchanted toadstools and crystal lakes. Heroes and heroines in these stories have supernatural assistance in solving problems. *Snow White and the Seven Dwarfs* is a typical fairy tale.

Animal tales

Folktales are often told with animals that have human characteristics as the main characters. *The Little Red Hen* falls into this category of folktale. One of the most ancient types of story, fables, are animal tales. In these stories, the animals symbolize humans, often to make a specific point or teach a moral lesson, which is explicitly stated at the end of the fable. *Aesop's Fables* are among the best-known fables in the Western culture, and *Jataka Tales* are well known in the Eastern culture.

Trickster tales are also animal tales. The principal character in these stories is amoral, neither good nor bad. Tricksters laugh when they should not and are always

	TABLE 8.1	
	Common types of traditional literature.	
Type	Characteristics	Example
Folktales	giants, witches, magic, tasks, ogres	*Jack and the Beanstalk* *Goldilocks and the Three Bears*
Cumulative folktales	repeat actions, refrains in sequence	*Henny Penny, Johnny Cake*
Fairy tales	magic and wonder	*Cinderella, Beauty and the Beast*
Animal tales	animals who outwit enemies	*Little Red Hen, Three Billy Goats Gruff*
Fables	animal stories that teach a lesson	*The Hare and the Tortoise*
Trickster tales	tales in which characters are able to dupe other characters (especially rabbits and coyotes)	*Brer Rabbit*
Noodlehead tales (humorous folktales)	silly humans, stupid characters	*The Princess and the Pea, Simple Simon*
Myths	explain the origin of the world and natural phenomena	Greek myths
Pourquoi tales	explain why certain things are the way they are	*How the Snake Got Its Rattles* *How the Rabbit Got a Short Tail*
Legends	often based on historical figures with embellished deeds	*Robin Hood, King Arthur*
Tall tales	larger-than-life characters	*Daniel Boone, Paul Bunyan*
Ballads	rhyme and rhythm set to music	*Granny, Will Your Dog Bite, and Other Mountain Rhymes*

"up to" something, but tricksters are charming and likable and tend to escape punishment. The trickster's function in folk literature is to keep us from taking ourselves too seriously (Lester, 1988). Trickster tales appear in every culture, although the trickster animal varies among cultures. Brer Rabbit is a well-known trickster character for children in the United States. Native Americans identify the coyote as a trickster, and tales from the African tradition have a spider as trickster.

Noodlehead tales, drolls, and simpleton tales

The principal character in these stories is an engaging fool. They are popular because they represent the underdog who wins, the good-hearted fool who triumphs. A common theme in noodlehead stories is the simpleton or fool who trades something of value for a worthless object. Lazy Jack, one of the most famous of these characters, trades a cow for some worthless beans in one popular story. Of course, in the end the worthless objects turn out to be valuable—they grow a giant beanstalk.

Myths

Myths are stories about gods and supernatural beings. Myths explain human origins and events in nature, and tie relationships between humans and the supernatural. Myths occur in all cultures. Perhaps the best-known myths are pourquoi tales, also called *why stories.* These myths explain why the rabbit has a short tail, why the elephant has a long trunk, and so forth.

Legends

Legends are closely related to myths, but the main characters are frequently based on actual historical figures, such as religious saints, rather than supernatural beings. Although usually based in truth about a person, place, or event, legends tend to embellish and embroider the truth in order to showcase a particular virtue so that the character's wonderful feats grow more amazing with each telling. For instance, King Arthur and his knights of the Round Table exemplify chivalrous behavior; Joan of Arc exemplifies courage and conviction; Robin Hood and his Merry Men exemplify taking care of the poor. A famous U.S. legend involves George Washington, who refused to lie about chopping down a cherry tree despite the fact that he would be punished for admitting the crime. Other types of legend explain rocks, mountains, and other natural features, as do the Australian writer Oodgeroo's stories about Mother Earth's features as well as her legends about trees.

Published and unpublished legends exist throughout the United States, and local and regional legends are especially interesting to students. Charles Harry Whedbee collected stories about the North Carolina coast in *Outer Banks Mysteries & Seaside Stories.* Another legend appears in *The Legend of Sleeping Bear,* by Kathy-Jo Wargin, which tells the story of the Sleeping Bear Dune in Michigan.

Tall tales

Tall tales are based on lies and exaggerations about larger-than-life characters such as Fin M'Coul, John Henry, Mike Fink, Davy Crockett, Johnny Appleseed, and Daniel Boone. As with legends, some of the characters in tall tales actually lived, whereas others may be a composite of several people; many are entirely fiction. These stories are probably the precursors of the larger-than-life characters in modern novels (Saxby & Winch, 1987) such as Crocodile Dundee of movie fame, Pocahontas made famous by the Disney movie, and *Swamp Angel.*

Ballads

Ballads are essentially dramatic poems that tell stories handed down from one generation to the next through song. These narrative poems have marked rhythm and rhyme. They may include passages of dialogue, a chorus or refrain and formalized phrases that recur from ballad to ballad. Ballads usually tell stories about heroes, murders, love, tragedies, and feuds. "The Streets of Laredo" is a ballad that tells of a cowboy's exploits (Sutherland & Livingston, 1984). "Stagolee" is an African-American hero who is the subject of both ballads and folktales (Lester, 1969). The Australian ballad "Waltzing Matilda," which American children enjoy, tells about life in the Australian bush. Traditional ballads can serve as a good introduction to literature in general and to poetry in specific: Ballads introduce children to the themes of great literature and tune their ears to the rhythms of poetry.

Clio, a cat, wrote about her lives in nine different historical times.

Selecting and Evaluating Traditional Literature

The factors to consider when selecting and evaluating traditional literature are basically the same as for all literature. Some specific guidelines to keep in mind as you add to your collection are:

1. Does the book tell a good story?
2. Does the dust jacket or the foreword identify the book as traditional literature and tell the original cultural source of the selection? Does the reteller identify the source of the tale?
3. What characteristics of traditional literature does it have (e.g., formulaic beginning or ending, universal setting stated briefly, little or no description, etc.)?
4. Does the story have rapid plot development?
5. Are the characters symbolic? Can children relate to them?
6. Is the style simple and direct?
7. Does the story express universal values?

MODERN FANTASY

Modern fantasy is the literature of imagination, which is so important that Albert Einstein is quoted as saying, "Imagination is more important than knowledge" (Shlain, 1990, p. 119). "Fantasy allows authors to create extraordinary worlds and to people them with characters who challenge and expand our sense of the norm" (Greenlaw, 1995, p. 236). These imagined worlds permit authors to explore the basic truths of our world. In this way, good fantasy can help readers understand reality. According to Eisner (1992), "We cannot know through language what we cannot imagine. The image—visual, tactile, auditory—plays a crucial role in the construction of meaning through text. Those who cannot imagine cannot read" (p. 125).

Authors of fantasy effortlessly use imaginary elements to create a seamless story so real that the reader cannot avoid accepting it. The story cannot "clank," jarring the reader back to reality (Greenlaw, 1995). Readers willingly suspend disbelief to join in the magic and believe this story could actually happen. Then, they accept the magic that enables pigs to fly, animals to talk, entire villages to appear and disappear, and clocks to strike 13.

Modern fantasy is richly varied, ranging from simple stories of magic to profoundly complex stories such as the *Star Wars* movies. These films are elaborate stories of good versus evil, a theme that appears in an extraordinary fantasy series from Great Britain, the Harry Potter series.

Many modern fantasies are metaphors about life. For instance, animals such as those in *Cabbage Moon* by Tim Chadwick and Helen Lester's *Three Cheers for Tacky* represent children's qualities. The tiger in *The Tiger Who Lost His Stripes* by Anthony Paul has a case of "stripelessness." While searching for his stripes, he discovers selfishness, which he overcomes with ingenuity and intuition. Stories such as these make children feel secure and loved. Dick King-Smith also uses animals to parallel human nature in his books. The pig, dog, and sheep in *Babe: The Gallant Pig* have many human qualities. King-Smith's affectionate understanding of the creatures he writes about enable him to develop parallels with human nature (Townsend, 1990). Modern fantasy takes for granted not only the physical world and the real world that we see and feel, but also the supernatural world with all sorts of possibilities. Fantasy has special qualities distinguishing it from other genres. It concerns things that cannot happen, worlds that cannot exist, yet each story has a self-contained logic that creates its reality such as the otherworld fantasy that appears in C. S. Lewis's *The Chronicles of Narnia* and the land of unicorns that Bruce Coville created when he wrote *Into the Land of the Unicorns.* In some fantasy, visitors can come from other worlds as in Alexander Key's *The Forgotten Door.* These visitors may cause us to see ourselves in new ways and to discover the importance of kindness and love.

The Historical Roots of Fantasy

Traditional literature communicates universal truth, values, and mores in the ancient oral tradition, whereas modern fantasy is an art form that communicates the truth of contemporary life. Both folktales and modern fantasy have elements of magic that are contrary to life as we know it.

Modern fantasy inherits its common themes such as the struggle between good and evil, basic human values, and perseverance in the face of adversity from traditional literature. Many of its characters are symbols of good, beauty, and wisdom or of ugliness, bad, and evil. Fantasy and traditional literature share the quality of make-believe as well as many of their stylistic features. Some authors of modern fantasy make extensive use of the folktale style. For example, Jane Yolen chose this style in *The Girl Who Cried Flowers,* a collection of five tales of magic with a formulaic beginning ("Far to the North where the world is lighted only by softly flickering snow") and a "happily ever after" ending.

The first author of modern fantasy was Hans Christian Andersen. His stories, written in the early 1800s, were first translated into English in 1846 and were a mixture of folktale adaptations and fantasies that grew out of his own troubled childhood. Jacob and Wilhelm Grimm's tale *The Six Swans* was probably the stimulus for his popular story *The Wild Swans. The Ugly Duckling* and *The Steadfast Tin Soldier* are make-believe stories that are based on Andersen's experiences. *The Emperor's New Clothes* comments on the falseness he observed in society.

George MacDonald is another early author of fantasy. *At the Back of the North Wind,* published in 1871, was one of the foundations of modern fantasy. Illustrators, including Maurice Sendak, have interpreted MacDonald's *The Golden Key* and *The Light*

VIGNETTE

The only sounds in Will Livingston's fourth-grade classroom were those of pages turning. Reading workshop had this effect on his students; they really enjoyed reading. When he told them it was time to stop reading, Sarah groaned. Finally, Mr. Livingston tapped her on the shoulder.

"Your group is waiting."

"But I don't want to stop! This is the best book I ever read in my whole life!" she said.

"What are you reading?"

"*Harry Potter and the Prisoner of Azkaban;* a friend of mine bought it in England for me because I couldn't wait until it came out here. Then my mom made me go to bed at midnight."

"What do you like about it?" Tom asked.

"It is a fabulous, wonderful, awesome, terrific book, " Sarah answered.

"What genre is it?"

Sarah said, "Fantasy and I never really read fantasy before, but Harry is a wizard who has to live with his aunt, uncle, and cousin who detest him. He goes to school at Hogwarts School of Witchcraft and Wizardry, but he isn't allowed to cast spells in the world of Muggles. He is so cool."

Tom asked, "What is the world of Muggles?"

"You'll have to read it and find out."

Princess. Modern writers of fantasy build on folktales and on the work of authors such as these. Among the most popular stories of all time are fantasies such as *Charlotte's Web* by E. B. White, *Winnie-the-Pooh* by A. A. Milne, *A Wrinkle in Time* by Madeleine L'Engle, *A Bear Called Paddington* by Michael Bond, *Charlie and the Chocolate Factory* by Roald Dahl, and *The Wonderful Wizard of Oz* by Frank Baum.

Children and Fantasy

Fantasy stimulates students to look at life and the problems of life in new ways (Britton, 1977). In fantasy, children develop more open-minded attitudes that enable them to understand others' points of view. Fantasy stretches the imagination and encourages

dreams, stimulating creative thinking and problem-solving abilities. Nevertheless, some students such as those in the vignette on this page think fantasy is not for them. Perhaps they realize that it is a demanding genre or they lack experience with it. Fantasy, of all the genres of writing for children, offers the greatest challenge and the greatest rewards to both readers and writers (Smith, 1988).

Through fantasy children verify their understanding of the external world they share with others: Fantasy helps children construct a coherent picture of their immediate world (Smith, 1987). Fantasy also gives children a way of examining their inner world and comparing it with the inner worlds of others (Britton, 1977). People vary in imaginative ability. Some readers take pleasure in the ingenuity of fine fantasy, whereas others read fantasy simply because it tells a good story. Readers may reject fantasy because it is not real. However, gifted children choose to read fantasy more frequently than children who are not gifted (Swanton, 1984). Experienced teachers recognize that they need to cultivate children's taste for fantasy. Book selection and classroom activities stimulate students' interest in fantasy.

Activities such as reading aloud from fine fantasy develop children's appreciation for this genre; choose fantasies that have the broadest appeal and that are a good "read." A delightful read-aloud for younger listeners is *The Fortune-Tellers* by Lloyd Alexander. They like the witty characters and the fortune-teller's interesting prophesies, as well as looking at the vivid, detailed illustrations. Another great read-aloud is Deborah and James Howe's *Bunnicula.* Harold, a dog who was a spectator of this story, wrote this hilarious book. After a rabbit arrives in the home, vegetables begin to appear that have been drained of their juices. The plot thickens when Chester the cat concludes that Bunnicula is a vampire rabbit and sets out to protect the family from vampire attack.

Readers in the fifth and sixth grades enjoy the originality of plot and character in William J. Brooke's short stories in *Untold Tales.* One of the stories is a clever play, "A Prince in the Throat." The science-fiction piece "Into the Computer" is an entertaining and challenging story. Middle-grade readers who like ghost stories will like Patricia McKissack's *The Dark-Thirty: Southern Tales of the Supernatural.* These stories stir the imagination but are not so gruesome as to make children fearful.

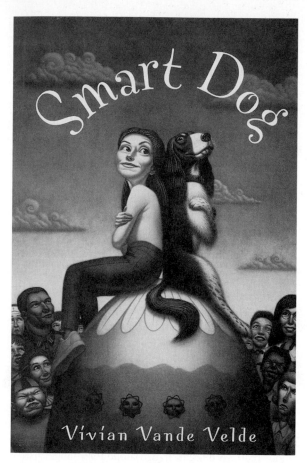

Amy saved Sherlock, a talking dog, who helped Amy solve a problem.

The Nature of Fantasy

Two things set excellent fantasy apart from other genres. First, the author must have a strongly realized personal vision, a perspective or belief about the meaning, significance, symbolism, allegory, a moral, message, or lesson in the fantasy, which is the second aspect (Langton, 1977). For instance, L'Engle addresses the theological meaning of the role of love in the conflict between good and evil in *A Wrinkle in Time*. Despite this moral or lesson, the author must avoid moral pronouncements; children do not tolerate them any better than do adults. Instead, these truths must emerge naturally from the story, providing insights about the human condition without preaching (Smith, 1988).

"The best stories are like extended lyrical images of unchanging human predicaments": life and death, love and hate, good and evil, courage and despair are dramatized (Cook, 1969, p. 2). Fantasy communicates a sense of truth, as well as tells us something about our world and ourselves. For example, in *The Forgotten Door* by Alexander Key, readers confront their fear of the unknown and different. A truth clothed in the fantastic is often easier to understand and accept than a baldly stated fact.

The images, ideas, and possibilities in fantasy must, however, remain essentially true to life and good and evil; the fantasy must maintain a consistent logic throughout to allow readers to believe that magic and impossible happenings are plausible. Obviously, fantasy always includes at least one element of the impossible, one element that goes against the laws of the physical universe, as we currently understand them (Alexander, 1965); it concerns things that cannot really happen, people or creatures that do not really exist. Nevertheless, each story must have its own self-contained logic that creates its own reality (Cameron, 1993). They need to draw boundary lines outside which the fantasy may not wander. For example, in *Charlotte's Web* the animals talk among themselves, but not to the human beings. White created this logic at the outset of the story, and it is never violated. Although the author is free to create any specific boundaries or logic, writers of fantasy must be hardheaded realists. "What appears gossamer is, underneath, solid as prestressed concrete. Once committed to his imaginary kingdom, the writer is not a monarch but a subject" (Alexander, 1965, p. 143).

Elements of Fantasy

As with traditional literature, authors of fantasy use all of the normal stylistic devices to make readers believe in fantasy. They skillfully craft language that will cause readers to suspend their disbelief and enjoy fantasy, inviting readers to enter their fanciful worlds.

Characters

Well-rounded, believable characters are essential in fantasy. To be believable they must be multidimensional characters who grow and develop through their experiences in the story. Meg, the protagonist in *A Wrinkle in Time,* is such a character. She is fearless at times and falters at others; nevertheless, she is courageous and determined to find her father at any cost. Meg learns lessons, changes, and develops throughout the book.

Readers come to know characters' personalities through their dialect, vocabulary, and speech rhythms. For instance, in *Eva*, Peter Dickinson creates much of the principal character's personality by revealing her thoughts. Eva awakens from a coma induced by an accident, thinking:

> Waking . . . strange . . . dream about trees? Oh, come back! Come. . . . Lost. . . . But so strange. . . . Oh, darling, said Mom's voice, farther away now. There was something in it—had been all along, in spite of the happiness in the words. A difficulty, a sense of effort. (p. 35)

Dickinson creates mood through what is not said. Eva senses that something is not normal long before she or the readers realize exactly what has happened: Eva survived the accident because her brain was placed in the body of a chimpanzee. After Eva realizes that she is living in a chimpanzee's body, she thinks:

> Okay, it was better than dying, but that wasn't enough. You had to awaken and open your eyes and see your new face and like what you saw. You had to make the human greeting and the chimp greeting and mean them. (p. 31)

The principal character in a fantasy establishes the logic of the fantasy and helps readers enter into the make-believe by expressing a confidence and belief in the unbelievable events and characters. Eva recognizes her dilemma and suffers as she becomes more aware and must adjust to her situation. The fact that she is living in a chimpanzee's body is logical because her father is a researcher who studies them. Both the masterful characterization and Eva's reactions to the situation make readers believe.

Another technique authors use to entice readers into accepting make-believe is through characters who refuse to believe in fantasy, despite the fact that they may be fantasies themselves or at least taking part in a fantasy. In *Tom's Midnight Garden* by Philippa Pearce, strange events defy the laws of time. However, Tom has a difficult time finding a friend to discuss the words "Time No Longer" on the face of the grandfather clock. When the clock strikes 13, he finds a friend who convinces him to suspend disbelief until the mystery unfolds.

Setting

Detailed settings make readers believe in fantasy. The author's use of sensory imagery helps readers hear, smell, and taste the sounds, odors, and tastes of the

Preston, the pig, outwits the wily, Mr. Wolf, but readers are kept guessing when Red Riding Hood and the three little pigs show up.

imaginary place. E. B. White uses sensory imagery in his descriptions of the barn in which Charlotte and Wilbur lived. Readers who are well acquainted with farms can smell the barn when reading about it in *Charlotte's Web*. Peter Dickinson invites readers to believe in his stories by describing unusual characters, places, and events in detail. His skill is illustrated in *A Box of Nothing*:

> It took a whole day for the Burra's green arm to come to life again. In the meanwhile it made do with a monkey arm, which wasn't as useful. The table set firm at the same time, and the fridge out on the slope had "gone fossil." . . . By then James was almost used to eating food that cooked itself and watching a TV that switched itself off and on when it felt like it and sleeping on a living bed. (p. 47)

Plot

Characters and setting come together in an original plot to create excellent fantasy. Natalie Babbitt does this in *Tuck Everlasting*. In this story, the central characters drink from a secret spring, which allows anyone who drinks from it to live forever. The carefully drawn characters are as convincing as the setting of this make-believe world, creating a tightly wound novel.

One of the most common strategies that authors use for making a fantastic plot believable is beginning the story in reality and gradually moving into fantasy. Readers may not even realize the book is fantasy until the second or third chapter. E. B. White used this technique in *Charlotte's Web* to draw readers into the plot.

Authors sometimes choose to convince us to believe in their fantasy by having characters move back and forth between their real environment and the make-believe environment. In *Fog Magic,* Julia Sauer creates a character who lives in a normal home but she visits a make-believe village, Blue Cove, only when it is foggy. Philippa Pearce also uses this strategy effectively in *Tom's Midnight Garden.* Tom lives in a present-day house, but he visits in a long-ago garden and plays with an imaginary character when the old hall clock strikes 13, thus defying the natural laws of time. Tom does not realize the fantasy until he is leaving the house and garden to return.

This technique is useful in books for younger children as well. Chris Van Allsburg begins the picture book *Jumanji* in a realistic setting. The fantasy starts when the children begin playing a game that cannot be stopped before the entire game is completed. In this potentially dangerous game many unbelievable events seem real. For example, a hippopotamus crashes through the living room and a python slithers onto the mantel.

Authors must make their plots credible and consistent, retaining their inner logic, if readers are to believe in their fantasy.

Theme

Theme is a significant aspect of fantasy. Universal themes such as wishes and dreams, the struggle between good and evil, and the importance of lore are most common in modern fantasy. Symbolism is often used to help further the theme of a fantasy. In *Tuck Everlasting,* Babbitt uses Ferris wheels and other wheels in the story as symbols of the cycle of the seasons and of life and death. The point of symbolism is that the hub of a wheel is a fixed point that is best left undisturbed, and this supports Babbitt's major theme: "everlasting life can be a burden."

Style

The language authors use, one of the major components of style, is especially important in fantasy because authors must find a way to tell about places, things, and people that do not exist in such a way that readers will see them in their imagination. William Steig's elegant language easily accomplishes this. His animal fantasy *The Amazing Bone* tells about a "succulent" pig that "dawdled" on the way to school and seemed "destined" to become dinner for a fox. Steig always stays within the logic of his story. Pearl may talk to amazing bones, but she always remains a pig. Steig's language styling is superb.

The point of view, determined by the person telling the story, is in fantasy as in other genres, another aspect of style. A 12-year-old girl who travels back 100 years in time narrates *The Root Cellar.* The author, Janet Lunn, researched how people lived at that time. In *The Battle for the Castle* by Elizabeth Winthrop, two boys travel back in time to battle huge rats in order to save a palace. In the process, they learn about different kinds of courage.

The point of view, in some stories, switches from one character to another or to an omniscient storyteller. In *Wonderful Alexander and the Catwings* Ursula K. Le Guin uses an omniscient point of view to tell about kittens who are born with wings that permit them to escape the slums of a city. The point of view changes when they go to the country and find children who will cherish them.

Types of Fantasy

All forms of fantasy are important in children's lives. Classroom experiences with fantasy cultivate children's imaginations. Two forms of modern fantasy are high fantasy and science fiction.

High fantasy

High fantasy is a complex, philosophical form of literature that focuses on themes such as the conflict between good and evil. The complexity and abstractness of high fantasy make it most popular with a middle school audience. Creators of fantasy write of myth and legend, of science and technology, and of human life as it is lived, might be lived, and ought to be lived (Le Guin, 1979). The characters in high fantasy are often symbolic of good people who are entangled in an endless battle between good and evil, which occurs in each book of the popular Harry Potter series.

The theme of Jackie Koller's *The Dragonling* is peace. At the beginning of the story, Darek hopes to slay a dragon, but instead he finds a baby dragon in the pouch of a dragon his brother killed. This discovery leads him to see the dragons in a new light. In this high fantasy, the protagonist's goal changes and he strives to make peace between his people and the surviving dragons.

Science fiction

What will life be like in 2050? How will we travel? Will there be colonies of earth people on Mars or some newly discovered planet? These are the kinds of themes explored in science fiction. In this imaginative literature, plausible events are depicted that are logical extrapolations from known facts. The story builds around events and problems that would not have happened at all without the scientific content (Gunn, 1975). This is illustrated in Sylvia Engdahl's *Beyond the Tomorrow Mountains,* which tells about rebuilding a life in a different world after the protagonist escapes an earth doomed to destruction. *The Giver* by Lois Lowry is an excellent example of science fiction. In this book, Jonas lives in a time when everything is under control. Children are the same until they become Twelves, and then they are assigned to their adult jobs. Jonas is selected to receive the true memories of the pain and joy of life. The book *Eva,* which was discussed earlier in this chapter, is another example of fine science fiction.

We find some crossover between high fantasy and science fiction: Much, although not all, science fiction is also high fantasy. Vivien Alcock's *The Monster Garden* is a science fiction story that is also high fantasy.

In this story, matter produced in a lab grows into a monster that is kind-hearted and wise. But, Monny the monster has to go away because she is different, which makes her unacceptable to people in the community.

Selecting Fantasy

When selecting fantasy for your classroom consider the following factors in addition to the guidelines for all literature.

1. Does it tell a good story?
2. What are the elements of fantasy in this story (e.g., setting, magic powers, time, etc.)?
3. How is this story different from the real world?
4. How has the author made the story believable?
5. What is the theme of this fantasy?

Classroom Activities: Traditional Literature

Traditional stories are quite compatible with classroom activities and teaching. Their brevity, simplicity, and directness make them particularly well suited to teaching children the elements and structures of literature. Furthermore, their oral quality and universal appeal make superior materials for learning activities.

Classroom Activities: Fantasy

More than other genre, fantasy needs to be introduced and read aloud. Introductions explain the context of the story and encourage listeners to predict story events.

Classroom Activities

ACTIVITY 8.1   CHANTING

Folktales are ideal vehicles for teaching students to chant refrains. *The Little Red Hen* works well for this activity because it has repetitive events and repeated, rhythmic phrases. Write the repeated phrases on the chalkboard or on charts and encourage the children to join in on repeated parts as you read aloud. Show them the charts that will guide their part of the activity. Read the story with the children's assistance several times. Vary this activity by having them prepare to read the story and the other children join in on the refrain.

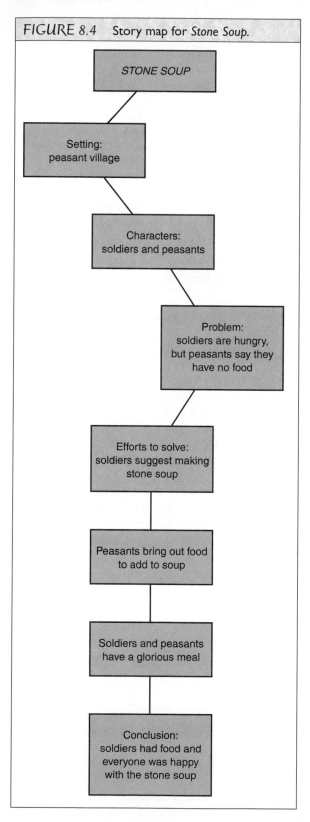

FIGURE 8.4 Story map for *Stone Soup*.

STONE SOUP

Setting:
peasant village

Characters:
soldiers and peasants

Problem:
soldiers are hungry,
but peasants say they
have no food

Efforts to solve:
soldiers suggest making
stone soup

Peasants bring out food
to add to soup

Soldiers and peasants
have a glorious meal

Conclusion:
soldiers had food and
everyone was happy
with the stone soup

ACTIVITY 8.2   MAPPING

Mapping is a good activity for developing understanding, even if the students will not be telling a story. This activity summarizes and organizes students' understanding of stories. You may have the students create their own maps using the model given in Figure 8.4.

ACTIVITY 8.3   STORYTELLING

Storytelling, a natural activity to use with traditional literature, develops children's oral language and communication.

1. Let the children choose stories. Tell them to choose ones that they especially enjoy.
2. Have them learn their stories, but not memorize them. Tell them to be concerned with the outline of the story initially. After identifying the basic plot, they can list, map, or outline these elements with drawings. A story map is a graphic display showing the organization of events and ideas in the story (see Figure 8.4).
3. After the students have a map or plan for their stories, group them in pairs so that the pairs can tell their stories to each other from the map or plan.
4. Once they can remember their story outlines, ask them to elaborate on their storytelling using these techniques:

   a. Visualize the setting, the people, and the action. Think about what you would see, hear, and feel if you were there. Choose words that will make the story more vivid so that your listeners can visualize it as you do. Retell the story with the more vivid language.
   b. Think of ways that you can make the story more exciting for the audience and get them more involved.

ACTIVITY 8.4   COMPOSING FOLKTALES

Students can compose their own folktales. This activity is a variation of one suggested by Livo and Rietz (1986). Write setting, character, and problem or conflict ideas on slips of paper and put each in a separate pile (all the settings together, all the characters together, etc.). Place students into groups of two or three and let each group draw one idea from each pile of slips. Then ask them to develop a spontaneous story using the setting, characters, and problem or conflict they selected. Once they are used to working this way, the activity can be varied by giving the students one slip of paper only so that they have a part of the story and must build the rest of it. On the slips of paper you might write ideas such as:

1. Characters: mean witch, spider, trickster rabbit, good fairy.
2. Setting: enchanted forest, a peasant hut, a giant toadstool, a castle.
3. Problem: cannot break evil witch's spell, lost in a forest, cannot find family, hungry.

ACTIVITY 8.5   PREDICTION

Folktales are quite predictable, so anticipation and prediction are good ways to involve children with the stories. Select a story such as *Henny Penny* or *The Three Billy Goats Gruff* by Paul Galdone, *Who's in Rabbit's House* by Verna Aardema, or *Fin M'Coul: The Giant of Knockmany Hill* by Tomie dePaola. Introduce the story to the children. Ask them to predict what the story will be about from the title and the book cover. Then read the story aloud, stopping at various points in the story to ask them to predict what will happen next. After they predict, tell them to listen to determine whether their predictions were correct. When teaching *The Little Red Hen* you might stop for predictions after each of these points in the story:

1. The hen asks for help planting the wheat.
2. The hen asks for help watering the wheat and pulling the weeds.
3. The hen asks for help cutting the ripe wheat.
4. The hen asks someone to take the wheat to be ground into flour.
5. The hen asks for help making the wheat into bread.
6. The hen asks for help eating the bread.

A variation of this activity might be to have the children write their predictions and then discuss them after the story is completed.

ACTIVITY 8.6   ILLUSTRATING FOLKTALES

Children enjoy creating their own illustrations for their favorite folktales, many of which have variants that have been interpreted in various ways. Prepare them for this activity by presenting several picture book versions of the same folktale (see Figure 8.5 for a sample list). After the students examine the tales, ask them to identify the medium, style, colors, and lines used to illustrate the various tales and to think about the way they will illustrate the tale and why they chose these colors, lines, and so forth. They may like to add the text to their illustrations and bind the stories to make their own books.

> FIGURE 8.5   Illustrated folktales to compare.

Brer Rabbit	*The Tales of Uncle Remus: The Adventures of Brer Rabbit* by Julius Lester, illustrated by Jerry Pinkney *The People Could Fly: American Black Folktales* by Virginia Hamilton, illustrated by Leo and Diane Dillon
The Three Billy Goats Gruff	*The Three Billy Goats Gruff* by Peter Asbjornsen, illustrated by Marcia Brown *The Three Billy Goats Gruff* by Paul Galdone
Jack and the Beanstalk	*Jim and the Beanstalk* by Raymond Briggs *Jack and the Beanstalk* by Tony Ross *Jack and the Bean Tree* by Gail E. Haley
Cinderella	*Yeh-Shen* by Ai-Ling Louie *Cinderella* by Charles Perrault, illustrated by Errol Le Cain *Cinderella* by Charles Perrault, illustrated by Marcia Brown *Cinderella* by the Brothers Grimm, illustrated by Nonny Hogrogian *Cinderella* by Paul Galdone

ACTIVITY 8.7   WRITING FOLKTALES

Folktales are exceptional models for writing. Folktale studies can teach story parts (beginning, middle, end), story form, and story structure as well as the elements of story grammar (i.e., setting, problem, actions, and resolution). Folktales also provide models of story content. Through studying legends, myths, animal tales, fairy tales, and other folktales, students can learn to understand and to write them.

Introduce each type of folktale to the students (i.e., fables, pourquoi tales, trickster tales, legends, myths, etc.) and give examples of each. Then have the students identify additional examples of each type, specifying the characteristics that helped them identify the various types of folktales. Ways of applying this activity to specific types of folktales are listed below.

1. Have the students identify cumulative stories structured around repetition: *Bringing the Rain to Kapiti Plain* by Verna Aardema, *The Gingerbread Boy* by Paul Galdone, and *The House That Jack Built* by Janet Stevens are examples. Read or have the students read the tales aloud, then discuss the cumulative aspects of the stories. Write the repeated portions on the chalkboard or charts. They may want to act out the repeated lines. Have them identify these elements of cumulative stories.
   - The stories are short.
   - The stories have a strong rhythmic pattern.

   - The story events are in a logical order and related to the preceding events.
   - All of the story events are repeated and accumulated until a surprise ending is reached.

   Once students learn the structure of cumulative stories, they may write their own cumulative tales, conforming to the story elements identified earlier. This activity is a variation of one suggested by Kennedy and Spangler (1986).

2. A journey story is one in which characters set out to travel to a specific place and have adventures along the way. *The Bremen Town Musicians* by Janet Stevens and *The Fat Cat* by Jack Kent are examples of this story type. Use the pattern developed in the preceding activity as a basis for having children write journey stories. Have them identify these elements of cumulative stories: In journey stories characters go on a journey far from home, and they mature as a result of their experiences. They may also draw a line that illustrates the route taken on the journey (Kennedy & Spangler, 1986).

3. Fables are especially easy to write because they are short and moralistic. After reading fables such as *Aesop's Fables* by Heidi Holder, *Fables* by Arnold Lobel, and *Three Aesop Fox Fables* by Paul Galdone, children may write their own fables. Have them identify these elements of fables:

- Fables contain a moral or lesson.
- Fables have animals as the main characters.
- The animals act like humans.
- Fables are short with fast action.
- The last line of the story contains the moral.

4. Wishing stories are common in traditional literature. One of the most popular is *The Fisherman and His Wife.* Other wish stories teachers might choose to use in the classroom are *The Rainbow-Colored*

Horse by Pura Belpré and *The Three Wishes* by Paul Galdone. Have students identify these elements of wishing stories:

- Character receives wishes, usually three.
- Character misuses the wishes.
- Character discovers the wishes were not so important.
- Character often learns to rely on himself or herself.

ACTIVITY 8.8   COMPARING VARIANT FOLKTALES

Several variants exist for many popular tales, often as many as 900 interpretations of a single tale. (For example, see the list of Noah and the Flood variations at the end of the Children's Literature References and Recommended Books section at the end of this chapter.) Compare variants by noting the similarities and differences in the various aspects of the story structure (e.g., setting, character, problem, resolution, conclusion) and the way they are written or illustrated.

Read variants of a folktale aloud, and let students individually prepare charts to compare them, such as the one shown in Table 8.2. Other elements that can be compared are the differences in language in folktales from different countries, the differences in formulaic beginnings and endings, and themes. Another possibility is comparing the text, illustrations, and cultural characteristics in the variants.

TABLE 8.2 Comparison chart for folktale variants.						
Author/ illustrator	Main character	Setting	Other characters	Beginning	Problem	Ending
Jakob and Wilhelm Grimm Nonny Hogrogian Greenwillow, 1981	Cinderella	Germany	Stepmother Doves Hazel tree	Invitation to ball	Cinderella mistreated	Marries prince
Charles Perrault Marcia Brown Scribner's 1954	Cinderella	France	Stepmother Stepsisters	Invitation to ball	Cinderella mistreated	Marries prince

ACTIVITY 8.9   COMPARING WRITTEN AND FILM VERSIONS OF FOLKTALES

Many traditional stories have been made into films, which children will enjoy watching as a class after having heard or read the book version. Class discussion after viewing the film can focus on questions such as:

1. What scenes were in the book that were not in the film?
2. Why did the filmmaker omit these scenes?
3. Were the characters the same in the book and the film?

4. How did the colors and art style vary between the two media?
5. Describe the overall differences between the two versions.
6. Why did these differences occur?

If a video recorder is available, students can film their own versions of the story.

ACTIVITY 8.10   READING JOURNALS

Reading journals are important vehicles to facilitate children's response to fantasy and other genres as well. At the close of each reading session, the students summarize and respond to the reading completed that day by writing in their journals. In addition to writing about what they read and responding to the reading, students should include any questions they have for subsequent discussions and identify words and phrases that are new to them or that need further exploration. Reading journals can be used during discussions to refresh their memory.

ACTIVITY 8.11   INQUIRY UNITS

Inquiry units can develop children's response to fantasy. A unit may explore the fantastic elements such as time travel, miniature worlds, futuristic settings, and other strange happenings. Through comparing the plot, theme, characterization, setting, and style, students achieve a greater understanding and appreciation for fantasy. Other units may be developed around books with themes of peace, good versus evil, or other common ideas in fantasy. Group or class charts can compare thematic development in different works. An example of a topical unit about dragons follows.

We selected the topic of dragons because it can be developed with children of different ages. Additionally, most dragon books are in the fantasy genre, which is the focus of this unit. The objective of this study is to identify the element or elements of the impossible that the author created. Intermediate-grade students will extend this goal to include the strategy that authors use to make readers believe the impossible.

Introduction
Preview the read-alouds by asking what the children know about dragons. Show the students pictures of dragons, which you can locate in art books and from various museums' Web sites. The CD-ROM *The Dragon in Chinese Art* (CDR Software ed., 1998; C\W95\ww) is very useful. Ask primary-grade children if they have ever discovered anything exciting on a walk or while they were playing. Ask intermediate-grade students if they have ever seen a dragon dance or a dragon in art. After discussion, read aloud *Raising Dragons* for primary-grade students and *Behold . . . the Dragons!* to intermediate-grade students.

Discussion Questions: Primary Grades
1. What is the best part of this story? Why do you think that?
2. Which character is your favorite? Why?
3. Do you think you could find a dragon egg?

4. Would you like to have a dragon of your own? Why or why not?

5. How do you know this story is make-believe (fantasy)?

6. What did you learn from this story?

7. How did the author make you like the story?

8. Art and writing:

   a. The children could draw pictures of their own dragons and dragon eggs.

   b. They could write about the things they would do with a dragon as a friend.

   c. They could draw pictures of ways that dragons could help them.

9. Music and dance: Look up Chinese dragon dancing on the Internet.

Books for Further Study: Primary Grades

- *Dragon School* by Cara J. Cooperman.
- *Aja's Dragon* by Diane Fisher.
- *Dragon Poems* by John Foster.
- *Custard the Dragon and the Wicked Knight* by Ogden Nash.
- *Dragon's Fat Cat: Dragon's Fourth Tale* by Dav Pilkey.
- *Elvira* by Margaret Shannon.
- *Chin Chiang and the Dragon's Dance* by Ian Wallace.

Discussion Questions: Intermediate Grades

1. Do you believe in dragons? Why or why not?

2. Where do dragons come from?

3. What new facts did you learn from *Behold . . . the Dragons!*?

4. Why are dragons so popular?

5. Why do you think dragons are important in so many cultures?

6. What mechanical things can be compared to dragons?

7. Do you think dragons are real? Why or why not?

8. Art and music: After studying dragon dancing, have the children do a dragon dance.

9. Social Studies: Discuss the types of dragons found in the art, dance, and music of different cultures. How do they differ? How are they similar? Have the children create their own artistic expressions of dragons.

10. Inquiry: Ask the students to brainstorm and come up with questions they would like to study about dragons.

11. Literature: Have the students read at least one additional book about dragons. Then discuss the fantasy in the book and the writer's strategies for creating fantasy.

Books for Further Study: Intermediate Grades

- *The Dragonslayers* by Bruce Coville.
- *Dragon's Milk* by Susan Fletcher.
- *The Book of Dragons* by Michael Hague.
- *The Dragon of Lonely Island* by Rebecca Rupp.
- *The Care and Feeding of Dragons* by Brenda Seabrooke.
- *Backyard Dragon* by Betsy and Samuel Sterman.
- *American Dragons: Twenty-Five Asian American Voices* by Laurence Yep.

ACTIVITY 8.12 DISCUSSION

Class discussion of fantasy is important to building children's understanding and response. Through discussion students achieve a greater understanding and appreciation for fantasy.

Instead of leading the discussion, you may prefer to participate as a group member and let the students take turns starting the discussion, using significant questions such as, "What do you think?" and, "Why do you think this?" The students may have enough questions in their journals to stimulate the discussion or may need help in coming up with good open-ended discussion questions such as:

- What do you predict will happen next in the story?

- What did you learn about the characters, setting, and other parts of the story in today's reading?
- What experiences of your own did you remember in relation to today's reading?

- What other books could you compare this one to?

Another approach is for students to complete individually discussion webs such as the one shown in Figure 8.6.

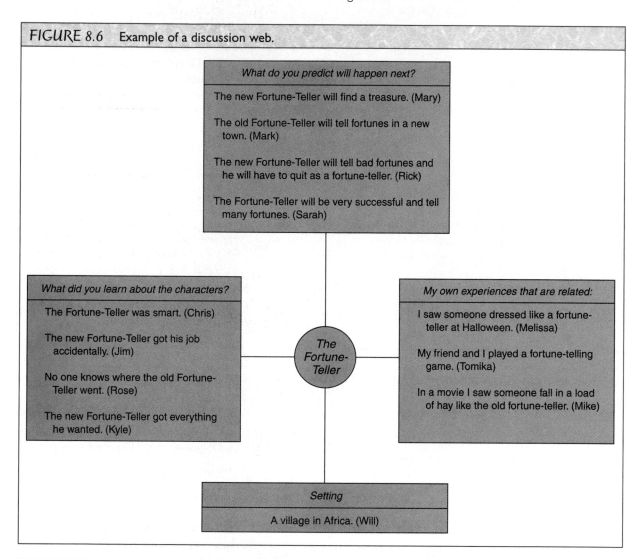

FIGURE 8.6   Example of a discussion web.

What do you predict will happen next?

The new Fortune-Teller will find a treasure. (Mary)

The old Fortune-Teller will tell fortunes in a new town. (Mark)

The new Fortune-Teller will tell bad fortunes and he will have to quit as a fortune-teller. (Rick)

The Fortune-Teller will be very successful and tell many fortunes. (Sarah)

What did you learn about the characters?

The Fortune-Teller was smart. (Chris)

The new Fortune-Teller got his job accidentally. (Jim)

No one knows where the old Fortune-Teller went. (Rose)

The new Fortune-Teller got everything he wanted. (Kyle)

My own experiences that are related:

I saw someone dressed like a fortune-teller at Halloween. (Melissa)

My friend and I played a fortune-telling game. (Tomika)

In a movie I saw someone fall in a load of hay like the old fortune-teller. (Mike)

The Fortune-Teller

Setting

A village in Africa. (Will)

ACTIVITY 8.13   AUTHOR PROFILES AND STUDIES

Choosing an author to focus on in traditional literature and fantasy is difficult. John Bierhorst has written exceptional Native American folktales, Gale Haley is recognized for her interpretations of folktales, and Ed Young has retold Asian folktales. These are just a few of the fine authors in this genre. However, we finally selected John Bierhorst. His biographical profile, as well as Chris Van Allsburg's, follows.

A Biographical Profile: John Bierhorst

John Bierhorst is an American folklorist and adapter of Native American literature for children. Many of his books have been recognized as Notable Books by the American Library Association.

As a child he never encountered Native American culture in any of the books he read. He discovered his interest in writing while attending college, and his interest in anthropology contributed to his desire to study native cultures. These interests led him to create an anthology of songs, prayers, orations, and languages in *The Hungry Woman: Myths and Legends of the Aztecs.* He concentrates on the Iroquois in *The Woman Who Fell from the Sky: The Iroquois Story of Creation.* He has also translated eight Charles Perrault tales. The books identified in this profile are merely representative of his work.

A Biographical Profile: Chris Van Allsburg

Chris Van Allsburg's books have established this author–illustrator as one of the premier creators of picture books. He enjoys creating books that combine humor, mystery, and imagination. When asked where his ideas come from, he often says, "I steal them from the neighborhood kids," or "They are beamed to me from outer space" (Van Allsburg, 1995, p. 661). He says that he really does not know because each story starts out with a vague idea that materializes as a completed concept. He believes that the people who believe in the fantastic have a gift. One of his own fantasies is that a miraculous machine exists that could be hooked up to his brain and instantly produce finished art from the images in his brain. Some of his very popular books are: *The Polar Express, Jumanji, The Mysteries of Harris Burdick, The Wreck of the Zephyr, The Widow's Broom,* and *The Sweetest Fig.*

SUMMARY

Both traditional literature and modern fantasy are make-believe, and both are important in children's lives as well as adults' lives. For young and old they serve the function of play, dreaming, and imagining better worlds and solutions to problems. Lloyd Alexander (1965) shares his view of this genre:

> Fantasy touches our deepest feelings, and in so doing, it speaks to the best and most hopeful parts of ourselves. It can help us learn the most fundamental skill of all—how to be human. (p. 43)

Traditional literature is based on the oral tradition. The stories, ballads, and tales in this genre are descendants of the original oral stories, created by storytellers around campfires long ago. These stories have traveled all over the world from storyteller to storyteller, teaching listeners about life and about people. The favorites of the past continue to be popular today. The characters, settings, and events in folktales are symbolic, and they differ from other forms of fiction in that they teach more direct lessons. Other forms of literature develop themes more subtly, but even the more direct teachings of folktales must avoid preachy-teachy stories.

Modern fantasy is modern make-believe. It usually has more developed characters and plots than traditional stories, but the make-believe is still developed through magic events, characters, time, and places. The themes of fantasy are often concerned with the age-old battle between good and evil. The abstract, imaginative nature of fantasy educates children's imagination, but children are more likely to appreciate it when teachers introduce the stories and read them aloud.

Thought Questions

1. How are fantasy and traditional literature alike?
2. How are fantasy and traditional literature different?

3. What are the major characteristics of high fantasy?

4. Why is traditional literature so popular?

5. Why is motivating children to read fantasy important for teachers?

6. How does traditional literature relate to culture?

Research and Application Experiences

1. Develop a booktalk for introducing folktales or fantasy to a group of children.

2. Interview children at various grade levels and ask them to identify which fantasy books they have enjoyed. Ask them what they like about the particular books they enjoy.

3. Interview teachers asking them to tell how many fantasies they read in one year to their class and the number of traditional literature stories they read. What conclusions can you draw from this information?

4. Read a fantasy to a group of children or a class and then discuss the book. Tape the discussion so you can analyze its strengths and weaknesses.

5. Students who are interning in a school classroom may experiment with having the students or a group of students keep a reading journal for a month and analyze how the journal influences their reading response.

6. Create a bibliography of fantasies for a selected grade level.

7. Identify various versions of a single folktale that students could compare in a classroom.

Children's Literature References and Recommended Books

Note: Books designated with an asterisk (*) are recommended for reluctant readers.

Aardema, V. (Reteller). (1977). *Who's in rabbit's house?* (L. Dillon & D. Dillon, Illus.). New York: Dial. (2–4). TRADITIONAL LITERATURE.

The story of how rabbit and his friends save his house.

Aardema, V. (Reteller). (1981). *Bringing the rain to Kapiti Plain* (B. Vidal, Illus.). New York: Dial. (1–3). TRADITIONAL LITERATURE.

An African cumulative tale, this book describes a delightful day of rain.

Alcock, V. (1988). *The monster garden.* New York: Delacorte. (4–6). MODERN FANTASY.*

Frankie discovers an experimental sample that she grows into a baby monster. She has to be responsible for its well-being.

Alexander, L. (1992). *The fortune-tellers* (T. S. Hyman, Illus.). New York: Dutton. (K–5). TRADITIONAL LITERATURE.*

The fortune-teller prophesies bright futures for his customers.

Andersen, H. C. (1986). *The emperor's new clothes* (D. Duntze, Illus.). New York: North South Books. (2–5). MODERN FANTASY.

The king shows off his new clothes, but only one boy points out that he has no clothes on.

Andersen, H. C. (1991). *Thumbelina* (D. Johnson, Illus.). New York: Picture Book Studio. (K–3). MODERN FANTASY.

A tiny girl has many adventures.

Andersen, H. C. (1992). *The steadfast tin soldier* (F. Marcellino, Illus.). New York: HarperCollins. (K–3). MODERN FANTASY.

The story of a tin soldier's love for a paper doll.

Andersen, H. C. (1999). *The ugly duckling* (J. Pinkney, Illus.). New York: Morrow. (K–5). MODERN FANTASY.

In this story, an ugly duckling becomes a swan.

Asbjornsen, P. C. (1957). *The three billy goats gruff* (M. Brown, Illus.). San Diego, CA: Harcourt. (K–3). TRADITIONAL LITERATURE.

Three goats want to eat grass, but a troll threatens them.

Babbitt, N. (1975). *Tuck everlasting.* New York: Farrar, Straus & Giroux. (4–7). MODERN FANTASY.

Winnie Foster runs away from her parents and meets the Tucks, all of whom have drunk from the spring of everlasting life.

Babbitt, N. (1998). *Ouch! A tale from Grimm* (F. Marcellino, Illus.). New York: HarperCollins. (K–3). TRADITIONAL LITERATURE.

This is the story of Marco, who is born into an unremarkable family, but becomes King by using his wits.

Baum, L. F. (1987). *The wonderful wizard of Oz.* New York: Morrow. (4–8). MODERN FANTASY.

Originally published in 1900, this book has been called the "first American fantasy." The Land of Oz is inhabited by the Tin Man, the Scarecrow, the Cowardly Lion, and Dorothy.

Begay, S. (1992). *Ma'ii and cousin horned toad.* New York: Scholastic. (1–3). TRADITIONAL LITERATURE.

A traditional Navajo trickster tale.

Belpré, P. (1978). *The rainbow-colored horse* (A. Martorell, Illus.). New York: Frederick Warne. (1–6). TRADITIONAL LITERATURE.

A collection of Spanish folktales.

Bernhard, E., & Bernhard, D. (1994). *The girl who wanted to hunt.* New York: Holiday House. (K–4). TRADITIONAL LITERATURE.

Birdseye, T. (1993). *Soap! Soap! Don't forget the soap! An Appalachian folktale* (A. Glass, Illus.). New York: Holiday House. (K–3). TRADITIONAL LITERATURE.*

The boy in this story has a poor memory, which leads to humorous situations.

Bond, M. (1960). *A bear called Paddington* (P. Fortnum, Illus.). Boston: Houghton Mifflin. (K–2). MODERN FANTASY.

A bear from darkest Peru visits London.

Boston, L. M. (1955). *The children of Green Knowe* (P. Boston, Illus.). New York: Harcourt. (4–8). MODERN FANTASY.

In this part of a fantasy series set in the past and the present, a lonely child is sent off to live with his great-grandmother in an ancient manor house.

Briggs, R. (1970). *Jim and the beanstalk.* New York: Coward-McCann. (K–2). TRADITIONAL LITERATURE.

Brooke, W. J. (1992). *Untold tales.* New York: HarperCollins. (5–9). MODERN FANTASY.

A collection of short stories that build on clever word play and traditions.

Casler, L. (1994). *The boy who dreamed of an acorn* (S. Begay, Illus.). New York: Philomel. (3–6). TRADITIONAL LITERATURE.

In this Native American folktale, a boy who dreamed about an acorn discovers that small, weak things can have great power.

Chadwick, T. (1994). *Cabbage moon* (P. Harper, Illus.). New York: Orchard. (K–2). MODERN FANTASY.*

A curious rabbit explores the world, asking questions. He hates the cabbage his mother serves, but he learns about it on a trip to the "cabbage moon."

Climo, S. (1993). *The Korean Cinderella* (R. Heller, Illus.). New York: HarperCollins. (K–4). TRADITIONAL LITERATURE.

Cooperman, C. J. (1997). *Dragon school* (J. Pierard, Illus.). New York: Pocket Books. (K–4). MODERN FANTASY.

Coville, B. (1994). *Into the land of the unicorns.* New York: Scholastic. (3–6). MODERN FANTASY.

Cara's grandmother convinces her to jump into space and into the land of the unicorns where she discovers that she must save the unicorns from extinction.

Coville, B. (1995). *The Dragonslayers* (K. Coville, Illus.). New York: Pocket. (3–6). MODERN FANTASY.

Dahl, R. (1964). *Charlie and the chocolate factory* (J. Schindelman, Illus.). New York: Knopf. (2–6). MODERN FANTASY.

These unusual characters have vices that lead to their downfall.

Day, N. R. (1995). *The lion's whiskers: An Ethiopian folktale* (A. Grifalconi, Illus.). New York: Scholastic. (K–3). TRADITIONAL LITERATURE.

A loving stepmother is willing to risk death to win the love of her stepson. The illustrations show the lifestyle of the Amhara people.

dePaola, T. (1981). *Fin M'Coul: The giant of Knockmany Hill.* New York: Holiday House. (1–3). TRADITIONAL LITERATURE.

This is an Irish folktale.

Dickinson, P. (1985). *A box of nothing.* New York: Delacorte. (3–5). MODERN FANTASY.

James purchases a box of nothing for $0.00 in the Nothing Shop.

Dickinson, P. (1988). *Eva.* New York: Delacorte. (6–9). MODERN FANTASY.

The principal character survives an accident when her brain is implanted in the body of a chimp.

Engdahl, S. L. (1973). *Beyond the Tomorrow Mountains* (R. Cuffari, Illus.). New York: Atheneum. (4–8). MODERN FANTASY.

The story of a young man who is born after the earth is doomed to destruction.

Fisher, D. (1999). *Aja's dragon* (M. Levy, Illus.). New York: Mercury. (K–2). MODERN FANTASY.

Fletcher, S. (1996). *Dragon's milk.* New York: Aladdin Paperbacks. (3–6). MODERN FANTASY.

Foster, J. (Ed.). (1997). *Dragon poems* (K. Paul, Illus.). New York: Oxford University Press. (K–4). POETRY.

Galdone, P. (1971). *Three Aesop fox fables.* New York: Clarion. (1–3). TRADITIONAL LITERATURE.

Fables teach lessons with foxy characters.

Galdone, P. (1978). *Cinderella.* New York: McGraw-Hill. (1–4). TRADITIONAL LITERATURE.

The classic French version of Cinderella.

Galdone, P. (1979). *The three billy goats gruff.* New York: Clarion. (PreK–1). TRADITIONAL LITERATURE.

Galdone, P. (1980). *The three wishes.* New York: Clarion. (K–2). TRADITIONAL LITERATURE.

Galdone tells a traditional three-wish story.

Galdone, P. (1983). *The gingerbread boy.* New York: Clarion. (PreK–1). TRADITIONAL LITERATURE.

Galdone, P. (Reteller). (1984). *Henny Penny.* New York: Houghton Mifflin. (PreK–1). TRADITIONAL LITERATURE.

Henny Penny is an alarmist.

Gibbons, G. (1999). *Behold . . . the Dragons!* New York: Morrow. (1–3). INFORMATIONAL BOOK.

The author presents dragons from cultures all over the world. Dragons in mythology and folktales are explored.

Grimm, Jacob & Wilhelm. (1981). *Cinderella.* New York: Greenwillow. (1–3). TRADITIONAL LITERATURE.

An older version of the well-known folktale.

Haddix, M. P. (1998). *Among the hidden.* New York: Simon & Schuster. (4–6). MODERN FANTASY.

In a society where families are allowed to have only two children, a third child is born, but he must live in the attic to avoid being seen by authorities.

Hague, M. (Selector). (1995). *The book of dragons.* New York: Morrow. (3–6). MODERN FANTASY.

Haley, G. E. (1986). *Jack and the bean tree.* New York: Crown. (PreK–4). TRADITIONAL LITERATURE.

An Appalachian version of the traditional tale.

Hamilton, V. (Reteller). (1985). *The people could fly: American Black folktales* (L. Dillon & D. Dillon, Illus.). New York: Knopf. (4–8). TRADITIONAL LITERATURE.

A superb collection of tales.

Holder, H. (1981). *Aesop's fables.* New York: Viking. (3–6). TRADITIONAL LITERATURE.

A collection of the best-known Aesop's fables.

Howe, D., & Howe, J. (1979). *Bunnicula* (A. Daniel, Illus.). New York: Atheneum. (3–5). MODERN FANTASY.

A dog narrates this hilarious fantasy about a well-read cat and a vampire bunny.

Isaacs, A. (1995). *Swamp angel* (P. O. Zelinsky, Illus.). New York: Dutton. (1–4). TRADITIONAL LITERATURE.

This is a tall tale about a larger-than-life woman who performs amazing feats.

Jacobs, J. (Collector). (1989). *Tattercoats* (M. Tomes, Illus.). New York: Putnam. (K–2). TRADITIONAL LITERATURE.

Jaffe, N. (1998). *The way meat loves salt: A Cinderella tale from the Jewish tradition* (L. August, Illus.). New York: Henry Holt. (K–4). TRADITIONAL LITERATURE.

Kent, J. (1971). *The fat cat.* Chicago: Parents. (1–3). TRADITIONAL LITERATURE.

A traditional tale translated from Danish.

Key, A. (1965). *The forgotten door.* Philadelphia: Westminster. (4–6). MODERN FANTASY.*

A strange boy with unusual powers appears in a farming community. He seems to have come out of nowhere.

King-Smith, D. (1983). *Babe: The gallant pig.* New York: Crown. (3–6). MODERN FANTASY.

This fantasy has elements that are both funny and serious. Babe the pig does not realize that she is to become a part of the farmer's menu, then she thinks she is a dog.

King-Smith, D. (1989). *Martin's mice* (J. Alborough, Illus.). New York: Crown. (3–6). MODERN FANTASY.

Martin, a cat, decides to raise mice to avoid the taxing job of catching them, but he gets in deeper than he planned.

Koller, J. F. (1990). *The dragonling* (J. Mitchel, Illus.). New York: Little Brown. (3–5). MODERN FANTASY.

Darek hopes to slay a dragon until he discovers a baby dragon and nurtures it.

Lattimore, D. N. (1990). *The dragon's robe.* New York: Harper. (2–4). TRADITIONAL LITERATURE.

A traditional Chinese tale about a weaver who saves her people from disaster.

Le Guin, U. (1988). *Wonderful Alexander and the catwings* (S. D. Schindler, Illus.). New York: Orchard. (1–3). MODERN FANTASY.

These unusual kittens use their wings to escape the inner city and find a home in the country.

L'Engle, M. (1962). *A wrinkle in time.* New York: Farrar, Straus & Giroux. (5–8). MODERN FANTASY.

Meg and her brother set out to find their lost father and discover they must journey through time to find him.

Lester, H. (1994). *Three cheers for Tacky* (L. Munsinger, Illus.). Boston: Houghton Mifflin. (1–3). MODERN FANTASY.*

Tacky the penguin is a bumbling character who tries to achieve greater skill through practice. His friends appreciate his individuality.

Lester, J. (1969). *Black folktales* (T. Feelings, Illus.). New York: Baron. (3–12). TRADITIONAL LITERATURE.

A variety of folktales including pourquoi and hero tales.

Lester, J. (Reteller). (1988). *More tales of Uncle Remus: Further adventures of Brer Rabbit, his friends, enemies, and others* (J. Pinkney, Illus.). New York: Dial. (3–6). TRADITIONAL LITERATURE.

A new interpretation of the well-known tales.

Lewis, C. S. (1950). *The lion, the witch and the wardrobe* (P. Baynes, Illus.). New York: Macmillan. (5–8). MODERN FANTASY.

The classic fantasy of four children who discover the enchanted land of Narnia.

Lobel, A. (1980). *Fables.* New York: Harper & Row. (K–2). TRADITIONAL LITERATURE.

These tales are given new twists.

Louie, A.-L. (Reteller). (1982). *Yeh-Shen: A Cinderella story from China* (E. Young, Illus.). New York: Philomel. (K–2). TRADITIONAL LITERATURE.

Lowry, L. (1993). *The giver.* Boston: Houghton Mifflin. (4–7). MODERN FANTASY.

This science fiction story is about a world where everything is under control. When the children become Twelves, they are assigned their adult jobs.

Lunn, J. (1983). *The root cellar.* New York: Scribner's. (4–8). MODERN FANTASY.

Twelve-year-old Rose is sent to live with her aunt in a country home on the shores of Lake Ontario where she discovers an overgrown root cellar.

Lurie, A. (Reteller). (1999). *The black geese: A Baba Yaga story from Russia* (J. Souhami, Illus.). New York: DK Publishing. (K–8). TRADITIONAL LITERATURE.

A mother who is going to market tells her daughter to take care of her brother so that Baba Yaga's black geese will not steal him.

MacDonald, G. (1989). *At the back of the North Wind* (J. W. Smith, Illus.). New York: Morrow. (4–6). MODERN FANTASY.

The story of a boy who seeks help from the cold north wind.

Martin, R. (1992). *The rough-face girl* (D. Shannon, Illus.). New York: Putnam. (K–4). TRADITIONAL LITERATURE.

McKissack, P. C. (1992). *The dark-thirty: Southern tales of the supernatural* (B. Pinkney, Illus.). New York: Knopf. (2–6). TRADITIONAL LITERATURE.*

A collection of scary stories.

Milne, A. A. (1926). *Winnie-the-pooh* (E. H. Shepard, Illus.). New York: Dutton. (PreK–4). MODERN FANTASY.

Classic stories of a bear who gets into great difficulties.

Milnes, G. (Collector). (1990). *Granny, will your dog bite, and other mountain rhymes.* New York: Knopf. (3–6). TRADITIONAL LITERATURE.

Rhymes, ballads, and jokes are collected in this book.

Nash, O. (1999). *Custard the dragon and the wicked knight* (L. Munsinger, Illus.). Boston: Little Brown. (K–2). POETRY.

Naylor, P. R. (1991). *Shiloh.* New York: Atheneum. (4–7). CONTEMPORARY REALISTIC FICTION.

A boy tries to prevent abuse to a dog that he befriends.

Nolen, J. (1998). *Raising dragons* (E. Primavera, Illus.). New York: Silver Whistle. (K–3). MODERN FANTASY.

During a Sunday before-supper walk, a little girl discovers an egg that hatches into a baby dragon and becomes her best friend.

Oodgeroo. (1994). *Dreamtime: Aboriginal stories* (B. Bancroft, Illus.). New York: Lothrop, Lee & Shepard. (3–8). TRADITIONAL LITERATURE.

Aboriginal folklore that Oodgeroo heard as a child.

Paul, A. (1995). *The tiger who lost his stripes* (M. Foreman, Illus.). New York: Harcourt. (PreK–2). TRADITIONAL LITERATURE.

General MacTiger awakens from a nap to discover that Python has stolen his stripes, and he must bargain with various animals to get them back.

Pearce, P. (1958). *Tom's midnight garden* (S. Einzig, Illus.). Philadelphia: Lippincott. (4–7). MODERN FANTASY.

A time fantasy that won the British Carnegie Medal. Tom is visiting in an old house and discovers a clock that strikes 13 and a mysterious garden.

Perrault, C. (1997). *Cinderella.* (M. Brown, Illus.). New York: Aladdin. (K–2). TRADITIONAL LITERATURE.

Pilkey, D. (1992). *Dragon's fat cat: Dragon's fourth tale.* New York: Orchard. (K–2). MODERN FANTASY.

Pollock, P. (Reteller). (1996). *The turkey girl: A Zuni Cinderella story* (E. Young, Illus.). Boston: Little Brown. (K–2). TRADITIONAL LITERATURE.

Rohmer, H. (Adapter). (1989). *Uncle Nacho's hat* (V. Reisberg, Illus.). San Francisco: Children's Book Press. (1–3). MODERN FANTASY.

Uncle Nacho cannot get rid of his old hat in this tale.

Rowling, J. K. (1999). *Harry Potter and the prisoner of Azkaban.* New York: Levine. (4–8). MODERN FANTASY.

Harry Potter, a wizard, attends Hogwarts School of Witchcraft and Wizardry and is forced to spend summer vacations with his aunt, uncle, and cousin who detest him. The preceding books in this series are *Harry Potter and the Chamber of Secrets* and *Harry Potter and the Sorcerer's Stone*, and the latest volume is *Harry Potter and the Goblet of Fire.*

Rupp, R. (1998). *The dragon of Lonely Island* (W. Minor, Illus.). New York: Candlewick. (3–6). MODERN FANTASY.

San Souci, R. D. (1998). *Cendrillon: A Caribbean Cinderella* (B. Pinkney, Illus.). New York: Simon and Schuster. (K–4). TRADITIONAL LITERATURE.

Sauer, J. L. *Fog magic* (L. Ward, Illus.). New York: Viking. (4–6). MODERN FANTASY.

Ten-year-old Greta discovers the village of Blue Cove, only to realize that it exists only in the fog.

Scieszka, J. (1989). *The true story of the 3 little pigs* (L. Smith, Illus.). New York: Viking. (K–6). MODERN FANTASY.

Scieszka, J. (1991). *The frog prince, continued* (S. Johnson, Illus.). New York: Viking. (K–4). MODERN FANTASY.

Scieszka, J. (1992). *The stinky cheese man and other fairly stupid tales* (L. Smith, Illus.). New York: Viking. (K–6). MODERN FANTASY.

Seabrooke, B. (1998). *The care and feeding of dragons.* New York: Cobblehill. (K–4). MODERN FANTASY.

Selden, G. (1960). *The cricket in Times Square* (G. Williams, Illus.). New York: Ariel. (2–4). MODERN FANTASY.

Chester Cricket catches a train to the city and finds a whole new world.

Service, P. F. (1985). *Winter of magic's return.* New York: Atheneum. (4–7). MODERN FANTASY.

Set 500 years after a nuclear holocaust that humanity survived.

Shannon, M. (1993). *Elvira.* New York: Ticknor & Fields. (1–3). MODERN FANTASY.

Elvira is an unusual dragon who prefers to avoid eating people.

Steig, J. (1998). *A handful of beans: Six fairy tales* (W. Steig, Illus.). New York: Harper. (K–3). TRADITIONAL LITERATURE.

These well-illustrated stories are retellings of traditional tales.

Steig, W. (1976). *The amazing bone.* New York: Farrar, Straus & Giroux. (2–4). MODERN FANTASY.

A succulent pig and a talking bone outwit a wily fox.

Sterman, B., & Sterman, S. (1993). *Backyard dragon* (D. Wenzel, Illus.). New York: HarperCollins. (3–6). MODERN FANTASY.

Stevens, J. (1985). *The house that Jack built.* New York: Holiday House. (PreK–2). TRADITIONAL LITERATURE.

A cumulative tale about building a house.

Stevens, J. (Reteller). (1992). *The Bremen town musicians.* New York: Holiday House. (K–2). TRADITIONAL LITERATURE.

A scraggly group of animals take a trip to meet some robbers.

Stevens, K. (1994). *Aunt Skilly and the stranger* (R. A. Parker, Illus.). New York: Ticknor & Fields. (K–2). TRADITIONAL LITERATURE.

Aunt Skilly entertains a stranger for dinner. He thanks her and leaves, but returns to rob her.

Van Allsburg, C. (1981). *Jumanji.* Boston: Houghton Mifflin. (1–3). MODERN FANTASY.

A jungle adventure game gets out of hand when two children ignore their parents' admonitions.

Wallace, I. (1984). *Chin Chiang and the dragon's dance.* New York: Atheneum. (K–2). INFORMATIONAL BOOK.

Wargin, K. (1998). *The legend of Sleeping Bear* (G. Van Frankenhuyzen, Illus.). Chelsea, MI: Sleeping Bear Press. (K–3). TRADITIONAL LITERATURE.

This legend tells of a mother bear whose twin cubs are lost, so the mother waits for them and becomes the Sleeping Bear Dunes.

Wells, R. (1998). *The fisherman and his wife: A brand new version* (E. Hubbard, Illus.). New York: Dial. (PreK–3). TRADITIONAL LITERATURE.

This classic is retold with a spin.

White, E. B. (1952). *Charlotte's web* (G. Williams, Illus.). New York: Harper & Row. (2–4). MODERN FANTASY.

A spider saves her friend, Wilbur the pig, from being eaten.

Winthrop, E. (1993). *The battle for the castle*. New York: Holiday House. (4–6). MODERN FANTASY.

Two boys travel back to medieval times where they help battle large rats to save the castle.

Yep, L. (Ed.). (1995). *American dragons: Twenty-five Asian American voices*. New York: HarperCollins. (5–8). CONTEMPORARY REALISTIC FICTION, POETRY.

Yolen, J. (1974). *The girl who cried flowers* (D. Palladini, Illus.). New York: Crowell. (4–6). MODERN FANTASY.

Five tales of magic written in the style of traditional literature.

Young, E. (1994). *Little Plum*. New York: Philomel. (1–3). TRADITIONAL LITERATURE.

A modern version of Tom Thumb in picture book format.

Zelinsky, P. O. (Reteller). (1998). *Rapunzel*. New York: Dutton. (1–4). TRADITIONAL LITERATURE.

Zelinsky has interpreted the Grimm tale with exquisite illustrations.

Noah and the Flood Variations

Baynes, P. (1988). *Noah and the Ark*. New York: Henry Holt. (K–3)

Bollinger, M. (1972). *Noah and the rainbow*. (Helga Aichinger, Illus.). New York: Crowell. (K–3)

dePaola, T. (1983). *Noah and the Ark*. New York: Harper. (K–3)

Diamond, J. (1983). *Noah's Ark*. Englewood Cliffs, NJ: Prentice-Hall. (K–3)

Eborn, A. (1984). *Noah and the Ark and the animals*. (Ivan Gantschev, Illus.). Natick, MA: Picture Book Studio. (K–3)

Fischetto, L. (1989). *Inside Noah's Ark*. (Laura Fischetto, Illus.). New York: Viking Kestrel. (K–3)

Fussennegger, G. (1982). *Noah's Ark*. (Annegert Fuchshuber, Illus.). Philadelphia: Lippincott. (K–3)

Geisert, A. (1988). *The Ark*. Boston: Houghton Mifflin. (K–3)

Haley, G. E. (1971). *Noah's Ark*. New York: Atheneum. (K–3)

Hogrogian, N. (1971). *Noah's Ark*. New York: Atheneum. (K–3)

Hutton, W. (1977). *Noah and the Great Flood*. New York: Atheneum. (K–3)

Lenski, L. (1948). *Mr. and Mrs. Noah*. New York: Crowell. (K–3)

Mee, C. L., Jr. (1978). *Noah*. (Ken Munowitz, Illus.). New York: Harper. (K–3)

Ray, J. (1990). *Noah's Ark*. New York: Dutton Children's Books. (K–3)

Rounds, G. (1985). *Washday on Noah's Ark*. Holiday House. (K–3)

Singer, I. B. (1974). *Why Noah chose the dove*. (Eric Carle, Illus.). New York: Farrar, Straus & Giroux. (2–5)

Spier, P. (1977). *Noah's Ark*. New York: Doubleday. (K–3)

Wildsmith, B. (1980). *Professor Noah's spaceship*. New York: Oxford. (K–3)

References and Books for Further Reading

Alexander, L. (1965). The flat-heeled muse. *Horn Book, 14,* 143–144.

Alexander, L. (1991). The grammar of story. In B. Hearne & M. Kaye (Eds.), *Celebrating children's books* (pp. 3–13). New York: Lothrop, Lee & Shepard.

Applebee, A. (1978). *The child's concept of story.* Chicago: University of Chicago Press.

Bettelheim, B. (1975, December 8). The uses of enchantment. *New Yorker,* p. 5.

Britton, J. (1977). The role of fantasy. In M. Meek, A. Worlow, & G. Barton (Eds.), *The cool web: The pattern of children's reading.* London: Bodley Head.

Cameron, E. (1993). *The seed and the vision: On the writing and appreciation of children's books.* New York: Dutton.

Chukovsky, K. (1963). *From two to five.* Los Angeles: University of California Press.

Cook, E. (1969). *The ordinary and the fabulous.* Cambridge, England: Cambridge University Press.

Dundes, A. (1965). *The study of folklore.* Englewood Cliffs, NJ: Prentice Hall.

Eisner, E. (1992). The misunderstood role of the arts in human development. *Phi Delta Kappan, 8,* 591–595.

Frye, N. (1964). *The educated imagination.* Bloomington, IN: Indiana University.

Greenlaw, M. J. (1995). Fantasy. In A. Silvey (Ed.), *Children's books and their creators* (pp. 234–236). Boston: Houghton Mifflin.

Gunn, J. (1975). *Alternative worlds: The illustrated history of science fiction.* Englewood Cliffs, NJ: Prentice Hall. A&W Visual Library.

Harms, J. (1972). *Children's responses to fantasy in relation to their stages of intellectual development.* Unpublished doctoral dissertation, Ohio State University, Columbus, Ohio.

Hearne, B. (1990). *Choosing books for children: A commonsense approach.* New York: Delacorte.

Hunter, M. (1975). *Talent is not enough.* New York: Harper.

Kennedy, D., & Spangler, S. (1986). Story structure 3: The how or why story. *The Reading Teacher, 39,* 365.

Langton, J. (1977). The weak place in the cloth: A study of fantasy for children. In P. Heins (Ed.), *Crosscurrents of criticism: Horn Book essays 1968–1977* (pp. 143–159). Boston: Horn Book.

Le Guin, U. K. (1979). National book award acceptance speech. In S. Wood (Ed.), *The language of the night: Essays of fantasy and science fiction* (pp. 60–61). New York: Putnam.

Lester, J. (1969). *Black folktales.* New York: Pantheon.

Lester, J. (1988, Summer). The storyteller's voice: Reflections on the rewriting of Uncle Remus. *New Advocate, 1,* 143–147.

Livo, N. J., & Rietz, S. A. (1986). *Storytelling process and practice.* Littleton, CO: Libraries Unlimited.

Miller, S. (1995). American folklore. In A. Silvey (Ed.), *Children's books and their creators* (pp. 22–24). Boston: Houghton Mifflin.

Opie, I., & Opie, P. (1974). *The classic fairy tales.* London: Oxford University Press.

Pitcher, E., & Prelinger, E. (1963). *Children tell stories: An analysis of fantasy.* New York: International Universities.

Rothman, R. (1990, February 21). Experts warn of attempts to censor classic texts. *Education Week,* p. 5.

Saxby, M., & Winch, G. (1987). *Give them wings: The experience of children's literature.* South Melbourne, Australia: Macmillan.

Schwartz, A. (1977). Children, humor, and folklore. In P. Heins (Ed.), *Crosscurrents of criticism: Horn Book essays 1968–1977* (pp. 214–215). Boston: Horn Book.

Shlain, L. (1990). *Art and physics: Parallel visions in space, time and light.* New York: Morrow.

Smith, F. (1988). *Joining the literacy club: Further essays into education.* Portsmouth, NH: Heinemann.

Smith, G. (1987). Inner reality: The nature of fantasy. In M. Saxby and G. Winch (Eds.), *Give them wings: The experience of children's literature.* (pp. 259–276). South Melbourne, Australia: Macmillan.

Sutherland, Z., & Livingston, M. C. (1984). *The Scott/Foresman anthology of children's literature* (8th ed.). Chicago: Scott Foresman.

Swanton, S. (1984, March). Minds alive! What and why gifted students read for pleasure. *School Library Journal, 30,* 99–102.

Thompson, S. (1951). *The folktale.* New York: Holt Rinehart & Winston.

Townsend, J. R. (1990). *Written for children.* New York: HarperTrophy.

Van Allsburg, C. (1995). Voices of the creators: Chris Van Allsburg. In Anita Silvey (Ed.), *Children's books and their creators* (pp. 660–662). Boston: Houghton Mifflin.

People Now: Contemporary Realistic Fiction

9

KEY TERMS

alternative family   realistic fiction
    structures   series books
didacticism   values clarification

GUIDING QUESTIONS

As you read, think about whether you strongly identify with the story characters and their problems. Keep the following questions in mind as you read through this chapter.

1. Can you see relations between the issues and problems presented in these realistic books and issues and problems that you experienced growing up?

2. Are these problems related to young people who are currently growing up?

3. Can you think of any reasons for putting contemporary characters in such a wide variety of settings?

4. Many cultural groups are represented in this genre. Why might this be so?

5. Why is realistic fiction so popular with children?

OVERVIEW

Contemporary realistic fiction and historical fiction (which is presented in chapter 10) both describe events, people, and relationships as they might have happened. In these stories, problems are solved through hard work, persistence, and determined efforts rather than magic, as in fantasy. No fantastic elements, no magical spells, and no supernatural powers appear in this type of fiction. However, we do find occasional serendipities—because truth is often stranger than fiction.

The protagonists succeed or fail as a result of their own strengths or weaknesses. As children read contemporary realistic fiction, they have opportunities:

- to gain insights about people and events that occur in the current time;
- to learn how current events may influence young people;
- to become aware of the similarities of the human spirit in all contexts; and
- to experience the ways that people have survived and learned from their challenges.

INTRODUCTION

Protagonists learn about the problems and the tragedies—and sometimes the comedies—of growing and living in today's world. Readers can walk in another person's shoes to learn what that person thinks and feels about experiences.

Contemporary realistic fiction addresses the problems that are often faced in the real world. Avi's contemporary character Philip Malloy in *Nothing But the Truth* grapples with rights and issues in current life, as does Ryan Walker in Phyllis Reynolds Naylor's *Walker's Crossing*. Ryan wants just one thing: to be a cowboy. But his older brother belongs to a local militia group that is convinced that the U.S. government, foreign immigrants, and people who are racial minorities are going to take over the area. Ryan is forced to make a decision that is at odds with his brother's beliefs.

VIGNETTE

Jeff McKenzie held up Frances Temple's *Tonight, by Sea* so his fifth graders could see the cover.

Jennifer groaned, "Oh no! Another multicultural book, I'm tired of reading about people from other countries so that we can learn how they live."

"Jennifer, why do you think this is a multicultural book?"

"Because the kids look like they are from some other country."

Mr. McKenzie replied, "Well, you're right in a way, but this story is really about courage. The people in this story are Haitian boat people who are trying to escape hunger and terror of their government. You could call this a 'quest' story, but these people became refugees in order to survive, so it is a survival story."

"What's a refugee?" asked Sheila.

"A homeless person," said Randolph.

"No it isn't! I've never heard anyone call the people at the homeless shelter refugees," Gina said.

Cameron said, "Well, refugees wander around because they don't have a place to go. Isn't that being homeless?"

After several minutes of discussion, Mr. McKenzie changed his plans and asked, "Have you decided what a refugee is?"

"No, no," they answered and said, "We don't know what a quest is either."

The unit Mr. McKenzie created based on the students' questions is presented in the last section of this chapter.

CONTEMPORARY REALISTIC FICTION

The challenge for writers of realistic fiction is to combine characters, contemporary events, and actions in such a way as to create a memorable story with a theme that appeals to readers. The most memorable stories have characters that are real enough that readers can identify with their feelings. Perhaps most important, they are characters that readers care about. The events and settings must also be believable so that readers are drawn into seeking resolution to the problems presented. The themes need to be ones that we care about; in other words, they need to be universal so readers can connect them with their own lives.

Furthermore, authors of children's realistic fiction are committed to telling the truth. Fine literature portrays honest interpretations of actual events, characters, and conflicts. After all, "The world has not spared children hunger, cold, sorrow, pain, fear, loneliness, disease, death, war, famine, or madness. Why should we hesitate to make use of this knowledge when writing for them?" (Steele, 1973, p. 290). A growing number of people, however, believe that books for children and young adults need to be censored—or at least rewritten—to protect the children from the harsh realities portrayed or because the ideas conflict with their view of the world. Robert Burch (1973) disagrees, stating:

> If we could guarantee children that the world out there would be completely safe, then fine, we could afford to give them only stories that leave the impression. But until we can, in whatever we present as being realistic, is it not cheating for it to be otherwise? (p. 284)

Well-written realistic fiction gives an honest depiction of life as perceived by the author.

Children no less than adults experience the effects of cruelty, war, segregation, separation, and a multitude of stresses. How they deal with these issues can give them insight for recognizing and dealing with conflicts that they may face in their lives. Books can give them a vision of a better world as well as a vision of how they can be a part of changing their world. One of the distinguishing characteristics of children's realistic fiction is the message of hope and possibility that is always present. Even though life may be hard, survival and the possibility of better things are never out of the question. People, especially children, need hope to be able to sustain the will to live, and children's realistic fiction encourages positive expectations of fulfillment. "Writings for young people are about maturing in the real world.

The important thing is that things do change; whatever is can be made better" (Hamilton, 1992, p. 678).

Realistic fiction does not only deal with "heavy" issues. This genre also includes many books with non–life-threatening problems that authors deal with sensitively and with compassion but often with a touch of humor and lightheartedness. For example, Betsy Byars, who draws on experiences with her own children, writes about real life while capturing the absurdities of situations with her special talent for looking at situations from a good-humored perspective. *The Burning Questions of Bingo Brown* not only addresses first love between two classmates, but also takes a serious look at a teacher's integrity. Beverly Cleary's book *Ramona's World* is superb realistic fiction that focuses on the ever feisty Ramona, a fourth grader adjusting to a baby sister.

In this genre also are some of the series books, which satisfy the needs of many readers to simply relax and enjoy a good read. Some examples of series books include Bill Cosby's popular Little Bill series, Karen Hesse's fine Red Feather series (*Lavender* is an example), the Animorphs series by K. A. Applegate, the Goosebumps series by R. L. Stine, and the Baby-sitters Club series by Ann Martin.

Similarities and Differences in Contemporary and Historical Realistic Fiction

Although historical fiction and contemporary realistic fiction are different genres, they have many common features, and understanding these shared features is important because of the difficulty in classifying some books into one genre or the other. (See the section When Does the Present Become the Past? in chapter 10.) Their shared characteristics include:

1. The plot contains events and incidents that could actually occur in the particular setting of the book. These events and incidents are *possible,* but need not be *probable* (Russell, 1994).

2. The characters demonstrate both strengths and weaknesses in their actions. They are not perfect.

3. The language used is typical of the language used in the setting, either in the past or the present.

4. The theme is one that readers can relate to. They can make connections between the ideas in the book and their own lives.

ISSUES IN REALISTIC FICTION

As we mentioned, many adults do not understand the use of graphic reality portrayed in some realistic fiction, and this is an important issue to consider for those who choose literature for children and young adults. Certainly, no books are "right" or "wrong" in and of themselves; the issue is whether a specific book is right or wrong for a specific reader. This implies that before purchasing or recommending a book for a reader, the adult should be familiar with both.

Didacticism

Didacticism, presenting obvious, heavy-handed moral messages or instructions, alienates many readers. Some authors find realistic fiction an irresistible platform for sharing their beliefs and values. Some believe young people lack values and should be taught through didactic literature. The issue here is not a concern for the specific values espoused, but the way in which they are presented. One of the differences between well-written fiction and poorly written fiction is the way beliefs and values are expressed. In well-written fiction, the beliefs and values are implicit. They emerge from the characters' actions, conversations, and decisions. In poorly written fiction, the theme or message gets in the way of the story itself.

Susan Sharp (1992) suggests, "it is the values and ideas we think children might miss if we don't assert them that leads us into didactic stories, [however,] in the works of the greatest writers, unresolved issues can make the best stories" (p. 696). Because didacticism usually alienates readers, we recommend avoiding didactic books when selecting or recommending literature.

Anne Devereaux Jordan (1997a) sums up the important issues relating not only to didacticism but also to realistic fiction in general:

> While realistic fiction is useful in conveying messages to readers, the reason to choose a particular book should be because it is well-written and pleasing to read; it enhances the reading experience. If we review the history of realistic fiction, we see that these are the books that have claimed the hearts of children generation after generation. Similarly, the books we have carried with us into adulthood are those that still delight us and reveal insights into our humanity at any age rather than being a sermon about a particular problem topical only during our youth. This is not to say that the moral tale, or, today, the problem novel does not have

a place, but that it must be recommended—unlike the rod of earlier days—sparingly if we are to develop a love of reading in young people. (p. 57)

The Value of Realism

Values portrayed in many books of realistic fiction can be a major issue in children's literature. In chapter 1 we introduced this issue, which cannot be resolved in a simple fashion. Certainly authors express values one way or another every time they write. Knowing this places greater responsibility on the adults who guide children's reading. An open marketplace of ideas encourages children to think critically and express their own values. Certainly this is a multifaceted issue that is an ongoing concern, and values are an especially important issue in realistic fiction. The depiction of families has moved from the *Ozzie and Harriet* and *Leave It to Beaver* types to single-parent families, unwed mothers, and alcoholic parents. Should we pretend that these families do not exist or should authors present a realistic picture of society today? Should authors allow the characters in children's books to use profanity? Would Gilly, the foster child in *The Great Gilly Hopkins,* be the same character if she did not use some profanity? The author, Katherine Paterson, is a minister's wife and the daughter of missionaries. The use of profanity is a way to demonstrate Gilly's characteristics; any amount of description would not be as effective. No matter what the arguments are in favor of such realism or who writes it, some parents may be very upset if their children are allowed to read such things.

Violence

Violence is an issue throughout our society and the depiction of violence in realistic fiction is a concern in selecting literature. Although violence appears in all genres of children's literature, it seems to appear most frequently in realistic fiction and traditional literature. (See chapter 8 for a discussion of violence in traditional literature.)

Can children's books exclude violence while portraying realistic contemporary life? Walter Dean Myers includes guns, gangs, and violence in the *Scorpions* and depicts teachers and principals in a negative light. Nevertheless, this is a too-good-to-miss book that raises important issues for children in

Grades 4 through 8. The author writes out of his own experience and a reality for many youngsters in contemporary society.

TYPES OF REALISTIC FICTION

The categories of realistic fiction in this section emerged from the literature itself as we read thousands of books for children and young adults and asked this question: Is the struggle one in which the focus is on the main character's growth and development and in which the setting is almost incidental, or is the reason for the problem the result of societal events? Three broad categories emerged from the literature: (a) families, (b) challenges from outside the family, (c) books to meet special interests. We developed subcategories based on the types of problems or themes within the books. We also found books that describe children with challenges—learning problems, emotional disabilities, physical handicaps, and so forth, and we address these in chapter 13.

Families

Stories grow out of authors' experiences and are greatly influenced by the times and values of the society in which they write. Taxel (1994) states, "Like other cultural artifacts, children's literature is a product of convention that is rooted in, if not determined by, the dominant belief systems and ideologies of the times in which they are created" (p. 99). Family structure in books, both past and present, gives evidence of these belief systems and values.

Nuclear families

Although many families no longer consist of two parents with their children, this is still society's norm. Not surprisingly, then, we see this structure mirrored in numerous books. For some children and adults, these books confirm the belief that families provide needed support and guidance as children mature.

Books in which the family interactions are the focus of the story have many variations. They range from "happily ever after" books to those with less optimistic endings. Beverly Cleary's books have a long-standing popularity with children and adults, and children can easily identify with many of the situations in her books. In *Beezus and Ramona,* Beezus learns that having bad thoughts about a pesky little sister who always seems to get her own way is quite normal. The entire Quimby family learns to adjust to Mr. Quimby's unemployment in *Ramona and Her Father,* and the feelings of unease, irritation, and worry are eventually resolved and replaced with joy, understanding, and insight. Some readers may think the solutions are too easy; others gain a sense of relief and comfort as problems are solved.

Lensey Namioka's book *Yang the Youngest and His Terrible Ear* tells the story of the Yang family who moved from China to the United States. All of the Yangs are musicians except for Yingtao, who discovers that he is more successful at baseball than music. The cooperation of an older sister during a recital convinces the family that Yingtao really cannot make beautiful music but that he can be successful in other ways.

The Abernathy family, six children, two parents, and a host of relatives are embroiled in many family kinds of activities, including many practical jokes. As expected, after brother Brad dies, the family has a hard time recovering. In *Fig Pudding,* Ralph Fletcher demonstrates his insight into how this family is able to learn to laugh again—not only at outside events but at themselves.

Sometimes siblings do not have similar interests and goals. Twins Dee and Dezzy, just turning 13, seem to be on the opposite ends of almost any continuum of interests and abilities. Dezzy appears to be *Thirteen Going On Seven* and has difficulty because she is not the smart, outgoing person her sister is. After their grandmother dies however, Dezzy is the one who is able to create a cohesive family again. Marilyn Sachs helps us understand that each member of a family plays a unique role and each is important.

Family misfits. Finding one's place in a nuclear family can be difficult. Louise Fitzhugh portrays this problem in *Nobody's Family Is Going to Change.* Emma Sheridan wants to be a lawyer like her father, and her brother Willie wants to be a dancer like his Uncle Dipsey. But their parents want them to choose more traditional careers. The father is particularly upset because as an African American he has fought prejudice to become an attorney.

Betsy Byars tells the story of another misfit in *The Glory Girl.* Anna Glory is the misfit in her family, the Glory Gospel Singers, because she cannot carry a tune:

There are lots of people who didn't fit into their families. Anna reminded herself of this all the time—the dumb one in a family of brains, the ugly one in a family of beauties. But no one—Anna was sure of this—felt as left out as she did when her family sang together. (p. 29)

Anna's family is portrayed as quite artificial. Only after Anna and another family misfit, Uncle Newt, save the rest of the family does the reader (and the family) realize that each person is important.

Family problems.   Members of intact families do not escape serious problems either. In *I See the Moon* by C. B. Christiansen, 12-year-old Bitte cannot understand the tension occurring in her family. When she learns that her older sister, Kari, is pregnant, Bitte confidently makes plans for helping to care for the baby. When Kari decides not to get married and to put the baby up for adoption, Bitte is sent to live with her Uncle Axel because of her negative attitude. Bitte matures while she is away and learns to accept that families are linked in many ways. The book is Bitte's "letter" to her niece.

In *Francesca, Baby,* Joan Oppenheimer vividly describes the family illness of alcoholism. Francesca and Mary Kate's mother begins drinking heavily after their brother's death. Their father escapes by traveling more and more. Francesca has to assume most of the family responsibilities. A teacher intervenes and helps Francesca seek assistance through Alateen. As she learns about alcoholism, she is able to confront the serious problems involved. Readers who are unfamiliar with programs such as Alateen and Alcoholics Anonymous may find the solutions contrived and simplistic, but those who are familiar with these programs will recognize that the events are not unusual or exceptional.

In *Kidnapping Kevin Kowalski,* a young man faces mental and physical difficulties making normal life impossible, compounded by an overprotective mother. Through the courage of his sister and friends, who "kidnap" him, he begins his real recovery. Mary Jane Auch's book *Kidnapping Kevin Kowalski* presents a unique view of family and friends.

For a variety of reasons, some families lose their homes and become homeless. *Shelter Folks* by Virginia Kroll describes the feelings that 9-year-old Joelle has about living in a neighborhood shelter. She begins to accept the situation when she learns that a classmate also lives in the shelter. Joelle also learns that it is a community when some of the others living in the shelter come to her school function.

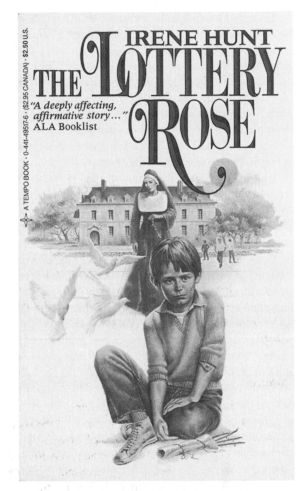

Georgie, an abused child who dreams of flowers, slowly learns to give—and to receive—love.

Extended families.   More and more books of realistic fiction are including relationships with grandparents, aunts, uncles, and other extended family members. Research by Janice S. McElhoe (1999) found that although grandparents are often presented stereotypically in picture books, many excellent books are available that include grandparents more realistically, which means that they are presented with both strengths and weaknesses.

Lester Laminack creates a sensitive portrayal of a difficult subject, Alzheimer's disease, in *The Sunsets of Miss Olivia Wiggins.* In this story, Miss Wiggins's great-grandson talks to her although she does not react; however, he does notice a twitch of a smile when he hugs her good-bye.

Lacey's Grandmom in *Return to Bitter Creek* by Doris Buchanan Smith is a controlling person. She had wanted to control Lacey's mother, Campbell, after Lacey was born so the two of them left Bitter Creek under unpleasant circumstances. Ten years later when Lacey, Campbell, and Campbell's boyfriend, David, return, Grandmom is still trying to control. Not until David's death does the family come together, learning to respect each person without trying to impose anyone's will on another family member.

In another story, Elizabeth is forced to spend the summer with her artist grandmother on an island in Maine. Elizabeth is upset because she believes that her parents want her out of the house so they can spend the summer alone with her new baby brother. Elizabeth and Gran settle in together, and Elizabeth develops a relationship with her as well as with Aaron, the peculiar son of their only neighbors. When Aaron is lost, Gran and Elizabeth find him, but the excitement is too much for Gran's heart and she collapses. Paula Fox has written an insightful book about the importance of learning about life and death and the importance of family interactions in *Western Wind*.

Ruth White has written an incredible story describing the importance of family support in the Newbery Honor book *Belle Prater's Boy*. When Woodrow's mother, Belle, disappears, he moves in with his grandparents. His next door neighbors are his aunt, uncle, and cousin, Gypsy. As their friendship develops, both Gypsy and Woodrow learn to depend on each other and in the process come to terms with Belle's disappearance and the death of Gypsy's father.

Ariel and her grandmother make a quilt using one of Ariel's drawings in *The Canada Geese Quilt*. Making the quilt gives Grandma the will to live after she has a stroke, and it helps Ariel learn to accept her grandmother's disability. Natalie Kinsey-Warnock's book will help younger readers recognize the special relationships that can occur between grandparents and grandchildren.

Sharon Creech describes Zinny's house:

> Strolling from our kitchen through the passage into Aunt Jessie and Uncle Nate's kitchen was like drifting back in time. On our side was a zoo of noises: . . . But when you stepped through the passage, suddenly you'd be in the Quiet Zone of Aunt Jessie's and Uncle Nate's house. . . . (p. 3)

Aunt Jessie gives the book its title, *Chasing Redbird*, a wonderful story of discovering self and others.

Alternative family structures

In many books published prior to the 1960s, the typical family structure included two parents, children, and perhaps a few close family members. Alternative structures were the result of a parent's death, often the mother. Contemporary realistic fiction published today portrays alternative family structures much more frequently, and death is not the sole reason for these changes. Divorce, desertion, or sexual preference of parents all create families that are not "typical." Homelessness, single-parent families, children raised by family members rather than parents, foster children, and families with stepparents are all portrayed with increasing frequency as family structures in this genre. The children and young people in these books struggle as they learn to survive. For some of the children, the struggle is physical; for others, it is emotional. In addition to the normal challenges of growing up, these children have extra responsibilities, different expectations, and circumstances over which they have no control. The ways they cope with these life conditions give readers insights about life.

Most of the characters in these books have some sort of family structure or adult support. Through their experiences, the characters begin to develop an understanding of themselves and those around them. They come to realize that they are not the only people in the world facing these problems, a realization that helps them feel connected to the world. Connectedness to others is a major theme in many of these books.

Single parents. Being a member of a single-parent family is often not easy. Money is often in short supply, and the family members often go without things they want or need. Thursday is the worst day of the week in *Gettin' through Thursday* by Melrose Cooper because that is the day before payday. Andre worries that even though Mama has promised to have a party for him if he makes the honor roll, it will not occur because it happened on Thursday. What a surprise is in store for him. This is a celebration that he will not forget.

Alice Mead writes with sensitivity and hope about *Junebug,* who lives with his mother, younger sister, and Aunt Jolita in the Auburn Street projects. Junebug has to contend with pressure from his friends and others to get involved in activities he should avoid. Aunt Jolita, who is supposed to be watching Junebug and his 5-year-old sister, is irresponsible, so Junebug must assume responsibility for himself and his sister. For his tenth birthday, Junebug puts messages into 50 bottles; a ferry captain gets one of the bottles, and the opportunities that Junebug dreamed about begin to take place.

Quinella Ellerbee's mother left the family to play in a Kentucky bluegrass band. Pa-Daddy does his best to keep the family together, even though the family has to move to the swamps. This causes great dissention among the children and their father, and the conflicts increase after he loses his job in the mines. Quin wonders how things will ever be right again. Joyce McDonald does not provide any easy answers, but readers are left with the feeling that *Comfort Creek,* even if it is a made-up place, is a safe place.

Jane Leslie Conly tells the story of Shana and Cody, whose father left the family when he met the new waitress at the Peter Pan Inn. After the children and their mother move to the suburbs, they realize how much they all missed the green of their small town. Only by spending time with a "ranger" during *Trout Summer* and facing death does Shana begin to accept that truth: Losses are a part of life.

Paula Danziger has written five books about Amber Brown and the changes that take place in her life. In *Forever Amber Brown,* once Amber learns to accept her mother's divorce, she needs to adjust to the fact that her mother decides to get engaged.

Divorce and stepfamilies.
Beverly Cleary tells the story of a child of divorce in *Strider,* and its predecessor *Dear Mr. Henshaw.* The main character, Leigh Botts, writes in his diary about his life. He is concerned with his dog, his peers, and school.

Divorce and remarriage place many children into stepfamilies. Children must struggle to make sense, first, of the divorce, and then, of becoming a member of a different family. In *What Hearts,* Bruce Brooks introduces Asa, an excited 7-year-old coming home to share the prizes he has won in first grade. When he arrives home, his mother is sitting on a suitcase on the porch, the house is empty, and his parents have separated. Almost immediately he is introduced to his mother's friend, David, who soon becomes Asa's stepfather. Asa and David are not two of a kind and at times life is almost unbearable. By the time Asa and his stepfather have made the first step toward what might be a good relationship, his mother has decided to divorce David and once again Asa is set adrift.

Although not a life-threatening situation, when 11-year-old Erin Mitchell finds that she may have to change her name when she is adopted by her stepfather, she has a dilemma. She loves Leo, her stepfather, but doesn't want to give up her own name. She finally decides that she will stay Erin Mitchell. Mary Jane Miller has written a believable story, *Me and My Name,* about a conflict that other young people may be experiencing.

Maggie visits her father, stepmother, and baby half-sister in Avi's *Blue Heron.* She anticipates tensions when she arrives, but does not realize the actual problems she will face. Her sick father has lost his job, he refuses to take his medicine, and then he has a serious car accident. Maggie's only peace during the summer comes from observing a blue heron. As she works with her stepmother to save her father, they begin to develop a positive relationship. In the end, all of the main characters develop greater self-awareness.

Long-distance fathers.
Jim Ugly by Sid Fleischman deals with the unfortunate topic of absentee fathers. Jake Bannock's father supposedly dies and Jake is to live with his cousin, Aurora. The only reminder Jake has of his father is his dog, Jim Ugly. When Jake overhears Aurora planning to kill Jim Ugly, he runs away. After he gets away he comes to the conclusion that his father is not really dead. Eventually Jake and Jim Ugly are reunited with his father.

Unlike Jake, Jimmy Little in *Somewhere in the Darkness* by Walter Dean Myers never really knew his father, who is in jail. After his mother's death, Jimmy lives with Mama Jean. Then Crab, his father, escapes from a hospital and insists that Jimmy accompany him so they can escape from the authorities. During the escape, he hears his father's side of the incident for which he was imprisoned. Crab is captured and dies; Jimmy returns to live with Mama Jean, but he has learned the importance of parent-and-child relationships.

Although Marion Dane Bauer's focus in *Face to Face* is the relationship between father and son, the conflict also is between stepfather and stepson. Michael's stepfather adopts him. But when his biological father calls for a visit, Michael is more than ready to go. He is angry because his stepfather took the new rifle Michael received for his birthday. During the visit, Michael's father, Dave, constantly tests him for bravery. Even when he "wins" a test, it is not a good feeling. The situation deteriorates, and Michael returns home early. At home, he finds his gun and tries to commit suicide. His stepfather finds him and helps him finally understand that his father truly does care for him but not in the way that Michael would like him to.

Living with foster parents or family members other than a parent.   Many times children must live with foster parents or relatives who are not their parents. Sometimes parents die, some parents are dysfunctional, or war or military careers may separate children from either or both parents. In *The Cookcamp,* Gary Paulsen writes about a boy living with his grandmother because his father is a soldier in World War II and his mother is unable to cope. The boy learns to help his grandmother, who cooks for nine road builders. He learns to love his grandmother and gets used to the men, who become a part of his life. When his mother is able to take him, he returns with a mixture of happiness and sadness.

In *Child of the Owl* by Laurence Yep, Casey's father is always planning "big deals" that will make him rich. After he is hospitalized as a result of a beating, he sends Casey to live with her uncle, but streetwise Casey and her big-shot lawyer uncle don't hit it off. He sends Casey to live with her eccentric Chinese grandmother, Paw-Paw. From her grandmother, Casey learns about the discrimination her father has faced. She also learns about her culture and comes to love her grandmother.

Although *Journey,* the title of a Patricia MacLachlan book and the name of the main character, is from a different cultural background than Casey, he has some of the same types of problems. Journey and his sister live with their grandparents. They wait for promised letters from their mother that never come. Grandfather takes many photographs that chronicle the family, and through studying these photos, Journey comes to realize that his grandparents love him deeply. He also realizes that his mother is not likely to return. In the end, Journey develops an interest in photography.

Summer, the main character in *Missing May* by Cynthia Rylant, has lived with a series of relatives. Finally, elderly Aunt May and Uncle Ob find her and take her home to their trailer in the mountains of West Virginia. When Aunt May dies 6 years later, Summer faces another crisis because she loses the security she finally had developed. Eventually, both Summer and Uncle Ob gain the strength to accept May's death.

Truman Capote writes a sensitive story about Buddy, a second grader who goes to live with a collection of elderly relatives because of a custody battle. His best friend becomes Miss Sook, the elderly aunt in charge of the household. At school, Buddy is bullied incessantly by Odd Henderson. Miss Sook, who always looks for the best in everyone, invites Odd to be *The Thanksgiving Visitor.* When Miss Sook lies to protect Odd, Buddy is heartbroken. Only by seeing Odd from Miss Sook's perspective is Buddy able to accept the affront and to learn from it.

Fifteen-year-old Sara was abandoned by her parents when she was born. She has lived in many foster homes and has learned to keep her feelings tight inside herself. When she is sent to the Huddlestons, things change. Sara begins to open up. When The Woman (Sara's biological mother) comes, Sara stays with her foster family. Julie Johnston has written a story that exposes the process of coming to terms with one's feelings in *Adam and Eve and Pinch-Me.*

Generations of families.   Some excellent literature follows generations of the same family, giving readers insight into a family over many years. They are given the rare opportunity to see the positive changes that occur over decades. Other times, however, readers see the changes and are dismayed by them.

In *Jericho,* Janet Hickman presents the lives of four generations of women, focusing primarily on GrandMin, the great-grandmother, and Angela, the great-granddaughter. GrandMin's mind is back in Jericho, the town where she grew up. She has only fleeting periods of living in the present and requires the help of her daughter, granddaughter, and Angela. Through a series of flashbacks, we see GrandMin's life from childhood through adulthood and we develop an understanding of the family.

Walter Dean Myers portrays the generations of survivors that make up the Lewis family in *The Glory Field.* He traces the family from 1753 on the coast of Sierra Leone, West Africa, to present-day Harlem, New York. They were slaves in 1864 during the Civil War. By 1900, they lived on 8 acres of land called the Glory Field. By 1964, the Civil Rights Movement had started, and the family joined in this battle. Tommy finds the shackles that were on the legs of the first family member brought to this country and chains himself to the sheriff. In the final section, the Lewis family gathers for a last reunion at Glory Field; a resort is going to be built there. Malcolm, a family member, attends the reunion and becomes custodian of the shackles that symbolize the common bond among all generations.

Challenges from Outside the Family

As children grow up, the family—whether nuclear or alternative—may come to assume less importance in children's lives and the peer group takes on greater importance. These changes represent children's growing need for independence. Parents, siblings, extended family members, and other adults who have been the focus of a child's interactions may begin to fade into the background. A common theme in books dealing with this period of life is problems within the family: family members who "do not understand" or who try to interfere with peer relations. In general, however, despite conflicts, the characters still see their families, especially parents, as integral partners in resolving problems. Other books address problems outside the family with peers, school, and nonfamily adults; the family is less involved as the characters seek to define who they are becoming. In these books, the characters need support, which they may receive from peers or other adults or, in some circumstances, an understanding family. A third kind of problem occurs as the characters face emotional or physical challenges that they must meet by themselves, without family or peers. Their ultimate survival depends on how they overcome the hardships. They may not have the support of adults or others; they may be alone by choice or because of circumstances beyond their control. The books for children and young adults reviewed here reflect these three kinds of problems or conflicts. Of course, readers may place a book in a different category than is done here. As is true in life, many books cannot be neatly pigeonholed.

Families and Peers

All of the families portrayed in this section are supportive of their children, although this support is not always appreciated. As youngsters begin to identify more closely with their peers and develop some independence, conflicts begin to arise among their parents and their siblings. In *Planning the Impossible* by Mavis Jukes, River's parents are planning to go out of town to celebrate her aunt's birthday. This trip will have disastrous consequences because it conflicts with the school's Fourth Annual Powwow. River and her best friend, Margaret, have made elaborate schemes to hang out with the boys they like and even more important, they have devised a way to match up Margaret's father with one of their favorite teachers. All is in jeopardy because of River's family!

Paula Danziger has written a series of books that follow Matthew as he moves from fourth grade through junior high: *Everyone Else's Parents Said Yes, Make Like a Tree and Leave, Earth to Matthew,* and *Not for a Billion, Gazillion Dollars.* These books show the changing patterns of peer and family relationships as Matthew develops. In the early years, Matthew has almost exclusive interactions with boys; over time girls gradually are included in the activities. The major emphasis in this series of books is peer relationships, but it also addresses issues such as conservation, ecology, and responsibility.

Bobby moves to upstate New York from Illinois in *Spider Boy.* He misses his old friends and has difficulty making new ones. His passion for learning about and studying spiders earns him the name of Spider Boy, but it also provides an opportunity to make friends. We learn about Bobby's feelings not only through the description that Ralph Fletcher writes but also through Bobby's journal.

When Palmer LaRue turns 10, he is expected by his father, the boys in his class, and the community in general to become a *Wringer,* one who finishes killing the pigeons that were not killed by gunfire in the annual pigeon shoot. Palmer is taunted by the boys who see his aversion to wringing as a weakness they can use to their advantage. After Palmer adopts a pigeon, he knows that he must take a stand against tradition and defy his father and the others. In doing so, he develops a sense of respect for himself and begins to change the perspective of his father and some others in the community. Jerry Spinelli creates a realistic picture of pressures peers and family members inflict on children.

Walter Dean Myers uses an urban setting for *Won't Know Till I Get There,* portraying different situations through 14-year-old Steve's diary entries. Steve's parents believe that they have a responsibility to share their home and love with a child who is less fortunate. They choose Earl, a 13-year-old who has a criminal record. When Steve and his friends spray paint a train to show off for Earl, they are caught and sentenced to spend the summer working in a senior citizens' home. Over the course of the summer, the children learn to respect each of the seniors as individuals. They also learn about the harm that stereotypes can cause and that personal values can make life worthwhile. Steve's parents support both boys. Although

Earl's birth mother refuses to sign the adoption papers, the family assumes legal custody of him.

Betsy Byars addresses abusive behavior through an 11-year-old boy in *Cracker Jackson*. Cracker seeks to help his former babysitter, Alma, convinced that she is in trouble because she has bruises. Finally she agrees to go to a battered women's shelter, but changes her mind halfway there and insists that Cracker take her home. Later, when Cracker's mother goes to Alma's house she finds that both Alma and Alma's baby have been badly beaten and takes them to the hospital. When the two recover, Cracker and his parents take Alma and her baby to a shelter so they can begin a new life.

For some young people whose family is from a different culture, the expectations of the cultures makes developing independence doubly hard. In *April and the Dragon Lady* Lensey Namioka describes this conflict with sensitivity. How can one become independent and develop an identity that is appropriate for the new style of life when tradition is so powerful?

Peers

Phyllis Reynolds Naylor has written a series of four books that describe the interactions among the three girls in the Malloy family and the four boys of the Hatford family. The Malloy family has not even moved in yet and *The Boys Start the War*. It does not take long before *The Girls Get Even*. As the children get older, the rivalry continues but changes occur and all of them must make some hard decisions that involve sibling loyalty as well as obedience to their teachers and parents. Even so, both *Boys Against Girls* and *The Girls' Revenge* continue to describe the desire of each group to have the upper hand in the ongoing feud.

The theme of Katherine Paterson's *Flip-Flop Girl* is friendship between two misfits. Vinnie moves to a new school after her father's death. During the difficult first days in school she meets Lupe, a fellow misfit, and the two form a tenuous relationship. After Lupe helps Vinnie in a crisis, she learns to accept responsibility for her own actions and she begins to mature.

Ten-year-old Blaze faces major life changes after his mother's death in Kevin Henkes's *Words of Stone*. Blaze is a fearful child who is easily upset. He is very disturbed to see his mother's name written in stones on the hillside. Then he learns that Joselle, who is visiting her own grandmother, did it. He also learns that she

embellishes the truth, but she does help him get over some of his fears. He realizes that she too feels lonely and abandoned.

Lois Ruby describes Greta's life at home as being miserable because of *This Old Man*. Not until she moves to San Francisco to a group home and becomes friends with Wing, a Chinese-American boy, is she able to begin to put her life into perspective. The friendship is also important for Wing, whose grandfather's culture is a dominating force in his life.

Friendships make a positive contribution to growing up, but they can have negative consequences as well. In *Out of Control*, Norma Fox Mazer describes a friendship among three boys that begins in elementary school and continues into high school. These three popular boys are accustomed to impressing girls, but Valerie is not impressed with their behavior and confronts them. They decide to get even and attack her in the hall. They are surprised when she reports the attack and they are suspended from school. Valerie explains why she goes public about the attack: "Because you guys did what you wanted to me and you're home free" (p. 216). Rollo begins to question himself, his actions, and his friends. He breaks with his friends at the end of the story.

It is always a difficult experience when one's best friend moves away. Paula Danziger (author of many well-written books, including the Amber Brown books) and Ann M. Martin (author of the Baby-Sitters Club series) have captured the essence of what this is like in their book, *P.S. Longer Letter Later*. Through the letters that Tara and Elizabeth write, readers learn about how changes affect families and individuals. Their friendship is strong, supportive, and long lasting, even if their primary interactions are through their writing.

Survival

The young people in these books must rely on their own wits, intelligence, and strength to survive. Except for occasional intervals, they may not have family, peer, or other adult support. Survival may include a number of elements. The characters learn to pay attention to and take cues from animals, from those around them, and from the environment as well. They must learn not to panic but to keep calm. In most of the stories that follow, characters may learn to trust them-

Literature circles give students opportunities to discuss the books they've read.

selves and often selected other people. They also need resilience and hope (Poe, 1999).

Clay Garrity, abandoned by his parents, is befriended by homeless men in Paula Fox's *Monkey Island*. After some hoodlums trash the park, Clay becomes ill and goes to the hospital. While there, a social worker comes to interview him and places Clay in a foster home. His foster parents are kind, but Clay depends on his street friends. Then social services locates his mother and reunites Clay with her.

Harley Nunn's mother has regularly abandoned him since he was a young child. His saga is revealed in *Out of Nowhere* by Ouida Sebestyen. At the beginning of the story, Harley's mother is living with a man who will not take Harley with them. When Harley is abandoned in a roadside park, an old woman offers him food. Then he finds a dog and the three form an unlikely trio. They travel to the old woman's home and add two more people to the group. Over time they build a kind of dependence and trust among themselves, and Harley experiences the responsibilities and stability of love.

In a book by Jerry Spinelli, Jeffrey becomes *Maniac Magee* when he runs away from his aunt and

uncle's dysfunctional family at age 11 to the town where he lived before his parents' death. He receives the nickname Maniac Magee because of the outrageous things he does: He borrows a book from Amanda Beale, which he carries around with him; intercepts a pass at the varsity football game; saves a child from the Finsterwalds; runs on the railroad rails; hits every one of John McNab's pitches; and hits the Little League team bully. He lives with the animals at the zoo; with the Beales, a Black family in a segregated town; with a groundskeeper at the band shell; and with the racist McNabs. In a completely unconventional manner, Maniac becomes a bridge between the White and Black sides of town. The book ends as Maniac follows Amanda, knowing "that finally, truly at long last, someone was calling him home" (p. 184).

Kirkpatrick Hill introduces us to *Toughboy and Sister,* two Athabascan children who live in a village along the Yukon. After their mother dies, the village women decide to place the children in different families because their father is drunk most of the time. However, the father does not allow this to happen and with some support from Natasha, the "medicine woman," they manage. In the spring, the father and children go to the fish camp for the summer. The father gets drunk, dies, and the children are left to fend for themselves. When they do not return to the village when school starts, Natasha knows something is wrong and comes to find them.

In the following books, the main characters have families but their survival still depends in large part on what they themselves do.

Jean Craighead George has written many wonderful books for older children. *My Side of the Mountain,* a favorite of adults and children alike, is an account of how Sam creates a house in the roots of a tree to survive the winter and tames a falcon to help him gather food. Although Sam has a family and occasional guests, he is self-sufficient. In the sequel *On the Far Side of the Mountain,* Sam's sister Alice joins him on the mountain. Alice has her own tree house, but she and Sam work together on projects. Sam's falcon has disappeared, but Alice is able to free it, and Sam contacts the sheriff who arrests the men who stole the bird to sell it illegally. Through their experiences, Sam and Alice learn to appreciate not only each other but other people as well.

Gary Paulsen has written a number of survival books with young men as protagonists. In *Tracker,*

John Borne's grandfather is dying of cancer and John must go deer hunting alone. He knows his grandparents need the food to survive the winter, but he has a hard time killing an animal. He tracks a doe, thinking about life, death, and dying, and he is unable to kill the deer. He returns and tells his grandparents that he could not kill. Sam is surprised at his grandfather's pride in him. At this point, he is able to accept the inevitability of death.

In another of Paulsen's books, *Hatchet,* Brian Robeson is stranded in a wilderness after the pilot of a small plane dies and the plane crashes in a lake. Brian is injured but survives, and he is forever changed by his experience. In the sequel to *Hatchet,* entitled *The River,* the story is continued.

Paulie and her family live in Haiti where there is much political conflict among the villagers who support President Aristide and those who support the coup d'etat. Reporters come in to get their stories, and Paulie, her family, and friends are in danger of being killed. They choose a different danger—escape by boat to Florida. Frances Temple tells a compelling story of survival in *Tonight, by Sea.*

SPECIAL INTERESTS AND SERIES BOOKS

Many children develop interests during the elementary years that they retain throughout their lives; others explore a different interest each month. Whichever is true of the children you are working with, literature is a means of exploring and expanding children's interests.

When one goes into the children's and young adult section of many bookstores, the series books may comprise the majority of books found on the shelves; in fact, you may find special sections devoted only to series books. What are series books? Anne Devereaux Jordan (1997b) suggests that these are the books that are read while in the bathtub: They are "usually not particularly well-written or intellectually taxing, but are heavy in suspense or action and cheap in cost so that it doesn't matter if they accidentally fall in the water" (p. 22). The characteristics of series books are that they follow a set formula, have predictable plots with stereotypic characters who are often one-sided but who are able to solve all problems, and often are short and easy to read. These books tend to be episodic. They obviously appeal to readers, both boys and girls, and are worthwhile in that these books often are the ones that will encourage reluctant readers to start reading other books that may be more substantial. Although

they are popular with a range of ages of children, they serve a particular need for second- and third-grade readers, who are moving from learning to read to gaining fluency.

Sports

This section identifies books that help readers look at sports from a broader perspective than that of who wins or loses. The games and game practice create events and contexts that show readers the importance of telling the truth, racial appreciation, and accepting one's weaknesses as well as strengths. Older readers will enjoy these stories even if they are not involved in sports.

We seemed to find more excellent books about baseball than about any of the other sports. As is true with other topics, baseball is the vehicle to create a story that demonstrates a significant theme. In *Dean Duffy* by Randy Powell, 17-year-old Dean must make some hard decisions about what direction he wants his life to take. Although he has been a baseball star in high school, he has had a two-year slump. His mentor has been able to get him a baseball scholarship, but Dean does not know if he is willing to take advantage of it to try to get out of his slump. His friends have a variety of other kinds of dilemmas, and he sees other alternatives. Only because of these situations is he finally able to come to some resolution about his future.

Baseball is the focus in two of Walter Dean Myers's books, *Me, Mop, and the Moondance Kid* and *Mop, Moondance, and the Nagasaki Knights.* The first book describes the lives of two adopted children and their experiences before adoption. Through baseball they learn to share both good and bad times. They also learn to deal with people they do not respect. In the second book, the same children are playing teams from other countries. The team members find communicating with the other teams difficult, but they meet these challenges with the strategies of 12-year-olds. When the problems grow too big, their parents help.

Two books by Will Weaver, *Striking Out* and *Farm Team,* chronicle the tensions that occur between responsibilities to oneself and responsibilities for work. Keeping a balance while growing up is difficult; it is even more difficult when there is not as much support as one really needs. Fourteen-year-old Billy Baggs makes difficult decisions and readers learn about both baseball and farm life.

Some children learn to cope with failure through sports. Jason Ross is despondent when he is cut from the baseball team. He seeks coaching assistance from a school custodian in *Finding Buck McHenry* by Alfred Slote. This story includes some interesting history of players in the old Negro leagues.

Dean Hughes helps us understand a foster child's feelings through his interest in baseball in *Team Picture*. David puts his energy into his pitching in his Pony League. However, he is struggling with the fact that his foster father, Paul, might start drinking again. This fear translates into unacceptable behaviors with his teammates until finally David begins to talk with, and trust, Paul. As he begins to get support from others, he is able to accept both friendship and the weaknesses within himself.

We found two exceptional books about running: *Runner's Song* by Frank McLaughlin and *The Runner* by Cynthia Voigt. In the first, Jeannie is persistent about her goal of becoming a track champion, even though she has more than her share of trouble. After her father deserts her and her mother, they have little money to live on or to buy her special track shoes; she has trouble passing several of her classes; she confronts a family illness. However, with the support of her coach and her poetry, she is able to reach many of her goals.

In *The Runner*, Bullet Tillerman, the best runner on the school track team, has become a loner. He consistently feels boxed in by his father's unreasonable demands. When he finally learns a little about being a team player, he drops out of high school and joins the army. Running away did not solve his problems.

Basketball from a coach's perspective is the theme of *The Rebounder* by Thomas I. Dygard. The coach, Doug Fulton, encounters a natural basketball player, Chris Patton, who refuses to play because he is afraid of injuring other players. Of course, Chris has a reason for these fears and eventually the student manager is able to help Chris work through them. Chris finally is able to join the team, having come to accept the fact that accidents do happen.

Mysteries

Mysteries are popular with children, although teachers, librarians, and parents have often regarded them with suspicious eyes, concerned about literary quality. Fortunately, children's mysteries include those by several notable authors such as Betsy Byars, Joan Lowery Nixon, Gary Paulsen, Phyllis Reynolds Naylor, and Virginia Hamilton, and adults can be assured of the quality of children's books by these authors.

Betsy Byars writes about Herculeah Jones, whose father is a police detective and mother is a private investigator in *Dead Letter*. Herculeah finds a letter in the lining of the pocket of a coat she bought from a thrift shop. She and her friend, Meat, discover who the coat belonged to and discover who killed her.

Joan Lowery Nixon is a well-known mystery writer and the only three-time winner of the Edgar Allan Poe Award. In *Search for the Shadowman,* Andy investigates his family history for a school assignment. His interactions with elderly family members and their friends lead him to ask questions about the mysterious Joe Conley, who had been disowned generations earlier. The reasons for the refusal to discuss him are an integral part of the plot.

Paul and Taryn's parents have been having whispered battles for a long time. Both children worry that their parents may divorce. In school, Taryn has difficulty paying attention in class, gets yelled at by her teacher, and at lunch jokingly suggests that pizzas should be sent to the offending teacher's house. The pizzas really are sent with unexpected consequences, and Taryn is blamed. Taryn and her friends trick the person who really ordered the pizzas to confess in *The Pizza Puzzle* by Susan Beth Pfeffer.

In addition to all the other books he writes in different genres, Gary Paulsen writes a mystery series. In the Culpepper Adventures series, Duncan Culpepper and his best friend, Amos, embroil themselves in mysterious situations. In *The Case of the Dirty Bird* they search for hidden treasure but find a building filled with gunpowder instead.

The Cam Jansen Adventure series, written by David Adler, are books for readers who are making the transition from easy-to-read books to chapter books. Both Cam, who has a photographic memory, and her friend, Eric, are willing to take chances to solve the mysteries they seem to attract. For example, in *Cam Jansen and the Mystery of the Dinosaur Bones,* they discover that the museum guide and a friend are stealing bones. They also are able to keep an older person from winning the photography contest in *Cam Jansen and the Mystery of the U.F.O.*

Animal Stories

Foxy is a stray dog living near a campground. Both Jeff and Amber want the dog, but Foxy bonds with Jeff.

Several accidents occur, many of which are life threatening, before Jeff and Foxy are together. Helen V. Griffith has written a very believable book, which won Florida's Sunshine State Young Readers Award.

Rodman Philbrick writes books that are memorable; *The Fire Pony* is no exception. Joe Dilly and his younger brother, Roy, are running away when they find the Bar None Ranch. Joe's talent is working with horses, but he also drinks too much and likes fires. Both work for Mr. Jessup at the ranch and Roy begins to put down roots. When a fire is started, Joe dies, leaving Roy an orphan. Mr. Jessup signs the necessary papers so that Roy will not have to return to foster homes.

The Pony Pals, Anna, Lulu, and Pam, always seem to be having adventures—or adventures find them. In *Detective Pony*, the seventeenth book in this series by Jeanne Betancourt, a fire breaks out in the animal clinic, and Anna and her horse find the stray cat that was missing.

Other Series Books

We can recommend several other series books that are written for readers who are beginning to read chapter books. Some of them follow.

The Spencer's Adventures books by Gary Hogg relate the zany ideas that Spencer has and that all seem to have happy endings. For example, in the series' fourth book, *The Great Toilet Paper Caper*, Spencer decides to get his name into the Gigantic Book of World Records by walking backward longer than anyone else has. When his teacher and the principal of the school recognize the fun of "Backwards Day" at school, the class decides to make the world's biggest roll of toilet paper so the principal will also get an award. Everyone has fun and wins awards.

David A. Adler writes about a fourth grader in his series about Andy Russell. In *The Many Troubles of Andy Russell*, Andy's gerbils have escaped, creating many problems for him both in school and out of school. This situation has occurred to enough children to make the story very realistic.

Several of the Bailey School Kids series books by Debbie Dadey and Marcia Thornton Jones deal with the almost supernatural. In both *Gargoyles Don't Drive School Buses* and *Vampires Don't Wear Polka Dots* inferences are made, but not confirmed, about the teacher and the bus driver not being quite real. Younger readers enjoy the ambiguity.

Classroom Activities

Fiction in contemporary settings is particularly useful in developing children's understanding of themselves, their families, their cultural backgrounds, their values, and issues addressed in the curriculum. Trade books provide children with multiple human perspectives that textbooks do not. Moreover, literature permits readers to experience a variety of current and cultural events in a very personal way. This is why more and more teachers are incorporating trade books, reader's theater, literature study groups, read-alouds, storytelling, and informal drama in their classes.

Unit Suggestions

ACTIVITY 9.1   LITERATURE-BASED TEACHING: REFUGEES

Teachers who use literature as a basis for their teaching use the same principles as those used when literature is the basis for learning to read. Instead of textbooks, trade books are the primary sources of information. Textbooks become reference material, just the way encyclopedias are. Although the teacher must still meet certain objectives, much of the direction for learning comes from the students' interests and motivation. They share the responsibility for planning with the teacher, and they help decide on activities and projects

The fifth-grade students described in the opening vignette generated questions about refugees, and the teacher, Mr. McKenzie, decided to create a literature-based unit around their curiosity. One student realized that three refugees attended their school and asked to invite them into the classroom. After talking with these children, the class decided they wanted to know more, and they chose to read Frances Temple's *Tonight by Sea* and Margy Burns Knight's *Who Belongs Here?* They studied formal definitions that identified refugees as people who flee from one place to another for safety. Through discussion, the students heard one another's questions, which stimulated more thinking and questioning. At this point, they had a better concept of what a refugee was, but they wanted to know more. They generated additional questions to study such as, "Could we ever become refugees?"

Mr. McKenzie believes that learning is social inquiry and that students who investigate real questions are truly learning (Copenhaver, 1993). He works to structure, guide, and coach his students as they investigate. In this instance, he created a set of readings (the list follows) that would provide a diverse view of refugees. The students formed literature circles (Daniels, 1994) and each group selected questions to study and books to read.

Reading List

- Cormier, Robert. *Other Bells for Us to Ring.*
- Dillon, Eilis. *Children of Bach.*
- Gregory, Kristina. *Earthquake at Dawn.*
- Hesse, Karen. *Letters from Rifka.*
- Karr, Kathleen. *It Ain't Always Easy.*
- Kerr, Judith. *When Hitler Stole Pink Rabbit.*
- Leighton, Maxine. *An Ellis Island Christmas.*
- Levitin, Sonia. *Silver Days.*
- Lutzeier, Elizabeth. *The Coldest Winter.*
- Turner, Ann. *Katie's Trunk.*

Reading, discussion, writing, and meeting with actual refugees were the major activities the cooperative groups used for learning. Each group wrote papers that summarized the things they had learned about refugees. They added the concepts of *displaced person* and *immigrant* to their discussions. After they answered the original questions (listed in the opening vignette), each student wrote an explanation of refugees.

Each group summarized everything they had learned and created a way of sharing their conclusions with the class. One group created a frieze that showed the countries many refugees came from and a large papier-mâché globe with flags identifying the countries of origin. Another group made and illustrated a chart that showed the problems that refugees face and a list of organizations that help refugees. Another group focused on the parts of the United States that were home to refugees, exploring why refugees chose those particular places to live. Another presented a skit to the class that gave reasons for people becoming refugees, such as war or natural disasters. The students concluded that they, too, could become refugees through no fault of their own. Indeed, some members of the class even learned that their ancestors came to this country as refugees.

SUMMARY

Realistic fiction is a "tell it like it is" genre that deals with a broad range of topics that are enjoyable to read, provide insights about oneself and others, and increase understanding of events and issues. This genre plays an important role in the curriculum because it puts the reader in the shoes of the characters who have different experiences than they have had. Such experiences help children understand themselves and others. Trade books motivate students to read more than textbooks do and give readers a feeling of the emotions, the time, and the place so they have a deeper understanding than they would from reading only facts.

Because of the range of topics and the controversial issues these books address, questions are regularly raised about their suitability for children. However, the issues addressed are the very reasons that realistic fiction can be the backbone of personal, school, and public libraries. Children can read them simply for enjoyment or for supplementing and enriching curricular material. Realistic fiction encourages readers to reflect on themselves and on contemporary issues in ways that few other genres do.

Thought Questions

1. What preparations will you make as you select books to be used in your classroom? Does your school district have written guidelines for book selection? Does the district have an approved book list? Does the district have a policy that addresses what to do if a book is challenged by a parent or other adult? Is censorship an issue?

2. What policy, if any, exists in your school district about using specific textbooks or basal readers? If you are required to use a basal reader, how will you adapt it so your students can read authentic literature?

3. How can you integrate literature with a social studies textbook?

4. What are your favorite contemporary realistic fiction books?

Enrichment Activities

1. Find movies that have been adapted from realistic fiction. After reading the books, make Venn diagrams that illustrate the similarities and differences in the book and film version of the story.

2. Identify an issue or topic. Using one of the resource books cited or other sources, identify books that are available on that topic. Compile an annotated bibliography for current or future use.

3. Read several of the contemporary fiction works that have received the Newbery or Newbery Honor Award. Explain why you think these books received the award.

4. Collect several books that are written in the form of journals or letters such as *Spider Boy, Dear Mr. Henshaw,* and *Strider.* Plan ways that you could use these as models for your students' journals.

5. Many realistic fiction books refer to school and school experiences as an integral part of the plot. Identify several of these books, such as some of the series books or *Earth to Matthew, Scorpions,* and *Flip-Flop Girl,* and analyze the portrayal of the school. Is it positive or negative? What are the implications of the portrayal?

Children's Literature References and Recommended Books

Note: Books designated with an asterisk (*) are recommended for reluctant readers.

Adler, D. A. (1980). *Cam Jansen and the mystery of the U.F.O.* (S. Natti, Illus.). New York: Viking. (1–3). CONTEMPORARY REALISTIC FICTION.*

Cam and Eric discover that the mysterious UFO is a trick.

Adler, D. A. (1981). *Cam Jansen and the mystery of the dinosaur bones* (S. Natti, Illus.). New York: Viking. (1–3). CONTEMPORARY REALISTIC FICTION.*

Cam and Eric discover that the museum guide is stealing dinosaur bones.

Adler, D. A. (1998). *The many troubles of Andy Russell* (W. Hillenbrand, Illus.). New York: Harcourt. (1–3). CONTEMPORARY REALISTIC FICTION.*

Andy has gerbils loose in the house and a neighbor who wants to move in with him.

Applegate, K. A. (1996–2000). *The Animorphs series.* New York: Scholastic. (3–6). CONTEMPORARY REALISTIC FICTION.*

More than 20 books in which children and animals "morph."

Auch, M. J. (1990). *Kidnapping Kevin Kowalski.* New York: Holiday House. (4–7). CONTEMPORARY REALISTIC FICTION.

After Kevin's accident, he is "kidnapped" from his overprotective mother so he can begin to recover.

Avi. (1992). *Blue heron.* New York: Bradbury. (4–7). CONTEMPORARY REALISTIC FICTION.

Maggie visits her father, stepmother, and baby half-sister and discovers problems she did not expect.

Bauer, M. D. (1991). *Face to face.* New York: Clarion. (4–6). CONTEMPORARY REALISTIC FICTION.

Michael has a difficult time establishing a relationship with his stepfather as well as with his father.

Betancourt, J. (1998). *Detective pony.* New York: Scholastic. (2–4). CONTEMPORARY REALISTIC FICTION.*

Anna, Lulu, and Pam have a variety of adventures in the Pony Pals series.

Brooks, B. (1992). *What hearts.* New York: HarperCollins. (4–8). CONTEMPORARY REALISTIC FICTION.

This Newbery honor book addresses four major problems that Asa, the protagonist, faces: divorce, moving, a stepfather, and learning about love.

Byars, B. (1983). *The glory girl.* New York: Viking. (5–8). CONTEMPORARY REALISTIC FICTION.

Anna is the family misfit and is unappreciated until she and her uncle, also a misfit, are able to save all of them.

Byars, B. (1985). *Cracker Jackson.* New York: Viking. (4–7). CONTEMPORARY REALISTIC FICTION.

Eleven-year-old Cracker helps his former babysitter, who is the victim of beatings.

Byars, B. (1988). *The burning questions of Bingo Brown.* New York: Viking. (4–6). CONTEMPORARY REALISTIC FICTION.*

This is a funny story about first love between classmates, and a teacher who has some serious problems.

Byars, B. (1996). *Dead letter.* New York: Viking. (4–6). CONTEMPORARY REALISTIC FICTION.*

Herculeah Jones finds a letter from a dead woman and with help finds out who killed her.

Capote, T. (1996). *The Thanksgiving visitor* (B. Peck, Illus.). New York: Knopf. (5–8). CONTEMPORARY REALISTIC FICTION.

Buddy learns that there are more perspectives about life than his own.

Christiansen, C. B. (1994). *I see the moon.* New York: Atheneum. (5–8). CONTEMPORARY REALISTIC FICTION.

Bitte's older sister Kari is pregnant; all involved have different ways of dealing with the pregnancy. Hard decisions must be made and accepted.

Cleary, B. (1968). *Beezus and Ramona* (L. Darling, Illus.). New York: Morrow. (2–5). CONTEMPORARY REALISTIC FICTION.*

Another old favorite—how do siblings work out appropriate relationships?

Cleary, B. (1977). *Ramona and her father* (A. Tiegreen, Illus.). New York: Morrow. (2–5). CONTEMPORARY REALISTIC FICTION.*

Ramona and her father have some problems to work out—each has difficulty looking at other perspectives.

Cleary, B. (1983). *Dear Mr. Henshaw* (P. O. Zelinsky, Illus.). New York: Morrow. (4–7). CONTEMPORARY REALISTIC FICTION.*

Leigh Botts writes a series of letters to his favorite author in an attempt to deal with his parents' divorce.

Cleary, B. (1991). *Strider* (P. O. Zelinsky, Illus.). New York: Morrow. (4–7). CONTEMPORARY REALISTIC FICTION.*

Leigh Botts and a friend find a dog and agree on joint custody.

Cleary, B. (1999). *Ramona's world* (A. Tiegreen, Illus.). New York: Morrow. (2–5). CONTEMPORARY REALISTIC FICTION.*

Ramona adjusts to the birth of a new sibling.

Conly, J. L. (1995). *Trout summer.* New York: Scholastic. (5–8). CONTEMPORARY REALISTIC FICTION.

Shana and Cody test all of their physical and mental resources as they spend a summer in the woods.

Cooper, M. (1998). *Gettin' through Thursday* (N. Bennett, Illus.). New York: Lee & Low. (4–6). CONTEMPORARY REALISTIC FICTION.

Being poor is not easy and Thursday, the day before payday, is worst of all, especially if a party has been promised.

Cosby, B. (2000). *The day I saw my father cry.* (V. P. Honeywood, Illus.). Cartwheel Books. (4–8). CONTEMPORARY REALISTIC FICTION.

Creech, S. (1997). *Chasing Redbird.* New York: HarperCollins. (5–9). CONTEMPORARY REALISTIC FICTION.

Setting and attaining a personal goal is an important part of growing up. However, Zinny's goal may be impossible to achieve.

Dadey, D., & Jones, M. T. (1997). *Vampires don't wear polka dots* (J. S. Gurney, Illus.). New York: Scholastic. (2–4). CONTEMPORARY REALISTIC FICTION.*

The Bailey School kids hypothesize that their new teacher is a vampire.

Dadey, D., & Jones, M. T. (1996). *Gargoyles don't drive school buses* (J. S. Gurney, Illus.). New York: Scholastic. (2–4). CONTEMPORARY REALISTIC FICTION.*

The Bailey School kids are sure that the new bus driver looks just like one of the gargoyles on a building.

Danziger, P. (1989). *Everyone else's parents said yes.* New York: Delacorte. (3–6). CONTEMPORARY REALISTIC FICTION.*

Matthew Martin is planning big things for his birthday, but his plans go awry.

Danziger, P. (1990). *Make like a tree and leave.* New York: Delacorte. (3–6). CONTEMPORARY REALISTIC FICTION.*

Matthew is serving as the chair of the Mummy Committee on the Egypt Unit Project.

Danziger, P. (1991). *Earth to Matthew.* New York: Delacorte. (3–6). CONTEMPORARY REALISTIC FICTION.*

Matthew is beginning to experience the pangs of love.

Danziger, P. (1992). *Not for a billion, gazillion dollars.* New York: Delacorte. (3–6). CONTEMPORARY REALISTIC FICTION.*

Matthew's peer relationships as well as issues of responsibility are the focus of this story.

Danziger, P. (1996). *Forever Amber Brown* (T. Ross, Illus.). New York: Putnam. (3–6). CONTEMPORARY REALISTIC FICTION.*

After Amber has learned to accept her parents' divorce, her mother considers getting engaged.

Danziger, P., & Martin, A. M. (1998). *P.S. Longer letter later.* New York: Scholastic. (4–8). CONTEMPORARY REALISTIC FICTION.

When a best friend moves away, the friendship survives through letters.

Dygard, T. J. (1994). *The rebounder.* New York: Morrow. (5–9). CONTEMPORARY REALISTIC FICTION.

A basketball coach is perplexed about why a "natural" player refuses to be on the team.

Fitzhugh, L. (1974). *Nobody's family is going to change.* New York: Farrar, Straus & Giroux. (4–6). CONTEMPORARY REALISTIC FICTION.

Although children want very much to have an "ideal" family, that rarely happens; too many conflicting needs and desires arise.

Fleischman, S. (1992). *Jim Ugly* (J. A. Smith, Illus.). New York: Greenwillow. (4–7). CONTEMPORARY REALISTIC FICTION.

After his father's death, the only thing Jake has of his father's is his dog, Jim Ugly.

Fletcher, R. (1995). *Fig pudding.* New York: Clarion. (3–6). CONTEMPORARY REALISTIC FICTION.

A family experiences tragedy when one of the children dies, but they eventually learn to laugh at themselves again.

Fletcher, R. (1997). *Spider boy.* New York: Clarion. (4–6). CONTEMPORARY REALISTIC FICTION.

Bobby's intense interest in spiders creates problems as well as opportunities.

Fox, P. (1991). *Monkey Island.* New York: Orchard Books. (4–7). CONTEMPORARY REALISTIC FICTION.

Clay's parents abandon him and street people befriend him. Only after his illness is he reunited with his mother.

Fox, P. (1993). *Western wind.* New York: Orchard Books. (4–8). CONTEMPORARY REALISTIC FICTION.

Living with Grandmother on an island in Maine is not Elizabeth's first choice of how to spend her summer.

George, J. C. (1959). *My side of the mountain.* New York: Dutton. (4–7). CONTEMPORARY REALISTIC FICTION.

In this enduring favorite, Sam becomes self-sufficient in the house he creates in the roots of a tree.

George, J. C. (1990). *On the far side of the mountain.* New York: Dutton. (4–7). CONTEMPORARY REALISTIC FICTION.

The sequel to *My Side of the Mountain* tells what happens when Sam's sister joins him on the mountain.

Griffith, H. V. (1997). *Foxy.* New York: Beech Tree. (4–6). CONTEMPORARY REALISTIC FICTION.

While camping in the Florida Keys, Jeff finds a stray dog and befriends it.

Henkes, K. (1993). *Words of stone.* New York: Puffin. (3–7). CONTEMPORARY REALISTIC FICTION.

Two children who have serious problems learn from each other and begin to address the issues in their lives.

Hesse, K. (1993). *Lavender* (A. Glass, Illus.). New York: Holt. (1–4). CONTEMPORARY REALISTIC FICTION.

Codie wonders if she will still be special after her aunt has a baby.

Hickman, J. (1994). *Jericho.* New York: Greenwillow. (4–7). CONTEMPORARY REALISTIC FICTION.

Four generations of girls and women learn about and from one another.

Hill, K. (1990). *Toughboy and sister.* New York: McElderry. (3–6). CONTEMPORARY REALISTIC FICTION.

Two Athabascan children spend the summer by themselves after their father dies. They are finally rescued when they do not return for the beginning of school.

Hogg, G. (1997). *The great toilet paper caper* (C. Slack, Illus.). New York: Scholastic. (2–4). CONTEMPORARY REALISTIC FICTION.

Spencer and his friends have a variety of very humorous adventures in the Spencer's Adventures series.

Hughes, D. (1996). *Team picture.* New York: Atheneum. (4–7). CONTEMPORARY REALISTIC FICTION.

David cannot control events around him; he concentrates on his pitching.

Hunt, I. (1976). *The lottery rose.* New York: Scribners. (4–8). CONTEMPORARY REALISTIC FICTION.

Georgie, an abused child, is sent to a private school where he begins to heal and build some permanent relationships.

Johnston, J. (1994). *Adam and Eve and Pinch-Me.* New York: Little, Brown. (4–8). CONTEMPORARY REALISTIC FICTION.

After Sara moves in with her new foster family, she begins to feel like she is a real family member.

Jukes, M. (1999). *Planning the impossible.* New York: Delacorte. (4–6). CONTEMPORARY REALISTIC FICTION.

A family event and a school event scheduled for the same day cause many problems.

Kinsey-Warnock, N. (1989). *The Canada geese quilt* (L. W. Bowman, Illus.). New York: Cobblehill/Dutton. (3–5). CONTEMPORARY REALISTIC FICTION.

Ariel and her grandmother become even closer than they had been after Grandmother's stroke.

Knight, M. B. (1993). *Who belongs here?* (A. S. O'Brien, Illus.). New York: Tilbury House. (2–5). CONTEMPORARY REALISTIC FICTION.

This picture book portrays the confusion of a Cambodian child who struggles to come to the United States, only to be rejected by his classmates.

Kroll, V. (1995). *Shelter folks* (J. N. Jones, Illus.). New York: Wm. B. Eerdmans. (4–6). CONTEMPORARY REALISTIC FICTION.

Having to live in a shelter house for homeless people is a difficult situation, but when 9-year-old Joelle does so, she learns to like the people with whom she is living.

Laminack, L. L. (1998). *The sunsets of Miss Olivia Wiggins.* New York: Peachtree. (1–4). CONTEMPORARY REALISTIC FICTION.

Portrays an Alzheimer's patient in a nursing home interacting with her great-grandson.

MacLachlan, P. (1991). *Journey.* New York: Delacorte. (2–5). CONTEMPORARY REALISTIC FICTION.

Journey and his sister live with their grandparents; they learn to accept the fact that their mother has deserted them.

Martin, A. M. (1983–2000). *The Baby-Sitters Club series.* New York: Scholastic. (3–5). CONTEMPORARY REALISTIC FICTION.

A series of books about young girls growing up together.

Mazer, N. F. (1993). *Out of control.* New York: Morrow. (6–10). CONTEMPORARY REALISTIC FICTION.

Three male high school friends who always have things their way are stunned when Valerie rebuffs them. They attack her and are surprised when she reports the attack.

McDonald, J. (1996). *Comfort Creek.* New York: Delacorte. (5–8). CONTEMPORARY REALISTIC FICTION.

Moving to the swamp area is especially hard on Quinn, who was supposed to edit the school newspaper. After Pa-Daddy loses his job in the mines, things seem even more difficult.

McLaughlin, F. (1998). *Runner's song.* New York: Northbush. (7–10). CONTEMPORARY REALISTIC FICTION.

Deserted by her father, Jeannie and her mother must make sacrifices. A runner, Jeannie tries to concentrate on becoming a champion and discovers new interests and purposes.

Mead, A. (1995). *Junebug.* New York: Farrar, Straus & Giroux. (3–5). CONTEMPORARY REALISTIC FICTION.

Junebug is carrying a lot of responsibilities for a 9-year-old. For his tenth birthday, he asks for little, but surprisingly gets more than he asked for.

Miller, M. J. (1990). *Me and my name.* New York: Viking. (3–6). CONTEMPORARY REALISTIC FICTION.

Erin must decide if she is going to change her last name after her stepfather adopts her.

Myers, W. D. (1982). *Won't know till I get there.* New York: Viking. (5–8). CONTEMPORARY REALISTIC FICTION.

Fourteen-year-old Steve's family takes in a street-tough foster child named Earl and both boys get in trouble. The author uses a humorous style.

Myers, W. D. (1988a). *Me, Mop, and the Moondance Kid* (R. Pate, Illus.). New York: Delacorte. (3–7). CONTEMPORARY REALISTIC FICTION.*

Two adopted children must make adjustments to their new family.

Myers, W. D. (1988b). *Scorpions.* New York: Harper & Row. (4–8). CONTEMPORARY REALISTIC FICTION.

Jamal is forced into taking on the leadership of a Harlem gang when his brother goes to jail. He finds he is treated with respect when he has a gun, but tragedy forces him to realize the dangers of guns and gangs.

Myers, W. D. (1992a). *Mop, Moondance, and the Nagasaki Knights.* New York: Delacorte. (3–7). CONTEMPORARY REALISTIC FICTION.*

In this sequel to *Me, Mop, and the Moondance Kid,* the baseball team plays against teams of children from other countries. The parents support it in many ways.

Myers, W. D. (1992b). *Somewhere in the darkness.* New York: Scholastic. (5–9). CONTEMPORARY REALISTIC FICTION.

Jimmy Little never knew his father, who is in jail. His father escapes and comes to take Jimmy with him. Although his father is recaptured and eventually dies, Jimmy gains insight about him and his life.

Myers, W. D. (1994). *The glory field.* New York: Scholastic. (5–9). HISTORICAL FICTION, CONTEMPORARY REALISTIC FICTION.

This book traces the Lewis family from 1753 in Sierra Leone, West Africa, to present-day Harlem, New York.

Namioka, L. (1992). *Yang the youngest and his terrible ear* (K. de Kiefte, Illus.). Boston: Joy Street. (3–5). CONTEMPORARY REALISTIC FICTION.

Not being musical in a musical family is difficult, especially when the family does not understand the importance of baseball.

Namioka, L. (1994). *April and the dragon lady.* San Diego: Browndeer. (4–7). CONTEMPORARY REALISTIC FICTION.

Cultural expectations create many problems for young people.

Naylor, P. R. (1993a). *The boys start the war.* New York: Delacorte. (4–6). CONTEMPORARY REALISTIC FICTION.

The girls in the Malloy family have not even moved in when the boys in the Hatford family plan pranks to play on them.

Naylor, P. R. (1993b). *The girls get even.* New York: Delacorte. (4–6). CONTEMPORARY REALISTIC FICTION.

The Malloy girls give as good as they get!

Naylor, P. R. (1994). *Boys against girls.* New York: Delacorte. (4–6). CONTEMPORARY REALISTIC FICTION.

The rivalry between the Malloys and the Hatfords reaches new heights.

Naylor, P. R. (1998). *The girls' revenge.* New York: Delacorte. (4–6). CONTEMPORARY REALISTIC FICTION.

Difficult choices must be made between loyalty to family, obedience to teachers and parents, and the desire to best the other side.

Naylor, P. R. (1999). *Walker's crossing.* New York: Atheneum. (4–8). CONTEMPORARY REALISTIC FICTION.

Ryan makes a decision that conflicts with his brother's involvement with a local militant group.

Nixon, J. L. (1996). *Search for the shadowman.* New York: Delacorte. (5–8). CONTEMPORARY REALISTIC FICTION.

Trying to find out about one's ancestors reveals an unexpected mystery.

Oppenheimer, J. L. (1976). *Francesca, baby.* New York: Scholastic. (4–9). CONTEMPORARY REALISTIC FICTION.

Francesca must assume adult responsibilities as a result of her mother's alcoholism. Alateen helps her understand herself and her mother better.

Paterson, K. (1978). *The great Gilly Hopkins.* New York: Crowell. (4–7). CONTEMPORARY REALISTIC FICTION.

Gilly is a hardened child of the foster care system until she lives with Trotter, a foster parent. She finally meets her biological mother and comes face-to-face with reality.

Paterson, K. (1994). *Flip-flop girl.* New York: Dutton. (4–7). CONTEMPORARY REALISTIC FICTION.

Two girls, neither of whom has learned to fit in with others, find that they can become friends.

Paulsen, G. (1984). *Tracker.* New York: Bradbury. (4–8). CONTEMPORARY REALISTIC FICTION.*

John is expected to kill a deer to provide meat for the winter. He is unable to do so but learns much about both living and dying.

Paulsen, G. (1987). *Hatchet.* New York: Viking. (4–7). CONTEMPORARY REALISTIC FICTION.*

The plane Brian was on crashes and he must survive in the wilderness with nothing but his hatchet.

Paulsen, G. (1991a). *The cookcamp.* New York: Orchard Books. (3–6). CONTEMPORARY REALISTIC FICTION.

A boy is left with his grandmother who cooks for a group of loggers. All "adopt" him, but he misses his family.

Paulsen, G. (1991b). *The river.* New York: Delacorte. (4–7). CONTEMPORARY REALISTIC FICTION.

In this sequel to *Hatchet,* Brian returns to the wilderness with a psychologist and they are both hit by lightning. Brian again has to fight for his survival.

Paulsen, G. (1992). *The case of the dirty bird.* New York: Dell. (3–5). CONTEMPORARY REALISTIC FICTION.

In the Culpepper Adventure series, Duncan and Amos have a variety of adventures. In this one, they search for treasure but find gunpowder instead.

Pfeffer, S. B. (1996). *The pizza puzzle.* New York: Delacorte. (3–6). CONTEMPORARY REALISTIC FICTION.

Sometimes even when a suggestion is made jokingly, unexpected consequences result. Don't ever order pizzas in someone else's name!

Philbrick, R. (1996). *The fire pony.* New York: Blue Sky. (6–10). CONTEMPORARY REALISTIC FICTION.

Joe Dilly and his brother, Roy, find work on ranches; Joe has a way with horses. However, fires always seems to blaze in the areas where the boys have been.

Powell, R. (1995). *Dean Duffy.* New York: Farrar, Straus & Giroux. (6–10). CONTEMPORARY REALISTIC FICTION.

Dean Duffy must make some hard decisions about his future. Will he be able to overcome his slump and learn to play baseball professionally?

Ruby, L. (1984). *This old man.* New York: Houghton. (6–9). CONTEMPORARY REALISTIC FICTION.

Greta is able to put her life into a realistic perspective only after moving away from her family.

Rylant, C. (1992). *Missing May.* New York: Orchard Books. (4–6). CONTEMPORARY REALISTIC FICTION.

Both Summer and her Uncle Ob mourn Aunt May's death, but with difficulty they learn to accept it.

Sachs, M. (1993). *Thirteen going on seven.* New York: Dutton Children's Books. (4–6). CONTEMPORARY REALISTIC FICTION.

Twin sisters are very different from each other, especially as they become teenagers. Not until each learns to respect the other do they come to terms.

Sebestyen, O. (1994). *Out of nowhere.* New York: Orchard Books. (4–8). CONTEMPORARY REALISTIC FICTION.

His mother and her boyfriend have abandoned Harley, but he learns to develop trust and stability when he lives with an old woman and a collection of other characters.

Slote, A. (1991). *Finding Buck McHenry.* New York: HarperCollins. (5–8). CONTEMPORARY REALISTIC FICTION.

When Jason is cut from the baseball team, he seeks coaching assistance from the school's custodian.

Smith, D. B. (1986). *Return to Bitter Creek.* New York: Viking Penguin. (4–7). CONTEMPORARY REALISTIC FICTION.

Lacey and her mother leave Bitter Creek under unpleasant circumstances when Lacey is 2. They return 10 years later and little has changed, but a sudden death requires everyone to change.

Spinelli, J. (1990). *Maniac Magee.* New York: Little, Brown. (4–7). CONTEMPORARY REALISTIC FICTION.

After running away from his dysfunctional home, Jeffrey becomes "Maniac" and in so doing makes an impact on many lives, especially his own.

Spinelli, J. (1997). *Wringer.* New York: HarperCollins. (5–8). CONTEMPORARY REALISTIC FICTION.

LaRue knows that when he is 10, he will be expected to take part in the annual pigeon shoot; he does so in an unexpected manner.

Stine, R. L. (1997–1999). *The Goosebumps series.* New York: Scholastic. (3–6). CONTEMPORARY REALISTIC FICTION.

A series of mystery books for intermediate readers.

Temple, F. (1995). *Tonight, by sea.* New York: Orchard. (4–7). CONTEMPORARY REALISTIC FICTION.

Haiti is no longer a safe place for many families to live; Paulie and her family make the dangerous boat trip to Florida.

Voigt, C. (1985). *The runner.* New York: Atheneum. (7–10). CONTEMPORARY REALISTIC FICTION.

A powerful book in which family conflicts are intense. Bullet takes much of his frustration out by running, which ultimately leads to his death.

Weaver, W. (1993). *Striking out.* New York: Harper-Collins. (5–8). CONTEMPORARY REALISTIC FICTION.

This book addresses the way Billy balances baseball with responsibilities for work.

Weaver, W. (1995). *Farm team.* New York: Harper-Collins. (5–8). CONTEMPORARY REALISTIC FICTION.

With Billy's father in jail, the balance between work and baseball is even more crucial.

White, R. (1996). *Belle Prater's boy.* New York: Farrar, Straus & Giroux. (4–8). CONTEMPORARY REALISTIC FICTION.

When Belle Prater disappears, her son Woodrow goes to live with his grandparents, next door to his cousin. The cousins develop a close and supportive relationship.

Yep, L. (1977). *Child of the owl.* New York: Harper-Collins. (5–8). CONTEMPORARY REALISTIC FICTION.

Casey's father sends her to live with her uncle who sends Casey to live with her Chinese grandmother.

References and Books for Further Reading

Burch, R. (1973). The new realism. In V. Haviland (Ed.), *Children and literature: Views and reviews.* Glenview, IL: Scott Foresman.

Copenhaver, J. (1993). Instances of inquiry. *Primary Voices, K–6,* pp. 6–12.

Daniels, H. (1994). *Literature circles: Voice and choice in the student-centered classroom.* York, ME: Stenhouse.

Hamilton, V. (1992). Planting seeds. *The Horn Book, 57,* 674–680.

Jordan, A. D. (1997a). *Follow the gleam: Teaching and learning genre with children and young adults, Part I.* Brandon, VT: Esmont.

Jordan, A. D. (1997b). *Follow the gleam: Teaching and learning genre with children and young adults, Part II.* Brandon, VT: Esmont.

McElhoe, J. S. (1999). Images of grandparents in children's literature. *New Advocate, 12,* 249–258.

Poe, E. A. (1999). Reading to survive. *Signal, 23,* 3.

Russell, D. L. (1994). *Literature for children: A short introduction* (2nd ed.). White Plains, NY: Longman.

Sharp, S. (1992). Why didacticism endures. *The Horn Book, 68,* 694–696.

Steele, M. (1973). Realism, truth and honesty. In V. Haviland (Ed.), *Children and literature: Views and review.* Glenview, IL: Scott Foresman.

Taxel, J. (1994). Political correctness, cultural politics, and writing for young people. *New Advocate, 1,* 93–107.

People Then: Historical Fiction

KEY TERMS

historical fiction   issues
historical periods   KWL charts
immigration   war

GUIDING QUESTIONS

1. Can you see similarities between the problems presented in contemporary realistic fiction (see chapter 9) and the problems presented in historical fiction books?

2. Are the problems presented in historical fiction related to those currently faced by young people?

3. Why is the setting so important for books of historical fiction?

4. Why might some books in this genre be challenged or banned?

OVERVIEW

Simply stated, historical fiction is the genre in which the story takes place long enough ago that the setting is considered "historical." The story must also be realistic, with events and actions that could have actually occurred. As is true for contemporary realistic fiction, it must have no magical or make-believe elements that allow problems to be solved. (See chapter 9 for a de-

scription of the similarities between contemporary and historical fiction.) The characters, although imagined, must act realistically in a manner consistent with how individuals might have thought and acted at the time. They may interact with actual historical figures, but no made-up conversations can occur with those figures. The setting, including the language used, must accurately represent the time period. The attitudes and behaviors must reflect those of the historical times rather than those of the present. This means that some readers may regard aspects of a particular story as racist, stereotyped, or condescending, an unfair criticism if what is described would have been realistic in that time and setting. The themes in historical fiction are similar to the themes of any good literature: They must connect with the life, dreams, and heart of the reader.

Experts do not always agree about which books to categorize as historical fiction. Anne Devereaux Jordan (1997) suggests that for historical fiction, an author must write about a time and place other than his or her own time. Adamson (1987) is even more specific, believing that the author should be writing about a period in time in which he or she has not lived—or if writing about one's own experiences, that the story should be no more recent than one generation before the present. "For example, fiction written in 1987 must be set, at the latest, in 1967 to be considered historical. Fiction written in 1930 but set in 1925 does not fulfill this criterion for legitimate historical fiction" (p. ix). The problem with these criteria is that they do not take into account the reader, and ultimately the reader must decide whether a book is historical fiction. For example, most of us would probably consider the book written in 1930 set in 1925 historical fiction because the book is not about our times—and if the events described were related to events in 1925, it certainly would not be considered contemporary realistic fiction.

INTRODUCTION

"The more things change, the more they stay the same." This familiar quotation is a good description of the genre discussed in this chapter. When reading these books of historical fiction, you may be struck by the similarities in the themes and events found in contemporary realistic fiction. Often only the details and the contexts have changed; the events remain parallel.

Katherine Paterson (1992), author of many award-winning books for children, notes:

I've been writing a chapter this year for a book entitled *The World in 1492*. My assignment is "Asia in 1492." What I discovered about the world in 1492 and Asia in 1492 was that it looked depressingly like the world in 1992. (p. 165)

In both historical and contemporary realistic fiction, events reflect what has happened or could have happened. The similarities exist because throughout time the same kinds of events occur again and again.

The interactions among people are also similar. Some people in the past were governed by greed and self-interest just as some people are today. Mean-spiritedness and the desire to take advantage of those who may be weaker are not limited to any historical era—and these characteristics certainly are evident in historical fiction as well as in contemporary realistic fiction. On the other hand, one reads about characters in past and present settings who exemplify many positive characteristics. They are compassionate, unselfish, and benevolent. Characters are most realistic when they have a reasonable mix of good and not-so-good characteristics—because then they are most like real people.

VIGNETTE

Donna Alexander had finished reading the first few chapters of *Once on This River* by Sharon Dennis Wyeth. As usual, the sixth graders were eager to talk about the events in the book.

"I didn't know the slave trade was going on in 1760."

"Why were they taking the slaves to New York? I thought that slaves were used only in the South."

"Did they really have slave auctions in the North, too?"

"How could a newborn baby be a slave?"

As the questions continued, Ms. Alexander recognized that her students were genuinely curious about slavery, who was involved, when and where it occurred; in addition, they had misconceptions about it. Taking advantage of their interest, she thought that the study of slavery would not only be a fruitful area of investigation for all of them, but it would also accomplish many of the curriculum goals for the year.

The next day, after reading another chapter, Ms. Alexander had each student generate a KWL (know–want to know–learned) chart in which students wrote what they knew about slavery, what they wanted to learn about slavery, and leaving blank the column regarding what they would learn about slavery. Following this, the class put together all of their ideas for a class KWL chart. This was the beginning of a year's exploration of slavery, the events that led to the Civil War, to the Civil Rights Movement in the 1960s, and related current events.

223

A brave man saved many lives when he helped people escape the Nazis.

HISTORICAL FICTION

What makes historical fiction unique? The major difference between this genre and that of contemporary realistic fiction is the setting, which of course includes the particular time period described. The setting and time period are very important to the story because they influence the language used, the interactions among people, the social traditions displayed, the cultural behaviors, and the conflicts that occur. Rosemary Sutcliff (1973) suggests that "the way people act is conditioned by the social custom of their day and age—even the way they think and feel" (p. 308). When writing about a setting that is historically quite different from the present, authors obviously must include more details about the context. The integration of these details into the story is a distinguishing characteristic between well-written historical fiction and that which is merely mediocre.

Choice of characters, both the main characters and those who support them, is particularly important. If an author uses actual people from a period of the past and creates conversations and actions in which those people did not participate, then the work is not historical realistic fiction. Placing fictional characters in actual events and creating actions and conversations for them is acceptable; doing the same with actual historical people is not acceptable. An author must have documentation of the characters' actions and conversations in order to use them in historical realistic fiction.

Historical fiction then has additional characteristics that distinguish it from realistic fiction:

1. The details describing the historical setting are portrayed so that readers are drawn into the times.
2. The actions, thoughts, conversations, and feelings accurately reflect the historical period.
3. Although actual historical events may be used, no conversations or actions of actual people are included unless the conversations or actions can be documented.
4. There are descriptions of, or references to, historical events that are documented or events that could have occurred in the time period.

Some of the events in the books in this genre are unpleasant, but they reflect real life in a particular historical era. Many of the books deal with the uglier side of life. Death and dying, cruelty and abuse, racism and sexism are integral elements of many plots. Hester Burton (1973), author of several books of historical fiction, reflects:

> History is not pretty. The Nazi concentration camps aside, I think people were far more cruel to each other in times past than they are today. The law was certainly more cruel. So was poverty. So was the treatment of children. The brutality of times past may shock the oversensitive. (p. 303)

As you read books in this genre, you will discover that addressing sensitive subjects in a historical setting is often more acceptable, thus removing the immediacy of the abuse. For example, in two of Avi's books, *Night Journeys* and *Encounter at Easton,* written about events in the late 1700s, the community is trying to find two runaway bondsmen. Twelve-year-old Peter wants to help find them to get the reward; then he finds out that the runaways are children his own age. Elizabeth was branded with an "M" on her thumb because she stole food; Robert was sentenced because he helped her. Elizabeth died trying to escape; Robert survived. Clearly, this is not a pretty picture.

Not all books of this genre, however, are so intense; many present life experiences that have to do with the everlasting conflicts inherent in growing up, of relationships in families, and the problems of peer relationships. For example, the well-loved Laura Ingalls Wilder Little House series recounts what moving and living in frontier America was like. Although life was filled with many difficulties, the emphasis is on the positive and lighthearted aspects of their challenges.

An Issue

Because of the realistic nature of historical fiction, some parents and educators may try to limit the choices of books available for children to read. They may feel that they have a duty to screen readers from what they believe is objectionable. This happens in large part because as Sutcliff (1973) suggests, the "child is liable to absorb ideas from books which may remain with him for the rest of his life, and even play some part in determining the kind of person that he is going to become" (p. 306). When adults decide the content is unsuitable for a group of readers, this is an overt form of censorship.

A more subtle form of censorship in both contemporary and historical realistic fiction occurs when authors write about societal issues and events. For example, during World War II, little quality literature for children was written about the war that was occurring (Hunt, 1994). "Pulp war stories" appeared in which "war is reduced to a simple adventure story in which good is pitted against evil" (p. 199). Not until the mid-1960s, when authors who grew up during World War II began to write, did readers have opportunities to identify with characters who experienced the events and interactions that could have occurred during the war years.

> Writers for children mirror very accurately the mood and expectations of the country. Although most adults (including writers) were aware the inevitability of U.S. involvement in the war, a reluctance to think about the implications kept even distant echoes of it out of most children's books except for propagandistic adventures. . . . It was only when those children grew up that they wrote, for the next generation after them, about the experiences of the 1940s—perhaps because it was only then, a quarter of a century and more later, that their readers were ready to hear about it. (p. 205)

The contention might be made, however, that only then were the adults ready for the children to hear about these experiences.

When Does the Present Become the Past?

Readers are often confused when attempting to classify books as realistic fiction or historical fiction: Just when does the present become the past? Books that were contemporary when they were published, may, over time, become historical. Children who are currently in the third grade think of the historical past as any time before they were born. Adults have very different perspectives regarding the historical past.

Many books are easy to classify. Scott O'Dell places *My Name Is Not Angelica* in 1733; in *Waiting for Anya,* Michael Morpurgo uses a World War II setting. Both of these books are obviously historical fiction. On the other hand, Paula Danziger obviously puts *Not for a Billion, Gazillion Dollars* in the present day, as does Betsy Byars in her Herculeah Jones mystery series. These books are clearly contemporary fiction.

Various children's literature experts employ different schemes for categorizing books as historical or contemporary fiction. Some authors classify anything set after World War II as contemporary fiction (Norton, 1995; Russell, 1994), whereas other authors classify everything up until the Gulf War as historical fiction (Cullinan & Galda, 1994; Huck, Hepler, & Hickman, 1993; Reed, 1994). Perhaps the most sensible solution is for readers to decide whether the book is contemporary or historical, which permits them to use their experience and judgment as they respond to a book. As long as readers can support a classification, it should be honored.

ORGANIZING THE CATEGORIES OF HISTORICAL FICTION

To be most easily used, books of historical fiction need to be in categories. Readers who want to read about a particular era need to be able to find those books quickly and efficiently. However, this genre also has many books that have important themes that may not be related to a particular time; their themes are more universal in nature. Although most of the subcategories in this chapter are based on a modification of the historical periods Crabtree, Nash, Gagnon, and Waugh (1992) describe, two other categories emerged: families and friends, and survival and growing up. The themes and events in these categories are not dependent on any specific time era, even though the setting is long ago. The books in these two categories typify the idea that the more things change, the more they stay the same.

Recently, a variation of traditional historical fiction books has been published—historical fiction series books. The series books share many of the characteristics of the series books as described in chapter 9. However, a notable difference between these series books and the other series books is that each is written by a different author, all of whom have earned a reputation for quality writing. Although these books are set in several historical periods, they will be described here rather than in the historical eras.

The Dear America series is written in the format of diaries of young adolescent girls who could have lived during particular times of history. Included in each book is an epilogue so that readers have an idea of "what happened next," a historical note that provides factual information about the times, and pictures of original documents, maps, and pictures. Readers gain insight about what life might have been like for girls their own ages long ago. Some of the books in this series include the following. *A Journey to the New World: The Diary of Remember Patience Whipple* by Kathryn Lasky chronicles the journey on the *Mayflower.* The time period is from 1620 to 1621. *The Winter of Red Snow: The Revolutionary War Diary of Abigail Jane Stewart* by Kristiana Gregory spans December 1, 1777, to July 4, 1778. Kristiana Gregory also describes 1847 in *Across the Wide and Lonesome Prairie: The Oregon Trail Diary of Hattie Campbell. When Will This Cruel War Be Over? The Civil War Diary of Emma Simpson* by Barry Denenberg describes events for the last year of the war. Ann Rinaldi writes of what life may have been like for a Native American girl who is taken from her reservation in 1880 to go to school in Pennsylvania in *My Heart Is on the Ground: The Diary of Nannie Little Rose, a Sioux Girl. West to a Land of Plenty: The Diary of Teresa Angelino Viscardi* by Jim Murphy describes the trek from New Jersey to Idaho in 1883. The excitement and the boredom of many days' traveling are made clear. Sherry Garland describes what life in the Alamo was like in *A Line in the Sand: The Alamo Diary of Lucinda Lawrence.* What might life have been like for a traveling companion to a rich passenger on the *Titanic*? Ellen Emerson White lets us see the events in *Voyage on the Great Titanic: The Diary of Margaret Ann Brady,* an accounting of four incredible days. The Dear America series is written to appeal to girls in middle school.

The My Name Is America series is written to appeal to boys in this same age group. Many of the time periods are the same but the books are the journals kept by boys. This series also includes historical notes, including illustrations and maps. Barry Denenberg describes the life of an apprentice in a Boston tavern in 1770 in *The Journal of William Thomas Emerson, a Revolutionary War Patriot.* Perspectives of the Civil War period are included in *The Journal of James Edmond Pease, a Civil War Union Soldier* by Jim Mur-

phy. *The Journal of Joshua Loper: A Black Cowboy* by Walter Dean Myers lets readers see what life was like driving a herd of 1,200 cattle across the Chisholm Trail to Kansas in 1871.

Families and Friends

Holidays are an integral part of all types of families. Virginia Hamilton writes about a traditional family Christmas in *The Bells of Christmas,* set in southwest Ohio in 1890 with aunts, uncles, and cousins joining in the celebration: caroling, eating, exchanging gifts, and attending church. Hamilton gives the readers a picture of a warm family celebration of this special holiday.

In *A Bride for Anna's Papa,* Isabel Marvin emphasizes the interactions of the characters within the context of the setting, which is 1907 in the iron range of Minnesota. After Anna's mother dies, Anna must take responsibility for the house and for her younger brother, which prevents her from attending school until the new teacher convinces her to come for a few hours each week. Anna and her brother decide their father needs a wife, but when the teacher and their father marry, Anna is resentful. When a great fire destroys the surrounding area, Anna begins to change her attitude:

> She would always mourn her mother, but Mae was now an important part of their family, someone she had come to accept and even to love. Their house might not be standing after this fire, but they were together, a family. (p. 136)

Bette Bao Lord gives us insight into how one little girl overcomes prejudice and stereotyping in the book *In the Year of the Boar and Jackie Robinson.* Shirley Temple Wong and her mother move to the United States to join her father in 1947. Shirley's adjustment to school is difficult. She gets two black eyes from Mabel, one of the biggest girls in fifth grade, but refuses to tell who hit her. After that, Mabel becomes Shirley's guide and guard. With her help, Shirley learns to play baseball and becomes a fan of Jackie Robinson. In sixth grade, she makes another friend, Emily, and helps her get elected to class president. When Jackie Robinson comes to the school, Shirley presents him with the key to the school. It is a proud moment for Shirley when she meets her hero and recognizes the opportunities that are available to her.

Darcy and her mother move to Frenchtown, Massachusetts, when her father joins the army. Darcy has moved so often and is so shy that she has never had a best friend. Kathleen Mary O'Hara decides that they will be best friends. Darcy, a Unitarian, is over-whelmed by Kathleen Mary, a Catholic. The difference in religion is an ongoing part of the plot of this very believable story of how two very different personalities complement each other. When Darcy's father is missing in action and presumed dead, Darcy needs a miracle. Robert Cormier has written a believable story about love and miracles in *Other Bells for Us to Ring.*

Survival and Growing Up

Millie Jewett was born in Nantucket in 1907. She is soon abandoned by her mother and is sent to live with her grandmother, where she grows up to be a local legend. She assumed the responsibilities of guardian of the coastal waters and in so doing would often beat the Coast Guard to rescues. *Madaket Millie* by Frances Ward Weller is not only strong but intelligent; Millie is a good model for children.

Elspet Mary was born in Scotland in 1832. When she was not yet 4, her mother is killed. Her father is a sailor, so Elspet goes to live with her aunt and uncle, where she is warmly welcomed. Elspet Mary settles in but soon the family is uprooted to move to the New World. She wonders if she will ever have *The Belonging Place* that she wants. Author Jean Little makes connections between her own family's move to Canada and Elspet Mary's move to the New World.

Casey does not want to spend the summer with her grandmother while her father is fighting in the Korean War. However, she is in for some surprises as she makes friends with a mentally disabled man, various relatives, and meets people her own age. Sue Ellen Bridgers writes a story, *All Together Now,* that readers who have experienced fights, races, baseball, and other events will appreciate.

In a very different setting, Jan Hudson tells about the challenges of growing up in the Native American culture in *Sweetgrass,* the story of a 15-year-old Blackfoot girl. She and her friends are beginning to have their marriages arranged. They face constant problems in finding food, and another Nation attacks them. The greatest challenge occurs when the family is exposed to smallpox during the coldest part of the winter. Sweetgrass is spared the smallpox, but the entire responsibility for her family's care falls to her. She must find food as well as bury the dead. She copes so well with these challenges that her father recognizes her as an adult.

Jean Fritz brings to life the explorers who changed the map of the world.

Two survival stories by Arthur Roth are set in the 1800s. In *The Iceberg Hermit,* 17-year-old Allan Gordon signs on to a whaling ship working north of Greenland. The captain is a stubborn man and does not start the return trip until bad weather sets in. The ship hits an iceberg and sinks; Allan is the sole survivor. The ship surfaces and provides him with food, but he lives in a cave well away from the ship. A young polar bear adopts him and helps him find food. Later Eskimos discover him, and he lives with them for several seasons. After 7 years he returns to Scotland via a whaling ship.

Roth uses a very different setting for a survival theme in *The Castaway.* Daniel has a misunderstanding with his brother and runs away to sea. His ship crashes, and Daniel washes up on a small rock reef in the southern Pacific Ocean. He learns how to get food and shelter, and he makes friends with some of the animals. Five years later, he is rescued when a ship is blown off course.

Lucas Whitaker has been orphaned. He leaves the family farm and becomes apprenticed to Doc Beecher, a college-trained doctor. Cynthia DeFelice has written a fascinating story in which readers not only see Lucas grow up but also learn about eighteenth-century attitudes and practices about health and illness. *The Apprenticeship of Lucas Whitaker* demonstrates that some orphans have opportunities for success even under difficult circumstances.

HISTORICAL PERIODS

(Note: See the section on series books above for titles that also fit in these time periods.)

The story characters in this section face many of the same challenges as those in the previous section—growing up with or without families, establishing relationships with peers and adults, and surviving on their own. However, these young people have no control over the events that affect them. Slavery, war, economic hardships, and political upheavals change their entire way of life and create new challenges.

The books in this section are organized chronologically, but considerable overlap occurs in the years included in the various categories. History resists neat categorization.

Pre-Colonial Era

Pedro's Journal by Pam Conrad and *I Sailed with Columbus* by Miriam Schlein both tell about Columbus's voyages from a cabin boy's point of view. In both books, the cabin boy is aware that Columbus is keeping two sets of records, and each is ashamed of the mistreatment of the natives. Overall, each writer gives a relatively positive view of Columbus and his goals. We find similarities in the authors' descriptions of events, although they differ in the emphasis placed on some events, so both books suggest interesting possibilities for critical comparison reading.

Jane Yolen offers a very different perspective of Columbus in *Encounter.* A native boy dreams of strangers who are coming to the village and the problems they will bring with them, but because he is only a child, the elders ignore him. When the strangers arrive, he and several others are taken captive. He is able to escape, but disease and colonization doom his people.

Being a member of a tribe in which members get an adult name by demonstrating ability to use a bow and arrow is not a good thing—especially if one's vision is poor. Walnut cannot count the number of fingers on a upraised hand but learns that by listening, he is able to know more about the setting than those who can see. He earns the name *Sees Behind Trees* and as he supports other tribe members, he grows in confidence and strength. Michale Dorris has written a book that makes the reader ponder the issues presented.

Colonial Era

Two books for younger readers describe the life of the Pilgrims soon after coming to the New World. Gary Bowen uses the diary of 13-year-old Christopher Seals, an indentured orphan who stays with the Brewster family in *Stranded at Plimoth Plantation, 1626,* to describe the challenges endured. Cheryl Harness presents an interesting account of a fictional family, carefully researched to be representative of the Pilgrims who arrived on the *Mayflower* and their struggles. The detailed drawings and bibliography make *Three Young Pilgrims* a particularly interesting book.

By the late 1600s, Salem, Massachusetts, was the setting for the ugly events known as the Salem witch trials. Ann Rinaldi writes graphically of the context in which they occurred and about the effects on the accusers, those accused, and those who were part of this community. *A Break with Charity: A Story about the Salem Witch Trials* is fascinating reading for older readers.

Another book for older readers, set in the same time period, is *The Witch of Blackbird Pond* by Elizabeth George Speare. When Kit befriends the "wrong" people, she is one of those named as a witch and is nearly killed. With the help of some friends, she is finally acquitted and eventually gains acceptance in the community.

In Kathryn Lasky's book *Beyond the Burning Time,* Mary Chase's widowed mother is named a witch and sentenced to hang. Although they are terrified, Mary and her brother are determined to save their mother, who is imprisoned under terrible conditions, awaiting execution. In the end, their mother must have her foot amputated, but she escapes and the family starts a new life in Bermuda. This is a very carefully researched book and includes interesting documentation.

Slavery is an integral part of the history of our country. Although we tend to think of slavery in terms of the Civil War, it began much earlier. Scott O'Dell develops the reader's sensitivity to this in *My Name Is Not Angelica,* the story of Raisha and Konje, prominent members of their African tribe who were to marry in three years' time. After they are taken captive and sold on St. John Island in 1733, they suffer cruel treatment as slaves. Konje is treated so badly that he joins the other runaway slaves who jump off a cliff rather than go back to the plantations when they are discovered. Raisha is later taken to Martinique where, according to the law there, she is no longer a slave.

Monday and her mother come to New York from their home in Madagascar in 1760 to prove that Uncle Frederick, who has been sold as a slave, is actually a free man. Sharon Dennis Wyeth did extensive research about the African Americans who were living at that time; *Once on This River* is a spectacular book with a surprising ending.

Sally Keehn carefully documented *I Am Regina,* which is based on a fascinating true story. Regina is captured by Indians during the French and Indian War. During the 8 years of her captivity, she grows to love the woman with whom she lives. Eventually she is returned to her real mother, who identifies her through a song she sang to Regina when she was a child.

Revolutionary War Era

Children's authors have written about many of the dimensions of the Revolutionary War, including the colonists, the loyalists, the Native Americans, adults, children, and many others. Literature helps children understand complex periods of history such as this by helping them identify with the characters and their emotions as they hear or read the stories of this period.

Avi documents a 24-hour period of the Revolutionary War in *The Fighting Ground*. In this story, 13-year-old Jonathan runs away to join the fighting, but three Hessians capture and imprison him in a house with the bodies of a small boy and his parents. After burying them, Jonathan escapes, only to be recaptured. He is finally able to return home, wiser than when he left.

James Lincoln Collier and Christopher Collier present a Tory point of view of the Revolutionary War in *My Brother Sam Is Dead*. Tim witnesses his Tory father's imprisonment and the massacre of his neighbors by British troops; then his brother, a Continental soldier, is convicted of a crime he did not commit. This story shows the human cost of war and that everyone loses in war.

The Native American perspective on the Revolutionary War is portrayed in *The Valley of the Shadow* by Janet Hickman. This story is based on the Delaware Nation in Ohio, which converted to Christianity and tried to remain neutral in the war. Tobias and the group experience a daily struggle to live; eventually all but Tobias and his friend, Thomas, are captured and methodically murdered.

When the Revolutionary War began, both the British and the colonists wanted the Native Americans to fight with them. This caused great problems for Coshmoo, a Delaware Indian boy, and Daniel, a young settler, who are best friends. Sally Keehn clearly illustrates in *Moon of Two Dark Horses* that taking sides in any conflict often means making life-threatening decisions.

The difficulties of African Americans during the Revolutionary War period is the theme of *Jump Ship for Freedom* by James Lincoln Collier and Christopher Collier. The main character of this story, Dan, is trying to buy his family's freedom. His maturation and growing confidence are an important aspect of the theme. He does finally achieve freedom.

Ann Rinaldi has written several books for older readers about the Revolutionary War era. All of these books have strong female characters who provide insights that may allow a clearer understanding of the times. *The Fifth of March: A Story of the Boston Massacre* shows that every issue has at least two perspectives. Rachel Marsh is a patriot and an indentured servant girl for John Adams, but she falls in love with a young British soldier. Her conflicting feelings require her to make very difficult decisions. In *The Secret of Sarah Revere,* readers are given a picture of the tensions that occur in the family of Paul Revere before and during the war. In *Finishing Becca: A Story About Peggy Shippen and Benedict Arnold,* 14-year-old Becca serves as the personal maid of Peggy Shippen. Historical evidence suggests that Peggy may have manipulated Arnold into becoming a traitor. When most of us think about the Revolutionary War, we think of events that took place in Boston and the Northeast. *Cast Two Shadows: The American Revolution in the South* helps readers understand that the war had great impact on people living in other parts of the colonies, not just in the North.

Building and Expansion

Following the Revolutionary War and continuing well into the 1900s, the United States expanded and grew in remarkable ways. Some of these expansions were the result of events that today's Americans are not proud of; others demonstrate the best qualities that we still celebrate. For many people, America was a land of opportunity, and with hard work and persistence, people could have better lives. Other families and groups were discriminated against and their ways of living were destroyed. This category of books covers a large span of time and cuts across more well-defined historical eras.

We sometimes tend to forget that some people remained to put down roots where their families had settled originally, whereas others moved westward to settle the frontier. Barbara Cooney portrays life in New England in *Island Boy.* Matthias's father built the first house on Tibbets Island and Matthias returns to the island again and again during his long life.

For many years children and adults have loved the Laura Ingalls Wilder Little House series based on Wilder's family life. These books tell of her family moving and living in frontier America. The family is introduced in *Little House in the Big Woods* and follows the moves of her family to frontier America, ending with Laura's adulthood in *The First Four Years.*

The exploits of Laura and her family have become a real part of Americana. A popular television series, *Little House on the Prairie,* was based on one of her books by the same name. More recently, T. L. Tedrow (1992) has written another series of books, The Days of Laura Ingalls Wilder. He states in the foreword of *Good Neighbors,* "While this book is a fictional account of Laura's exploits, it retains the historical integrity of her columns, diary, . . . and the general history of the times in which she lived" (p. 10). Roger Lea MacBride has also written a series about the Wilders from the perspective of Laura's daughter, Rose. MacBride was Rose's only heir and has her books, diaries, and letters, which serve as the basis for his series of books, called the Little House Rocky Ridge Years. Titles include *Little House on Rocky Ridge* and *Little Farm in the Ozarks,* and *New Dawn on Rocky Ridge,* in which Rose, who is not yet 16, must make some decisions about marriage and further education.

As the pioneers moved west, they often fought with the Native Americans who had been living on the land for generations. This is the theme of *Thunder Rolling in the Mountains* by Scott O'Dell and Elizabeth Hall, which tells about the westward movement from the Native American perspective. When Sound of Running Feet and her friends see a White family's cabin, they know there is danger from the White settlers and their soldiers. The community is forced to move, and they battle the soldiers as they are moved from camp to camp and eventually to a reservation in Idaho.

Elisabeth J. Stewart tells the story of 9-year-old Meli, a Cherokee whose family has either been killed or lost when the soldiers had driven them out of their homes. When she sees her wounded brother, they escape and make their way back to the Appalachians. *On the Long Trail Home* is based on the life of the author's great-grandmother.

Runs With Horses is one of the last group of Apaches to be captured by the U.S. Army. This book recounts the passion, tragedy, and betrayal of the Apaches. Brian Burks provides a bibliography of books used in researching the events, which could be useful for further study.

After her parents' deaths in 1839, Lucy moves from Detroit to live with her aunt and uncle who run a school for Indian children. Aunt Emma is a hard woman who believes that the Indian children should give up their native ways and adopt the ways of the White settlers. Not until Aunt Emma learns to love Matthew (Star Face) is she able to respect the Indian ways or to give any affection to Lucy. *The Indian School* by Gloria Whelan gives insight into the attitudes of the times, although in reality the Aunt Emmas of the world still may not have learned to respect the Indian culture.

California Whipple certainly did not want to move from her comfortable life in Massachusetts to California, even if her mother and siblings reveled in the challenges and new lifestyle. To express her irritation with all concerned, California changes her name to Lucy, attempts to do as little as possible, and writes long, complaining letters to her grandparents. When her mother remarries and moves away, Lucy is lonely and has to decide what to do with her life. Her decision reflects her growing maturity, which we read about in *The Ballad of Lucy Whipple* by Karen Cushman.

Civil War Era

The themes of slavery and the Civil War are inextricably tied together and influence the entire history of our nation. Slavery was a pivotal force before, during, and after the Civil War. Understanding this period in history allows readers to understand current events better. The attitudes and interactions among the people living during this time, the risks they took for themselves and others, and the decisions they made have had long-term affects on all of us.

Escaping from slavery is an important element in many books written about this time period. Jip tumbled off a wagon when he was a young boy. He could never understand why his mother never stopped to pick him up. He lives in the town's poor farm, doing what is expected of him, but always wondering about his past. A stranger inquires about Jip, which raises more questions about who he is and where he comes from. With the help and support of Teacher and her friend, Jip goes to safety and finds the answers to his questions. Katherine Paterson has created a fascinating book describing *Jip: His Story.*

Jennifer Armstrong takes us on a very different journey in *Steal Away.* Susannah lives in Vermont, but after her parents' deaths she must live with her uncle's family in Virginia. In his household, she meets a young slave, Bethlehem Reid, with whom she becomes friends. The two girls decide to dress as boys and escape to Vermont. This exciting story is told through journals and letters and follows the two girls from 1855 through 1896.

Two Tickets to Freedom by Florence B. Freedman is based on the true story of William and Ellen Craft. They escaped from slavery when Ellen dressed like a White Southern gentleman and her husband was her slave. Overcoming many challenges, they successfully make their way to England and safety. Many years later, they return to Georgia where they buy a plantation and establish the Woodville Cooperative Farm School.

Mary Lyons uses letters to tell about the life of an African-American child born into slavery in *Letters from a Slave Girl: The Story of Harriet Jacobs.* She portrays a life of great injustice, hope, and courage. As an adult, Harriet runs away and hides in an attic crawlspace for 7 years. Although this book shows slavery's brutality, the main character's spirit is uplifting.

In *Nightjohn* and *Sarny: A Life Remembered,* Gary Paulsen describes how the human spirit survives even under the greatest adversity. Dismemberment was the punishment for teaching slaves how to learn to read and write. Nightjohn is tortured but still his mission is to teach others to read. Sarny learns to read and when she finally becomes a free woman, she passes on the gift of literacy that she received from Nightjohn.

Paul Fleischman interprets *Bull Run,* a famous battle of the Civil War. He tells about this battle from the perspectives of eight Southern characters and eight Northern characters. Each of these individuals shares his or her expectations and hopes of what will happen when the two armies meet. This book is an excellent one for reader's theater.

Katie is a kitchen maid in a wealthy household in 1863. When plans emerge that her employers are willing to pay $300 to Katie's family so that her brother would take the place of the wealthy son, the war becomes very personal. Being Irish adds to the problems that Katie encounters, but she learns to take risks and do what she knows is right. Isabelle Holland helps readers ask hard questions of themselves in *Behind the Lines.*

Industrialization

The Civil War forwarded the movement toward industrialization and the peace made raw materials available. The industrial movement, however, was built on the labor of men, women, and even children who were in many ways enslaved to the factory owners and managers. In *Lyddie,* Katherine Paterson shows readers the life of a girl working in the weaving room of a factory. When Lyddie defends a friend from the advances of the overseer, she is fired. Her strong character prevails through hard work and perseverance, and she eventually goes to Oberlin College.

In another story of this period, *The Bobbin Girl,* Emily Arnold McCully writes about 10-year-old Rebecca who is a bobbin girl in a textile mill. Working conditions are awful, and when the owners of the mill plan to lower the already too-low wages, she must decide whether to join the strike or continue working.

Joan Aiken shows readers a horrifying view of mill workers' lives in *Midnight Is a Place.* In this instance, the owner of a mill teaches Lucas, his ward, how to run the mill so that Lucas can take over when he is older. Lucas, however, is appalled by the lack of regard for human life. Lucas and a friend are able to gather enough evidence to displace the people in control.

Mining was often a way of life for the men and boys in Appalachia. When a cave-in traps James and his father, they are able to survive by working together. Ian Wallace describes incidents from the life of his grandfather in *Boy of the Deeps.*

Immigration

Many of the immigrants who came to the United States fled lives of injustice and poverty to come to work in the factories and farms of this country, as did Rebekah

Levinsky and her Jewish family, who fled Russia with only the clothes they could carry. Joan Lowery Nixon tells their story in *Land of Hope*. Through Rebekah's eyes we see the pain of families whose members were denied admittance to this country. As the story unfolds, Rebekah is denied an education so that her older brother can go to school. When he refuses an education, she is finally able to realize her dream.

Laurence Yep writes a powerful story, *Dragon's Gate*, which recounts the experiences of the Chinese who built the transcontinental railroad in the mid-1800s. The focus is on Otter, a Chinese boy who joins his father and uncle in California. When realities shatter his dreams, Otter endures many hardships to attain his goals.

An immigration story set in the present time is Eve Bunting's *How Many Days to America? A Thanksgiving Story*. A family from an unnamed Caribbean country leave their country and head for America and freedom. They crowd into a small fishing boat and set off under the cover of night, encountering thieves and soldiers, but finally reach the shores of the United States.

The Twentieth Century: Wars, Issues, and Events

Wars

The twentieth-century wars are the subjects of many books, but many more of these books focus on World War II than World War I, the Korean War, the Vietnam War, or the more recent Gulf War. Perhaps this is because during World War II everyone living at that time was involved at some level, and it so drastically changed people's lives. Also, authors tend to write about their childhood experiences and memories, so this far-reaching event became the subject of many books. This section includes a sampling from several of these wars, but consult a card catalog or a computer database to locate books that fit your educational needs.

World War I.   Gloria Skurzynski portrays life in the United States of World War I through the lives of two boys in *Goodbye, Billy Radish*. In a steel town of 1917, the men who are not soldiers work 12 hours a day, 7 days a week. Boys as young as 14 work these long shifts as well. The heavy work schedule leads to factory accidents and deaths, but accidents are not the only threat to life: The dreaded flu epidemic sweeps through the United States and takes Billy's life.

Pieter Van Raven's *Harpoon Island* explores the hysteria in the United States about Germans during World War I. The main character is Frank, whose grandfather was German. When a submarine is sighted, the islanders assume Frank is a German sympathizer. After the island dwellers learn the truth, they vote for Frank to stay on the island.

World War II.   Choosing the books for this section was difficult because of the many fine pieces of literature focusing on this period. We have tried to choose books that show the war's impact on different people. The themes in this section are concerned with the prejudice that fear creates, the importance of freedom, and the courage to prevail in the face of great difficulty.

The prejudice against Germans during World War I was prevalent throughout the United States during World War II as well, and that prejudice extended to the Japanese living on the West Coast. Because of fear and prejudice, Japanese Americans were interned in camps located in remote areas of the United States. Yoshika Uchida brings these events to life in *The Bracelet, Journey to Topaz,* and *Journey Home,* fictional accounts based on her own family's experiences. In *The Bracelet,* a book for younger readers, Emi, a second grader, and her Japanese-American family are sent to an internment camp. They first live in a horse stall at a former racetrack; later they are transferred to an internment camp in Utah. Both *Journey to Topaz* and *Journey Home* are for older readers. *Journey to Topaz* describes life in the internment camp through Yuki's eyes. She vividly describes their fears, the privations of living in the camp, and their desire to prove their loyalty to the United States. *Journey Home* tells about the mistreatment the Japanese Americans faced once they were released and returned home. This great injustice in our history is commemorated in a mural that depicts the internment of 120,000 Japanese Americans, which in turn inspired Sheila Hamanaka to write the picture book *The Journey: Japanese Americans, Racism, and Renewal.* The text accompanying the dramatic illustrations in this book describes the indignities and degradation suffered by these innocent people.

The prejudice against Japanese Americans does not end with the end of the war. Virginia Wolff describes two teams of sixth-grade girls who play a baseball game, called *Bat 6,* each spring. Sazam's father was killed at Pearl Harbor; Aki is of Japanese descent.

Even in 1949, the tensions, fears, and hate all influence the game and the girls.

Until the bomb was dropped on Nagasaki, Mieko's life has been fairly predictable. After the bomb, she is sent to live on her grandparents' farm and her hand is badly injured. Mieko is devastated because she wants to become an artist. With the prodding of her family and friends, she begins to paint again. *Mieko and the Fifth Treasure* by Eleanor Coerr lets readers see that recovery is possible.

Graham Salisbury won the Scott O'Dell Award for his book *Under the Blood-Red Sun*. It is the story of a Japanese-American family told from Tomi's perspective. With the support of Tomi's eighth-grade friends, the family is able to survive after Tomi's father and grandfather are arrested.

The United States was not the only country affected by World War II, of course. Vilna, Poland, and Siberia are the sites of *The Endless Steppe*, a true story by Esther Hautzig based on her family's trials during the war. This powerful book about human survival and adaptability tells the story of a close-knit Jewish family transported to Siberia when the Russian army occupies their country. They survive transportation in a cattle car, degrading work, and a starvation-level existence. Esther Hautzig now lives in the United States.

Lois Lowry set *Number the Stars* in Copenhagen during the war. In this story, the Johansen family "adopts" Ellen, a 10-year-old Jewish child. They are able to do this because an older daughter was killed working for the Resistance Movement, and the Jewish girl takes her place in the family. Eventually, Ellen is able to sail to Sweden and freedom.

Hide and Seek by Ida Vos (translated by Terese Edelstein and Inez Smidt) is the fictionalized account of the author's life, beginning when she was 8 and the Nazis invaded Holland. To be safe, Rachel and her sister, Esther, go to live in a variety of places with different families. Other family members have been in the concentration camps, and many have died. The survivors struggle, even after the war.

Nine-year-old Anna and her family flee their comfortable home and life in Berlin to escape from the Nazis in 1933. They reach England and safety three years later. This book, *When Hitler Stole Pink Rabbit,* is based on the experiences of the author, Judith Kerr.

Laura E. Williams describes the changing attitudes of Korinna, a loyal member of the local Nazi youth group. Until she interacts with a Jewish mother and her young daughter who are being hidden by Korinna's parents, Korinna believes that what the Nazis are doing is right. Finally she must make a life-and-death decision about what she believes and what is right. *Behind the Bedroom Wall* helps readers understand the difficulty of these kinds of decisions.

Michael Morpurgo sets *Waiting for Anya* in France. The theme is a village's response to the killing of Jews. When the Germans become suspicious that villagers are helping Jewish children escape to Spain, the entire town becomes involved. Only two of the children are unable to escape, but they survive.

During World War II, men drafted as soldiers who refused to fight because of conscientious objections were assigned to noncombat positions. Other soldiers went AWOL (absent without leave from the army) for various reasons. Men in both of these categories were often the victims of prejudice during this extremely patriotic period. Mary Downing Hahn writes about these conflicts in *Stepping on the Cracks*. Margaret and Elizabeth are angry with Gordy, the meanest boy in their class. They decide to get even and in the process they discover that his brother is AWOL, which they use against him. Then Margaret's family receives word that her brother has been killed. After they learn that Gordy's alcoholic father abuses the entire family, they realize that many human elements affect judgments about people.

Vietnam War. The Vietnam War is a little-understood chapter in U.S. history; nevertheless, it influenced all of our lives. Katherine Paterson in *Park's Quest* gives one perspective on this war. Park cannot understand why his mother will not talk about his father, who died in Vietnam. Finally, during a brief visit with his father's family, he discovers that his father had another family in Vietnam and Park has a half-sister, Thanh. The other family lives near his grandparents, and Park becomes acquainted with Thanh; gradually they come to accept each other.

In *The Wall,* Eve Bunting portrays a boy and his father searching for a name at the Vietnam Veterans Memorial. This picture book helps young children understand the significance of the wall as a disabled veteran, a mourning couple, and children on an outing visit it.

Minfong Ho in *The Clay Marble* presents another context for Vietnam. The story is set in a refugee camp on the border of Thailand and Cambodia. Countless refugees have fled to the camp in search of free food and farming supplies. The children quickly become acquainted and try to create a peaceful world although a peaceful life is so dim and distant that they can scarcely remember it. All too soon, the fighting and destruction move near the camp. Families are separated and family members struggle to reunite with the people they love.

Events and Issues

Natural events, over which we have little control, happen all the time, as do events caused by human error or mistaken judgment and events caused by attitudes and tradition that impact what individuals and groups may or may not be allowed to do. These types of events are reflected in the literature in this genre.

Barbara Williams's book *Titanic Crossing* tells the story of the *Titanic* from the perspective of 12-year-old Albert Trask. He, his younger sister, mother, and uncle are going back to the United States at the bidding of his controlling grandmother. His mother and uncle die; Albert and his sister survive. Albert promises his sister that he will stay with her even if it means that he will not have the opportunities he would like.

Events leading up to and included in the Civil Rights Movement are some of the most significant in our country's history. Many books have been written on the issues involved, the effects on people, and the results of the efforts taken by individuals, families, and institutions. Books by Mildred D. Taylor chronicle the struggles of the Logan family and their friends and the discrimination they faced beginning in the 1930s. Many of the books are told from Cassie's perspective over a period of years. All of these books—*Song of the Trees; Roll of Thunder, Hear My Cry* (which won the Newbery Award); *Let the Circle Be Unbroken; The Friendship; The Gold Cadillac;* and *Mississippi Bridge*—allow today's readers to better understand events that occurred during this time period.

By 1957, the U.S. Supreme Court had ordered that schools be desegregated. In *The Girl on the Outside,* Mildred Pitts Walter looks at what happened when a school is to be integrated. This story is told from the perspective of two girls who go to the school, Sophia who is White and Eva who is African American.

In a thoroughly enjoyable story, Christopher Paul Curtis lets readers become a part of the Watson family on a trip to see their grandparents in Alabama. This was a difficult time—1963—for an African-American family to travel south, where schools, parks, playgrounds, as well as hotels and restaurants were segregated. *The Watsons Go to Birmingham—1963* helps readers experience the social conditions at that time and appreciate the changes that have been made.

In a book for younger readers, 7-year-old Anna has a Black teacher at her Catholic school. Sister Anne is a wonderful teacher who helps the second graders confront the issues of racism in an appropriate way. Marybeth Lorbiecki writes of events in her own life in *Sister Anne's Hands.*

REALISTIC FICTION IN THE CLASSROOM

Books of realistic fiction are frequently used to develop social studies concepts, cultural studies, and geography. Historical fiction turns facts and statistics into living human experience (Tunnell & Ammon, 1993). They help create emotional connections so that readers understand the realities of times other than their own; they can feel the joys, triumphs, and hopes, as well as the pain, suffering, and despair of others. Trade books can be used as the primary resource with textbooks used as supplementary materials when integrating curriculum studies.

The National Council of the Social Studies and the National Center for History in the Schools (1994) have developed standards for children in kindergarten through Grade 12. These standards include teaching suggestions and trade book examples such as using "historical fiction such as *Trouble at the Mines* by Doreen Rappaport to investigate the strikes in the coal mines and the organizing efforts of Mother Mary Jones" (1993, p. 154). The Web site for the National Council of the Social Studies *www.NESS.org* is very helpful, offering suggestions for teachers and updated lists of trade books for the social studies.

An increasing number of excellent books of realistic fiction have been put on audiotapes, which can be used several ways. First, students whose reading levels may not match their interest levels are able to listen to the stories for purely recreational purposes. These same students will be able to participate in Literature Circles if they are able to listen to the tapes while they read the books. Second, if teachers recommend these audio books and share titles with the parents of their students, families can listen to them while on car trips and can discuss the ideas they hear. Third, using these books as models, students can record their favorite books to be shared with audiences of their choice. Audio books are a very flexible teaching resource.

Suggested Audio Books

- *Catherine, Called Birdy* by Karen Cushman and read by Kate Maberly (BDD Audio, 1966; ISBN 0–553–47669–6).
- *The Midwife's Apprentice* by Karen Cushman and read by Jenny Sterlin (Recorded Books, 1996; ISBN 0–7887–0577–6).
- *The Devil's Arithmetic* by Jane Yolen and read by Barbara Rosenblat (Recorded Books, 1996; ISBN 0–7887–0541–5).

Resource Guides for Using Trade Books in Classrooms

The increasing use of trade books in classrooms has encouraged publishers to provide excellent resources for teachers.

Guides That Provide Multiple Approaches to Integrating Literature in Classrooms

- The Exploring the United States Through Literature series, published by Oryx Press, includes books, periodicals, and videos. Two of the titles included in this series are *Exploring the Great Lakes Through Literature* (Latrobe, 1994) and *Exploring the Southeast States Through Literature* (Veltze, 1994).
- *The Story of Ourselves: Teaching History Through Children's Literature* (Tunnell & Ammon, 1993) is a practical resource that provides a rationale for understanding history and integrating literature and history in the classroom.
- *War and Peace: Literature for Children and Young Adults* (Walter, 1993) describes techniques for sharing books, suggestions for classroom activities, and comprehensive bibliographies.
- *Using Literature to Teach Middle Grades About War* (Kennemer, 1993) includes 6 units about the major U.S. wars.

- *History Workshop: Reconstructing the Past with Elementary Students* (Jorgensen, 1993) uses the strategies and structure of reading/writing workshops to help students learn about history. Part I gives the rationale for using a history workshop; Part II tells how to do it; Part III presents 4 case studies in which the history workshop is used.
- *Understanding American History Through Children's Literature* (Perez-Stable and Cordier, 1994) focuses on U.S. history. The authors include lesson plans and activities.

As teachers, we want to help our students make connections with other time periods and cultures. Using historical fiction is one way to do this, of course. These books can provide emotional links between readers, events, and people of other times and places. A recently published series of books, not designed for use by young people but by adults who are going to write about particular time periods of the past, certainly presents clear pictures of these historical times. These books describe foods and drinks, how to furnish a house, how much things cost, employment, and language as it was used at the time. These books could most effectively be used with older students—perhaps sixth grade and up—because they give accurate presentation of the way life really was. For example, common slang terms and their definitions are given—and these include some words some people might find objectionable. Nonetheless, they are well worth while for teachers' use, even those who might not feel comfortable sharing them with their students.

- *The Writer's Guide to Everyday Life in Renaissance England: From 1485–1649* (Emerson, 1996)
- *The Writer's Guide to Everyday Life in the 1800s* (McCutcheon, 1993)
- *The Writer's Guide to Everyday Life in the Middle Ages: The British Isles from 500 to 1500* (Kenyon, 1995)
- *The Writer's Guide to Everyday Life in Regency and Victorian England: From 1811–1901* (Hughes, 1997)
- *The Writer's Guide to Everyday Life in the Wild West: From 1840–1900* (Moulton, 1998)
- *The Writer's Guide to Everyday Life in Colonial America: From 1607–1783* (Taylor, 1997)

Classroom Activities

ACTIVITY 10.1   FROM SLAVERY TO CIVIL RIGHTS

Beginning with the KWL charts developed in the opening vignette, Ms. Alexander and her class participated in an ongoing theme cycle. They read widely from a variety of genres—including biography, informational books, poetry, realistic fiction, and historical fiction, as well as reference books such as encyclopedias and textbooks. Based on the information they found, they created a time line and added dates throughout the year as they discovered significant events. The book *Oh, Freedom! Kids Talk About the Civil Rights Movement With the People Who Made It Happen* was an important source of dates for the time line as well as a resource for other books, series books, and videos about the times. One group of students decided that they would do interviews as the students did in this book, but instead of a book format, they wrote their own newspaper.

In order to accomplish district objectives, all students wrote letters; some to public figures to determine if discriminatory practices were happening in their city, others to solicit information about the proposed upcoming Underground Railroad Museum, others to family members who lived out of town to collect their remembrances. The letter writing was a continuing project for the whole year.

When a group of students found the book *Bull Run* by Paul Fleischman, they did a reader's theater presentation for the other sixth-grade classes. They did read-alouds of biographies to younger classes during Black History Month, which inspired them to write their own autobiographies.

These students read, discussed, wrote, shared, did interviews, listened to people—recorded and in person—and asked questions for which they wanted answers. They self-evaluated the information they got and made decisions about the quality of their own work and the work of their peers. In doing all of these activities, they learned about themselves, how to conduct investigations, and the process of inquiry as well as improving their literacy abilities—all of which will serve them well as life-long learners.

The titles of some of the books used in this unit, which were found not only by Ms. Alexander but by the students themselves, meet a variety of reading levels and interests. When doing a theme cycle, including many kinds and levels of books is possible.

- *Steal Away* by Jennifer Armstrong.
- *Barefoot: Escape on the Underground Railroad* by Pamela Duncan Edwards.
- *The Last Safe House* by Barbara Greenwood.
- *Oh, Freedom!* by Casey King and Linda Barrett Osborne.
- *...If You Traveled on the Underground Railroad* by Ellen Levine.
- *Christmas in the Big House, Christmas in the Quarters* by Patricia McKissack and Fredrick L. McKissack.
- *The Glory Field* by Walter Dean Myers.
- *Once on This River* by Sharon Dennis Wyeth.

ACTIVITY 10.2   WAGON WHEELS

Third graders reading Barbara Brenner's historical fiction *Wagon Wheels* can explore a variety of social issues, including interdependence, friendship, disasters, life after the Civil War, life on the frontier, and racism, as well as exploring the literary element of setting. In this story, the Muldie family is traveling to Nicodemus, Kansas, because Black families can homestead land there. The family encounters many difficulties in attaining their goal.

1. Introduce the book to the children, perhaps using a map so they can trace the route the Muldie family

traveled. Create a bulletin board with pictures of prairies, dugouts, and other scenes from the areas they traveled through.

2. Have students read the story silently.

3. Discuss the story with the children, stimulating them to think about the various elements of the story. Discuss the reasons the family traveled to Nicodemus, Kansas. Possible focus questions for discussion include:

   a. Why did the boys not travel with their father? How would you feel if you were the boys?

   b. Why do you think Johnny told the ladies that the boys could take care of themselves?

   c. Why did the Osage Indians help the settlers?

   d. Would your parents allow you to travel 150 miles by yourself?

   e. What problems did the boys face in making the trip? Which was the most difficult problem?

   f. How is racism related to this story?

4. Discuss the setting with the children. Questions related to setting include:

   a. What was the time of this story?

   b. What was the place of the story?

   c. How was life different in the time and place of this story than it is today?

   d. What were the difficulties of living in a dugout house? What were the good things about this kind of house?

   e. What kind of research would a writer have to do to create this setting?

5. Use extension activities to allow students to respond to the story. For example:

   a. Students can make models of a dugout.

   b. Students can make a model of Nicodemus, Kansas.

   c. Cook cornmeal mush for the students to taste.

   d. Study the Osage Indians and their way of life. Create a frieze that shows the information gathered.

   e. Have each student identify one difficulty the brothers faced and write about the way he or she would overcome it.

   f. Compare this story with another book. Other stories that can be included in this unit are the following:

      ■ Freedman, Russell. *Children of the Wild West.*

      ■ Rowan, James P. *Prairies and Grasslands.*

      ■ Wilder, Laura Ingalls. *Little House on the Prairie.*

      ■ Wilson, Terry. *The Osage.*

SUMMARY

Historical fiction books are read and enjoyed by most people because of the connections that they can make between their life and the lives of people in other times and places. We can relate to the characters' problems, joys, and sorrows because these are the feelings of the human condition. In addition, teachers find this to be a very useful genre because there are so many connections that can be made in the curriculum.

Teachers should exercise care, however, when choosing these books. Parents need to be informed of the books their children may be reading because many of these books depict events and conditions that may be considered violent, racist, or stereotyped. Parents can be involved in the activities in the classroom, listening and discussing the books and the ideas in the books with their children.

Thought Questions

1. What policy, if any, exists in your school district about using specific textbooks or reference books? If you are required to use a textbook, how will you adapt it so that it can be used as a reference book?

2. How can you integrate literature with a social studies textbook?

BY Marianna Dengler ILLUSTRATED BY Sibyl Graber Gerig

Fiddlin' Sam loved to fiddle and the folks around him loved to hear him.

3. What are your favorite historical fiction books?
4. Why do you think that some historical periods have many more books written about them than other periods? What are the implications for children and teaching?
5. What subject do you think is most neglected in historical fiction? Why might this be so?

Children's Literature References and Recommended Books

Aiken, J. (1974). *Midnight is a place.* New York: Viking. (4–8). HISTORICAL FICTION.

The owner of a mill teaches his ward about running a mill, but his ward is horrified by the lack of regard for human life that he observes.

Armstrong, J. (1992). *Steal away.* New York: Orchard Books. (4–6). HISTORICAL FICTION.

Susannah and a new friend, Bethlehem, a slave, escape to the North and become lifelong friends.

Avi. (1984). *The fighting ground.* New York: Lippincott. (4–8). HISTORICAL FICTION.

Jonathan has a romanticized view of war. When he runs away to join in the fighting, he learns some very difficult lessons.

Avi. (1994a). *Encounter at Easton.* New York: Beech Tree. (4–7). HISTORICAL FICTION.

The sequel to *Night Journeys* tells what happened to the bondsmen.

Avi. (1994b). *Night journeys.* New York: Beech Tree. (4–7). HISTORICAL FICTION.

This story is set in the late 1700s and focuses on the search for and treatment of two escaped bondsmen, who happen to be young children.

Bowen, G. (1994). *Stranded at Plimoth Plantation, 1626.* New York: HarperCollins. (2–4). HISTORICAL FICTION.

This historical fiction portrays the daily life of an indentured orphan boy at Plimoth Plantation.

Brenner, B. (1978). *Wagon wheels.* (D. Bolognese, Illus.). New York: Harper & Row. (1–3). HISTORICAL FICTION.

An African-American family moves from Kentucky to Kansas after the Civil War.

Bridgers, S. E. (1979). *All together now.* New York: Knopf. (5–8). CONTEMPORARY REALISTIC FICTION.

Casey has to live with her grandmother in a small southern town "where nothing ever happens" while her father is fighting in the Korean War.

Bunting, E. (1988). *How many days to America? A Thanksgiving story* (B. Peck, Illus.). New York: Clarion. (K–3). CONTEMPORARY REALISTIC FICTION.

Even today immigrants come to the United States to escape repression and danger in their own countries.

Bunting, E. (1990). *The wall.* (R. Himler, Illus.). New York: Clarion. (4–8). CONTEMPORARY REALISTIC FICTION.

A boy and his father visit the Vietnam Veterans Memorial to search for a name. During the visit they encounter many other people looking for names.

Burks, B. (1995). *Runs With Horses.* New York: Harcourt Brace. (5–9). HISTORICAL FICTION.

Runs With Horses, a young Apache boy, struggles to grow up in an environment that is constantly changing.

Byars, B. (1996). *Dead letter.* New York: Viking. (4–6). CONTEMPORARY REALISTIC FICTION.

Coerr, E. (1993). *Mieko and the fifth treasure* (C. Urehara, Illus.). New York: Putnam. (3–5). HISTORICAL FICTION.

Mieko, whose hand was injured when the bomb fell on Nagasaki, must learn to regain confidence in her artistic ability.

Collier, J. L., & Collier, C. (1974). *My brother Sam is dead.* New York: Four Winds. (5–8). HISTORICAL FICTION.

The Revolutionary War is tearing a family apart because loyalties lie with both sides.

Collier, J. L., & Collier, C. (1981). *Jump ship to freedom.* New York: Delacorte. (4–8). HISTORICAL FICTION.

Dan, a young African American, presents a different perspective on the Revolutionary War than readers usually get.

Conrad, P. (1991). *Pedro's journal.* Honesdale, PA: Boyds Mill. (4–6). HISTORICAL FICTION.

Pedro is a cabin boy on Columbus's ship. His journal reveals his observations and feelings about the adventure.

Cooney, B. (1988). *Island boy.* New York: Viking. (K–3). HISTORICAL FICTION.

The book tells of Matthias's growth from child to grandfather in the context of his home.

Cormier, R. (1990). *Other bells for us to ring* (D. K. Ray, Illus.). New York: Delacorte (3–6). HISTORICAL FICTION.

When Darcy's father is missing in action, she needs a miracle.

Curtis, C. P. (1995). *The Watsons go to Birmingham—1963.* New York: Delacorte. (5–7). HISTORICAL FICTION.

The story of an African-American family who visit their parents in the segregated South.

Cushman, K. (1996). *The ballad of Lucy Whipple.* New York: Clarion. (4–7). HISTORICAL FICTION.

California (Lucy) Whipple did not want to move to California with her family; now they are moving again. Lucy decides to stay behind and finds out that "home" is not what she expected.

Danziger, P. (1992). *Not for a billion, gazillion dollars.* New York: Delacorte. (3–6). CONTEMPORARY REALISTIC FICTION.

Matthew's peer relationships and issues of friendship are at the center of this book.

DeFelice, C. (1996). *The apprenticeship of Lucas Whitaker.* New York: Farrar. (4–7). HISTORICAL FICTION.

Lucas is lucky to become the apprentice of a college-trained doctor, a rather unusual person in the mid-1800s.

Denenberg, B. (1996). *When will this cruel war be over? The Civil War diary of Emma Simpson.* New York: Scholastic. (4–8). HISTORICAL FICTION.

In her diary entries, Emma describes the horror of life in Virginia during 1863–1864.

Denenberg, B. (1998). *The journal of William Thomas Emerson, a Revolutionary War patriot.* New York: Scholastic. (4–8). HISTORICAL FICTION.

An apprentice at a tavern writes about the events that lead to the Revolutionary War in his journal.

Dorris, M. (1996). *Sees behind trees.* New York: Hyperion. (5–8). HISTORICAL FICTION.

Having poor vision presents a variety of obstacles for Walnut, a Native American boy, until he learns how to "see" with his ears.

Edwards, P. D. (1997). *Barefoot: Escape on the Underground Railroad* (H. Cole, Illus.). New York: HarperCollins. (1–4). HISTORICAL FICTION.

Animals help an escaped slave on the Underground Railroad.

Fleischman, P. (1993). *Bull Run* (D. Frampton, Illus.). New York: HarperCollins. (4–7). HISTORICAL FICTION.

Both Northern and Southern perspectives on this battle are presented.

Freedman, F. B. (1971). *Two tickets to freedom* (E. J. Keats, Illus.). New York: Simon & Schuster. (4–6). HISTORICAL FICTION.

Two slaves, a husband and wife, escape to England by relying on disguises and bravery in the face of challenges.

Freedman, R. (1983). *Children of the wild west.* New York: Clarion. (3–6) INFORMATIONAL BOOK.

The book documents life in the American West from 1840 to the early 1900s.

Garland, S. (1998). *A line in the sand: The Alamo diary of Lucinda Lawrence.* New York: Scholastic. (4–8). HISTORICAL FICTION.

This book presents a girl's perspective about the events at the Alamo.

Greenwood, B. (1998). *The last safe house.* (H. Collins, Illus.). San Francisco: Kids Can. (3–6). HISTORICAL FICTION, INFORMATIONAL BOOK.

This book, a combination historical fiction and informational book, describes the Underground Railroad.

Gregory, K. (1992). *Earthquake at dawn.* New York: Harcourt Brace Jovanovich. (4–8). HISTORICAL FICTION.

A fictionalized account of two young women witnessing the San Francisco earthquake of 1906.

Gregory, K. (1996). *The winter of red snow: The Revolutionary War diary of Abigail Jane Stewart.* New York: Scholastic. (4–8). HISTORICAL FICTION.

Abigail learns not to complain about her problems after soldiers, wearing no shoes in December and leaving blood in the snow, pass by her home.

Gregory, K. (1997). *Across the wide and lonesome prairie: The Oregon Trail diary of Hattie Campbell.* New York: Scholastic. (4–8). HISTORICAL FICTION.

This book gives insight to the difficulties families had to overcome on their 2,000-mile, 6-month westward journey.

Hahn, M. D. (1991). *Stepping on the cracks.* New York: Clarion. (5–8). HISTORICAL FICTION.

When a soldier goes AWOL during World War II, the whole family suffers.

Hamanaka, S. (1990). *The journey: Japanese Americans, racism, and renewal.* New York: Orchard. (5–8). HISTORICAL FICTION, INFORMATIONAL BOOK.

This book depicts the mural commemorating the internment of Japanese Americans during World War II.

Hamilton, V. (1989). *The bells of Christmas.* New York: Harcourt Brace Jovanovich. (4–7). HISTORICAL FICTION.

This book describes the Christmas celebration of an African-American family in 1890.

Harness, C. (1992). *Three young Pilgrims.* New York: Bradbury. (1–4). HISTORICAL FICTION.

A fictionalized account of a family who comes to America on the *Mayflower* and their struggles to survive as well as their pleasures.

Hautzig, E. (1968). *The endless steppe.* New York: Crowell. (4–7). HISTORICAL FICTION.

A close-knit Jewish family is transported to Siberia during World War II.

Hesse, K. (1992). *Letters from Rifka.* New York: Henry Holt. (5–8). HISTORICAL FICTION.

Rifka and her family flee the oppression against Jews in Russia. The details of her journey are written in letters to her cousin.

Hickman, J. (1974). *The valley of the shadow.* New York: Macmillan. (4–7). HISTORICAL FICTION.

During the Revolutionary War, soldiers murder members of the Delaware Nation. Tobias, a survivor, gets help from missionaries.

Ho, M. (1991). *The clay marble.* New York: Farrar, Straus & Giroux. (4–8). HISTORICAL FICTION.

A refugee camp on the Thailand and Cambodian border is authentically portrayed in this novel.

Holland, I. (1994). *Behind the lines.* New York: Scholastic. (5–7). HISTORICAL FICTION.

Katie struggles with the injustice of her wealthy employers' paying $300 to hire her brother to fight in place of their son in the Civil War.

Hudson, J. (1989). *Sweetgrass.* New York: Philomel. (3–6). HISTORICAL FICTION.

A 15-year-old Blackfoot Indian girl must assume the responsibility for her family after they are attacked and a smallpox outbreak kills many people.

Karr, K. (1990). *It ain't always easy.* New York: Farrar, Straus & Giroux. (4–6). HISTORICAL FICTION.

In this story, two orphans travel from New York City to Pennsylvania, searching for love and for a family.

Keehn, S. M. (1991). *I am Regina.* New York: Philomel. (4–7). HISTORICAL FICTION.

Regina is captured by Native Americans during the French and Indian War. Regina's mother recognizes Regina because of a song they used to sing together when Regina was young.

Keehn, S. M. (1995). *Moon of two dark horses.* New York: Philomel. (4–6). HISTORICAL FICTION.

Cooshmoo, a Delaware Indian boy, and Daniel, a young settler, have been friends a long time. Their friendship is severely tested during the Revolutionary War.

Kerr, J. (1972). *When Hitler stole pink rabbit.* New York: Coward, McCann & Geoghegan. (4–6). HISTORICAL FICTION.

Anna and her family flee from Berlin to escape from the Nazis.

King, C., & Osborne, L. B. (1997). *Oh, freedom! Kids talk about the Civil Rights Movement with the people who made it happen* (J. Brooks, Illus.). New York: Knopf. (3–8). INFORMATIONAL BOOK.

Factual descriptions of aspects of the Civil Rights Movement and interviews of those who were involved.

Lasky, K. (1994). *Beyond the burning time.* New York: Blue Sky. (5–8). HISTORICAL FICTION.

The widow Virginia Chase is named a witch and sentenced to hang. Her children succeed in saving her life.

Lasky, K. (1996). *A journey to the New World: The diary of Remember Patience Whipple.* New York: Scholastic. (4–8). HISTORICAL FICTION.

The book, in diary format, describes the events of the *Mayflower* crossing and the first year at the Plimoth settlement.

Leighton, M. R. (1992). *An Ellis Island Christmas* (D. Nolan, Illus.). New York: Viking. (2–4). HISTORICAL FICTION.

This is a story of a family of immigrants who have to spend Christmas on Ellis Island.

Levine, E. (1988). *...If you traveled on the Underground Railroad.* (L. Johnson, Illus.). New York: Scholastic. (3–5). INFORMATIONAL BOOK.

Questions and answers about the Underground Railroad.

Levitin, S. (1989). *Silver days.* New York: Atheneum. (3–6). HISTORICAL FICTION.

This book tells about the further adventures of a Jewish family who escapes Nazi Germany.

Little, J. (1997). *The belonging place.* Toronto: Viking. (3–6). HISTORICAL FICTION.

Elspet Mary lives with her aunt and uncle; they move to Canada from Scotland.

Lorbiecki, M. (1998). *Sister Anne's hands.* (K. W. Popp, Illus.). New York: Dial. (K–3). CONTEMPORARY REALISTIC FICTION.

The second graders confront racism because their teacher is black.

Lord, B. B. (1984). *In the year of the boar and Jackie Robinson* (M. Simont, Illus.). (3–6). HISTORICAL FICTION.

Shirley Temple Wong and her family move to the United States in 1947. She is not easily accepted by the other children but develops some strong friendships by being a friend to her peers.

Lowry, L. (1989). *Number the stars.* Boston: Houghton Mifflin. (4–6). HISTORICAL FICTION.

This Newbery Award winner tells of a Danish family helping a Jewish girl escape the Nazis.

Lutzeier, E. (1991). *The coldest winter.* New York: Oxford University Press. (4–8). HISTORICAL FICTION.

The story is set in the Irish Potato Famine of the 1840s. An Irish family is evicted from their farm in the dead of winter because the landlord wants more grazing land.

Lyons, M. E. (1992). *Letters from a slave girl: The story of Harriet Jacobs.* New York: Scribner's. (4–8). HISTORICAL FICTION.

A fictionalized account, this story is told through letters written by an African-American child born into slavery.

MacBride, R. L. (1993). *Little house on Rocky Ridge* (D. Gilleece, Illus.). New York: HarperCollins. (3–5). HISTORICAL FICTION.

This is the first in a series of books about Rose Wilder, daughter of Laura Ingalls Wilder.

MacBride, R. L. (1994). *Little farm in the Ozarks* (D. Gilleece, Illus.). New York: HarperCollins. (3–5). HISTORICAL FICTION.

Another story of Rose and her family, based on her diaries and papers.

MacBride, R. L. (1997). *New dawn on Rocky Ridge* (D. Andreasen, Illus.). New York: HarperCollins. (3–5). HISTORICAL FICTION.

Rose Wilder is growing up and must decide if she wants to fall in love or further her education.

Marvin, I. R. (1994). *A bride for Anna's papa.* Minneapolis, MN: Milkweed Editions. (3–7). HISTORICAL FICTION.

Anna's widowed father marries her teacher and Anna has mixed feelings. Not until they have faced dangers together does she accept Mae as an integral part of the family.

McCully, E. A. (1996). *The bobbin girl.* New York: Dial. (K–4). HISTORICAL FICTION.

Ten-year-old Rebecca works in a textile mill, where she must decide whether to go on strike when the owners threaten to lower wages.

McKissack, P. C., & McKissack, F. L. (1994). *Christmas in the big house, Christmas in the quarters* (J. Thompson, Illus.). New York: Scholastic. (5–9). HISTORICAL FICTION.

A recounting of what Christmas was like for white people and black slaves in 1859 in the South.

Mochizuki, K. (1998). *Passage to freedom.* (D. Lee, Illus.). New York: Lee & Low Books. (2–5). BIOGRAPHY.

The author's father was a diplomat to Lithuania during WWII. He signed the papers that allowed many Jews to escape persecution.

Morpurgo, M. (1991). *Waiting for Anya.* New York: Viking. (4–8). HISTORICAL FICTION.

French villagers help Jewish children escape the Nazis during World War II.

Murphy, J. (1998a). *The journal of James Edmond Pease, a Civil War Union soldier.* New York: Scholastic. (4–8). HISTORICAL FICTION.

As this book describes, being a soldier during the Civil War was a most difficult experience.

Murphy, J. (1998b). *West to a land of plenty: The diary of Teresa Angelino Viscardi.* New York: Scholastic. (4–8). HISTORICAL FICTION.

The book details the journey from New Jersey to Idaho on rail and wagon train in 1883, which was both dangerous and boring.

Myers, W. D. (1994). *The glory field.* New York: Scholastic. (6–10). HISTORICAL FICTION, CONTEMPORARY REALISTIC FICTION.

The book traces generations of an African-American family from 1753 in Sierra Leone to the present.

Myers, W. D. (1999). *The journal of Joshua Loper: A black cowboy.* New York: Scholastic. (4–6). HISTORICAL FICTION.

This book is a good reminder that many of the cowboys of the West were African-American, and they often had special challenges.

Nixon, J. L. (1992). *Land of hope.* New York: Bantam. (4–8). HISTORICAL FICTION.

After Rebekah and her family immigrated to the United States, life was not easy for them. They face discrimination in a variety of ways.

O'Dell, S. (1989). *My name is not Angelica.* Boston: Houghton Mifflin. (5–8). HISTORICAL FICTION.

Raisha and Konje are captured in Africa and sold into slavery. Their treatment is so bad that Konje jumps off a cliff rather than go back into slavery. Raisha is taken to Martinique where she is no longer a slave.

O'Dell, S., & Hall, E. (1992). *Thunder rolling in the mountains.* Boston: Houghton Mifflin. (4–7). HISTORICAL FICTION.

Trouble happens when the settlers move onto Indian lands. The tribe must move and eventually settles on a reservation in Idaho.

Paterson, K. (1988). *Park's quest.* New York: Lodestar. (5–7). HISTORICAL FICTION.

Park learns about his father, who died in Vietnam, and meets his half-sister whose mother was Vietnamese.

Paterson, K. (1991). *Lyddie.* New York: Lodestar. (5–8). HISTORICAL FICTION.

Lyddie's mother hires Lyddie out to work in the textile mills in Lowell, Massachusetts. When Lyddie confronts the overseer, she is fired. Through her determination and courage, she is able to succeed, and eventually goes on to college.

Paterson, K. (1996). *Jip: His story.* New York: Lodestar. (4–6). HISTORICAL FICTION.

Jip is abandoned as a small child, and finding out who he is presents grave dangers for his safety.

Paulsen, G. (1993). *Nightjohn.* New York: Delacorte. (5–9). HISTORICAL FICTION.

When Nightjohn is caught teaching slaves to read, which is illegal, he is tortured.

Paulsen, G. (1997). *Sarny: A life remembered.* New York: Delacorte. (5–9). HISTORICAL FICTION.

Sarny, whom Nightjohn taught to read, becomes a free woman. She helps other people become literate.

Rappaport, D. (1987). *Trouble at the mines* (J. Sandin, Illus.). New York: Crowell. (5–7). HISTORICAL FICTION.

Families and children get involved in a strike in Arnot, Pennsylvania, in 1898.

Rinaldi, A. (1992). *A break with charity: A story about the Salem witch trials.* San Diego: Harcourt Brace. (6–10). HISTORICAL FICTION.

When Susanna finds out why people are accused of being witches, she must decide if she wants to share what she knows and put her family in danger, or if she should not say anything and let the hysteria continue.

Rinaldi, A. (1993). *The fifth of March: A story of the Boston Massacre.* San Diego: Harcourt Brace. (6–10). HISTORICAL FICTION.

Rachel Marsh, an indentured servant for John Adams, falls in love with a British soldier.

Rinaldi, A. (1994). *Finishing Becca: A story about Peggy Shippen and Benedict Arnold.* San Diego: Harcourt Brace. (4–6). HISTORICAL FICTION.

Benedict Arnold may have become a traitor to the country because of the influence of Peggy Shippen.

Rinaldi, A. (1995). *The secret of Sarah Revere.* San Diego: Harcourt Brace. (6–10). HISTORICAL FICTION.

Sarah, daughter of Paul Revere, takes on the responsibility of keeping her family together while her father is away.

Rinaldi, A. (1998). *Cast two shadows: The American Revolution in the South.* (4–8). HISTORICAL FICTION.

Caroline, who lives in South Carolina, has difficulty coming to terms with the deaths, the takeover of their land, and the imprisonment of her father during this war.

Rinaldi, A. (1999). *My heart is on the ground: The diary of Nannie Little Rose, a Sioux girl.* New York: Scholastic. (4–8). HISTORICAL FICTION.

With good intentions, sometimes terrible things are done to children, especially when a culture is not respected.

Roth, A. (1974). *The iceberg hermit.* New York: Four Winds. (5–8). HISTORICAL FICTION.

Allan is the only survivor of a whaling ship that sinks after hitting an iceberg. He lives alone near Greenland for 7 years.

Roth, A. (1983). *The castaway.* New York: Scholastic. (5–8). HISTORICAL FICTION.

Daniel runs away to sea and his ship wrecks. He is the only survivor and survives for 5 years by himself on an island in the Pacific.

Rowan, J. P. (1983). *Prairies and grasslands.* New York: Children's Press. (1–3). INFORMATIONAL BOOK.

Salisbury, G. (1994). *Under the blood-red sun.* New York: Delacorte. (5–8). HISTORICAL FICTION.

Because his Japanese father and grandfather were arrested after Pearl Harbor was bombed, Tomi must help his mother and sister survive. His friends on his ball team support him.

Schlein, M. (1991). *I sailed with Columbus* (T. Newsom, Illus). New York: HarperCollins. (4–7). HISTORICAL FICTION.

A cabin boy tells his story about sailing with Columbus.

Skurzynski, G. (1992). *Goodbye, Billy Radish.* New York: Bradbury. (4–7). HISTORICAL FICTION.

During World War I even boys had to work long hours in steel factories. They were not safe places for workers of any age.

Taylor, M. D. (1975). *Song of the trees* (J. Pinkney, Illus). New York: Dial. (5–9). HISTORICAL FICTION.

Readers are introduced to Cassie Logan and her family and the difficulty African Americans had in surviving.

Taylor, M. D. (1976). *Roll of thunder, hear my cry.* New York: Dial. (5–9). HISTORICAL FICTION.

During the 1930s, the members of the Logan family faced overt racism and hostility.

Taylor, M. D. (1981). *Let the circle be unbroken.* New York: Dial. (5–9). HISTORICAL FICTION.

This is the sequel to *Roll of Thunder.*

Taylor, M. D. (1987a). *The friendship* (M. Ginsburg, Illus.). New York: Bantam. (4–8). HISTORICAL FICTION.*

African American boys observe the hostile treatment of an old African American man by a store clerk.

Taylor, M. D. (1987b). *The gold Cadillac* (M. Hays, Illus.). New York: Dial. (3–6). HISTORICAL FICTION.*

Driving in the segregated South was a hazardous undertaking, especially for a black family driving an expensive car.

Taylor, M. D. (1990). *Mississippi bridge* (M. Ginsburg, Illus.). New York: Dial. (3–6). HISTORICAL FICTION.

African-American bus riders must get off the bus when white passengers arrive.

Tedrow, T. L. (1992). *Good neighbors.* Nashville, TN: Thomas Nelson. (3–6). HISTORICAL FICTION.

This fictionalized account of Laura Ingalls Wilder retains historical integrity.

Turner, A. (1992). *Katie's Trunk* (R. Himler, Illus.). New York: Macmillan. (2–4). HISTORICAL FICTION.

Set during the Revolutionary War, this book tells the story of a young Tory girl whose home is threatened by the colonists.

Uchida, Y. (1971). *Journey to Topaz* (D. Carrick, Illus.). New York: Scribner's Sons. (4–7). HISTORICAL FICTION.

This story of a Japanese-American family sent to an internment camp shows how they prove their loyalty to the United States.

Uchida, Y. (1978). *Journey home* (C. Robinson, Illus.). New York: Atheneum. (4–7). HISTORICAL FICTION.

The sequel to *Journey to Topaz* describes the mistreatment the Japanese Americans faced once released from the internment camps.

Uchida, Y. (1993). *The bracelet* (J. Yardley, Illus.). New York: Philomel. (2–5). HISTORICAL FICTION.

Emi and her family are moved to internment camps after the bombing of Pearl Harbor.

Van Raven, P. (1989). *Harpoon Island.* New York: Scribner's. (5–8). HISTORICAL FICTION.

American hysteria about the Germans reaches unacceptable heights in this story.

Vos, I. (1991). *Hide and seek* (T. Edelstein & I. Smidt, Trans.). New York: Scholastic. (4–6). HISTORICAL FICTION.

As Rachel and her family escape from the Nazis, they live with a variety of families who hide them.

Wallace, I. (1999). *Boy of the deeps.* New York: DK Publishing. (4–7). HISTORICAL FICTION.

Boys as well as men worked underground in the mines; when a cave-in occurs, James survives because he and his father work together.

Walter, M. P. (1982). *The girl on the outside.* New York: Lothrop, Lee & Shepard. (4–7). HISTORICAL FICTION.

Two girls, one white, the other African American, tell the story of school desegregation.

Weller, F. W. (1997). *Madaket Millie* (M. Sewall, Illus.). New York: Philomel. (4–6). HISTORICAL FICTION.

An abandoned child uses her strength and brains to become a member of the Coast Guard.

Whelan, G. (1996). *The Indian school* (G. Dellosso, Illus.). New York: HarperCollins. (3–6). HISTORICAL FICTION.

Lucy lives with her aunt and uncle at their school for Indians. She cannot understand why the Indians are the ones expected to change when their way of life is inappropriate.

White, E. E. (1998). *Voyage on the great Titanic: The diary of Margaret Ann Brady.* New York: Scholastic. (4–6). HISTORICAL FICTION.

An account of 4 days on the *Titanic.*

Wilder, L. I. (1932). *Little house in the big woods* (H. Sewell, Illus.). New York: Harper & Row. (4–7). HISTORICAL FICTION.

The story tells of the Ingalls family during their years on the prairie.

Wilder, L. I. (1953). *Little house on the prairie* (G. Williams, Illus.). New York: Harper & Row. (4–7). HISTORICAL FICTION.

The first book in the series describing the Ingalls family.

Wilder, L. I. (1971). *The first four years* (G. Williams, Illus.). New York: Harper & Row. (4–7) HISTORICAL FICTION.

This is the story of the first four years of Laura's marriage.

Williams, B. (1995). *Titanic crossing.* New York: Dial. (3–5). HISTORICAL FICTION.

Albert and his family return to the United States on the *Titanic.*

Williams, L. E. (1996). *Behind the bedroom wall* (A. N. Goldstein, Illus.). Minneapolis: Milkweed Editions. (4–6). HISTORICAL FICTION.

Korinna is an active member in a Nazi youth group during World War II. When she finds out that her family is hiding a Jewish mother and her daughter, she faces some hard decisions.

Wilson, T. P. (1998). *The Osage.* New York: Chelsea House. (5–9). INFORMATIONAL BOOK.

Describes the history and the present situation of the Osage tribe.

Wolff, V. E. (1998). *Bat 6.* New York: Scholastic. (4–7). HISTORICAL FICTION.

Prejudice and hate, left over from the war with Japan, interfere with an annual girls' softball game.

Wyeth, S. D. (1998). *Once on this river.* New York: Knopf. (5–9). HISTORICAL FICTION.

Monday learns about the horrors of slavery as she and her mother try to win the freedom of her uncle who has been enslaved even though he is a free man.

Yep, L. (1993). *Dragon's gate.* (1993). New York: HarperCollins. (4–7). HISTORICAL FICTION.

Otter, a Chinese boy, joins his father and uncle as they work on the transcontinental railroad at the time of the Civil War.

Yolen, J. (1992). *Encounter* (D. Shannon, Illus). New York: Harcourt Brace Jovanovich. (4–9). HISTORICAL FICTION.

A young Taino boy has a nightmare about the arrival of Columbus to the island where his tribe lives. The future fulfills his worst fears.

References and Books for Further Reading

Adamson, L. G. (1987). *A reference guide to historical fiction for children and young adults.* Westport, CT: Greenwood Press.

Burton, H. (1973). The writing of historical novels. In V. Haviland (Ed.), *Children and literature: Views and reviews.* Glenview, IL: Scott Foresman.

Copenhaver, J. (1993). Instances of inquiry. *Primary Voices K–6,* pp. 6–12.

Crabtree, C., Nash, G. B., Gagnon, P., & Waugh, S. (Eds.). (1992). *Lessons from history: Essential understandings and historical perspectives students should acquire.* Los Angeles: University of California.

Cullinan, B., & Galda, L. (1994). *Literature and the child* (3rd ed.). Fort Worth, TX: Harcourt Brace.

Emerson, K. L. (1996). *The writer's guide to everyday life in renaissance England: From 1485–1649.* Cincinnati, OH: Writer's Digest Books.

Huck, C., Hepler, S., & Hickman, J. (1993). *Children's literature in the elementary school* (5th ed.). Dubuque, IA: Wm. C. Brown.

Hughes, K. (1997). *The writer's guide to everyday life in Regency and Victorian England: From 1811–1901.* Cincinnati, OH: Writer's Digest Books.

Hunt, C. C. (1994). U.S. children's books about the World War II period: From isolationism to internationalism, 1940–1990. *The Lion and the Unicorn, 18,* 190–208.

Jordan, A. D. (1997). *Follow the gleam: Teaching and learning genre with children and young adults, Part II.* Brandon, VT: Esmont.

Jorgensen, K. (1993). *History workshop: Reconstructing the past with elementary students.* Portsmouth, NH: Heinemann.

Kennemer, P. K. (1993). *Using literature to teach middle grades about war.* Phoenix, AZ: Oryx.

Kenyon, S. (1995). *Writer's guide to everyday life in the middle ages: The British Isles from 500 to 1500.* Cincinnati, OH: Writer's Digest Books.

Latrobe, K. H. (1994). *Exploring the Great Lakes through literature.* Phoenix, AZ: Oryx.

McCutcheon, M. (1993). *The writer's guide to everyday life in the 1800s.* Cincinnati, OH: Writer's Digest Books.

Moulton, C. (1998). *The writer's guide to everyday life in the Wild West: From 1840–1900.* Cincinnati, OH: Writer's Digest Books.

National Council of the Social Studies and National Center for History in the Schools. (1994). *Social studies standards.* Los Angeles: University of California.

Norton, D. (1995). *Through the eyes of a child* (2nd ed.). Englewood Cliffs, NJ: Merrill/Prentice Hall.

Paterson, K. (1992). Daughters of hope. *Horn Book, 69,* 164–170.

Perez-Stable, M. A., & Cordier, M. H. (1994). *Understanding American history through children's literature.* Phoenix, AZ: Oryx.

Reed, A. (1994). *Reaching adolescents: The young adult book and the schools.* New York: Merrill/Macmillan.

Russell, D. L. (1994). *Literature for children: A short introduction.* (2nd ed.).White Plains, NY: Longman.

Sutcliff, R. (1973). History is people. In V. Haviland (Ed.), *Children and literature: Views and reviews* (pp. 305–312). Glenview IL: Scott Foresman.

Taylor, D. (1997). *The writer's guide to everyday life in colonial America: From 1607–1783.* Cincinnati, OH: Writer's Digest Books.

Tunnel, M., & Ammon, R. (Ed.). (1993). *The story of ourselves: Teaching history through children's literature.* Portsmouth, NH: Heinemann.

Veltze, L. (Ed.). (1994). *Exploring the southeast states through literature.* Phoenix, AZ: Oryx.

Walter, V. A. (1993). *War and peace: Literature for young children.* Phoenix, AZ: Oryx.

Truth Is Stranger than Fiction: Biography and Informational Books

KEY TERMS

biographical fiction
biography
concept books
experiment and
    activity books

exposition
informational book
life cycle books

GUIDING QUESTIONS

1. What kinds of information interested you as an elementary student? Did you find books in the library on this subject?

2. What biographies of famous people did you read as a child?

3. What are the major characteristics of nonfiction? How do informational books and biographies differ from the other genre?

OVERVIEW

We live in an information age fueled by a flood of knowledge. Information drives our society. We gulp and gobble it and wait for the next wave to come. Moreover, information quickly grows obsolete. This means that nonfiction is more important in all our lives than ever before. Today's children will have to read and understand massive amounts of information throughout their lives.

Informational books are a tool for satisfying children's curiosity about their environment (Hearne, 1990). Moreover, nonfiction provides the answers to children's questions. It whets their appetites for more study, as is demonstrated in the opening vignette where the children demonstrate how factual content fascinates and motivates children's interests. Well-written nonfiction holds a genuine fascination for children. To capitalize on this compelling interest, teachers, librarians, and parents must put the right books into children's hands at the right moment, something that requires a solid knowledge of children's informational books.

INTRODUCTION

Informational literature for children is flourishing to-day—in fact, it is edging out textbooks in classrooms as thematic and inquiry studies assume a larger role. Librarians and teachers must be most selective with the genre of nonfiction because the many new well-written and beautifully designed informational books should replace the out-of-date and poorly written titles of yesteryear remaining in some collections of literature.

VIGNETTE

We began our visit in a kindergarten classroom. An eager kindergarten boy greeted us: "Hi, my name's Daniel. I'm your host. See our shoes!"

He guided us around the classroom, identifying shoes of every size, color, and description, including jogging shoes, football shoes, ballet shoes, tap shoes, tennis shoes, baby shoes, clogs, moccasins, safety toe work shoes, and golf shoes.

Daniel explained, "We're reading books about shoes, too."

"Which books are your favorites?" I asked.

He showed us *Shoes from Grandpa* by Mem Fox, *Shoes* by Elizabeth Winthrop, and *My Two Feet* by Alice Schertle. Daniel said that Ms. Greene read all of the books aloud and then put them on the reading table for the children to read.

As we walked around the kindergarten, we saw Ms. Greene and her students engaged in a wide range of activities. They studied shoes from many cultures. The children engaged in free reading, wrote in journals, created posters and paper sculptures, and dramatized events they thought the shoes would have experienced. They counted the shoes displayed in the classroom, discussed the shoes required for different occupations, and drew pictures of shoes they designed for special purposes. The children's interest in shoes was evident as they explained their activities.

In another corridor of the school, we found a fourth/fifth-grade combination classroom, in which cooperative groups were working at tables around the classroom. Each group of students had a stack of informational books and a list of questions the group had generated about reptiles. I joined a group of students who were deeply involved in a discussion of snakes. They referred to 10 different books as they completed their questions. As the group put the finishing touches on their work, I asked one of the students, "What was the most interesting thing that you learned about snakes?"

He pointed to an illustration in the book he was reading and said, "Did you know snakes used to have feet?"

"No, I didn't!"

He enthusiastically explained that, during one period of the evolutionary history of snakes, they had feet, which gradually disappeared because they didn't need them. Then snakes developed into the form we recognize today.

THE CHANGING PERSPECTIVE ON NONFICTION

Nonfiction has often been treated as a poor relative in children's literature in spite of the fact that creating a nonfiction book requires the same quality of imagination as is essential to the writing of fiction. Imagination, invention, selection, language, and form are just as important in making a good volume of biography, history, or science as they are to the making of a piece of fiction (Meltzer, 1994). Russell Freedman (1988) addressed this issue in his acceptance speech for the Newbery Award:

> Nonfiction has never been completely ignored; for a long time it was brushed off and pushed aside, as though factual books were socially inferior to the upper crust stuff we call literature. . . . If a nonfiction book were talented and ambitious enough, it could rise above its station. But for the most part, children's nonfiction was kept in its place. (p. 422)

Several developments have contributed to the changing place of nonfiction in children's literature. First, the quality of children's nonfiction is impressive. Today's nonfiction is characterized by effective writing and attractive layouts, and it addresses a wide range of subject matter. In addition, librarians and educators have realized that children truly enjoy nonfiction and some even prefer nonfiction to fiction. As a result, nonfiction is assuming a place of greater prominence in the world of children's literature, evidenced by such developments as the Horn Book Graphic Gallery competition to honor outstanding nonfiction books for excellence in design. The National Council of Teachers of English bestows the Orbis Pictus Award to an outstanding children's nonfiction book each year. The lists of honor books for such prestigious awards as the Newbery Award, the Caldecott Medal, and the Boston Globe/Horn Book Awards are including nonfiction books more frequently than before.

When nonfiction is used in many elementary classrooms, it is used exclusively in content areas to help children acquire information about specific topics (Duthie, 1994), but educators have good reasons for using it throughout elementary schools. It is an important read-aloud for all grade levels. Good expository text is born of deep investment and passion (Meltzer, 1994). Well-written, well-researched nonfiction is exciting and creative. Excellent nonfiction makes readers want to know more, inviting them to reexamine the topic at hand, be it history, geography, the arts, or whatever area it deals with.

Extensive use of nonfiction establishes children's familiarity with this genre early, permitting them to read nonfiction with confidence (Duthie, 1994). Research shows that students who lack these experiences exhibit more difficulty comprehending expository text than narrative text and are less sensitive to important information in expository text (Ballantyne, 1993). Children who are exposed to various genres of literature recognize the differences among the genres as young as age 4, and children who have experiences with nonfiction enjoyed it and chose to read more nonfiction than their peers (Stoodt & Amspaugh, 1994). Young children who read nonfiction can grow to be excited, competent, creative readers and writers of nonfiction across all curriculum areas (Duthie, 1994). Nonfiction not only provides rich experiences but also has implications for lifelong learning (Walmsley, 1994).

Trends in Current Nonfiction

James Cross Giblin (1987), author and publisher of numerous nonfiction children's books, identifies four factors that characterize recent nonfiction: (a) a clear focus on a single aspect of the subject, (b) tightly written text designed to hold children's interest, (c) emphasis on illustration, and (d) careful attention to book design.

These elements are apparent in Aliki's *William Shakespeare and the Globe.* Aliki maintains a clear focus on the topic of Shakespeare and the Globe Theatre—while creating clearly written, engaging prose that holds intermediate-grade children's attention. Detailed descriptions of the Globe Theatre, relevant quotes from Shakespeare's plays, and a list of words and expressions that Shakespeare invented add dimension to the book. Detailed illustrations with informative captions contribute to the clean design. Moreover, the author brings readers into the present with a discussion of the rebuilding of the Globe Theatre in London.

THE VALUE OF NONFICTION

Nonfiction literature is valuable for children of today. Nonfiction is the most widely read genre. According to William Zinsser (1990), the preponderance of what writers write and sell is nonfiction. Book and magazine publishers publish nonfiction and readers demand nonfiction. Nevertheless, children's nonfiction has had the

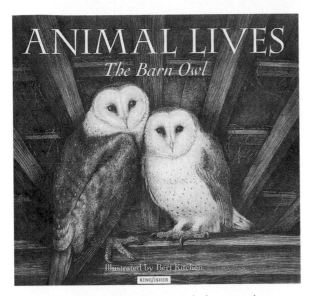

Owls sound and act mysteriously because they are nocturnal birds.

reputation of being so dull that it would put an owl to sleep (Harvey, 1998), but newer nonfiction, such as *Red-Eyed Tree Frog* by Joy Cowley and illustrated with exquisite photos by Nic Bishop, demonstrates how well-written and well-illustrated nonfiction can entice readers.

Provides information.   Informational books *provide up-to-date facts.* Students can explore timely topics as global warming in books such as Laurence Pringle's *Global Warming.* The color illustrations, maps, graphs, and text present this topic in ways that children can comprehend, as well as increasing their awareness of these issues as they impinge on the global community.

Expands background knowledge.   Through wide reading on content area topics, children learn the concepts and terms associated with these topics. Nonfiction books present topics in greater depth and detail than textbooks can. Social studies textbooks mention Eleanor Roosevelt only in passing, but the library has entire books devoted to her life. Moreover, trade books are usually written in a more interesting style. Nonfiction books provide children with a rich context for understanding many aspects of some real time, place, animal, person, or event, thus enhancing their schemata.

Promotes exploration.   A good book simulates direct experience—it makes the child want to go out and experience the observation or discovery firsthand (Harvey,

1998). Many of today's nonfiction books for young readers promote that kind of firsthand discovery by explaining how to participate in particular activities through clear, easy-to-follow directions. For example, in *Simple Simon Says: Take One Magnifying Glass,* Melvin Berger provides easy directions for a variety of fascinating experiments whereby children examine fingerprints, dollar bills, and crystals with a magnifying glass.

Enhances emotional development.   Nonfiction promotes the emotional development of its readers (Hearne, 1990). Books such as *Dinosaurs Divorce,* by Marc and Laurene Krasny Brown, can help children understand some of the emotions they experience when parents separate. Nonfiction, as well as fiction, helps children realize they are not the only ones in the world facing problems and gives them characters with whom they can identify.

Nonfiction books summarize and organize information. *Ghost Liners: Exploring the World's Greatest Lost Ships* by Ballard and Archbold summarizes and organizes information about ocean liners that sank and examines the circumstances of each wreck. Books that organize and summarize information help students understand and respond to nonfiction.

Immersing children in well-written nonfiction helps them learn to read nonfiction with understanding and appreciation. Moreover many experiences with nonfiction give children a basis for organizing ideas and writing in the nonfiction genre. For example, *Red-Eyed Tree Frog* by Joy Cowley follows an engaging red-eyed tree frog's search for something to eat, which will stimulate children to read and write about their interests.

BIOGRAPHY

Biography is the story of a life, the "history of the life of an individual" (Lukens, 1995). When biography is working, it sparks the reader's interest—even for a reader who initially had no interest in the subject. Reading a well-written biography becomes an absorbing human encounter with a person whose achievement is out of the ordinary. Children's fascination with this phenomenon is no different from that of adults. In addition, biographies allow children to identify with people of the past and the present.

> Readers learn about life by tapping the experiences of others. If it is possible for the people described in biographies to overcome obstacles such as ignorance,

poverty, misery, fear and hate, then it must be possible for the rest of us. This is the very optimistic message that children find in biographies. (Zarnowski, 1990, p. 9)

Children can see others' lives as models of achievement and career goals; they may learn about courage and tenacity in the face of adversity and difficulty.

Biographers do not simply tell the stories of individual lives, because their subjects do not live isolated lives. Their lives, are shaped through their interactions with other people and through events that form the backdrop of their story. Certainly, describing the subjects of children's biographies without considering the personal and historical contexts of their lives would be impossible. "When you write biography, you present history through the prism of a single life, a life, that is, of course, connected to other lives" (Meltzer, 1981, p. 15). Thus, when children read biographies, they learn about not just one but many lives, as well as about different times and places.

Some biographies reveal a great deal about the times and places in which an individual or individuals lived. In *Boss of the Plains,* Laurie Carlson explains how John Batterson Stetson invented the hat now identified with the West when he saw that the hats men had worn in the East were useless in the heat and wind of the West. Jerry Stanley illuminates a little-examined aspect of the U.S. frontier in *Frontier Merchants: Lionel and Barron Jacobs and the Jewish Pioneers Who Settled the West.* In rich detail, Stanley describes how Lionel and Barron Jacobs converted a canned goods business into a thriving bank.

Writing Biography

The first requirements of a good biography are that it be accurate, up-to-date, and authentic. Objective biographers research their subjects carefully. They also, however, assume an attitude or theme in writing toward the subject, which guides them in selecting the events and details to include. Once the research has been done and the attitude decided, the writer shapes the biography to make the subject come alive.

Biography may appear to be a simple writing task, essentially a reporting of actual people, events, and life stories. Biographers, however, must decide on a style of writing appropriate to the subject, a theme, a point of view, how much detail to include about the subject's life, whether to use illustrations, which friends or ene-

mies of the subject to write about, and many other details. Biographers use many of the same techniques as other storytellers: They "set their scenes descriptively, develop their characters completely, and give us the impression of life unfolding" (Zarnowski, 1990, p. 6). Because children have experienced these literary techniques, "biographies are a comfortable, somewhat familiar type of material for children" (p. 6).

When writing a biography of any type, the author must determine which facts are appropriately omitted or included in telling the subject's story. Sometimes they elect to omit or to mention only particular facts about a person that may be controversial or deemed inappropriate for children. For example, in his biography of *Charles A. Lindbergh: A Human Hero,* James Cross Giblin chose to recognize this man's Nazi sympathies that impacted on his brief time in the world spotlight.

Types of Biography

One of the most important decisions a biographer must make is the type of biography to write: complete or partial, single or collective.

Complete versus partial biography

Complete, or cradle-to-grave, biographies describe a subject's life from birth to death. In *Lost Star,* Patricia Lauber traces Amelia Earhart's life from her birth in Atchison, Kansas, in 1897, to her disappearance in 1937. Partial biographies, on the other hand, focus on a particular time or specific event in a subject's life. In *Leonardo da Vinci: The Artist, Inventor, Scientist,* Alice and Marten Provensen describe the events of the year 1492 in da Vinci's life. During this year he developed a flying machine, created a statue, studied the heavens, and painted the *Mona Lisa.* William Miller's picture book *Zora Hurston and the Chinaberry Tree* tells of a little-known episode in the childhood of the renowned writer Zora Neale Hurston. Another picture book, Edith Kunhardt's *Honest Abe,* depicts only major events in the life of Abraham Lincoln through unforgettable primitive paintings and simple language. The text and illustrations are uniquely suited to the subject's life.

Single versus collective biography

Single biographies such as Russell Freedman's award-winning *Eleanor Roosevelt: A Life of Discovery* and James Cross Giblin's exceptional picture biography of

Thomas Jefferson focus on the life of one individual. On the other hand, a collective biography describes in a single book several subjects with some connection among them that addresses the theme of the book. Brent Ashabranner's *People Who Make a Difference* profiles ordinary people who made a difference in the lives of the needy, in the environment, through community service, and through personal example. In *Seven Brave Women,* Betsy Hearne tells the history of seven ancestors who exhibited bravery.

Autobiography

Many autobiographies are written for children as well. For example, Tomie dePaola's autobiography, *26 Fairmount Avenue* tells about his childhood and the beginning of his career writing picture books.

Authentic versus fictionalized biography

How to interpret an individual's life is a very important decision on the biographer's part. The author may adhere to the facts in authentic biography or dramatize the subject's life through fictionalized biography. In authentic biography, the only facts included are those verifiable through research. Any dialogue is substantiated by historical documents (Russell, 1991). Biographer Jean Fritz (1990) explains her stance: "I would make up nothing, not even the dialogue, and I wouldn't even use dialogue unless I had a source. I would be honest. If there was a fact I wasn't sure of, or if it was unknown, I would say so" (p. 25).

Most children's biography, however, is fictionalized. This style, often called biographical fiction, *represents a middle position between strict adherence to known facts and completely invented narrative:* The "facts are the bricks with which a biographer builds" (Coolidge, 1974, p. 141). In fictionalized biography, dialogue and events can be invented based upon historical documents (Sutherland & Arbuthnot, 1991). Margery Fisher (1972) points out that "to draw a line too sharply between known fact and reasonable deduction would be to deny [children] a great deal of persuasive detail" (p. 304). Barbara Brenner's *On the Frontier with Mr. Audubon,* for example, records the story of Audubon's journey down the Mississippi in 1821. She uses the character of his real-life assistant, Joseph Mason, to create imaginary journal entries, as though he were recording their trip.

Selecting and Evaluating Biography

Biography has not enjoyed the popularity with children that other literary genres, such as realistic fiction, has in the past (Meltzer, 1987). Part of this lack of enthusiasm may be a relic of the poor quality of many children's biographies of the past (Carr, 1982; Fisher, 1972), which were often characterized by inaccuracies, poor writing, and overglorification of historical figures. For instance, Russell Freedman (1988) cites an older Lincoln biography that includes this exchange between 11-year-old Abe and his father: "Books!" said his father. "Always books! What is all this studying going to do for you? What do you think you are going to be?" "Why," said Abe, "I'm going to be President" (p. 424).

This contrived dialogue illustrates the writing commonly found in older biographies. Moreover, this author made it appear that Lincoln was different from other 11-year-old children—that he was somehow predestined for the presidency. This is not an uncommon style of writing in older biographies; today, however, children's biographies of excellent quality are available. When selecting excellent biography, consider the subject of the biography, the accuracy of the information, the characterization, the theme, and the writing style.

Subject

For many years, the subjects of children's biographies were historical figures considered worthy of emulation. More and more writers and others are realizing that people who have made significant impact on their world may or may not have been admirable or commendable (Lukens, 1995).

Jean Fritz has written about both types of characters. In *You Want Women to Vote, Lizzie Stanton?* she wrote about an admirable character who strove to realize her potential against great odds. Jean Fritz chose the telling details that created an accessible, fascinating portrait of Stanton's accomplishments, her decisive, impatient, outspoken personality, as well as her indomitable spirit. Moreover, Fritz has depicted the greater society that Stanton hoped to change.

Members of minority cultures have often been omitted from biography and history. "Not that long ago . . . American children learned American history minus Black people. The same is certainly true of women, Hispanics, and Native Americans" (Hearne, 1990, p. 136). One of the most visually striking biographies to break this color barrier is *Story Painter: The Life of Jacob Lawrence* by Duggleby. The use of Lawrence's paintings to illustrate significant points in his life as well as to illustrate his artistic accomplishments makes this a stunning book. Faith Ringgold's painted quilts illustrate her autobiographical picture book, *Tar Beach.* Jeanette Winter's biography of Georgia O'Keeffe, *My Name is Georgia,* show her independent spirit and her development as a woman and an artist. Chapter 15 includes biographies of outstanding people from many cultures.

Accuracy

Accuracy is the linchpin of excellent biography. The best biographers conduct exhaustive research to document their books. Russell Freedman began his research for the Newbery Award–winning *Lincoln: A Photobiography* at the Abraham Lincoln Bookshop in Chicago. He read widely from the many books on Lincoln's life, examined original documents, and conducted eyewitness research at sites in Kentucky, Indiana, Illinois, and Washington, D.C. (Freedman, 1988). He documents his research in three sections of the book, "In Lincoln's Footsteps," "Books About Lincoln," and in the acknowledgments and credits, so that others can find the same facts he did while doing his research.

Today's biographers, however, create realistic portraits of their subjects, as Freedman did in *Lincoln: A Photobiography:*

> His untidiness followed him home from the office. He cared little for the social niceties that were so important to his wife. He was absent-minded, perpetually late for meals. He was away from home for weeks at a time. . . . And he was moody, lapsing into long, brooding silences. (p. 41)

Freedman explained that recognizing Lincoln's weaknesses throws his strengths and his greatness into sharper relief.

Characterization

Biographers often choose to use the main characteristic of a subject as a focal point and a theme for their writing. Freedman has done this in his biographies of Lincoln and Eleanor Roosevelt. Jean Fritz focused on Revere's compulsive activities in *And Then What Happened, Paul Revere?* Her theme and style in this biography meld together seamlessly: Her short sentences and informal tone mimic Revere's compulsive, breathless speech.

The goal of biographers is to create characters who come alive for children. To achieve this, a biographer selects facts that effectively tell the subject's story and help children feel they know the character described. Authors use various devices to help us understand their subjects. In *The Librarian Who Measured the Earth,* Kathryn Lasky depicts Eratosthenes's extremely curious nature, a trait with which many children can identify, because they too are filled with wonder and questions.

Another stylistic technique for helping readers "see" a subject is telling the story from a child's point of view. Allen Say compares his life and his grandfather's life in the Caldecott Award–winning book *Grandfather's Journey,* telling about his grandfather's journey to the United States and his return to Japan. His grandfather loved both countries, and when he was in one country he yearned for the other. Say explains that he feels the same way. Although Say is not a child, his point of view makes his grandfather's biography warm and personal.

Theme

Biographers identify a unifying thread or theme to bind the characterization of their subject together. Different authors go about this in various ways. In some instances, research into the subject's accomplishments reveals an obvious theme, but in most cases so much research exists the biographer must select the most prominent or appropriate theme from several possibilities. This then determines the facts to include and exclude and shapes the authors' interpretation of their subjects. Freedman's biography of Eleanor Roosevelt focuses on her discoveries about herself and her own strengths. He chose to exclude extensive discussion of her husband's infidelity.

Style

A lively, interesting style makes the subject of a biography come alive for readers. Children generally enjoy facts woven into narrative style (Russell, 1991). They find it easier to understand biography that reads like a story, albeit a real-life story. Adopting narrative style, however, does not excuse the biographer from the research needed to create authenticity in daily life, food, games, clothing, and conversation. For example, the language created in conversation should be appropriate to the era, and discussions must reflect the issues of the time. Some of the vocabulary used may be foreign to young readers and impede their understanding. Jean Fritz (1990) explains that in her biographies she limits vocabulary to make the books readable, but she does not omit important words just because they may be strange to young readers. Some authors include glossaries to help children.

INFORMATIONAL BOOKS

One of the most exciting trends in children's literature today is the burgeoning informational book market. Outstanding writers are creating exemplary nonfiction. At their best, these books show the authors' deep-seated interest in their chosen subjects. The authors' personal interest in their subjects is contagious for young readers, who want to know more and more. Their hours of research, thoughtful writing, well-chosen graphics, and balance between fact and narrative result in books that are truly literature (Elleman, 1991).

England and Fasick (1987) suggest these books are written for at least three purposes. One purpose is to introduce young children to specific ideas and concepts. Such books are designed to engage "browsers" and as a result have large print, colorful illustrations, and simple, clearly explicated text. Joy Masoff's *Emergency!* is an example of such a book. In this book children learn about the many people involved in emergency work. Another purpose of nonfiction is to supply information; this type of book is intended for children already interested in a particular topic or area of study. Gail Gibbons's book *Exploring the Deep, Dark Sea* is an excellent example. In it, she explains one of the world's most complicated ecosystems with lucid language and lush illustrations. She shares information about tropical rain forests, such as the fact that 240 inches of rain may fall there in a single year. The third purpose of a nonfiction book is to summarize and organize information. Laurence Pringle's book, *Living Treasure: Saving Earth's Threatened Biodiversity,* summarizes and organizes information about our planet's unique organisms.

Types of Informational Books

Informational books appear in a variety of formats: concept books, nature identification books, life-cycle books, experiment and activity books, books derived from original documents and journals, photographic

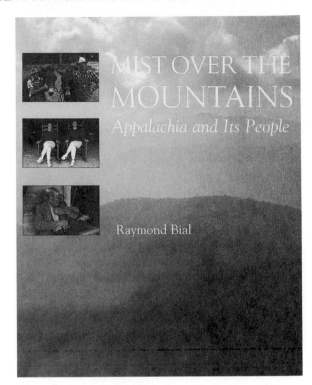

The beauty and warmth of Appalachian mountain life are shown in this book.

essays, and reference books and periodicals. They focus on many subjects, including the arts, animals, mathematics, man-made objects, language, sex, the life cycle, and every other topic imaginable (Stewig, 1988). Many nonfiction books cannot easily be categorized because they deal with specialized information that does not obviously belong to a specific type.

Concept books

Concept books explore abstract ideas and categories of ideas. For example, *Hottest, Coldest, Highest, Deepest* by Steve Jenkins explores global geography to identify record-breaking places and make the numbers tangible with maps and collage illustrations. David Adler's *How Tall, How Short, How Far Away* examines units of measurement.

Nature identification books

Nature identification books, as the name implies, focus children's attention on the natural world. Primary-grade students will enjoy Joy Cowley's *The Red-Eyed*

Tree Frog and the magnificent photographs that illustrate the book. The title *Exploding Ants: Amazing Facts About How Animals Adapt* by Joanne Settel is bound to attract children to this fascinating book.

Life-cycle books

Life-cycle books trace the growth of animals and plants. *Beaver* by Glen Rounds examines the life and daily habits of an interesting animal. The author has been observing beavers and drawing and writing about them most of his life, so he brings extraordinary authenticity to the subject.

Experiment and activity books

Experiment and activity books, another category of nonfiction, provide children with hands-on exploration of a variety of concepts. Such books include safety precaution statements, lists of sequential steps to follow, list of required materials or equipment, and an illustration of the finished project. A good example of this category of books is *You Gotta Try This! Absolutely Irresistible Science* by Vicki Cobb, which includes several dozen experiments with observations and clear warnings about potential problems.

Books from original documents and journals

Books derived from research involving original documents and journals interest children because of their authenticity. Julius Lester's *To Be a Slave* is a touchstone for this type of book. To learn about the slavery experience, Lester consulted many sources, including especially valuable interviews with slaves recorded by members of the Federal Writers Project in the late 1930s and early 1940s. This was a part of Roosevelt's Works Progress Administration (WPA). The actual words of the former slaves were used to describe their experiences.

Photographic essays

Photographic essays are an increasingly important form of informational book. Sally Ride and Susan Okie's *To Space and Back,* Patricia Lauber's *Hurricanes,* and Russ Kendall's *Eskimo Boy* are outstanding examples of books in which color photography lends an air of authenticity to the information. Caroline Arnold, a notable author of informational books, also effectively uses color photographs to illustrate her ideas, conveying a real sense of desert life in *Watching Desert Wildlife.* Richard Wormser uses black-and-white photographs to illustrate *Hoboes,* which are just right for the tone of the book and the subject. In *Comets, Meteors, and Asteroids,* Seymour Simon combines drawings, photographs, and simple language to create an informational book that elementary school children can understand.

Reference books and periodicals

Reference works, available for virtually all areas of information, include encyclopedias, bibliographies, dictionaries, atlases, and almanacs for all age groups. These resources are important for their content and for teaching students how to search for information (England & Fasick, 1987). *The Children's Animal Atlas* by David Lambert explains how animals have evolved, where they live today, and why so many are in danger. *The Children's Atlas of Exploration,* by Antony Mason, enables readers to follow in the footsteps of the great explorers. Mason's *The Kingfisher First Picture Atlas* represents the trend to publish reference books for younger students. Arthur Yorinks's *The Alphabet Atlas,* intended for kindergarten and first-grade students, examines where and how people live all over the world; its pictorial table of contents makes it especially useful. Encyclopedias on CD–ROM are an exciting addition to traditional reference works. When using these reference materials, students may actually listen to a speech or piece of music, they can see people and machines moving, and many other exciting innovations.

Some reference works are recommended for all age groups. *Exploring Your World: The Adventure of Geography* (Donald Crump, Ed.) has 334 encyclopedia entries on a variety of geographical topics, with more than 1,000 photographs, diagrams, and charts. Specialized bibliographies such as Mary Anne Pilger's *Science Experiments Index for Young People* includes science activities and experiments drawn from 700 books.

Kingfisher publishes a variety of reference works. *The Kingfisher First Picture Atlas* includes information about map scale as well as reading and making maps. This book was written as a first atlas for young readers. *The Kingfisher Young People's Encyclopedia of the United States* (William Shapiro, Ed.) has 1,200 entries that reflect the school curriculum. *The Kingfisher First Encyclopedia of Animals* (Burnie & Gamlin) has 450 entries about animals. Kingfisher also publishes an *Illustrated Thesaurus,* by George Beal.

Dorling Kindersley publishes a variety of reference works as well, including *The Dorling Kindersley Children's Illustrated Dictionary.*

Innovative Informational Books

The Magic School Bus series is well known among schoolchildren and teachers for a humorous approach to science for children. Joanna Cole, the author, is the winner of the 1991 Washington Post/Children's Book Guild Nonfiction award for the body of her work. In *The Magic School Bus: In the Time of the Dinosaurs* and *The Magic School Bus on the Ocean Floor* as well as other Magic School Bus titles, readers meet Ms. Frizzle, an unusual teacher who wears outrageous clothes and drives a magic school bus on incredible journeys. Although the bus trips are fanciful, the science reported is accurate and carefully documented. These books are also available on CD–ROM.

J. Young's *The Most Amazing Science Pop-Up Book* is an interactive book with a working record player, compass, microscope, camera, sundial, kaleidoscope, and periscope. This book is rich with accurate information as well.

In its Voyages of Discovery series, Scholastic Books also offers an interactive approach to information. For example, *Exploring Space* has movable maps of the constellations, plastic overlays, fold-out maps, 3-D glasses, and a sky clock students can rotate to tell time as sixteenth-century astronomers did. A time line and extensive references for further reading are included, and the information is up-to-date and accurate.

Selecting and Evaluating Informational Books

What standards distinguish excellent informational books from mediocre ones? Most of all, the best informational books make us think. Facts abound in our information-dense world, but books that make readers think are not as prevalent. Several criteria guide the evaluation of informational books: the literary style and technique; the authority of the author; and the accuracy, appropriateness, and attractiveness of the book.

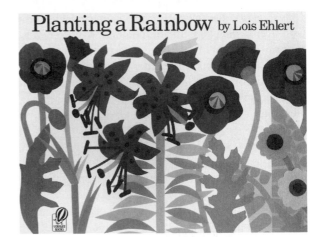

Flowers make a rainbow.

Style

Literary style refers to an author's use of language, sometimes called *voice.* A distinctive, interesting voice is crucial to informational books. Clarity, accuracy, organization, scope, currency, objectivity, honesty, authority, illustration, documentation, holistic treatment, and readability are all important factors in informational books, but without voice, nonfiction too often goes unheard (Hearne, 1993).

Karen Wallace's *Think of an Eel* is a book that does have a voice, one "that is a distinctive blend of verbal and artistic styles that shapes the subject, from the selection of facts to the progression with which they're presented. The end papers depict developmental stages of eel growth in eye-catching watercolors and suggest a mysterious dynamic about to unfold" (Hearne, 1993, p. 273). Readers are involved with the subject from the first line, but the author never romanticizes the subject. She includes information about the gulls who eat eels and about the worn-out and wasted bodies of the eels after they lay their eggs. *Think of an Eel* is a part of the Read and Wonder series published by Candlewick.

A concise style that presents facts in simple, direct language is appropriate for most informational books. Quality nonfiction authors use correct terminology, present information simply, and do not talk down to their readers. Books of this quality inspire readers in the same ways that great teachers do (Stodart, 1987).

They present the subject in an understandable form while remaining true to the content. A good voice, however, consists of more than conveying information as a "basket of facts," no matter how accurate and direct the information is. The best nonfiction is literature; it combines factual information with literary devices that make the ideas come alive. The writing in these books has an aesthetic dimension similar to good fiction (Purves & Monson, 1984). Jane Yolen (1973), who writes fiction, poetry, and nonfiction, says, "It is the . . . writer's problem to turn . . . data into information. Data is useful only to the trained ear and eye. As information it speaks to anyone who takes the time to listen. Changing data into information is a creative process. It is the first of a series of processes that make the writing of nonfiction as creative as the writing of fiction" (p. 69).

The best writers of informational books convey an enthusiasm and passion about their subject that is passed on to their readers. This transformation from data to information through literary style distinguishes the writing typical of textbooks from that of quality informational trade books. Compare the quality of writing on the same topic from a textbook and a trade book:

Textbook.   "So the Pilgrims decided to look for a place where they could have their own church and also live as English men and women.

After thinking about a number of places, the Pilgrims decided to go to North America. . . .

In 1620, about a hundred people crowded onto a small ship called the *Mayflower*" (McAuley & Wilson, 1987, p. 69).

Trade book.   "The *Sparrowhawk's* crew set sail from London in hopes of reaching Jamestown, Virginia. Amongst the 26 passengers, mostly Irish servants, were Masters Fells and Sibsey. I was indentured to Captain Sibsey by my unscrupulous uncle. On November 6 our ship crashed in fog on what the captain told us was a New England shore" (Bowen, *Stranded at Plimoth Plantation, 1626,* p. 1).

The textbook description is factually accurate, but it does not make the past come alive in ways that children can understand. The trade book, however, gives a vivid and lively portrayal of this period in U.S. history. Moreover, the trade book stimulates children to read more of the book. Bowen's writing creates the sense of adventure that those early settlers must have felt in coming to a new land.

Technique

Closely related to style is the literary technique authors employ to make their subjects interesting. All of the techniques used by authors of fiction books are employed by authors of nonfiction: narrative, metaphor and simile, relating known information to new information, imagery, and "hooks" to engage readers' interest.

Karla Kuskin combines narrative and exposition in *Jerusalem, Shining Still* to tell the 3,000-year history of Jerusalem through text, prose, and poetry. She explains, "The Moslems, like the Christians and the Jews, thought that Jerusalem was a special place in the world, a holy city" (p. 16).

In *Think of an Eel,* Karen Wallace compares eels to familiar things to help children who probably have never seen an eel to understand what they are like:

> *Think of an eel.*
> *He swims like a fish.*
> *He slides like a snake. . . .*
> *He looks like a willow leaf,*
> *clear as a crystal. . . .*
> *He eats like a horse.*

Visual imagery helps readers see the sod houses that settlers built in Freedman's book *Children of the Wild West.* He describes the inside of a sod house: "During heavy rains, water seeped through the roof and dripped down on the settlers and their furnishings" (p. 33).

Authors often use the journalistic device of a "hook" to capture children's interest. For example, "Launch morning. 6. . . 5. . . 4. . . The alarm clock counts down. 3. . . 2. . . 1. . . Ring! 3:15 A.M. Launch minus four hours" (Ride & Okie, *To Space and Back,* p. 14). The countdown, juxtaposed with the alarm-clock ring, draws children's interest. It also relates the unfamiliar countdown with the familiar ring of an alarm clock.

Authority

The author's qualifications for writing an informational book are usually given on the back flap of the book jacket or the book itself. When this information is not available, readers can consult reviews in journals such as the *Horn Book,* the *New Advocate, Language Arts,* and the *Bulletin of the Center for Children's Books* to learn more about an author's expertise.

Some children's authors are themselves authorities on the subjects about which they write, as are Jean Craighead George, a naturalist, and Millicent E. Selsam, a botanist. Many authors of informational books, however, are not experts in the fields they have chosen to write about. Instead, these authors thoroughly research the topic and consult with experts to ensure accuracy and credibility in their text. They usually credit the authorities who assisted them in their research in the opening or closing pages of the book. For example, on the copyright page of the book *Volcano: The Eruption and Healing of Mount St. Helens,* Patricia Lauber acknowledges the help of 13 individuals, including geologists, naturalists, and foresters.

Accuracy

Accuracy is essential in nonfiction. Clear, correct, and up-to-date facts and concepts are the hallmarks of fine children's nonfiction, and illustrations, diagrams, charts, maps, and other material in the book should meet these requirements as well. Accuracy includes more than correct factual information, however. Effective authors of informational books distinguish between theories and facts and make clear that various points of view exist regarding controversial subjects. Recency of information, illustrations, and examples in the book are also important considerations because information in older books may have been revised by current research; check the copyright date to ensure obtaining the most up-to-date information possible.

David Macaulay's *The Way Things Work,* winner of the Boston Globe/Horn Book Award for Nonfiction, received praise for its attention to detail and accuracy. The text is lucid and clear, and he uses a limited number of words.

Accuracy of information can be checked with a recent encyclopedia or a current textbook, but concern for accuracy is often a confusing issue. In *America Alive: A History,* Jean Karl has created an excellent informational book that gives children a sense of historical continuity in a narrative chain that reads like a story. However, we find a few small "bloopers," such as saying Sutter's Mill is west of San Francisco

instead of east as it should be. As Roger Sutton (1994) points out, however, "that's a quibble in a book filled with telling detail" (p. 3). Certainly, accuracy is essential in evaluating nonfiction, but in this book the inaccuracies are small and do not invalidate its quality.

Another consideration in selecting and evaluating nonfiction is the author's use of anthropomorphism, or attribution of human characteristics to animals or objects. Some authors use anthropomorphism because they think this will make their animal subjects more human and interesting to readers (Lukens, 1995). However, animal behavior is fascinating in and of itself and does not have to be obscured by ascribing human characteristics to animals. Anthropomorphism can confuse children and lead them to believe that animals think and behave in the same ways as human beings.

Appropriateness

The concept of appropriateness in informational books encompasses several issues. Excellent informational books suit their audience. They are organized well and include bibliographies and suggestions for further reading. The literary style corresponds to the subject and the audience for which the book is intended.

Clearly organized text enables children to understand the author's presentation of information. An author may organize the text by moving from the familiar to the unfamiliar, moving from the general to the specific, or through a question-and-answer format. A common organizational pattern is presenting facts in chronological order. Gail Gibbons uses this pattern in her informational book, *Sunken Treasure,* which details the discovery of the *Atocha,* a Spanish treasure ship. Seven sections organize the information: the sinking, the search, the find, the recording, the salvage, the restoration and preservation, and the cataloging and distribution.

Bibliographic data, which includes tables of contents, indices, glossaries, appendices, and lists of related readings, help children understand the information presented. These aids can help readers locate specific information within a book without having to read the entire book. Effective bibliographic aids provide the starting point for gathering additional information on a particular topic. Whetting children's appetite for further study does little good if they cannot proceed to locate more information on the topic.

Attractiveness

Attractiveness or appeal is important to children. They are more likely to pick up a book that is attractive than one that is not. Modern children have been conditioned to visual images by television and computers and expect a fast pace and dramatic impact. Informational books can include attractive, colorful illustrations that range from photographs to paintings to line drawings. Attractiveness cannot remain the sole criterion, however. Illustrations, charts, and diagrams must be accurate and should mesh with the text, faultlessly depicting the ideas, concepts, and facts presented in the book. Moreover, although illustrations can be used to enhance the text and attract readers, illustrations cannot replace strong organization and well-written text to present information.

Leonard Everett Fisher (1988), who has illustrated many nonfiction books, explains his purpose in illustrating nonfiction:

> Today what interests me . . . is giving youngsters a visual memory of a fact rather than just the fact. I am trying to present a factual mood. The Tower of London, for instance, is a creepy place, and if I can establish the creepiness of the place so that the youngster gets an unsettled feeling about the tower. . . . I'm trying to create the emotion of the history, the dynamics of history, together with the facts of history. I'm trying to communicate what events in history felt like. (p. 319)

Photography is increasingly common in children's nonfiction. Stodart (1987) points out that photographs add a sense of direct reporting and are very important in documenting history and biography. Effective use of photographs in scientific informational books is one hallmark of Seymour Simon's work. The photographs he obtained from the *Viking I* and *Mariner I* space probes give his readers a sense of "being there" in the book *Mars*.

Both illustrations and layout are instrumental in guiding children's response to nonfiction. Appropriate placement of the illustrations and text on the page influences the facts, ideas, and concepts readers will focus on and the importance they attribute to the information presented. Illustrations should prepare readers to understand the text. Innovative layouts such as the use of three-dimension in *The Human Body* by Jonathon Miller and David Pelham and the interactive format in *Exploring Space* are significant to readers' response to a nonfiction book.

CLASSROOM ACTIVITIES FOR ENHANCING NONFICTION EXPERIENCE

All literature is taking an increasingly important role in classrooms because of current views of teaching. Exploring a theme or topic through trade books permits students to discover the connections among the types of knowledge belonging to particular domains. These units help children understand how knowledge is organized, used, and related (Pappas, Kiefer, & Levstik, 1990). They contribute to children's fundamental understanding of science, social studies, mathematics, art, and music. Informational books help promote children's critical thinking, suggest methods of study, and provide a writing model for children to use when reporting information.

Nonfiction literature has distinct benefits in developing students' knowledge, skills, and interests. Trade books permit teachers to use books of different reading levels that address the same subject so that all children can study materials at a level appropriate for their ability (Hillerich, 1987; Shanahan, 1992). Trade books are usually more up-to-date than textbooks, which appeals to students who are more interested in the present than the past. Trade books are more likely to depict the latest scientific and social science discoveries. Moreover, the writing styles used in trade books are more appealing to readers than textbook style. Nonfiction books have both content and visual appeal for students. Their interesting cover designs, graphics, and choice of topics appeal to children. Trade books provide greater depth of information whether they are exploring places, cultures, people, or science. They can address controversial issues and sensitive subjects. For example, trade books explore prejudice, the Holocaust, and Vietnam in depth, whereas textbook authors often give such topics superficial attention. Finally, trade books tend to arrange information in a more logical and coherent fashion than textbooks (Fielding, Wilson, & Anderson, 1986).

Trade Books and Science

Many of today's students spend most of their science class time engaged in hands-on experiences. They ask questions, make observations, infer, measure, and think. They record their work, their thinking, their observations, and their conclusions in science journals. For homework, they may read from a textbook or trade book and answer teacher- or student-generated questions that tap reasoning skills. Nontextbook science experiences predominate today. Both the National Science Teachers Association and the American Association for the Advancement of Science endorse a scientific-inquiry-based approach to instruction. Both organizations recognize the importance of scientific literacy.

Trade books, both nonfiction and fiction, play an important role in current concepts of teaching science. Children can learn basic science concepts, scientific thinking, the relation of science to their lives, the excitement of the new and unknown, and the beauty of nature from trade books. The quality and readability of science trade books is increasing. Each year the *Science Teacher* publishes Outstanding Science Tradebooks for Children, a list selected by a committee from the National Science Teachers Association. A number of excellent authors write science trade books: Aliki, Caroline Arnold, Jim Aronsky, Barbara Bash, Melvin Berger, Lynne Cherry, Joanna Cole, Helen Cowcher, Margery Facklam, Jean Craighead George, Patricia Lauber, Laurence Pringle, and Seymour Simon are just a few.

To get a sense of what makes a science trade book outstanding, read some that are identified as exemplary, such as those listed below. The quality of an individual book depends upon the author of that book, so if the book is part of a series, evaluate the quality of each book in the series.

- The Sierra Club publishes children's nonfiction books related to the study and protection of the earth's scenic and ecological resources—mountains, wetlands, woodlands, wild shores, rivers, deserts, and plains. These books, such as Barbara Bash's *Shadows of Night,* are consistently high-quality trade books for children in Grades 4 and higher.
- The Let's-Read-and-Find-Out Science series, published by HarperCollins, has been researched and validated by authorities in the field. This series is divided into Stage 1 books, which explain simple and easily observable science concepts for preschool and kindergarten children, and Stage 2 books, which explore more challenging concepts for children in the primary grades and include hands-on activities that children can do themselves. *My Five Senses* by Aliki and *What Lives in a Shell?* by Kathleen Weidner Zoehfeld are Stage 1 books. *The Planets in Our Solar System* by Franklyn M. Branley is an example of a Stage 2 book.
- Thomson Learning publishes a variety of interesting hands-on books. The Make It Work! series includes titles such as *Insects, Body, and Machines.* The Science Activities series includes such titles as *Electricity, Heat, and Light.*
- Joanna Cole's Magic School Bus series, illustrated by Bruce Degen and published by Scholastic, is popular with children and teachers. The majority of her titles are concerned with science, as in *The Magic School Bus at the Waterworks.*
- Each of the books in the Read and Wonder series, published by Candlewick, has been carefully developed. The writing style and illustrations are superb. You will enjoy titles such as *A Piece of String Is a Wonderful Thing* and *The Wheeling and Whirling-Around Book,* both by Judy Hindley.
- The Real Kids/Real Science series of children's science trade books includes such titles as *Ornithology, Vertebrate Zoology,* and *Woods, Ponds, and Fields.* These books are produced in association with the Children's School of Science in Woods Hole, Massachusetts, and Thames and Hudson publishing house.
- Additionally, many excellent individual science trade books not associated with a series exist; these too will develop children's scientific literacy and their understanding of the interdependence of science, mathematics, and technology.
- *Twister* by Darleen Bailey Beard
- *A River Ran Wild* by Lynne Cherry
- *I Took a Walk* by Henry Cole
- *Wildlife Rescue: The Work of Dr. Kathleen Ramsay* by Jennifer Owings Dewey

- *Tree Trunk Traffic* by Bianca Lavies
- *Whales and Dolphins* by Steve Parker

Trade Books and Social Studies

Milton Meltzer (1994), a master of nonfiction, not only believes that young readers need to learn how houses are built, how trucks run, how flowers grow, how birds fly, how weather is formed, and how physical handicaps are overcome, but he also believes they need to know how character is shaped and how the world works. Moreover, he believes that disasters of nature (hurricanes, floods, droughts) and of human society (Vietnam, the Holocaust, poverty) are worthy of attention as causes of suffering to human victims. He believes that all children will encounter fundamental problems of race and class and tyranny in their lifetime and that they should prepare for this by reading about such things.

Literature contains all the great stories of humanity and can be used in social studies to help students develop a sense of history, a sense that the past influences the present, and a sense that various cultures each contribute in an important way to the global society (Cullinan, 1989). Social studies curricula are moving toward this idea of global education, of helping students understand the relations in their immediate environment and in the world. Nonfiction writers can create an awareness of society and culture that reaches beyond mere facts, helping children understand this country and others in the light of their historical development. Nonfiction writers can create a vision of what might be, which excites the imagination and stretches the mind. This is why trade books are a rich resource for teaching social studies; they enable children to develop social studies concepts in a memorable way.

The books mentioned in the "Notable Children's Tradebooks in the Field of Social Studies" offer interesting alternatives to textbooks. This compilation of books is selected each year by the National Council for the Social Studies in conjunction with the Children's Book Council and appears in *Social Education.* Margy Burns Knight has written several good examples of the exciting trade books available for social studies. *Talking Walls* tells the story of 14 walls that exist in our world. Each of the walls gives teachers

opportunities to integrate social studies with all areas of the curriculum in a fascinating study. The walls included in this book are:

- The Great Wall of China
- Aborigine Wall Art
- The Western Wall
- Great Zimbabwe
- Canadian Museum of Civilization
- Taos Pueblo
- Nelson Mandela's Prison Walls
- Mahabalipuram's Animal Walls
- The Lascaux Cave
- Muslim Walls
- Cuzco
- The Vietnam Veterans Memorial
- Mexican Murals
- The Berlin Wall

Knight's *Who Belongs Here?* is based on the true story of Nary, a Cambodian child who dreamed of coming to the United States but who was rejected when he arrived. This book, like *Talking Walls,* invites young readers to explore the implications of intolerance. The author asks, "What if every American whose ancestors came from another country was forced to leave the United States? Who would be left?" She includes a compendium of detailed information at the end of the book. Both *Talking Walls* and *Who Belongs Here?* are picture books that young children can enjoy as a story, and middle-grade children can do detailed studies of the ideas, concepts, and information.

Many books can serve to enhance the social studies. Farris and Fuhler (1994) suggest a variety of picture books for the social studies in an article in the *Reading Teacher.* The guidelines shown in Figure 11.1 for selecting picture books for teaching social studies concepts are adapted from those suggested by Farris and Fuhler. A list appears on page 266 of the Children's Literature References and Recommended Books section at the end of this chapter.

Trade Books and the Arts

The arts are enjoying increasing attention in many elementary schools. Fortunately, a wide range of trade books is available to promote children's interest in the

FIGURE 11.1 Picture books for social studies.	
Guideline	Example
The text and illustrations should appeal to readers.	Osband, G., & Andrew, R. (1991). *Castles*. New York: Clarion.
The facts and information are accurate, authentic, and current.	Towle, W. (1993). *The Real McCoy: The Life of an African-American inventor* (W. Clay, Illus.). New York: Scholastic.
The content extends the social studies topic under study.	Burleigh, R. (1991). *Flight*. (M. Wimmer, Illus.). New York: Philomel.
The illustrations are accurate.	Cherry, L. (1992). *A river ran wild: An environmental history*. San Diego: Harcourt Brace Jovanovich.
The books is free of stereotypes.	Myers, W. D. (1999). *At her majesty's request: An African princess in Victorian England*. New York: Scholastic.
The language is rich and clear.	Bruchac, J., & London, J. (1992). *Thirteen moons on turtle's back* (T. Locker, Illus.). New York: Philomel.
The book motivates further reading, thinking, and studying.	Ancona, G. (1999). *Charro: The Mexican cowboy*. New York: Harcourt.

arts. The arts help children create their own visions of things through carving, painting, dancing, singing, and writing (Greene, 1992). The world of fine arts includes paint, clay, and pastels—but language, poems, stories, and riddles are arts as well. Music is an art, too: musical sounds, melody, harmony, and dissonance. Movement is art: It is the body in motion, making shapes, exerting effort, articulating visions, moving in space and time (Greene, 1992). A special list of books to help to integrate the arts into the curriculum is given in the Recommended Books section at the end of this chapter.

Teaching Strategies for Nonfiction

Trade books cover topics from multiple perspectives with imagination and interesting detail. They communicate the feelings, personal associations, imagination, and attitudes related to a topic; therefore they are excellent materials for developing higher order thinking. Higher order thinking can be developed with specific strategies (Holmes & Ammon, 1985) such as the one in Activity 11.2 on page 263, which is developed over several days and includes three stages: readiness, reading, and responses. The example in the activity is based on a study of the Middle Ages because this topic is commonly studied in the elementary grades.

Illustrations

Nonfiction books are usually illustrated with photographs, paintings, drawings, and prints, just as fiction is, although more photographs are used in nonfiction than other genres. The illustrations in nonfiction are especially important because they help readers understand the subject. Activity 11.3 on page 264 presents a guide for studying photographs and other forms of illustration as well.

Drama and role playing

Creative drama is an excellent follow-up for students who are reading biographies. Children can learn a great deal from role playing or dramatizing biographies and even some informational literature as well. They may act out events in the biography; playing the part of a historical figure helps them develop a better understanding of that character and his or her role in history. Another activity is conducting television interviews. One student prepares questions while another prepares to be the character, considering the style of dress, issues of the day, and so forth. A camcorder or a tape recorder will add to the feeling of conducting a television interview.

FIGURE 11.2 Data chart for summarizing data from different sources.

BOOK TITLE	QUESTIONS			
	What kinds of elephants are there?	What do elephants eat?	How large do elephants grow?	How dangerous are elephants?
Elephant Crossing by Toshi Yoshida				
Kingfisher Animal Atlas				
Zoo magazine				

Summarizing important events

Patricia Lauber summarizes the information about Stone Age culture and cave paintings in *Painters of the Caves*.

Data charts

One of the problems children encounter when using multiple sources to gather information and write reports is how to integrate the information they collect. Several authors present the concept of a data chart to help summarize information (Hennings, 1994; Stoodt, 1989). The steps in preparing a data chart are:

1. Identify the topic or problem.
2. Brainstorm questions, which become the labels for each column.
3. Identify the sources of information in the left-hand column.
4. Have the students complete the chart.

   Figure 11.2 shows a sample data chart.

Unit Suggestions

ACTIVITY 11.1   WHAT ABOUT BATS? (4TH GRADE)

This unit was the outcome of a student's question about the bat houses he saw while on vacation. He asked, "Why do people want to have bats in their yards? They're dirty, they drink blood, and they get in your hair and give you rabies." Several of the students in the class agreed with him, so this is the unit the teacher and the students planned.

1. Objective: Students will develop these basic concepts:

   a. Bats are the only mammals that fly.

   b. Nearly 1,000 kinds of bats are found in the world.

   c. Some bats navigate by sight and some use sound waves.

Books such as Stellaluna, which is about bats, help correct children's incorrect notions about certain topics.

d. Bats eat vast quantities of insects every night.

e. Some bats are essential for the pollination and reseeding of important plants—bananas, cashews, avocados, and figs, to name a few.

f. Bats are some of the most helpful and fascinating creatures in the world.

g. Bats need to be protected because through ignorance and fear many of them are being destroyed.

h. Bats, whose wings are very much like human hands, belong to the scientific order Chiroptera, which means "hand-wing" in Latin.

2. Objective: Students will research the questions posed by their classmates.

a. Do bats drink blood?

b. Do bats get in humans' hair?

c. Why are bats considered dirty?

d. Do bats carry rabies?

e. How well can bats see? Is it accurate to say someone is as blind as a bat?

The students learned so much from researching these questions that they wanted to learn more about bats and protecting them. They generated additional research questions and projects.

1. Build a model of a bat's wing to show the fingers and thumb.

2. Build models of various kinds of bats.

3. Research the bat as a symbol of good fortune and wisdom in China. Paint illustrations and be prepared to explain why the bat is a symbol of good fortune.

4. Find out about the construction of bat houses and build one.

5. Choose your favorite bat and find out all you can about this particular bat. Write a report, a story, or a poem about your bat.

6. Write a newspaper article about bat protection. Why do bats need protection? What can we do to protect bats? How can we spread the word about protecting bats?

Suggested Books

- *Shadows of Night: The Hidden World of the Little Brown Bat* by Barbara Bash
- *Bats: Night Fliers* by Betsy Maestro and illustrated by Giulio Maestro
- *Bats: Mysterious Flyers of the Night* by Dee Stuart
- *Stellaluna* by Janell Cannon

ACTIVITY 11.2   DEVELOPING HIGHER ORDER THINKING THROUGH READINESS, READING, AND RESPONSES

1. *Readiness.* In the readiness stage, children brainstorm words related to the topic. For example, children in one sixth-grade class came up with *armor, moat, castle, lords, ladies, jester, king, duke,* *prince,* and *knight.* They posed questions— Where did the people live? Were they slaves? What did they eat? How did they travel?—and categorized them.

2. *Reading.* Next, they selected trade books for sustained silent reading in order to collect and summarize data to answer their questions. Once they chose their resource books, they wrote their bibliography of the topic using data charts (see discussion on page 262). Some children made their own notes. Some of the books the students chose were *A Medieval Feast* by Aliki, *Quest for a King: Searching for the Real King Arthur* by Catherine Andronik, *The Truth About Castles* by Gillian Clements, and *Castle* by David Macaulay. As the children proceed with their research, discrepant information may emerge. They can reread, review, and check additional resources to resolve the discrepancies. In the process, they may generate new questions they wish to answer.

3. *Response.* In the response stage, children express their feelings and thoughts through writing, oral presentations, art, music, dance, and drama.

ACTIVITY 11.3   STUDYING ILLUSTRATIONS

This sample activity provides a guide to developing visual literacy with illustrations. This experience is based on ideas in "Visual Interpretation of Children's Books" (Goldstone, 1989), as well as *Stop, Look, and Write* (Leavitt & Sohn, 1964) and *Images in Language, Media, and Mind* (Fox, 1994). The visual literacy guide is applied to *Prairie Visions* by Pam Conrad.

1. Introduce the selected photograph or illustration to the students. Explain its significance and its source. After the students acquire some experience with this strategy, they can choose their own photographs or illustrations.

2. State questions to guide students' thinking. For example: Where do you think this picture was taken or what does it illustrate? What does the picture tell about the lives of the people in the book? Why were the horses on the roof of the house? What else would you like to know about the people and the way they lived?

   Students may work in pairs, small groups, or individually; they may write their answers or make notes for class discussion.

3. Describe the overall impression of the illustration. Is it dark and dreary or light and colorful, sad or happy, lively or quiet?

4. Ask students to label the people, animals, and objects in the photograph or illustration. For example, students could label different individuals, the shelter, and the horses in *Prairie Visions: The Life and Times of Solomon Butcher.*

5. Then ask students to describe the items, people, activities, structures, and so forth in the photograph or illustration. A detailed list for a photograph in *Prairie Visions* would include many items because the photographs are crowded with many objects.

6. Ask students to think about the things they have catalogued in steps 3 through 5 and use their lists and labeled items to draw inferences about the lives of the people in the book. How did they live? Where did they go to school? What did they eat? What were their homes like? What did they do for recreation?

7. When the students complete their inferences, read the text aloud.

8. The students can synthesize their thoughts with the text and the illustrations. They may decide to study the topic further. In fact, fine illustrations motivate students to further study. The students may write a paragraph about their conclusions and support them with references to the illustrations and text or their further study.

ACTIVITY 11.4   PROFILING AN AUTHOR

Learning about authors and their interests helps readers understand how they get story ideas. After studying an author or illustrator through one of the methods described in previous activities, students can write biographical profiles to summarize their research. The profile of Caroline Arnold (see box) demonstrates some of her strategies for selecting and developing writing ideas.

Author Profile: Caroline Arnold

Caroline Arnold has an outstanding body of literary work, most of which is nonfiction. Her favorite subjects are nature and the out-of-doors. Her childhood in Minnesota and the summers she spent in a small, northern Wisconsin camp contributed to her lifelong interest in these subjects. Many of Arnold's books are illustrated with photographs, which are appropriate to her subjects. In addition to nonfiction books for children, she has written for television and for interactive CD–ROMS.

Many awards and honors have come to Arnold for her work. Among her most widely recognized works are: *Trapped in Tar; The Ancient Cliff Dwellers of Mesa Verde; A Walk on the Great Barrier Reef; Saving the Peregrine Falcon; Fox; Bat; Cheetah;* and *Hippo.* Arnold's Web site tells about herself, her family, and her books; she also has activities for children to do after reading her books.

SUMMARY

Nonfiction includes biography and informational literature. In the past, this genre has often been overlooked, but its quality is improving and its quantity is increasing. Children show a greater interest in nonfiction when they have opportunities to experience excellent nonfiction.

Nonfiction trade books are often more up-to-date and detailed than textbooks. Children find these books interesting because they answer the natural questions that children have about the world around them. Children can learn about people who have been leaders and people who have made contributions to all aspects of life from biography. They can learn about math, science, social studies, and the fine arts from informational books. These books also give them the background necessary to understand the facts presented and to relate these facts to their experiences.

Thought Questions

1. Why is nonfiction particularly appealing to many children?

2. What standards would you apply in choosing nonfiction for your library or classroom?

3. Why do you think some authors specialize in the nonfiction genre?

4. How can a nonfiction author ensure accuracy and authenticity in a work?

Research and Application Experiences

1. Compare three informational books on the same topic. What are the differences in the facts presented? What are the similarities?

2. Compare three biographies of the same person's life. What are the similarities? What are the differences?

3. Identify a topic you would like to know more about. Then identify the types of information you would collect about the topic. Create a data chart for the topic.

4. Read a nonfiction book and write a synopsis of it. Then evaluate it and list the standards you used. What were the book's strong points? What were its weak points?

5. Prepare a booktalk for a nonfiction book you enjoy. Give the booktalk to a group of children or to a group of classmates.

6. Find a nonfiction author on the Web and learn why he or she chooses to write nonfiction. Find out how the author chooses his or her topics. Write an author profile.

7. Find Caroline Arnold's Web site and ask her questions that you or your students would like to have answered.

8. Select a topic that you would like to explore in a classroom and use the Internet to identify books and create a bibliography.

Children's Literature References and Recommended Books

Note: Books designated with an asterisk (*) are recommended for reluctant readers.

Adler, D. A. (1999). *How tall, how short, how far away* (N. Tobin, Illus.). New York: Holiday. (1–3). PICTURE BOOK, INFORMATIONAL BOOK.

An interesting introduction to measurement.

Aliki. (1962). *My five senses.* New York: Crowell. (PreK–1). INFORMATIONAL BOOK.

This is a Stage 1 book in the "Let's-Read-and-Find-Out" science series.

Aliki. (1993). *A medieval feast.* New York: Crowell. (4–8). INFORMATIONAL BOOK.

Modern children get a glimpse of authentic medieval living in this book.

Aliki. (1999). *William Shakespeare & the Globe.* New York: HarperCollins. (4–6). INFORMATIONAL BOOK.

The author/illustrator provides detailed information and descriptions of Shakespeare, his work, and the Globe Theatre.

Ancona, G. (1999). *Charro: The Mexican cowboy.* New York: Harcourt. (1–3). INFORMATIONAL BOOK.

Andronik, C. M. (1989). *Quest for a king: Searching for the real King Arthur.* New York: Atheneum. (4–8). INFORMATIONAL BOOK.

The author portrays the various efforts to locate King Arthur.

Arnold, C. (1985). *Saving the Peregrine falcon* (R. Hewett, Photog.). Minneapolis, MN: Carolrhoda. (3–8). INFORMATIONAL BOOK.

The peregrine falcon was near extinction, and this book tells about the bird and efforts to save it from extinction.

Arnold, C. (1987). *Trapped in tar* (R. Hewett, Photog.). New York: Clarion. (3–up). INFORMATIONAL BOOK.

Collecting rocks as a child ignited the author's interest in fossils. Later she visited the La Brea tar pits and wrote about those fossils.

Arnold, C. (1988). *A walk on the Great Barrier Reef* (A. Arnold, Photog.). Minneapolis, MN: Carolrhoda. (3–8). INFORMATIONAL BOOK.

The Great Barrier Reef is in Australia, and this book shows why so many people visit it.

Arnold, C. (1989a). *Cheetah* (R. Hewett, Photog.). New York: Morrow. (3–8). INFORMATIONAL BOOK.

The author offers a study of this very fast traveling animal.

Arnold, C. (1989b). *Hippo* (R. Hewett, Photog.). New York: Morrow. (3–8). INFORMATIONAL BOOK.

The water pig is an African animal.

Arnold, C. (1992). *The ancient cliff dwellers of Mesa Verde* (R. Hewett, Photog.). New York: Clarion. (3–8). INFORMATIONAL BOOK.

The author's text and photographs show how the ancient Anasazi lived 1,000 years ago.

Arnold, C. (1994). *Watching desert wildlife* (A. Arnold, Photog.). Minneapolis: Carolrhoda. (2–5). INFORMATIONAL BOOK.

The author takes readers on a guided tour of desert life.

Arnold, C. (1996a). *Bat* (R. Hewett, Photog.). New York: Morrow. (3–8). INFORMATIONAL BOOK.

The author describes this fascinating animal, which has had an interesting life, and its importance to ecology.

Arnold, C. (1996b). *Fox* (R. Hewett, Photog.). New York: Morrow. (3–8). INFORMATIONAL BOOK.

The author describes the fox and the fox's life.

Ashabranner, B. (1989). *People who make a difference* (P. Conklin, Photog.). New York: Dutton. (3–8). BIOGRAPHY.*

Stories about everyday people who make a difference.

Ballard, R. D., & Archbold, R. (1998). *Ghost liners: Exploring the world's greatest lost ships.* (K. Marschall, Illus.). New York: Little, Brown. (4–8). INFORMATIONAL BOOK.

A true life mystery that examines actual shipwrecks and missing ships.

Bash, B. (1993). *Shadows of night: The hidden world of the little brown bat.* San Francisco: Sierra Club Books for Children. (1–3). INFORMATIONAL BOOK.*

The author provides interesting bat facts illustrated with color photographs.

Batten, M. (1992). *Nature's tricksters: Animals and plants that aren't what they seem* (L. Lovejoy, Illus.). Boston: Little, Brown. (1–4). INFORMATIONAL BOOK.*

The author documents the unusual protective devices of plants and animals.

Beard, D. B. (1999). *Twister* (N. Carpenter, Illus.). New York: Farrar, Straus & Giroux. (PreK–2). INFORMATIONAL BOOK.

Berger, M. (1989). *Simple Simon says: Take one magnifying glass.* New York: Scholastic. (K–3). INFORMATIONAL BOOK.

This activity book helps children use magnification to get a different view of the world.

Blos, J. W. (Adapter). (1994). *The days before now: An autobiographical note by Margaret Wise Brown* (T. B. Allen, Illus.). New York: Simon & Schuster. (1–3). BIOGRAPHY.

The life of Margaret Wise Brown told in her own words.

Blumberg, R. (1989). *The great American gold rush.* New York: Bradbury. (4–8). INFORMATIONAL BOOK.

The author explains gold fever and its lure for Easterners and immigrants.

Bourne, B., & Saul, W. (1994). *Exploring space: Using Seymour Simon's astronomy books in the classroom.* New York: Morrow. (3–9). INFORMATIONAL BOOK.

Space-related projects that will extend students' knowledge of astronomy.

Bowen, G. (1994). *Stranded at Plimoth Plantation, 1626* (G. Bowen, Illus.). New York: HarperCollins. (2–5). INFORMATIONAL BOOK, HISTORICAL FICTION.*

This story is told through the journal entries of a 13-year-old boy who is stranded at Plimoth Plantation until he can find passage to Jamestown.

Branley, F. M. (1993). *The planets in our solar system.* New York: HarperCollins. (1–3). INFORMATIONAL BOOK.*

A Stage 2 book in the Let's-Read-and-Find-Out Science series.

Brenner, B. (1977). *On the frontier with Mr. Audubon.* (G. Lippincott, Illus.). New York: Coward, McCann, and Geoghegan. (4–8). BIOGRAPHY.

Audubon's experiences as told by his apprentice.

Brown, L. K., & Brown, M. (1984). *Dinosaurs divorce.* Boston: Little Brown. (1–5). INFORMATIONAL BOOK.*

An informational book about divorce.

Bruchac, J., & London, J. (1992). *Thirteen moons on turtle's back* (T. Locker, Illus.). New York: Philomel. (2–5). TRADITIONAL LITERATURE.

Burleigh, R. (1991). *Flight: The Journey of Charles Lindbergh* (M. Wimmer, Illus.). New York: Philomel. (1–3). INFORMATIONAL BOOK, BIOGRAPHY.

Burnie, D., & Gamlin, L. (1999). *The Kingfisher first encyclopedia of animals.* New York: Kingfisher. (2–5). INFORMATIONAL BOOK.

This reference includes 450 entries about animals.

Cannon, J. (1993). *Stellaluna.* New York: Harcourt Brace Jovanovich. (1–3). MODERN FANTASY, INFORMATIONAL BOOK.*

This is the story of a little fruit bat who is separated from her mother. She lands in a bird's nest and grows up with birds.

Carlson, L. M. (1998). *Boss of the plains: The hat that won the West* (H. Meade, Illus.). New York: DK Publishing. (1–4). INFORMATIONAL BOOK.*

The story of John Batterson Stetson and how he invented a hat.

Cherry, L. (1992). *A river ran wild: An environmental history.* San Diego: Harcourt. (1–4). INFORMATIONAL BOOK.

This picture book begins with Native Americans and traces the environmental history of a river.

Clements, G. (1990). *The truth about castles.* Minneapolis, MN: Carolrhoda. (K–6). INFORMATIONAL BOOK.

This information book tells about life in real castles.

Cobb, V., & Darling, K. (1999). *You gotta try this! Absolutely irresistible science* (T. Kelley, Illus.). New York: Morrow. (3–6). INFORMATIONAL BOOK.

Experiments for students accompanied by appropriate warnings and observations.

Cole, H. (1998). *I took a walk.* New York: Greenwillow. (PreK–2). INFORMATIONAL BOOK.

Cole, J. (1986). *The magic school bus at the waterworks* (B. Degen, Illus.). New York: Scholastic. (K–4). INFORMATIONAL BOOK, MODERN FANTASY.

The magic school bus travels to the waterworks.

Cole, J. (1989). *The magic school bus: Inside the human body* (B. Degen, Illus.). New York: Scholastic. (K–4). INFORMATIONAL BOOK, MODERN FANTASY.

Ms. Frizzle's class takes an unusual field trip on their magic school bus.

Cole, J. (1992). *The magic school bus on the ocean floor* (B. Degen, Illus.). New York: Scholastic. (K–4). INFORMATIONAL BOOK, MODERN FANTASY.

The indomitable Ms. Frizzle takes her class to the ocean floor.

Cole, J. (1994). *The magic school bus: In the time of the dinosaurs* (B. Degen, Illus.). New York: Scholastic. (K–4). INFORMATIONAL BOOK, MODERN FANTASY.

Ms. Frizzle's class visits a dinosaur dig.

Cone, M. (1992). *Come back, Salmon* (S. Wheelwright, Illus.). San Francisco: Sierra Club. (3–6). INFORMATIONAL BOOK.

This book documents an actual event. The children adopt a creek and bring it back to life.

Conrad, P. (1989). *Prairie visions: The life and times of Solomon Butcher.* New York: HarperCollins. (4–8). BIOGRAPHY.

This book is based on the life of a frontier photographer in Nebraska during the 1800s.

Cowley, J. (1999). *Red-eyed tree frog* (N. Bishop, Illus.). New York: Scholastic. (1–3). INFORMATIONAL BOOK.

Brilliantly colored photographs provide detailed views of the tree frog and its eating habits.

Crump, D. (Ed.). (1994). *Exploring your world: The adventure of geography.* New York: National Geographic Society. (3–6). INFORMATIONAL BOOK.

A reference for geographical topics.

dePaola, T. (1999). *26 Fairmount Avenue.* New York: Putnam. (1–3). BIOGRAPHY.

The author's story of his early life and how he became interested in creating picture books.

Dewey, J. O. (1994). *Wildlife rescue: The work of Dr. Kathleen Ramsay.* Honesdale, PA: Boyds Mills. (4–8). INFORMATIONAL BOOK.

This book documents Dr. Ramsay's work saving wild animals.

Dodds, D. A. (1994a). *The Dorling Kindersley children's illustrated dictionary.* New York: Dorling Kindersley. (1–6). INFORMATIONAL BOOK.

A useful reference book.

Dodds, D. A. (1994b). *The shape of things* (J. Lacome, Illus.). Cambridge, MA: Candlewick. (PreK–1). INFORMATIONAL BOOK.

Explores the shapes of things through photographs and drawings of everyday things.

Duggleby, J. (1998). *Story painter: The life of Jacob Lawrence.* New York: Chronicle. (3–6). BIOGRAPHY.*

A striking, well-researched biography of Jacob Lawrence.

Exploring space. (1994). New York: Scholastic. (3–6). INFORMATIONAL BOOK.

Movable maps of constellations, plastic overlays, fold-out maps, 3-D glasses, and so forth make this an interactive informational book.

Fox, M. (1992). *Shoes from Grandpa* (P. Mullens, Illus.). New York: Orchard Books. (PreK–2). CONTEMPORARY REALISTIC FICTION.

A cumulative story tells how Jessie is clothed by all the members of her family.

Freedman, R. (1983). *Children of the wild West.* New York: Clarion. (4–8). INFORMATIONAL BOOK.

This book documents life in the American West from 1840 to the early 1900s.

Freedman, R. (1987). *Lincoln: A photobiography.* New York: Clarion. (4–8). INFORMATIONAL BOOK, BIOGRAPHY.

This work is a superb portrayal of Abraham Lincoln.

Freedman, R. (1993). *Eleanor Roosevelt: A life of discovery.* New York: Clarion. (4–8). INFORMATIONAL BOOK, BIOGRAPHY.

The author depicts Eleanor Roosevelt as a "late bloomer" who was late in finding herself, but who continued to grow.

Fritz, J. (1973). *And then what happened, Paul Revere?* (M. Tomes, Illus.). New York: Coward, McCann & Geoghegan. (2–5). BIOGRAPHY.

A humorous tribute to Paul Revere's character that focuses on his skills of reporting what happened to him.

Fritz, J. (1995). *You want women to vote, Lizzie Stanton?* (D. Di Salvo-Ryan, Illus.). New York: Putnam. (3–6). INFORMATIONAL BOOK, BIOGRAPHY.*

The author has captured the spirit of Elizabeth Stanton in this fascinating portrait.

Gibbons, G. (1988). *Sunken treasure.* New York: Crowell. (1–4). INFORMATIONAL BOOK.*

The book details the discovery of the *Atocha,* a Spanish treasure ship.

Gibbons, G. (1990). *Beacons of light: Lighthouses.* New York: Morrow. (1–4). INFORMATIONAL BOOK.*

The work explains how technology has changed lighthouses.

Gibbons, G. (1994). *Nature's green umbrella.* New York: Morrow. (K–4). INFORMATIONAL BOOK.*

The author explains one of the world's most complex ecosystems.

Gibbons, G. (1999). *Exploring the deep, dark sea.* Boston: Little, Brown. (PreK–2). INFORMATIONAL BOOK.

Giblin, J. C. (1994). *Thomas Jefferson* (M. Dooling, Illus.). New York: Scholastic. (3–6). BIOGRAPHY.

This is a superb portrayal of Jefferson.

Giblin, J. C. (1997). *Charles A. Lindbergh: A human hero.* New York: Clarion. (4–7). BIOGRAPHY.

A well-balanced biography of the American hero who had human weaknesses.

Haslam, A., Baker, W., & Wyse, L. (2000). *Insects* (J. Barnes, Photog.). Chicago: World Book/Two-Can. (4–7). INFORMATIONAL BOOK.

This is one of the Make It Work series.

Haslam, A., & Glover, D. (2000). *Machines* (J. Barnes, Photog.). Chicago: World Book/Two-Can. (4–7). INFORMATIONAL BOOK.

This is one of the Make It Work series.

Haslam, A., & Wyse, L. (2000). *Body* (J. Barnes, Photog.). Chicago: World Book/Two-Can. (4–7). INFORMATIONAL BOOK.

This is an activity book that helps students understand how the body works.

Hearne, B. (1997). *Seven brave women* (B. Andersen, Illus.). New York: Greenwillow. (2–5). BIOGRAPHY.

This collective biography tells about the bravery of seven women in the same family.

Hindley, J. (1993). *A piece of string is a wonderful thing* (M. Chamberlain, Illus.). Cambridge, MA: Candlewick. (1–3). INFORMATIONAL BOOK.

This informational book is part of the Read and Wonder series.

Hindley, J. (1994). *The wheeling and whirling-around book.* Cambridge, MA: Candlewick. (1–3). INFORMATIONAL BOOK.

This informational book is part of the Read and Wonder series.

Jenkins, S. (1998). *Hottest, coldest, highest, deepest.* Boston: Houghton Mifflin. (K–3). INFORMATIONAL BOOK.*

This book presents a global geography tour to locate record-setting locations.

Karl, J. (1994). *America alive: A history.* New York: Philomel. (3–8). INFORMATIONAL BOOK.*

The author gives a balanced, inclusive overview of U.S. history.

Kendall, R. (1992). *Eskimo boy: Life in an Inupiaq Eskimo village.* New York: Scholastic. (2–4). INFORMATIONAL BOOK.

The author tells the story of a 7-year-old Inupiaq Eskimo boy and his family.

Knight, M. B. (1993). *Who belongs here? An American story* (A. S. O'Brien, Illus.). Gardiner, ME: Tilbury House. (1–5). BIOGRAPHY.

This is the story of Nary, who escaped Cambodia and encounters intolerance in the United States.

Knight, M. B. (1996). *Talking walls* (A. S. O'Brien, Illus.). Gardiner, ME: Tilbury House. (1–8). INFORMATIONAL BOOK.

Fourteen different walls around the world are the subject of this book.

Kunhardt, E. (1993). *Honest Abe* (M. Zeldis, Illus.). New York: Greenwillow. (1–4). BIOGRAPHY.

Primitive paintings illustrate this biography.

Kuskin, K. (1987). *Jerusalem, shining still* (D. Frampton, Illus.). New York: Harper & Row. (4–6). INFORMATIONAL BOOK.

Text, prose, and poetry tell the 3,000-year history of Jerusalem.

Lambert, D. (1992). *The children's animal atlas.* Brookfield, CT: Millbrook (2–5). INFORMATIONAL BOOK.

Documents animal evolution and the danger of extinction for animals.

Lasky, K. (1994). *The librarian who measured the earth* (K. Hawkes, Illus.). Boston: Joy Street. (2–4). BIOGRAPHY, INFORMATIONAL BOOK.

A biography of Eratosthenes, who lived more than 2,000 years ago.

Lauber, P. (1986). *Volcano: The eruption and healing of Mount St. Helens.* New York: Bradbury. (3–6). INFORMATIONAL BOOK.

Photographs and text describe the events before, during, and after the eruption of Mount St. Helens.

Lauber, P. (1988). *Lost star.* New York: Scholastic. (3–6). INFORMATIONAL BOOK, BIOGRAPHY.

This book recounts Amelia Earhart's life.

Lauber, P. (1998). *Painters of the caves.* New York: National Geographic. (4–8). INFORMATIONAL BOOK.

The author tells about the murals painted by cave dwellers at Chauvet, Lascaux, and Trois-Frères.

Lauber, P. (1999). *Hurricanes.* New York: Scholastic. (3–6). INFORMATIONAL BOOK.*

The author offers a superb discussion of hurricanes with excellent illustrations.

Lavies, B. (1989). *Tree trunk traffic.* New York: Dutton. (K–4). INFORMATIONAL BOOK.

Describes the living things going up and down a tree.

Lester, J. (1968). *To be a slave* (T. Feelings, Illus.). New York: Dial. (4–8). INFORMATIONAL BOOK.*

This work, a compilation of interviews with former slaves, offers insight into their lives as slaves.

Levinson, R. (1986). *I go with my family to Grandma's* (D. Goode, Illus.). New York: Dutton. (2–5). HISTORICAL FICTION.

This book is based on family life in New York City in the late 1800s.

Little, J. (1988). *Little by Little: A writer's education.* New York: Viking Penguin. (3–5). BIOGRAPHY.

Jean Little, the Canadian author who is nearly blind, tells her story.

Macaulay, D. (1977). *Castle.* Boston: Houghton, Mifflin. (3–8). INFORMATIONAL BOOK.

This book details the construction of a castle.

Macaulay, D. (1988). *The way things work.* Boston: Houghton, Mifflin. (3–8). INFORMATIONAL BOOK.

The author describes and illustrates more than 500 machines.

Maestro, B. (1994). *Bats: Night fliers* (G. Maestro, Illus.). New York: Scholastic. (1–3). INFORMATIONAL BOOK.*

The author includes interesting bat information for the younger reader.

Masoff, J. (1999). *Emergency!* New York: Scholastic. (3–6). INFORMATIONAL BOOK.*

The author identifies the modes of emergency transportation and the people involved.

Mason, A. (1994). *The Kingfisher first picture atlas.* New York: Kingfisher. (1–4). INFORMATIONAL BOOK.

A picture-book atlas for younger students.

Mason, A., & Lye, K. (1993). *The children's atlas of exploration.* Brookfield, CT: Millbrook. (3–6). INFORMATIONAL BOOK.

Documents the routes of great explorers.

Miller, J., & Pelham, D. (1983). *The human body.* New York: Viking. (2–5). INFORMATIONAL BOOK.

A three-dimensional pop-up book describing the human body.

Miller, W. (1994). *Zora Hurston and the Chinaberry tree* (C. Van Wright & Y. Hu, Illus.). New York: Lee & Low. (1–3). BIOGRAPHY.

The book focuses on one incident in the early life of African American writer Zora Hurston.

Morgan, S. (1994). *Circles and spheres.* New York: Thomson Learning. (1–3). INFORMATIONAL BOOK.

The book explores the shapes of things through photographs and drawings of everyday activities and objects.

Musical instruments. (1993). New York: Scholastic. (3–8). INFORMATIONAL BOOK.*

A part of the Voyages of Discovery series. *Paint and Paintings* is another title in this series.

Myers, W. D. (1991). *Now is your time!* New York: Harper. (4–8). INFORMATIONAL BOOK.

The author traces the history of African Americans and their struggle for freedom.

Myers, W. D. (1999). *At Her Majesty's request: An African princess in Victorian England.* New York: Scholastic. (3–6). BIOGRAPHY.

Osband, G., & Andrew, R. (1991). *Castles.* New York: Orchard. (2–5). INFORMATIONAL BOOK.

Parker, S. (1994). *Whales and dolphins.* New York: Sierra Club and Little Brown. (3–6). INFORMATIONAL BOOK.

This book gives information and photographs of these fascinating creatures.

Pilger, M. A. (1988). *Science experiments index for young people.* Englewood, CO: Libraries Unlimited (3–8). INFORMATIONAL BOOK.

The book is a specialized biography of science activities and experiments.

Pringle, L. (1990). *Global warming.* New York: Arcade. (4–6). INFORMATIONAL BOOK.

The author offers a detailed explanation of global warming.

Pringle, L. (1991). *Living treasure: Saving Earth's threatened biodiversity* (I. Brady, Illus.). New York: Morrow. (4–6). INFORMATIONAL BOOK.

This informational book summarizes and organizes information about our planet's unique organisms.

Provenson, A., & Provenson, M. (1984). *Leonardo da Vinci: The artist, inventor, scientist.* New York: Viking. (3–7). BIOGRAPHY.

This book describes one year in the life of Leonardo da Vinci.

Ride, S., with Okie, S. (1986). *To space & back.* New York: Lothrop, Lee & Shepard. (2–5). INFORMATIONAL BOOK.

This book documents an astronaut's life.

Ringgold, F. (1991). *Tar beach.* New York: Crown. (1–4). BIOGRAPHY.

The author tells the story of her childhood.

Rounds, G. (1999). *Beaver.* New York: Holiday. (K–3). INFORMATIONAL BOOK.

The subjects of this authentic treatment are beavers and their constructions.

Say, A. (1993). *Grandfather's journey.* Boston: Houghton Mifflin. (3–6). BIOGRAPHY.

Say compares his life to his grandfather's life in this book.

Schertle, A. (1985). *My two feet* (M. Dunham, Illus.). New York: Lothrop, Lee & Shepard. (K–2). INFORMATIONAL BOOK.

This is a book about shoes.

Settel, J. (1999). *Exploding ants: Amazing facts about how animals adapt.* New York: Atheneum. (4–9). INFORMATIONAL BOOK.

Informational book about the ways animals and insects adapt.

Shapiro, W. E. (Ed.). (1994). *The Kingfisher Young People's Encyclopedia of the United States.* New York: Kingfisher. (3–6). INFORMATIONAL BOOK.

This work features 1,200 entries that reflect the school curriculum.

Simon, S. (1987). *Mars.* New York: Morrow. (3–8). INFORMATIONAL BOOK.

NASA photographs illustrate the information in this book.

Simon, S. (1994). *Comets, meteors, and asteroids.* New York: Morrow. (3–8). INFORMATIONAL BOOK.

Basic information, photographs, and drawings explain these subjects to readers.

Stanley, J. (1992). *Children of the dust bowl.* New York: Crown. (4–12). INFORMATIONAL BOOK.

A compelling book about the "Okie" migration to California in the 1930s.

Stanley, J. (1998). *Frontier merchants: Lionel and Barron Jacobs and the Jewish pioneers who settled the West.* New York: Crown. (4–7). INFORMATIONAL BOOK.

The story of merchandising on the frontier and how the Jacobs turned canned goods into a bank.

Stuart, D. (1994). *Bats: Mysterious flyers of the night.* Minneapolis: Carolrhoda. (1–4). INFORMATIONAL BOOK.

This is an informative book about bats.

Towle, W. (1993). *The Real McCoy: The life of an African-American inventor* (W. Clay, Illus.). New York: Scholastic. (2–5). BIOGRAPHY.

Wallace, K. (1993). *Think of an eel* (M. Bostock, Illus.). Cambridge, MA: Candlewick Press. (1–4). INFORMATIONAL BOOK.

The author describes the characteristics and life cycle of the eel.

Winter, J. (1991). *Diego* (J. Winter, Illus.). New York: Knopf. (1–4). BIOGRAPHY.*

The book chronicles the life of Diego Rivera, the Latino painter, and shows how his early life influenced his art.

Winter, J. (1998). *My name is Georgia.* New York: Harcourt Brace. (2–4). BIOGRAPHY.

The work is a biography of Georgia O'Keeffe, an artist who saw the world in her own way.

Winthrop, E. (1986). *Shoes* (W. Joyce, Illus.). New York: HarperCollins. (K–2). CONTEMPORARY REALISTIC FICTION.

The author explores the pleasure children derive from new shoes.

Wormser, R. (1994). *Hoboes: Wandering in America, 1870–1940.* New York: Walker. (5–9). INFORMA-TIONAL BOOK.

The book explores the hobo culture of the early 1900s.

Young, J. (1994). *The most amazing science pop-up book.* New York: Scholastic. (4–6). INFORMATIONAL BOOK.

This is an interactive information book that is rich with accurate information.

Zoehfeld, K. W. (1994). *What lives in a shell?* (H. K. Davie, Illus.). New York: HarperCollins. (1–3). IN-FORMATIONAL BOOK.

This is a Stage 1 book in the Let's-Read-and-Find-Out Science series.

References and Books for Further Reading

Ballantyne, M. M. (1993). The effects of narrative and expository discourse on the reading comprehension of middle school-aged good and poor readers (University Microfilms No. 94-06, 749). *Dissertation Abstracts International 54,* 4046.

Carr, J. (1982). What do we do about bad biographies? In *Beyond fact: Nonfiction for children and young people* (pp. 45–63). Chicago: American Library Association.

Coolidge, O. (1974). *The apprenticeship of Abraham Lincoln.* New York: Scribner's.

Cullinan, B. (1989). *Literature and the child* (2nd ed.). New York: Harcourt.

Cullinan, B. (1992). Leading with literature. In B. Cullinan (Ed.), *Invitation to read: More children's literature in the reading program.* Newark, DE: International Reading Association.

Duthie, C. (1994). Nonfiction: A genre study for the primary classroom. *Language Arts, 71,* 588–595.

Elleman, B. (1991, September). Paula Fox's *The village by the sea. Book Links, 1,* 48–50.

England, C., & Fasick, A. (1987). *Child view.* Littleton, CO: Libraries Unlimited.

Farris, P., & Fuhler, C. (1994). Developing social studies concepts through picture books. *Reading Teacher, 47,* 380–387.

Fielding, L., Wilson, P., & Anderson, R. (1986). A new focus on free reading: The role of trade books in reading instruction. In T. Raphael (Ed.), *The contexts of school-based literacy* (pp. 149–160). New York: Random House.

Fisher, L. E. (1988). The artist at work: Creating nonfiction. *Horn Book, 64,* 315–323.

Fisher, M. (1972). *Matters of fact: Aspects of nonfiction for children.* New York: Crowell.

Fox, S. (1994). *Media and mind.* Alexandria, VA: ASCD.

Freedman, R. (1988). Newbery acceptance speech. *Journal of Youth Services in Libraries, 1,* 421–427.

Fritz, J. (1990). The teller and the tale. In W. Zinsser (Ed.), *Worlds of childhood: The art and craft of writing for children* (pp. 21–46). Boston: Houghton Mifflin.

Giblin, J. (1987). A publisher's perspective. *Horn Book, 63,* 104–107.

Goldstone, F. (1989). Visual interpretation of children's books. *Reading Teacher, 42,* 592–595.

Greene, M. (1992). Texts and margins. In M. Boldberg & A. Phillips (Eds.), *Arts as education.* Cambridge, MA: Harvard Educational Review. Reprint Series No. 24, 1–18.

Harvey, S. (1998). *Nonfiction matters.* York, ME: Stenhouse.

Hearne, B. (1990). *Choosing books for children: A commonsense approach.* New York: Delacorte.

Hearne, B. (1993). Review of *Think of an eel. Bulletin of the Center for Children's Books, 46,* 347.

Hennings, D. (1994). *Language arts.* Boston: Houghton Mifflin.

Hillerich, R. (1987). Those content areas. *Teaching K–8, 17,* 31–33.

Holmes, B. C., & Ammon, R. I. (1985). Teaching content with trade books. *Childhood Education, 61,* 166–170.

Leavitt, J., & Sohn, D. (1964). *Stop, look, and write!* New York: Bantam.

Lukens, R. (1995). *A critical handbook of children's literature* (4th ed.). Glenview, IL: Scott Foresman.

McAuley, K., & Wilson, R. H. (1987). *The United States: Past to present.* Lexington, MA: D. C. Heath.

Meltzer, M. (1981). Beyond the span of a single life. In B. Hearne and M. Kaye (Eds.), *Celebrating children's books* (pp. 87–96). New York: Lothrop, Lee, & Shepard.

Meltzer, M. (1987). The reader and the writer. In C. Bauer (Ed.), *The best of the Bulletin*. Urbana, IL: National Council of Teachers of English.

Meltzer, M. (1994). *Nonfiction for the classroom*. New York: Teachers College Press.

Pappas, C. C., Kiefer, B., & Levstik, L. (1990). *An integrated language perspective in the elementary school*. White Plains, NY: Longman.

Purves, A., & Monson, D. (1984). *Experiencing children's literature*. Glenview, IL: Scott Foresman.

Russell, D. L. (1994). *Literature for children: A short introduction*. White Plains, NY: Longman.

Shanahan, T. (1992). Nine good reasons for using children's literature across the curriculum. In T. Shanahan (Ed.), *Distant shores resource packages, IV* (pp. 10–22). New York: McGraw Hill School Division.

Stewig, J. (1988). *Children and literature*. Boston: Houghton Mifflin.

Stodart, E. (1987). Wings of fact: Non-fiction for children. In G. Saxby & M. Winch (Eds.), *Give them wings: The experience of children's literature* (pp. 247–257). South Melbourne, Australia: Macmillan.

Stoodt, B. (1989). *Reading instruction* (2nd ed.). New York: HarperCollins.

Stoodt, B., & Amspaugh, L. (1994, May). *Children's response to nonfiction*. A paper presented to the Annual Meeting of the International Reading Association, Toronto, Canada.

Sutherland, Z., & Arbuthnot, M. H. (1991). *Children and books* (8th ed.). Chicago: Scott Foresman.

Sutton, R. (1994). Editorial. *Bulletin of the Center for Children's Books, 47*, 3.

Walmsley, S. A. (1994). *Children exploring their world: Theme teaching in elementary school*. Portsmouth, NH: Heinemann.

Yolen, J. (1973). *Writing books for children*. Boston: The Writer.

Zarnowski, M. (1990). Learning about biographies. Urbana, IL: National Council of Teachers of English.

Zinsser, W. (Ed.). (1990). *Worlds of childhood: The art and craft of writing for children* (pp. 1–21). Boston: Houghton Mifflin.

Books About the Arts

Anholt, L. (1994). *Camille and the sunflowers: A story about Vincent Van Gogh*. New York: Barrons. (1–3).

Carratello, J. & Carratello, P. (1993). *Focus on composers*. Chicago: Teacher Created Materials. (4–8).

Chertok, B., Hirshfeld, G., & Rosh, M. (1994). *Learning about ancient civilizations through art*. New York: Scholastic. (3–6).

DesJarlait, P. (1995). As recorded by N. Williams. *Conversations with a Native American artist*. Minneapolis: Runestone Press.

Hart, A. & Mantell, P. (1994). *Kids make music!* Charlotte, VT: Williamson. (K–4).

Hart, K. (1994). *I can paint!* Portsmouth, NH: Heineman. (2–5).

Hastings, S. (1993). *The firebird*. (R. Cartwright, Illus.). Cambridge, MA: Candlewick. (3–6).

Howard, N. (1992). *William Sidney Mount: Painter of rural America*. Worcester, MA: Davis. (3–6).

Hughes, A. (1994). *Van Gogh*. New York: Barrons. (3–8).

Jenkins, J. (1992). *Thinking about colors*. New York: Dutton. (1–3).

Martin, B. (1994). *The Maestro plays*. New York: Henry Holt. (1–3).

Micklethwait, L. *A child's book of art*. New York: Dorling Kindersley. (1–5).

Musical Instruments. (1993). Scholastic Voyages of Discovery Series. New York: Scholastic. (All ages).

Paint and Painting. (1993). Scholastic Voyages of Discovery Series. New York: Scholastic. (All ages).

Prokofiev, S. (1987). *Peter and the wolf*. (R. Cartwright, Illus.). New York: Holt. (1–5).

Rachlin, A. (1994). *Beethoven*. New York: Barrons. (1–5).

Thompson, K. & Loftus, D. (1995). *Art connections*. New York: Goodyear. (4–8).

Turner, R. (1992a). *Dorothea Lange*. Boston: Little, Brown. (4–8).

Turner, R. (1992b). *Portraits of women artists for children: Mary Cassatt*. Boston: Little, Brown. (3–8).

Oral and Silent Literature 12

KEY TERMS

antiphonal choral
   reading
booktalking
choral reading
creative drama
cumulative stories

line-a-child choral
   reading
reader's theater
refrain choral reading
storytelling
unison choral reading

GUIDING QUESTIONS

1. Why is reading aloud to children important in developing literary experiences?

2. How do oral and silent reading differ?

3. What should you consider when selecting a book to read aloud to your class?

OVERVIEW

Sharing excellent children's literature through oral language and language play is one of the most delightful and appropriate ways to foster children's construction of story understanding and appreciation of literary language (Labbo & Field, 1996). By inviting children to listen, savor, envision, read chorally, engage in creative movement, tell stories, dramatize, and booktalk during group, individual, and whole group experiences, oral language allows the rhythm of the story and the cadence of the words to pull listeners in. Oral projects enrich children's responses to literature, contributing images that escape the devices of written language, as well as making texts accessible to both readers and nonreaders.

Oral and silent reading processes are complementary. Readers rely on a foundation of silent reading to prepare for oral interpretation. Silent reading permits readers to understand text more rapidly and to think at higher cognitive levels. This chapter explores oral and silent reading strategies. In the following vignette, the complementary nature of oral and silent reading are made apparent.

INTRODUCTION

Discussion gives readers a chance to intertwine their own life "stories" with the story the author created. It also allows them to reflect on and revise the meaning they derived from the text by hearing and considering others' views about the story's meaning. Moreover such activities stimulate children to respond emotionally to text.

For children of all ages, oral literary activities such as hearing stories, reading aloud, dramatizing, storytelling, choral reading, and reader's theater serve important purposes. These activities enhance readers' understanding of literature, story action, and story characters. Oral literature activities also enrich children's understanding of the special conventions, devices, and effects of spoken language. They develop an ear for written language and a sense for the differences between the sound of book language and everyday speech.

The term *literature* generally brings the thought of books, but literature is much more than just books. Storytelling is the oldest form of literature. Reading aloud is also rooted in the past, when it was a major source of entertainment and news. Young children begin their journey to literacy with listening to nursery rhymes their parents or caregivers recite aloud. Acting out favorite characters extends children's literary experiences, which also gives them opportunities to see the world from another person's perspective.

VIGNETTE

Sally Richmond's fourth graders had just finished reading Gardiner's *Stone Fox* and the class was discussing the death of Willie's dog, Searchlight. The children were experienced with reader's theater, and they suggested *Stone Fox* for a production.

Denise said, "I cried my eyes out when Searchlight died! . . . It made me think about the time my dog died. We had to take her to the vet to be put to sleep. The story is so real for me. . . . I think Willie hurt just like I did when my dog died."

"You could feel the tension. You wanted Willie to win. Then when his dog died, it was so sad. The ending just left me sitting there believing that his dog just couldn't die," added Tina.

Chris agreed. "The ending was a real shocker. I don't think I've ever read a book with such a powerful ending before. When I look back on the book I feel different about it than when I was reading it. Now I see that Willie's grandpa had no will to live, but Willie had enough will for two people. Willie was so strong for a 10-year-old."

The children agreed that the strong emotional response they all had in reading the book would be beneficial in the reader's theater they planned. They all wanted to portray the striking aspects of the story.

READING ALOUD TO CHILDREN

Listening to stories read aloud allows children to experience the enjoyment of books, as well as to learn to love literature. When young children curl up in a parent's lap for a good book, they share an atmosphere of trust and the reading is a pleasurable experience. Such enjoyable activities present natural opportunities for learning without formal instruction. When reading aloud a book such as Michael Rosen's *We're Going on a Bear Hunt,* parents and children discuss stories, ask and answer questions, and chant the refrain together: "We're going on a bear hunt. We're going to catch a big one. What a beautiful day! We're not scared." In this warm, supportive environment, children associate reading with pleasure; they begin to see reading as an activity to be enjoyed and valued. They also acquire a foundation for learning to read (Naylor & Borders, 1993).

Listening to stories helps children understand structures of literature, which not only enhances their understanding of story, but also provides structure for later writing of stories. Hearing stories read aloud builds literary understandings—children can listen to memorable characters and plots that they might not be able to read for themselves. It also builds a foundation for learners' response to literature. Listening to stories frees children from thinking about word identification and word meaning, permitting them to think, feel, and respond to the stories, poems, or information they hear. They find thinking critically about literature is easier when it is read aloud, and daily listening to stories improves children's ability to talk about and retell stories (Morrow, 1988).

Reading aloud gives listeners of all ages opportunities for shared responses to literature—whether social, emotional, or intellectual. Perfect (1999) points out the sense of community that develops when a group shares the experience of listening to a book read aloud. Two texts exist in a read-aloud situation, the text of the book and the text the oral reader creates. Listeners experience both texts and make meaning from both texts. The reader is sharing a love of the story by giving the book to listeners.

As children grow in their ability to read and understand for themselves, hearing a story read aloud may motivate them to seek out stories by the same author or on the same topic. In this way, the experience of hearing a well-crafted story is not unlike throwing pebbles into a pond; the impact of the story creates an impetus for reading more and more books from an expanding variety of genres. After hearing Mildred Taylor's *Roll of Thunder, Hear My Cry,* which describes an African-American family's plight in Mississippi during the Great Depression, middle school children may elect to read this book on their own. Read-alouds may attract children to other books by Mildred Taylor such as *The Friendship* or *The Gold Cadillac.* They may wish to explore a topic such as racial prejudice by reading Paula Fox's *The Slave Dancer* or Julius Lester's *To Be a Slave.*

Reading Aloud in the Classroom

Providing time to read aloud to children in the school setting is just as vital as parents reading to their children at home. Children at all grade levels, including high school, should hear good literature read aloud daily. These highly motivating activities are often an afterthought in the curriculum if time permits. This is particularly disturbing considering several studies (Cohen, 1968; Cullinan, Jaggar, & Strickland, 1974; Purcell-Gates, 1988; Teale & Martinez, 1987) indicating that children whose teachers read to them have higher reading and writing achievement than children who lack these experiences.

Reading to students creates openings for positive student–teacher interactions. Sharing warmth, laughter, interest, and emotion—all will tell your class something. A reader gives listeners the text that is being read aloud, that read-aloud time is a time when all children, regardless of reading ability, are equally able to appreciate the wonder of a good story or information book.

Selecting Material for Reading Aloud

Some stories are for reading aloud and some are for telling. Storytelling is discussed in a later section of this chapter. Stories are for reading when the "style of the writing is so intrinsically a part of the story that it would be difficult to get the words together right by telling" (Ross, 1972, p. 217). For example, changing the words in A. A. Milne's *Winnie-the-Pooh* would cause the charm of the story to vanish.

Read-alouds give teachers and parents a chance to read quality literature that children might not choose for themselves or that they might be unable to read for themselves. Read-aloud materials are not confined to books. They can include magazine articles, short stories, poems, newspaper articles, or anything of interest to reader and listener. Read-aloud materials should be chosen carefully, however, to introduce children to motivating literature that gives them the benefits identified earlier in this chapter. Criteria for good read-aloud materials mandate that the work:

1. be of high literary quality from a variety of genres;
2. be appropriate to the age and developmental level of children;
3. be interesting enough to hold children's attention;
4. have strong plot lines and characters with which children can identify in fiction;
5. if nonfiction, have accurate information;
6. have a concrete subject related to children's experiences in poetry; and
7. be at reading levels of up to two or more grade levels above the grade level of the children as long as the material interests them.

Read-aloud literature is often confined to fiction or poetry, but all genres may be used as read-alouds for all ages. Many picture books are appropriate for older children or adults. Biographies and informational books make excellent read-alouds as well. Traditional literature is, of course, always a favorite read-aloud because these stories lend themselves to oral presentation due to their traditional roots; moreover, they explore human foibles and are usually action-packed stories.

Many adults and children enjoy the humor in a book such as *The Secret Knowledge of Grown-Ups* by David Wisniewski, and the laughter can continue with *Swine Divine* by Jan Carr and *Minnie and Moo Go Dancing* by Denys Cazet. Laughter is definitely the product of reading the poems in *Laugh-eteria* by Douglas Florian. Young children will enjoy the rhyming text in Mem Fox's *Boo to a Goose*. Children in grades 2 through 4 will enjoy *The Shaman's Apprentice* by Lynne Cherry and Mark Plotkin because the suspense and mystery will appeal to them. Lloyd Alexander's *Gypsy Rizka* generates laughter with its perils-of-Pauline type story. In this episodic chapter book, one chapter sets up the joke and the next one resolves it.

Teachers' read-aloud choices are most often confined to fiction or poetry. Popular primary-grade read-alouds include *Charlotte's Web* by E. B. White, *Little House on the Prairie* by Laura Ingalls Wilder, and the Amelia Bedelia books by Peggy Parish. Works by Leo Lionni, Tomie dePaola, Arnold Lobel, and poems by Shel Silverstein and Jack Prelutsky are popular read-alouds. Common intermediate grade read-alouds include *Island of the Blue Dolphins* by Scott O'Dell, *James and the Giant Peach* by Roald Dahl, and *Mrs. Frisby and the Rats of NIMH* by Robert C. O'Brien.

However, biographies and information books also make excellent read-alouds for every grade level. Informational books do not have to be read straight through; instead, the reader may choose parts that are related to classroom activities or interests. Some biographies also can be read by selecting pertinent episodes. Although, biographies, such as Robert Burleigh's *Black Whiteness: Admiral Byrd Alone in the Antarctic,* are ideal for reading aloud. Russell Freedman's *Martha Graham, a Dancer's Life* is another great read-aloud for middle-grade students. Both of these biographies are best read straight through.

The lively text of the informational book *Red-Eyed Tree Frog* by Joy Cowley makes this a riveting read-aloud adventure for children in grades 1 through 3. Nonfiction read-alouds for primary children also might include books such as Candace Fleming's *The Hatmaker's Sign: A Story by Benjamin Franklin,* which may be considered historical fiction but is based on an anecdote found in Thomas Jefferson's papers and has a wonderful read-aloud quality. In *Water* by Frank Asch children learn about water and what it means to them. These informational books lend themselves to reading straight through. Middle-grade children will enjoy Michael Tunnel and George Chilcoat's *The Children of Topaz,* which is based on a classroom diary of a teacher in a Japanese American internment camp. *This Land Is My Land* is a nonfiction book by George Littlechild, a member of the Plains Cree Nation. Littlechild is a renowned artist who tells about his art in this wonderful book. Children will enjoy looking at the art as well as hearing about it. In reading these books aloud, teachers may prefer to select parts to read and return to the books over a period of time.

Traditional literature interests a wide age range of listeners. Steven Kellogg's *I Was Born About 10,000 Years Ago* is a well-loved tall tale that appeals to many children. The Uncle Smoke Stories by Roger Welch are Native American stories about Coyote the trickster that appeal to children from third grade to junior high school. *The Corn Woman* by Angel Vigil is a collection of stories and legends of the Hispanic Southwest.

These traditional stories share the beauty of family life before television when families passed the time by talking to each other for hours. The stories in these books are presented as separate stories, so teachers may choose to read one or more short stories aloud.

Planning a Read-Aloud Session

Reading aloud is an occasion for sharing stories, jokes, and excerpts from newspapers and nonfiction. The reader selects the material, arranges the physical setting, and looks over the materials. In classrooms or libraries, the physical setting should be arranged to permit readers to see and hear. When reading picture books, show the illustrations at the same time that you are reading.

A read-aloud session has three major components. First, introduce the book and identify the author and illustrator. Second, the first reading of the selection should be for understanding and appreciation, however, teachers or librarians may stop reading at predetermined points to encourage prediction or to connect a character, an incident, or a problem to literature they have previously experienced. Third, depending upon the particular book in question, the teacher may conduct a follow-up discussion during which the children may raise questions or the teacher may introduce points for discussion. Figure 12.1 illustrates this read-aloud model.

READER'S THEATER

"Reader's theater is a great way to develop children's meaningful and fluent reading" (Martinez, Roser, & Strecker, 1998–1999). Reader's theater is oral delivery of stories, poetry, biography, or information by two or more readers who characterize and narrate clearly and expressively. The performers must understand the literature they are presenting so that they can structure the development of character and plot. "Reader's theater is neither lecture nor play; rather it is a staged program that allows the audience to create its own images through the skilled performance of the readers" (McCaslin, 1990, p. 263). The simplicity of reader's theater makes it appealing and effective because it does not require rehearsal or elaborate staging, yet it is so motivating that students enjoy practicing their oral reading.

The cast may be large or small. In situations with a small cast, one individual may read several parts. During the presentation, the entire cast remains on

---

FIGURE 12.1   Read-aloud example for third grade.

The Little Ships: The Heroic Rescue at Dunkirk in World War II
BY LOUISE BORDEN
ILLUSTRATED BY MICHAEL FOREMAN

Introduction: Louise Borden has written a number of books, including *Goodbye, Charles Lindbergh: Based on a True Story* and *A. Lincoln and Me.* The illustrator of *The Little Ships,* Michael Foreman, has also illustrated other books about war.

This is a true story that happened during World War II. Soldiers from the United States and other Allied countries were stranded on the beaches at Dunkirk. Teachers could bring in a map of Europe and place a star by Dunkirk so children can see where this happened. The book tells how the troops were saved.

During reading: The reader may choose to stop and ask children to predict future events, although this is not necessary with every book. The teacher might ask the children to identify who is telling the story.

Following reading: The teacher should conduct a discussion using the following questions:

- Why do you think the author called this book *The Little Ships* when many of these vessels were boats rather than ships?
- Who were the heroes in this story? What kind of heroism did they demonstrate?
- Can you think of any other books or characters that are similar to *The Little Ships*? How are they similar?
- What was the "miracle of Dunkirk"?
- What image does the phrase "silent parade over the waters" bring to your mind?

---

stage, reading the various assigned portions (McCaslin, 1990). Movement is minimal, and actions are suggested through simple gestures and facial expressions. Readers usually take formal positions behind lecterns or sit on stools, often turning their backs to the audience to show that they are absent from a scene. Readers may turn around or lower their heads when not participating in a scene.

Selecting Material

Students who are becoming fluent readers need manageable texts in which to practice. The reading selection itself is an important element in building fluency (Martinez, Roser, & Strecker, 1998–1999). Many types of literature are well suited to reader's theater presentations including modern literature and traditional tales, including all kinds of fiction, poetry, history, biography, and unpublished materials. In some instances, related materials may be mixed in a presentation. For example, a poem and a story with related themes can be performed together. Manna (1984) suggests that reader's theater stories should have these characteristics:

1. an interesting, fast-paced story with a strong plot;
2. a lot of dialogue;
3. recognizable and believable characters;
4. plausible language; and
5. a distinct style.

Clearly, teachers may choose from among many appropriate pieces of literature, including the following suggestions.

- *The Princess and the Pea,* by Hans Christian Andersen and illustrated by Paul Galdone
- *A Bear for Miguel* by E. M. Alphin
- *The Golly Sisters Ride Again,* by Betsy Byars
- *My Brother Ant,* by Betsy Byars
- *Henny Penny* by Paul Galdone
- *The Ballad of Belle Dorcas* by William Hooks
- *King of the Playground* by P. R. Naylor
- *Rolling Harvey Down the Hill* by Jack Prelutsky
- *The Relatives Came* by Cynthia Rylant
- *Fa Mulan: The Story of a Woman Warrior* by Robert San Souci
- *I Am the Cat* by Alice Schertle and illustrated by Robert Buehner
- *Raising Sweetness* by Diane Stanley
- *Horton Hatches the Egg* by Dr. Seuss
- *Bartholomew and the Oobleck* by Dr. Seuss
- *Bremen Town Musicians* by Janet Stevens
- *Many Moons* by James Thurber

Planning a Reader's Theater Performance

After selecting a piece for the performance, the next step is identifying who will read which part. If the piece is too long, the readers will choose the scenes that convey the concept or theme of the piece rather than read the entire selection. After making these decisions, plan and decide on the details of staging. A common staging device is to have the readers sit on stools in a circle, turning around on the stools so their backs face the audience when they are not participating in a scene. In somewhat more elaborate staging, a spotlight may be focused on the individual who is reading at the moment. Students may also sit or stand side by side, with the narrators at one side and closer to the audience.

A colored marking pen or magic marker can be used to identify the various parts to be read by individuals. Readers should practice reading in a comfortable, relaxed manner at a pace that moves the scene along, but not so rapidly that the audience is lost. Careful reading and discussion of the text during preparation is essential because a piece of literature cannot be interpreted without understanding. The accompanying box illustrates a fifth-grade class preparing for a reader's theater performance.

A Report on a Reader's Theater Performance

The students chose to read *Where the Lilies Bloom* by Vera and Bill Cleaver. Eight readers took the parts of Mary Call, the protagonist; Devola, her older sister; Roy Luther, the father; Kiser Pease, the landlord and neighbor; Mary Call's younger brother and sister; the storekeeper who buys herbs from Mary Call; and a neighbor. The readers used stools in a circle so they could turn their backs to the audience when not participating.

They identified the following scenes as key to understanding the story.

1. Mary Call and Roy Luther discuss his impending death and burial in the grave he has prepared.
2. Mary Call and the children pretend their father is ill when a neighbor comes to call.
3. Mary Call and Devola care for Kiser Pease when he is ill.
4. Mary Call and the storekeeper interact when Mary Call sells herbs.
5. Kiser Pease brings his car to the Luther's so that Devola can sit in it.
6. Kiser Pease asks Devola to marry him.
7. Mary Call pretends she wants to marry Kiser.
8. Devola takes charge and decides to marry Kiser.

The readers decided to serve herb tea after their performance because Mary Call earns a living for her family by gathering herbs. They also planned to read the sequel to this story, *Trial Valley.*

STORYTELLING

Storytelling is a powerful, magical way of introducing and exploring literature. Storytellers make stories come to life. Oral literature includes stories, poems, and information told aloud to another person or persons. The first written description of storytelling appears in the Egyptian papyrus known as the Westcar Papyrus, recorded sometime between the twelfth and eighteenth dynasties (2000–1300 B.C.), describing a storytelling encounter between Khufu (Cheops) and his sons. Historically, storytellers have preserved our past and transmitted it orally to new generations.

Ruth Sawyer (1962), who traveled around the world to discover stories and storytellers, calls storytelling a folk art. She believes enduring stories are a sharing of mind, heart, and spirit. Northrup Frye (1964) is convinced that traditional literature, stories in the oral tradition, is the basis of all modern stories. Cooper and Collins (1992) believe stories are the part of us that makes us human and that stories are at the heart of the teaching and learning process. Storytellers in widely different cultures tell stories with common threads running through them. Traditional stories even appear to be the basis for television shows; daytime dramas probably owe their appeal to ancient tales such as *Cinderella* and *Snow White.*

Storytellers have a live, listening audience with whom to interact, whereas writers do not have a chance to interact directly with their readers. Listeners hear voice effects and see their storyteller move, bend, and breathe. The oral story is soft and malleable, yielding to the pleasures of the audience. Its language is not the precise and unchanging form of the written story created by a single author, but the evolving, flowing language of the community (Barton, 1986). Many authors were storytellers before they became writers.

Storytelling is natural to human beings because it helps us remember and understand things that have happened, it teaches us how to behave, as well as how not to behave. It stimulates our imagination: As the storyteller spins a tale, the listeners create pictures in their minds of the characters, the setting, and the story events. Storytelling develops an awareness of and sensitivity to the thoughts and feelings of the listeners. We can laugh and cry. Our feelings are valid and storytelling allows us to express them (Cooper & Collins, 1992). "As the teller looks right at the listeners, eyes meet and an interactive communication exists between

Twelve Lizards Leaping is a different kind of Christmas story.

them" (Livo & Rietz, 1986, p. xi). Storytelling can bring people of all ages together for a shared experience actively involving both storyteller and listeners.

The Roots of Storytelling

Traditional literature, a common source of material for storytellers, is the product of a community. One storyteller tells a story; another hears it and retells it, reshaping it in the retelling. A detail may be deleted and a new one added because of the new storyteller's personal style or perhaps to tailor the story for a particular audience (Lester, 1988). This is how versions of the same story develop throughout the world.

We find literally hundreds of versions of popular stories such as *Cinderella.* The most common version may be the one written by Charles Perrault and retold by Marcia Brown. In this version, Brown creates a fairy-tale quality with ruffles and flourishes. Margaret Greaves's *Tattercoats* is a British version in which the prince falls in love with a dirty girl wearing a torn petticoat. The prince invites Tattercoats, her gooseherd friend, and his geese to come to the king's ball, where the gooseherd plays a magic pipe, which changes Tattercoats's rags to beautiful robes and the geese to pages. *Yeh-Shen* by Ai-Ling Louie is based on the oldest written version of *Cinderella.* Yeh-Shen, the protagonist in this Chinese folktale, must serve her stepmother and stepsister. She has one friend, a fish whom she feeds and talks with each day. After her stepmother kills the fish, Yeh-Shen discovers that its magic powers can provide fine clothes and feathers to attend a festival where she loses a slipper that the king uses to claim her hand in marriage. In this version, a shower of flying stones crushes the stepmother and stepsister.

Another form that storytellers use is the cumulative format because these stories accumulate, with events building on events and phrases building on phrases, building to a climax when the accumulation falls apart. A modern tale, *The Napping House,* by Audrey Wood introduced in chapter 1, is a cumulative tale. It begins with one character taking a nap, then additional characters and animals join the nap. Cumulative stories are highly predictable, with events and phrases repeated as new ones are added. Cumulative stories probably descended from early primitive efforts at conscious storytelling consisting of a simple chant set to the rhythm of some daily occupation such as grinding corn, paddling a canoe or kayak, sharpening weapons for hunting or war, or ceremonial dancing (Sawyer, 1962).

Storytelling in the Classroom

Oral language precedes written in children's development. They learn to talk and to explain, a form of storytelling, before they learn to read and write stories. Therefore, beginning children's literary experiences with oral activities and using these activities as a basis for subsequent experiences with written language makes sense.

Storytelling develops positive attitudes toward literature, reading, and writing (Roney, 1989). It motivates children to read and write themselves, as shown in the accompanying box, and provides a model for children's own writing. Children enjoy participating in storytelling through telling their own stories and joining in on repeated phrases when others are telling stories. Hearing and telling different types of stories develops their awareness and comprehension of the various forms of narrative (Golden, 1984). Storytelling develops thinking abilities (Roney, 1989). Teachers can tell stories to introduce literature, to help children learn about stories, to develop children's listening and speaking skills, and to model storytelling behavior. Teachers who are storytellers can help their students learn to tell stories.

A Storytelling Experience

Jim Phillips told his first graders to make a story circle on the rug in his classroom; then he sat down on a low chair and opened the book *Brown Bear, Brown Bear* by Bill Martin. He held the book so the children could see it, told them the title and the author's name, and started reading.

"Brown Bear, Brown Bear, What do you see?" "I see a red bird looking at me."

Mr. Phillips read through the entire cumulative tale, in which each animal or bird sees another. When he finished, the children pleaded for him to read it again and he did. After the second reading, Mr. Phillips told the children they were going to make a story. They immediately asked how.

He answered, "You are going to think of new animals for the *Brown Bear, Brown Bear* story. I'll begin with 'Blue Jay, Blue Jay, What do you see?' Now, Lauren, tell us what the Blue Jay sees."

After thinking for a few moments, Lauren said, "I see a pink butterfly looking at me."

Mr. Phillips said, "Pink butterfly, pink butterfly, What do you see? Tony, tell us what the pink butterfly sees."

Tony said, "I see a striped zebra looking at me!"

Mr. Phillips and the children continued until they had completed a story, then they retold it. Afterward, Mr. Phillips said, "I am going to write your story on this chart, so you can remember it. While I am writing your story on a chart, you can draw pictures of the animals and birds that you thought of for the story and we will paste them to the chart pages."

Later in the day, he noticed that a number of the children were writing and illustrating their own *Brown Bear* stories. When the children completed their individual stories, they read them to their classmates.

The Internet is a rich source of storytelling ideas and suggested materials. Students can hear storytellers sharing their favorite stories. For example, *www.themoonlitroad.com* is an excellent site and *The Storytelling FAQ* at *www.lilliput.co.uk/storytel.html* is another helpful site.

Selecting Material

The first step in storytelling is selecting a story to learn. Traditional literature is a good starting point. *Teaching Through Stories: Yours, Mine, and Theirs* (Roe, Alfred, & Smith, 1998) is a helpful reference in finding good traditional stories. Begin with an appealing version of a traditional story that you already know, such as *Cinderella, Three Billy Goats Gruff,* and *Stone Soup.* The most important factor in choosing a story for telling is that you enjoy the story so that you will also enjoy the telling. As a beginning storyteller, a simple story will give you security as you begin. You will find the following authors helpful because they retell traditional stories and write stories in a traditional literature style.

- *Why Mosquitoes Buzz in People's Ears* by Verna Aardema
- *Dichos: Proverbs and Sayings from the Spanish* by Charles Aranda
- *I, Houdini: The Autobiography of a Self-Educated Hamster* by Lynne Reid Banks and illustrated by Terry Riley
- *Latin American Tales: From the Pampas to the Pyramids of Mexico* by Genevieve Barlow
- *The Jack Tales* retold by Richard Chase
- *The Three Little Pigs* by Jean Claverie
- *Look What Happened to Frog: Storytelling in Education* by Pamela Cooper and Rives Collins
- *The Literature of Delight* by Kimberly Olson Fakih
- *Hairyman* by David Holt
- *Tailybone* by David Holt
- *Jack and the Beanstalk* by Steven Kellogg
- *Black Folktales* by Julius Lester
- *The Tales of Uncle Remus: The Adventures of Brer Rabbit* by Julius Lester
- *The Storyteller's Sourcebook: A Subject, Title and Motif Index to Folklore Collections for Children* by Margaret Read MacDonald
- *The Boy Who Loved Frogs* by Jay O'Callahan
- *Little Heroes* by Jay O'Callahan
- *Stories and Songs for Little Children* by Pete Seeger
- *Baseball in April and Other Stories* by Gary Soto

Storytellers need not feel confined to traditional stories, however. Modern tales such as *Alexander and the Terrible, Horrible, No Good, Very Bad Day* by Judith Viorst is a delightful story that has broad appeal.

Planning Storytelling

The main ingredient in planning storytelling is learning the story. Storytelling confidence comes with story familiarity. Storytellers should know their story well, but learning it verbatim is not necessary. Learning the framework of a story is important, however, to provide a skeleton to follow in telling it and to learn any phrases that are repeated or important to the story. Once these elements are learned, practice telling the story several times helps polish the presentation.

Learning the framework of a story is easy, but storytellers use some tools to help them recall the story. As mentioned in chapter 2, stories have structure; they are orderly and conform to structure rules recognized as story structure or story grammar (Livo & Rietz, 1986). Stories that conform to the expected structure are easier to recall and to understand (Downing & Leong, 1982). Story patterns help readers comprehend literature; they also give form to writing. Story patterns can be mapped or diagrammed to assist storytellers in recalling and interrelating the ideas and events of a story. Story patterns and maps are especially helpful in teaching children to prepare stories for storytelling. Figure 12.2 illustrates a structural map of the story "The Wide-Mouthed Frog."

Some storytellers choose to use story maps to help them learn their stories. The following techniques will help teachers and children with storytelling.

1. When preparing to learn a story for storytelling, read several stories a week or so in advance. The story that comes back to you most frequently is the one to learn.

2. Divide the story into beginning, middle, and end. Learn it in segments, such as separate scenes or units of action. Learn the story structure in order, but do not memorize it. The ways of dividing a story differ from storyteller to storyteller. One way of dividing *The Three Little Pigs* is:

- Part 1: The three little pigs set out to find their fortune. One builds a house of straw, the next builds a house of sticks, and the third builds a brick house.
- Part 2: The wolf eats pigs one and two and goes after the third one.
- Part 3: The pig sends the wolf to an apple orchard and a fair and then outwits him. The wolf ends up in the kettle.

FIGURE 12.2   Story grammar for "The Wide-Mouthed Frog."

Setting:

The wide-mouthed frog and his wife live beside a pond with their newborn babies.

The Problem:

The wide-mouthed frog babies are hungry. Mrs. Wide-Mouthed Frog sends her husband out to get food for the babies.

The Events:

1. Mr. Wide-Mouthed Frog meets a goat and asks him what his babies eat. The goat recommends tin cans, which the wide-mouthed frog rejects.
2. He meets a cat who recommends mice.
3. He meets a duck who recommends milk.
4. He meets a horse who recommends grain.
5. He meets an owl who recommends wide-mouthed frogs.

Resolution:

The wide-mouthed frog narrows his mouth and says, "Oooooooohhhhhh."

3. Do not memorize the exact words of a story, but do learn any special catch phrases and use them in telling the story. Catch phrases are phrases that may appear several times within the story or that the story hinges on, such as "I'll huff and I'll puff and I'll blow your house down" in *The Three Little Pigs*.

4. Don't worry about using the same words every time you tell the story.

5. Be expressive in storytelling, but do not be so dramatic that you overshadow the story itself (Morrow, 1988).

6. Practice telling the story several times before actually telling it to an audience to get comfortable with saying the story aloud and with the sound of your own voice.

7. Practice by tape recording yourself. Wait a day or two to listen to the tape so you can be objective. When you evaluate the tape think about the parts of the story and identify those that need changing or expanding. Does your voice sound pleasing? Do you speak at a speed that is appropriate to the story?

8. Look directly at your audience when you are telling the story.

9. The story should not be longer than 10 minutes.

You will find helpful materials through the Internet and storytelling associations. The National Storytelling Network (NTN) is located in Jonesborough, Tennessee, and it has a Web site, *www.storynet.org*. It has a magazine, many storytelling materials, and sponsors storytelling events such as "Tellabrations" on the Saturday before Thanksgiving. This international event takes place in elder hostels, on airplanes, in schools and colleges, in museums, and wherever people gather. Whenever you access the NTN Web site, you will discover a plethora of storytelling sites from around the world. East Tennessee State University has a storytelling program with coursework. It also publishes *Storytelling World*.

Storytelling Variations

Sitting in front of an audience and using only voice and expressions is not the only way to tell a story. Storytelling can be varied in many ways to give novelty to tried-and-true stories. Variations also can be used cooperatively with children to give them greater involvement with the literature presented.

Flannel board stories

When telling stories with flannel boards, the teller sits or stands by a board covered with flannel. Cutouts of characters backed with flannel are placed on the board as they appear in the story. Some storytellers may lay the flannel board on a table to prevent the figures from falling. Children can also use flannel boards and will enjoy taking turns telling stories with a flannel board.

Stories told with a flannel board should not have large numbers of characters or complex actions. After selecting a story, the teller decides which parts to show and which to tell. For example, in preparing *Goldilocks and the Three Bears* the teller or students could make figures for Goldilocks, the three bears, three sizes of bowls, three sizes of chairs, and three sizes of beds; some tellers may like to have a broken bowl and a broken chair to illustrate the story further. These figures can be used to present the entire story; details and actions do not have to be portrayed.

The characters can be drawn or painted on cardboard, construction paper, or any other convenient material. After cutting them out, back them with flannel or sandpaper so they will stick to the flannel board. Use yarn, buttons, or fabric to decorate and develop the characters. The board can be covered with flannel, although indoor-outdoor carpeting makes a very satisfactory backing. Figures cling to it and it wipes clean.

Prop stories

Props such as hats, canes, stuffed animals, boxes, rocks, toys, and fruit can enhance storytelling. Beans, a small harp, and a china or plastic hen are excellent props for *Jack and the Beanstalk*. The props give the storyteller and the audience a focal point and help the storyteller remember the story.

Mouse Count

Ellen Stoll Walsh

The mice count and uncount themselves.

Music stories

Some stories are excellent when told with background music. For example, *Jack and the Beanstalk* sounds wonderful when told with the music "In the Hall of the

A Storyteller's Version of "The Wide-Mouthed Frog"

Mr. and Mrs. Willie T. Wide-Mouthed Frog lived beside a pretty pond with blue water and white lily pads. They were thrilled to have three beautiful green babies. But the babies were always hungry and crying. Mrs. Wide-Mouthed Frog was tired of hunting for food, so she told her husband to go out and hunt food for their hungry babies. Mr. Willie T. Wide-Mouthed Frog set out to find food. He hopped around the beautiful blue pond.

He met a goat and stopped. "Hello, Goat, I'm a wide-mouthed frog, and I'm hunting food for my babies. What do your babies eat?"

"My babies eat tin cans. They chew them right up."

"Oh! Wide-mouthed frog babies can't eat tin cans. Thank you."

The frog hops on. He meets a cat.

"Hello, Cat, I'm a wide-mouthed frog, and I'm hunting food for my babies. What do your babies eat?"

"My babies eat mice. They chew them up bones and all."

"Wide-mouthed frog babies can't eat mice. Thank you."

The frog hops on. He meets a horse and stops.

"Hello, Horse, I'm a wide-mouthed frog and I'm hunting food for my babies. What do your babies eat?"

"My babies eat grain. They grind it up with their teeth."

"Wide-mouthed frog babies can't eat grain. Thank you."

The frog hops on. He meets a duck and stops.

"Hello, Duck, I'm a wide-mouthed frog, and I'm hunting food for my babies. What do your babies eat?"

"My babies eat worms. They wash them down with water."

"Wide-mouthed frog babies can't eat worms. Thank you."

The frog hops on. He sees an owl in a tree and stops.

"Hello, Owl, I'm a wide-mouthed frog, and I'm hunting food for my babies. What do your babies eat?"

"My babies eat wide-mouthed frogs."

The frog sucks his mouth into a narrow little circle and says, "Oooohhhh!" and then hurries home.

Mountain King" playing in the background. This piece is from Legends in Music by Bowmar Orchestral Library. RCA Victor has an Adventures in Music record library for elementary schools that includes excellent selections for story background music. Musical storytellers can play their own accompaniment.

Cut stories

Cut stories are stories told while the storyteller cuts out a piece of paper to form a character or object in the story. The figures may be drawn ahead of time on construction paper to make the cutting easier (Morrow, 1979). Some teachers are sufficiently skilled to fold the paper and cut multiple figures while storytelling. Many picture books and folktales are good choices for cut stories because the teller can cut objects to accompany the story. For example, a gingerbread boy cutout could accompany the story *The Gingerbread Boy,* or a pancake could accompany *The Pancake.*

CHORAL READING

Choral reading is an oral literary activity in which several readers read a selection in unison with the direction of a leader. This ancient technique has been in use for centuries. Choral reading was an important element of Greek drama. Researchers found evidence of choral speaking in ancient religious ceremonies and festivals, and it is still used for ritualistic purposes in church services and on patriotic occasions (McCaslin, 1990). Ross (1972) points out that choral reading was used in early schools because there were not enough books.

Choral reading involves listening and responding to language. Through participating in choral reading, students become aware of the sounds of language, predictable language patterns, and the rhythm and melody of language, which helps them understand the meaning of text (Miccinati, 1985). After choral reading experiences, children are better able to predict the words and phrases that follow one another. The purpose of choral reading is to convey meaning through sound, stress, duration, and pitch. Choral reading also develops diction and enunciation of speech sounds.

Choral reading is a group activity that gives students opportunities for social cooperation because individuals focus on a common goal. In a group activity such as this, students can participate without feelings of self-consciousness. Choral reading knows no age limits—kindergarten children enjoy it, as do high school students and adults.

Selecting Material

Choral reading in the elementary classrooms can begin with short nursery rhymes in kindergarten. Rhythm and rhyme are the important factors in nursery rhymes, which help children remember them. Material for choral reading should be meaningful and have a strong rhythm and an easily discernible structure. The following list includes only a few of the materials that make interesting choral readings.

- *Baby-O* by Nancy Carlstrom and illustrated by Susie Stevenson
- "So Long as There's Weather" by Tamara Kitt
- "The Umbrella Brigade" by Laura Richards
- "Godfrey, Gordon, Gustavus Gore" by William B. Rand
- *Laughing Time: Collected Nonsense* by William Jay Smith
- *Train Song* by Diane Siebert
- *Truck Song* by Diane Siebert
- *I Know an Old Lady Who Swallowed a Fly* by Glen Rounds
- *Peanut Butter and Jelly* by Nadine Westcott

Planning a Choral Reading

When initiating a choral reading activity, prepare the students by giving them time to read the material silently and then aloud to themselves or their peers. After reading, lead a discussion to develop students' understanding of the selection. Once the students understand the selection, they can practice reading orally. Teachers can help young children respond to language rhythms by clapping or tapping to the rhythm. Initially, the teacher may chant most of the rhyme and have the children chime in only on the last line or a repeated refrain. Use a single selection with various choral reading methods so students learn about the various ways of expressing meaning. After students have experiences with the various choral reading types, they can choose selections and plan their own choral readings.

Four common types of choral reading exist: refrain, line-a-child, antiphonal, and unison. The easiest to learn is *refrain,* in which the teacher reads most of the lines and the students read the refrain. In *line-a-child reading,* individual students read specific lines while the entire group reads the beginning and ending of the selection. *Antiphonal* or *dialogue choral reading* is most appropriate for middle- or intermediate-level students. It enables readers to explore pitch and duration of sound. Boys, girls, and groups vary their pitches and sound duration for different parts of the selection. *Unison* is the most difficult choral reading approach because the entire group speaks all of the lines. Without seeking perfection, the participants must practice timing so that they are producing words and sounds simultaneously. Combinations of all of these types may be used for a single selection.

Tamara Kitt's poem "So Long as There's Weather" is a fine children's choice for choral reading. The spare use of words, frequent pauses, sound effects, emphasized words, and short lines ranging from 1 to 5 syllables create a feeling of changing weather and a child's joy in all kinds of weather. The appeal of this poem for children makes it an excellent choice for choral reading. Alert the students to the fact that dashes in the text represent pauses and that the emphasized words and pauses make the choral reading more interesting. A choral reading experience involving "So Long as There's Weather" for primary-grade children might proceed as indicated in the following:

1. Begin with crashing cymbals to simulate thunder or with water poured from container to container to simulate rain.
2. The teacher reads the first verse.
3. The children read the second verse in unison from a chart.
4. The teacher or a child who has practiced reads the third verse.
5. The children read the fourth verse in unison from a chart.
6. On the emphasized words in the fourth verse, designated children crash cymbals together.

As children develop their understanding of chanting in unison, they can move to longer selections. *Peanut Butter and Jelly* by Nadine Westcott is an excellent longer piece for choral reading. After children learn to chant this play-rhyme, the teacher can introduce the hand-clap and knee-slap motions that accompany it. Later, the teacher may choose to divide the poem into parts to be read by different groups.

CREATIVE DRAMA

Creative drama is informal drama created by the participants (McCaslin, 1990). This kind of drama is improvisational and process-centered rather than exhibitional. It may be based on a story with a beginning, a middle, and an end. It may, on the other hand, be an original plot that explores, develops, and expresses ideas and feelings through dramatic enactment. The players create the dialogue whether the content is a well-known story or an original plot. "With each playing, the story becomes more detailed and better organized, but it remains extemporaneous and is at no time designed for an audience," which avoids rehearsal and memorization (McCaslin, 1990, p. 5).

Reenactments allow each member of the group an opportunity to play various parts and to be part of the audience for others. Scenery and costumes have no place in creative drama, although an occasional prop or piece of costume may be permitted to stimulate the imagination (McCaslin, 1990). Similarly, readers have no written script to follow. Creative drama emphasizes spontaneity and improvisation, although involvement in creative drama may lead students to write a script for a play later. When dialogue is written, the nature of the drama changes. Written drama can be very rewarding and children enjoy the creative writing involved in such enterprises.

Creative drama is done for fun, understanding, and learning, and yields many benefits. It is a way of learning and knowing; the actors become participants instead of merely observers (Heathcote, 1983). As children improvise in acting out a story they have read, an episode from a story, or an experience of their own, they participate in the literature or the incident. They comprehend and express the important details of plot, character, word meanings, story sequence, and cause-and-effect relations (Miccinati, 1985). This makes story characters and story action more concrete and comprehensible for children. In acting out stories, they use their bodies, voices, and movements to enact literature; translating words into action encourages children to interpret and respond to literature. Dramatization also increases vocabulary, syntactic flexibility, and the ability to predict aspects of story.

Creative drama also makes strong contributions to the growth of children's communication effectiveness (Busching, 1981). It requires logical and intuitive thinking; it personalizes knowledge and yields aesthetic pleasure (Siks, 1983). Drama gives children opportunities to experiment with words, emotions, and social roles. Heathcote (1983) believes that drama expands children's understanding of life experiences and that it leads them to reflect on particular circumstances and to make sense out of their world in a deeper way.

The poet and songwriter helps us appreciate the beauty of our country.

Creative drama is one of the best ways of discovering and learning to appreciate literature. Other creative drama activities include pantomime, puppets, and story creation (discussed later in this section).

Selecting Material

A dramatized story can make a lasting impression. Therefore, the opportunity to become well acquainted with good literature through dramatizing it is a major value of creative drama. Both folktales and modern stories provide fine opportunities for acting. Believable characters, a well-constructed plot, and a worthwhile theme make for engrossing drama. Any story, episode, or event that children have enjoyed is a likely candidate for dramatization. Students of all ages enjoy acting out versions of the same story and comparing the versions. For example, they might act out three versions of *Cinderella* and compare the characterization, plot, and setting. Perhaps a few suggestions of specific stories for dramatization will stimulate you to think of others.

Young children enjoy dramatizing many traditional stories they have heard again and again, such as Gail Haley's *Jack and the Bean Tree,* or a version of *Little Red Riding Hood* for grades 1–3. Many of John Burningham's cumulative tales such as *Mr. Gumpy's Outing* for preschoolers and first graders lend themselves to dramatization. Middle-grade students enjoy stories such as *Bunnicula* by Deborah and James Howe, *The Pushcart War* by Jean Merrill, and *The Book of Three* by Lloyd Alexander.

Planning Creative Drama

Teachers should create many opportunities for children to participate in short, unstructured drama. The following guidelines are helpful in creating these opportunities:

1. Although props are not necessary, many teachers gather a collection of props for dramatic plays. Jewelry, fabric, hats, canes, clothing, and Halloween costumes are useful props.
2. Select a story or have the children select a favorite story. A book that includes a large number of characters gives more children opportunities to participate.
3. Discuss the main events with the students. Identify and sequence the events to be included. You may wish to outline the events using a story map.
4. Identify the characters in the story. Discuss their actions, attitudes, and feelings. Explain that the children should act the way they think the character walked, talked, and so on.
5. Discuss the action in each scene and give the children opportunities to practice it. They may need to pretend to walk in heavy boots or need to practice expressive gestures such as walking happily, sadly, or so forth. Pantomime (discussed next) is a way of preparing children to move in expressive ways.
6. Assign character roles to class members. Ask the participants to think about and visualize the characters. Children who do not want to participate can be directors or stage managers.
7. Give the audience a purpose for watching the play. For example, ask them to observe characterization and character development or plot development.
8. Dramatize the story.
9. Discuss the dramatization.
10. Recast the characters and play the story again.

Pantomime

"Pantomime is the art of conveying ideas without words"; it sharpens children's perceptions and stimulates the imagination as the players try to remember actions and characters (McCaslin, 1990, p. 71). Children can pantomime stories as another child or the teacher reads them. They may create a character from literature or one of their own invention. Pantomime is an excellent way to begin creative drama because it is a natural means of expression for primary-grade children.

In kindergarten, basic movements such as walking, running, skipping, and galloping prepare for the creative use of rhythms. Music can set the mood for people marching in a parade, horses galloping, toads hopping, cars racing on a track, or children skipping on a sunny spring day (McCaslin, 1990). Older children also enjoy pantomime and children who have limited knowledge of English or who have speech and hearing problems can participate in it.

Puppets

Puppet shows are dramas in which the actors are puppets that come to life with the assistance of a puppeteer. Children enjoy making puppets and becoming puppeteers. Puppets are excellent for children who are shy because they can express themselves through the puppet. They also work well with children who are reluctant to participate in creative drama.

A puppet show allows children to dramatize their favorite books or scripts they have written. Puppetry stimulates the imagination of the children who are creating puppets and planning to dramatize a story. Children practice cooperation as they work with others to make puppets and puppet productions.

The stage can be quite simple—a youngster kneeling behind a table and moving an object along the edge of it—or as elaborate as imagination and skill can make or buy it. Similarly, you can provide commercially produced puppets, or children can make their own. They can create a puppet with nothing more than a bandanna wrapped around the first three fingers so that the thumb and little finger are the arms (McCaslin, 1990). The following are some of the puppets students can construct (Stoodt, 1988, p. 119; see Figure 12.3).

- *Stick puppets:* Draw the character on tagboard, cardboard, or construction paper and decorate it with yarn, sequins, and tissue paper. Cut out the figure and attach it to a stick, tongue depressor, or dowel for manipulation.
- *Paper-plate puppets:* Draw faces on paper plates and decorate them with yarn for hair. Glue the plates on sticks, dowels, or rulers for manipulation.
- *Sock puppets:* Add yarn hair, button eyes, and felt bits for a nose, ear, or other features to the toe end of a sock. Put your hand inside the sock for manipulation.
- *Styrofoam-cup puppets:* Decorate a cup as a character and attach the completed puppet to a stick or dowel for manipulation.

FIGURE 12.3   Student-made puppets.

Stick puppet   Paper plate puppet

Sock puppet   Styrofoam-cup puppet

Cloth or hand puppet   Paper-bag puppet

- *Cloth puppets:* Sew fabric to fit over a child's hand. Decorate it to create a character.
- *Paper-bag puppets:* Draw the character on the bag and put the bag over your hand to manipulate it, using the folded bottom of the bag for the mouth area; or decorate the bag as the character, stuff it with newspaper or cotton, and put a stick, dowel, or ruler into the neck of the bag and tie it shut, turning it upside down and using the stick for manipulation.

Some helpful puppeteering references include *Storytelling with Puppets* by Connie Champlin and Nancy Renfro (1985), *Making Puppets Come Alive* by Larry Engler and Carol Fijan (1973), and *The Consultant's Notebook* by Puppeteers of America (1989).

BOOKTALKS

Booktalks are akin to storytelling but have a somewhat different purpose: motivating children to read. Both children and teachers should regularly share their favorite books through booktalks.

Booktalks should be based on books the teller really enjoys, otherwise, attracting readers for the book will be difficult. To prepare for the booktalk, read the book, think about the things that make it work, and listen to the voice of the book. Put the book aside and do other things. The parts that come back to you over the next few days will be the ones to include in your talk.

Booktalks may include one or more books. A common subject or theme—animals, war, survival, terror, love, secrets, outsiders—can link multiple books. A variety of reading levels, genre, and cultures will appeal to a wide range of reading interests and push readers a little beyond where they might go on their own (Rochman, 1989).

Booktalks usually follow one of three styles: (a) tell highlights of the book, (b) read highlights from the book, (c) combine telling and reading. For instance, a booktalk on *Eva* by Peter Dickinson might begin by telling about the hospital scene with the sobbing mother and Eva's confusion as she comes out of a coma, followed by reading a quotation in which Eva talks about living in a chimpanzee's body: "You had to awaken and open your eyes and see your new face and like what you saw. You had to make the human greeting and the chimp greeting and mean them."

EVALUATING ORAL STORY EXPERIENCES

"Experience without reflection is hollow" (Cooper & Collins, 1992, p. 3). Guided discussion gives children an opportunity to reflect on oral experiences, respond to them, offer support to their classmates, and think about future experiences. They can also be used to elicit constructive criticism. For instance, questions such as the following, partially suggested by Cooper and Collins, could be used to evaluate a creative drama:

1. What did you like best about this playing?
2. When was the imagination really at work?
3. When were the characters most believable?
4. What did you learn from the playing that you did not know from the telling?
5. What did you learn about the important ideas in this story?
6. Did we leave out anything in this playing?
7. What would you like to try in our next playing of the scene?

8. What other things could our characters do or say?
9. How can we make our playing even more believable?

SILENT READING

Understanding is the goal of all reading, whether being read aloud to, reading silently, or reading aloud for an audience. All reading is an interactive process. Reading aloud to children gives them a model for reading and language development, which they use during silent reading to increase their reading and language skills. With practice, silent reading becomes more fluent and readers can readily perceive ideas in the text. Children who read more show large differences in their reading abilities as a result of their practice (Fractor, Woodruff, Martinez, & Teale, 1993). Silent reading, which precedes reading aloud to others, permits readers to focus on meaning without being overly involved with pronouncing words. Oral reading requires readers to think ahead of their voices and prepare to pronounce the next word or phrase, a skill that develops over time with extensive practice in silent reading.

Literature Circles

Literature circles are small, temporary discussion groups who have chosen to read the same story, poem, article, or book. Each group member prepares to take specific responsibilities in the discussion and the participants come to group with the notes they have taken to help them with their responsibilities. The reading circles have regular meetings with the discussion roles rotating for each meeting. After they finish a book, the circle members plan to share the highlights of their reading with others in the classroom or school. Then they form different groups, select another reading, and begin a new cycle. After the readers learn to sustain their discussions, they may drop the specific roles in the discussion (Daniels, 1994).

The goal of reading circles is to create open, natural conversations about books students have read. Divergent, open-ended, interpretive questions and critical reading questions encourage reader response and discussion. Questions such as the following encourage readers to read, process, savor, and share their personal response. When organizing literature circles, teachers give students sample questions to help them begin, but teachers point out that the best discussion questions come from their own thoughts, feelings, and concerns. The following are sample questions (Daniels, 1994).

A big sister likes to read to her brothers.

- What was going through your mind while you read this?
- What was discussed in this (a specific) part of the book?
- Can someone summarize briefly?
- Did today's reading remind you of any real-life experiences?
- What questions did you have when you finished this section?
- Did anything in the book surprise you?
- What are the one or two most important ideas?
- Predict some things you think will be talked about next.

Children participating in reading circles may choose passages to be shared using these guidelines: important, surprising, funny, confusing, informative, controversial, well written, thought-provoking (Daniels, 1994). We recommend that you read Harvey Daniels's book because it provides excellent ideas based on teachers' experiences developing reading circles. Another helpful book for students in middle school is *You Gotta Be the Book* by Jeffrey D. Wilhelm.

Book and Breakfast

Book and Breakfast has been implemented in Chesterfield County, Virginia, schools. Participants in this program read designated books and discuss them with volunteer mothers leading the discussion. The volunteer leaders read the book and are provided a discussion guide. The discussions take place before school and the students have breakfast while talking about their books. Both students and volunteer discussion leaders enjoy Book and Breakfast.

Uninterrupted Sustained Silent Reading (USSR-DEAR-SSR)

Uninterrupted sustained silent reading (USSR), also known as DEAR (drop everything and read) or SSR (sustained silent reading), is usually regarded as a logical counterpart to daily oral reading. USSR is predicated on the idea that teachers regularly involve children in learning the skills of reading, but they often overlook giving children time to practice reading, thereby developing reading fluency. USSR also makes children aware that reading and books are important; it allows them to experience whole books rather than fragments, and it gives them practice in sustaining attention, thinking, and reading.

Effective USSR programs require a foundation of reading materials that is broad enough to include materials appropriate to the age, development, and reading levels of all the children involved. These materials may include books, periodicals, magazines, newspapers, reference books, and any other type of reading material that might interest the children. They should be in the classroom library where children can readily obtain them. Select books from the school library and obtain extended loans from the local public library to stock classroom shelves.

When developing a USSR program, teachers should first explain the purpose and procedures. The students should understand that they may bring reading material to class or select from the classroom library, but they are not to move around the room, draw, talk, or do anything other than read. Everyone reads; teachers should allow no interruptions and require no reports on their reading.

At the outset, allocate 5 to 10 minutes for first and second graders and 10 to 15 minutes for third through sixth graders. The time can gradually be increased as children grow more comfortable with the process. The time of day varies among schools and teachers. Some schools have schoolwide programs that involve everyone in the school reading at the same time. In other schools individual teachers schedule USSR when it fits best in their schedules. Some teachers have students maintain records of their reading through a log of titles or number of pages read or through a reading journal. Some teachers give the students time to share poems or excerpts from their reading.

Fostering Silent Reading

The best way teachers can foster silent reading is to provide many opportunities for silent reading such as USSR. Silent reading, however, is not a directly observable skill. Teaching children how to read silently through guided silent reading is important, as is providing opportunities for readers to respond to silent reading through discussion and other activities.

Guided silent reading

Teachers should begin by guiding children to read silently or "read with their eyes." Then encourage them to think about what they read as they read it. Demonstrate the thinking that occurs during silent reading by means of a "think-aloud," in which the teacher or a fluent reader verbalizes what occurs in their minds while they read silently. For example, reading "A treasure hunt—today's the day. Come on in and you can play!" (Cauley, *Treasure Hunt*) might lead a reader to think of questions such as:

- What kind of a treasure hunt?
- What is the treasure?
- Is it a Saturday or summer vacation, because these children should be in school?
- Who are they inviting to the treasure hunt?

These demonstrations guide students toward understanding how to think as they read silently—which simply admonishing them to think does not do—and enhance their response to literature.

Perhaps most important to developing silent reading skill is helping readers develop authentic reasons, or purposes, for silent reading. Silent reading that is active and purposeful enhances understanding and response. Again, purpose in reading is not directly observable, so teachers must guide readers' understanding and development of purpose. All students learn best when they create purposes for themselves. In the same way that thinking in reading can be modeled through think-alouds, a teacher or good reader can model or talk about authentic purposes. In this way, others can understand what purposes in silent reading are and can learn to develop their own purposes. Another way of modeling purpose in silent reading is to work with a group as a whole to develop purposes in listening to a story that is read aloud, as shown here with *Splash!* by Ann Jonas:

1. Introduce the book to the children by reading the title, *Splash,* and asking what they think the story will be about. Such anticipation activities will give the students something to think about as they read—a purpose.

2. Write their responses on the chalkboard and ask them to think, as they hear the story, whether the splash in the story is what they expected. This will develop their sense of listening purpose and help them to actively and purposefully listen as you read.

3. Ask the children which character in the story they liked best. Answering this question develops purpose because readers see the story through the eyes of characters they like, which focuses their attention.

4. Ask them why they think Ann Jonas wrote this book. Thinking about why the author wrote the book will allow them to compare the author's purpose in writing with their purpose in listening and will develop their understanding of purpose.

Prereading discussions and purposeful listening activities such as these connect readers and books. They will be most useful and understandable for the children when they are based on the children's own questions. (Figure 12.4 shows a web of student questions generated from the title of *All Pigs Are Beautiful* by Dick King-Smith. As they begin to develop their own purposes and read silently, encourage them to read the entire story, poem, or informational piece because they can respond more fully to a complete work than to a fragment. Questions and activities for silent reading should encourage this by focusing on the entire piece.

Responding to silent reading

Students can respond to and organize their silent reading in many ways. Class discussion is a tried-and-true method of allowing some children to respond to their reading. Prompts (discussed in chapter 3) are useful in eliciting oral and written responses. Reflecting about a story and participating in written dialogues and discussions develop comprehension. Participating in a community of readers, dramatizing a story, or preparing for literature circles also give opportunities for response and peer feedback. Individual response could include completing a story grammar of the book or choosing a character and explaining why this individual is their favorite. Figure 12.4 illustrates a third-grade reader's response to *All Pigs Are Beautiful.*

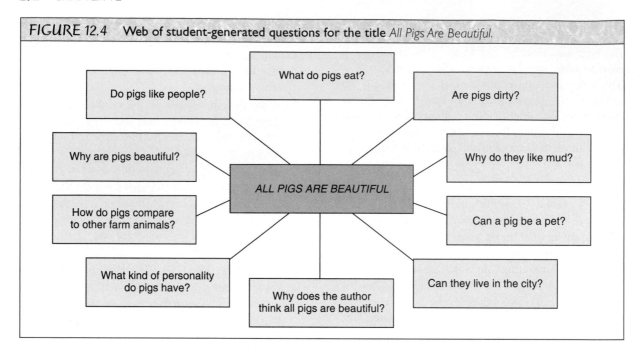

FIGURE 12.4 Web of student-generated questions for the title *All Pigs Are Beautiful.*

Unit Suggestions

ACTIVITY 12.1 RAINY'S POWWOW

Introduction

In this tale of self-discovery and acceptance, a young girl learns that she must listen to and follow her own heart.

The Thunderbird Powwow is about to begin and Rainy still does not know what style of dance to choose so that she can be given her own special name. She asks Grandmother White Hair (who had been a traditional dancer), the Powwow Princess (who is a shawl dancer), and her friend Celeste (who is a jingle dancer) what it feels like to dance in their chosen styles. But none of these seem right for Rainy. As the dancing begins, Rainy enters the arena, but she is too shy to move. Then, listening to the drumbeats, Rainy moves with the rhythm and keeps on dancing even when the music stops. The sound of laughter gradually reaches Rainy, who flees the dance floor, embarrassed and humiliated. Grandmother White Hair's words comfort her, but it is the eagle's gift

that gives Rainy her special name and the inspiration to choose her own dance.

Quality children's books are enjoyable just for their stories and pictures. However, activities such as those here can help teachers develop the themes of a book in a more complete way. This guide highlights things from nature, a major theme in *Rainy's Powwow.*

Soaring with the Eagles

This activity can be an individual project, incorporated into cooperative grouping, or completed with partners working together. For younger students, show pictures of eagles and orally lead a fact-finding discussion about the birds. As a class, brainstorm the facts chosen to be included in the eagle books, then have students write the same facts in their booklets. The layered booklets must be made ahead of time and distributed when the students have chosen their six facts. Ask students to write a title for their booklets and illustrate the covers.

Developed by rising Moon Books from Northland Publishing, Flagstaff, Arizona, for *Rainy's Powwow* by Linda Theresa Raczek.

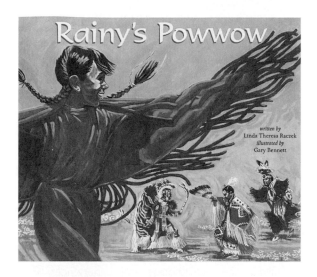

Book Connection   "Little Sister," Saleen said. "An eagle circled the arbor during the dance and dropped this in your path. In this way the eagle has honored you with a name. White Plume Dancing, this is your eagle feather."

Information   Eagles are very important to the spiritual traditions of Native North Americans. The birds are celebrated as animals of power, strength, and grace. The symbolism of eagles can be seen throughout the United States. As in the book, the eagle feather is honored in Native American headdresses as well as eagle totems, arrows, myths, and dances. Eagle feathers are cherished and celebrated.

Activity   Research information about eagles. Create your own "layered" eagle fact book complete with illustration.

- Research information about eagles from books, movies, magazines, and the Internet.
- After reviewing your newfound information, create a booklet by choosing six of your favorite facts about eagles and listing them on separate pieces of paper. You'll need a paper cutter, stapler, and ruler.
- Each eagle fact should be written in sentence form on the bottom of each layered page. Regular 8 1/2″ × 11″ paper works well if complete sentences are used. The remainder of the page is used for illustrations; thus, the last page of the booklet has the most room for illustrations. There will be a total of seven pieces of white pa-

per stapled together at the top. The cover will be 4 inches in length, and the attached pages will be increased in length by 1 inch from the previous page. Each flap will lift up to reveal the illustration underneath. (Smaller versions of this layered booklet are also fun for students!)

- When the booklet is complete, you should be able to read all the eagle facts without lifting the pages!
- Share your book with a friend!

Powwow Headpieces

Book Connection   "They watched the soldiers march by solemnly, holding flags high over their heads. Then came the traditional dancers slowly, in buckskin and feathers, porcupine quills, shells, beads—all things from nature."

Activity   Create your own powwow headpiece using items found on a nature walk.

- Before starting out on a nature scavenger hunt, make a list of the items you will be searching for. (Keep in mind you will need small, light objects.)
- Discuss the possibilities of what you may find on your walk.
- Discuss the difference between litter and objects in nature.
- Review the necessary safety rules before beginning your nature walk. Try to plan your walk outside of the school playground where you are more likely to find things in their natural state.
- Bring a paper lunch sack with you to collect your items.
- Upon returning from the nature walk, list your newfound treasures on paper. Compare both the prediction list and the new list. Were you surprised by some of the items you found? Were you unable to find any items on your prediction list?
- Choose one or two items from your bag and describe it to a classmate using as many descriptive words as possible.
- Use a 2-inch-wide tag board band as a basic pattern for the headpiece. Make sure the band will fit around your head, but do not staple the ends together until the project is complete. Use your items from nature, as well as additional materials to create a unique and colorful headpiece!

Sample list of things found in nature:

- feathers
- dirt
- shells
- flowers
- quills
- bark
- pebbles
- leaves

- seeds
- grass
- thorns
- berries
- sticks
- nuts
- sand
- bone

Suggested additional materials:

- construction paper
- glue
- stapler
- crayons
- string
- ribbon
- craft feathers

- paint
- scissors
- yarn
- tag board
- sequins
- rulers
- beads

Further Activities

1. Lorraine admires the powwow princess. "If I were the powwow princess," Lorraine boasted, "my shawl would glitter like gold. When I danced, people would admire my steps. I would win every contest." Complimenting another person is a rewarding experience; it makes you feel good about yourself. Whom do you admire and why? Think of a person you admire and list five kind things about him. Write a letter to a person you admire, telling him why you feel this way. Send the letter if possible.

2. Lorraine is embarrassed during her first attempt at powwow dancing. "I feel so ashamed," she said. "I will never learn to dance!" Her Grandmother encourages her to try again. What activities have you tried that were difficult at first? Did you keep trying, or give up easily? When you finally succeeded, how did you feel? Ask your parents about a time when they felt discouraged but kept practicing until the skill was mastered.

3. Grandmother, Lorraine, and Raymond have a close relationship and show respect for each other. How do you and your family members show you care about each other? Tell about a day when you did something kind for a family member. Write the definition of respect in your own words.

4. Native Americans treat their elders with deep respect and honor. Honor your grandparents by holding a "Grandparent Tea" and invite them to tell about their childhoods and experiences. Treat them to snacks and a homemade gift.

5. Make your own powwow drum using an empty cylindrical oatmeal container. Cover with colored construction paper and decorate.

6. Native Americans use herbs for various purposes. Research this topic and grow your own herb garden in the classroom.

7. Powwows encourage intertribal communication and enhance common interest among Native Americans. They are festivals of culture, tradition, celebration, and reflection. Think of other times when families and friends gather together during the year: family reunions, birthdays, religious occasions, weddings, picnics, and parties. Name various traditions that take place during these occasions: blowing out the candles on a cake, hitting a piñata, gift giving, dancing, games, eating, and firework displays. Discuss the importance of these social gatherings. Why are they important?

SUMMARY

Oral and silent reading strategies give students opportunities to experience literature and to respond to it in highly motivating situations. Both oral and silent reading strategies focus on the meaning of literature. Both are appropriate approaches to all genre. In many instances, oral and silent reading are integrated because children who are preparing for oral performances read silently in anticipation of oral reading. One of the major differences between oral and silent reading is that oral readers must think of word pronunciation and produce the appropriate sounds for a word. This makes oral reading a slower process than silent reading.

Oral reading concerns interpreting written literature for the appreciation of listeners, thus it is related to its artistic dimension. Oral reading serves other needs as well. For example, in the early years of schooling, children have limited reading abilities, which restrict their experiences with books, but oral reading, storytelling, choral reading, flannel board stories, dramatization, puppets, and booktalking give them a wide variety of literary experiences. Children who have experiences such as these come to books with greater understanding and appreciation, which enable children to develop an ear for the sound of written language and to understand a great deal about literature before they can read for themselves. In choosing literature for oral presentations, therefore, teachers need to consider the "sound" of the language.

Silent reading activities occur more often after children have acquired some reading abilities. USSR is an important silent reading activity, during which students read materials of their own choosing for their own purposes. The central focus is a period of time during which everyone reads, including any adults present.

should add color and dramatic appeal to the story when it is told aloud.

5. Choose a story for a flannel board presentation, prepare a script, and make the flannel board and the characters. Then present it to a group of children. Write about your experiences.

6. Choose a story for a puppet dramatization. Plan the script, make the puppets, practice the presentation. Present it to a group of children. Write about your experiences.

7. Listen to a recording of a professional storyteller and identify the strengths of the storyteller. List the ways that you could use this recording in the classroom.

8. Find storytelling on the Internet and listen to a story told by a professional storyteller.

Thought Questions

1. Why are the oral strategies so motivating for children?

2. How do these activities develop literacy?

3. Which of these activities will you use most often? Why?

4. Why do some teachers rarely if ever use activities such as those presented in this chapter?

5. Write a letter to convince a teacher to use the activities described in this chapter.

6. Is reading aloud to children important? Why or why not?

Research and Application Experiences

1. Choose a poem and plan a choral reading for it that involves individual and unison reading.

2. Prepare *Alexander and the Terrible, Horrible, No Good, Very Bad Day* by Judith Viorst for oral reading. Then make a tape of your reading for your own analysis.

3. Make a story map for *The House That Jack Built* by Nadine Westcott. This map can serve as your guide for telling this story.

4. Invent five descriptive phrases for the characters in *Goldilocks and the Three Bears*. These phrases

Children's Literature References and Recommended Books

Note: Books designated with an asterisk (*) are recommended for reluctant readers.

Aardema, V. (Reteller). (1975). *Why mosquitoes buzz in people's ears* (L. Dillon & D. Dillon, Illus.). New York: Dial. (PreK–3). TRADITIONAL LITERATURE.

Alexander, L. (1964). *The book of three.* New York: Holt, Rinehart & Winston. (4–8). MODERN FANTASY.

A story of magic and amazing feats.

Alexander, L. (1999). *Gypsy Rizka.* New York: Dutton. (3–6). MODERN FANTASY.*

A funny perils-of-Pauline type story. The episodic chapters will lend themselves to reading over several days.

Alphin, E. M. (1996). *A bear for Miguel* (J. Sandin, Illus.). New York: HarperCollins. (1–3). CONTEMPORARY REALISTIC FICTION.*

Andersen, H. C. (1978). *The princess and the pea* (P. Galdone, Illus.). New York: Seabury. (1–3). MODERN FANTASY.

Aranda, C. (1993). *Dichos: Proverbs and sayings from the Spanish.* Santa Fe, NM: Sunstone. (4–8). TRADITIONAL LITERATURE.

Asbjornsen, P. C., & Moe, J. (1982). *Norwegian folk tales.* New York: Pantheon. (K–6). TRADITIONAL LITERATURE.

Asch, F. (1995). *Water.* New York: Harcourt Brace. (K–3). INFORMATIONAL BOOK.*

The book tells about water and its importance.

Banks, L. R. (1988). *I, Houdini: The autobiography of a self-educated hamster* (T. Riley, Illus.). New York: Doubleday. (3–6). MODERN FANTASY.

Barlow, G. (1966). *Latin American tales: From the Pampas to the pyramids of Mexico* (W. M. Hutchinson, Illus.). Chicago: Rand McNally. (3–8). TRADITIONAL LITERATURE.

Borden, L. (1997). *The little ships: The heroic rescue at Dunkirk in World War II* (M. Foreman, Illus.). New York: McElderry. (3–5). HISTORICAL FICTION.*

The story of Dunkirk.

Burleigh, R. (1998). *Black whiteness: Admiral Byrd alone in the Antarctic* (W. L. Krudop, Illus.). New York: Atheneum. (3–8). BIOGRAPHY.

This is a biography told through entries in Admiral Byrd's journal written while he was alone. Beautifully illustrated.

Burningham, J. (1971). *Mr. Gumpy's outing.* New York: Macmillan. (PreK–1). PICTURE BOOK.

A cumulative tale with Mr. Gumpy and animals.

Byars, B. (1994). *The Golly sisters ride again* (S. Truesdell, Illus.). New York: HarperCollins. (1–3). HISTORICAL FICTION.*

Carlstrom, N. W. (1986). *Jesse Bear, what will you wear?* (B. Degen, Illus.). New York: Macmillan. (PreK–2). POETRY.

A young bear's activities are described in rhymes.

Carlstrom, N. W. (1992). *Baby-O* (S. Stevenson, Illus.). New York: Little, Brown. (Pre–K). POETRY.

Carr, J. (1999). *Swine divine* (R. Bender, Illus.). New York: Holiday House. (1–4). MODERN FANTASY.*

Farmer Luke bathes Rosie the pig and takes her to town, but she prefers mud.

Cauley, L. B. (1994). *Treasure hunt.* New York: Putnam. (1–3). CONTEMPORARY REALISTIC FICTION.*

In this clever mystery for younger children, the reader must go from clue to clue to solve the mystery.

Cazet, D. (1998). *Minnie and Moo go dancing.* New York: DK Publishing. (1–4). MODERN FANTASY.*

Minnie and Moo are cows who wish they could dance, so they dress up and put on makeup. When they get to the dance, the story really gets funny.

Chase, R. (Reteller). (1943). *The Jack tales.* Boston: Houghton Mifflin. (3–8). TRADITIONAL LITERATURE.

Cherry, L., & Plotkin, M. J. (1998). *The shaman's apprentice.* New York: Harcourt Brace. (2–5). CONTEMPORARY REALISTIC FICTION.

Kamanya lives in the Amazon rain forest. When he is sick, his mother takes him to the shaman. Kamanya never forgets the shaman who saves him.

Claverie, J. (Reteller). (1989). *The three little pigs.* New York: North South. (K–3). TRADITIONAL LITERATURE.

Cleaver, V., & Cleaver, B. (1969). *Where the lilies bloom* (J. Spanfeller, Illus.). New York: Harper & Row. (5–8). CONTEMPORARY REALISTIC FICTION.*

Mary Call is a very strong 14-year-old who takes care of her family after her father's death. The landlord wants to marry her older sister, Devola, who is "cloudy headed."

Cleaver, V., & Cleaver, B. (1977). *Trial valley.* Philadelphia: Lippincott. (5–8). CONTEMPORARY REALISTIC FICTION.

In this sequel to *Where the Lilies Bloom,* Devola and Kiser are married. They discover a child in a cave in the woods and decide to adopt him, but he prefers to stay with Mary Call.

Cowley, J. (1999). *Red-eyed tree frog* (N. Bishop, Illus.). New York: Scholastic. (1–3). INFORMATIONAL BOOK.

A nonfiction book providing a lively text with exquisite photographs of the red-eyed tree frog.

Dahl, R. (1996). *James and the giant peach* (L. Smith, Illus.). New York: Knopf. (3–6). MODERN FANTASY.

A mistreated boy escapes in a flying peach.

Dickinson, P. (1988). *Eva.* New York: Delacorte. (6–9). MODERN FANTASY.

Eva's body is destroyed in an accident, so her brain is implanted in the body of a chimpanzee. This science fiction story has a fascinating plot and characterization.

Fleming, C. (Reteller). (1998). *The hatmaker's sign: A story by Benjamin Franklin* (R. A. Parker, Illus.). New York: Orchard. (1–3). HISTORICAL FICTION.

Benjamin Franklin tells his friend Thomas Jefferson a story about a hatmaker.

Florian, D. (1999). *Laugh-eteria.* New York: Harcourt. (3–6). POETRY.

A collection of hilarious poems.

Fox, M. (1998). *Boo to a goose* (D. Miller, Illus.). New York: Dial. (K–2). PICTURE BOOK, CONTEMPORARY REALISTIC FICTION.

The child in this story would do almost anything except say "boo" to a goose.

Fox, P. (1973). *The slave dancer* (E. Keith, Illus.). New York: Bradbury. (6–10). HISTORICAL FICTION.

Jessie plays his flute on a slave ship.

Freedman, R. (1998). *Martha Graham, a dancer's life.* New York: Clarion. (4–8). BIOGRAPHY.

A well-written biography of dancer Martha Graham.

Galdone, P. (Reteller). (1984). *Henny Penny.* Boston: Houghton Mifflin. (1–2). TRADITIONAL LITERATURE.*

Gardiner, J. R. (1988). *Stone fox* (M. Sewall, Illus.). New York: Crowell. (3–6). CONTEMPORARY REALISTIC FICTION.

A boy enters a race to win money to help his grandfather.

Greaves, M. (Reteller). (1990). *Tattercoats.* New York: Potter. (1–3). TRADITIONAL LITERATURE.

A version of the *Cinderella* story.

Guthrie, W. (1998). *This land is your land* (K. Jakobsen, Illus.). (K–4). PICTURE BOOK.

Haley, G. E. (1986). *Jack and the bean tree.* New York: Crown. (1–4). TRADITIONAL LITERATURE.

An Appalachian version of Jack and the beanstalk.

Holt, D. (1994a). *Hairyman.* Fairview, NC: High Windy Audio. (All ages). TRADITIONAL LITERATURE.

Holt, D. (1994b). *Tailybone.* Fairview, NC: High Windy Audio. (All ages). TRADITIONAL LITERATURE.

Hooks, W. H. (1990). *The ballad of Belle Dorcas* (B. Pinkney, Illus.). New York: Knopf. (2–4). TRADITIONAL LITERATURE.

Howe, D., & Howe, J. (1979). *Bunnicula* (A. Daniel, Illus.). New York: Atheneum. (2–4). MODERN FANTASY.

A dog wrote this story about a vampire rabbit.

Jonas, A. (1995). *Splash!* New York: Greenwillow. (K–2). PICTURE BOOK, MODERN FANTASY.

Animals and children splash in a pool while adding and subtracting.

Kellogg, S. (Reteller). (1991). *Jack and the beanstalk.* New York: Morrow. (K–4). TRADITIONAL LITERATURE.

Kellogg, S. (Reteller). (1996). *I was born about 10,000 years ago.* New York: Morrow. (K–5). TRADITIONAL LITERATURE.*

This exuberant tall tale is based on an American folk song.

King-Smith, D. (1993). *All pigs are beautiful* (A. Jeram, Illus.). Cambridge, MA: Candlewick. (1–4). PICTURE BOOK.

The author shares his love of pigs by telling the details of their lives.

Kitt, T. (1988). So long as there's weather. In B. S. de Regniers, E. Moore, M. M. White, & J. Carr (Eds.), *Sing a song of popcorn.* New York: Scholastic. (K–6). POETRY.

Lester, J. (1968). *To be a slave* (T. Feelings, Illus.). New York: Dial. (5–12). INFORMATIONAL BOOK.

Descriptions of slave life based on interviews with former slaves.

Lester, J. (1969). *Black folktales* (T. Feelings, Illus.). New York: Baron. (3–12). TRADITIONAL LITERATURE.

Lester, J. (1987). *The tales of Uncle Remus: The adventures of Brer Rabbit* (J. Pinkney, Illus.). New York: Dial. (3–6). TRADITIONAL LITERATURE.

Littlechild, G. (1993). *This land is my land.* San Francisco: Children's Book Press. (3–6). BIOGRAPHY.

The author tells about his life through his art.

Louie, A.-L. (Reteller). (1982). *Yeh-Shen: A Cinderella story from China* (E. Young, Illus.). New York: Philomel. (1–3). TRADITIONAL LITERATURE.

Martin, B. Jr. (1967). *Brown Bear, Brown Bear, what do you see?* (E. Carle, Illus.). New York: Holt. (P–1). PICTURE BOOK.

A repetitive tale.

Merrill, J. (1964). *The pushcart war* (R. Solbert, Illus.). New York: Scott. (4–8). CONTEMPORARY REALISTIC FICTION.

The story of a war between pushcarts and trucks in New York.

Milne, A. A. (1926). *Winnie-the-Pooh* (E. H. Shepard, Illus.). New York: Dutton. (1–5). MODERN FANTASY.

Christopher Robin is part of the adventures of Pooh and his friends.

Naylor, P. R. (1991). *King of the playground* (N. L. Malone, Illus.). New York: Atheneum. (3–5). CONTEMPORARY REALISTIC FICTION.

O'Brien, R. C. (1974). *Mrs. Frisby and the rats of Nimh* (Z. Bernstein, Illus.). New York: Atheneum. (4–8). MODERN FANTASY.

Intelligent rats escape the National Institute of Mental Health.

O'Callahan, J. (1994a). *Little heroes.* Fairview, NC: High Windy Audio. (1–3).

O'Callahan, J. (1994b). *The boy who loved frogs.* West Tisbury, MA: Vineyard Video. (1–3).

O'Dell, S. (1960). *Island of the blue dolphins.* Boston: Houghton Mifflin. (4–6). HISTORICAL FICTION.

The story of a girl who survives alone on a Pacific island.

Perrault, C. (1997). *Cinderella*. New York: Aladdin. (K–2). TRADITIONAL LITERATURE.

This is Brown's retelling of Perrault's *Cinderella*.

Prelutsky, J. (1980). *Rolling Harvey down the hill* (V. Chess, Illus.). New York: Greenwillow. (K–2). POETRY.

Raczek, L. T. (1999). *Rainy's Powwow* (G. Bennett, Illus.). Flagstaff, AZ: Rising Moon. (2–5). CONTEMPORARY REALISTIC FICTION.

Rand, W. B. (1951). Godfrey, Gordon, Gustavus Gore. In M. H. Arbuthnot (Comp.), *Time for poetry*. Glenview, IL: Scott Foresman. (K–6). POETRY.

Richards, L. (1951). The umbrella brigade. In M. H. Arbuthnot (Comp.), *Time for poetry*. Glenview, IL: Scott Foresman. (K–6). POETRY.

Rosen, M. J. (Ed.). (1989). *We're going on a bear hunt* (H. Oxenbury, Illus.). New York: McElderry. (PreK–2). MODERN FANTASY.

The interesting, repetitious language in this story encourages participation by listeners as this old chant is told.

Rounds, G. (1990). *I know an old lady who swallowed a fly*. New York: Holiday. (1–6). TRADITIONAL LITERATURE.*

An old cumulative rhyme, which tells of an old lady who swallows all sorts of impossible things until she swallows a horse and "dies of course."

Rylant, C. (1985). *The relatives came* (S. Gammell, Illus.). New York: Bradbury. (2–4). CONTEMPORARY REALISTIC FICTION.

San Souci, R. D. (1998). *Fa Mulan: The story of a woman warrior* (J. Tseng & M. Tseng, Illus.). New York: Hyperion. (2–4). TRADITIONAL LITERATURE.

Schertle, A. (1999). *I am the cat* (M. Buehner, Illus.). New York: Lothrop, Lee & Shepard. (1–4). POETRY.

Seeger, P. (1994). *Stories and songs for little children*. Fairview, NC: High Windy Audio. (PreK–2).

Seuss, Dr. (1940). *Horton hatches the egg*. New York: Random House. (1–4). MODERN FANTASY.

Seuss, Dr. (1949). *Bartholomew and the Oobleck*. New York: Random House. (1–4). MODERN FANTASY.

Siebert, D. (1984). *Truck song* (B. Barton, Illus.). New York: Crowell. (1–4). POETRY.

Siebert, D. (1990). *Train song* (M. Wimmer, Illus.). New York: Crowell. (1–4). POETRY.

Smith, W. J. (1990). *Laughing time: Collected nonsense* (F. Krahn, Illus.). New York: Farrar, Straus & Giroux. (1–5). POETRY.

Soto, G. (1990). *Baseball in April and other stories*. New York: Harcourt Brace Jovanovich. (3–5). CONTEMPORARY REALISTIC FICTION.

Stanley, D. (1999). *Raising Sweetness* (G. B. Karas, Illus.). New York: Putnam. (1–4). CONTEMPORARY REALISTIC FICTION.*

Stevens, J. (Reteller). (1992). *The Bremen town musicians*. New York: Holiday House. (K–3). TRADITIONAL LITERATURE.

Stevens, J. R. (1999). *Twelve lizards leaping* (C. Mau, Illus.). Flagstaff, AZ: Rising Moon. (K–2). PICTURE BOOK.

A take-off on the traditional Christmas carol.

Taylor, M. D. (1976). *Roll of thunder, hear my cry*. New York: Dial. (5–9). HISTORICAL FICTION.

During the 1930s African-American families seek to retain their pride and integrity.

Taylor, M. D. (1987a). *The friendship* (M. Ginsburg, Illus.). New York: Scholastic. (4–8). HISTORICAL FICTION.*

The friendship between a black child and a white child causes problems when they are adults.

Taylor, M. (1987b). *The gold Cadillac* (M. Hays, Illus.). New York: Dial. (3–6). HISTORICAL FICTION.*

Driving in the segregated South was a hazardous undertaking, especially for a black family driving an expensive car.

Thurber, J. (1990). *Many moons* (M. Simont, Illus.). New York: Harcourt Brace Jovanovich. (4–6). MODERN FANTASY.

Tunnell, M. O., & Chilcoat, G. W. (1996). *The children of Topaz*. New York: Holiday House. (4–7). INFORMATIONAL BOOK.

This nonfiction book is based on a classroom diary that tells the story of a Japanese American internment camp.

Vigil, A. (Reteller). (1994). *The corn woman*. Englewood, CO: Libraries Unlimited. (5–8). TRADITIONAL LITERATURE.

Stories from the southwestern United States.

Viorst, J. (1972). *Alexander and the terrible, horrible, no good, very bad day* (R. Cruz, Illus.). New York: Atheneum. (K–6). PICTURE BOOK, CONTEMPORARY REALISTIC FICTION.

Alexander encounters most of the things that he dislikes in a single day. He wants to go to Australia to escape, but his mother says these things happen there, too.

Westcott, N. B. (1987). *Peanut butter and jelly.* New York: Dutton. (PreK–2). POETRY.

This traditional play-rhyme is based on a magic chef who makes peanut butter with the assistance of elephants who mash the peanuts and stomp the grapes for jelly.

Westcott, N. (1990). *I know an old lady who swallowed a fly.* New York: Dutton. (1–6). POETRY.

White, E. B. (1952). *Charlotte's web* (G. Williams, Illus.). New York: Harper. (2–5). MODERN FANTASY.

A spider saves the pig's life.

Wilder, L. I. (1953). *Little house on the prairie* (G. Williams, Illus.). New York: Harper. (4–7). HISTORICAL FICTION.*

The story of the Wilder family.

Wisniewski, D. (1998). *The secret knowledge of grown-ups.* New York: Lothrop, Lee & Shepard. (K–4). MODERN FANTASY.*

This book opens secret files, hidden from kids for thousands of years. Are you ready for the real reasons that grown-ups tell children to drink their milk and other things?

Wood, A. (1984). *The napping house* (D. Wood, Illus.). New York: Harcourt. (K–2). PICTURE BOOK.

A cumulative tale about a rainy afternoon nap.

References and Books for Further Reading

Barton, B. (1986). *Tell me another.* Portsmouth, NH: Heinemann.

Busching, B. (1981, March). Readers theater: An education for language and life. *Language Arts, 58,* 330–338.

Champlin, C., & Renfro, N. (1985). *Storytelling with puppets.* Chicago: American Library Association.

Cohen, D. (1968). The effect of literature on vocabulary and reading achievement. *Elementary English, 45,* 209–213, 217.

Cooper, P., & Collins, R. (1992). *Look what happened to frog: Storytelling in Education.* Scottsdale, AZ: Gorsuch Scarisbrick.

Cullinan, B., Jaggar, A., & Strickland, D. (1974). Language expansion for Black children in the primary grades: A research report. *Young Children, 29,* 98–112.

Daniels, H. (1994). *Literature circles: Voice and choice in the student-centered classroom.* York, ME: Stenhouse.

Downing, J., & Leong, C. K. (1982). *Psychology of reading.* New York: Macmillan.

Engler, L., & Fijan, C. (1973). *Making puppets come alive.* New York: Taplinger.

Fakih, K. O. (1993). *The literature of delight.* New Providence, NJ: R. R. Bowker.

Fractor, J. S., Woodruff, M. C., Martinez, M. G., & Teale, W. H. (1993). Let's not miss opportunities to promote voluntary reading: Classroom libraries in the elementary school. *Reading Teacher, 46,* 476–484.

Frye, N. (1964). *The educated imagination.* Bloomington, IN: Indiana University.

Golden, J. M. (1984). Children's concept of story in reading and writing. *Reading Teacher, 37,* 578–584.

Heathcote, D. (1983). Learning, knowing, and languaging in drama: An interview with Dorothy Heathcote. *Language Arts, 60,* 695–701.

Labbo, L., & Field, S. (1996). Bookalogues: Oral language and language play. *Language Arts, 73,* 8.

Lenz, L. (1992). Crossroads of literacy and orality: Reading poetry aloud. *Language Arts, 69,* 597–603.

Lester, J. (1988). The storyteller's voice: Reflections on the rewriting of Uncle Remus. *New Advocate, 1,* 143–147.

Livo, N. J., & Rietz, S. A. (1986). *Storytelling process and practice.* Littleton, CO: Libraries Unlimited.

MacDonald, M. R. (1982). *The storyteller's sourcebook: A subject, title and motif index to folklore collections for children.* Detroit: Neal-Schuman.

Manna, A. L. (1984). Making language come alive through reading plays. *Reading Teacher, 37,* 713–717.

Martinez, M., Roser, N., & Strecker, S. (1998–1999). I never thought I could be a star: A readers' theater ticket to fluency. *Reading Teacher, 52,* 326–334.

McCaslin, N. (1990). *Creative drama in the classroom* (5th ed.). New York: Longman.

Miccinati, J. (1985). Using prosodic cues to teach oral reading fluency. *Reading Teacher, 39,* 206–212.

Morrow, L. M. (1979). *Super tips for story telling.* New York: Scholastic.

Morrow, L. M. (1988). Young children's responses to one-to-one story readings in school settings. *Reading Research Quarterly, 23,* 89–107.

Naylor, A., & Borders, S. (1993). *Children talking about books.* Portsmouth, NH: Heinemann.

Perfect, K. A. (1999). Rhyme and reason: Poetry for the heart and head. *Reading Teacher, 52,* 728–737.

Puppeteers of America. (1989). *The consultant's notebook.* Chicago: Puppeteers of America.

Purcell-Gates, V. (1988). Lexical syntactic knowledge of written narrative held by well-read-to kindergartners and second graders. *Research in Teaching English, 22,* 128–160.

Rochman, H. (1989). "Booktalking: Going global." *Horn Book, 58,* 30–35.

Roe, B., Alfred, S., & Smith, S. (1998). *Teaching through stories: Yours, mine, and theirs.* Norwood, MA: Christopher-Gordon.

Roney, R. C. (1989). Back to the basics with storytelling. *Reading Teacher, 42,* 520–523.

Ross, R. R. (1972). *Storyteller.* Columbus, OH: Merrill.

Sawyer, R. (1962). *The way of the storyteller.* New York: Viking.

Siks, G. (1983). *Drama with children (2nd ed.).* New York: Harper & Row.

Stoodt, B. D. (1988). *Teaching language arts.* New York: Harper & Row.

Teale, W. H., & Martinez, M. (1987). *Connecting writing: Fostering emergent literacy in kindergarten children.* Technical Report No. 412. San Antonio, TX: University of Texas at San Antonio.

Wilhelm, J. D. (1997). *You gotta be the book.* New York: Teachers College Press.

Literature for Children with Real-Life Challenges

13

KEY TERMS

challenged students

diverse background

exceptional students

inclusion

individual differences

individualized
  education plan
  (IEP)

mainstreaming

GUIDING QUESTIONS

As you read this chapter, think about the following questions and answer them after you complete the chapter.

1. What principles should you consider when selecting literature that addresses the challenges that children encounter?

2. How important is literature for and about children with special challenges? Why?

3. How is inclusion related to this chapter?

OVERVIEW

The typical all-American family simply does not exist today. The family image of years past—two middle-class White parents, a stay-at-home mom with an apron, and a go-to-work dad with a briefcase, two children, a dog and a cat, and a single-family dwelling with a picket fence—is gone forever. That is not to say that people in the past had no challenges, but their problems reflected the simpler society and the morality of the times. In books, many characters were portrayed as simplistic stereotypes of good or bad behaviors that failed to convey the true complexity of children's personalities and of their lives. However, children's literature has evolved, leading to a depiction of reality that resonates with children's lives today. Real-life literature addresses families facing many challenges: children with disabilities, abused children, substance abuse, divorce, and other difficulties (Peck, 1983). Children's lives have changed, as have their books, and as their lives changed, the demographics of the student population in the United States changed.

INTRODUCTION

Real-life literature addresses families facing many different challenges, children with disabilities, abused children, substance abuse, divorce, and other difficulties (Peck, 1983). Children's lives have changed, as have their books, and as their lives changed, the demographics of the student population in the United States changed.

These changes are in fact accelerating. Schools today embrace a diverse student population including hearing and sight impairments, impaired mobility, economic disadvantages, cultural differences, giftedness, emotional disabilities, and mental disabilities. These students are no longer segregated because society is becoming more sensitive to the special needs of all people. Current educational philosophy encourages each individual to realize his or her full potential.

Sensitivity to the special needs of students escalated when Public Law 94–142 was passed in 1978. This law provides for the education of all children with disabilities and requires that these students be taught in the least restrictive educational environment possible, which often involves mainstreaming. In mainstreaming, exceptional students spend a large part of the school day in regular classrooms. Each of these students is provided with an individualized education plan (IEP) to map out the most suitable education for the student with special needs. Parents are invited to participate in the planning process, and the IEP is not implemented until the student's parents have approved it. Inclusion of exceptional students is a major movement in education: the goal is to place challenged students in classrooms with fewer students and to provide an aide or assistant who will work to help the child participate in the regular classroom. However, the implementation of these laws differs among schools due to local administration and funding; the wide range of implementation makes generalizing about educating challenged students impossible.

VIGNETTE

Principal Mary Allison hailed Steve Liu as he signed in for the day.

"Hi! How are you this fine morning?"

"Good," replied Mr. Liu.

"We need to chat for a few minutes about a new student you'll be getting in a few weeks," Mrs. Allison said.

"This is a lot of notice," Mr. Liu responded.

"You'll probably need it because this student is legally blind. He can see only the difference between light and dark and will have a tutor. You'll need time to create a good learning environment for everyone," Mrs. Allison replied.

Mr. Liu looked thoughtful. "This should be interesting. I've just started reading Jean Little's autobiography, *Little by Little*. She is virtually blind and lives a full life. The children enjoyed her book *Different Dragons* so much I decided to read her autobiography to them. They were appalled at the way she was treated by other children."

"Good! Do you think your students could find additional literature, films, and Web sites about blind and partially sighted people?" Mrs. Allison asked.

"I'm sure we can. The media specialist will help," he answered.

"Then we can prepare the entire school. This could be the beginning of a schoolwide study of people with special challenges," Mrs. Allison said.

Mr. Liu nodded his agreement, then stopped short. "Say, I just had a thought! Would it be all right with you if the fifth graders dramatized some of the incidents in *Little by Little?*"

Belle Prater's boy lived a mysterious life and his friend was determined to solve his mystery.

THE VALUE OF REAL-LIFE LITERATURE

Literature, as this book has emphasized many times, can be a powerful influence in children's lives. Many children who had special challenges growing up can now write about their childhood. Sandra Wilde (1989) provides an example in the following quotation.

> My reason for telling this story is to celebrate the power of literature in helping us to know who we really are, and the power of the human spirit to recognize and remember that true self despite pain and adversity. . . .
>
> Many years ago, I looked like any other little girl on the outside, but there was something different about me on the inside. My parents were two needy people who didn't know how to love, and I spent much of my childhood being either bullied or casually ignored. . . . Fortunately, I had the public library. (p. 49)

Many people do not intend to be insensitive, but they unwittingly contribute to children's feelings of inadequacy. However, children's books enable students to understand and appreciate themselves and others. Reading about characters who face challenges gives children who have special needs opportunities to identify with them. Equally important, such literature can cultivate in other students an understanding, empathy, and appreciation of challenged people. Children who have never interacted with disabled persons and who are not challenged themselves lack exposure to or experience with life's challenges. The way children view such challenges of living is based on the values learned in their homes and schools.

Teaching values is a controversial educational issue, yet liberals and conservatives alike decry a "moral crisis" among young people. They attribute increased school violence to youngsters who do not know right from wrong. Influential educators such as Thomas Lickona and Nel Noddings have studied these issues. Contentious issues surround values clarification; to wit: Can we actually teach values? What values should be taught? When should values be taught? Who should teach values? How should values be taught? Although this book cannot resolve these thorny issues, literature can serve as a context for inquiry into values. Books such as Lickona's *Educating for Character* (1992), Noddings's *The Challenge to Care in Schools* (1992), and Andrews's *Teaching Kids to Care* (1994) are helpful resources. For instance, in *Teaching Kids to Care,* Andrews includes units of study and lists of literature for an inquiry approach to values. She includes topics such as appreciation of differences, empathy, compassion, homelessness, consequences of doing right and wrong, gentleness, obedience, self-concept, individuality and independence, honesty, honor, patience, and many others.

These values are apparent in Karen Hesse's books; she is profiled on page 305.

SELECTING AND EVALUATING REAL-LIFE LITERATURE

When selecting appropriate literature, teachers should consider character portrayal, as well as literary quality (Sage, 1977). Unfortunately, many folktales depict people with physical deformities as villains or use them to frighten and menace other story characters (Rudman, 1993). Teachers and media specialists must analyze literature with great sensitivity to avoid presenting books that express insensitive attitudes and to

Author Profile: Karen Hesse

Immersing myself in Karen Hesse's writing was a rewarding experience. After reading her extraordinary books, I focused on her books addressing the problems that youngsters must endure in the past, present, and future. In *Letters from Rifka,* she wrote about 12-year-old Rifka Nebrot and her family who fled the anti-Semitism of postrevolutionary Russia. On Ellis Island, she was held in quarantine because ringworm had left her bald. Nyle in the book *Phoenix Rising* faces problems of future life. A leak in a Vermont nuclear plant has spread contamination throughout New England, leaving death and ruination in its wake. The plot raises important issues—environmental disaster, friendship, first love, loss, and death. A dramatically different plot and character are introduced in *The Music of Dolphins,* which revolves around a girl who was reared by dolphins. After scientists discover her, they plan to teach her how to live in human society, which she quickly learns is not as honest and gentle as dolphin society. Karen Hesse received the Newbery Medal for *Out of the Dust,* which is set in Midwest America's dustbowl of the 1930s. Billie Jo Kelby, the protagonist, faces terrible problems because her mother and the infant she was carrying were killed by an accident for which Billie Jo is blamed. She must mature to the point of forgiving each one who contributed to her problems.

The children I interviewed from grades 4 through 8 recommended these books without reservation (Stoodt-Hill, 1999). Many of them volunteered that one or the other of these books was the best they had ever read. Another interesting comment from the majority of readers was their plan to reread one or more of the books. When asked to identify the feature they liked best about Karen Hesse's writing, they responded that they liked her characters and really cared about them. They also said that her books were true; the author wrote truth, not that the stories had actually happened.

In her Newbery acceptance speech Karen Hesse (1998) said, "I never make up any of the bad things that happen to my characters. I love my characters too much to hurt them deliberately. . . . It just so happens in life, there's pain; sorrow lives in the shadow of joy, joy in the shadow of sorrow." She also said that "we have to decide—do we let the pain reign triumphant, or do we find a way to grow, to transform, and ultimately transcend our pain?" (p. 435).

---

present literature that addresses the problems many children experience.

However a literary work portrays characters with disabilities, each poem, story, or informational piece must have literary merit, or it will not attract readers. Books that are written to teach or preach rarely capture readers' interest. In *Stay Away from Simon!* Carol Carrick creates an excellent adventure story set on Martha's Vineyard in the 1830s. Lucy and her friend Desire are afraid of Simon, a handicapped boy they see laughing and playing in the schoolyard snow. When snow closes the school, Lucy and her little brother start home together, but lose their way in the snow. When they hear a deep voice, they are afraid it is Simon, but he appears and saves them by guiding them home. This story is an exciting, suspenseful one that is enhanced with well-drawn characters that include a boy with physical disabilities. The disabled character in this story is an active participant in the plot.

Another example of sensitive character portrayal is found in Barbara Corcoran's *Child of the Morning,* in which Susan suffers a skull fracture in a volleyball game at school. Her dizzy "spells" continue so long that everyone in the small town, including her own sister, considers her strange. Her sister believes that Susan's strange behavior has caused a decline in the family business. Everyone in town refused to give Susan a summer job. Finally, she finds work with a summer theater, and she is given a small part in a play where she is treated with respect rather than pity. Nevertheless, Susan is concerned about her future. Her character is fully developed through her interactions with other characters, her actions, and her thoughts. This book develops children's awareness of the emotional aspects of physical disabilities.

As in all quality literature, story characters in real-life literature are portrayed as complex personalities with strengths, flaws, problems, feelings, and responses. Any characters with disabilities should be clearly integral to the plot and not an expendable part of the background. Characters with disabilities are capable of helping others and of having loving family relationships and friendships. The characters with disabilities develop through their experiences, just as individuals without disabilities do. Authors, however, need to avoid stereotypical behavior in characters with disabilities and avoid superhuman portrayals, a device often used by authors to make handicapped characters more acceptable (Rudman, 1993). Characters with disabilities must be permitted to have ordinary flaws and to be average, nonspectacular people, although characters should be people that readers will care about. The plot in a good book focuses on what they can do (Landrum, 1998–1999).

The major characters in Karen Hesse's *Just Juice* are complex and multidimensional: Juice is her daddy's girl and like him she cannot read. His illiteracy is a factor in his unemployment and his tax problems. Hesse portrays an out-of-the mainstream existence that many Americans do not know about. However, readers will recognize Juice's strength and determination in the face of adversity. Gary also has a learning problem in Cutler's *Spaceman.* He has dyslexia and experiences the dilemma facing many children because he is misplaced and misunderstood.

Fiction and nonfiction should provide honest, up-to-date, realistic information and advice about any disabling condition. Miracle cures are not possible for all handicapping conditions. Some authors portray a disability as something that positive thinking, prayer, and hard work will overcome. This has the effect of making it seem as if the disability is somehow the person's own fault and that good behavior or wishing can cure the condition (Rudman, 1993).

Two books are of particular value when choosing books that have characters with disabilities. One volume, *Portraying Persons with Disabilities: An Annotated Bibliography of Fiction for Children and Teenagers,* by Joan Friedberg, June Mullins, and Adelaide Sukiennik, addresses nonfiction works (1992), while the other, *Portraying Persons with Disabilities: An Annotated Bibliography of Nonfiction for Children and Teenagers,* by Debra Robertson, addresses fiction (1992). Two references that describe books written before 1990 are *Notes From a Different Drummer* by Baskin and Harris (1977) and *More Notes From a Different Drummer* by Baskin and Harris (1984).

Landrum (1998–1999) has developed an excellent guide for evaluating novels for adolescent readers about challenged characters. We found that many of her items were similar to ours, and were appropriate for children's books as well. The following criteria summarize our standards.

Character development

1. Challenged characters are strong or become stronger and more competent through the plot events.
2. Challenged characters are portrayed through what they can do.
3. Challenged characters are multidimensional characters whose emotions, strengths, and weaknesses are portrayed.
4. Challenged characters are not portrayed as overly heroic or as victims.
5. Challenged characters are portrayed as participating in a family and having friends.
6. Challenged characters' handicaps are accurately portrayed.

Plot

7. The plot is realistic and avoids contrived events and miracle cures.
8. The challenged characters experience events similar to the experiences and conflicts of their peer group.
9. All of the story events are realistic and uncontrived.

Tone

10. The story avoids terms that label the challenged characters.
11. The story should leave the challenged characters with hope.

The following discussions of children's books featuring characters with special problems is categorized by the specific problems of the characters, including hearing impairments, visual impairments, health problems, abuse, substance abuse, physical handicaps, emotional handicaps, and mental handicaps. The majority of books with handicapped characters fall into the categories of realistic fiction, historical fiction, and informational books. Example selections from the various genres are included in this discussion.

Hearing Challenges

Children with hearing impairments exhibit a full range of individual differences. Their experiences, families, interests, intelligence, and motivation are as diverse as those of other children. Their impairments may range from moderate to severe: Some live in a silent world whereas others may hear a few sounds. Hearing aids may help some people with hearing impairments to perceive as much sound as possible. However, children whose hearing is impaired usually have distorted or incomplete auditory input even with hearing aids and have difficulty producing and understanding speech sounds; words such as *Dan* and *tan* can confuse anyone with impaired hearing. Deaf children, therefore, require special instruction to learn language.

Moses Goes to a Concert by Issac Millman depicts the complex life of children with hearing impairments. In this book, Moses and his deaf classmates enjoy a young people's concert when their teacher gives them balloons so they can feel the vibrations of the music. After the concert, they meet the percussionist, who is also deaf.

Another deaf child, Mark, demonstrates the difficulty of connecting with his classmates in the book, *Going with the Flow* by Claire Blatchford. He does finally establish a friendship, which rings true because his friend does not allow him to hog the ball when they play basketball. This book includes author's notes about deafness and sign language.

Laura Rankin's beautiful picture book *The Handmade Alphabet* presents a striking interpretation of the manual alphabet. Her stepson, who is deaf, communicated through lipreading for the first 18 years of his life. Then he learned American Sign Language, which allowed him to share ideas fully. Through it he gained understanding and communication. This book is especially useful in introducing the manual alphabet to children who can hear.

Although they are commonly thought of as being only for persons with visual impairments, guide dogs are sometimes trained to interpret sounds for people with hearing impairments as well. Patricia Curtis tells about the training of such a dog in *Cindy, A Hearing Ear Dog.*

Vision Challenges

Children with visual impairments or blindness do not have the visual input necessary to learn about their world, so they need special instruction. The book *Seeing Things My Way* by Alice Carter tells the story of second-grader Amanda who has a brain tumor that caused her to lose some of her vision. She received therapy to learn new skills. Books such as this help children understand that visual impairment does not

always mean blindness. Children who are blind often learn to read Braille and listen to "talking" or recorded books. Fortunately, many more recorded books are available today than ever before. Listening to recorded books extends their experiential background and prepares them to learn to read, either Braille or print if they can see large print.

Children with visual impairments need many opportunities to explore concrete objects with their senses of smell, touch, taste, and hearing. Tactile books made from fabric, yarn, buttons, and zippers are excellent learning tools for young children with impaired vision. Pockets in these books can hold cardboard or plastic shapes. Discussion and descriptions of these concrete experiences are essential to building background knowledge and experience.

Some people with visual impairments use guide dogs to achieve greater independence, a skill that requires education for the person as well as the dog. *A Guide Dog Puppy Grows Up* by Caroline Arnold follows Honey, a golden retriever, through her training from puppy to guide dog. Each stage of her training is explained with text and photographs.

Several genres include books about children with visual challenges and the ways they have adjusted. These authors sensitize readers to the individual differences among people with this disability whose lives are as varied as individuals who do not have this disability. In *Through Grandpa's Eyes,* Patricia MacLachlan introduces John, who really learns to see from his blind grandfather. MacLachlan helps readers appreciate the creativity of John's grandfather, who plays the cello, and his grandmother, who is a sculptor. Both grandparents are shown as capable and able to take care of themselves.

Jean Little, who has visual impairments, writes sensitively about this condition. In *From Anna* she tells about Anna, whose family escapes to Canada from Nazi Germany. Anna is awkward and unsure of herself and feels rejected. After her disability is identified, she has opportunities to develop competence and confidence, which enable her to overcome her difficulties in a realistic fashion.

Mobility Challenges

People with impaired mobility are sometimes identified as orthopedically disabled. They may have impaired legs, arms, or both, or may even have paralyzed body parts. Mobility impairments may originate at birth, through accident, or through illness. Some children are born with cerebral palsy, which can impair mobility quite seriously or very mildly. Injury to the spinal cord often causes paralysis below the injury.

Mobility for people with physical impairments usually requires special equipment such as wheelchairs, walkers, braces, prostheses, and canes. Of course, using this equipment requires therapy and training. In recent years, ramps have been added to buildings to permit better access by people who use this equipment. Likewise, many public places now have restrooms that are accessible to wheelchairs. In the nonfiction book *What Do You Do When Your Wheelchair Gets a Flat Tire? Questions and Answers About Disabilities,* Douglas Biklen and Ellen Barnes answer the questions that most children ask about many types of disabilities. Black-and-white photographs help explain physical handicaps in *A Look at Physical Handicaps* by Maria Forrai and Margaret Pursell.

Seeing eye dogs and hearing ear dogs are not the only animals that help people with disabilities. Recently animals have been trained to assist people with impaired mobility as well. Researchers have trained monkeys to prepare food, to feed people, to pick up the telephone when it rings, to pick up things that have been dropped, and even to brush teeth. Suzanne Haldane tells about some of the ways that monkeys assist people in *Helping Hands: How Monkeys Assist People Who Are Disabled.* The photographs in this book help readers understand how useful monkeys can be.

Many excellent books address the topic of mobility for people with disabilities and help children understand and accept differences in themselves and others. Marguerite de Angeli's *The Door in the Wall* is set in medieval times. Robin has physical impairments in his legs and is mistreated by other children. The monks help Robin learn to read, write, whittle, and use crutches, and eventually he shows his mettle and becomes a hero. This book has retained its popularity for many years, probably because Robin overcomes his handicap and becomes a hero in the story. *The Balancing Girl* by Berniece Rabe shows a first grader who adeptly adjusts to her braces, crutches, and wheelchair to do many things. Maxine Rosenberg's *My Friend Leslie* is a kindergartner with multiple handicaps. This photographic essay shows her classmates acceptance of her handicaps.

Some parents are so concerned about their children with disabilities that they overprotect them, a topic addressed by Jan Slepian in *The Alfred Summer.* Alfred has an overprotective mother and a father who ignores him, but during a very special summer he is able to make friends. *Wheelchair Champions* focuses on activities for people in wheelchairs. Harriet Savitz tells about real people in wheelchairs who excel in various sports. Marie Killilea's *Karen* is about a baby born with cerebral palsy whose family recognizes that she must learn to do things for herself and that she has to struggle to walk with braces. Sally in Jean Little's *Mine for Keeps* has a different problem. She has always attended a special school for children with disabilities, but she leaves the school to attend regular school. The changes in her life frighten her and make her anxious, but she gets a puppy that matures along with her.

Health Challenges

Children experience many of the same health challenges as adults. Epilepsy, diabetes, childhood arthritis, leukemia, cystic fibrosis, and heart malfunction are only a few of the physical conditions that can affect a child's life. Although medication is helpful for some of these conditions, serious side effects can alter the lives of people who take it. Children who depend upon medication must become responsible for taking it. In *Edith Herself* Ellen Howard shows the attitude toward seizures before medication was commonly available. Edith and her family have to accept and adjust to her problem without the aid of modern medicine.

Leukemia often requires extensive medical treatment and can be life threatening. Bone marrow transplants are sometimes used in its treatment, as Diana Amadeo demonstrates in *There's a Little Bit of Me in Jamey.* Brian tells about his concern for his younger brother Jamey, a leukemia victim. He has ambivalent feelings about the situation because he is worried about his brother's terrible illness, yet at the same time he resents the fact that his parents have very little time for him. Then the doctor discovers that Brian's bone marrow is a good match for Jamey. The book is very realistic because Brian observes that the transplant is a hope not a cure.

Many diabetics must take insulin, and they have to control their diet. In *You Can't Catch Diabetes from a Friend* Lynn Kipnis and Susan Adler explain diabetes with simple text and photographs. Ron Roy's *Where's Buddy?* approaches diabetes from the point of view of a boy who must become responsible for taking his medication and who must deal with the problem of overprotective parents.

AIDS is a health problem of recent origin, but the numbers of AIDS victims are increasing. *Ryan White: My Own Story* is a good book for youngsters because it tells about AIDS from a child's point of view. In Paula McGuire's book *AIDS,* intermediate-grade children can learn the basic facts focusing on how HIV is and is not spread. In *Fighting Back: What Some People Are Doing About AIDS,* also a nonfiction piece, Susan Kuklin speaks with candor about the facts of living with AIDS. *Children and the AIDS Virus* by Rosmarie Hausherr is a different treatment of this subject. The book is written at two levels, large print for younger children and smaller print for older children, and looks at the ways children can and cannot contract AIDS. Linda Walvoord Girard wrote a fiction story about AIDS: *Alex, the Kid with AIDS.* This superb story is so well written that Alex's illness almost seems incidental to the story. Alex acts very much like any fourth-grade boy—he even speculates about taking advantage of the fact that he has AIDS. When the school nurse explains his illness and the appropriate precautions, she does so without overdramatizing them.

Allergies are a great problem for many people today. Some physicians believe they are increasing due to the pollution in our atmosphere. Judith Seixas has written an easy-to-read book, *Allergies: What They Are, What They Do,* which discusses the causes of allergic reactions. Doris Buchanan Smith's novel *A Taste of Blackberries* is built around the death of a boy who is allergic to bee stings and his best friend's reaction to the tragedy.

Emotional Challenges

Emotional challenge is an aspect of the human condition that afflicts many people from time to time. Emotional ups and downs are a fact of life with the stresses, fast pace, and high expectations of contemporary life. Many of the challenges with which children must cope have emotional dimensions. Reading about characters with emotional disturbances helps readers empathize with their problems and in some instances with the problems their children and families face because of the character's emotional difficulties. In Cynthia Voigt's *Homecoming* and its sequel *Dicey's Song,* the mother's mental breakdown forces Dicey to take the responsibility for her younger siblings. She eventually seeks assistance from the grandmother she does not know, and her mother dies in the mental hospital. In *Notes for Another Life* by Sue Ellen Bridgers, a father is emotionally ill and the mother is unable to cope. The grandparents in this story support Wren and her brother as they cope with these problems.

Learning Challenges

Challenges to learning take many forms, from mild learning disabilities to severe mental retardation. Quality literature that addresses this issue is hopeful with characters who adjust to their circumstances or make progress through education, therapy, schools, rehabilitation, or determination.

Learning disabilities arise from a number of sources, some of which are unidentifiable. However, learning disabilities prevent many children from experiencing success in school. Doris Buchanan Smith writes about a 9-year-old boy in *Kelly's Creek* who cannot read, write, or draw circles. Kelly experiences success for the first time when studying marsh life in a nearby creek, and his success is recognized by peers and adults. In *Just One Friend,* Lynn Hall writes about a learning disabled girl who fears mainstreaming into a regular classroom. She hopes to have just one friend. Another picture of mainstreaming is provided in *Dustin's Big School Day* by Alden Carter. Second-grader Dustin has Down syndrome, and this photoessay shows his productive school day. Some students with learning difficulties have specialized teachers and they are mainstreamed into regular classrooms as well.

In Vera and Bill Cleaver's *Me Too,* Lydia tries to help her twin Lorna, who has a disability, do simple tasks so that their father will find her more acceptable, but she is not successful. Marlene Fanta Shyer has a similar theme in *Welcome Home, Jellybean.* Twelve-year-old Neil's father leaves when his sister returns home from an institution for the retarded. This author communicates the family torment arising from a handicapped child's problems and helps readers see the love and compassion that Neil feels for his sister.

Harriet Sobol writes a sister's feelings about her retarded brother in *My Brother Steven Is Retarded.* She is honest to say that he embarrasses her sometimes, but that she is very happy when he laughs. Megan has to

A mixed race child is really more than half.

take care of her disabled brother in *A Real Christmas This Year* by Karen Lynn Williams, but her struggling family is doing the best they can in raising a severely disabled child. In *Radiance Descending,* by Paula Fox, Paul's brother with Down syndrome embarrasses him, but he discovers that Jacob is lovable.

A mentally retarded adult is a major character in Sue Ellen Bridger's *All Together Now.* The major character becomes friends with him, and her grandmother demonstrates understanding for him. *My Friend Jacob* by Lucille Clifton is also about a friendship between two people. Sam is sensitive to the problems of his friend who has Down syndrome, and they discover that they are able to teach each other different things.

Mags, Karen Hesse's main character in *Wish on a Unicorn,* is like many siblings of disabled children. She must grow up fast because she must take care of her little brother and her sister, who has brain damage, while her mother works. This means that she cannot do the things that sixth graders like to do, and she cannot make friends because she must constantly attend to the younger children.

Abused Children

Abuse of children, a painful subject, has been addressed very little until recent times. Abuse takes various forms: some children are physically abused, some are sexually abused, some are emotionally abused, and some are neglected. Giving children opportunities to read or hear books about abused characters is impor-

tant because abused children usually feel they are to blame. Many abused children react with shame and try to protect their abuser. In Betsy Byars's *The Pinballs,* Harvey, a foster child, lies to protect his father who runs him down with a car while in a drunken rage. Some abused children think they imagined the abuse. Til, in *The Girl Who Lived on the Ferris Wheel* by Louise Moeri, is not sure whether she is abused or whether it is her imagination until she is almost killed by her mother. Only after she discusses the situation with a friend does she realize her mother is not normal. Literature can help youngsters realize that abuse is real and undeserved.

Literature about abused children must not blame the victim or excuse the abusers, although it may offer insight about the abuse. Some abusive adults are also substance abusers who hurt children when they are under the influence of alcohol or drugs. In Irene Hunt's *The Lottery Rose* the mother and her boyfriend beat Georgie when they drink. After a savage beating, Georgie spends time in the hospital and goes to a Catholic school, where he experiences the first kindness in his life. This powerful story ends with hope for Georgie's future, an important aspect of literature about abused children.

Abuse takes many forms and is a complex issue. Virginia Hamilton's compelling story *Sweet Whispers, Brother Rush* conveys this concept. Dabney has a congenital illness that impairs his capacity and causes him to die prematurely. Dabney's mother confines him to his bed and leaves his younger sister to care for him. The mother is not a substance abuser nor is she a disturbed character; she is trying to protect him in her own way. Virginia Hamilton's fine book sensitizes readers to the complex issues surrounding the issue of child abuse.

Cynthia Voigt takes on the challenge of writing about a difficult subject in *When She Hollers:* a stepfather's sexual abuse and a mother who will not believe it. The protagonist struggles with her problem and tries to talk with a school counselor, and eventually consults with her best friend's father, a lawyer, who cannot give her easy answers. After this she takes control of the situation; she makes clear to her stepfather that he is to leave her alone, and she takes a knife to bed with her. The resolution is not pat or clear, but it is realistic. The book *I Hadn't Meant to Tell You This* by Jacqueline Woodson portrays a friendship between Lena and Dion who flee their sexually abusive father. Although the girls' journey is a sad one, the story is a loving story in which they discover much goodness in the world. Their story continues in Lena.

Some nonfiction books also address abuse. Books help both children and adults recognize children's behaviors that indicate abuse and offer advice about what to do if one is the victim of abuse. Margaret Hyde's *Cry Softly! The Story of Child Abuse* provides lists of organizations that help abused children and their parents. This book helps readers understand the many types of people who abuse children.

Some children are neglected by their parents or caregivers, which is a form of abusive behavior. Ten-year-old Kitty in Vera Cleaver's *Moon Lake Angel* is abandoned by her father, who has a new family; then her mother remarries and Kitty ends up in a boarding house. She spends her time plotting revenge, but when the chance for revenge comes she finds that she has changed. In *Dr. Dredd's Wagon of Wonders* by Bill Brittain, Calvin is in bondage to Dr. Dredd, who takes him from an orphanage because of his rainmaking talent. Dr. Dredd uses him but does not provide for his basic needs. Calvin escapes Dr. Dredd, but his freedom is in the hands of a community that vacillates about what to do.

Joan Lowery Nixon writes about the lives of children sent west on an orphan train in 1860 in *A Family Apart*. The parents of these children are unable to care for them and believe their children will be better off adopted by others who can provide for them, but the children feel abandoned by their parents. Charlene Talbot also writes about the orphan train in *An Orphan for Nebraska*.

Substance Abuse

Substance abuse may involve drugs or alcohol, and it is an issue addressed in both fiction and nonfiction literature. Authors of informational books on this subject focus most often on the ways that drugs and alcohol change the brain and the body, as do Catherine O'Neill in *Focus on Alcohol*, Jeffrey Shulman in *Focus on Cocaine and Crack*, and Paula Klevan Zeller in *Focus on Marijuana*. These nonfiction books are part of a series that provides a factual approach to substance abuse.

Walter Dean Myers writes about a gang of friends who join a basketball team at a youth center and unexpectedly become involved with drugs in *Fast Sam, Cool Clyde, and Stuff*. Alice Childress, author of *A Hero Ain't Nothin' But a Sandwich*, takes a somewhat different approach to this issue by depicting different points of view of the various characters.

Lifestyle Challenges

Children whose family life is different from the traditional two-parent family are apt to feel that they are different. They may feel responsible for the changes in their family, and they often feel unloved. These children may be the victims of divorce, they may be in foster care, or they may be adopted.

Many children today experience pain and unhappiness as a result of their parents' separation: Approximately 50% of marriages today end in divorce. Some children live with one parent and have no memory of ever living with both; others live with neither parent. Literature can help them and their friends understand their difficulties. Books such as Peggy Mann's *My Dad Lives in a Downtown Hotel* show characters learning about the realities of living with a single parent and visiting with the other parent. They feel awkward with the situation and wonder if anything will ever be right again.

Middle-grade children, as well as younger children, experience pain and confusion when their parents separate. Paula Danziger's *The Divorce Express* depicts an all-too-common situation: children shuffling back and forth between parents. During holiday times, airplanes, trains, and buses are filled with youngsters who must divide their time between parents. Betsy Byars writes about children spending a vacation with their father in *The Animal, the Vegetable and John D. Jones*. Readers learn that life goes on after divorce in the story *Lost Summer* by Elizabeth Feuer. Lydia goes to camp after her parents divorce and discovers that she has more in common with her sister than she thought as she is drawn into camp life.

Learning to get along with stepparents is a fact of modern life. Mavis Jukes has written two books focusing on this situation. In *Like Jake and Me* a young boy is learning to get along with his stepfather and preparing to live with the twins his mother is expecting. *No One Is Going to Nashville* by Mavis Jukes focuses on the relationship Sonia has with her father and stepmother.

Children live with foster parents for a variety of reasons. Some are abandoned, others are waiting to be adopted, and some have suffered abuse and have been removed from the abuser's care. Foster children often find their own means of survival in foster care. In Shirley Gordon's *The Boy Who Wanted a Family*, 7-year-old Michael has been in many foster homes, but he finally finds the mother of his dreams. Chad in C. S. Adler's *The Cat That Was Left Behind* finds relating to

This noted Hispanic artist creates pottery.

Unusual family situations arise from a variety of circumstances. *Mom, the Wolf Man, and Me* by Norma Klein is the story of an unmarried mother. These stories shock some people, but this story shows warmth and love in unconventional situations.

Homeless Children

Homelessness is a prevalent problem today. In some places, homeless children cannot attend school. When they can attend school, they cannot check books out of a library, and homework is usually out of the question. And these are just the beginning of their problems. Carol Fenner portrays Ian and his father, a Vietnam War veteran, who are homeless in *The King of Dragons*. But the father simply fails to return one day, and Ian is completely on his own.

The nonfiction book *No Place to Be: Voices of Homeless Children* by Judith Berck is based on interviews of the homeless children that she got to know. She presents their experiences through their own words and poems, interwoven with her narrative. Iareem speaks about being homeless in this quotation, "The shelter is only another home, it's not another life. It's not like I just moved into another life like an alien . . . the shelter doesn't control who you are" (99–100).

Classroom Activities

A good way to help children who do not have disabilities learn about the difficulties faced by their peers with disabilities is through units that focus on the universal problems they face. These units are also important to students who do have disabilities, because they can identify with the story characters and realize they are not the only people in the world who have encountered problems.

an old fisherman and a cat easier than relating to his foster family. He learns how to relate to his foster family as a result of understanding the abandoned cat.

Children who are adopted and their new parents must make many adjustments. Jeanette Gaines writes about the loving relationship between Abby and her adopted family in *Abby.* Maxine Rosenberg writes about adoption in the informational book *Being Adopted.*

Classroom Activities

ACTIVITY 13.1 ADJUSTING FOR THE PROBLEMS OF STUDENTS WITH DISABILITIES

Purpose
This activity, designed for grades K–4, introduces the kinds of adjustments that can be made to help classmates who have sensory or physical disabilities. It can

help students understand the feelings of their peers who have disabilities and learn appropriate ways to be their friends. The outcome of this activity is a discussion of disabilities, the feelings of people about their disabilities, and ways to treat people who have disabilities. Middle-grade students can prepare a written handbook of ways that students can help students with disabilities in their classes and those they meet in other places.

Introduction

Before this activity students should participate in a literature-based unit to acquaint them with physical disabilities.

1. Ask children to explain the terms *disability, physical disability,* and *sensory disability.* Create a language-experience chart about the information they volunteer. For fourth graders, ask the children to write their own meanings for these words.

2. Ask the students to make a list of all the physical and sensory disabilities they can think of.

3. Discuss the things that people who have physical and sensory disabilities need to have or do to compensate for their disabilities. For example, ask why some people wear glasses, why some people wear hearing aids, and why others use wheelchairs.

4. Explain that some people make additional adjustments, such as learning Braille, sign language, and so forth, and that the class will be studying about these for the next few weeks.

5. Let the children use some of the equipment used by people who have disabilities so that they can experience the difficulties involved. Bring to class a collection of items such as eye patches, drugstore nonprescription glasses, a wheelchair, a walker, ear plugs, bandages for eyes, arm braces, a boot cast, braces, and crutches. Let them attempt to take the wheelchair into the bathroom and through doors, use a walker while their legs are in casts, walk with casts, leave ear plugs in for an hour, cover one eye and then both eyes with patches or bandages, and use any other equipment available.

6. After using the equipment, have students write about their feelings and experiences. They may choose to write a letter to a friend, parent, or grandparent or to write a journal entry about their feelings. Younger children can dictate rather than write. The students could write and illustrate a class book about their experiences as handicapped people.

7. Students can learn to communicate through the manual alphabet. They may visit with deaf children and try their new skills in communication. Books such as the following are helpful in developing this skill:

- *Handmade ABC: A Manual Alphabet* by Linda Bourke
- *The Handmade Alphabet* by Laura Rankin
- *Handtalk School* by Mary Beth Miller and George Ancona
- *Handtalk Birthday: A Number and Story Book in Sign Language* by Remy Charlip, Mary Beth Miller, and George Ancona

SUMMARY

Every classroom has individuals who vary in social and emotional background, language ability, cultural background, physical ability, and intellectual ability. These differences are acknowledged and accepted in contemporary schools more than ever before. The variability in the school population carries with it the responsibility for making appropriate adjustments in the curriculum and materials. Presenting literature that portrays people with disabilities in a well-balanced manner enables students who do not have disabilities to understand and identify with their peers with disabilities better, and it helps students who do have disabilities to identify with the characters and understand themselves better.

A wide variety of excellent literature is available for educating students about individual differences. All students are individuals, and those who have disabilities are as varied and individual as students without disabilities. Quality literature depicts this individuality and does not stereotype characters. Any characters with disabilities are integral to the book; they are not just stuck in to make a point.

Thought Questions

1. Why do you think the portrayal of people with disabilities has changed?

2. What trends do you predict in this kind of literature?

3. This subject has more informational books than any other discussed in this book. Why do you think this is true?

4. What kinds of books should be written about people with disabilities?

5. What kinds of books need to be written about the children who face universal problems?

Research and Application Experiences

1. Make a card file of books about people facing universal problems or disabilities. Each book should meet the standards identified earlier in this chapter.

2. Compare the treatment of a child with disabilities in two books. How are they alike? How are they different?

3. Visit a class that has mainstreamed students and find out how often the teacher introduces literature with characters who have disabilities.

4. Write a short story about a person who has a disability.

5. How has the portrayal of people with disabilities and those facing universal problems changed?

Children's Literature References and Recommended Books

Note: Books designated with an asterisk (*) are recommended for reluctant readers.

Adler, C. S. (1981). *The cat that was left behind.* New York: Clarion. (4–6). CONTEMPORARY REALISTIC FICTION.

Chad goes to a new foster home where the parents welcome him, but he finds it hard to warm up to them. However, after he makes friends with a cat, he is able to accept his foster family.

Amadeo, D. M. (1989). *There's a little bit of me in Jamey* (J. Friedman, Illus.). Morton Grove, IL: Whitman. (3–6). CONTEMPORARY REALISTIC FICTION.

Brian tells this story about his younger brother Jamey, a leukemia victim. Brian gives his brother a bone marrow transplant, which gives Jamey his best chance to live.

Arnold, C. (1991). *A guide dog puppy grows up* (R. Hewett, Photog.). New York: Harcourt Brace Jovanovich. (2–5). INFORMATIONAL BOOK.*

This book follows Honey, a golden retriever, through her training from puppy to guide dog. Each stage of training is explained with text and photographs.

Berck, J. (1992). *No place to be: Voices of homeless children.* Boston: Houghton Mifflin. (3–8). INFORMATIONAL BOOK.*

An informational book based on interviews with homeless children; illustrated with photographs.

Biklen, D., & Barnes, E. (1978). *What do you do when your wheelchair gets a flat tire? Questions and answers about disabilities.* New York: Human Policy Press. (2–5). INFORMATIONAL BOOK.

This book tells about children with various disabilities and how they feel about their disabilities, as well as their likes and dislikes and how they would like to be treated.

Blatchford, C. H. (1998). *Going with the flow* (J. L. Porter, Illus.). Minneapolis, MN: Carolrhoda. (2–4). CONTEMPORARY REALISTIC FICTION.

Fifth-grader Mark, who is deaf, has a difficult time making friends in his new school.

Bourke, L. (1978). *Handmade ABC: A manual alphabet.* New York: Harvey House. (1–5). INFORMATIONAL BOOK.

This book uses pictures of hands to demonstrate sign language.

Bridgers, S. E. (1979). *All together now.* New York: Knopf. (4–6). CONTEMPORARY REALISTIC FICTION.

Casey, who is 12, goes to visit her grandmother and discovers a neighbor who is 30, but who has the mind of a 12-year-old. This man spends his days playing baseball. This is a good story with well-rounded characters.

Bridgers, S. E. (1981). *Notes for another life.* New York: Knopf. (4–6). CONTEMPORARY REALISTIC FICTION.

Wren's father has an incurable mental illness and her mother is unable to cope with the situation. Fortunately, their grandparents are able to give Wren and her brother emotional support.

Brittain, B. (1987). *Dr. Dredd's wagon of wonders* (A. Glass, Illus.). New York: Harper & Row. (5–7). HISTORICAL FICTION.*

Calvin is in bondage to Dr. Dredd who took him from an orphanage because of his rainmaking talent. Calvin escapes Dr. Dredd, but his freedom is in the hands of a community.

Byars, B. (1977). *The pinballs.* New York: Harper & Row. (4–6). CONTEMPORARY REALISTIC FICTION.

Harvey lies to protect his father, who ran him down with a car in a drunken rage.

Byars, B. (1982). *The animal, the vegetable, and John D. Jones* (R. Sanderson, Illus.). New York: Delacorte. (4–6). CONTEMPORARY REALISTIC FICTION.

Clara and her older sister are looking forward to vacationing with their father until they discover that his girlfriend and her son are coming too.

Caines, J. F. (1973). *Abby* (S. Kellogg, Illus.). New York: Harper & Row. (PreK–2). CONTEMPORARY REALISTIC FICTION.

Abby is adopted and finds a special place in her family.

Carrick, C. (1985). *Stay away from Simon!* (D. Carrick, Illus.). New York: Clarion. (3–6). HISTORICAL FICTION.

Lucy is afraid of Simon, who has a mental disability. One snowy day he follows her and her brother after school and helps them find their way home.

Carter, A. (1998). *Seeing things my way* (C. S. Carter, Photog.). Morton Grove, IL: Whitman. (K–3). INFORMATIONAL BOOK.

A second grader learns to cope with a brain tumor that is affecting her vision.

Carter, A. (1999). *Dustin's big school day* (D. Young & C. S. Carter, Illus.). Morton Grove, IL: Whitman. (PreK–2). CONTEMPORARY REALISTIC FICTION.

A boy with Down syndrome has an exciting school day.

Charlip, R., Miller, M. B., & Ancona, G. (1987). *Handtalk birthday: A number & story book in sign language.* New York: Four Winds. (K–4). INFORMATIONAL BOOK.

At her surprise birthday party, a deaf woman and her guests communicate using sign language. The book uses photographs for illustrations.

Childress, A. (1973). *A hero ain't nothin' but a sandwich.* New York: Coward McCann. (5–8). CONTEMPORARY REALISTIC FICTION.

This novel focuses on drug abuse as 13-year-old Benjie is in the process of becoming a heroin addict.

Cleaver, V. (1987). *Moon Lake angel.* New York: Lothrop, Lee & Shephard. (4–8). CONTEMPORARY REALISTIC FICTION.*

Ten-year-old Kitty is abandoned by her father, who has a new family. Her mother remarries and Kitty is sent to stay in a boarding house. She plots revenge, but cannot carry out her plans.

Cleaver, V., & Cleaver, B. (1973). *Me too.* Philadelphia: Lippincott. (5–7). CONTEMPORARY REALISTIC FICTION.

Lydia tries to help her twin, Lorna, who has a disability, do simple tasks so their father will find her more acceptable, but she is not successful.

Clifton, L. (1980). *My friend Jacob* (T. Di Grazia, Illus.). New York: Dutton. (1–4). CONTEMPORARY REALISTIC FICTION.*

Sam has a friend, Jacob, with Down syndrome. This story tells how the two friends help each other.

Corcoran, B. (1982). *Child of the morning.* New York: Atheneum. (4–6). CONTEMPORARY REALISTIC FICTION.

After a skull fracture, Susan experiences odd "spells" that cause her sister and the townspeople to treat her differently. Then she learns that she has epilepsy and fears for the career in dance that she hopes to have.

Curtis, P. (1981). *Cindy, a hearing ear dog* (D. Cupp, Photog.). New York: Dutton. (2–4). INFORMATIONAL BOOK.

This nonfiction book shows how dogs are trained to interpret sounds for people with hearing impairments. The photographs are appealing and instructive.

Cutler, J. (1997). *Spaceman.* New York: Dutton. (4–6). CONTEMPORARY REALISTIC FICTION.

Gary, a fifth grader, has dyslexia, and he is misplaced and misunderstood.

Danziger, P. (1982). *The divorce express.* New York: Delacorte. (5–7). CONTEMPORARY REALISTIC FICTION.

Phoebe must ride the divorce express every weekend because she lives with her interior decorator mother and visits her painter father each weekend.

de Angeli, M. (1949). *The door in the wall.* New York: Doubleday. (4–9). HISTORICAL FICTION.

Robin has physical impairments in his legs and is mistreated by other children. Eventually he learns to read.

Fenner, C. (1998). *The king of dragons.* New York: McElderry. (4–6). CONTEMPORARY REALISTIC FICTION.

Ian and his father, a Vietnam War veteran, have been homeless for years. When Ian's father fails to return one day, Ian is on his own.

Feuer, E. (1995). *Lost summer.* New York: Farrar. (3–6). CONTEMPORARY REALISTIC FICTION.

After Lydia's parents divorce, she is sent to camp where her sister is a counselor. She learns to make friends and appreciate her sister.

Forrai, M., & Pursell, M. S. (1976). *A look at physical handicaps* (M. Forrai, Photog.). Minneapolis: Lerner. (K–3). INFORMATIONAL BOOK.

This book explains physical disabilities, their causes, and ways of adjusting.

Fox, P. (1997). *Radiance descending.* New York: DK Ink. (3–8). CONTEMPORARY REALISTIC FICTION.

Paul is embarrassed by his brother who has Down syndrome, but he discovers Jacob is lovable.

Girard, L. W. (1991). *Alex, the kid with AIDS* (B. Sims, Illus.). Morton Grove, IL: Whitman. (3–5). CONTEMPORARY REALISTIC FICTION.

Alex is the new kid in fourth grade, and he has AIDS. This good story entertains without overdoing the informative aspect of his illness.

Gordon, S. (1980). *The boy who wanted a family* (C. Robinson, Illus.). New York: Harper & Row. (1–5). CONTEMPORARY REALISTIC FICTION.

Seven-year-old Michael has been in many foster homes. In this story with a happy ending, he finally finds the mother of his dreams.

Haldane, S. (1991). *Helping hands: How monkeys assist people who are disabled.* New York: Dutton. (3–7). INFORMATIONAL BOOK.

Through this nonfiction book illustrated with photographs, children learn about the ways that monkeys can help disabled people.

Hall, L. (1985). *Just one friend.* New York: Scribner. (4–6). CONTEMPORARY REALISTIC FICTION.

In this book a girl with learning disabilities faces her fears of being mainstreamed. Her greatest fear is that she will not have a friend.

Hamilton, V. (1982). *Sweet whispers, brother Rush.* New York: Philomel. (6–8). CONTEMPORARY REALISTIC FICTION.

This story is about Dabney, who is "slow" and "different." He has a rare illness and eventually dies. The mother confines Dabney to bed and his 14-year-old sister must care for him until he dies.

Hausherr, R. (1989). *Children and the AIDS virus.* New York: Clarion. (3–6). INFORMATIONAL BOOK.*

This book looks at AIDS and the ways that children can and cannot get the disease. The book is written at two levels, with big print for young children and smaller print for older children.

Hesse, K. (1991). *Wish on a unicorn.* San Diego: Holt. (4–6). CONTEMPORARY REALISTIC FICTION.

Mags must take care of her younger brother and her sister, who has brain damage, while their mother works.

Hesse, K. (1992). *Letters from Rifka.* New York: Holt. (4–8). HISTORICAL FICTION.

Rifka writes letters to her cousin in Russia.

Hesse, K. (1994). *Phoenix rising.* New York: Holt. (6–10). MODERN FANTASY.

Set in the future, this story explores radiation contamination throughout the United States. The characters make the issues real for readers.

Hesse, K. (1996). *The music of dolphins.* New York: Scholastic. (4–7). MODERN FANTASY.

A girl who grew up with dolphins is the central character. When she is discovered by scientists, they try to teach her to live in human society.

Hesse, K. (1997). *Out of the dust.* New York: Scholastic. (4–8). HISTORICAL FICTION.

Billie Jo Kelby survives living in the dust bowl, her mother's death, and her father's reaction to these problems in this Newbery Award book.

Hesse, K. (1998). *Just Juice* (R. A. Parker, Illus.). New York: Scholastic. (4–7) CONTEMPORARY REALISTIC FICTION.

Juice is her daddy's girl, but his illiteracy has created enormous family problems.

Howard, E. (1987). *Edith herself* (R. Himler, Illus.). New York: Atheneum. (3–7). HISTORICAL FICTION.

Edith is orphaned and goes to live with her older sister, but then she begins to have seizures. This story is set in the 1890s, before people with epilepsy received much medical help.

Hughes, D. (1996). *Team picture.* New York: Atheneum. (5–9). CONTEMPORARY REALISTIC FICTION.

David lives in a makeshift family; his legal guardian, Paul, is the bellman who is struggling with alcoholism.

Hunt, I. (1976). *The lottery rose.* New York: Scribner's. (4–7). CONTEMPORARY REALISTIC FICTION.

His mother and her boyfriend have abused Georgie since he was born. They beat him savagely when they drink. Finally Georgie has an opportunity to enroll in a Catholic school.

Hyde, M. O. (1980). *Cry softly! The story of child abuse.* Louisville, KY: Westminster Press. (3–6). INFORMATIONAL BOOK.

This book provides a list of organizations that help abused children and their parents. It also helps concerned people to understand that child abuse is not confined to any particular people or class of people in society.

Jukes, M. (1983). *Like Jake and me* (L. Bloom, Illus.). New York: Knopf. (1–3). CONTEMPORARY REALISTIC FICTION.

This story portrays a young boy who is learning to understand his stepfather. His mother is expecting twins, and he obviously has a warm, loving relationship with her.

Jukes, M. (1984). *No one is going to Nashville* (L. Bloom, Illus.). New York: Knopf. (3–6). CONTEMPORARY REALISTIC FICTION.*

This book tells about the relationship between Sonia and her father and stepmother. She is adjusting to the new relationships that resulted from her parents' divorce.

Killilea, M. (1954). *Karen.* New York: Dodd Mead. (2–6). INFORMATIONAL BOOK.

Karen is born with cerebral palsy. This book addresses her family's adjustment to her disability.

Kipnis, L., & Adler, S. (1979). *You can't catch diabetes from a friend* (R. Benkof, Photog.). Gainesville, FL: Triad Scientific Publishers. (2–6). INFORMATIONAL BOOK.

In simple text and photographs, this book explains diabetes and the daily routines of diabetic children.

Klein, N. (1972). *Mom, the wolf man, and me.* New York: Pantheon. (5–7). CONTEMPORARY REALISTIC FICTION.

Brett is afraid life with her unwed mother will change if her mother marries.

Kuklin, S. (1988). *Fighting back: What some people are doing about AIDS.* New York: Putnam. (6–12). INFORMATIONAL BOOK.

This nonfiction book tells what living with AIDS is like. The author writes factual material with candor.

Lacapa, K., & Lacapa, M. (1994). *Less than half, more than whole.* Flagstaff AZ: Northland. (2–5). CONTEMPORARY REALISTIC FICTION.

A child of mixed race has difficulties.

Little, J. (1962). *Mine for keeps* (L. Parker, Illus.). New York: Little, Brown. (4–6). CONTEMPORARY REALISTIC FICTION.

Sally has always attended a special school for the disabled. Now she transfers to a regular school, and she fears the change. A puppy helps her make the adjustment.

Little, J. (1972). *From Anna* (J. Sandin, Illus.). New York: Harper & Row. (4–6). HISTORICAL FICTION.

Anna and her family escape from Nazi Germany. In Canada, her family discovers that Anna's vision difficulties are responsible for her clumsy, awkward behavior. She overcomes her problems by getting eyeglasses.

Little, J. (1986). *Different dragons* (L. Fernandez, Illus.). New York: Viking. (3–6). CONTEMPORARY REALISTIC FICTION.

The story of a boy's battle with his fears of darkness, thunderstorms, and dogs. In the process of facing his fears he learns about his brother's and father's fears.

Little, J. (1987). *Little by Little: A writer's education.* New York: Viking. (3–6). BIOGRAPHY.

Jean Little's own story about her extraordinary life. She has been nearly blind from birth, but overcame ridicule, rejection, and bullying to find friends and to write poetry and stories.

MacLachlan, P. (1980). *Through Grandpa's eyes* (D. Ray, Illus.). New York: Harper & Row. (1–3). CONTEMPORARY REALISTIC FICTION.

John's grandfather is blind, but John learns to see better from his grandfather, who also plays the cello.

Mann, P. (1973). *My dad lives in a downtown hotel* (R. Cuffari, Illus.). New York: Doubleday. (1–5). CONTEMPORARY REALISTIC FICTION.

Joey learns about life in a divorced family in this book. He finds visiting his dad in a hotel awkward and uncomfortable.

McGuire, P. (1998). *AIDS.* Austin, TX: Raintree Steck-Vaughn. (4–6). INFORMATIONAL BOOK.

This book focuses on the basic facts about HIV and AIDS.

Miller, M. B., & Ancona, G. (1991). *Handtalk school.* New York: Four Winds. (1–3). INFORMATIONAL BOOK.

Color photographs illustrate this book based on an actual school, its teachers, and its students.

Millman, I. (1998). *Moses goes to a concert.* New York: Farrar, Straus & Giroux. (1–3). INFORMATIONAL BOOK.

Moses and his deaf classmates attend a concert and discover they can feel the instruments' vibrations through balloons.

Moeri, L. (1979). *The girl who lived on the Ferris wheel.* New York: Dutton. (5–8). CONTEMPORARY REALISTIC FICTION.

Til is not sure if she is being abused or is just imagining it until her mother almost kills her. After she discusses the situation with a friend, she realizes her mother is not normal.

Myers, W. D. (1975). *Fast Sam, cool Clyde, and Stuff.* New York: Viking. (6–12). CONTEMPORARY REALISTIC FICTION.

Stuff and his friends join a basketball team and inadvertently become involved with drugs.

Nixon, J. L. (1987). *A family apart.* New York: Bantam. (4–6). HISTORICAL FICTION.

This book tells about the lives of a family of children sent West on an orphan train because their families could not care for them. The children struggle with their parents' decision because they feel abandoned.

O'Neill, C. (1990). *Focus on alcohol* (D. Neuhaus, Illus.). New York: 21st Century Books. (4–7). INFORMATIONAL BOOK.

This is one of a series of books that examines drug abuse. This one looks at the impact of alcohol on the brain.

Rabe, B. (1981). *The balancing girl* (L. Hoban, Illus.). New York: Dutton. (K–3). INFORMATIONAL BOOK.

Margaret, a first grader, is able to balance many things while wearing braces and using crutches. She also gets around easily in a wheelchair.

Rankin, L. (1991). *The handmade alphabet.* New York: Dial. (1–4). PICTURE BOOK.

This is an alphabet picture book that features the manual alphabet used in sign language. The author explains that her stepson is deaf.

Rosenberg, M. (1983). *My friend Leslie* (G. Ancona, Photog.). New York: Lothrop, Lee & Shepard. (K–3). INFORMATIONAL BOOK.

This book is a photoessay about Leslie, who has multiple handicaps, and her kindergarten classmates' acceptance of her.

Rosenberg, M. (1984). *Being adopted* (G. Ancona, Photog.). New York: Lothrop, Lee & Shepard. (3–6). INFORMATIONAL BOOK.

An informational book, illustrated with photographs, that provides straightforward information about adoption.

Roy, R. (1982). *Where's Buddy?* (T. Howell, Illus.). New York: Clarion. (2–5). CONTEMPORARY REALISTIC FICTION.

Seven-year-old Buddy has diabetes. While his older brother is babysitting, Buddy disappears. He is found in a cave and has not taken his medicine.

Savitz, H. M. (1978). *Wheelchair champions: A history of wheelchair sports.* New York: Crowell. (3–6). INFORMATIONAL BOOK.

This book is about real people who are in wheelchairs and compete in sporting events.

Seixas, J. S. (1991). *Allergies—What they are, what they do* (T. Huffman, Illus.). New York: Greenwillow. (2–4). INFORMATIONAL BOOK.*

This easy-to-read book addresses the causes of allergic reactions. It is illustrated with cartoons.

Shulman, J. (1990). *Focus on cocaine and crack* (D. Neuhaus, Illus.). New York: 21st Century Books. (4–6). INFORMATIONAL BOOK.*

This is one of a series of books that examines the impact of drugs on the body and the brain.

Shyer, M. F. (1978). *Welcome home, Jellybean.* New York: Scribner's. (4–6). CONTEMPORARY REALISTIC FICTION.

Twelve-year-old Neil has a sister who has lived in an institution for people with mental retardation, but when she returns home the family members have problems adjusting.

Slepian, J. (1980). *The Alfred summer.* New York: Macmillan. (4–6). CONTEMPORARY REALISTIC FICTION.

Alfred has an overprotective mother and a father who ignores him. He makes two friends during the summer and his independence grows.

Smith, D. B. (1973). *A taste of blackberries* (C. Robinson, Illus.). New York: Crowell. (3–5). CONTEMPORARY REALISTIC FICTION.

Jamie dies of an allergic reaction to a bee sting, and his best friend blames himself for his death. After the funeral, he offers to become Jamie's mother's son.

Smith, D. B. (1975). *Kelly's creek* (A. Tiegreen, Illus.). New York: Crowell. (2–5). CONTEMPORARY REALISTIC FICTION.

Nine-year-old Kelly knows that he is not like other children. He cannot read, write, or even draw circles. He develops an interest in marsh life and becomes successful.

Sobol, H. L. (1977). *My brother Steven is retarded* (P. Agre, Photog.). New York: Macmillan. (1–4). CONTEMPORARY REALISTIC FICTION.

This story is told from the point of view of Beth, who has a brother with mental retardation. She expresses her embarrassment with his behavior and her pleasure when he laughs.

Talbot, C. (1979). *An orphan for Nebraska.* New York: Atheneum. (2–5). HISTORICAL FICTION.

This historical fiction is based on the actual orphan trains that carried children from the East to be adopted by families in the West and Midwest.

Voigt, C. (1981). *Homecoming.* New York: Atheneum. (3–6). CONTEMPORARY REALISTIC FICTION.

Dicey's mother has a mental breakdown and goes to a mental hospital in this book. Dicey manages to take care of her younger siblings and to get them to their grandmother, who is virtually unknown to all of the children.

Voigt, C. (1982). *Dicey's song.* New York: Atheneum. (3–6). CONTEMPORARY REALISTIC FICTION.

In this sequel to *Homecoming,* Dicey and her younger siblings are living with their grandmother during their mother's confinement in a mental hospital. Dicey and her grandmother build a relationship, and then the children's mother dies.

Voigt, C. (1994). *When she hollers.* New York: Scholastic. (4–8). CONTEMPORARY REALISTIC FICTION.

This is a sensitive book about sexual abuse by a stepfather and about a mother who will not believe it is happening.

White, R., & Cunningham, A. M. (1991). *Ryan White, My own story.* New York: Dial. (6–12). INFORMATIONAL BOOK.

In this account, coauthored by Ryan White, he tells about his battle with AIDS, the discrimination he suffered, and dying. Nevertheless, this is an upbeat treatment.

Williams, K. L. (1995). *A real Christmas this year.* New York: Clarion. (3–6). CONTEMPORARY REALISTIC FICTION.

Megan has to look after her disabled younger brother, which interferes with her life, but her low-income family is doing the best they can.

Woodson, J. (1994). *I hadn't meant to tell you this.* New York: Delacorte. (6–9). CONTEMPORARY REALISTIC FICTION.

In this book, Lena and her sister face the fact that they must flee their sexually abusive father.

Woodson, J. (1999). *Lena.* New York: Delacorte. (6–9). CONTEMPORARY REALISTIC FICTION.

Lena and her sister, Dion, flee their sexually abusive father. Lena is a protective big sister seeking a place in the world.

Zeller, P. K. (1990). *Focus on marijuana* (D. Neuhaus, Illus.). New York: 21st Century Books. (4–7). INFORMATIONAL BOOK.

This is one of a series of books that explores the influence of drugs on the body and brain.

References and Books for Further Reading

Andrews, S. (1994). *Teaching kids to care.* Bloomington, IN: ERIC Clearinghouse.

Baskin, R., & Harris, J. (1977). *Notes from a different drummer.* New York: R. R. Bowker.

Baskin, R., & Harris, J. (1984). *More notes from a different drummer.* New Providence, NJ: R. R. Bowker.

Friedberg, J., Mullins, J., & Sukiennik, A. (1992). *Portraying persons with disabilities, Vol. 1* (2nd ed.). New Providence, NJ: R. R. Bowker.

Hesse, K. (1998). The Newbery Acceptance Speech. *Horn Book, 74,* 432–440.

Landrum, J. (1998–1999). Adolescent novels that feature characters with disabilities: An annotated bibliography. *Journal of Adolescent & Adult Literacy, 42,* 284–295.

Lickona, T. (1992). *Educating for character.* New York: Bantam Doubleday Dell.

Noddings, N. (1992). *The challenge to care in schools.* New York: Teachers College Press.

Peck, P. (1983, winter). The invention of adolescence and other thoughts on youth. *Top of the News, 39*(2), 45–47.

Robertson, D. (1992). *Portraying persons with disabilities.* New Providence, NJ: R. R. Bowker.

Rudman, M. K. (1993). *Children's literature: Resource for the classroom.* Norwood, MA: Christopher-Gordon.

Sage, M. (1977). A study of the handicapped in children's literature. In A. S. MacLeod (Ed.), *Children's literature: Selected essays and bibliographies.* College Park: University of Maryland College of Library and Informational Service.

Stoodt-Hill, B. (1999). A survey of children's reading preferences. Richmond, VA: Unpublished.

Wilde, S. (1989, November). The power of literature: Notes from a survivor. *New Advocate, 2,* 49–52.

Unit Studies: Literature, Response, and Learning

14

KEY TERMS

character frames	skills-based themes
classroom sets	story frames
connections	story grammar
core literature	student-generated themes
fact frames	teacher-generated themes
inquiry	theme cycle
integrated units	theme immersion
plot frames	unit

GUIDING QUESTIONS

Have you been a student in a classroom or observed in a classroom where literature was widely used to enrich reading instruction or the teacher used literature-based instruction?

1. What are the benefits of literature-based instruction?

2. What problems might a teacher encounter in developing literature-based instruction?

3. How can literature enrich content studies?

4. What are the basic components of a literature unit?

OVERVIEW

The focus throughout this book has been to encourage children's response to literature. Children who read and

respond to literature have a better understanding of the world they live in (Walmsley, 1994). Readers who find beauty in stories and poems, in the sounds of words, and who relate their feelings to the books they read are responding to the aesthetic nature of literature (Rosenblatt, 1983).

This chapter synthesizes and organizes the understandings developed in the preceding chapters. Reflecting on this material will help you create experiences that facilitate children's growth into life-long readers. When reading to students and encouraging their own reading, you have just begun to create their literary experiences. Unit experiences enrich and expand their literary growth through the focus, goals, and experiences that are a part of the unit and materials (Hughes, 1993).

This text is a resource for identifying books in the various genres that interest children and that address the subject matter or theme. It is also a resource for exploring literature in classrooms, media centers (libraries), and homes. This chapter provides practical, usable guides and units that classroom teachers have developed, used, and refined. These units are organized around a variety of formats, reflecting the different ways teachers think about them.

INTRODUCTION

Careful planning of literature-based units and themes will maximize children's understanding of, response to, and appreciation of literature. The literature and materials and teaching strategies are benchmarks to guide your development of literature-based curricula or to add literature experiences to basal textbooks or programs.

The opening vignette portrays a third-grade teacher who incorporated integrated instruction. The students in her classroom have opportunities to find patterns and connections through inquiry, or collaborative research, which enables them to create meaning from the books they read. Students learn through building connections among books and ideas that facilitate their understanding (Hartman, 1992; Peterson, 1991). As integrated studies unfold, students construct connections among subjects and topics, which occur as they reflect on the subject in relation to their experiences.

VIGNETTE

A Day in Mary Scott's Third Grade Classroom

The students work individually or in small groups. Their activities include writing in response journals, reading independently, and doing fine arts activities.

First block of the day: Language arts

These third graders are in the midst of a unit focusing on the geography and life in various regions of the United States during the first half of the twentieth century. The major books for this unit are *In Coal Country* by Judy Hendershot, *Letting Swift River Go* by Jane Yolen, *The Year of the Perfect Christmas Tree: An Appalachian Story* by Gloria Houston, and *Celebrate America: In Poetry and Art* edited by Nora Panzer.

They are expanding language arts abilities while exploring geography and the ways authors use language to create setting. In analyzing setting and description, they also refer to the illustrations created for these books. Their learning experience includes writing daily in response journals. Comparing the various sections of the United States as portrayed in these stories develops comprehension and critical thinking. The teacher reads aloud each day from *Celebrate America: In Poetry and Art* to expand their understanding and appreciation.

After language arts, the students have physical education or recess.

Mathematics

As a part of this unit, the students explore the concepts of centuries, time, and history.

Social Studies and Science

Students compare the physical geography and descriptions of the three regions depicted in the books they are reading through photographs, illustrations, and written language. They also identify regional foods and recipes for the county fair, which will be the culminating activity for the unit.

Fine Arts

The students read about regional arts in the areas they are studying in *Celebrate America: In Poetry and Art*. Exploring the arts in the various regions involves contacting regional and local art museums to order prints and slides for classroom display. Their art focus is primitive painting and the art teacher explores the techniques used in primitive paintings so that the students can create their own primitive paintings.

Closure

At the end of each day, students discuss their experiences and write in their learning logs.

Carlos shows readers how he and his Latino friends celebrate Carnival.

UNITS OF STUDY

A *unit of study* is a collection of lessons that motivates students toward in-depth study of a topic, issue, person, idea, or theme. These studies give students a chance to focus on the topic or theme to discover relations and connections. Well-developed units encourage students to become active, involved learners. Units may focus on a single book, an author, or a group of books that addresses the same topic or theme. Students use reading, writing, talking, listening, and thinking as tools to discover relations and to link new connections with prior understandings.

In unit teaching, important aspects of two or more subjects are deployed to achieve goals that focus on substantial themes such as a specific disaster, racial tension, loneliness, survival, the solar system, the water cycle, and endangered species. Terry Johnson and Daphne Louis (1990) found they could sensibly and productively integrate some subject areas for some of the time. Language arts, social studies, and science offer numerous opportunities for integration with art and music. The language arts processes of reading, writing, speaking, and listening are best learned in relation to content areas. Learning across the curriculum is a natural outcome of literature-based instruction. Units may be whatever you choose to make them—there is no right or wrong way to conceptualize these studies. The way teachers use literature in their classrooms or media centers may change many times during their professional life.

Literature in the Curriculum

Teaching with literature is not a specific method or process based on hard-and-fast rules. Uses of literature can be molded and adapted to fit local curricula and students. Teachers grow and change in their philosophies of teaching as they experience schools, children, and educational philosophies. Moreover professional teachers continue reflecting, evolving, and learning throughout their careers.

Literature, however, can be brought into classrooms no matter what the prevailing philosophy, and the goal of this chapter is to explore ways to do this. This chapter presents a variety of ideas that can be adapted to many classrooms. Unit teaching, integrated teaching, thematic teaching, and child-centered classrooms coexist with many approaches to education. For example, many elementary teachers modify basal reader lessons by drawing on their students' experiences and interests. Basal readers are often organized in units that facilitate literature connections. These teachers develop concepts and vocabulary that are critical to understanding lessons and ask questions that stimulate higher order thinking. Teachers may offer students a wide range of extension activities.

These guidelines are helpful in developing a literature emphasis in literacy programs:

1. Read aloud to students every day at every grade level. Read fiction, poetry, and nonfiction.

2. Find out about students' interests: what they know and have experienced and what they need to know. This will help in planning extensions and selecting literature.

3. After completing a unit or lesson in a basal program, develop a unit on the same theme or topic that permits students to read whole books rather than the abridged, edited versions of literature that appear in most basal readers. For example, after

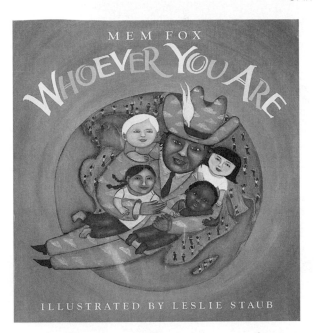

Mem Fox shows readers that every one of us is important.

reading a basal unit on dreams, develop a dreams unit. Discuss the basal selections the students have read. They could discuss dreams from many perspectives. What are their dreams about growing up? What do they dream about? What is the importance of dreams?

4. Ask the students to think of questions that they would like to have answered about dreams. Write the questions on a chart or chalkboard.

5. Give booktalks on the books selected for the unit and give the children choices about the questions they will research and the books they will read. For 4 or 5 groups of 5 to 7 students, 7 or 8 sets of books are adequate. The children should read their books individually.

6. Have the students participate in literature discussion groups after they have completed the book. Students who are accustomed to reading page by page in the basal, however, may do better at the outset by reading half of the book and participating in discussion, then completing the book and participating in another discussion. Develop the students' reading fluency and confidence so they can read the entire book first, because they will have an understanding of plot, characterization, and other story elements only after reading the entire book.

7. Have the students keep literature logs as they read their books. An alternative is to write a letter to a friend or their teacher about their book.

8. Have the students select extensions that express their response to the literature they read.

Making Connections Through Inquiry

Units provide a framework for inquiry in the classroom; inquiry is one of the processes through which children learn. Knowledge only gives the illusion of residing in books: In reality knowledge is connections among people in particular times and contexts (Harste, 1993). Learners help one another learn and respond because learning is social inquiry (Copenhaver, 1993), which means that social processes such as talking with others help readers make sense of new information. Although they can arrive at a meaning alone, they do so more often in collaboration (Barnes, 1995). This is why creating classrooms of inquirers is essential to learning (Harste, 1993).

The beginning or access point for inquiry is what students already know about a topic. Creating a web that shows what students already know about the topic or theme can initiate a unit. Construct a class or group web on a large sheet of paper with the topic in the center. Then have students brainstorm what they know about the subject, and write the information around the topic. Students can create individual webs of their own knowledge. Figure 14.1 shows a web of prior knowledge for the topic of friends that a group of second graders created for a Being Friends unit. The teacher of this class chose to begin the inquiry with "things we do with friends" because this was the most frequent response given on the map of knowledge.

Inquiry focuses on authentic learning because the questions students focus on have meaning for them. Moreover, they are actively engaged in finding the answers. They are learning through doing. Inquiry is based on students' questions and their investigations to answer their questions. Some teachers ask students to think of questions about curriculum topics that are personally important. Both student-generated questions and teacher-generated questions focus inquiries. Students may spend a week or so thinking of questions, writing them in journals, and explaining why the particular

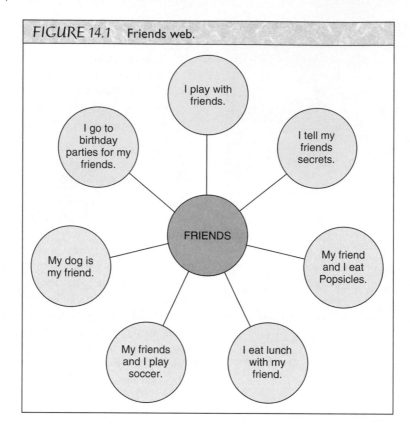

FIGURE 14.1   Friends web.

questions are personally powerful enough to sustain a period of inquiry (Copenhaver, 1993).

To investigate their questions, students discuss, listen, read, write, view films and television, and consult with people who have special knowledge related to the questions. They may conduct their own experiments, such as a group of kindergarten students did when investigating insects. They experimented to find out which insects crawled fastest. All of these approaches to investigation and more can be applied during integrated instruction.

DEVELOPING THEMES AND UNITS

Defining themes and units is difficult because the applications of this concept are so varied. Some educators use the terms synonymously, whereas others differentiate between them (Walmsley, 1994). This book uses *theme* to identify the meaning, focus, or central idea of a unit of study, such as "ocean life" or "courage," and *unit* to identify the organizing framework for a thematic study. A unit for ocean life identifies the goals, experiences, activities, and materials the teacher plans to de-

velop through the theme. In addition to theme units, teachers can devise structural units. The box on page 326 shows a theme unit that identifies the focus and the framework of a given topic.

In theme unit learning, students and teachers investigate topics, themes, and concepts in various ways. Students who are independent readers can study books, magazines, and reference books, and emergent readers can rely on stories and information read aloud. Discussion contributes to examining a topic, as does writing about it. Many teachers encourage students to maintain learning logs about their units. Students participate in individual or group activities and projects related to the topic. Frequently teachers incorporate the arts (music, drama, and visual arts) into the unit. In many instances, science, math, and social studies are relevant to the unit. These connections offer opportunities for both direct and indirect teaching of the skills and strategies that we expect students to accomplish.

A theme unit is an intensive learning experience for students and teachers. Teachers may choose theme units or students may select theme units. Some educators call student-generated units *theme cycles* (Altwerger & Flores, 1994). Both types of units are a part of classroom experiences. The suggested theme topics in the box on page 328 can be used for many grade levels because these inquiries can develop in various ways and at several levels.

Students use their language-arts abilities as they learn through theme units. Jean Dickinson (1995) reports that her fifth- and sixth-grade students, who used picture books, novels, and textbooks to explore World War II, developed these reading strategies:

1. to visualize while reading
2. to use prior knowledge
3. to reread interesting and exciting parts and parts with especially interesting language
4. to ask questions about what they read
5. to make predictions
6. to discuss books with friends
7. to find ideas for writing
8. to look beyond the cover
9. to relate books to other books they have read and to books by the same author
10. to put themselves in the story
11. to know when they do not understand something in the book
12. to read the rest of a paragraph to figure out a word meaning

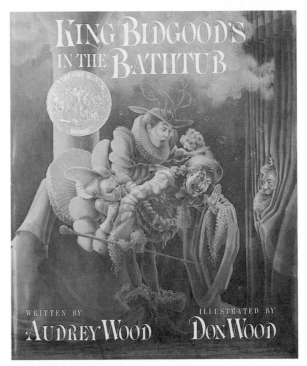

The author's lyric text with its repetitive style conveys the merry mood of King Bidgood's court. Together the author and illustrator have created an unforgettable bathtime story.

Shared Book Experiences

Teachers can manage book sharing for a unit in at least five ways. The approach depends on the age and maturity of the students and the availability of materials. Regardless which system of managing book sharing teachers use, they must give the students time to discuss and share their ideas about the books that they read.

1. Read the book or books aloud, encouraging the students to discuss what is happening. Read books more than once: Children's responses increase and deepen with each rereading of a book (Jacque, 1993).
2. Read each book aloud and have the students respond in a response journal, literature log, or interactive journal.

3. Obtain a class set of one title and have all the students read that book independently. This is probably the least-favored approach because it easily leads to reading and analyzing the book in the same way that a basal reader selection is analyzed. This fragmentation interferes with the benefits of integrating literature in the reading program.
4. Divide the class into four cooperative groups and have each group read a different book. Conduct a booktalk for each of the books in advance to help children choose a book that appeals to their interests.
5. Have various groups or individuals read a book and retell the high points of the parts they read.

Planning Units

When choosing the unifying theme or focus of each unit, the teacher should consider several factors. Curriculum goals and objectives are central to the units.

Theme Unit

Focus: Time Fantasy for Upper Elementary

Objectives: To develop students' concepts of fantasy and the rules of well-written fantasy

To develop students' concepts of time and space as they are related to time fantasy

To develop students' ability to compare and contrast

PART I. TEACHER-PLANNED WHOLE-CLASS READING AND VIEWING

Teacher Read-Aloud:	*A Wrinkle in Time* by Madeleine L'Engle
Group or Partner Reading:	*Tom's Midnight Garden* by Philippa Pearce
	Playing Beatie Bow by Ruth Park
	The Root Cellar by Joyce Lunn
	"Flying Saucers" nonfiction magazine article
Music:	appropriate to the past or future
Art:	art of the period

PART II. OVERVIEW OF LITERATURE PRESENTATION

Introduce the unit with a discussion of time travel. Ask the students questions such as:

1. Do you think people can travel through time?
2. If you could travel through time where would you go and what time period would you choose?
3. What are the advantages of time travel?
4. What are the disadvantages of time travel?

In addition to discussion have students write their thoughts about these questions. Then have them think of questions they would like to have answered. Create time capsules with paper towel rollers or some similar container. Seal the containers and store them until the unit is complete.

The teacher will read *Wrinkle in Time* aloud over a three-week period. When the book is finished, have students read in small groups or in pairs one of the titles listed for group or partner reading in Part I. Additional related reading is listed at the end of this unit.

The beginning point when devising a literature unit is to determine the focus of the project. Next, locate and sequence relevant material and develop appropriate experiences. Choosing the focus may be the most difficult aspect of the process because it demands a fairly broad familiarity with the world of children's literature and an understanding of the structure of the discipline. Units can be formulated around topic, form, structure, or theme (Johnson and Louis, 1990).

Have students work in small groups or pairs and assign a novel to be read by a specified date. Ask each group or pair of students to prepare analyses of their novels to share with the rest of the class. All students should be prepared to contribute to the comparison chart in Figure 14.2.

RELATED READINGS

- *Stonewords* by Pam Conrad
- *Eva* by Peter Dickinson
- *A Swiftly Tilting Planet* by Madeleine L'Engle
- *A Traveler in Time* by Alison Uttley
- *Ella Enchanted* by Gail Levine

CURRICULAR CONNECTIONS

Math. Have students discuss the role of math in space travel and how math relevant to space relates to their current math instruction.

Social studies. Describe the lifestyle and values of the people in the various stories. Have the students identify what kinds of things they need to consider when describing a society and its values.

Writing. Instruct students to keep reading journals in which they write a response to a novel they read.

Students also may use art, or music, or both to express their responses to the novels.

FIGURE 14.2   Comparison chart of novels

COMPARISON CHART				
Novel	*Stonewords*	*Ella Enchanted*	*Playing Beatie Bow*	
Main character				
Age				
Gender				
Friend or companion				
Setting 1				
Setting 2				
Theme				
Historical connections				
Climax				
Plot resolution				

THE NOVEL ANALYSIS

1. Plot   Is the plot interesting? _____

             Does the plot explain time travel in a logical fashion? _____

             How does the author convince you this story could have happened? _____,

             _____

2. Characters   Are the characters convincing? _____

             Do you care about the characters? _____

             What made them seem like real people? _____

3. Setting   How does the author convince readers that the setting is a real place? _____

             _____

             How does the author convince readers the time setting is real? _____

             _____

Theme Topics for Units

HOLIDAYS ACROSS CULTURES

New Year's	Flag Day
Christmas	Memorial Day
Kwanzaa	Arbor Day
Hanukkah	

CONCEPTS

being a friend/having friends	journeys around the world
what do your senses tell you?	journeys around our state
how many kinds of courage are there?	journeys around our country
heroes	what makes you laugh?
superheroes	what is a family?
space	conservation
communities	growing

ARTISTS AND WRITERS

Steven Kellogg	Trina Schart Hyman
Avi	Lois Ehlert
Pam Conrad	Katherine Paterson
Marc Brown	Tomie dePaola

CURRENT EVENTS

disasters	hurricanes
floods	blizzards
earthquakes	random acts of kindness
senseless acts of beauty	senseless acts of violence

CURRICULUM TOPICS (CONSULT YOUR OWN CURRICULUM)

addition	multiplication
great sentences from literature	great paragraphs from literature
water cycle—where has all the rain gone?	nutrition—you are what you eat
interpreting maps—where in the world are you going?	rain forests—what do rain forests have to do with me?
weather—it's raining cats and dogs	genre (traditional literature, poetry, biography, etc.)

For instance, first-grade teachers are usually accountable for emergent reading and writing and for developing concepts of family, friends, and holidays, among others. These concepts can be developed through units that focus on many topics or themes.

Once the curriculum goals and objectives are accounted for, consider what the students already know and what they need to know about the selected topic. In addition to prior knowledge, teachers usually consider the students' interests when planning units because they will be more motivated and have a greater sense of ownership when pursuing their own interests. Other considerations regarding choice of topic include the students' learning needs, developmental levels, and previous experiences. Teachers and librarians need to build background experiences for the theme or topic with students who lack them.

The available resources are an important consideration when planning units. A good supply of well-written books is essential. The books must, of course, address the unit topic or theme, but they also must match the students' range of reading levels. Both print and nonprint media develop children's knowledge base and understanding. Videos, films, pictures, computer programs, and Web sites are useful in developing units. Guest speakers or people who can demonstrate skills or materials add interest to unit studies. For example, a study of Britain is more lively when someone from that country visits the classroom. The Internet offers many sites that take students to Great Britain; they may visit museums and many fascinating places. Students can take field trips in their hometown to look for products imported from England.

When planning units, teachers need to include opportunities for art, music, writing, and similar experiences for students to respond to the literature they read, which enable readers to develop, refine, and personalize their understandings (Weston, 1993). The box on page 330 shows some of the possibilities for response experiences with literature-based units. The box on page 329 provides a form to summarize the unit plan.

Unit Plan

- Unit topic, theme, concept:
- Concepts (goals, objectives—include adopted curriculum, student interests, and student needs):
- Science:
- Social Studies:
- Math:
- Language Arts:
- Others (e.g., art, music, physical education, dance):

- Response experiences:
- Literature and textbooks used:

- Resources used (e.g., experts, references, film, experiments, field trips, media center):

- Describe processes used:
  inquiry:
  discussion:
  cooperative groups:
  paired activities:
  writing:
  observation:
  models:
  whole group:

- Response activities:
  storytelling:
  writing:
  art:
  music:
  dance:
  drama:
  response journal:
  other:

- Evaluation:
  portfolios:
  booklist:
  products:
  checklists:
  journals:

Response Experiences for Literature-Based Units

Language Arts

LISTENING

- Listening exercises using passages with outstanding language
- Visualize scenes from the book
- Listen for sensory images
- Identify book's structures
- Retell a story
- Speakers on special subjects

SPEAKING

- Discuss the book in a group
- Discuss the book using student-generated questions
- Tell the story as a news report
- Tell a student-composed story

READING

- Use reader's theater for all or part of a story or poem
- Read cultural variations of a traditional story
- Read and compare to other books

WRITING

- Write an original story with the same pattern
- Write the story as a play
- Write more about a character or add a new character
- Write song lyrics based on the story
- Keep a journal of feelings, ideas, parallels evoked as a result of story reading or listening

SCIENCE

- Study the habitat of the story
- Create an experiment to solve a story problem or mystery
- Think about how science is related to the book
- Relate scientific method to book

SOCIAL STUDIES

- Research the country, people, geography, history, anthropology of the setting
- Study the descriptions of places

PHYSICAL EDUCATION

- Create a dance of a scene in a story or a poem

MATH

- Discuss the math concepts that appear in the story

FINE ARTS

- Create a mural depicting scenes from the story
- Draw a picture story map
- Make puppets
- Dramatize one character

Assessing Unit Experiences

Assessment is an integral part of instruction and one means of gathering information regarding students' growth in understanding and appreciating literature. Teachers use assessment to determine whether students have learned what they are trying to teach. Assessment may reveal that students need additional practice and experience, or they may need to reteach concepts, skills, and processes. Moreover, teachers monitor progress because they are responsible for knowing students' progress and reporting their progress to the school and parents.

Literature-based reading programs usually do not have standardized tests to evaluate student achievement. The portfolio method of assessment (discussed later) is one means of effectively evaluating many areas of stu-

dents' reading achievement. Some school systems have adopted reading assessments or reading inventories to gather additional information, which can be combined with portfolio assessment. Other sources of information regarding student progress include work samples, journal entries, projects and displays, individual conferences, oral presentations, and student assessment forms. Teachers' observations and documentation are viable alternatives to testing, especially when combined with work samples: The goal is to develop readers who understand and respond to literature, as well as to accomplish content goals when appropriate. An excellent assessment of goal achievement is to hand a child a book and listen to him read and discuss the text; this will reveal to both teacher and child whether they are meeting their goals.

Informal observations are the basis for teacher-created anecdotal records of children's reading and literature experiences. To document their assessments, teachers record their observations. They may keep a running record or use a checklist that identifies the key curriculum, understandings, and skills. For instance, a literature checklist might include items such as:

- identifies the beginning, middle, and ending of stories,
- recognizes the central character in a story,
- follows the sequence of events in a story,
- understands and follows plot, and
- chooses to read for pleasure.

Teachers who collect varied materials and observations develop more complete pictures of children's reading, which facilitates their planning.

Portfolio assessment is a form of informal evaluation in which the student and the teacher gather information about each student's progress (Kimeldorf, 1994). Student input is a critical component of this assessment. A more complete picture of an individual's strengths and weaknesses is assembled through a reflective portfolio process. Reviewing portfolios collaboratively gives teachers and students opportunities to analyze what has been taught and learned and to plan for the future. Regardless of how valuable this process is, however, it is individualized and time-consuming for teachers.

Portfolio assessment falls into the following three common types (Meinback, Rothlein, & Fredericks, 1995):

1. *Showcase portfolios.* The student selects the work samples to be placed in the portfolio. Some teachers have the student explain the context of the work and why the work is exemplary from the student's perspective.
2. *Descriptive portfolios.* The teacher assigns projects and selects completed work to place in the portfolio.
3. *Evaluative portfolios.* Students include qualitative materials, such as tests, in the portfolio.

CLASSROOM ACTIVITIES

This section of the chapter is devoted to actual units that classroom teachers have developed, used, and refined. These units are organized around different formats, some narrative and others outlined, reflecting the different ways teachers think about them. Experienced teachers, beginning teachers, and those in the mid-career may approach units and use literature in the classroom differently.

Unit Suggestions

ACTIVITY 14.1   DAY AND NIGHT (KINDERGARTEN)

When planning a thematic unit, I usually consider the students' interests and the activities they have previously enjoyed. I also consult the Standard Course of Study for our grade level and identify specific curricular goals and objectives from each of the content areas that corresponds to the unit I plan to teach. Often the units selected come from the area of social studies or science. It is very important when using an integrated approach that materials selected teach skills in reading/language arts, mathematics, social studies, science, fine arts, and physical education.

When planning this type of unit, I first identify my goals related directly to the content area in which the unit was selected. In this particular unit on day and night, I want the students to be able to explain both verbally

and nonverbally why we have day and night. Many other skills can be developed during this time. I plan to introduce the concept of telling time to the hour and half-hour; review counting and number identification 0–12; and review seasons, months of the year, and days of the week. Children will experience using a sundial for the first time and will create a crude sundial for themselves. Children will have fun discovering shadows and measuring their own shadows during different times of day. These are the goals I identified.

Topic: Day and Night

Goals

1. To help children understand that day and night are caused by the rotation of the earth.

2. To introduce the concepts of the sun, moon, stars, and the planet Earth.

3. To introduce the concept of telling time using various instruments (sundial, clock, calendar).

Skills to Develop

Mathematics

- counting 0–12 (review)
- telling time—compare/contrast a clock, calendar, and sundial
- number identification 0–12 (review)
- telling time to the hour and half-hour (introduction)

Reading

- sequencing (story events)
- letter identification: Mm, Ss, Dd, Nn
- rhyming words (continued)
- phonemic awareness: m, s, d, n

Writing

Stories for dictation. Children dictate stories to their teacher based on their responses to these books: *Sounds All Around; Night in the Country; Me and My Shadow;* and *Stella and Roy Go Camping.*

Literature

- journals
- logs
- shared writing

Science

- day/night
- constellations
- earth, sun, stars, moon
- rotation or turning
- shadows
- seasons with respect to day/night

Social Studies

- things we do during the day/night
- days of the week
- birthdays
- careers that require working at night
- months of the year
- culture

Fine Arts

- tracing shadows
- nighttime pictures using black wash paint
- daytime pictures
- constellation patterns

Physical Education

Focus on circle games that move clockwise ("Duck, Duck, Goose"; "With Stars"; "Farmer in the Dell"; "London Bridge")

Introduction

Thought Question

Why do we have day and night? Record student responses on chart paper.

Circle Time

Use the book *I Have a Friend* by Keiko Narahashi to introduce the concept of shadows. After reading, have children go out and find their shadows. With a friend, they can use a nonstandard unit of measurement (jump ropes or blocks) to measure one another's shadows. Compare the height of the shadow with the child's actual height. Repeat this activity at another time of day. Discuss concepts of taller and shorter. Ask the children why they have shadows and record responses.

Small-Group Activities

Read the story *Bear Shadow* by Frank Asch.

Discussion Questions

- Why did the bear want to lose his shadow?
- What things did he do to lose his shadow?
- How would you lose your shadow?
- Draw a picture of where you might go so your shadow would not find you.

Activities

- Have children dictate a story about losing their shadow.
- Trace children's shadows outside on butcher paper. Have the children come inside and paint their shadows to show the clothing they are wearing.
- Have children write a story about something they and their shadow like to do together.
- Share the poem *My Shadow* by Robert Louis Stevenson and ask students to compare the

poem with the activities they and their shadow like to do together.

- Using paper clocks, show the children the time they went outside to trace their shadows.
- Play the recording "Paper Clocks" by Hap Palmer.
- Discuss the events of a school day. Using the clock, show the time children get up in the morning, eat breakfast, start school, have circle time, go outside to play, and so forth. Let children experiment with clocks to show when they do certain things at home. *The Grouchy Ladybug* by Eric Carle may be read in a small group and then placed in the mathematics or exploration center with clocks for the children to use.

Learning About Daytime

Circle Time

Discuss why we are able to see our shadows. Ask the children if they think they would see their shadows if it were cloudy or raining outside. Encourage the children to deduce that we see our shadows because of the sun. discuss that the sun is a star, that we live on a planet called Earth, and why we are able to see the sun part of the day. Discuss why we have day and night.

Read *Rooster Crows* by Ragnhild Scamell. Discuss why the rooster could not get the sun to come up at the stroke of midnight, and show this time on the clock. Explain that we have day and night because the earth rotates or turns. When the earth turns, part of it is exposed to the sun and the other part is not. Using a globe, help the children locate your state and mark it with a sticker. Gently turn the globe so that the children can see the earth rotate or turn. Let the children practice rotating the globe. Have one child hold a flashlight on the part of the globe with the students' state. Explain that the sun is a star and it does not move; rather the earth slowly rotates or turns. As it turns and the sun is no longer pointing directly at the state, it is becoming afternoon. As the earth turns we no longer face the sun and it is nighttime. The other part of the world is facing the sun and therefore having daytime. As the earth continues to turn, the part that is far away from the sun gets closer, creating dawn, then morning. Let children take turns holding the flashlight (the sun) and turning the globe (Earth).

Circle Time

Share *The Napping House* by Audrey Wood with the students. After several readings students will enjoy pre-

dicting what is coming next. The children can dramatize the story with puppets. Read *Grandfather Twilight* by Barbara Berger to the students. Discuss what the pearl in the story represents (the moon). This will lead into the study of night.

Writing. Have the children do a shared writing activity. For example, the children can write to their parents explaining their experiences and what they learned.

Learning About Nighttime

Circle Time

Have the children observe the night sky. Ask them to record everything they see. They can do this for several evenings. During circle time have the children tell what they saw and record their information. Categorize and count the different things. Discuss what the moon looked like. Introduce the phases of the moon with Frank Asch's book *Moon Bear*. Have children compare the moon they saw with the one in the story. Have children draw the phases of the moon on the calendar as they observe them in the night sky.

Small-Group Activities

Share picture books of constellations. Show the children that the constellations make patterns in the sky. Tell them how long ago people used these patterns to help find their way. Help children recreate the pattern of the Big Dipper and Little Dipper. Place glue-backed stars on black paper as they appear in the night sky (copy pattern from constellation book). Use chalk to connect the stars so that children can see the pattern. Repeat using other stars.

Have children cut out pictures of activities that are done during the day and others that are done at night; then sort and paste the pictures onto poster board. Record words and phrases that are dictated about the pictures. (One half of the poster board can be yellow and the other half black to simplify the sorting process for students. It also helps to have some pictures already available for cutting for children who are unable to locate any pictures in magazines.)

Introduce /Ss/ for stars. Have children look for /s/ on stars. Use sand trays to trace the letter/s/. Discuss the /s/ sound. Help children identify words beginning with the /s/ sound. Use a dictionary to help children associate pictures with the letter and sound. (Repeat this activity with other letters when appropriate.)

Circle Time

Introduce *Goodnight Moon* by Margaret Wise Brown. Read the story several times. Begin leaving out the final word in the second sentence and have children supply it. Pull out pairs of rhyming words and illustrate each on an index card. Have children practice putting the pairs of words together.

Small-Group Activities

Read *Time for Bed* by Mem Fox. Study the end papers. Listen for pairs of rhyming words. Help the children find the rhyming words. Create a book of rhyming words with things associated with day and night. Encourage the students to make end papers for their books. Make nighttime pictures using crayons. Use a tempera paint wash to cover the pictures. Have children dictate sentences about things they like to do at night.

Read *Happy Birthday, Moon* by Frank Asch. Help the children learn their birthdays. Discuss the book, asking what kind of present the children would give the moon. Discuss the idea of an echo, which is introduced in this story. Then have children make a birthday board with their birthdays and the birthdays of family members.

Circle Time

Read Cynthia Rylant's *Night in the Country*. Have the children listen to and record the night sounds of the city. Share these during circle time. Compare the night sounds of the city and the night sounds of the country.

Small-Group Activities

Share *Good-night, Owl!* by Pat Hutchins. Have the animals that keep the owl awake cut out to use on the flannel board. Have the children practice retelling the story using the flannel board animals to sequence the retelling.

Other Books to Use in Unit

- *Ladybird First Facts About Space* by Caroline Arnold
- *What the Moon Is Like* by Franklin M. Branley
- *While I Sleep* by Mary Calhoun
- *Turtle Day* by Douglas Florian
- *Star, Little Star* by Lonnie George
- *The Moon and You* by E. C. Krupp
- *Under the Moon* by Joanne Ryder
- *Nine O'Clock Lullaby* by Marilyn Singer

ACTIVITY 14.2   RECYCLING (FIRST OR SECOND GRADE)

The students in this classroom had already had experiences with big books prior to this unit. They had many experiences with *Raffi Songs to Read* and had listened to Raffi tapes. They had big book experiences with books like Ruth Krauss's *The Happy Day,* which has a simple, repetitive text that children enjoy. They dramatized some of these stories and thoroughly enjoyed reading and rereading or singing their big books. See chapter 5 for more information on big books.

The unit described here was planned in response to the schoolwide recycling project suggested by the principal. After my initial panic at the thought of first graders and recycling, I remembered a new book I had seen at my favorite children's bookstore and ran to the phone to put a hold on *Round and Round Again* by Nancy Van Laan. One way home from school, I picked up the book and started planning.

Topic: Recycling

Objectives

- to learn the meaning of recycling
- to identify things that can be recycled
- to identify language repetition and predict it
- to identify rhyming words

Literature

- *Round and Round Again* by Nancy Van Laan. This is a predictable book.
- *Mother Earth's Counting Book* by Andrew Clements

Background Information for the Teacher

Recycling means reusing. The mother recycles everything in Van Laan's story. The refrain in the book is: "Round and round and round again, over yonder and back again." The story is told in couplets and the rhymes will be easy for first graders to find.

The key points are:

1. the meaning of recycling
2. the materials that are usually recycled
3. the recycling symbol
4. local recycling and how the children can help
5. yard sales are a form of recycling and so is giving one's clothes to a younger brother or sister

Materials
- recycling decal
- recycling bin
- picture of the recycling truck
- student journals
- chart paper

Language Arts
Read the story aloud twice and ask the children to join in on the repeated parts. After the second reading, ask the children to chant the refrain and show them it in print on the chart.

Ask these questions to start discussion:

1. Why do you think the title of this book is *Round and Round Again?* (Relate to recycle and reuse.)
2. What was your favorite of all the things that mother made in this story?
3. What were the funniest things that mother recycled?
4. How do you recycle things at your home?
5. (Show the recycling symbol.) Why do you think it looks like this? Can you think of any ways this symbol is related to the book we just read?
6. Think of some questions you would like to ask about the story or about recycling. Then we will discuss your questions.

Science
Discuss the fact that Styrofoam is permanent garbage. Think of things made of Styrofoam and materials that could be used instead.

ACTIVITY 14.3   COUNTING (SECOND, THIRD, OR FOURTH GRADE)

This unit, which focuses on various ways of counting, is presented in a unit map.

Questions
- What do you want or need to count?
- What is the best way to count that thing?

Math
- Why do we need to count things?
- What kinds of things need to be counted?
- What is one-to-one correspondence?

Writing
- Think of a new way to count and write it down.

Art
- Make illustrations and art to go with the project.

Social Studies
- Why is counting people important?
- What do we call it when we count people?
- What is a poll?
- Why do we conduct polls?

Literature
- *The King's Commissioners* by Ann Friedman
- *The Search for Delicious* by Natalie Babbitt
- *Only One* by Marc Harshman
- *The Librarian Who Measured the Earth* by Kathryn Lasky
- *The Toothpaste Millionaire* by Jean Merrill
- *Counting Jennie* by Helena Clare Pittman
- *Chestnut Cove* by Tim Egan
- *Turtle Time* by Sandol Stoddard

ACTIVITY 14.4   NATIVE AMERICAN FOLKTALES (THIRD GRADE)

Topic: Native American Folktales

Objectives
- to learn the characteristics of the folktale genre
- to identify Native American values through their folktales
- to develop vocabulary related to the Native American culture

Background Information
Originally folktales were told around campfires, which is why their structure differs from other genres. Folktales were told by people who did not read or write. They were used to entertain, to teach lessons, and to teach listeners about their culture. Folktales were very important in transmitting culture. These tales help us know how Native Americans lived and what is important to them.

Literature
- *Baby Rattlesnake* by Te Ata. This teaching tale is written at an independent reading level for third grade.
- *Iktomi and the Berries: A Plains Indian Story* by Paul Goble. Read aloud to introduce Native American storytelling. Trickster tales such as this one appear in the traditional literature of all cultures.
- *The Great Buffalo Race: A Seneca Tale* retold by Barbara Juster Esbensen. This pourquoi tale explains how the buffalo got its hump. It is a good read-aloud.
- *Sky Dogs* by Jane Yolen. This read-aloud explains why Native Americans first thought horses were dogs.
- *Ma'ii and Cousin Horned Toad* by Shonto Begay. The author, a Navajo, tells his own favorite childhood tale in this book.
- *The Mud Pony: A Traditional Skidi Pawnee Tale* by Caron Cohen. This story shows the importance of horses in the Native American culture. Children can read this one.
- *The Legend of the Bluebonnet* by Tomie dePaola. This picture book is one children can read for themselves.
- *Rainbow Crow: A Lenape Tale* by Nancy Van Laan. A read-aloud.
- *The Rough-Face Girl* by Rafe Martin. This is a tale from both the Algonquin and Comanche. It is a Native American version of *Cinderella*. Good for oral reading, discussion, and comparison with other Cinderella versions.
- *Navajo: Visions and Voices Across the Mesa* by Shonto Begay. The talented Navajo artist combines his art with his prose and poetry in this book.

Before the Unit
Have the students make a web of words they associate with Native Americans.

Vocabulary
The students can make an illustrated dictionary of words from the books they read or listen to. They may choose words from the web and the stories they read. These words can be done on cards, charts, or notebooks.

Discussion Questions

Prereading
- What do you think a "teaching tale" is?
- Have your parents ever told you a teaching tale? What about?
- As you read one of these stories, think about who is teaching something and who is supposed to learn something.

Postreading
- What lesson do you think the characters were supposed to learn?
- What did you notice in these stories?
- Did any of the stories remind you of other books you have read or television shows you have seen?
- What questions would you like to ask the characters in these stories?

Extensions for Response:
- Summarize one of the stories orally or in writing.
- Describe the setting of one of the stories.
- Tell what you learned about Native Americans from these tales. Tell or write what makes you think this.

- Look at the Seneca page borders in *The Great Buffalo Race* and create the borders you would like if you were a Native American.
- Have the children draw numbers and participate in small-group sharing according to the number they drew. In the small groups, ask them to:

1. Retell a favorite part of the story.
2. Identify the words that describe the main character.
3. Tell two new things learned from one story.
4. Summarize the story.
5. Complete the following chart for each story.

Title and author: _____

Problem: _____

Resolution: _____

Main character: _____

What was the reward? _____

Who received the reward? _____

What did you learn about Native Americans? _____

_____

ACTIVITY 14.5   PIRATES (THIRD OR FOURTH GRADE)

Topic: Pirates

Goals

- to study oceans through pirate routes
- to study the difference between salt water and fresh water
- to learn about the importance of vitamin C and how sailors got vitamin C
- to learn why pirates needed math to figure out where they were and to plot their route
- to learn pirate songs
- to learn pirate words and language

Questions

1. Why did pirates live on ships? Did they always live on ships? Can you be a pirate if you do not live on a ship?
2. Why do pirates wear funny clothes?
3. How did they get their treasure?
4. Did they help other people?
5. How do you become a pirate?

Dan keefer '99

Dan drew this fierce pirate after reading Treasure Island.

6. Why do they use funny words?
7. Did all the pirates live long ago? Do pirates exist today?

8. Why did people become pirates?
9. Can girls be pirates?

Literature
- *Tough Boris* by Mem Fox

- *Pirates: Robbers of the High Seas* by Gail Gibbons
- *One-Eyed Jake* by Pat Hutchins
- *Do Pirates Take Baths?* by Kathy Tucker
- *The Ballad of the Pirate Queens* by Jane Yolen

ACTIVITY 14.6 INVENTORS (FOURTH OR FIFTH GRADE).

Topic: Inventors

Questions
- What is the best invention in the world?
- What is an invention that changed the world?
- What is creativity?

Math
- measurement
- computers
- probability

Art
- make drawings of inventions
- make a model of your favorite invention

Thinking
- classify inventions

Science
- identify important scientific inventions

Writing
- Write to the U.S. Patent Office to get information about obtaining patents.
- Write about a needed invention that would improve your life.

Social Studies
- How did these inventions change life in the United States: automobiles, telephones, computers, computer chips?

Reading
- Review biographies of famous inventors and some not so famous—what made these people creative?

Sarah drew this lighthouse after reading Birdie's Lighthouse as part of a lighthouse unit. She also visited some lighthouses on the Web.

Literature
- *100 Inventions That Shaped World History* by Bill Yenne
- *The Wright Brothers: How They Invented the Airplane* by Russell Freedman
- *Walt Disney* by Barbara Ford
- *Outward Dreams: Black Inventors and Their Inventions* by Jim Haskins

- *The Many Lives of Benjamin Franklin* by Mary Osborne
- *Pinkerton: America's First Private Eye* by Richard Wormser
- *Mistakes That Worked: 40 Familiar Inventions and How They Came to Be* by Charlotte Foltz Jones
- *The Toothpaste Millionaire* by Jean Merrill

ACTIVITY 14.7   COURAGE (FIFTH GRADE)

Topic: Courage

Objectives
- to develop students' concept of courage
- to develop students' understanding of the ways authors develop historical setting
- to develop students' understanding of the kinds of conflict that lead to exceptional expressions of courage
- to develop a time line that shows the time period of the wars in this unit
- to relate the time periods studied to the music of those periods

Background
The students will read books set in the Civil War; World War II; the 1950s in Montgomery, Alabama; and in the present day. The goal is to develop their understanding of courage and to recognize different kinds of courage.

Materials
- journals
- *Star Wars* video
- tape recorders and tapes
- tape or records of music for the various eras
- other materials as students develop ways to express their response to the books they read

Literature
- *Mountain Valor* by Gloria Houston
- *Rosa Parks: My Story* by Rosa Parks with Jim Haskins
- *Shades of Gray* by Carolyn Reeder
- *Letters from a Slave Girl: The Story of Harriet Jacobs* by Mary E. Lyons
- *Number the Stars* by Lois Lowry
- *Waiting for Anya* by Michael Morpurgo
- *Hatchet* by Gary Paulsen

Beginning
Ask the students to write a definition of *courage* in their journals and date it. Explain that they will write in their journals after each reading session. Their journal entries will focus on their response to the books they are reading.

Guiding Questions
1. What kind of courage is expressed in this book?
2. Did you notice any symbols of courage in this book? If so, what were they?
3. What kinds of conflict appeared in the book that caused a character to demonstrate courage?
4. How did the author build tension in the book you read?
5. How did the author create an historical setting in your book?
6. How did the events in the book change the lives of the characters, particularly the main character?

Extensions
1. Write a new definition of *courage* in your journal and date it.
2. Collect newspaper stories about people who demonstrate courage.
3. Listen to the music of this time period and compare it to the ideas expressed in the book you read. What similarities and differences can you identify?
4. Create a time line for the story you have read.
5. Prepare interview questions that you would like to ask the main character in your book.
6. Read another book from the list and compare it with the first one you read.

SUMMARY

This chapter guides readers' synthesis of their learning about children's literature. Using literature in the classroom, reading aloud daily, integrated curriculum, inquiry learning, units, and assessment are the focus of this chapter. Units are intensive learning experiences that help students make connections as they learn. Integrated units develop language skills within a context that may involve social studies, math, science, the arts, music, and physical education. Inquiry learning focuses on students' questions as powerful stimulators of learning. Units may focus on curriculum topics, themes, authors/illustrators, current events, concepts, or student-generated ideas.

A unit includes these components: goals or objectives, resources, science, social studies, math, language arts, the arts, music, physical education, literature, and textbooks. A unit plan serves as a road map for teachers, which may be revised as it is used.

Thought Questions

1. What components should teachers consider when developing units? Can you think of any additional considerations?
2. Describe a unit in your own words.
3. How do teachers use portfolios to assess literature-based instruction?
4. How are reading aloud to children and their own silent reading related to inquiry units?

Research and Application Experiences

1. Prepare a complete integrated unit for a grade level of your choice. Teach your unit if possible.
2. Prepare a unit that could be integrated with a specific unit in a basal reader of your choice.
3. Consult a curriculum guide for a local school district and list the unit topics or themes appropriate for the grade level you teach or hope to teach.
4. Read a unit ideas book and decide which units you would be interested in using and why you would use these.
5. Write a narrative plan for inquiry instruction and getting children to raise important questions.
6. Determine what literature-related items you think should be included in a portfolio for your class or the class you plan to teach. Explain why you would choose these items.

Children's Literature References and Recommended Books

Arnold, C. (1990). *Ladybird first facts about space.* New York: Ladybird. (1–3). INFORMATIONAL BOOK.

The book develops space concepts for young children.

Asch, F. (1978). *Moon bear.* New York: Scribner's. (PreK–1). PICTURE BOOK.

Bear thinks he sees a bear in the moon.

Asch, F. (1985). *Bear shadow.* Englewood Cliffs, NJ: Prentice Hall. (PreK–1). PICTURE BOOK.

Little Bear sees his shadow and he is fascinated.

Asch, F. (2000). *Happy birthday, moon.* New York: Simon & Schuster. (PreK–1). PICTURE BOOK.

In this book, a birthday celebration leads to a discussion of moons.

Ata, T. (1989). *Baby rattlesnake* (L. Moroney, Adapt.; V. Reisberg, Illus.). San Francisco: Children's Book Press. (1–2). TRADITIONAL LITERATURE.

This is a Native American teaching tale.

Babbitt, N. (1969). *The search for delicious.* New York: Farrar, Straus & Giroux. (3–6). MODERN FANTASY.

The king searches for the meaning of *delicious.*

Begay, S. (1992). *Ma'ii and cousin horned toad.* New York: Scholastic. (1–3). TRADITIONAL LITERATURE.

This is a traditional Navajo story about the coyote trickster.

Begay, S. (1994). *Navajo: Visions and voices across the Mesa.* New York: Scholastic. (2–6). POETRY, PICTURE BOOK.

Shonto Begay combines his art with his prose and poetry in this book.

Berger, B. (1984). *Grandfather Twilight.* New York: Philomel. (K–2). PICTURE BOOK.

Grandfather Twilight is a gentle person and a storyteller children enjoy.

Branley, F. M. (1986). *What the moon is like* (T. Kelley, Illus.). New York: Harper & Row. (1–3). INFORMATIONAL BOOK.

This is a simple, informational book.

Brown, L. K., & Brown, M. (1992). *Dinosaurs to the rescue! A guide to protecting our planet*. New York: Little, Brown. (2–6). INFORMATIONAL BOOK.

This informational book is a guide to conservation.

Brown, M. W. (1947). *Goodnight moon* (C. Hurd, Illus.). New York: Harper & Row. (PreK–1). PICTURE BOOK.

A young child wishes goodnight to everything in his room and to the moon.

Calhoun, M. (1992). *While I sleep* (E. Young, Illus.). New York: Morrow. (PreK–1). PICTURE BOOK.

A child asks where various animals and toys live.

Carle, E. (1977). *The grouchy ladybug*. New York: Thomas Crowell. (K–2). PICTURE BOOK.

The grouchy ladybug tries to fight with everyone she meets but makes a friend.

Clements, A. (1994). *Mother Earth's counting book* (L. S. Johnson, Illus.). New York: Clarion. (K–2). PICTURE BOOK.

Mother Earth counts plants, animals, lakes, oceans, and continents.

Cohen, C. L. (Reteller). (1988). *The mud pony: A traditional Skidi Pawnee tale* (S. Begay, Illus.). New York: Scholastic. (1–3). TRADITIONAL LITERATURE.

A Pawnee boy makes a pony from mud, which comes to life.

Conrad, Pam. (1990). *Stonewords*. New York: HarperCollins. (4–6). MODERN FANTASY.

In this suspense story, Zoe and Zoe Louise are best friends in spite of the fact that one of them is a ghost from the past. Zoe must discover the mystery of Zoe Louise and her ghostly presence.

dePaola, T. (1983). *The legend of the Bluebonnet*. New York: Putnam. (K–2). TRADITIONAL LITERATURE.

This is a Comanche tale in which selfishness is punished and unselfishness is rewarded.

Dickinson, P. (1988). *Eva*. New York: Delacorte. (6–9). MODERN FANTASY.

This science fiction story has a principal character who survives an accident when her brain is implanted into the body of a chimp.

Dorros, A. (1990). *Me and my shadow*. New York: Scholastic. (1–3). CONTEMPORARY REALISTIC FICTION.

The author explores the concepts of shadows.

Egan, T. (1995). *Chestnut Cove*. Boston: Houghton Mifflin. (K–2). CONTEMPORARY REALISTIC FICTION.

Portrays a friendly community in which people help one another.

Esbensen, B. J. (Reteller). (1994). *The great buffalo race: How the Buffalo got his hump; A Seneca tale*. New York: Little, Brown. (1–3). TRADITIONAL LITERATURE.

This pourquoi tale explains how the buffalo got its hump.

Florian, D. (1989). *Turtle day*. New York: Crowell. (1–3). INFORMATIONAL BOOK.

This book helps children learn about turtles and reptiles.

Ford, B. (1989). *Walt Disney*. New York: Walker. (4–8). BIOGRAPHY.

This biography of Walt Disney provides children with insight.

Fox, M. (1989). *Night noises* (T. Denton, Illus.). New York: Harcourt Brace Jovanovich. (K–2). PICTURE BOOK.

This story is about the sounds of animals at night.

Fox, M. (1994). *Tough Boris* (K. Brown, Illus.). New York: Harcourt Brace Jovanovich. (2–4). PICTURE BOOK.

This book is about Boris, a pirate who is not so tough.

Fox, M. (1997a). *Time for bed* (J. Dyer, Illus.). New York: Harcourt Brace Jovanovich. (PreK–1). PICTURE BOOK.

All of the animals are ready for bed in this book.

Fox, M. (1997b). *Whoever you are*. (L. Straub, Illus.). New York: Harcourt. (K–4). PICTURE BOOK.

Freedman, R. (1991). *The Wright brothers: How they invented the airplane* (W. Wright & O. Wright, Photog.). New York: Holiday House. (3–8). BIOGRAPHY.

A description of the contest and the Wright brothers' quest to fly. Photographs from the time add realism to the presentation.

Friedman, A. (1994). *The king's commissioners*. New York: Scholastic. (2–5). MODERN FANTASY.

Commissioners of the king find a mathematical solution to their problems.

George, L. (1992). *Star, little star*. East Rutherford, NJ: Grosset and Dunlap. (K–2). POETRY.

This is a book of poetry about night and sleeping.

Gibbons, G. (1992). *Recycle! A handbook for kids*. New York: Little, Brown. (2–5). INFORMATIONAL BOOK.

This book suggests specific recycling projects.

Gibbons, G. (1993). *Pirates: Robbers of the high seas*. New York: Little, Brown. (2–5). INFORMATIONAL BOOK.

Facts are presented about pirates in this descriptive book.

Goble, P. (Reteller). (1989). *Iktomi and the berries: A Plains Indian story.* New York: Orchard. (K–6). TRA-DITIONAL LITERATURE.

A trickster story from the Lakota Sioux.

Harshman, M. (1993). *Only one.* New York: Cobble-hill. (K–2). PICTURE BOOK.

This counting book is different from others in that it focuses on counting multiples such as one hive of bees.

Haskins, J. (1991). *Outward dreams: Black inventors and their inventions.* New York: Walker. (5–8). INFOR-MATIONAL BOOK.

This book details significant accomplishments of African Americans that have been omitted from tra-ditional history books.

Hendershot, J. (1987). *In coal country* (T. B. Allen, Il-lus.). New York: Knopf. (2–4). HISTORICAL FICTION.

A girl tells about growing up in a miner's family in Ohio during the 1930s.

Houston, G. (1990). *Littlejim* (T. B. Allen, Illus.). New York: Philomel. (3–5). HISTORICAL FICTION.

Littlejim is a Civil War story about one of the au-thor's ancestors.

Houston, G. (1994). *Mountain Valor* (T. B. Allen, Illus.). New York: Philomel. (5–7). HISTORICAL FICTION.

Twelve-year-old Valor dresses like a boy to help her family during the Civil War.

Hutchins, P. (1972). *Good night, owl!* New York: Macmillan. (K–2). PICTURE BOOK.

A cumulative tale about night and going to sleep.

Hutchins, P. (1979). *One-eyed Jake.* New York: Green-willow. (1–3). PICTURE BOOK.

This book is about one-eyed Jake, a mean-looking pirate.

Jones, C. F. (1991). *Mistakes that worked: 40 familiar inventions and how they came to be* (J. O'Brien, Illus.). New York: Doubleday. (4–8). INFORMATIONAL BOOK.

This book presents the stories behind 40 things that were invented or named by accident.

Krauss, R. (1949). *The happy day* (M. Simont, Illus.). New York: Harper. (PreK–1). PICTURE BOOK.

The forest animals find a spring flower.

Krulik, N. E. (1991). *My picture book of the planets.* New York: Scholastic. (1–3). INFORMATIONAL BOOK.

This book introduces the planets to young children.

Krupp, E. C. (1993). *The moon and you* (R. R. Krupp, Illus.). New York: Macmillan. (1–3). CONTEMPO-RARY REALISTIC FICTION.

A bedtime story about a child and the moon.

Lasky, K. (1994). *The librarian who measured the earth* (K. Hawkes, Illus.). New York: Joy Street. (1–4). INFORMATIONAL BOOK, BIOGRAPHY.

This story tells about an actual person who was a li-brarian, and how he measured the earth before we had modern technology.

L'Engle, M. (1962). *A wrinkle in time.* New York: Far-rar, Straus & Giroux. (5–8). MODERN FANTASY.

Meg and her brother set out to find their father who has disappeared. They learn that they must journey through time in order to find him.

L'Engle, M. (1978). *A swiftly tilting planet.* New York: Farrar, Straus & Giroux. (5–8). MODERN FANTASY.

Levine, G. C. (1997). *Ella enchanted.* New York: Harper. (3–7). MODERN FANTASY.

A blundering fairy gives Ella an undesirable enchantment.

Lowry, L. (1989). *Number the stars.* Boston: Houghton Mifflin. (4–7). HISTORICAL FICTION.

A Jewish girl is "adopted" by her neighbors who hide her from the Nazis.

Lunn, J. (1983). *The root cellar.* New York: Scribner's. (4–8). CONTEMPORARY REALISTIC FICTION.

Twelve-year-old Rose is sent to live with her aunt in a country home on the shores of Lake Ontario. Rose is not very happy in her new situation until she dis-covers an overgrown root cellar.

Lyons, M. E. (1992). *Letters from a slave girl: The story of Harriet Jacobs.* New York: Scribner's. (4–7). HISTORICAL FICTION.

The experiences of a slave girl are written in the form of letters.

Martin, Jr., B. (1967). *Brown bear, brown bear what do you see?* (E. Carle, Illus.) New York: Holt Rinehart & Winston. (PreK–1). PICTURE BOOK.

This predictable story about large colorful animals is good for the youngest readers.

Martin, R. (1992). *The rough-face girl* (D. Shannon, Illus.) New York: Putnam. (K–4)). TRADITIONAL LIT-ERATURE.

This tale, from both the Algonquin and Comanche Indians, is the Native American version of *Cin-derella.*

Merrill, J. (1972). *The toothpaste millionaire.* Boston: Houghton Mifflin. (4–7). CONTEMPORARY REALISTIC FICTION.

A homemade toothpaste project becomes very profitable.

Morpurgo, M. (1991). *Waiting for Anya.* New York: Viking. (4–7). HISTORICAL FICTION.

Jewish children are taken to an isolated farm and then across the border to escape from the Germans during World War II.

Narahashi, K. (1987). *I have a friend.* New York: McElderry. (PreK–3). CONTEMPORARY REALISTIC FICTION.

Some children have dolls or pets or toys as friends; this boy has a shadow as a friend.

Osborne, M. P. (1990). *The many lives of Benjamin Franklin.* New York: Dial. (4–8). BIOGRAPHY.

The author focuses on Franklin as a scientist, statesman, diplomat, and inventor.

Panzer, N. (Ed.). (1994). *Celebrate America: In poetry and art.* New York: Hyperion. (3–8). PICTURE BOOK.

Art and poetry are arranged thematically. The art is from the National Museum of American Art at the Smithsonian.

Park, R. (1982). *Playing Beatie Bow.* New York: Atheneum. (3–6). MODERN FANTASY.

Parks, R., with Haskins, J. (1992). *Rosa Parks: My story.* New York: Dial. (6–10). BIOGRAPHY.

Rosa Parks tells her story of defying Jim Crow laws in Montgomery, Alabama.

Paulsen, G. (1987). *Hatchet.* New York: Viking. (5–7). CONTEMPORARY REALISTIC FICTION.*

Brian survives a plane crash and survives the wilds of Canada.

Pearce, P. (1958). *Tom's midnight garden* (S. Einzig, Illus.). Philadelphia: Lippincott. (4–7). MODERN FANTASY.

This time fantasy won the British Carnegie Medal. Tom stays in an apartment in an old house with his aunt and uncle when his brother is ill. He discovers a clock that strikes 13 and a mysterious garden that appears at midnight with a young girl in it.

Pfeffer, W. (1999). *Sounds all around* (H. Keller, Illus.). New York: HarperCollins. (K–3). INFORMATIONAL BOOK.

Teaches young children the science of sound and how we use sound.

Pittman, H. C. (1994). *Counting Jennie.* Minneapolis: Carolrhoda. (1–3). PICTURE BOOK.

In this picture book, Jennie counts everything she sees.

Raffi. (1992). *Raffi songs to read.* New York: Crown. (PreK).

This is a cassette tape containing songs to help children learn the rhythm of language. Printed text for the tape is available.

Reeder, C. (1989). *Shades of gray.* New York: Macmillan. (4–7). HISTORICAL FICTION.

This story is set during the Civil War.

Ryder, J. (1989). *Under the moon* (C. Harness, Illus.). New York: Random House. (PreK–K). PICTURE BOOK.

Mama mouse teaches her child special things such as how to use his nose.

Rylant, C. (1986). *Night in the country* (M. Szilagyi, Illus.). New York: Bradbury. (1–3). PICTURE BOOK.

This is a beautifully illustrated exploration of night.

Scamell, R. (1994). *Rooster crows* (J. Riches, Illus.). New York: Tambourine. (1–3). PICTURE BOOK.

A placid rooster bets he can crow the sun up.

Singer, M. (1991). *Nine o'clock lullaby* (F. Lessac, Illus.). New York: HarperCollins. (PreK–K). PICTURE BOOK.

A poetic lullaby for young children.

Stevens, J. R. (1999). *Carlos and the carnival* (J. Arnold, Illus.). Flagstaff, AZ: Rising Moon. (K–4). CONTEMPORARY REALISTIC FICTION.

Stevenson, R. L. (1989). *A child's garden of verses.* New York: Chronicle. (K–6). POETRY.

Stoddard, S. (1995). *Turtle time* (L. Munsinger, Illus). Boston: Houghton Mifflin. (PreK–K). PICTURE BOOK.

When climbing into bed a young child is reminded of her pet turtle.

Tucker, K. (1994). *Do pirates take baths?* (N. B. Westcott, Illus.). Morton Grove, IL: Albert Whitman. (1–3). PICTURE BOOK.

In this humorous story, children learn that even pirates take baths.

Uttley, A. (1964). *A traveler in time* (C. Price, Illus.). New York: Viking. (3–6). MODERN FANTASY.

Van Laan, N. (Reteller). (1989). *Rainbow crow: A Lenape tale* (B. Vidal, Illus.). New York: Knopf. (1–3). TRADITIONAL LITERATURE.

A traditional tale about a smart crow.

Van Laan, N. (1994). *Round and round again* (N. B. Westcott, Illus.). New York: Hyperion. (1–3). PICTURE BOOK.

This delightful story of an unusual mother who cannot waste anything is told in couplets with a refrain that children will immediately join in with.

Wolff, A. (1999). *Stella and Roy go camping*. New York: Dutton. (K–2). PICTURE BOOK.

A brother and sister go camping and identify animal footprints.

Wood, A. (1984). *The napping house* (D. Wood, Illus.). New York: Harcourt Brace Jovanovich. (K–2). PICTURE BOOK.

A child and a number of animals go to sleep in Granny's bed.

Wood, A. (1985). *King Bidgood's in the bathtub* (D. Wood, Illus.). New York: Harcourt. (K–2). PICTURE BOOK.

Wormser, R. (1990). *Pinkerton: America's first private eye*. New York: Walker. (5–8). INFORMATIONAL BOOK.

This book begins with Pinkerton growing up in the slums of Glasgow.

Yenne, B. (1993). *100 inventions that shaped world history*. San Francisco: Bluewood Books. (3–6). INFORMATIONAL BOOK.

Identifies and tells about 100 important inventions.

Yolen, J. (1990). *Sky dogs* (B. Moser, Illus.). New York: Harcourt Brace Jovanovich. (K–4). TRADITIONAL LITERATURE.

The story is about how the Blackfoot Indians got horses.

Yolen, J. (1992). *Letting swift river go* (B. Cooney, Illus.). New York: Little, Brown. (2–4). HISTORICAL FICTION.

This book tells about changing the course of a river by flooding a town.

Yolen, J. (1995). *The ballad of the pirate queens* (D. Shannon, Illus.). New York: Harcourt Brace Jovanovich. (3–8). MODERN FANTASY.

This picture book is about two women pirates and their exploits.

References and Books for Further Reading

Altwerger, B., & Flores, B. (1994). Theme cycles: Creating communities of learners. *Primary Voices K–6, 2*, 2–6.

Barnes, D. (1995). Talking and learning in classrooms: An introduction. *Primary Voices K–6, 3*, 2–7.

Copenhaver, J. (1993). Instances of inquiry. *Primary Voices K–6, 1*, 6–12.

Dickinson, J. (1995). Talk and picture books in intermediate classrooms. *Primary Voices K–6, 3*, 8–14.

Fredericks, A. (1991). *Social studies through children's literature*. Englewood, CO: Teachers Ideas Press.

Harste, J. (1993). Inquiry-based instruction. *Primary Voices K–6, 1*, 2–5.

Hartman, D. K. (1992). Eight readers reading: The intertextual links of able readers using multiple passages. *Reading Research Quarterly, 27*, 122–123.

Hughes, S. (1993). The impact of whole language on four elementary school libraries. *Language Arts, 70*, 521–530.

Jacque, D. (1993). The judge comes to kindergarten. In *Journeying: Children responding to literature* (pp. 43–53). Portsmouth, NH: Heinemann.

Johnson, T., & Louis, D. (1990). *Bringing it all together: A program for literacy*. Portsmouth, NH: Heinemann.

Kimeldorf, M. (1994). *A teacher's guide to creating portfolios*. Minneapolis, MN: Free Spirit.

Laughlin, M., & Swisher, C. (1990). *Literature-based reading*. Phoenix, AZ: Oryx Press.

Meinback, A., Rothlein, L., & Fredericks, A. (1995). *The complete guide to thematic units: Creating the integrated curriculum*. Norwood, MA: Christopher-Gordon.

Peterson, B. (1991). Selecting books for beginning readers. In D. Deford, C. A. Lyons, and G. S. Pinnell (Eds.), *Bridges to literacy: Learning from reading recovery*. Portsmouth, NH: Heinemann.

Rosenblatt, L. M. (1983). *Literature as exploration*. New York: Noble and Noble.

Walmsley, S. (1994). *Children exploring their world*. Portsmouth, NH: Heinemann.

Weaver, C., Chaston, J., & Peterson, S. (1993). *Theme exploration*. Portsmouth, NH: Heinemann.

Weston, L. (1993). The evolution of response through discussion, drama, writing, and art in a fourth grade. In K. Holland, R. Hungerford, and S. Ernst (Ed.), *Journeying: Children Responding to Literature* (pp. 137–150). Portsmouth, NH: Heinemann.

Culturally Conscious Literature

15

KEY TERMS

culturally conscious   diversity
culture

GUIDING QUESTIONS

1. What factors are important when selecting literature to build cultural consciousness?

2. How can literature contribute to cultural consciousness?

3. Can a person be an individual and a member of a cultural group?

OVERVIEW

Our country is a mosaic of cultures, which gives our society a richness and patina that we need to respect and cultivate. Culture is a design for living—ways of acting, believing, and valuing; it is a shared set of ideas, behaviors, discourses, and attitudes that internally and externally define a social group (Shanahan, 1994). Cultural consciousness is awareness of and sensitivity to cultural diversity and its contribution to our lives. Cultural diversity manifests in our lives every day—in voice mail systems that offer messages in the language of our choice and information and directions that are printed in several languages. Restaurants and groceries feature foods from all over the world. The music and art from many cultures are found in our museums and concert halls. No one can stand apart from culture, and each is a member of many subcultures within her or his social contexts. All readers are cultural beings—part of multiculturalism. Literature can help children become conscious of culture, cultural traditions, and values.

In this chapter, we explore books that will help children acquire sensitivity to and respect for the many cultures comprising this country. To this end, we have organized culturally conscious children's literature around themes and experiences that unite cultures.

The following vignette illustrates how cultural consciousness can be cultivated.

INTRODUCTION

Children reflect the culture into which they are born and they express cultural attitudes early in life. They can only express the attitudes their experiences have provided. One can only imagine the cultural consciousness of a two-year-old who yelled a racial epithet at an African-American friend of ours. And consider the cultural consciousness of a seven-year-old who used the same language with a Puerto Rican friend. These anecdotes illustrate the concepts of culture that some children bring to school. They already have concepts of family, morality, rules, time, gender roles, dress, safety, and values that are part of their cultural heritage. However, cultural consciousness can develop through experiences with the cultural heritage of other individuals. In the process of becoming culturally conscious, children can also develop pride in belonging to a particular racial, ethnic, cultural, or economic group, and they can learn to value other people. Literature contributes to children's cultural consciousness (Wong, 1997; Reimer, 1992).

VIGNETTE

On a snowy January day I drove into a school parking lot to visit student-teachers. Just ahead a bicycle rider carrying a passenger pedaled up to the school. An Asian child wearing a pink robe and fuzzy pink slippers hopped off. I followed her into the school; she went to a kindergarten classroom as I proceeded to the office. A few minutes later, I entered the same kindergarten to observe a frustrated student-teacher. The following discussion was under way.

Adam demanded, "What's wrong with that new kid, Miss Jefferson?"

"Yeah!" Antoine said. "She wears bed clothes to school, she's weird."

Diego added, "She eats funny stuff and she won't eat what we eat and she don't talk right."

The student-teacher explained that Kim came from Cambodia, a country far away where people dress differently, speak a different language, and their parents take them to school on a bicycle. Miss Jefferson also told the children that Kim had learned English, and she went on to explain that Kim's parents thought they were buying school clothes when they purchased the robe and slippers because they looked like Cambodian clothes.

Then Miss Jefferson asked the children how they would feel if they moved to a new country where they did not know the language and people laughed at them. She explained that her family came from Africa long ago. Then Dwan, Darcella, and Jerome proudly said their families came from Africa. Diego said that his family came from Mexico when he was a baby. After some discussion, Miss Jefferson asked the children to find out where their ancestors came from. In the meantime, she asked the children to be kind and helpful to Kim.

Later in our conference, we talked about the fact that new ideas become meaningful to children when they relate directly to them. The student-teacher consulted an article in *Childhood Education* entitled "Authentic Multicultural Activities" (Boutte & McCormick, 1992), the book *Building Bridges with Multicultural Picture Books* by Janice J. Beaty (1997), and *Educating Young Children in a Diverse Society* by E. W. King, M. Chipman, & M. Cruz-Janzen (1994). She selected the children's books listed in Figure 15.1 as a basis for the unit.

FIGURE 15.1   Children's books for a culturally conscious unit.

Clothing

Aunt Elaine Does the Dance from Spain by L. Komaiko (Multicultural)
Ayu and the Perfect Moon by D. Cox (Balinese)
My Best Shoes by M. Burton (African American)
Two Pairs of Shoes by E. Sanderson (Native American)
Uncle Nacho's Hat by H. Rohmer (Hispanic)

Food

Dumpling Soup by J. K. Rattigan (Hawaiian, Asian)
Everybody Cooks Rice by N. Dooley (Multicultural)
Feast for 10 by C. Falwell (African American)
Halmoni and the Picnic by S. Choi (Korean)
Itse Selu, The Cherokee Harvest Festival by D. Pennington (Cherokee)
Mel's Diner by M. Moss (Multicultural)
Potluck by S. Shelby (Multicultural)
Three Stalks of Corn by L. Politi (Hispanic)
The Tortilla Factory by G. Paulsen (Hispanic)
Where Are You Going Manyoni? by C. Stock (African)

CULTURAL STUDIES

The phrase *multicultural literature* does not appeal to many people today, perhaps because we have heard it so often and assume that it is "taken care of." Moreover, many people think multicultural refers to "other people" because they believe they are culture-free and normal (Shanahan, 1994). Children's literature itself demonstrates the complexity of multiculturalism and the inescapable conclusion that all readers are cultural beings (Shanahan, 1994).

Librarian Susan Lempke (1999) discovered that a formerly single culture (White) neighborhood library became so diverse that it served Ethiopian, Indian, Swedish, half White/half Black, and half Jewish/half Filipino children. The census Web site *www.census.gov/population/www/socdeo/foreign.html* shows that almost one third of the total foreign-born population entered the United States between 1990 and March 1997. These figures do not include the children born since their parents came to the United States, nor does it include the minority populations who have lived here for generations.

In her study Lempke identified 216 current picture books in four review journals. Then she analyzed the books to identify those portraying a diverse world. Only 21 picture books achieved this, and she questioned how well some of these books actually depicted diversity. For instance, she was concerned that African Americans were depicted as people with heavy problems and big responsibilities to the exclusion of other aspects of their cultures. However, Costello's (1992) research indicated that parents, teachers, and others in the African American community she studied viewed such books as authentic.

However, our reviews of current children's picture books indicate subtle changes. We can identify some picture books in which the protagonist's race is irrelevant to the story. For example, Nolen's *Raising Dragons* is a delightful imaginative picture book that shows an African American girl whose magnificent imagination is the basis for a wonderful story. Some culturally conscious teachers think that we should not forget the pain and sorrow of the African American experience, but we would do well to remember the times of joy and happiness.

Hazel Rochman (1993), herself an immigrant, is vehement about cultural studies and what she considers the essentials of these studies: (a) multiculturalism means across cultures, against borders, and (b) multiculturalism does not refer only to people of color. However, Rudine Sims Bishop (1994) and Violet Harris (1994) point out that people of color have been outside mainstream America, and for this reason they focus on the portion of multicultural literature that is concerned with people of color.

Obviously, immigrants account for some of our cultural diversity, but Native Americans, the original Americans, have cultures that are little known to many of us. Many Asian Americans, African Americans, and Latinos have maintained cultural traditions, although they have lived their entire lives in this country. Moreover, cultural groups such as the Amish, Appalachian Mountain folks, Latter Day Saints, and the Jewish have strong cultural traditions and they, too, have experienced prejudice for their beliefs.

Many cultures should be included in cultural studies, although our overall goal is to become culturally

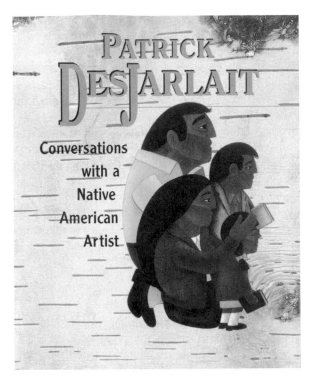

DesJarlait's paintings demonstrate some of the traditional customs central to the Red Lake Chippewa way of life.

1. Cultural studies help children recognize the humanity they share with all people. They learn that all people feel love, fear, and joy.

2. Cultural studies help children change their perspectives so they view themselves as members of various groups rather than seeking identity based solely on race, gender, or socioeconomic status. For example, an individual may be Black, American, a first grader, and so forth.

3. Cultural studies increase children's understanding, appreciation, and respect for different cultures and their contributions to the quality of life in the world.

4. Cultural studies foster positive group identity and understanding of many lifestyles. This encourages a broad range of social relationships, openness, and interest in others.

Cultural consciousness is "caught" rather than "taught"; it is developed through everyday experiences (Boutte & McCormick, 1992). Cultural consciousness should be integrated throughout all activities every day. These activities foster children's social, emotional, and cognitive development. When children recognize the humanity that all people share no matter what their cultural heritage, they learn that racism, discrimination, and prejudice are unacceptable in a just world.

LITERATURE AND CULTURAL STUDIES

Literature can affect not only how readers view children from other cultures, but it also influences how they view themselves and their own culture. Children's self-concepts are influenced by the images they see portrayed in media (Cohen, 1968; Miel & Kiesten, 1967). These images influence the way they see themselves, as well as the way they view people from various ethnic and cultural groups. Children respond well to stories that reflect situations they can identify within their own experiences.

Young children are especially susceptible to stereotypes because they have not yet developed critical thinking skills and accept information from books, television, and newspapers as factual. Books transmit messages to readers and listeners about minority groups. Unfortunately, these messages frequently encourage children to develop negative attitudes toward individuals who have a different physical appearance.

Books can also, however, foster feelings of pride in culture and an understanding of people who look

conscious. We can become aware of culture and sensitive to the impact of others' culture on our lives, as well as our own on their lives. However, the people within a cultural group are unique individuals with their own thoughts, goals, and values. We are each different from one another.

> From our fingerprints to our voices, from our toenails to our eyelashes, each of us is unique. But we are also alike. We eat. We sleep. We work. We play. We are born as babies, grow as children, and develop into mature human beings, the grand inheritors of Planet Earth. (Beaty, 1997, p. 3)

We cannot assume that all members of a cultural group think the same way. Within a cultural group, individuals are unique. Cultural studies help us focus on our similarities and celebrate our differences (Beaty, 1997). Through cultural studies, children explore literature, discuss, and participate to become more aware and accepting of one another. The following guidelines for cultural studies reflect some of the areas of common agreement (Ramsey, 1987; Stoodt, 1992).

different. In *My Song Is Beautiful*, Mary Ann Hoberman shows celebrations of childhood from many cultural perspectives. Eloise Greenfield's poems in *Night on Neighborhood Street* realistically describe African American families and their friends. Jan Spivey Gilchrist's illustrations enable children to see themselves and others realistically. After seeing this book, kindergarten children commented, "Hey, that baby looks just like me when I was little." An African American mother reading the book became tearful because it reminded her so much of her family growing up and her children when they were babies (Costello, 1992). Books such as these foster pride in one's own culture and understanding of other cultures. Reading about familiar experiences conveys the message that each person is valuable and important (Rasinski & Padak, 1990).

Literature provides vicarious experiences that expand understanding to give readers new lenses with which to view the world. "Books are an effective and powerful way to validate children's unique lifestyles and to expand their awareness beyond their immediate experiences" (Ramsey, 1987, p. 14). Stories can foster in children compassion and humanness, as well as the ability to feel joy about another person's happiness (Chukovsky, 1963). Writers use narrative to organize and interpret perceptions of the world, and fiction allows children to experience the lives of others. It can reconfirm one's own existence and humanity. When we recognize the power of stories, selecting the best ones for developing cultural sensitivity then becomes a paramount issue.

SELECTING CULTURALLY CONSCIOUS LITERATURE

The first consideration to address in choosing culturally conscious literature is choosing books that have authentic depictions of cultural groups and individuals. One problem in choosing excellent multicultural literature and finding literature with contemporary settings and lifestyles is the fact that many of the available multicultural books are in the traditional literature and historical fiction genre. Because stories provide a framework for interpretation of reality (Hardy, 1977), children need authentic multicultural literature that relates to their lives. Culture is affirmed when children discover that their own life experiences resonate with those in books.

The book *Bein' With You This Way* by W. Nikola-Lisa reflects the universal childhood joy of being together. This story is set in a park on a sunny day. The main character, an African American girl, rounds up a group of her friends for fun and playground games. They tell the story in a playground rap. Another book that depicts authentic experiences for children is *Barrio: Jose's Neighborhood* by George Ancona. Readers see the Barrio, the Mission District of San Francisco, through the eyes of young Jose Luis. The author communicates Jose's daily interests, his hopes, and his friends, as well as the people's abiding commitment to the Barrio.

Although no consensus exists regarding the issues involved in selecting culturally conscious literature, research and discussion suggest a few significant factors to consider in reviewing culturally sensitive literature. As you explore literature with children, you may think of additional factors that you believe should be added.

1. The book must be of excellent literary quality. Fiction should tell a good story, information must be interesting, and poetry excellent.
2. The book should be culturally accurate, reflecting cultural values and beliefs. Accurate information helps readers acquire a "true" sense of the culture. The dialogue and relationships should be authentic with in-depth treatment of any cultural issues (Yokota, 1993).
3. Cultural details enrich stories, poems, and informational pieces. These should be woven into literature in such a way that readers develop a sense of the culture (Reese, 1996).
4. The dialogue and relationships depicted in the books should be authentic.
5. Minority group characters should be distinct individuals whose lives are rooted in their culture (Yokota, 1993). These individuals should be depicted as three-dimensional characters with whom children can identify.

Books with characters of similar backgrounds, familial situations, living in familiar situations, and of a close age will help instill a motivation to read. The next section of this chapter is organized around themes and topics that focus on the common bonds that children share. Figure 15.2 identifies the themes and topics that are the focus of this section.

FAMILY BONDS

Every child comes first of all from a family. Families are as varied as individuals: Some may have a single

FIGURE 15.2   Developing cultural consciousness.

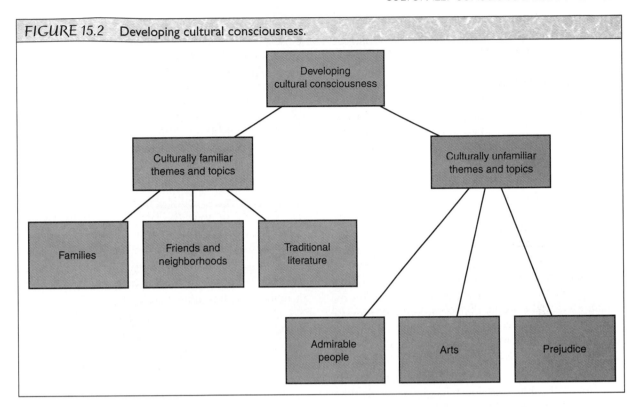

mother or a single father as the custodial parent, others may have both a mother and a father, or grandparents or aunts and uncles may be in the parenting role. Children of gay couples may have two mothers or two fathers. We cannot identify all of the possible variations of the family theme, but children can identify with characters in a family setting because they have related experiences. When books show children from another culture, they have an opportunity to put themselves in the roles of multicultural characters (Beaty, 1997). Many children enjoy a close relationship with their grandparents.

Grandparents of every background and ethnic group love their grandchildren. The book *Halmoni and the Picnic* by Choi tells about a Korean grandmother who finds adjusting to life in New York difficult until her granddaughter Yummi invites her to a school picnic. The children enjoy grandmother's delicious kimbap and invite her into their games and songs. The Spanish word for grandmother is *Abuela,* and the book *Abuela* by Arthur Dorros tells about Rosalba and her Abuela who have an imaginary flying trip over New York. The close relationship between a Hispanic boy and his grandfather is the theme of Pat Mora's book *Pablo's Tree.* In this story, the grandfather buys a tree and dec-

orates it with a different surprise every year on his adopted grandson's birthday. *Sam and the Lucky Money* by Karen Chinn portrays the story of a Chinese boy and his grandparents. Each of these books could be a superb beginning point for cooking, artwork, or storytelling.

Young children learn about all kinds of families from stories portraying everyday life. Rain is the setting for the gentle African American family story, *Silver Rain Brown* by M. Helldorfer. In this story, a boy and his pregnant momma swelter in summer heat. The baby and the rain arrive on the same evening. A celebration of fathers is the theme of the beautiful poetry in the book *In Daddy's Arms I Am Tall: African Americans Celebrating Fathers,* compiled and illustrated by Javaka Steptoe. Another family story, *Bird Boy* by Elizabeth Starr Hill, tells the story of young Chang who is mute, but that does not prevent him from helping his family earn a living by fishing on the Li River in southern China.

Cynthia Rylant and Barry Moser grew up in Appalachia, and they present a picture of Appalachian life in *Appalachia: The Voices of Sleeping Birds.* In words and images they portray homes, foods, dogs, and views of the world. *Coal Mine Peaches* by Michelle Dionetti provides an excellent portrayal of coal mining families in Appalachia. A Mexican American child describes a day in his life in Tricia Brown's book, *Hello Amigos!* Photographs illustrate his story about going to school, celebrating his birthday, and living with his family in the Mission District of San Francisco. *Down Buttermilk Lane* by Barbara Mitchell illustrates life in an Amish family. A photoessay, *Salmon Summer* by Bruce McMillan, portrays the cultural heritage of 9-year-old Alex, a Native Aleut, as he and his father fish for summer salmon. Linda Jacobs Altman's book, *Amelia's Road,* tells the story of a migrant child's dream.

All children will appreciate Walter Dean Myers's book *Brown Angels: An Album of Pictures and Verse.* He couples superb photographs of African American children with sensitive poetry to show their parents' pride and love. Combining *Brown Angels* with *Family Pictures* by Carmen Lomas Garza, *Snapshots from the Wedding* by Gary Soto, and *An Amish Wedding* by Richard Ammon could stimulate children from many cultures to find family albums and wedding albums to learn family stories. Perhaps they will be motivated to create photoessays.

In *Grandpa's Gamble* by Richard Michelson the grandchildren think Grandpa Sam spends all his time praying. Then one day they bump the credenza door and photographs come flying out, and they are shocked to discover what they do not know about Grandpa. Based on a true story, this family narrative depicts the Jewish culture while telling a great story. Research into her Ojibwa roots led Louise Erdrich to write *The Birchbark House.* She is a member of the Turtle Mountain Band of Ojibwa, and her story portrays traditional Ojibwa life. The protagonist, Omakayas, plays with the baby, fights with her brother, and tries to be like her beautiful sister. However, the satisfying rhythms of their lives are shattered forever when a visitor arrives.

When grandparents, cousins, and assorted relatives gather, family stories are told again and again. Cynthia Rylant creates a rollicking tale of family togetherness in *The Relatives Came.* Although the story is set in Appalachia, most people can relate to the excitement of a visit from relatives and perhaps tell their own stories about the time the relatives came. Stories are the focus of *The Sunday Outing* by Gloria Pinkney, which tells of the times Aunt Odessa and Ernestine spend at the train station telling stories. In *Letters from Rifka* by Karen Hesse, 12-year-old Rifka tells of her journey to the United States in letters to her cousin in Russia. The letters tell a story that everyone can enjoy. A collection of stories about Cuban life, *Under the Royal Palms: A*

Childhood in Cuba by Alma Flor Ada, gives readers a close look at an active and loving extended family.

Family members significantly influence our lives, but friends are very important, too. If we are very fortunate, we have friends with many cultural backgrounds.

Friends and Neighbors

Friends and neighbors often become lifelong sources of strength and support. The popular African adage, "It takes a village to raise a child," has become familiar to us in recent years, and it is demonstrated in the book *Down Home at Miss Dessa's.* Author Bettye Stroud tells a story set in a rural African American community in the 1940s and shows how neighbors benefited young and old in the community. This warm story tells how two young sisters offer to help care for an elderly neighbor who has injured her foot.

A dramatic true story, *Teammates,* by Peter Golenbock, describes the friendship of Jackie Robinson and his teammate Pee Wee Reese. When others could not see beyond the color of Robinson's skin, Reese stood by his friend, the first African American to play big league baseball. Bill Gutman writes about the cooperation and teamwork that are keys to the success of Michael Jordan and Scottie Pippen in the biography *Teammates: Michael Jordan, Scottie Pippen.* He tells their personal histories, as well as portraying their respectful relationship. Some friends help by standing up to be counted like Pee Wee Reese; others do it quietly.

Mary is a friend who cares for Mr. Hiroshi's beautiful garden after he is relocated to a war hostage camp in *Flags* by Maxine Trottier. Friends help a Vietnamese girl overcome her fears in the story *The Little Weaver of Thai-Yen Village* by Khanh Tuyet Tran. She is alone and frightened after her grandmother and mother are killed in the Vietnam War. Then she comes to the United States to have her wound treated, and new friends help her. Friends are prominent in Ruth White's powerful books. In *Belle Prater's Boy,* White writes about friendships in Appalachian settings. Woodrow, who is Belle Prater's son, comes to live in Coal Station after she disappears. Woodrow meets his cousin Gypsy who is curious about his mother, but she becomes his friend and supporter.

In a somewhat lighter vein, Yoko, a Japanese girl, makes a friend who helps her feel better after classmates jeer at her favorite sushi lunch in the book *Yoko* by Rosemary Wells. Karen Hesse depicts friends having fun as they dress in their bathing suits in anticipation of a summer storm in *Come on, Rain*. After the rain comes, neighborhood mothers join their daughters to enjoy a delicious summer rain. Friendship enables cultures to live together and enrich each other's lives in *Mama and Papa Have a Store* by Amelia Lau Carling. The store owners are Chinese who live in the heart of Guatemala City.

Friends in a Mexican American neighborhood enjoy a series of adventures after Lolo captures a tarantula. In Kirk Reeve's *Lolo & Red-Legs,* both girls and boys search for information about the care and feeding of this unusual pet. People work together in a very different setting in *Raising Yoder's Barn* by Jane Yolen. After lightening starts a fire that burns a family's barn, community spirit brings Amish neighbors together to rebuild the barn, and even 8-year-old Matthew helps. At the end of the day, the family gives thanks for their good neighbors and their new barn.

Patricia Polacco writes about the friendship between a Jewish lady and an African American boy in *Mrs. Katz and Tush.* Larnel, a black child, discovers that Mrs. Katz came from Poland where she experienced prejudice also. Friendship is also the theme of Patricia Polacco's book *Pink and Say,* which is based on a true story that occurred during the Civil War. During the war an African American soldier and a White soldier become friends and the African American soldier saves the other soldier's life. In another true story of friendship, Joseph Bruchac tells of a little-known incident that united Native Americans and Quakers in *The Arrow Over the Door.*

ADMIRABLE PEOPLE

Admirable people may be famous, but many people who are heroes, role models, and mentors are not famous; nevertheless, they are important in our lives and in our country's history. Many admirable, courageous people of color have been omitted from history books, and teachers and librarians can help overcome these omissions through literature.

Famous people such as Diego Rivera, a well-known Mexican artist who expressed his political philosophy in beautiful murals, helped give a voice to the inequities of life and the poverty of many people. Jeanette Winter portrays the story of his early life in *Diego*. Zora Hurston uses her art to celebrate black pride. The life story of this folklorist, writer, and anthropologist is the theme of *Sorrow's Kitchen: The Life and Folklore of Zora Neale Hurston* by Mary Lyons.

Unknown people, such as the Native American brothers who were forced to attend a government boarding school for Indians in 1930s California, are admirable people because they struggled with homesickness and dealt with a situation that was forced on them. Chiori Santiago tells their story in *Home to Medicine Mountain*. No doubt the free Black homesteaders who settled in Oklahoma also had to struggle with homesickness and fears. Joyce Thomas tells their story in *I Have Heard of a Land*. Navajo code talkers used their Navajo language, faith, and ingenuity to help win World War II. Sara Hoagland Hunter tells their story in *The Unbreakable Code*. Hiroki Sugihara, Japanese ambassador to Lithuania in 1940, was a virtually unknown hero. He risked his own safety to give visas to Jewish refugees in 1940. He was later imprisoned in a Soviet internment camp and then the Japanese asked him to resign from diplomatic service. Ken Mochizuki tells Sugihara's story in *Passage to Freedom*. The Jubilee Singers of Fisk University are the subject of Hopkinson's book, *A Band of Angels: A Story Inspired by the Jubilee Singers,* which tells the story of this powerful group of singers. They toured the country to support their university.

Iqbal Masih was certainly an admirable person. Susan Kuklin tells his story in *Iqbal Masih and the Crusaders Against Child Slavery*. Iqbal Masih was sold into slavery at age 4. He was later freed and became an activist who came to the United States in 1994, but upon his return to Pakistan, he was murdered at age 12. Lewis Hayden lived in a different time, but he, too, was a determined, quiet hero. Not much is known about this former slave who became an abolitionist, but Joel Strangis researched documents of the time when he wrote the book *Lewis Hayden and the War Against Slavery*. Sarah Forbes Bonetta's story is unusual as well. She was a young African captive who was freed, but she was given as a gift to Queen Victoria. Walter Dean Myers pieces together her life story in *At Her Majesty's Request: An African Princess in Victorian England.*

Some athletes are among the famous people whom children admire. Jackie Robinson was baseball's first Black major league player, and he has been a role model for many minority athletes. Kenneth Rudeen's biography *Jackie Robinson* tells his story. Michael Jordan is a hero to children from all racial and cultural groups. Eloise Greenfield's book of poetry, *For the Love of the Game: Michael Jordan and Me,* celebrates Jordan's admirable qualities. Another admirable athlete, Wilma Rudolph, overcame partial paralysis from polio. Kathleen Krull tells the story of her indomitable spirit and unlimited determination in *Wilma Unlimited: How Wilma Rudolph Became the World's Fastest Woman.* Rudolph overcame major obstacles to become a world-class runner and the first woman ever to win three gold medals in a single Olympics. Mexican American athlete Pancho Gonzales became a world champion tennis player in the 1950s at a time when other champions were White athletes from wealthy backgrounds. The author, Doreen Gonzales, tells about his working-class background and emphasizes the discrimination he overcame to win recognition and respect in the biography *Richard "Pancho" Gonzales.*

RACISM AND PREJUDICE

Prejudice occurs in the lives of all minorities. Racism and prejudice are negative experiences, but they do occur and we must confront them. Eve Bunting confronts prejudice and the rapport between races in *Smoky Night,* which depicts riots in Los Angeles. A Cambodian child gives prejudice a voice in the book *Who Belongs Here?* by Margy Burns Knight. He explains how he overcame many dangerous obstacles to get to the United States and then encountered prejudice. In a Native American story, *Less Than Half, More Than Whole* by Kathleen and Michael Lacapa, a boy experiences prejudice because he is of mixed races. Marguerite W. Davol explores the issue of mixed races in *Black, White, Just Right.* Mary Hoffman introduces both racism and sexism in *Amazing Grace:* friends tell Grace that she cannot have the role of Peter Pan because she is Black and she is a girl. Aekyung's classmates taunt her because of her "Chinese eyes" in *Aekyung's Dream* by Min Paek, but she develops the strength to survive. Faith Ringgold tells how prejudice affected her father's employment and its impact on her family in her autobiographical book *Tar Beach.*

A Mexican family joins "the circuit" of migrant workers in Francisco Jiménez's *The Circuit: Stories From the Life of a Migrant Child.* Multiple themes are woven into this superb book. The rich family culture and family customs give them love and endurance, but the central theme is the cruel reality of the migrant labor camps from which escape is nearly impossible. A compelling theme propels the book *Buried Onions* by Gary Soto. After dropping out of college, the protagonist, Eddie, struggles to survive in an inner-city environment characterized by the underemployment and racism that plagues many of the places Latinos live in the United States.

The Japanese internment during World War II demonstrates prejudice in a very concrete manner. Jerry Stanley writes about this period in his book *I Am an American: A True Story of Japanese Internment.* This incident is also the subject of *The Moon Bridge* by Marcia Savin in which the incident is viewed from the perspective of Ruthie Fox whose best friend is interned. However, the end of World War II did not solve the racism against Japanese. *Heroes* by Ken Mochizuki tells the story of Japanese American Donnie who always has to be the "bad guy" when he plays with his friends. He explains that his family served in the U.S. Army, but his friends laugh at him. His uncle and father help him learn about heroes.

An unusual perspective develops in Libba Gray's *Dear Willie Rudd.* In this story, a woman writes a letter to Willie Rudd, the housekeeper in her childhood home. In the letter, she describes and apologizes for the injustices directed toward African Americans when she was growing up. Native Americans have struggled for survival throughout history. Their struggles—with the earth, with one another, and with the White people—is the theme of *The People Shall Continue* by Simon Ortiz. In writing *Thunder from the Clear Sky* Marcia Sewall uses alternating "witness" voices so the Wampanoags and Pilgrims could air their disparate views of the intrigues, alliances, and betrayals among tribes and settlers. Ruth White's *Sweet Creek Holler* demonstrates prejudice in the Appalachian Mountains. The bread winner of a coal mining family has been shot in this story, so their lives change, but they find the courage to go on.

Prejudice among the Amish is the theme of *Family Tree* by Katherine Ayres. While completing a school assignment, Tyler Stoudt discovers her father's secret past; that he was Amish, and that his family disowned him when he married her mother.

Although we tend to believe that racism is declining, minority athletes face an ongoing struggle to achieve equality and respect. Their story is told in *A Level Playing Field: Sports and Race* by Evaleen Hu. Prejudice is also the theme of two of Mildred Taylor's books, *The Friendship* and *The Gold Cadillac.* In each of these stories, African Americans experience racism. In *The Friendship* three boys observe a southern store clerk mistreat an elderly man who had befriended the clerk when he needed help. A family traveling in *The Gold Cadillac* experience prejudice because they are traveling in an expensive car. Gideon, Pascal, and Nelly are slaves freed by President Lincoln, but they discover that freedom and land are difficult to keep even though they are free. Harriette Gillem Robinet tells their story in *Forty Acres and Maybe a Mule.*

THE ARTS

Art is not as focused on reproducing the world in which we live as with creating a world that we can imagine. The beautiful book *A Rainbow at Night* by Bruce Hucko was created so that a group of Navajo children could share their paintings and poems as an introduction to their culture. Rainbows and their colors are important to the Navajos. *Gathering the Sun: An Alphabet in Spanish and English* by Alma Flor Ada is a bilingual alphabet book that uses rich and deep hues of color in illustrations. The book tells the life of a migrant family working in the fields as one reads and explores the alphabet. Twenty-eight poems in Spanish and English are superimposed on the artwork. The continuity of culture, family, and friends is woven into the text and illustrations.

Faith Ringgold is an internationally renowned artist who creates autobiographical story quilts, soft sculptures, and African masks, all of which are displayed in major museums around the United States. She used story quilts to illustrate her book *Tar Beach.* Her book *Talking to Faith Ringgold* includes photographs of many of her works as well as a list of museums that display her works. Quilts are an art form of the Amish, but we cannot locate children's books regarding Amish quilts; you may be able to explore this facet of culture through quilt pictures from books. Additionally, the Smithsonian Institution maintains cultural exhibits and information that can be accessed through the Internet. Needlework has been part of Hmong culture for centuries, but only since the war in Vietnam and Laos has the new narrative form of "story cloths" emerged as a bridge between past and present. The book *Dia's Story Cloth: The Hmong People's Journey of Freedom* by Dia Cha, stitched by Chue and Nhia Thao Cha and published in cooperation with the Denver Museum of Natural History, tells of the Hmong people's search for freedom.

Carmen Lomas Garza used cut-paper art to explore her Mexican heritage, giving her book *Magic Windows* a unique perspective. African masks are the subject of *The Art of African Masks: Exploring Cultural Traditions* by Carol Finley. The author gives a brief description of the culture that produced each mask, then she describes the mask and its use in religion or ritual. In the book *Art of the Far North: Inuit Sculpture, Drawing, and Printmaking,* Carol Finley gives a brief history of the Inuit people, then she moves to detailed descriptions of drawings, prints, and sculpture shown in full-color photographs. George Littlechild, the Native American artist, uses his talent to tell about the important people, places, and symbols in his life in the book *This Land Is My Land.*

I See the Rhythm, illustrated by Michele Wood, portrays the musical roots of African heritages through today's beats. The stunning paintings that illustrate the book help readers visualize the music. The book *I, Too, Sing America: Three Centuries of African American Poetry,* edited by Catherine Clinton, includes poetry by 25 poets, biographical information, and a sense of the time in which he or she lived and wrote. The poems reflect the poets' struggles for an individual sense of self, anger at injustice, and a love of freedom. Moreover, the author discusses the contributions of African American poets to American letters. Full-page sepia-toned textile patterns are a repeated design element.

Christine Normandin has edited two beautifully designed books of stories written and illustrated by Chief Lelooska—*Echoes of the Elders* and *Spirit of the Cedar People.* The stories are Kwakiutl tales from the American northwest coast. Hoop dancing is the chosen art form of Lakota Kevin Locke (Tokeya Inajin). His story is told in the biographical photo-essay, *Lakota Hoop Dancer,* by Jacqueline Left Hand Bull and Suzanne Haldane, which begins with a description of one of Locke's cultural roots, his family history, and his commitment to preserving the Lakota culture. Through colored photographs readers get a sense of Locke's connection to his environment and the way this connection nurtures his artistic process.

Jacob Lawrence, one of the premier African American artists, is the subject of the book *Story Painter: The Life of Jacob Lawrence* by John Duggleby. Lawrence's paintings are used to illustrate significant points in his life as well as to show his artistic accomplishment. Japanese wood blocks, a popular art form, are the subject of *Art of Japan: Wood-Block Color Prints* by Carol Finley. *Talking with Tebe: Clementine Hunter, Memory Artist* by Clementine Hunter and Mary Lyons is a biography of an African American artist whose strength and pride shows in photographs, but her artwork best tells her stories.

Walls probably seem an usual art form, but the books *Talking Walls* and *Talking Walls: The Stories Continue* by Margy Burns Knight explore cultures through telling the stories of walls from all over the world. An audiocassette edition of the second book will be appreciated by children of all ages.

Dance is based in culture. George Ancona captures the movement and spirit of all types of dances, including an Afghan wedding dance and a Turkish Gypsy folk dance in *Let's Dance!* Bill T. Jones and Susan Kuklin portray the art of Bill T. Jones, the talented black dancer, in the book *Dance.*

In addition to books, the Web site *http://curry. edschool.Virginia.EDU:80/go/multicultural/arts.html* the Curry Education School developed and maintains at the University of Virginia site and entitled *Multiculturalism & the Arts* is invaluable. This site includes songs with multicultural themes, photo exhibits, art gallery, and arts links regarding multicultural education.

TRADITIONAL LITERATURE

The most common genre of cultural literature is traditional stories. Such tales are numerous and widely available for all age groups; therefore, we list them by themes and identify the culture of origin. These suggested titles will give teachers and librarians beginning points for enjoying them.

Cinderella tales

Raisel's Riddle by Erica Silverman and illustrated by Susan Gaber

The Way Meat Loves Salt: A Cinderella Tale from the Jewish Tradition by Nina Jaffe

Pourquoi tales

The Coming of Night: A Yoruba Tale from West Africa by James Riordan

How the Rooster Got His Crown by Amy Lowry Poole

The Legend of the Lady Slipper: An Ojibwe Tale by Lise Lunge-Larsen and Margi Preus and illustrated by Andrea Arroyo

Snail Girl Brings Water: A Navajo Story by Geri Keams and illustrated by Richard Ziehler-Martin

The Story of Colors by Subcomandante Marcos

Ten Suns: A Chinese Legend by Eric Kimmel and illustrated by Yongsheng Xuan

Why Leopard Has Spots; Dan Stories from Liberia by Won-Ldy Paye and Margaret H. Lippert and illustrated by Ashley Bryan

Trickster tales

Coyote in Love with a Star by Marty Kreipe de Montaño and illustrated by Tom Coffin

The Bossy Gallito: A Traditional Cuban Folktale by Lucia Gonzalez

The Golden Flower: A Taino Myth from Puerto Rico by Nina Jaffe

In the Time of the Drums by Kim Siegelson and illustrated by Brian Pinkney

The Magic Bean Tree: A Legend from Argentina by Nancy Van Laan and illustrated by Beatriz Vidal

Cultural collections

The Emerald Lizard: Fifteen Latin American Tales to Tell in English and Spanish by Pleasant DeSpain and illustrated by Don Bell

A First Book of Myths: Myths and Legends for the Very Young from Around the World by Mary Hoffman

Golden Tales: Myths, Legends and Folktales from Latin America by Lulu Delacre

Native American Animal Stories by Joseph Bruchac

The People Could Fly: American Black Folktales by Virginia Hamilton

Tales of Wonder and Magic by Berlie Doherty. (Includes familiar and unfamiliar tales from cultures around the world.)

Throw Your Tooth on the Roof: Tooth Traditions from Around the World by Selby Beeler

Authors of Culturally Conscious Literature

Authors express their own interests and life experiences in the types of book they write. Pat Mora is a Latino author who lived her early years in El Paso, Texas, a border town between the United States and Mexico. She explains that she has spent much of her writing life, both in poetry and essays, describing and questioning our national patterns of prejudice and discrimination (Mora, 1994). She reports that she chose to write picture books not only because she is drawn to the form, but also because she believes a great need exists for books written by Latinos describing their values, customs, and realities. She also states that, "Not only Latino youngsters need and deserve such books—all young people do in our multicultural society" (p. 298). You can learn more about her by visiting her Web site. You will find that other authors who focus on multicultural literature maintain Web sites.

Unit Suggestions

ACTIVITY 15.1 COMPARING CULTURES

A good way to introduce cultural studies is to discuss culture with children. Explain that *culture* includes manners, feelings about self and other people, religion, right and wrong, education, entering adulthood, holidays, foods, clothes, and games—all the things we learned from our parents, grandparents, friends, neighbors, churches, and schools (Stoodt, 1992).

Ask the children to brainstorm what they have learned from each aspect of their cultures. Make lists of their ideas on the chalkboard or on charts. Organize the material into a chart like the one in Figure 15.3. Older students can create individual charts.

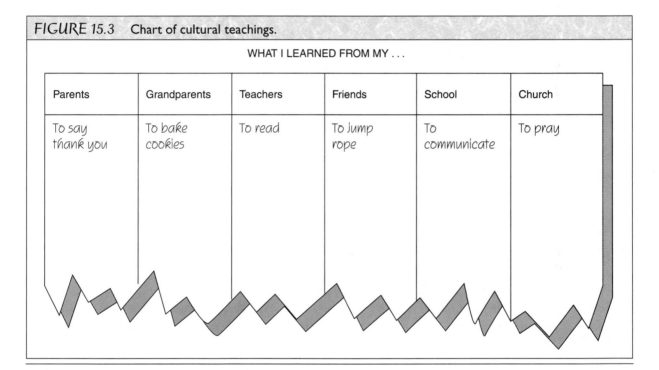

FIGURE 15.3   **Chart of cultural teachings.**

WHAT I LEARNED FROM MY . . .

Parents	Grandparents	Teachers	Friends	School	Church
To say thank you	To bake cookies	To read	To jump rope	To communicate	To pray

ACTIVITY 15.2 CONTEMPORARY STORIES

Read aloud a contemporary story from another culture and have the students compare the cultural information with their own lives. A Venn diagram is helpful in making this comparison.

ACTIVITY 15.3   MAPPING CULTURES

Have each student make a map of his or her culture using Figure 15.4 as a model. Culture maps can be the basis for bulletin boards. As students learn about culture, they can create culture maps for characters in stories.

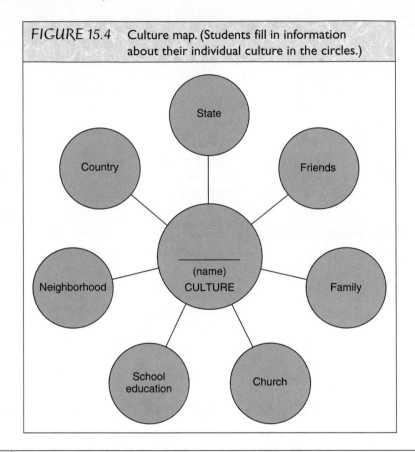

FIGURE 15.4   Culture map. (Students fill in information about their individual culture in the circles.)

ACTIVITY 15.4   CULTURAL COLLAGES

Discuss special family ways of celebrating holidays and birthdays, favorite colors, favorite foods, places they have lived, family size and composition, family education, religion, and values. Then students can make collages using magazine pictures (or those drawn by students), squares of colored paper, wallpaper, newspaper, cloth, and objects or symbols that are important to the individual to create collages representing their family's culture.

ACTIVITY 15.5   FAMILY TREES

Create family trees going as far back into family history as possible. Older students can learn how to research the family genealogy. Studies such as these sometimes give students clues about family ways of doing things that they did not realize had cultural implications. For example, this kind of research led one of the authors to Pennsylvania Dutch connections through family foods, names, and the stories her grandfather told. Faith Ringgold's book *Talking to Faith Ringgold* is very helpful.

ACTIVITY 15.6   COMPARING FOLKTALES

Students can compare the Cinderella story in various cultures, such as *Cinderella* (European), *The Rough-Face Girl* (Native American), and *Yeh-Shen* (Chinese). Figure 15.5 illustrates a comparison chart.

FIGURE 15.5   Chart for comparing traditional stories.

Title and Author	Main Character	Setting	Problem	How Solved	Conclusion
<u>Cinderella</u> Marcia Brown	Cinderella	European house and castle	Mean step-mother and stepsisters	The prince finds her and proposes.	They marry and live happily ever after.
<u>The Rough-Face Girl</u> Rafe Martin	An Algonquin girl with a rough face	Native American	The tribe rejects her scarred face.	She can see the Invisible Being.	She marries the Invisible Being.
<u>Yeh-Shen: A Cinderella Story from China</u> Ai-Ling Louie	Yeh-Shen	China	Her stepmother kills the fish that is Yeh-Shen's friend and eats it.	The fish's magic resides in its bones. The magic provides her with clothing for a festival.	She loses her slipper, and the King searches for her and marries her.
<u>Cendrillon: A Caribbean Cinderella</u> Robert D. San Souci	Cendrillon	Island of Martinique	Mean stepmother and stepsister	Godmother who is washer woman performs magic.	Cendrillon wears slipper and dances with bridegroom.
<u>The Golden Sanda: A Middle-Eastern Cinderella</u> Rebecca Hickox	Maha	Middle East	Mean stepmother and stepsister	Redfish is fairy godmother.	She is saved by a gold sandal; marries Tariq.
<u>The Turkey Girl: A Zuni Cinderella Story</u> Penny Pollock	Turkey girl	Zuni Indian, Western United States	Goes to great feast but does not return in time.	Turkeys	Turkeys are gone.

ACTIVITY 15.7   TRADITIONAL STORIES

Read aloud or have students read three traditional stories or poems from the same culture and identify the recurrent themes and details in these stories. A chart with headings such as those in Figure 15.5 will help them organize their ideas.

SUMMARY

The United States comprises diverse racial and cultural groups. Educators need to provide literary experiences that reflect the many backgrounds from which children come. Culturally conscious literature can play an important role in filling this need. In the past, minority cultures have been omitted or inaccurately portrayed in many children's books, which has a negative impact on children from all cultural groups. Quality literature permits children to experience others' lives, thus increasing their understanding and appreciation of cultures and people different from themselves. Children from minority cultures need books and characters to identify with because these books foster self-esteem and pride in ethnic heritage. Most important is encouraging children to recognize that people from different cultures share more similarities than differences. Moreover, children and adults need to recognize that racism and prejudice occur today.

Thought Questions

1. Develop your own definition of *culturally conscious education* and *multicultural literature* and explain why these definitions express your thoughts on the subject.
2. Why do so many people believe an abundance of multicultural books exists today when the data show otherwise?
3. What would you recommend to publishing companies regarding publishing multicultural literature?
4. Discuss the pros and cons of using children's literature to develop multicultural understanding.

5. Can someone who is not a member of a particular culture write a book about that culture? Discuss the pros and cons and your reasons for adopting the point of view that you have chosen.

Research & Application Experiences

1. Visit a school or public library and analyze the multicultural literature collection. Which cultures are best represented? Which are underrepresented? What books would you recommend they purchase?
2. Examine your own prejudices and stereotypes. How did you form these attitudes? What types of literature could you read to challenge these beliefs?
3. Identify criteria you feel are important when selecting multicultural literature for children.
4. Why are multicultural materials not readily available? Make a list of books you feel should be part of every school's collection.
5. Design a multicultural unit on a general topic such as families, transportation, pets, holidays, or friendships. Identify the books and activities that will help children develop a better understanding of a particular cultural group.
6. Develop a bibliography of excellent children's books for one culturally conscious unit based on a careful evaluation of each book. Different students may choose to research books for various cultural groups, so that you can exchange bibliographies.
7. Visit an Internet site that offers culturally conscious literature lists.

Children's Literature References and Recommended Books

Note: Books designated with an asterisk (*) are recommended for reluctant readers.

Ada, A. F. (1997). *Gathering the sun: An alphabet in Spanish and English* (S. Salva, Illus.). New York: Lothrop. (K–3). POETRY, PICTURE BOOK.

The author uses bright colors to illustrate this bilingual alphabet book, which tells about the life of a migrant family as one reads and explores the alphabet. Twenty-eight poems in Spanish and English are superimposed on the artwork.

Ada, A. F. (1998). *Under the royal palms: A childhood in Cuba.* New York: Atheneum. (3–5). CONTEMPORARY REALISTIC FICTION.*

A collection of stories that gives readers a close look at the active and loving extended family.

Altman, L. J. (1993). *Amelia's road* (E. O. Sanchez, Illus.). New York: Lee & Low. (K–2). CONTEMPORARY REALISTIC FICTION.

Amelia, the daughter of migrant farm workers, dreams of having a real home.

Ammon, R. (1998). *An Amish wedding.* New York: Atheneum. (K–3). CONTEMPORARY REALISTIC FICTION.

A younger sister describes the unique customs of the Amish people while telling about her sister's wedding.

Ancona, G. (1998a). *Barrio: Jose's neighborhood.* San Diego, CA: Harcourt Brace. (1–5). CONTEMPORARY REALISTIC FICTION.* (AVAILABLE IN SPANISH.)

The Barrio is the Mission District of San Francisco. Readers learn about the neighborhood through young Jose Luis.

Ancona, G. (1998b). *Let's dance!* New York: Morrow. (K–3). INFORMATIONAL BOOK.*

A simple text accompanies photographs of all types of dances, including an Afghan wedding dance and a Turkish Gypsy folk dance.

Ayres, K. (1996). *Family tree.* New York: Delacorte. (4–7). CONTEMPORARY REALISTIC FICTION.

Tyler Stoudt's class has to research their family tree, and she discovers her father's secret—he was Amish and his people disowned him when he married her mother.

Beeler, S. B. (1998). *Throw your tooth on the roof: Tooth traditions from around the world* (B. G. Karas, Illus.). Boston: Houghton Mifflin. (PreK–3). TRADITIONAL LITERATURE.

Brown, T. (1986). *Hello Amigos!* (F. Otiz, Photog.). New York: Henry Holt. (2–4). CONTEMPORARY REALISTIC FICTION.*

A Mexican American child describes a day in his life.

Bruchac, J. (1992). *Native American animal stories* (J. K. Fadden & D. K. Fadden, Illus.). Denver, CO: Fulcrum. (K–4). TRADITIONAL LITERATURE.

Bruchac, J. (1998). *The arrow over the door* (J. Watling, Illus.). New York: Dial. (3–6). HISTORICAL FICTION.*

This story, told in the alternating viewpoints of a Quaker boy and an Abenaki Indian, is based on a historical meeting of Quakers and Indians during the Revolutionary War.

Bunting, E. (1994). *Smoky night* (D. Diaz, Illus.). New York: Harcourt. (K–4). PICTURE BOOK, CONTEMPORARY REALISTIC FICTION.

The Los Angeles riots are portrayed in this story. A mother explains the violence to her son.

Carling, A. L. (1998). *Mama and Papa have a store.* New York: Dial. (PreK–4). CONTEMPORARY REALISTIC FICTION.

The story of a Chinese immigrant family living in Guatemala City. They operate a store and through the owners' and customers' interactions, readers see cultures living peacefully and enriching one another's lives.

Cha, D. (1994). *Dia's story cloth: The Hmong people's journey of freedom* (C. Cha & N. T. Cha, Illus.). New York: Lee & Low. (K–4). TRADITIONAL LITERATURE.

Tells the story of the Hmong people's search for freedom.

Chinn, K. (1995). *Sam and the lucky money* (C. Van Wright & Y. Hu, Illus.). New York: Lee & Low. (1–4). CONTEMPORARY REALISTIC FICTION.

Sam is excited about shopping with the lucky money that his grandparents gave him for Chinese New Year's Day. But he learns that giving is more important than receiving.

Choi, S. N. (1993). *Halmoni and the picnic* (K. M. Dugan, Illus.). Boston: Houghton Mifflin. (K–2). CONTEMPORARY REALISTIC FICTION.

When a Korean grandmother has difficulty adjusting to New York life, her granddaughter invites her to a school picnic.

Clinton, C. (1998). *I, too, sing America: Three centuries of African American poetry* (S. Alcorn, Illus.). Boston: Houghton Mifflin. (3–8). POETRY.

This is a collection of African American poetry.

Davol, M. W. (1993). *Black, white, just right!* (I. Trivas, Illus.). Morton Grove, IL: Whitman. (PreK–1). CONTEMPORARY REALISTIC FICTION.

A little girl tells about her black mother and white father, and herself, who is a little dark and a little light, which is just right.

Delacre, L. (Reteller). (1996). *Golden tales: Myths, legends, and folktales from Latin America.* New York: Scholastic. (2–6). TRADITIONAL LITERATURE.

de Montaño, M. K. (1998). *Coyote in love with a star* (T. Coffin, Illus.). New York: Abbeville Press. (2–5). TRADITIONAL LITERATURE.

A Potawatomi Indian Trickster tale.

DesJarlait, P. (1995). *Patrick DesJarlait: Conversations with a Native American artist.* Minneapolis: Runestone Press. (3–8). BIOGRAPHY.

DeSpain, P. (1999). *The emerald lizard: Fifteen Latin American tales to tell in English and Spanish* (D. Bell, Illus.). Little Rock, AK: August House. (4–8). TRADITIONAL LITERATURE.

Dionetti, M. (1991). *Coal mine peaches* (A. Riggio, Illus.). New York: Orchard. (1–4). HISTORICAL FICTION.

The work portrays the life of coal miners in Appalachia.

Doherty, B. (Collector). (1998). *Tales of wonder and magic.* Cambridge, MA: Candlewick. (4–8). TRADITIONAL LITERATURE.

Includes familiar and unfamiliar tales from cultures around the world.

Dorros, A. (1991). *Abuela.* New York: Dutton. (K–2). MODERN FANTASY.

Rosalba and her grandmother fly over New York in Rosalba's imagination. The book includes Spanish vocabulary.

Duggleby, J. (1998). *Story painter: The life of Jacob Lawrence.* San Francisco: Chronicle. (3–6). BIOGRAPHY.*

This work talks about the life of Jacob Lawrence.

Erdrich, L. (1999). *The Birchbark house.* New York: Hyperion. (4–7). HISTORICAL FICTION.*

This story of the Ojibwa portrays traditional life, which is shattered by outsiders.

Finley, C. (1998a). *Art of Japan: Wood-block color prints.* Minneapolis, MN: Lerner. (4–6). INFORMATIONAL BOOK.

This book explains wood-block prints and their importance.

Finley, C. (1998b). *Art of the Far North: Inuit sculpture, drawing, and printmaking.* Minneapolis, MN: Lerner. (4–6). INFORMATIONAL BOOK.

Part of the Art Around the World series, the book includes a brief history of the Inuit people and then moves to descriptions of the artwork shown in photographs.

Finley, C. (1999). *The art of African masks: Exploring cultural traditions.* Minneapolis, MN: Lerner. (4–6). INFORMATIONAL BOOK.

Part of the Art Around the World series. The author explains the cultural relation of each mask and how it is used.

Golenbock, P. (1990). *Teammates* (P. Bacon, Illus.). New York: Harcourt. (4–7). BIOGRAPHY.*

The theme of this book is the friendship of Jackie Robinson and teammate Pee Wee Reese.

Gonzales, D. (1998). *Richard "Pancho" Gonzales: Tennis champion.* New York: Enslow. (4–8). BIOGRAPHY.

The book is a biography of Pancho Gonzales, the tennis star.

Gonzalez, L. (Reteller). (1999). *The bossy gallito: A traditional Cuban folktale.* New York: Scholastic. (2–5). TRADITIONAL LITERATURE.

Gray, L. M. (1993). *Dear Willie Rudd* (P. M. Fiore, Illus.). New York: Simon & Schuster. (2–5). HISTORICAL FICTION.

A woman writes to a former housekeeper apologizing for the injustices she suffered.

Greenfield, E. (1991). *Night on neighborhood street* (J. S. Gilchrist, Illus.). New York: Dial. (K–5). POETRY.

This book is a collection of poems depicting the lives of African Americans and their families.

Greenfield, E. (1997). *For the love of the game: Michael Jordan and me* (J. S. Gilchrist, Illus.). New York: HarperCollins. (K–4). POETRY.

An inspirational poem encourages children to live with Michael Jordan's determination and passion.

Gutman, B. (1998). *Teammates: Michael Jordan, Scottie Pippen.* Minneapolis, MN: Millbrook. (4–6). BIOGRAPHY.

In alternating biographical chapters, readers learn about the cooperation and teamwork that are the keys to these players' success.

Hamilton, V. (1985). *The people could fly: American Black folktales* (L. Dillon & D. Dillon, Illus.). New York: Knopf. (3–10). TRADITIONAL LITERATURE.

Helldorfer, M. C. (1999). *Silver rain brown* (T. Flavin, Illus.). Boston: Houghton Mifflin. (PreK–2). CONTEMPORARY REALISTIC FICTION.

An African American boy and his pregnant momma are trying to keep cool during a drought.

Hesse, K. (1992). *Letters from Rifka.* New York: Holt. (4–7). HISTORICAL FICTION.

Twelve-year-old Rifka writes letters to her cousin in Russia.

Hesse, K. (1999). *Come on, rain* (J. J. Muth, Illus.). New York: Scholastic. (K–3). CONTEMPORARY REALISTIC FICTION.*

African American daughters and mothers enjoy a summer rain.

Hill, E. S. (1999). *Bird boy* (L. Liu, Illus.). New York: Farrar Strauss Giroux. (2–4). CONTEMPORARY REALISTIC FICTION.

A mute Chinese boy helps his family.

Hoberman, M. A. (Selector). (1994). *My song is beautiful.* New York: Little, Brown. (1–6). POETRY.

This book is a collection of multicultural poetry.

Hoffman, M. (1991). *Amazing Grace* (C. Binch, Illus.). New York: Dial. (K–3). PICTURE BOOK, CONTEMPORARY REALISTIC FICTION.

Grace loves stories and acting in plays, but a friend says that she cannot be Peter Pan because she is black and she is a girl.

Hoffman, M. (Reteller). (1999). *A first book of myths: Myths and legends for the very young from around the world.* New York: Dorling Kindersley. (K–3). TRADITIONAL LITERATURE.

Hopkinson, D. (1999). *A band of angels: A story inspired by the Jubilee Singers* (R. Colón, Illus.). New York: Atheneum. (2–6). HISTORICAL FICTION.

The inspiring story of the Fisk University Jubilee Singers, which is based on a real person's life.

Hu, E. (1995). *A level playing field: Sports and race.* Minneapolis, MN: Lerner. (3–6). INFORMATIONAL BOOK.

This book describes the ongoing struggle of minority athletes to achieve equality and gain respect.

Hucko, B. (1996). *A rainbow at night.* San Francisco: Chronicle Books. (3–8). POETRY.*

This book presents the world in words and pictures by Navajo children.

Hunter, C., & Lyons, M. E. (1998). *Talking with Tebe: Clementine Hunter, memory artist.* Boston: Houghton Mifflin. (3–8). BIOGRAPHY.

The story of an African American photographer.

Hunter, S. H. (1996). *The unbreakable code* (J. Miner, Illus.). Flagstaff, AZ: Northland. (2–6). CONTEMPORARY REALISTIC FICTION.

A Navajo grandfather explains how Navajo code talkers used their language, faith, and ingenuity to help win World War II.

Igus, T. (1998). *i see the rhythm* (M. Wood, Illus.). San Francisco: Children's Book Press. (4–8). INFORMATIONAL BOOK.

The book traces the African roots of today's musical beats.

Jaffe, N. (1996). *The golden flower: A Taino myth from Puerto Rico* (E. O. Sánchez, Illus.). New York: Simon & Schuster. (K–4). TRADITIONAL LITERATURE.

Jaffe, N. (1998). *The way meat loves salt: A Cinderella tale from the Jewish tradition* (L. August, Illus.). New York: Holt. (K–3). TRADITIONAL LITERATURE.

Jiménez, F. (1997). *The circuit: Stories from the life of a migrant child.* Albuquerque: University of New Mexico Press. (4–8). BIOGRAPHY.

This book, which won the CLASP Americas Award, follows the life of migrant workers who follow the crops to be picked.

Jones, B. T., & Kuklin, S. (1998). *Dance* (S. Kuklin, Photog.). New York: Hyperion. (3–6). INFORMATIONAL BOOK.

The poetic text describes photographs of the gifted African American dancer Bill T. Jones.

Keams, G. (Reteller). (1998). *Snail Girl brings water: A Navajo story* (R. Ziehler-Martin, Illus.). Flagstaff, AZ: Rising Moon. (K–3). TRADITIONAL LITERATURE.

This is a story of how Snail Girl gives drinking water to her people.

Kimmel, E. A. (Reteller). (1998). *Ten Suns: A Chinese legend* (Y. Xuan, Illus.). New York: Holiday House. (1–3). TRADITIONAL LITERATURE.

Knight, M. B. (1992). *Talking walls* (A. S. O'Brien, Illus.). Gardiner, MA: Tilbury House. (3–8). INFORMATIONAL BOOK, POETRY.

The text and illustrations explore walls around the world.

Knight, M. B. (1993). *Who belongs here?* (A. S. O'Brien, Illus.). Gardiner, MA: Tilbury House. (1–5). CONTEMPORARY REALISTIC FICTION.

Nary comes to this country from Cambodia. He and his grandmother overcome many dangerous obstacles to get here, but he is rejected in school.

Knight, M. B. (1996). *Talking walls: The stories continue* (A. S. O'Brien, Illus.). Gardiner, MA: Tilbury House. (3–8). INFORMATIONAL BOOK, POETRY.

This book explores cultures through the stories of walls from all over the world.

Krull, K. (1996). *Wilma unlimited: How Wilma Rudolph became the world's fastest woman* (D. Diaz, Illus.). New York: Harcourt Brace. (2–5). BIOGRAPHY.

Wilma Rudolph overcame her polio paralysis to become a world-class runner.

Kuklin, S. (1998). *Iqbal Masih and the crusaders against child slavery.* New York: Henry Holt. (4–8). INFORMATIONAL BOOK.

> Iqbal Masih, a Pakistani boy, is sold into slavery at age 4. After being freed, he becomes an activist against slavery. He was murdered at age 12.

Lacapa, K., & Lacapa, M. (1998). *Less than half, more than whole.* Flagstaff, AZ: Northland. (2–5). CONTEMPORARY REALISTIC FICTION.

> A mixed-race boy learns to be proud of his roots.

Left Hand Bull, J., and Haldane, S. (1999). *Lakota hoop dancer* (S. Haldane, Photog.). New York: Dutton. (3–6). INFORMATIONAL BOOK.

> Lakota hoop dancer Kevin Locke describes his art form and his life's work.

Littlechild, G. (1993). *This land is my land.* San Francisco: Children's Book Press. (3–6). BIOGRAPHY.

> Native American artist George Littlechild tells about the important things in life.

Lomas Garza, C. (1990). *Family pictures.* San Francisco: Children's Book Press. (3–6). INFORMATIONAL BOOK.

> A collection of folk art pictures portraying the life of a Latino family.

Lomas Garza, C. (1999). *Magic windows.* San Francisco: Children's Book Press. (K–3). INFORMATIONAL BOOK.

> Explores Mexican heritage.

Lunge-Larsen, L., & Preus, M. (Retellers). (1999). *The legend of the lady slipper: An Ojibwe tale* (A. Arroyo, Illus.). Boston: Houghton Mifflin. (1–3). TRADITIONAL LITERATURE.

Lyons, M. E. (1990). *Sorrow's kitchen: The life and folklore of Zora Neale Hurston.* New York: Scribner. (5–9). BIOGRAPHY.

> The book is the life story of Zora Neale Hurston.

Marcos, S. (1999). *The story of colors* (D. Domínguez, Illus.). El Paso, TX: Cinco Puntos. (K–3). TRADITIONAL LITERATURE.

McMillan, B. (1998). *Salmon summer.* Boston: Houghton Mifflin. (2–5). INFORMATIONAL BOOK.*

> In this photo essay, Alex, a Native Aleut, fishes with his father for summer salmon.

Michelson, R. (1999). *Grandpa's gamble* (B. Moser, Illus.). New York: Cavendish. (2–5). CONTEMPORARY REALISTIC FICTION.*

> The grandchildren think Grandpa Sam prays all of the time, until an accidental revelation shows his complex character.

Mitchell, B. (1993). *Down Buttermilk Lane* (J. Sanford, Illus.). New York: Lothrop Lee & Shepard. (K–3). CONTEMPORARY REALISTIC FICTION.

> The life of an Amish family is beautifully told and illustrated in this book.

Mochizuki, K. (1995). *Heroes* (D. Lee, Illus.). New York: Lee & Low. (1–4). CONTEMPORARY REALISTIC FICTION.

> Donnie is tired of playing the bad guy because he is Japanese American. He learns that heroes do not brag.

Mochizuki, K. (1997). *Passage to freedom* (D. Lee, Illus.). New York: Lee & Low. (3–6). HISTORICAL FICTION.

> The story of a brave Japanese man who helped Jews during World War II.

Mora, P. (1992). *A birthday basket for Tía* (C. Lang, Illus.). New York: Macmillan. (K–2). CONTEMPORARY REALISTIC FICTION.

> Cecilia prepares a surprise gift for her great-aunt's birthday, but her cat interferes.

Mora, P. (1994). *Pablo's tree* (C. Lang, Illus.). New York: Macmillan. (PreK–1). CONTEMPORARY REALISTIC FICTION.

> Grandfather buys a tree when his grandson is adopted. Each year he decorates the tree for Pablo's birthday.

Myers, W. D. (1993). *Brown angels: An album of pictures and verse.* New York: HarperCollins. (1–3). POETRY.

> A collection of photographs of African American children combined with sensitive poetry.

Myers, W. D. (1999). *At her majesty's request: An African princess in Victorian England.* New York: Scholastic. (4–6). BIOGRAPHY.

> The story of Sarah Forbes Bonetta, a young African captive who was freed and given as a gift to Queen Victoria.

Nikola-Lisa, W. (1994). *Bein' with you this way* (M. Bryant, Illus.). New York: Lee & Low. (1–3). CONTEMPORARY REALISTIC FICTION.*

> An African American girl visits the park and plays with her friends. The story is told in rap.

Nolen, J. (1998). *Raising dragons.* (E. Primavera, Illus.). New York: Silver Whistle/Harcourt. (K–3). MODERN FANTASY.

> A little girl discovers a dragon egg that hatches to become her pet.

Normandin, C. (Ed.). (1997). *Echoes of the elders* (Chief Lelooska, Author & Illus.). New York: Callaway/DK Ink. (4–6). TRADITIONAL LITERATURE.

Traditional Kwakiutl stories from the American northwest coast and illustrated with Chief Lelooska's artistic images.

Normandin, C. (Ed.). (1998). *Spirit of the Cedar People: More stories and paintings of Chief Lelooska* (Chief Lelooska, Author & Illus.). New York: Callaway/DK Ink. (4–6). TRADITIONAL LITERATURE.

These stories are Kwakiutl stories from the American northwest coast. All are creation myths, explaining how daylight and dark were divided.

Ortiz, S. J. (1977). *The people shall continue* (S. Graves, Illus.). San Francisco: Children's Book Press. (3–5). INFORMATIONAL BOOK.

The book portrays the Native American people's struggle for survival throughout history.

Paek, M. (1988). *Aekyung's dream.* San Francisco: Children's Book Press. (1–4). CONTEMPORARY REALISTIC FICTION.

Aekyung is taunted because of her Korean eyes.

Paye, W., & Lippert, M. H. (1998). *Why leopard has spots: Dan stories from Liberia* (A. Bryan, Illus.). Denver, CO: Fulcrum Kids. (K–5). TRADITIONAL LITERATURE.

Pinkney, A. D. (1998). *Duke Ellington: The piano prince and his orchestra* (B. Pinkney, Illus.). New York: Hyperion. (4–7). BIOGRAPHY.[*]

This is the life story of Duke Ellington and his music.

Pinkney, G. J. (1994). *The Sunday outing* (J. Pinkney, Illus.). New York: Dial. (2–4). CONTEMPORARY REALISTIC FICTION.

Ernestine and her Aunt Odessa spend the day at the train station telling stories.

Polacco, P. (1992). *Mrs. Katz and Tush.* New York: Bantam. (1–4). CONTEMPORARY REALISTIC FICTION.

Mrs. Katz, a Jewish lady, and Larnel, an African American boy, become friends, and she tells him about her experiences coming to this country from Poland.

Polacco, P. (1994). *Pink and Say.* New York: Philomel. (1–3). HISTORICAL FICTION.

Two 15-year-old Union soldiers become friends. The black soldier saves the life of the white soldier, and they are both sent to Andersonville Prison.

Poole, A. L. (Reteller). (1999). *How the rooster got his crown.* New York: Holiday House. (K–3). TRADITIONAL LITERATURE.

Reeve, K. (1998). *Lolo & red-legs.* Flagstaff, AZ: Rising Moon. (3–5). CONTEMPORARY REALISTIC FICTION.[*]

Eleven-year-old Lolo captures a tarantula, and he and his friends have a summer of adventures with their pet.

Ringgold, F. (1991). *Tar Beach.* New York: Crown. (K–4). BIOGRAPHY.

The author writes about her early life and illustrates it with her story quilts.

Ringgold, F. (1999). *If a bus could talk.* New York: Simon & Schuster. (K–3). BIOGRAPHY.[*]

This is the story of Rosa Parks, a black woman who refused to give up her bus seat for a white man. She is considered the mother of the Civil Rights movement.

Ringgold, F., Freeman, L., & Roucher, N. (1996). *Talking to Faith Ringgold.* New York: Crown. (3–6). INFORMATIONAL BOOK.

Faith Ringgold tells about her life and her art. She actually starts a conversation with the reader. Pictures of her art are included in the book.

Riordan, J. (1999). *The coming of night: A Yoruba tale from West Africa* (J. Stow, Illus.). Minneapolis, MN: Millbrook. (K–3). TRADITIONAL LITERATURE.

Robinet, H. G. (1998). *Forty acres and maybe a mule.* New York: Atheneum. (4–7). HISTORICAL FICTION.[*]

President Lincoln frees 12-year-old Pascal and his 8-year-old friend Nelly, but they find that staying free and keeping their land is difficult.

Rudeen, K. (1996). *Jackie Robinson* (M. Hays, Illus.). New York: HarperCollins. (2–6). BIOGRAPHY.

The biography of the first black man to play major league baseball.

Rylant, C. (1985). *The relatives came* (S. Gammell, Illus.). New York: Bradbury. (K–3). CONTEMPORARY REALISTIC FICTION.

A carload of relatives pay a visit to an Appalachian mountain family. When they leave, the family misses them.

Rylant, C. (1991). *Appalachia: The voices of sleeping birds* (B. Moser, Illus.). New York: Harcourt Brace Jovanovich. (2–5). POETRY, BIOGRAPHY.

The poetic text tells about life in Appalachia.

Santiago, C. (1998). *Home to Medicine Mountain* (J. Lowry, Illus.). San Francisco: Children's Book Press. (4–6). HISTORICAL FICTION.

Maidu brothers are forced to attend a government school for Indians.

Savageau, C. (1996). *Muskrat will be swimming* (R. Hynes, Illus.). Flagstaff, AZ: Northland. (2–4). CONTEMPORARY REALISTIC FICTION.

A Native American girl learns to be strong in the face of criticism.

Savin, M. (1992). *The moon bridge.* New York: Scholastic. (5–8). TRADITIONAL LITERATURE.

Schroeder, A. (Reteller). (1999). *The tale of Willie Monroe* (A. Glass, Illus.). New York: Clarion. (3–6). HISTORICAL FICTION.

Ruthie Fox's best friend, Mitsuko Fujimoto, is interned during World War II.

Sewall, M. (1995). *Thunder from the clear sky.* New York: Atheneum. (3–5). HISTORICAL FICTION.

Alternating "witness" voices tell of the intrigues, alliances, and betrayals between the Wampanoags and Pilgrims.

Siegelson, K. L. (1999). *In the time of the drums* (B. Pinkney, Illus.). New York: Jump at the Sun/Hyperion. (4–6). HISTORICAL FICTION.

Silverman, E. (1999). *Raisel's riddle* (S. Gaber, Illus.). New York: Farrar, Straus & Giroux. (1–3). TRADITIONAL LITERATURE.

Soto, G. (1997a). *Buried onions.* New York: Harcourt Brace. (4–8). CONTEMPORARY REALISTIC FICTION.

When Eddie drops out of college, he tries to find a place in the Latino inner city.

Soto, G. (1997b). *Snapshots from the wedding* (S. Garcia, Illus.). New York: Putnam. (K–3). CONTEMPORARY REALISTIC FICTION.

This picture book portrays a family wedding from a child's point of view.

Stanley, J. (1994). *I am an American: A true story of Japanese internment.* New York: Crown (4–8). INFORMATIONAL BOOK.

The history of the internment of West Coast Japanese citizens in relocation camps during World War II.

Steptoe, J. (Compiler & Illus.). (1997). *In Daddy's arms I am tall: African Americans celebrating fathers.* New York: Lee & Low. (K–4). POETRY.

This collection of poems celebrates and praises fatherhood. The book is dedicated to the illustrator's father, John Steptoe.

Strangis, J. (1999). *Lewis Hayden and the war against slavery.* New York: Linnet. (4–6). BIOGRAPHY.

Lewis Hayden, a former slave, became an abolitionist. He was a quiet, determined hero.

Stroud, B. (1996). *Down home at Miss Dessa's* (F. Marshall, Illus.). New York: Lee & Low. (2–4). CONTEMPORARY REALISTIC FICTION.

Two African American girls learn the joys of helping others.

Taylor, M. D. (1986). *The friendship* (M. Ginsburg, Illus.). New York: Dial. (5–8). HISTORICAL FICTION.

African American boys observe the hostile treatment of an old African American man by a store clerk.

Taylor, M. D. (1987). *The gold Cadillac* (M. Hays, Illus.). New York: Dial. (3–5). HISTORICAL FICTION.

A black family travels in a new gold Cadillac and encounters prejudice.

Thomas, J. C. (1998). *I have heard of a land* (F. Cooper, Illus.). New York: HarperCollins. (4–7). INFORMATIONAL BOOK.

This is the story of free black homesteaders who settled in the Oklahoma Territory.

Tran, K. T. (1987). *The little weaver of Thai-Yen village* (N. Hom, Illus.). San Francisco: Children's Book Press. (2–4). CONTEMPORARY REALISTIC FICTION.

Hien survives gunfire but must travel to the United States for medical care.

Trottier, M. (1999). *Flags* (P. Morin, Illus.). New York: Stoddart Kids. (K–3). HISTORICAL FICTION.

While staying with her grandmother, Mary admires Mr. Hiroshi. After he is sent to an internment camp, she cares for his garden.

Van Laan, N. (Reteller). (1998). *The magic bean tree: A legend from Argentina* (B. Vidal, Illus.). Boston: Houghton Mifflin. (K–3). TRADITIONAL LITERATURE.

Wells, R. (1998). *Yoko.* New York: Hyperion. (PreK–2). CONTEMPORARY REALISTIC FICTION.

Yoko is upset when the kids make fun of her sushi lunch.

White, R. (1988). *Sweet Creek Holler.* New York: Farrar, Straus & Giroux. (4–7). HISTORICAL FICTION.

A story of Appalachian life and the importance of friendship in our lives.

White, R. (1996). *Belle Prater's boy.* New York: Farrar, Straus & Giroux. (5–8). CONTEMPORARY REALISTIC FICTION.

This Newbery Honor Book is set in the Appalachia of the 1950s. Belle Prater's son must live with another family after his mother's disappearance. This story develops as a mystery and as one of friendship.

Winter, J. (1991). *Diego* (J. Winter, Illus.). New York: Knopf. (K–2). BIOGRAPHY.

This biography of artist Diego Rivera's early years shows his patriotism and his determination to paint.

Yolen, J. (1998). *Raising Yoder's barn* (B. Fuchs, Illus.). New York: Little Brown. (K–3). CONTEMPORARY RE-ALISTIC FICTION.

Amish neighbors rebuild a barn destroyed by lightning.

References and Books for Further Reading

Beaty, J. J. (1997). *Building bridges with multicultural picture books.* Upper Saddle River, NJ: Merrill/Prentice Hall.

Bishop, R. S. (1994). A reply to Shannon the canon. *Journal of Children's Literature, 20,* 6–8.

Boutte, G. S., & McCormick, C. (1992). Authentic multicultural activities. *Childhood Education, 68,* 140–144.

Cohen, D. (1968). The effect of literature on vocabulary and reading achievement. *Elementary English, 45,* 209–217.

Chukovsky, K. (1963). *From two to five.* Los Angeles: University of California Press.

Costello, J. (1992). *An inquiry into the attitudes of a selected group of African Americans towards the portrayal of African Americans in contemporary children's literature.* Unpublished doctoral dissertation, University of North Carolina, Greensboro.

Hardy, B. (1977). Narrative as primary act of mind. In M. Meek, A. Warlow, & G. Barton (Eds.), *The cool Web: The pattern of children's reading* (pp. 12–23). London: Bodley Head.

Harris, V. J. (1990). African American children's literature: The first one hundred years. *Journal of Negro Education, 59,* 540–555.

Harris, V. J. (1994). No invitations required to share multicultural literature. *Journal of Children's Literature, 20,* 9–13.

King, E. W., Chipman, M., & Cruz-Janzen, M. (1994). *Educating young children in a diverse society.* Boston: Allyn & Bacon.

Lempke, S. D. (1999). The faces in the picture books. *Horn Book, 75,* 141–147.

Madigan, D. (1993). The politics of multicultural literature for children and adolescents: Combining perspectives and conversations. *Language Arts, 70,* 168–176.

Miel, A., & Kiesten, E. (1967). *The shortchanged children of suburbia: What schools don't teach about human differences and what can be done about it.* New York: Institute of Human Relations Press.

Mihesuah, D. A. (1996). *American Indians: Stereotypes and specialties.* Atlanta, GA: Clarity.

Mora, P. (1994). A Latina in Kentucky. *Horn Book, 70,* 298–300.

Ramsey, P. (1987). *Teaching and learning in a diverse world: Multicultural education for young children.* New York: Teachers College Press.

Rasinski, T., & Padak, N. (1990). Multicultural learning through children's literature. *Language Arts, 67,* 576–580.

Reese, D. (1996). Teaching young children about Native Americans. *ERIC Clearing House on Elementary and Early Childhood Education.* Urbana, IL: University of Illinois.

Reimer, K. (1992). Multiethnic literature: Holding fast to dreams. *Language Arts, 69*(1), 14–21.

Rochman, H. (1993). *Against borders: Promoting books for a multicultural world.* Chicago: American Library Association.

Shanahan, P. (1994). I am the canon: Finding ourselves in multiculturalism. *Journal of Children's Literature, 20,* 1–5.

Stoodt, B. (1992, July). *Multicultural children's literature.* Paper presented at the World Congress on Reading, Maui, HI.

Wong, P. (1997, November). *Native American literature: It should be in every school's curriculum.* Paper presented to the 25th Southwest IRA Regional Conference, Orlando, Florida.

Wurzel, J. S. (1988). Multiculturalism and multicultural education. In J. S. Wurzel (Ed.), *Toward multiculturalism: A reader in multicultural education* (pp. 1–10). Yarmouth, ME: Intercultural.

Yokota, J. (1993). Issues in selecting multicultural children's literature. *Language Arts, 70,* 156–167.

Appendix

BOOK AWARDS

The Caldecott Medal

This award, sponsored by the Association for Library Service to Children, division of the American Library Association, is given to the illustrator of the most distinguished picture book for children published in the United States during the preceding year. Only U.S. residents or citizens are eligible for this award.

2000 *Joseph Had a Little Overcoat* by Simms Taback. Viking

1999 *Snowflake Bentley* by Jacqueline Briggs Martin. Illustrated by Mary Azarian. Houghton Mifflin.

1998 *Rapunzel* retold by Paul O. Zelinsky. Dutton.

1997 *Golem* by David Wisniewski. Clarion.

1996 *Officer Buckle and Gloria* by Peggy Rathmann. Putnam.

1995 *Smoky Night* by Eve Bunting. Illustrated by David Diaz. Harcourt.

1994 *Grandfather's Journey* by Allen Say. Houghton Mifflin.

1993 *Mirette on the High Wire* by Emily Arnold McCully. G. P. Putnam.

1992 *Tuesday* by David Wiesner. Clarion.

1991 *Black and White* by David Macaulay. Houghton Mifflin.

1990 *Lon Po Po: A Red-Riding Hood Story from China.* Translated and illustrated by Ed Young. Philomel.

1989 *Song and Dance Man* by Karen Ackerman. Illustrated by Stephen Gammell. Knopf.

1988 *Owl Moon* by Jane Yolen. Illustrated by John Schoenherr. Philomel.

1987 *Hey, Al* by Arthur Yorinks. Illustrated by Richard Egielski. Farrar.

1986 *The Polar Express* by Chris Van Allsburg. Houghton.

1985 *Saint George and the Dragon,* retold by Margaret Hodges. Illustrated by Trina Schart Hyman. Little, Brown.

1984 *The Glorious Flight: Across the Channel with Louis Blériot* by Alice and Martin Provensen. Viking.

1983 *Shadow* by Blaise Cendrars. Translated and illustrated by Marcia Brown. Scribner's.

1982 *Jumanji* by Chris Van Allsburg. Houghton Mifflin.

1981 *Fables* by Arnold Lobel. Harper.

1980 *Ox-Cart Man* by Donald Hall. Illustrated by Barbara Cooney. Viking.

1979 *The Girl Who Loved Wild Horses* by Paul Goble. Bradbury.

1978 *Noah's Ark* by Peter Spier. Doubleday.

1977 *Ashanti to Zulu: African Traditions* by Margaret Musgrove. Illustrated by Leo and Diane Dillon. Dial.

1976 *Why Mosquitoes Buzz in People's Ears* retold by Verna Aardema. Illustrated by Leo and Diane Dillon. Dial.

1975 *Arrow to the Sun* adapted and illustrated by Gerald McDermott. Viking.

The Newbery Award

This award, sponsored by the Association for Library Service to Children, division of the American Library Association, is given to the author of the most distinguished contribution to children's literature published during the preceding year. Only U.S. citizens or residents are eligible for this award.

2000 *Bud, Not Buddy* by Christopher Paul Curtis. Delacorte.

1999 *Holes* by Louis Sachar. Farrar Straus.

1998 *Out of the Dust* by Karen Hesse. Scholastic.

1997 *The View from Saturday* by E. L. Konigsburg. Atheneum.

1996 *The Midwife's Apprentice* by Karen Cushman. Clarion.

1995 *Walk Two Moons* by Sharon Creech. Harper-Collins.

1994 *The Giver* by Lois Lowry. Houghton Mifflin.

1993 *Missing May* by Cynthia Rylant. Jackson/Orchard.

1992 *Shiloh* by Phyllis Reynolds Naylor. Atheneum.

1991 *Maniac Magee* by Jerry Spinelli. Little, Brown.

1990 *Number the Stars* by Lois Lowry. Houghton Mifflin.

1989 *Joyful Noise: Poems for Two Voices* by Paul Fleischman. Harper.

1988 *Lincoln: A Photobiography* by Russell Freedman. Clarion.

1987 *The Whipping Boy* by Sid Fleischman. Greenwillow.

1986 *Sarah Plain and Tall* by Patricia MacLachlan. Harper.

1985 *The Hero and the Crown* by Robin McKinley. Greenwillow.

1984 *Dear Mr. Henshaw* by Beverly Cleary. Morrow.

1983 *Dicey's Song* by Cynthia Voigt. Atheneum.

1982 *A Visit to William Blake's Inn: Poems for Innocent and Experienced Travelers* by Nancy Willard. Illustrated by Alice and Martin Provensen. Harcourt.

1981 *Jacob Have I Loved* by Katherine Paterson. Crowell.

1980 *A Gathering of Days: A New England Girl's Journal, 1830–1832* by Joan Blos. Scribner's.

1979 *The Westing Game* by Ellen Raskin. Dutton.

1978 *Bridge to Terabithia* by Katherine Paterson. Crowell.

1977 *Roll of Thunder, Hear My Cry* by Mildred D. Taylor. Dial.

1976 *The Grey King* by Susan Cooper. McElderry/Atheneum.

1975 *M. C. Higgins, the Great* by Virginia Hamilton. Macmillan.

Coretta Scott King Awards

These awards, founded to commemorate Dr. Martin Luther King, Jr., and his wife, Coretta Scott King, for their work in promoting peace and world brotherhood, are given to an African American author and, since 1974, an African American illustrator whose children's books, published during the preceding year, made outstanding inspirational and educational contributions to literature for children and young people. The awards are sponsored by the Social Responsibilities Round Table of the American Library Association.

2000 Author: *Bud, Not Buddy* by Christopher Paul Curtis. Delacorte.
Illustrator: *In the Time of the Drums,* illustrated by Brian Pinkney. Text by Kim Siegelson. Hyperion.

1999 Author: *Heaven* by Angela Johnson. Simon & Schuster.
Illustrator: *i see the rhythm*, illustrated by Michele Wood. Text by Toyomi Igus. Children's Book Press.

1998 Author: *Forged by Fire* by Sharon M. Draper. Atheneum.
Illustrator: *In Daddy's Arms I Am Tall: African Americans Celebrating Fathers,* illustrated by Javaka Steptoe. Lee & Low.

1997 Author: *Slam!* by Walter Dean Myers. Scholastic.
Illustrator: *Minty: A Story of Young Harriet Tubman,* text by Alan Schroeder. Illustrated by Jerry Pinkney. Dial Books for Young Readers.

1996 Author: *Her Stories* by Virginia Hamilton. Illustrated by Leo and Diane Dillon. Scholastic/Blue Sky Press.
Illustrator: *The Middle Passage: White Ships Black Cargo* by Tom Feelings. Introduction by John Henrik Clarke. Dial.

1995 Author: *Christmas in the Big House, Christmas in the Quarters* by Patricia C. and Frederick L. McKissack. Illustrated by John Thompson. Scholastic.
Illustrator: *The Creation,* text by James Weldon Johnson. Illustrated by James E. Ransome. Delacorte.

1994 Author: *Toning the Sweep* by Angela Johnson. Orchard.
Illustrator: *Soul Looks Back in Wonder,* illustrated by Tom Feelings. Text edited by Phyllis Fogelman. Dial.

1993 Author: *The Dark-Thirty: Southern Tales of the Supernatural* by Patricia McKissack. Illustrated by Brian Pinkney. Knopf.
Illustrator: *The Origin of Life on Earth: An African Creation Myth,* illustrated by Kathleen Atkins Wilson. Retold by David Anderson. Sights Production.

1992 Author: *Now Is Your Time! The African-American Struggle for Freedom* by Walter Dean Myers. HarperCollins.
Illustrator: *Tar Beach* by Faith Ringgold. Crown.

1991 Author: *Road to Memphis* by Mildred D. Taylor. Dial.
Illustrator: *Aïda,* retold by Leontyne Price. Illustrated by Leo and Diane Dillon. Harcourt.

1990 Author: *A Long Hard Journey* by Patricia and Frederick McKissack. Walker.
Illustrator: *Nathaniel Talking* by Eloise Greenfield. Illustrated by Jan Spivey Gilchrist. Black Butterfly Press.

1989 Author: *Fallen Angels* by Walter Dean Myers. Scholastic.
Illustrator: *Mirandy and Brother Wind* by Patricia McKissack. Illustrated by Jerry Pinkney. Knopf.

1988 Author: *The Friendship* by Mildred D. Taylor. Illustrated by Max Ginsburg. Dial.
Illustrator: *Mufaro's Beautiful Daughters: An African Tale* retold and illustrated by John Steptoe. Lothrop.

1987 Author: *Justin and the Best Biscuits in the World* by Mildred Pitts Walter. Lothrop.
Illustrator: *Half a Moon and One Whole Star,* text by Crescent Dragonwagon. Illustrated by Jerry Pinkney. Macmillan.

1986 Author: *The People Could Fly: American Black Folktales* by Virginia Hamilton. Illustrated by Leo and Diane Dillon. Knopf.
Illustrator: *The Patchwork Quilt,* text by Valerie Flournoy. Illustrated by Jerry Pinkney. Dial.

1985 Author: *Motown and Didi* by Walter Dean Myers. Viking.
Illustrator: No award

1984 Author: *Everett Anderson's Goodbye* by Lucille Clifton. Holt.
Illustrator: *My Mama Needs Me* by Mildred Pitts Walter. Illustrated by Pat Cummings. Lothrop.

1983 Author: *Sweet Whispers, Brother Rush* by Virginia Hamilton. Philomel.
Illustrator: *Black Child* by Peter Magubane. Knopf.

1982 Author: *Let the Circle be Unbroken* by Mildred Taylor. Dial.
Illustrator: *Mother Crocodile: An Uncle Amadou Tale From Senegal,* adapted by Rosa Guy. Illustrated by John Steptoe. Delacorte.

1981 Author: *This Life* by Sidney Poitier. Knopf.
Illustrator: *Beat the Story-Drum, Pum-Pum* by Ashley Bryan. Atheneum.

1980 Author: *The Young Landlords* by Walter Dean Myers. Viking.
Illustrator: *Cornrows* by Camille Yarbrough. Illustrated by Carole Byard. Coward.

1979 Author: *Escape to Freedom* by Ossie Davis. Viking.
Illustrator: *Something on My Mind* by Nikki Grimes. Illustrated by Tom Feelings. Dial.

1978 Author: *Africa Dream* by Eloise Greenfield. Illustrated by Carole Byard. Crowell.
Illustrator: *Africa Dream.* Illustrated by Carole Byard. Text by Eloise Greenfield. Crowell.

1977 Author: *The Story of Stevie Wonder* by James Haskins. Lothrop.
Illustrator: No award

1976 Author: *Duey's Tale* by Pearl Bailey. Harcourt.
Illustrator: No award

1975 Author: *The Legend of Africana* by Dorothy Robinson. Johnson Publishing.
Illustrator: No award

Nonfiction Awards: Orbis Pictus Award

The Orbis Pictus Award for Outstanding Nonfiction for Children was established by the National Council of Teachers of English (NCTE) in 1990. The award was established to promote and recognize excellence in the field of nonfiction writing.

2000 *Through My Eyes* by Ruby Bridges. Edited by Margo Lundell. Scholastic.

Honor Books
 At Her Majesty's Request: An African Princess in Victorian England by Walter Dean Myers. Scholastic.
 Clara Schumann: Piano Virtuoso by Susanna Reich. Clarion.

Mapping the World by Sylvia A. Johnson. Atheneum.

The Snake Scientist by Sy Montgomery. Illustrated by Nic Bishop. Houghton Mifflin.

The Top of the World: Climbing Mount Everest by Steve Jenkins. Houghton Mifflin.

1999 *Shipwreck at the Bottom of the World: The Extraordinary True Story of Shackleton and the Endurance* by Jennifer Armstrong. Crown.

Honor Books

Black Whiteness: Admiral Byrd Alone in the Antarctic by Robert Burleigh. Illustrated by Walter Lyon Krudop. Atheneum.

Fossil Feud: The Rivalry of the First American Dinosaur Hunters by Thom Holmes. Messner.

Hottest, Coldest, Highest, Deepest by Steve Jenkins. Houghton Mifflin.

No Pretty Pictures: A Child of War by Anita Lobel. Greenwillow.

1998 *An Extraordinary Life: The Story of a Monarch Butterfly* by Laurence Pringle. Paintings by Bob Marstall. Orchard.

Honor Books

A Drop of Water: A Book of Science and Wonder by Walter Wick. Scholastic.

A Tree Is Growing by Arthur Dorros. Illustrated by S. D. Schindler. Scholastic.

Charles A. Lindbergh: A Human Hero by James Cross Giblin. Clarion.

Kennedy Assassinated! The World Mourns: A Reporter's Story by Wilborn Hampton. Candlewick.

Digger: The Tragic Fate of the California Indians from the Missions to the Gold Rush by Jerry Stanley. Crown.

1997 *Leonardo da Vinci* by Diane Stanley. Morrow.

Honor Books

Full Steam Ahead: The Race to Build a Transcontinental Railroad by Rhoda Blumberg. National Geographic Society.

The Life and Death of Crazy Horse by Russell Freedman. Holiday House.

One World, Many Religions: The Ways We Worship by Mary Pope Osborne. Knopf.

1996 *The Great Fire* by Jim Murphy. Scholastic.

Honor Books

Dolphin Man: Exploring the World of Dolphins by Laurence Pringle. Photographs by Randall S. Wells. Atheneum.

Rosie the Riveter: Women Working on the Home Front in World War II by Penny Colman. Crown.

1995 *Safari Beneath the Sea* by Diane Swanson. Sierra Club Books.

Honor Books

Wildlife Rescue by Jennifer Dewey. Boyds Mills.

Kids at Work by Russell Freedman. Clarion.

Christmas in the Big House, Christmas in the Quarters by Patricia and Frederick McKissack. Scholastic.

1994 *Across America on an Emigrant Train* by Jim Murphy. Clarion.

Honor Books

To the Top of the World: Adventures with Arctic Wolves by Jim Brandenburg. Walker.

Making Sense: Animal Perception and Communication by Bruce Brooks. Farrar, Straus & Giroux.

1992 *Flight: The Journey of Charles Lindbergh* by Robert Burleigh and Mike Wimmer. Philomel Honor Books.

Now Is Your Time! The African-American Struggle for Freedom by Walter Dean Myers. Harper Collins.

Prairie Vision: The Life and Times of Solomon Butcher by Pam Conrad. Harper Collins.

1991 *Franklin Delano Roosevelt* by Russell Freedman. Clarion.

Honor Books

Arctic Memories by Normee Ekoomiak. Holt.

Seeing Earth from Space by Patricia Lauber. Orchard.

1990 *The Great Little Madison* by Jean Fritz. Putnam.

Honor Books

The News About Dinosaurs by Patricia Lauber. Bradbury.

The Great American Gold Rush by Rhoda Blumberg. Bradbury.

Other nonfiction awards not listed are: the Boston Globe–Horn Book Award; the Carter B. Woodson Book Award; the Children's Book Guild Nonfiction Award; the Christopher Awards; and the Eva L. Gordon Award for Children's Science Literature.

Pura Belpré Award

The Pura Belpré Award is given every two years by the Association for Library Service to Children (ALSC) and the National Association to Promote Library Services to the Spanish Speaking (REFORMA).

The award honors Latino writers and illustrators whose work best portrays, affirms, and celebrates the Latino cultural experience in a work of literature for youth. Named in honor of Pura Belpré, the first Latina librarian of the New York Public Library. The first awards, given in 1996, were selected from books published 1990–1995.

2000 Text: *Under the Royal Palms: A Childhood in Cuba* by Alma Flor Ada. Atheneum.
Illustration: *Magic Windows: Cut Paper Art and Stories,* by Carmen Lomas Garza. Children's Book Press.

Text Honor Books
From the Bellybutton of the Moon and Other Summer Poems* by Francisco X. Alarcón. Illustrated by Maya Christina Gonzalez. Children's Book Press.
Laughing Out Loud, I Fly: Poems in English and Spanish by Juan Felipe Herrera. Illustrated by Karen Barbour. HarperCollins.

Illustration Honor Books
Barrio: Jose's Neighborhood by George Ancona. Harcourt Brace.
The Secret Stars by Joseph Slate. Illustrated by Felipe Dávalos. Cavendish.
Mama and Papa Have a Store by Amelia Lau Carling. Dial.

1998 Text: *Parrot in the Oven: Mi Vida* by Victor Martinez. Joanna Cotler Books/HarperCollins.
Illustration: *Snapshots from the Wedding* by Gary Soto. Illustrated by Stephanie Garcia. Putnam.

Text Honor Books
Spirits of the High Mesa by Floyd Martinez. Arte Público Press.

Laughing Tomatoes and Other Spring Poems/Jitomates Risueños y otros poemas de primavera by Francisco X. Alarcón. Illustrated by Maya Christina Gonzalez. Children's Book Press.

Illustration Honor Books
The Golden Flower: A Taino Myth from Puerto Rico by Nina Jaffe. Illustrated by Enrique O. Sánchez. Simon & Schuster Books for Young Readers.
In My Family/En mi familia by Carmen Lomas Garza. Children's Book Press.
Gathering the Sun: An Alphabet in Spanish and English by Alma Flor Ada; English translation by Rosa Zubizarreta. Illustrated by Simón Silva. Lothrop, Lee & Shepard.

1996 Text: *An Island Like You: Stories of the Barrio* by Judith Ortiz Cofer. Melanie Kroupa/Orchard.
Illustration: *Chato's Kitchen* by Gary Soto. Illustrated by Susan Guevara. Putnam.

Text Honor Books
The Bossy Gallito/El Gallo de Bodas: A Traditional Cuban Folktale by Lucia González. Illustrated by Lulu Delacre. Scholastic.
Baseball in April, and Other Stories by Gary Soto. Harcourt.

Illustrations Honor Books
Pablo Remembers: The Fiesta of the Day of the Dead by George Ancona. Lothrop. (Also published in a Spanish language edition: *Pablo Recuerda: La Fiesta de Día de los Muertos*).
The Bossy Gallito/El Gallo de Bodas: A Traditional Cuban Folktale retold by Lucia González. Illustrated by Lulu Delacre. Scholastic.
Family Pictures/Cuadros de Familia. Spanish language text by Rosalma Zubizarreta. Illustrated by Carmen Lomas Garza. Children's Book Press.

Glossary

Aesthetic reading   pleasurable, interesting reading, done for its own sake.

Antagonist   a character in a story who is in conflict with the main character or protagonist.

Authentic activities   activities that have meaning for the students engaged in them.

Author   the title given to the person who writes the text in books.

Autobiography   a category of biography written by the subject of the book.

Ballads   rhymes and rhythms set to music, centering on a single character in a dramatic situation.

Benchmark   a term describing an exemplary book that is used as a standard of quality for comparing other similar books.

Biography   tells the story of a particular person's life. In biography, authors conduct careful research in order to explore and record the lives and significant acts and accomplishments of a person. Three styles of biography are typical. For children (a) authentic biography is based on documented words, speeches, and writing of the subject; (b) the biographical fiction style of biography permits the author to create conversations and portray the everyday life of the subject, but these details are based on thorough historical research into the subject's character and life as well as the time in which the person lived; (c) when writing fictionalized biography, the author takes greater latitude in creating a story around the actual life of a subject.

Board books   books for young children that are printed on cardboard.

Booktalking   the act of telling or reading highlights of a book without revealing its entire plot. The purpose of booktalking is to motivate others to read a book.

Caldecott Medal   an award is presented by the American Library Association to the creator of an outstanding picture book each year.

Censorship   the act of controlling what literature is available to be read in any given setting. Censors may attempt to remove books from library shelves because they believe the works in question violate particular values, religious beliefs, or good taste.

Character frames   a strategy for developing students' understanding of character development in a story.

Characters   the people in a story, comparable to actors in movies or on stage. Their actions, thoughts, and conversations tell the story.

Choral reading   an oral literary activity in which a selection from literature is read by several persons in unison with the direction of a leader. The most common types of choral reading are: (a) refrain, in which the teacher reads most of the lines and the children read the refrain; (b) line-a-child choral reading, in which individual students read specific lines, while the entire group reads the beginning and ending of the selection; (c) antiphonal or dialogue choral reading, based on boys and girls (sometimes in groups) varying their voices to speak different parts of a selection.

Classroom sets   multiple copies of trade books for classroom use.

Community of response   term that denotes shared understandings within a group of readers who discuss ideas about the same books.

Concept books   books that explore the various facets of a particular concept and in the process develop a reader's understanding of it. Geometric shapes, nature, and maps are some of the subjects of concept books.

Concrete poetry   poetry written in the shape of the topic; a poem about a boat, for example, would be written in the shape of a boat.

Conflict   the result of difficulties or opposing views between characters in a story. Conflict gives a story the tension that makes it interesting. There are a number of types of conflict, such as conflict within an individual, between individuals, or between an individual and nature.

Connections   the process of identifying ways that books are related to one another and to the experiences of the reader.

Connotative meaning   inferred meaning as opposed to literal meaning. It is meaning deduced from "reading between the lines."

Contemporary   describes events and settings that readers recognize as being in the present.

Core literature   literature that is the focus of a unit study.

Creative drama   informal drama created by the participants in the drama. It is improvisational and process-centered: The players create the dialogue and there are no written scripts to follow.

Culturally conscious literature   recognizes the importance of culture and shows respect for people of all cultures and races.

Culture   the context in which children develop. Culture is comprised of the values and customs that form an identifiable heritage.

Cumulative stories   refers to stories that accumulate. Events build on events and phrases build on phrases, leading to a climax at which point the accumulation falls apart.

Developmentally appropriate   a phrase describing instruction that is compatible with the learner's stage of development.

Didacticism   consists of obvious moral messages or values that some authors believe should be taught directly.

Diversity variation   the student population of today's schools is more varied than in the past. Diversity arises from many sources, including ethnicity and emotional and physical development.

Early literacy experiences   experiences with literature that are had through listening to stories and handling books and writing materials.

Efferent reading   has a narrow focus and depends upon the reader's purpose; for example, efferent reading may be done to seek specific information such as directions.

Elements of literature   the structural elements of fiction that include plot, characterization, setting, style, and theme.

Emergent literacy   refers to the beginning stages of learning to read and write.

Emotional disability   a state in which feelings interfere with learning.

Engaging with literature   describes readers' response to reading in which readers' minds, interests, and feelings connect with the ideas in a text. It connotes an understanding and an emotional response to what is read.

Envisionment   the unique meaning each reader creates when reading; each reader has slight to significant differences in interpretation.

Epic   a story of a person's life and death told in poetic form.

Episode   the name given to a small plot within a larger one. It usually occurs in a single chapter within a book. In some books, each chapter is an episode.

Exceptional   a descriptive word for individual differences that fall outside the average, or bell curve. Exceptional students need adjustments in their instruction in order to achieve their potential.

Experiencing literature   reading with pleasure and with understanding.

Fable   a story about an animal that teaches a lesson.

Fact frames   a strategy for organizing the facts that one acquires from reading.

Family literacy   reading and writing that occur in the home.

Fantastic element   an impossible element in a story, something that could not really happen such as a person or animal that does not really exist, or an aberration of some other aspect of the laws of the real world.

Fantasy   a genre of literature that is based on make-believe elements; it may include such factors as characters, place, events, and time.

Figurative language   has a nonliteral meaning; it may include similes, metaphors, hyperbole, and personification.

Folktales   pieces of literature that mirror the mores and values of a culture; they are passed down from generation to generation and have no identifiable author.

Free verse   poetry that does not follow a traditional form in that it does not have a regular rhythm or meter, nor does it usually rhyme.

Genre   classifications of literature that share the same basic characteristics. The genre of children's literature includes picture books, poetry, fantasy, traditional literature, historical fiction, realistic (contemporary) fiction, biography, and nonfiction.

Great books those books that have lived through several generations, usually because they express universal truths; people in different situations and circumstances can relate to the way these truths are expressed.

Haiku a poetic form which originated in Japan and refers to nature and the seasons; it is patterned poetry of 17 syllables in which the first line contains 5 syllables, the second contains 7, and the third contains 5.

Historical fiction found in books in which the setting is in the past. Events and characters are realistic, and setting and background are true to a particular time period, but descriptions, and sometimes characters, are made up. Characters behave and react the way one would expect of people in the time period in which the story is set.

Illustrated books books in which illustrations are used to supplement the text.

Illustrators artists who create the illustrations for books. These artists create pictures that interpret the text; sometimes illustrations tell the whole story, as in wordless picture books.

Imagery images that are created in the mind through the use of language; imagery appeals to the senses of sight, sound, touch, and smell.

Inclusion a plan for teaching educationally handicapped students in the regular classroom rather than segregating them in special education classrooms.

Individual differences variations from one individual to another.

Individualized education plan (IEP) the plan developed by teachers, administrators, parents, and special educators to guide the education of students.

Infants children in the first year of life.

Inferencing interpretation of literature based on meanings that are not directly stated in a text; readers must "fill in the empty spaces."

Informational books books that explain, impart knowledge, or describe persons, places, things, or events.

Inquiry the process of searching for information, ideas, and truth about questions the student has raised.

Inside perspective a perspective of a culture from a member inside that culture.

Integrated units address various subjects and literacy processes included in the elementary curriculum.

Interests topics and experiences toward which individuals gravitate because they are motivated. Interests are usually developed and cultivated through experience.

Intertextuality the process of interpreting one text by connecting the ideas in it with the ideas in all other texts previously read.

Legends stories that are often based on an actual historical figure whose deeds and exploits have been embellished.

Literary quality describes well-written literature that has well-developed plots, themes, characterization, setting, and style. Nonfiction has literary quality when it is accurate, well-written, and interesting. It presents main ideas and supporting details, differentiates theories from facts, and has illustrations that are appropriate to the subject.

Literate environment a place where reading and writing are used for authentic purposes; many kinds of reading and materials are available in such a place.

Literature a body of written works, an art form in which language is used in creative, artistic ways.

Mainstreaming a practice that places exceptional students in the regular classroom.

Modern fantasy stories that take for granted not only the realities of the world that we see and feel, but also the supernatural aspects that lead to all sorts of possibilities; fantasies have identifiable authors.

Multiculturalism the process of developing sensitivity to the various cultures comprising a community, state, country, and world.

Multicultural literature portrays the diversity of the population.

Myths stories that explain the origin of the world and natural phenomena.

Narrative poetry tells a story; it includes the story elements of plot, character, setting, and theme.

Newbery the name given to a medal that is awarded annually by the American Library Association to an outstanding children's book.

Nonfiction books those in which all the information presented is true, such as a biography. No fictional elements are included in nonfiction.

Nonsense poetry composed in lyric or narrative form, it is playful and does not conform to what is expected; it pokes fun at what is usually taken seriously.

Partial biographies   focus on a particular part of a person's life. For example, a partial biography focuses on a subject's childhood or adult life.

Physical disability   refers to the condition of an individual who has learning challenges because of physical exceptionalities.

Picture books   tell stories by integrating language and pictures. Some picture books, however, are wordless.

Plot   the plan and structure of the story. Plots usually consist of introductory material, a gradual building of suspense, a climax, the falling of action, and the culmination.

Plot frames   strategies that help readers understand the plot line of a story.

Poetry   literature in its most intense, imaginative, and rhythmic form, which expresses and interprets the essence of experience through language; it is not the same as "verse."

Popular literature   in vogue at a particular time, it is usually characterized as a fad that enjoys a period of popularity and then disappears. Popular literature is produced very quickly and lacks the literary quality that would inspire readers to read and reread it.

Pourquoi   a story that explains why things are the way they are.

Preschool children   are those from ages three to four years. Preschool programs are usually designed for this age group.

Problem resolution   refers to the way conflicts and story problems are resolved.

Racial and ethnic stereotyping   based on the assumption that all members of a racial or ethnic group have the same characteristics. The characteristics assumed in stereotypes are usually negative views of people. Stereotyping interferes with the ability to see individuals as human beings.

Readability   the level at which a person can read a book (or other printed text) with comprehension.

Reader's theater   an oral presentation of literature—the oral delivery of stories, poetry, biography, or information by two or more readers who characterize and narrate clearly and expressively.

Realistic fiction   fiction that is written true to the physical and factual details of a particular time period. The problems that characters encounter are related to the realities of life during that time.

Response   what readers take to a text, what happens during reading, how they feel about what they have read, how it becomes alive and personal, and the ways these feelings are displayed.

Setting   the time and place of the story.

Sexual stereotyping   assumes that all men or all women behave in certain ways (for example, that all women are weak and all men are strong). Sexual stereotyping functions in a negative way and interferes with the ability to appreciate individuals as human beings.

Skills-based themes   those that focus on skills development; they are often the subject of unit studies. They may concentrate on literary skills such as the development of characters, sensory imagery, alliteration, and so forth.

Social studies   one of the primary content areas studied in schools; some of the subjects within this discipline are history, geography, and anthropology.

Stance   the purpose or purposes a reader has for reading. It gives form to the literacy experience as well as the mode for expressing a response.

Story frames   strategy for developing students' understanding of story structure.

Story grammar   refers to story structure.

Storytelling   the act of telling stories. Many storytellers tell traditional stories that they have heard from other storytellers, and they often read and memorize stories and retell them.

Student-generated themes   those that students identify or suggest.

Style   the way an author uses language and symbols to express ideas.

Survey nonfiction   a form of nonfiction that gives readers a broad overview of a topic rather than in-depth information.

Teacher-generated themes   those that teachers identify or suggest.

Theme   the universal meaning (big idea) that the author expresses through a literary work.

Theme cycle   a term some educators use to identify student-generated units.

Theme immersion   instruction that focuses on thematic units.

Theme unit   a unit of study that focuses on a specific theme.

Toddler   a term for a child who is in the second year of life. A toddler is usually walking or crawling and is able to explore the world to a greater extent than an infant.

Traditional literature   based on oral tradition. *Little Red Riding Hood* is an example of a traditional story.

Transaction   the interaction between a text and a reader in which both are modified and changed.

Unit   an organizing framework for children's inquiry and study.

USSR (uninterrupted sustained silent reading) sometimes called DEAR (drop everything and read) and is a specific period set aside for reading. Everyone in the class reads, including the teacher. In some schools, this is a school-wide reading time.

Visual art   evokes both cognitive and aesthetic understanding and response.

Visual literacy   a major avenue of communication in which understanding is gained visually by interpreting information presented on billboards, signs, television, pictures, and photographs.

Wordless picture book   describes a book in which the story is told entirely through the use of illustrations.

Young child   a term used to refer to children younger than age 6. Some authors describe young children as those in the primary grades.

Subject Index

Abused children, 310–311
Accuracy
  in biography, 252
  in nonfiction, 257
Admirable people, in culturally
    conscious literature, 353–354
Adolescent readers, and novels with
    challenged characters, 306
Aesthetic reading, 77
Aesthetics, 7
African Americans
  portrayal of, 55
  and racism, 354
Age. *See also* Young children
  and reading interests, 59
  and response to literature, 77
AIDS, 309
Alcohol abuse, 311
Allergies, 309
Alliteration, 148
Allusion, 36
Alternative family structures, in realistic
    fiction, 206
American Association for the
    Advancement of Science, 259
American Library Association, 51, 53,
    56–57
  web site of, 108
Americas Award, 51
Andersen, Hans Christian, 178
  and Hans Christian Andersen
    International Medal, 51
Animals
  for disabled people, 308
  in poetry, 159, 162
Animal tales or stories, 175–176,
    213–214
Antagonist, 27, 31
Anthropomorphism, 257
Antiphonal (dialogue) choral reading, 285
Appropriateness, in informational books,
    257–258
Arnold, Caroline, profile of, 265
Art concepts, 132–133
Artistic styles, in picture books, 124

Arts
  in culturally conscious literature,
    355–356
  stimulating interest in, 136
  and trade books, 260–261
Asian Americans, portrayal of, 55
Assessment, 330
  of unit experiences, 330–331
Assonance, 149
Attractiveness, of books, 258
Audio books, 235
Audiotapes, 65
Authentic literary experiences, 16
Author and illustrator studies, 89–92.
    See also Profiles
Author approach, 13
Authority, of informational-book author,
    256–257
Authors. *See also* profiles
  as attraction, 58
  of culturally conscious literature, 356
  and illustrators, 122
  need to know, 14–15
  for younger children, 109–110
Author style, 78
Author visit, vignette on, 38
Autobiography, 251
Awards for children's literature, 50–53
  criticism of, 53
  recipients of listed, 368–372

Balanced reading instruction, 10
Ballads, 176, 177
Basal readers, 10, 322
Bats, activity on, 262–263
Bees, in poetry, 159
Benchmarks, 5, 119
Bibliotherapy, 63–65
Bierhorst, John, profile of, 191
Big books, 111
Biographical fiction, 251
Biographical profile. *See* Profiles
Biography, 25, 249–253
  as read-aloud, 277
Birds, in poetry, 159

Book and breakfast, 290
Book awards. *See* Awards for children's
    literature
Books for children
  big, 111
  experiencing of, 83
  great number of, 14
  intended to be heard, 17
  introducing of, 82
  and literary thinking, 74
  physical characteristics of, 59
  of poetry, 154–156
Books for children, selection of. *See*
    Selection of books
Book sharing, 325
Booktalks, 288–289
Boston Globe/Horn Book Award, 51, 248

Caldecott Medal, 51, 52, 248, 368
Card files, on books read, 14, 15
Cartoon style, 124
Catharsis, 64
CD-ROMs, 65
Censorship, 48, 53–55
  and gender stereotyping, 56
  and racial or ethnic issues, 55
  and realistic fiction, 202, 225
  response to, 56–57
Challenged students and characters. *See*
    Exceptional students; Real-life
    literature
Chanting, of folktales, 183
Character(s), 15, 30–33, 42
  in fantasy, 180–181
  in traditional literature, 172–173
Characterization, in biography, 252
Character maps, 87
  based on *Amazing Grace,* 87
Charts, 86–89
Child-centered criticism, 57–65
Child development, and children's
    literature, 60–63
Children's Book Award, 51
Children's Book Council, 51–52, 91
Children's books. *See* Books for children

Children's Choices, 53, 58, 59
Children's literature, 2, 4–5, 17. *See also*
   Literature
   censorship of, 48, 53–57, 202, 225
   and curriculum, 16
   evaluation of, 50
   genre in, 24–26
   research and application experiences
      on, 17
   and teacher, 14–16
Children's Literature Web Guide, The,
   108, 128
Child Study Children's Book Committee
   of Bank Street College, 51
Choral reading, 157, 285–286
Cinderella tales, 356
Civil rights movement, in historical
   fiction, 234, 236
Civil War era, 230–231
Class discussion script, 94
Classics approach, 13
Climax, 29
Cognition, stimulation of, 9
Cognitive development
   and early literary experience, 103–104
   Piaget's levels of, 60, 104
Collaboration, in inquiry, 323
Colonial era, 228–229
Color, in picture books, 125–126, 137
Communication, and literature for young
   children, 106
Community of readers and writers, 16
Community of response, 79–80
Comparison chart, of novels, 327
Concept books, 253
Concrete poetry, 150–151
Conflict, 26, 28–29
Connections, knowledge as, 323
Connotation, 35
Consortium of Latin American Studies
   Programs (CLASP), 51
Contemporary realistic fiction. *See*
   Realistic fiction, contemporary
Contexts, as learned from literature, 74
Conversation, vs. literature, 9
Cooperative Children's Book Center, 53
Coretta Scott King Award, 51, 369–370
Council on Interracial Books for
   Children, 55
Counting, as thematic unit, 335
Courage, thematic unit on, 339
Creative drama, 286–288
Critical thinkers and readers, 83
   and open marketplace of ideas, 203
Criticism
   child-centered, 57–65

literary, 50
Cultural collages, 358
Cultural consciousness, 346, 347, 349
   vignette on, 347–348
Cultural literacy, and literature for young
   children, 106
Culturally conscious literature, 346
   admirable people in, 353–354
   and arts, 355–356
   authors of, 356
   family in, 350–352
   friends and neighbors in, 352–353
   racism and prejudice in, 354
   research and application experiences
      on, 360
   selecting of, 350
   traditional literature as, 356, 359, 360
   unit suggestions on, 357–360
Cultural studies, 348–349
   and literature, 349–350
Cultures
   comparing of, 357
   mapping of, 358
   understanding of, 7–8
Cumulative folktales, 176
Cumulative plots, 30
Cumulative stories, 281
Curriculum
   and children's literature, 16
   and literature, 10–13, 322–323
Cut stories, 285

Data charts, 262
Day and night, as thematic unit, 331–334
Day care environment, and emergent
   literacy, 107–108
Deafness, 306–307
DEAR (drop everything and read), 290
Denouement, 29
Design, in illustration, 126
Developmentally appropriate literature,
   60–63
   and response, 77
   for young children, 104, 105
Diabetes, 308–309
Dialogue (antiphonal) choral reading, 285
Didacticism, 203
Disabled students and characters. *See*
   Exceptional students; Real-life
   literature
Discussion
   on books read, 323
   and contexts, 74
   on fantasy, 189–190
   in first-grade literature experience, 82
   as literary experience, 38

on oral experiences, 289
   of poetry, 160
   as response, 84–85
      prompts for, 85
   script for, 94
Diverse background of students, 303.
   See also Exceptional students
Diversity, cultural, 346. *See also*
   Culturally conscious literature
Divorce, 311
   in realistic fiction, 207, 311
Documents, books from, 254
Dogs
   for disabled people, 308
   unit of study on, 130–131
Doll week, 136
Drama
   and biographies, 261
   creative, 286–288
Dramatic plots, 30
Dramatic poetry, 150
Drug abuse, 311
Dynamic (developed) characters, 31

Early childhood. *See* Young children
Early childhood programs, 108
Early Childhood Resource and
   Information Center (ECRIC),
   108–109
Early literary experience, value of,
   102–104
Echoing, in poetry, 157
Efferent reading, 77
Elements of literature. *See* Literary
   elements
Elitism, and book awards, 53
Emergent literacy, effect of environment
   on, 104, 106–109
Emotional challenges, 309
Emotions, in poetry, 146
Engagement activities, 80, 83–84
   author and illustrator studies, 89–92
   discussion, 84–85
   maps and charts, 86–89
   writing, 85–86
Enjoyment, from children's literature, 6–7
Environment
   and emergent literacy, 104, 106–109
   for reading, 15
   and reading interests, 60, 62
   and response to literature, 80
Envisionment, 75
Epics, 150
   folk, 175
Episodic plots, 30
Event response, 78

Exceptional students, 303
    classroom activities for, 312–313
    emotionally challenged, 309
    health challenged, 308–309
    hearing challenged, 306–307
    learning challenged, 309–310
    mobility challenged, 307–308
    overprotection of, 308
    vision challenged, 307
Experiencing of literature. *See* Literary
    experiences
Experiment and activity books, 254
Exploring books, classroom activities
    on, 40–41
Expressionism, 124
External environment, and emergent
    literacy, 108

Fables, 175, 176
Fairy tales, 175, 176
Families, 302. *See also* Parents
    and culturally conscious literature,
    350–352
    in realistic fiction, 204–208, 209–210
        historical fiction, 226–227
    in real-life literature, 302, 311–312
Family environment, and emergent
    literacy, 106–107
Family trees, 358
Fantasy, 22, 169
    and children, 179
    classroom activities on, 183–191
    elements of, 180–182
        historical roots of, 178–179
    modern, 24–25, 168, 170, 178, 179
    nature of, 180
    research and application experiences
        on, 192
    setting in, 33
    on time (theme unit), 326
    types of, 182–183
    vignette on, 23–24
Fathers, absentee, 207
Females, portrayal of, 56
Fiction, elements of, 42. *See also*
    Literary elements
Fiction, types of. *See* Historical fiction;
    Realistic fiction; Realistic fiction,
    contemporary; Science fiction
Fictionalized biography, 251
Figurative language (figures of speech),
    35–36, 149
Files, on books read, 14, 15
Fine arts
    and literature, 12–13
    response experiences for, 330
    in vignette, 321

First-grade literature experience, 82
Five senses activity, 112
Flannel board stories, 283–284
"Folk," 175
Folk art, 124
Folk literature, 175
Folklore, 168, 175. *See also* Traditional
    literature
Folktales, 8, 170–171, 176
    chanting of, 183
    comparing of, 359
    comparing variations of, 129, 187
    comparing written and film versions
        of, 188
    composing of, 185
    illustrating of, 185–186
    Native American (thematic unit),
        336–337
    negative character portrayal in, 304
    "new," 175
    and prediction, 185
    writing of, 186–187
Foreshadowing, 27
Foster parents, in realistic fiction, 208
Frame of reference, 26
Free verse, 150
Friends
    in culturally conscious literature,
        352–353
    in historical fiction, 226–227

Gender, and reading interests, 60
Gender stereotyping, and censorship, 56
Genre, 24
Genre(s), literary, 15, 22, 24–25
    developing understanding of, 38
    research and application experiences
        on, 42–43
    as teaching tool, 25–26
Genre patterns, 22
Genre understanding, vignette on, 23–24
Giblin, James Cross, biographical profile
    of, 92
Great books approach, 13
Growing up, in historical fiction, 227–228
Guided silent reading, 291

Haiku, 150
Hans Christian Andersen International
    Medal, 51
Harvard Preschool Project, 102
Health challenges, 308–309
Hearing challenges, 306–307
Hesse, Karen, profile of, 305
Higher order thinking, developing of,
    263–264
High fantasy, 182–183

Hines, Anna Grossnickle, profile of, 110
Historical fiction, 24, 25, 200, 222–225
    categories of, 225–226
        families and friends, 226–227
    survival and growing up, 227–228
    classroom activities on, 236–237
    and contemporary realistic fiction,
        202, 225
    and historical periods, 228–234
    sample book introduction for, 92–93
    setting of, 33
    vignette on, 223
Historical periods, U.S., 228
    pre-Colonial era, 228
    Colonial era, 228–229
    Revolutionary War era, 229
    building and expansion, 229–230
    Civil War era, 230–231
    industrialization, 231
    immigration, 231–232
    twentieth century, 232–234
Holidays
    across cultures, 328
    and poetry, 159
Homeless children, 312
Horn Book Graphic Gallery, 248
Household tales, 175
Humor, in poetry, 161
Hyperbole, 36

Identification, 64
Illusion, 37
Illustration(s)
    of folktales, 185–186
    in learning about stories, 137
    of nonfiction, 258, 261
    in picture books, 120, 122–126
    studying of, 264
Illustrators, 121–122
    as attraction, 58
    for younger children, 109–110
Illustrator studies, 89–92
Imagery, 36, 147, 148
Imagination, from literature, 8
Immigration, in historical fiction, 231–232
Impressionism, 124
Inclusion, 303
Individualized education plan (IEP), 303
Industrialization, in historical fiction, 231
Information, from children's literature, 8–9
Informational book(s), 25, 246–247, 249,
    253–255. *See also* Nonfiction books
    classroom activities on, 262–265
    as read-aloud, 277
    research and application experiences
        on, 265–266
    sample book introduction for, 94–95

selecting and evaluating of, 255–258
vignette on, 247
Inquiry units, 323–324
on fantasy, 188–189
Inquisition approach, 84
Insects, in poetry, 159
Insight, 64
Instruction
integrated, 10, 11, 49, 321
literature-based, 10–11
Integrated instruction, 10, 11, 49. *See also* Unit studies
vignette on, 321
Interest inventory, 63
International Reading Association
Children's Book award of, 51
Children's Choices award by, 53
Intellectual Freedom Committee of, 57
on literacy experiences, 10
trade books identified by, 51
Internet
authors' sites on, 13
The Children's Literature Web Guide on, 108
as information source, 53
storytelling ideas from, 281
and unit studies, 328
Intertextuality, 76
Intuitive stage, 104
Inventors, thematic unit on, 338–339
Issues, in historical fiction, 234

Journaling experiences, 95
Journals, books from, 254
Journals, response (reading journals), 85–86, 188

Kindergarten students. *See* Young children
Knowledge
from children's literature, 8–9
as connections, 323
through literary thinking, 74
Knowledge charts, 89
based on *Dinosaur Ghosts,* 90
KWL (know—want to know—learned) chart, 223

Language, poetic, 147–148
Language arts
and literature, 11
response experiences for, 330
and theme units, 325
in vignette, 321
Language charts, 87–88
Language devices, 35–36
Language experiences, 102
Language model, literature as, 9–10

Language to Literacy Program, 87
Latinos, portrayal of, 55
Laura Ingalls Wilder Award, 51
Learning across the curriculum, 322. *See also* Unit studies
Learning challenges, 309–310
Least restrictive educational environment, 303
Legends, 176–177
Leukemia, 308
Libraries, 108–109
Life-cycle books, 254
Lifestyle challenges, 311–312
Line, in illustrations, 126
Line-a-child reading, 285
Listening, response experiences for, 330
Listening Library, 65
Literacy
acquisition of, 101
visual, 127–128, 133
Literary activities, map of, 39
Literary convention, 24
Literary criticism, 50
Literary elements, 27
characters, 15, 30–33, 42, 172–173, 180–181
classroom activities on, 40
plot, 15, 27–30, 31, 42, 172, 181–182
research and application experiences on, 42–43
setting, 15–16, 33–34, 42, 172, 181
style, 35–37, 42 (*see also* Style)
theme, 13–14, 34–35, 42, 324
vignette on, 26
Literary experiences, 13–16
and children's development, 80
classroom activities on, 41
dimensions of creating, 79
early, 102–104
need for, 2
understanding enhanced by, 37–39
Literary genres. *See* Genres, literary
Literary quality, as selection standard, 50–53
Literary thinking, 74–76, 79
Literature, 4. *See also* Children's literature
and cultural studies, 349–350
and curriculum, 10–13, 322–323
engaging with, 80
experiencing of, 13–16 (*see also* Literary experiences)
and fine arts, 12–13
and language arts, 11
as means of knowing, 74
media-based, 65–66
oral, 275–289, 292–294, 295 (*see also* Oral literature)

power of, 6–10, 48–49
response to, 5, 15, 72–73, 320 (*see also* Response to literature)
and science, 12
and social science, 12
"using" vs. "receiving" (Lewis), 81
and writing, 11
Literature, selection of. *See* Selection of books
Literature-based instruction, 10–11
Literature Circles, and realistic fiction, 234
Literature experience, first-grade, 82
Literature response journals (reading journals), 85–86, 188
Love of literature, and emergent literacy, 107
Lyric poetry, 150

Mainstreaming, 303
in real-life literature, 309
Make-believe, 170. *See also* Fantasy
Maps and charts, 86–89
Mathematics
response experience for, 330
in vignette, 321
Meaning
construction of, 72
envisionment as, 75
in literature, 74
Media
experimenting with, 134
for young children, 111–112
Media-based literature, 65–66
Media centers, 108–109
Medium, 124–125
Metaphor, 149
Meter, 149
Misfits, family, 204–205
Mobility challenges, 307–308
Modern fantasy, 24–25, 168, 178
historical roots of, 178
origins of, 170
vignette on, 179
Monkeys, for disabled people, 308
Mood, 33–34
Movement, and poetry, 157–158
Multiculturalism, 346, 348
Multicultural literature, 55, 348
vignette on, 201
Music stories, 284–285
Mysteries, 213
Myths, 176

Narration, revealing characters through, 32
Narrative, and point of view, 36–37
Narrative poems, 150
Narrative style, 27

National Academy of Early Childhood Programs, 108
National Association for the Education of Young Children, 100
  on literacy experiences, 10
  Position Statement on Early Literacy of, 101
National Center for Children's Illustrated Literature, 128
National Center for History in the Schools, 234
National Coalition Against Censorship, 57
National Council of Teachers of English, 57, 248, 370
National Council of the Social Studies, 234
National Science Teachers Association, 51–52, 259
Native American folktales, as thematic unit, 336–337
Native American language chart, 88
Native Americans, in historical fiction, 230
Nature identification books, 253–254
Neighbors, in culturally conscious literature, 352–353
Newbery Award, 50–51, 52, 248, 368–369
"New folktales," 175
Nonfiction books, 9, 246, 247, 248. *See also* Informational books
  accuracy in, 257
  biography, 249–253, 277
  and disabling conditions, 306
  teaching strategies for, 261–262
  trade books as, 258–261
  value of, 248–249
Nonsense poetry, 151
Noodlehead tales, 176
Nostalgia, 35
Novels, comparison chart of, 327
Nursery rhymes, sound patterns of, 148

Older students, picture books for, 127
Onomatopoeia, 148
Oral language, 86, 274
Oral literature, 275
  and booktalks, 288–289
  choral reading, 157, 285–286
  and creative drama, 286–288
  discussion of, 289
  and reader's theater, 278–279
  and reading aloud, 276–278
  research and application experiences on, 295
  storytelling, 16, 37, 280–285 (*see also* Storytelling)
  unit suggestions on, 292–294
  vignette on, 275
Oral reading

  and silent reading, 274
  for young children, 110–111
Oral tradition, 25
Orbis Pictus Award, 370–372
Orthopedically disabled persons, 307–308

Pantomime, 287–288
Parallel plots, 30
Parents. *See also* Families
  of abused children, 310–311
  and censorship, 54, 57
    questionnaire for, 57
  of children with disabilities, 308
  and cognitive development, 104
  and literature for young children, 106
  and realistic fiction, 203
  as teachers, 100
Peer relations, in realistic fiction, 209, 210
Periodicals, 254
Personification, 149, 150
Perspective (point of view), 36–37
  in illustration, 126
Photographic essays, 254
Photography, and nonfiction, 258
Physical education, response experience for, 330
Piaget's levels of cognitive development, 60, 104
Picture books, 25, 118–119, 120, 137
  classroom activities for, 128–137
  contemporary, 121
  about dogs, 130–131
  history of, 120–121
  and illustrations, 120, 122–126
  and illustrators, 121–122
  for older students, 127
  research and application experiences on, 138
  selecting and evaluating of, 128
  types of, 118, 126–127
  vignette on, 119–120
  and visual literacy, 127–128, 133
Pirates, as thematic unit, 337–338
Planning, of units, 325, 328–330
Plot, 15, 27–30, 42
  and characters, 31
  in fantasy, 181–182
  in traditional literature, 172
Plot relationships charts, 88
  for *When Agnes Caws,* 89
Plot structure, attractive types of, 59
Poetry, 25, 144–145, 146
  and adults, 162
  categorization of, 147
  children's response to, 152
  classroom activities on, 161–162

  content of, 151–152
  elements of, 147–149
  emotional intensity in, 146
  enriching experience of, 156
    through discussion, 160
    through movement, 157–158
    through rhythm, 156–157
    through riddle-poems, 158
    through themes and topics, 159
    through writing, 160
  feelings expressed in, 146–147
  folk, 175
  research and application experiences on, 163
  and poets, 152–153
  selecting and evaluating of, 153–156
  types of, 149–151
  vignette on, 145
Point of view, 36–37
Portfolio assessment, 331
Pourquoi tales, 176, 356
Power of literature, 6–10, 48–49
Pre-Colonial era, 228
Preconceptual stage, 104
Prediction, and folktales, 185
Prediction charts, 89
  for *Three Names,* 90
Prejudice, and culturally conscious literature, 354
Prelutsky, Jack, profile of, 153
Preoperational stage of development, 104
Preschool environment, and emergent literacy, 107–108
Preschoolers. *See* Young children
Primitive art, 124
Profiles
  of Caroline Arnold, 265
  of John Bierhorst, 191
  of James Cross Giblin, 92
  of Karen Hesse, 305
  of Anna Grossnickle Hines, 110
  of Jack Prelutsky, 153
  of Chris Van Allsburg, 191
  of Rosemary Wells, 110
  of Paul O. Zelinsky, 134
Profiling, of author, 92
Prop stories, 284
Protagonist, 28, 29, 31
Public Law 94–142, 303
Puppets, 288
Pura Belpré Award, 51, 372
Purpose for reading (stance), 76–77, 291

Quality, as selection standard, 50–53

Race, and children's reading interests, 62
Racial and ethnic issues, in censorship, 55

Racism, and culturally conscious literature, 354
Readability, 62–63
Reader response, 5. *See also* Response to literature
Reader's theater, 278–279
  vignette on, 275
Reading
  choral, 157, 285–286
  environment for, 15
  oral, 110–111, 274
  reasons for, 76–77
  response experiences for, 330
  silent, 274, 289–292
Reading ability, and reading interest, 62
Reading aloud to children, 110–111, 276–278
  of picture books, 129
  of poetry, 153, 156
  and school success, 103
Reading interests, 58–59
  identifying of, 63
  and reading ability, 62
Reading journals (literature response journals), 85–86, 188
Realism
  in children's books, 7
  value of, 203
Realistic art, 124
Realistic fiction, 24, 25
  classroom use of, 234–235
  and disabling conditions, 306
  issues in, 203–204
Realistic fiction, contemporary, 24, 25, 200, 201, 202
  challenges in from outside family, 209–212
  classroom activities on, 214–215
  enrichment activities on, 216
  families in, 204–208, 209–210
  vs. historical fiction, 202, 225
  and special interests, 212–214
  vignette on, 201
Real-life literature, 302–303
  classroom activities on, 312–313
  research and application experiences on, 314
  selecting and evaluating of, 304–306
    and abused children, 310–311
    and emotional challenges, 309
    and health challenges, 308–309
    and hearing challenges, 306–307
    and homeless, 312
    and learning challenges, 309–310
    and lifestyle or family challenges, 311–312
    and mobility challenges, 307–308

    and substance abuse, 311
    and vision challenges, 307
  value of, 304
  vignette on, 303
Reasons for reading, 76–77
Reciting in unison, 135
Recycling, thematic unit on, 334–335
Reference books, 254–255
Refrain choral reading, 285
Refugees, literature-based teaching on, 214–215
Repetition, in poetry, 157
Research, reading interest, 58–59
Response journals (reading journals), 85–86, 188
Response to literature, 5, 72–73, 320
  classroom activities on, 92–95
  dimensions of, 77–78
  enhancing of, 83–84
    through author and illustrator studies, 89–92
    through discussion, 84–85 (*see also* Discussion)
    through maps and charts, 86–89
    through oral language activities, 86, 274
    through writing, 85–86, 330
  guiding of, 78–80
  and literary thinking, 74–76
  for literature-based units, 328, 330
  need to encourage, 15
  nurturing of, 80–83
  to poetry, 152
  and reasons for reading, 76–77
  research and application experiences on, 95
  and silent reading, 291–292
  understanding of, 77
  vignette on, 73
Revolutionary War era, 229
Rhyme, 148
Rhythm
  in poetry, 149, 156–157
  preparation for, 288
Riddle-poems, 158
Role playing, and biographies, 261

Schemata, 26
School environment, and emergent literacy, 107–108
School Library Journal, 52
School success, and early literary experience, 103
Science
  and literature, 12
  response experiences for, 330
  and trade books, 259–260

  in vignette, 321
Science and Children, 52
Science fiction, 25, 183
Science Teacher, 259
Selection of books, 48–49
  and censorship, 53–57 (*see also* Censorship)
  and child-centered criticism, 57–65
  for choral reading, 285
  for creative drama, 287
  for culturally conscious literature, 350
  and developmental stages, 60–63
  evaluation in, 50
    and literature awards, 50–53
  guidelines for, 63–65
  of informational books, 255–258
  and media-based literature, 65–66
  of picture books, 128
  of poetry, 153–156
  for reader's theater, 278–279
  for reading aloud, 276–278
  of real-life literature, 304–312
  research and application experiences on, 67
  for storytelling, 282
  in traditional literature, 177
  vignette on, 49
  for young children, 109–110
Sensory language, 148
Sentimental books, 35
Series books, 57–58, 212–214
  historical fiction, 225–226
  informational, 255
Setting, 15–16, 33–34, 42
  in fantasy, 181
  in traditional literature, 172
Shared book experiences, 325
Sierra Club, 259
Silent reading, 274, 289–292
Simile, 149
Simpleton tales, 176
Single parents, in realistic fiction, 206–207
Slavery, in historical fiction, 223, 228–229, 230–231, 236
Social Education, 52
Social science, and literature, 12
Social studies
  response experiences for, 330
  and trade books, 260, 261
  in vignette, 321
Sound, and response, 77
Sound patterns, in poetry, 148
Speaking, response experiences for, 330
Special interest books, 212–214
Sports, books on, 212–213
SSR (sustained silent reading), 290

Stages of development, 61, 77
Stance, 76–77
    aesthetic, 77
    efferent, 77
Static (delineated) characters, 32
Stepfamilies, in realistic fiction, 207, 311
Stereotypes, 55, 349
    in traditional literature, 128
Stories, 4
Story approach, 13
Story elements, 15
    and attractiveness, 59
Story grammars, 16, 23, 38–39
Story maps, 86–87
    for *Bloomability,* 86
    creating of, 135
    and fantasy, 184
Story pyramids, 89
Storytelling, 16, 37, 280–285
    with traditional literature, 184
    vignettes on, 3–4, 281
Structural units, 324
Structures, of children's literature, 15
Student-generated theme units, 324
Style, 35–37, 42
    author, 78
    in biography, 252–253
    in fantasy, 182
    of illustrations, 124
    in informational books, 255–256
    in traditional literature, 174
Subject-matter units, 14
Substance abuse, 311
Summarizing, of Stone Age culture, 262
Supporting characters, 31
Survival, in realistic fiction, 210–212
    in historical fiction, 227–228
Symbolism, 36

"Tale," 170
Tall tales, 176, 177
Teacher, and children's literature, 14–16
Teacher-generated theme units, 324
Teachers' Choices project, 51
Technique
    of illustrations, 125
        identifying of, 135
    in informational books, 256
Teddy bear week, 136
Textbook, 3
    trade-book writing compared with, 256
Theme(s), 13–14, 34–35, 42, 324
    in biography, 252
    in fantasy, 182
    in poetry, 159
    of traditional stories, 173–174
Theme cycles, 324

Theme unit learning, 324–325, 326, 327–328
Thinking
    stimulation of, 9
    ways of, 74
Time fantasy, theme unit on, 326
Titanic, in historical fiction, 234
Topics, in poetry, 159
Touchstone books, 14
Trade books, 3, 8–9, 16, 258
    and the arts, 260–261
    and children's interests, 62
    in classrooms, 235
    and science, 259–260
    and social studies, 260, 261
    textbook writing compared with, 256
Traditional literature, 25, 168, 170–171
    as basis of modern stories, 280
    classroom activities on, 183–191
    contemporary values of, 171
    as culturally conscious, 356, 359, 360
    elements of, 171–174
    vs. modern fantasy, 178
    as read-aloud, 277–278
    research and application experiences
        on, 192
    selecting and evaluating of, 177
    types of, 175
    vignette on, 169
Trickster tales, 175–176, 356
Truth, in children's books, 78. *See also*
        Realistic fiction

Understanding(s)
    children's construction of, 79
    and community of response, 79
    literary experiences as enhancing, 37–39
    from literature, 7–8, 12
    of real vs. make-believe, 170
    as response to literature, 77
    about structural elements, 23
Understatement, 36
Uninterrupted sustained silent reading
        (USSR), 290
Unison choral reading, 286
Unit, 324
Unit studies, 13–14, 322. *See also*
        Integrated instruction
    assessment of, 330–331
    book sharing in, 325
    classroom suggestions for, 331–340
    and culturally conscious literature,
        357–360
    on dogs, 130–131
    and inquiry, 323–324
    and oral literature, 292–294
    planning for, 325, 328–330

research and application experiences
        for, 340
    and role of literature, 322–323
    as theme units, 324–325, 326, 327–328

Values
    and censorship, 54
    teaching of, 304
Values clarification, 304
Van Allsburg, Chris, profile of, 191
Videos, 65
Vietnam War, in historical fiction, 233–234
Violence, in realistic fiction, 203–204
Vision challenges, 307
Visual literacy, 127–128, 133

Wars, in historical fiction, 232–234
Weather, in poetry, 161
Web sites, 128. *See also* Internet; World
        Wide Web
Webs of knowledge, 323
Wells, Rosemary, profile of, 110
Whole language, 10
Why stories, 176
Women (females), portrayal of, 56
Wonder tales, 175
Wordless picture books, 118, 126–127
Word play, in poetry, 149
World response, 78
World War I, historical fiction on, 232
World War II, historical fiction on, 225,
        232–233
World Wide Web
    authors' sites on, 13
    Companion Website, vii–viii
    multicultural arts site on, 356
Writing
    and emergent literacy, 107
    of folktales, 186–187
    and literature, 11
    of poetry, 160
    as response, 85–86, 330

Young children, 100–101. *See also* Age
    benefits of literature for, 106
    enhancement activities for, 110–112
    five senses activity for, 112
    importance of literary experiences
        for, 10
    research and application experiences
        on, 113
    selecting and evaluating literature for,
        109–110
    value of literary experience for, 102–104
    vignette on, 101–102

Zelinsky, Paul O., 134

Author/Title Index

A. B. See, 61
A. Lincoln and Me, 278
Aardema, Verna, 125, 138, 185, 186, 192, 282, 295
Aaron, I., 7
Abby, 312, 315
ABC Task Force, 109
Abercrombie, Barbara, 144
Abramson, R., 59
Abuela, 106, 114, 351, 362
Across the Wide and Lonesome Prairie: The Oregon Trail Diary of Hattie Campbell, 226, 240
Ada, Alma Flor, 352, 355, 360–361
Adam and Eve and Pinch-Me, 208, 218
Adams, J. J., 60
Adams, M. J., 10, 107
Adams, S. M., 26
Adamson, L. G., 222
Adler, C. S., 311–312, 314
Adler, David A., 213, 214, 216, 253, 266
Adler, Susan, 308–309, 317
Adoff, Arnold, 155
Adventures in Music (recording), 285
Adventures of Tom Sawyer, 50, 69
Adventuring with Books: A Booklist for PreK through Grade 6, 53
Advice for a Frog and Other Poems, 148, 166
Aekyung's Dream, 354, 365
Aesop's Fables, 175, 186, 194
Agre, P., 318–319
Ahlberg, A., 113
AIDS, 309, 317
Aiken, Joan, 231, 238
Airport, 61
Aja's Dragon, 189, 193
Alarcón, F. X., 147, 163
Alborough, J., 194
Alcock, Vivien, 30, 36–37, 43, 183, 192
Alcorn, S., 361
Alcott, L. M., 67
Alda, Arlene, 106, 113

Alex, the Kid with AIDS, 309, 316
Alexander, Lloyd, 27, 37, 179, 180, 191, 192, 277, 287, 295
Alexander, Martha G., 136, 138
Alexander and the Terrible, Horrible, No Good, Very Bad Day, 7, 9, 19, 282, 295, 298
Alfred, S., 282
Alfred Summer, The, 308, 318
Aliki, 61, 136, 138, 248, 259, 264, 266
Allen, T. B., 267, 342
Allergies—What They Are, What They Do, 309, 318
Alles, Hemesh, 133
All Pigs Are Beautiful, 291, 292, 297
All the Colors of the Race, 155
All Together Now, 227, 238, 310, 314
Almasi, J., 83, 84
Alphabet Atlas, The, 254
Alphin, E. M., 279, 295
Altman, Linda Jacobs, 352, 361
Altwerger, B., 324–325
Amadeo, D. M., 314
Amadeo, Diana M., 308
Amazing Bone, The, 182, 196
Amazing Grace, 78, 87, 96, 354, 363
Amelia Bedelia (series), 277
Amelia's Road, 352, 361
America Alive: A History, 257, 269
American Christmas, An, 159
American Dragons: Twenty-five Asian American Voices, 189, 197
American Girl (series), 57
American Sports Poems, 154, 164
Amish Wedding, An, 361
Ammon, R., 234, 361
Ammon, R. I., 261
Among the Hidden, 194
Amos Fortune: Free Man, 38
Amspaugh, L., 86, 248
Anapao, 65, 69
Ancient Cliff Dwellers of Mesa Verde, The, 265, 266

Ancona, George, 261, 266, 313, 315, 317, 318, 350, 355–356, 361
Andersen, B., 269
Andersen, Hans Christian, 178, 192, 279, 295
Anderson, G., 62
Anderson, R., 62, 258
Anderson, R. C., 10
And If the Moon Could Talk, 33, 43, 106, 113
Andrew, R., 261, 270
Andrews, S., 304
Andronik, Catherine M., 264, 266
And Then What Happened, Paul Revere?, 252, 269
Anglund, Joan Walsh, 35
Anholt, Laurence, 12–13, 17, 273
Animal, the Vegetable, and John D. Jones, The, 311, 315
Animal Lives: The Barn Owl, 249
Animals, Animals, 162
Animorphs, The (series), 202, 216
Ant Bully, The, 6, 19
Anthony, Joseph, 126, 138
Anti-Bias Curriculum: Tools for Empowering Young Children, 109
Appalachia: The Voices of Sleeping Birds, 351, 365
Appalachian Spring, 119
Applebee, A., 22, 170
Applegate, K. A., 202, 216
Apprenticeship of Lucas Whitaker, The, 227–228, 239
April and the Dragon Lady, 210, 219–220
Aranda, Charles, 282
Arbo, Chris, 126, 138
Arbuthnot, M., 148, 163
Arbuthnot, M. H., 251, 298
Archbold, R., 267
Ardizzone, E., 121
Ark, The, 197
Arlene Alda's 1 2 3, 106, 113

Arms, J., 166
Armstrong, Jennifer, 231, 236, 238
Arnold, A., 266
Arnold, Caroline, 61, 254, 259, 265, 266, 267, 307, 314, 334, 340
Arnold, Jeane, 322, 343
Arnosky, J., 67, 133
Aronsky, Jim, 259
Around the World in a Hundred Years: From Henry the Navigator to Magellan, 227
Arrow Book of Poetry, 155
Arrow Over the Door, The, 33, 43, 353, 361
Arrow to the Sun, 125, 140
Arroyo, A., 364
Art Connections, 273
Art Fundamentals, 132
Art Lesson, The, 133
Art of African Masks: Exploring Cultural Traditions, 355, 362
Art of Japan: Wood-Block Color Prints, 355, 362
Art of the Far North: Inuit Sculpture, Drawing, and Printmaking, 355, 362
Aruego, J., 96, 164
Asbjornsen, Peter C., 186, 192, 295
Asch, Frank, 106, 113, 277, 296, 332, 333, 334, 340
Ashabranner, Brent, 251, 267
Ata, Te, 336, 340
At Her Majesty's Request: An African Princess in Victorian England, 261, 270, 353, 364
A to Z: Access to Children's Picture Books, 53
At the Back of the North Wind, 178, 195
Auch, Mary Jane, 205, 216
Auden, W. H., 7
August, L., 194, 363
Aunt America (series), 58
Aunt Elaine Does the Dance from Spain, 348
Aunt Skilly and the Stranger, 196
"Authentic Multicultural Activities," 348
Avi, 207, 216, 224, 229, 238, 328
Ayres, Katherine, 354, 361
Ayu and the Perfect Moon, 348
Azarian, Mary, 97, 127

Babar's Little Circus Star, 61
Babbitt, Natalie, 61, 166, 171,

181–182, 192, 335, 340
Babe: The Gallant Pig, 178, 194
Baby Dances, The, 106, 114
Baby-O, 285, 296
Baby Rattlesnake, 336, 340
Babysitter's Club (series), 57, 202, 219
Baby Uggs Are Hatching, The, 153
Backyard Dragon, 189, 196
Bacmeister, Rhoda, 148–149, 163
Bacon, P., 362
Bagert, B., 150
Bailey, F. M., 76
Bailey School Kids (series), 214
Baker, K., 133
Baker, W., 269
Balancing Girl, The, 308, 318
Ballad of Belle Dorcas, The, 279, 297
Ballad of Lucy Whipple, The, 230, 239
Ballad of the Pirate Queens, The, 338, 344
Ballantyne, M. M., 248
Ballard, R. D., 267
Bamboo Flute, The, 49, 67
Bancroft, B., 195
Bandit's Moon, 59, 67
Band of Angels, A: A Story Inspired by the Jubilee Singers, 353, 363
Bang, Molly, 113, 133, 137, 138
Banks, Kate, 33, 43, 106, 113
Banks, Lynne Reid, 282, 296
Barefoot: Escape on the Underground Railroad, 236, 239
Barksdale-Ladd, M. A., 75
Barlow, Genevieve, 282, 296
Barnes, D., 323
Barnes, Ellen, 308, 314
Barnes, J., 269
Barnett, W. S., 100
Barn Owl, The, 126, 141
Barone, D., 85
Barrio: Jose's Neighborhood, 350, 361
Barthes, R., 76
Bartholomew and the Oobleck, 279, 298
Barton, Byron, 109, 166, 298
Baseball in April and Other Stories, 282, 298
Bash, Barbara, 259, 263, 267
Baskin, R., 306
Bat, 265, 266
Bat 6, 232–233, 244
Bats: Mysterious Flyers of the Night, 263, 271
Bats: Night Fliers, 263, 270
Batten, M., 267

Battle for the Castle, The, 182, 197
Bauer, C. J., 50, 53
Bauer, Marion Dane, 56, 67, 207, 216
Baum, L. Frank, 179, 192–193
Baylor, Byrd, 122, 133, 138, 150, 154, 155, 163
Baynes, P., 195, 197
Beach, R., 59
Beacons of Light: Lighthouses, 269
Beal, George, 254
Bean, 110, 115
Bean's Games, 110, 115
Bean's Night, 110, 115
Bear Called Paddington, A, 193
Beard, Darleen Bailey, 259, 267
Bear for Miguel, A, 279, 295
Bear Shadow, 332, 340
Beaty, Janice J., 348, 349, 351
Beauty and the Beast, 176
Beaver, 254
Beddows, E., 163
Bedtime!, 113
"Bedtime," 158, 164
Beeler, Selby B., 356, 361
Beethoven, 273
Beethoven Lives Upstairs (video), 65
Beezus and Ramona, 204, 217
Begay, Shonto, 193, 336, 340, 341
Behind the Bedroom Wall, 233, 244
Behind the Lines, 231, 240
Behold . . . the Dragons!, 188, 194
Being Adopted, 312, 318
Bein' With You This Way, 350, 364
Bell, Don, 356, 362
Belle Prater's Boy, 205, 221, 304, 352
Bells of Christmas, The, 226, 240
Belonging Place, The, 227, 241
Belpré, Pura, 187
Bender, R., 296
Benfield, C. M., 53
Benkof, R., 317
Bennett, Gary, 124, 141, 293, 298
Bennett, N., 217
Ben's Trumpet, 126, 140
Berck, Judith, 312, 314
Berger, Barbara, 333, 340
Berger, Melvin, 249, 259, 267
Berkus, Clara Widess, 7, 17
Bernhard, Emery & Durga, 169, 193
Bernstein, J. E., 63, 65
Bernstein, Z., 297
Berry, L. A., 97
Bertrand, Lynne, 61
Best Friends, 54, 68

Best Witches: Poems for Halloween, 159
Betancourt, J., 216
Bettleheim, B., 171
Between Earth & Sky, 124, 138
Bewell, D., 83–84
Beyer, B., 8
Beyond the Burning Time, 228, 241
Beyond the Tomorrow Mountains, 183, 193
Bial, Raymond, 253
Bierhorst, John, 190, 191
Biklen, Douglas, 308, 314
Binch, C., 96, 363
Bing Bang Boing, 149, 163
Birch, David, 12, 18
Birchbark House, The, 352, 362
Bird Boy, 351, 363
Birdie's Lighthouse, 73, 76, 96
Birds and Beasts, 159, 162, 166
Birdseye, T., 193
Birthday Basket for Tía, A, 364
Bishop, Nic, 249, 268, 296
Bishop, Rudine Sims, 348
Bissex, G., 11
Black, J. B., 38
Black, White, Just Right!, 354, 361
Black Cat, 25, 44, 122, 125, 140
Black Folktales, 195, 282, 297
Black Geese, The: A Baba Yaga Story from Russia, 171, 195
Black Whiteness: Admiral Byrd Alone in the Antarctic, 26, 43, 277, 296
Blake, R. W., 77
Blatchford, Claire H., 307, 314
Blatt, G., 62
Bloem, P. L., 84
Bloom, L., 165, 317
Bloomability, 7, 18, 86, 96
Bloome, D., 76
Blos, Joan W., 104, 113, 267
Blue Heron, 207, 216
Blumberg, R., 267
Bobbin Girl, The, 231, 241
Body, 259, 269
Bollinger, M., 197
Bolognese, D., 238
Bond, Michael, 136, 138, 193
Bond, N., 28
Bone, C., 118
Book Dragon, A, 33, 44
Bookfinder, The: A Guide to Children's Literature about the Needs and Problems of Youth Aged 2–15, 14, 53

Book of Dragons, The, 189, 194
Book of Three, The, 287, 295
Boone, Daniel, 176
Boorstin, Daniel, 2
Boo to a Goose, 277, 296
Borden, Louise, 278, 296
Borders, S., 84, 85, 276
Borrowers, The, 50, 68
Boshblobberbosh: Runcible Poems for Edward Lear, 151, 165
Boss of the Plains: The Hat that Won the West, 60, 250, 267
Bossy Gallito, The: A Traditional Cuban Folktale, 356, 362
Bostock, M., 19, 271
Boston, L. M., 193
Boston, P., 193
Bouncing on the Bed, 104, 115
Bourke, Linda, 313, 314
Bourne, B., 267
Boutte, G. S., 348, 349
Bowen, Gary, 228, 238, 256, 267
Bowman, L. W., 218
Bowmar Orchestral Library, 285
Box of Nothing, A, 181, 193
Boyajian, A., 113
Boy of the Deeps, 231, 244
Boy of the Three-Year Nap, 37, 45
Boys Against Girls, 210, 220
Boys Start the War, The, 210, 220
Boy Who Dreamed of an Acorn, The, 171, 193
Boy Who Loved Frogs, The, 282, 297
Boy Who Wanted a Family, The, 311, 316
Bracelet, The, 232, 244
"Brachiosaurus," 152
Brady, I., 271
Branley, Franklyn M., 259, 267, 334, 340
Break Dance Kids, The, 158, 165
Break with Charity, A: A Story about the Salem Witch Trials, 228, 242
Bremen Town Musicians, The (Stevens), 186, 196, 279, 298
Brenner, Barbara, 236–237, 238, 251, 267
Brer Rabbit, 176
Brett, Jan, 131, 138
Brickyard Summer: Poems, 154, 164
Bride for Anna's Papa, A, 226, 241
Bridge, E., 154
Bridgers, Sue Ellen, 227, 238, 309, 310, 314

Briggs, Raymond, 61, 127, 133, 138, 175, 186, 193
Bringing the Rain to Kapiti Plain, 186, 192
Brittain, Bill, 311, 314
Britton, J., 179
Bronfenbrenner, U., 104
Brooke, William J., 179, 193
Brooks, Bruce, 207, 216
Brooks, J., 240–241
Brown, Calef, 151, 163
Brown, K., 341
Brown, Laurene Krasny, 249, 267, 341
Brown, Marc, 11, 18, 109, 249, 267, 328, 341
Brown, Marcia, 133, 169, 171, 186, 192, 195, 359
Brown, Margaret Wise, 11, 18, 61, 101, 113, 267, 334, 341
Brown, Ruth, 61
Brown, Tricia, 352, 361
Brown Angels: An Album of Pictures and Verse, 352, 364
Brown Bear, Brown Bear, What Do You See?, 61, 281, 297, 342
Bruchac, Joseph, 33, 43, 124, 138, 261, 267, 353, 356, 361
Bruner, J., 12
Bryan, Ashley, 158, 166, 365
Bryant, M., 364
Buckley, Marilyn, 88
Buehner, M., 298
Buehner, Robert, 279
Building Bridges with Multicultural Picture Books, 348
Bulletin, The, 49
Bulletin of the Center for Children's Books, The, 257
Bull Run, 231, 236, 239
Bunnicula: A Rabbit Tale of Mystery, 24, 44, 61, 90, 96, 179, 194, 287, 297
Bunting, Eve, 120, 138, 232, 233, 238, 354, 361
Bunyan, Paul, 176
Burch, Robert, 202
Burgess, S. A., 59
Buried Onions, 354
Burkert, N. E., 67
Burks, Brian, 230, 238
Burleigh, Robert, 26, 43, 124, 138, 261, 267, 277, 296
Burnett, Frances Hodgson, 28, 43, 50, 67
Burnie, D., 254, 267

Burningham, John, 287, 296
Burning Questions of Bingo Brown, 202, 216
Burroughes, D., 43
Burton, Hester, 224
Burton, M., 348
Burts, D. C., 100
Busching, B., 286
Busy Town, 65, 69
But I'll Be Back Again, 147
Byars, Betsy, 37, 43, 202, 204–205, 210, 213, 216, 225, 239, 279, 296, 310, 311, 314

Cabbage Moon, 178, 193
Caine, G., 100
Caine, R., 100
Caines, J. F., 315
Cairney, T., 76
Caldecott, Randolph, 90, 120–121
Caldecott Celebration, A, 138
Calhoun, Mary, 334, 341
Calkins, L., 11
Cameron, E., 180
Camille and the Sunflowers: A Story About Vincent Van Gogh, 12–13, 17, 273
Cam Jansen and the Mystery of the Dinosaur Bones, 213, 216
Cam Jansen and the Mystery of the U.F.O., 213, 216
Camp, D. J., 127
Campbell, R., 59
Canada Geese Quilt, The, 205, 218
Canavan, D., 10
Candlewick Book of First Rhymes, The, 147, 163
Cane, Eric, 162
Cannon, Janell, 122, 138–139, 263, 267
Canyons (Paulsen), 65, 69
Capote, Truman, 208, 217
Care and Feeding of Dragons, The, 189, 196
Carle, Eric, 101, 112, 113, 133, 139, 197, 341, 342
Carling, A. L., 361
Carling, Amelia Lau, 353
Carlos and the Carnival, 322, 343
Carlson, G. R., 58
Carlson, Laurie M., 60, 250, 267
Carlstrom, Nancy White, 113–114, 136, 139, 285, 296
Carolina's Courage, 38

Carpenter, N., 267
Carr, Jan, 251, 277, 296, 297
Carratello, J. & P., 273
Carrick, Carol, 305, 315
Carrick, D., 243
Carson, Jo, 146, 163
Carter, Alden, 309, 315
Carter, Alice, 307, 315
Carter, C. S., 315
Cartwright, R., 273
Case of the Dirty Bird, The, 213, 220
Casler, Leigh, 171, 193
Castaway, The, 227, 243
Castle, 264, 270
Castles, 261, 270
Cast Two Shadows: The American Revolution in the South, 229, 243
Catalanotto, P., 96
Catch the Wind!, 73, 77, 96
Catherine, Called Birdy, 235
Cat Poems, 162
Cat That Was Left Behind, The, 311–312, 314
Cat Up a Tree, 106, 114
Cat Up a Tree: A Story in Poems, 150, 164
Cauley, L. B., 291, 296
Cazet, Dennis, 277, 296
Celebrate America: In Poetry and Art, 321, 343
Celebrations, 159
Cendrillon: A Caribbean Cinderella, 169, 196, 359
Cha, Chue & Nhia Thao, 355, 361
Cha, Dia, 355, 361
Chadwick, Tim, 178, 193
Challenge to Care in Schools, The, 304
Chamberlain, M., 269
Chambers, A., 5, 79, 80, 81
Champlin, Connie, 288
Changing Tunes, 7, 19
Chapman, Robert, 6, 124, 140
Charles A. Lindbergh: A Human Hero, 250, 269
Charlesworth, R., 100
Charlie and the Chocolate Factory, 179, 193
Charlip, Remy, 313, 315
Charlotte's Web, 7, 14, 19–20, 26, 32, 33, 35, 45, 53, 69, 179, 180, 182, 196, 277, 299
Charlsie's Chuckle, 7, 17
Charro: The Mexican Cowboy, 261, 266

Chase, Richard, 282, 296
Chasing Redbird, 205, 217
Cheetah, 265, 266
Cherry, Lynne, 122, 125, 139, 166, 259, 261, 267, 277, 296
Chertok, B., 273
Chess, V., 298
Chestnut Cove, 335, 341
Chicken Little, 137, 140
Chilcoat, George W., 9, 19, 277, 298
Childhood Education, 348
Child of the Morning, 305, 315
Child of the Owl, 208, 221
Children and the AIDS Virus, 316
Children of Bach, 215
Children of Green Knowe, 193
Children of the Dust Bowl, 271
Children of the Wild West, 239, 256, 268
Children of Topaz, The, 9, 19, 277, 298
Children's Animal Atlas, The, 254, 270
Children's Atlas of Exploration, The, 254, 270
Children's Book Council, 91
Children's Books and Their Creators, 153
Children's Catalog, 53
Children's Literature Web Guide, The, 13, 53, 65, 108, 128, 169
Children's Reference Plus, 49
Childress, Alice, 311, 315
Child's Book of Art, A, 273
Child's Garden of Verses, A, 343
Chimney Sweeps, 92, 96
Chin Chiang and the Dragon's Dance, 189, 196
Chinn, Karen, 351, 361
Chipman, M., 348
Choi, S. N., 348, 351, 361
Choosing Books for Children, 53
Chorao, K., 114
Christelow, E., 139
Christensen, Bonnie, 28
Christian, Frank, 106, 114
Christiansen, C. B., 205, 217
Christiansen, Candace, 125, 140
Christmas in the Big House, Christmas in the Quarters, 236, 241
Christmas Poems, 159
Chritelow, Eileen, 122
Chronicles of Narnia, The, 178
Chrysanthemum, 106, 114
Chukovsky, K., 170, 350
Cianciolo, P., 127

Ciardi, John, 161
Cinderella, 168, 170, 176, 280
    Galdone edition, 186, 194
Cinderella (Grimm Brothers), 25, 56,
    58, 67, 76, 127, 194
    Hogrogian edition, 186, 187
Cinderella (Perrault)
    Brown edition, 133, 169, 170, 171,
        186, 187, 195, 280, 298, 359
    Le Cain edition, 186
Cindy, A Hearing Ear Dog, 307, 315
Circle of Seasons, A, 150, 161, 165
Circles and Spheres, 270
*Circuit, The: Stories from the Life of a
    Migrant Child,* 354, 363
Circus! Circus!, 162
Clark, M., 103
Claverie, Jean, 282, 296
Clay, W., 261, 271
Clay Marble, The, 233–234, 240
Cleary, Beverly, 202, 204, 217
Cleaver, Vera, 311, 315
Cleaver, Vera and Bill, 279, 296,
    309, 315
Clement, Rod, 8, 18, 132, 139
Clements, Andrew, 334, 341
Clements, Gillian, 264, 268
Clemesha, D., 101, 116
Clifton, Lucille, 310, 315
Climo, Shirley, 169, 193
Clinton, C., 361
Coal Mine Peaches, 351–352, 362
Coastal Rescue, 97
Cobb, V., 268
Cobb, Vicki, 254
Coerr, Eleanor, 233, 239
Coffelt, Nancy, 131, 139
Coffin, Tom, 356, 362
Cohen, Caron L., 336, 341
Cohen, D., 276, 349
Coldest Winter, The, 215, 241
Cole, Henry, 239, 259, 268
Cole, Joanna, 255, 259, 268
Collier, Christopher, 229, 239
Collier, James Lincoln, 229, 239
Collins, A., 26
Collins, H., 240
Collins, Rives, 280, 282, 289
Colón, R., 363
Color Farm, 133
Coman, Carolyn, 31, 43, 81
Come Along, Daisy!, 109, 115
Come Back, Salmon, 268

Come on, Rain, 353, 363
Comets, Meteors, and Asteroids,
    254, 271
Comfort Creek, 207, 219
*Coming of Night, The: A Yoruba Tale
    from West Africa,* 356, 365
Complete Nonsense Book, The, 151,
    161, 165
Cone, M., 268
Conklin, P., 267
Conlin, A., 103
Conly, J. L., 7, 18
Conly, Jane Leslie, 207, 217
Conrad, Joseph, 27
Conrad, Pam, 228, 239, 264, 268, 326,
    328, 341
Consall, Crosby, 61
Consultant's Notebook, The, 288
*Conversations with a Native American
    Artist,* 273
Cook, E., 180
Cookcamp, The, 208, 220
Coolidge, O., 251
*Cool Melons–Turn to Frogs!: The Life
    and Poems of Issa,* 150, 163
Cooney, Barbara, 122, 125–126, 133,
    139, 230, 239, 344
Cooper, F., 366
Cooper, Melrose, 206, 217
Cooper, Pamela, 280, 282, 289
Cooperman, Cara J., 189, 193
Cooper-Mullin, A., 49
Copenhaver, J., 215, 323, 324
Copland, Aaron, 119
Corcoran, Barbara, 305, 315
Cordier, M. H., 235
Corduroy, 104, 114, 136, 139
Corfield, R. B., 165
Cormier, Robert, 215, 227, 239
Corn Woman, The, 277, 298
Cosby, Bill, 202, 217
Costello, J. H., 55, 348, 350
Cougar, 59, 67
Council on Interracial Books for
    Children, 55
Counting Jennie, 335, 343
Coville, Bruce, 178, 189, 193
Coville, K., 193
Cowboy Baby, 106, 114
Cowcher, Helen, 259
Cowley, Joy, 249, 253–254, 268,
    277, 296
Cox, D., 348

Cox, Judy, 37, 43
Coye, J. M., 49
Coyote, Peter, 65
Coyote in Love with a Star, 356, 362
Crabtree, C., 225
Cracker Jackson, 210, 216
*Crack in the Clouds and Other Poems,
    A,* 151, 165
Crane, Walter, 120
Creech, Sharon, 7, 18, 86, 96, 205, 217
Crews, Donald, 61, 160
Cricket in Times Square, The, 196
Crisp, S., 146, 154
Crist-Evans, Craig, 28
Critter Hunt (video), 112
Cruikshank, George, 90
Crump, Donald, 254, 268
Cruz-Jansen, M., 348
Cry Softly! The Story of Child Abuse,
    311, 316–317
Cuffari, R., 193, 317
Cullinan, B., 103, 108, 109, 144, 156,
    225, 260, 276
Culpepper Adventures (series), 213
Cummings, Pat, 121, 138
Cunningham, A. M., 319
Cunningham, J., 62
Cupp, D., 315
Curtis, Christopher Paul, 234, 239
Curtis, Patricia, 307, 315
Cushman, Karen, 230, 235, 239
*Custard the Dragon and the Wicked
    Knight,* 195
Cutler, J., 306, 315

Dadey, D., 217
Dahl, Roald, 179, 193, 277, 296
Dana Alliance for Brain Initiatives, 100
Dance, 356, 363
Dancin' in the Kitchen, 106, 114
Dandelion Seed, The, 126, 138
Daniel, A., 44, 194, 297
Daniels, H., 215, 289, 290
Danziger, Paula, 209, 210, 217, 225,
    239, 311, 315
Dark, Dark Tale, A, 61
*Dark-Thirty, The: Southern Tales of
    the Supernatural,* 179, 195
Darling, K., 268
Darling, L., 217
Davie, H. K., 272
Davol, Marguerite W., 354, 361
Day, Nancy Raines, 171, 193

Day I Saw My Father Cry, The, 217
Days Before Now, The: An Autobiographical Note, 267
Days of Laura Ingalls Wilder, The (series), 230
Dead Letter, 213, 216, 239
Dean Duffy, 212, 220
de Angeli, Marguerite, 308, 315
Dear America (series), 226
Dear Mr. Henshaw, 216, 217
Dear Willie Rudd, 354, 362
de Brunhoff, Laurent, 61
Deep in the Forest, 61
Deer at the Brook, 133
DeFelice, Cynthia, 59, 67, 227–228, 239
Defoe, Daniel, 50, 67
Deford, D., 11
Degen, Bruce, 74, 139, 152, 154, 166, 259, 268
de Kiefte, K., 219
Delacre, Lulu, 356, 361
de Lanux, E., 165
Dellosso, G., 244
de Montaño, Marty Kreipe, 356, 362
Denenberg, Barry, 226, 239
"Denson Dumm," 151
Denton, T., 341
dePaola, Tomie, 133, 155, 163, 185, 193, 197, 251, 268, 277, 328, 336, 341
de Regniers, Beatrice Schenk, 130, 139, 297
Derman-Sparks, L., 109
Desert is Theirs, The, 155
Desimini, L., 165
DesJarlait, P., 273, 349, 362
DeSpain, Pleasant, 356, 362
Detective Pony, 214, 216
Devil's Arithmetic, The, 235
DeVries, R., 102
Dewey, Jennifer Owings, 259, 268
DeWolf, M., 100
Diamond, J., 197
Dias, P., 26, 154
Dia's Story Cloth: The Hmong People's Journey of Freedom, 355, 361
Diaz, D., 361, 363
Dicey's Song, 309, 319
Dichos: Proverbs and Sayings from the Spanish, 282
Dickinson, D., 102, 103
Dickinson, Jean, 325
Dickinson, Peter, 25, 43, 181, 193, 289, 296, 326, 341

Did Adam Name the Vinegarron?, 154, 164
Didion, J., 9
Diego, 271, 353, 366
Different Dragons, 317
Digby (dog) adventures, 65, 69
Di Grazia, T., 315
Dillon, Eilis, 215
Dillon, Leo & Diane, 97, 121, 125, 140, 146, 164, 186, 192, 194, 295, 362
Dinosaur Dances, 74, 154, 166
"Dinosaur Dances," 152
Dinosaur Ghosts, 9, 18, 89, 90, 96
Dinosaurs Divorce, 249, 267
Dinosaurs to the Rescue! A Guide to Protecting Our Planet, 341
Dionetti, Michelle, 351–352, 362
DiSalvo-Ryan, DyAnne, 131, 139
Disher, G., 49, 67
Divorce Express, The, 311, 315
Dodds, D. A., 268
Dog Like Jack, A, 131, 139
Dogs Don't Wear Sneakers, 131, 140
Dogs & Dragons, Trees & Dreams: A Collection of Poems, 149, 155, 165
Dogs in Space, 131, 139
Doherty, Berlie, 356, 362
Domínguez, D., 364
"Don't Yell at Me," 151
Doodle Dandies: Poems That Take Shape, 151, 165
Dooley, N., 348
Dooling, M., 269
Door in the Wall, The, 308, 315
Do Pirates Take Baths?, 338, 343
Doppert, M., 18
Dorling Kindersley Children's Illustrated Dictionary, The, 255, 268
Dorothea Lange, 273
Dorris, M., 239
Dorros, Arthur, 106, 114, 341, 351, 362
Down Buttermilk Lane, 352, 364
Down Home at Miss Dessa's, 352, 366
Downing, J., 282
Dr. Dredd's Wagon of Wonders, 311, 314
Dr. Seuss's Alphabet (video), 112
Dragon in Chinese Art, The (CD-ROM), 188
Dragonling, The, 183, 194
Dragon of Lonely Island, 189, 196
Dragon Poems, 189, 193
Dragons are Singing Tonight, The, 153

Dragon School, 189, 193
Dragon's Fat Cat: Dragon's Fourth Tale, 189, 195
Dragon's Gate, 232, 244
Dragonslayers, The, 189, 193
Dragon's Milk, 189, 193
Dragon's Robe, The, 168, 194
Draw Me a Star, 139
Dream Keeper and Other Poems, The, 164
"Dreams," 149, 164
Dreamtime: Aboriginal Stories, 195
Dreyer, S. S., 53
Drop of Water, A: A Book of Science and Wonder, 12, 20
Du Bois, W. P., 142
Dugan, K. M., 361
Duggleby, John, 252, 268, 355, 362
Duke Ellington: The Piano Prince and His Orchestra, 365
Dumpling Soup, 348
Dundes, A., 171, 175
Dunham, M., 271
Duntze, D., 192
Durkin, D., 103
Dustin's Big School Day, 309, 315
Duthie, C., 248
Duvall, Shelley, 65, 69
Dyer, J., 45, 341
Dygard, Thomas J., 213, 217
Dyson, A. H., 100

Earthquake at Dawn, 215, 240
Earth to Matthew, 209, 216, 217
Easter Poems, 159
Eastman, P. D., 61
Eborn, A., 197
Echoes of the Elders, 355, 364–365
Eckhoff, B., 11
Edelstein, Terese, 233, 244
Edith Herself, 308, 316
Educating Young Children in a Diverse Society, 348
Education for Character, 304
Edwards, Pamela Duncan, 236, 239
Egan, Tim, 335, 341
Egielski, R., 121
Ehlert, Lois, 9, 18, 61, 101, 112, 114, 125, 128, 132, 133, 139, 255, 328
Eichenberg, Fritz, 161
18 Penny Goose, The, 24, 45
Einzig, S., 195, 343
Eisner, E., 178
Elbert's Bad Word, 11, 20

Eleanor Roosevelt: A Life of Discovery, 250, 268
Electricity, 259
Elementary School Library Collection, The: A Guide to Books and Other Media, 14, 53
Elephant Crossing, 262
"Eletelephony," 151, 166
Eliot, T. S., 150
Ella Enchanted, 326, 327, 342
Elleman, B., 81, 253
Ellis Island Christmas, An, 215, 241
Elvira, 168, 189, 196
Emerald Lizard, The: Fifteen Latin American Tales to Tell in English and Spanish, 356, 362
Emergency!, 253, 270
Emerson, K. L., 235
Emperor's New Clothes, The, 178, 192
Encounter, 228, 244
Encounter at Easton, 224, 238
Endless Steppe, The, 233, 240
Engdahl, Sylvia L., 183, 193
England, C., 253, 254
Englander, K., 18
Engler, Larry, 288
Erdrich, Louise, 352, 362
Ernst, S., 72
Errata: A Book of Historical Errors, 133, 142
Esbensen, Barbara Juster, 336, 341
Eskimo Boy: Life in an Inupiaq Eskimo Village, 254, 269
Estes, Clarissa, 4
Eva, 25, 43, 181, 183, 193, 289, 296, 326, 341
Evans, D., 49, 67
Everybody Cooks Rice, 348
Everyone Else's Parents Said Yes, 209, 217
Ewing, J. K., 102
Exploding Ants: Amazing Facts About How Animals Adapt, 254, 271
Exploring Space, 255, 268
Exploring Space: Using Seymour Simon's Astronomy Books in the Classroom, 267
Exploring the Deep, Dark Sea, 253, 269
Exploring the Great Lakes Through Literature, 235
Exploring the Southeast States Through Literature, 235
Exploring the United States Through Literature (series), 235

Exploring Your World: The Adventure of Geography, 254, 268
Eyes, Nose, Fingers, and Toes, 104, 114

Fables, 186, 195
Face to Face, 207, 216
Facklam, Margery, 259
Fadden, J. K. & D. K., 361
Faint Frogs Feeling Feverish, 161
Fakih, Kimberly Olson, 282
Falkner, J. M., 81
Falwell, C., 348
Family Apart, A, 311, 318
Family Pictures, 74, 96, 352, 364
Family Tree, 354, 361
Fa Mulan: The Story of a Woman Warrior, 279, 298
Fantasia (film), 65
Far and Few, Rhymes of the Never Was and Always Is, 149, 157, 165
Farest, C., 88
Farm Team, 212, 221
Farris, P., 260
Fasick, A., 253, 254
Fast Sam, Cool Clyde, and Stuff, 311, 318
Fat Cat, The, 186, 194
Feast for 10, 348
Feeley, J. T., 59, 62
Feelings, T., 195, 270, 297
Feiffer, Jules, 106, 114, 124, 127, 139
Feitelson, D., 103
Fenner, Carol, 312, 315
Fernandez, L., 317
Feuer, E., 315
Field, S., 274
Fielding, L. G., 62, 258
Fifth of March, The: A Story of the Boston Massacre, 229, 242
Fifty-One New Nursery Rhymes, 43, 96
Fighting Back: What Some People Are Doing About AIDS, 309, 317
Fighting Ground, The, 229, 238
Fig Pudding, 204, 218
Fijan, Carol, 288
Finding Buck McHenry, 213, 221
Finger Rhymes, 11, 18
Finishing Becca: A Story About Peggy Shippen and Benedict Arnold, 229, 242–243
Finley, Carol, 355, 362
Fin M'Coul: The Giant of Knockmany Hill, 185, 193

Fiore, P. M., 362
Firebird, The, 273
Fire Pony, The, 214, 220
First Book of Myths, A: Myths and Legends for the Very Young from Around the World, 356, 363
First Dog, The, 131, 138
First Flight, 160
First Four Years, The, 230, 244
Fischetto, Laura, 197
Fisher, Aileen, 155, 161
Fisher, C., 43, 44, 154
Fisher, Diane, 189, 193
Fisher, E., 60
Fisher, Leonard Everett, 133, 139, 165, 258
Fisher, Margery, 251
Fisherman and His Wife, The: A Brand New Version, 187, 196
Fish Eyes, 101, 114
Fitzhugh, Louise, 204, 218
Flags, 352, 366
Flavin, T., 362
Fleischman, Paul, 146, 148, 149, 154, 155, 159, 163, 231, 236, 239
Fleischman, Sid, 59, 67, 207, 218
Fleming, Candace, 88, 96, 277, 296
Fleming, Denise, 104, 106, 109, 112, 114, 125, 133, 139
Fletcher, Ralph, 204, 209, 218
Fletcher, Susan, 189, 193
Flight: The Journey of Charles Lindbergh, 261, 267
Flip-Flop Girl, 210, 216, 220
Flitterman-King, S., 85
Floca, B., 18
Flores, B., 324–325
Florian, Douglas, 149, 159, 163, 277, 296, 334, 341
Flying, 160
Focus on Alcohol, 311, 318
Focus on Cocaine and Crack, 311, 318
Focus on Composers, 273
Focus on Marijuana, 311, 319
Fog Magic, 25, 45, 182, 196
Ford, Barbara, 338, 341
Ford, E. A., 108
Foreman, Michael, 106, 114, 195, 278, 296
Forever Amber Brown, 207, 217
Forgotten Door, The, 178, 180, 194
Forrai, Maria, 308, 316
For the Love of the Game: Michael Jordan and Me, 353, 362

Fortnum, P., 193
Fortune-Tellers, The, 179, 192
Forty Acres and Maybe a Mule,
   354, 365
Foster, John, 189, 193
Foster's War, 29, 45, 59, 68
Fox, 265
Fox, Mem, 247, 268, 277, 296, 323,
   334, 338, 341
Fox, Paula, 29, 43, 81, 211, 218, 276,
   297, 310, 316
Fox, S., 264
Foxy, 213–214, 218
Fractor, J. S., 289
Fraim, S., 62
Frampton, D., 269
Francesca, Baby, 205, 220
Frasconi, A., 165
Fraser, B., 164
Freddi Fish and the Case of the
   Missing Kelp Seeds, 65, 69
Frede, E., 100
Fredericks, A., 328
Freedman, Florence B., 231, 239
Freedman, Russell, 239, 248, 250, 251,
   252, 256, 268, 277, 297, 338, 341
Freeman, Don, 104, 114, 136, 139
Freeman, L., 365
Fresh Paint: New Poems, 155, 165
Friedberg, Joan, 306
Friedman, Ann, 335, 341
Friedman, J., 314
Friendship, The, 97, 234, 243, 276,
   298, 354, 366
Fritz, Jean, 61, 227, 251, 252, 253, 269
"Frog," 149, 166
Frog and Toad, 61
Frog Prince, The, 175
From Anna, 307, 317
From Hand to Mouth, 92, 96
From the Bellybutton of the Moon and
   Other Summer Poems, 147, 163
Frontier Merchants: Lionel and Barron
   Jacobs and the Jewish Pioneers
   Who Settled the West, 250, 271
Frost, Robert, 150, 155
Frye, Northrup, 8, 24, 157, 168, 280
Fuchs, B., 367
Fuchshuber, Annegert, 197
Fufula, Karama, 155
Fuhler, C., 260
Fussennegger, G., 197
Fyleman, Rose, 43, 82, 96, 145

Gaber, Susan, 356, 366
Gagnon, P., 225
Gaines, Jeanette, 312
Galda, L., 225
Galdone, Paul, 135, 139, 186, 187,
   193–194, 279, 295, 297
Gallahue, D., 100
Gallo, D., 11
"Galoshes," 148–149
Gambrell, L., 83, 84
Gamlin, L., 254, 267
Gammell, S., 165, 298, 365
Gantos, J., 7, 18
Gantschev, Ivan, 197
Garcia, S., 366
Gardiner, J. R., 275, 297
Gargoyles Don't Drive School Buses,
   214, 217
Garland, Sherry, 226, 239–240
Gates, Frieda, 86
Gathering the Sun: An Alphabet in
   Spanish and English, 355,
   360–361
Geisert, A., 197
Gelsanliter, Wendy, 106, 114
Genishi, C., 100
Gentle Giant Octopus, 6, 19
George, Jean Craighead, 12, 18, 67,
   211, 218, 257, 259
George, Lonnie, 334, 341
Gettin' Through Thursday, 205, 217
Ghost Liners: Exploring the World's
   Greatest Lost Ships, 249, 267
Ghost of a Hanged Man, 8, 19
Gibbons, Gail, 73, 96, 125, 139, 194,
   253, 257, 269, 338, 341
Giblin, James Cross, 27, 28, 92, 96,
   248, 250–251, 269
Gift for Abuelita, A: Celebrating the
   Day of the Dead, 6, 124, 140
Gilchrist, Jan Spivey, 350, 362
Gillette, J. Lynett, 9, 18, 89, 90, 96
Gingerbread Boy, The, 186, 194, 285
Ginsburg, M., 97, 243, 298, 366
Girard, Linda Walvoord, 309, 316
Girl on the Outside, The, 234, 244
Girls Gets Even, The, 210, 220
Girls' Revenge, The, 210, 220
Girl Who Cried Flowers, The, 178, 197
Girl Who Lived on the Ferris Wheel,
   The, 310, 317
Girl Who Wanted to Hunt, The, 169, 193
Giver, The, 183, 195

Glanzman, L. S., 44
Glass, A., 193, 218, 314, 366
Glenn, C. G., 38
Global Warming, 271
Glory Field, The, 208, 219, 236, 242
Glory Girl, The, 204–205, 216
Glover, D., 269
Goble, Paul, 336, 342
"Godfrey, Gordon, Gustavus Gore,"
   157, 285, 298
Go Dog Go, 61
Going on a Whale Watch, 61
Going with the Flow, 307, 314
Gold Cadillac, The, 234, 243, 276,
   298, 354, 366
Golden, J. M., 281
Golden Flower, The: A Taino Myth
   from Puerto Rico, 356, 363
Golden Key, The, 178
Golden Sanda, The: A Middle-Eastern
   Cinderella, 359
Golden Tales: Myths, Legends, and
   Folktales from Latin America,
   356, 361
Goldilocks and the Three Bears,
   25–26, 127, 168, 172, 173, 176,
   283–284, 295
Goldstein, A. N., 244
Goldstein, Z., 103
Goldstone, F., 264
Golenbrock, Peter, 352, 362
Gollub, Matthew, 150, 163
Golly Sisters Ride Again, The, 279, 296
Gonzales, Doreen, 354, 362
Gonzalez, Lucia, 356, 362
Goodall, John, 127
Goodbye, Billy Radish, 232, 243
Goodbye, Charles Lindbergh: Based
   on a True Story, 278
Goode, Diane, 159, 270
Good Knight, 104, 115
Good Neighbors, 230, 243
Goodnight Moon, 11, 18, 61, 101,
   109, 113, 334, 341
Good-night Owl!, 334, 342
Goosebumps (series), 57, 202, 221
Gopher in the Garden and Other
   Animal Poems, A, 162
Gordon, Shirley, 311, 316
Gorey, Edward, 130, 139
Go Tell Aunt Rhody, 136, 138
Go with the Poem, 161
Graeber, Charlotte, 131, 139

Graham, J. B., 164
Gramma's Walk, 106, 112
Grandfather's Journey, 252, 271
Grandfather Twilight, 333, 340
Grandpa's Gamble, 352, 364
Granny, Will Your Dog Bite, and Other Mountain Rhymes, 175, 176, 195
Granstrom, B., 114
Granville Jones, Commando, 59, 68
Graves, D., 11
Graves, S., 365
Gray, Libba Moore, 15, 354, 362
Great American Gold Rush, The, 267
Great Books for Boys, 49
Great Buffalo Race, The: How the Buffalo Got His Hump; A Seneca Tale, 336, 337, 341
Great Gilly Hopkins, The, 10, 19, 26, 31, 35–36, 44, 68, 203, 220
Great Little Madison, The, 61
Great Toilet Paper Caper, The, 214, 218
Greaves, Margaret, 280, 297
Grebu, D., 18
Greek myths, 176
Green, N., 166
Greenaway, Kate, 120, 121
Greene, E., 101, 103, 104
Greene, M., 261
Greenfield, Eloise, 126, 139, 146, 154, 164, 350, 353, 362
Greenlaw, M. J., 58, 178
Greenwood, Barbara, 236, 240
Gregory, Kristiana, 215, 226, 240
Grey Lady and the Strawberry Snatcher, The, 133
Grifalconi, Ann, 171, 193
Griffith, Helen V., 59, 67, 214, 218
Grimm, Jacob & Wilhelm, 67, 170, 178, 194
Grouchy Ladybug, The, 133, 333, 341
Growing Vegetable Soup, 112, 114
Guard the House, Sam!, 141
Guide Dog Puppy Grows Up, A, 307, 314
Gunn, J., 183
Gurney, J. S., 217
Guthrie, Woody, 287, 297
Gutman, Bill, 352, 362
Gypsy Rizka, 277, 295

Haddix, M. P., 194
Hague, Michael, 142, 189, 194
Hahn, Mary Downing, 233, 240

Hairyman, 282, 297
Haldane, Suzanne, 308, 316, 355, 364
Haley, Gail E., 186, 194, 197, 287, 297
Haley, Gale, 190
Hall, Elizabeth, 230, 242
Hall, Lynn, 309, 316
Hallensleben, George, 33, 43, 113
Halloween A B C, 159
Halloween Poems, 159
Halmoni and the Picnic, 348, 351, 361
Halverson, C., 60
Hamanaka, Sheila, 232, 240
Hamilton, Virginia, 186, 194, 202, 213, 226, 240, 310, 316, 356, 362
Hammond, D., 89
Hancock, J., 83, 85
Handford, Martin, 133, 139
Handful of Beans, A: Six Fairy Tales, 171, 196
Handmade ABC: A Manual Alphabet, 313, 314
Handmade Alphabet, The, 307, 313, 318
Handtalk Birthday: A Number & Story Book in Sign Language, 313, 315
Handtalk School, 313, 317
Hansel and Gretel, 134, 140, 172
Hansen, J., 84
Happy Birthday, Moon, 334, 340
Happy Day, The, 126, 140, 334, 342
Hardy, B., 27, 350
Hare and the Tortoise, The, 176
Harmon, W., 14, 23, 28, 30, 34, 35, 36
Harms, J., 170
Harness, Cheryl, 228, 240, 343
Harper, P., 193
Harpoon Island, 232, 244
Harris, J., 306
Harris, Jim, 57, 75
Harris, Violet J., 55, 348
Harry Potter (series), 58, 178, 183, 196
Harry Potter and the Chamber of Secrets, 68
Harry Potter and the Prisoner of Azkaban, 179
Harshman, Marc, 335, 342
Harste, J., 11, 323
Hart, A., 273
Hart, K., 273
Hart, Kate, 133, 139
Hart, 100
Hartman, D. K., 76, 321
Harvey, S., 249
Haskins, Jim, 338, 339, 342, 343

Haslam, A., 269
Hassett, John and Ann, 106, 114
Hastings, S., 273
Hatchet, 28–29, 44, 49, 56, 68, 212, 220, 339, 343
Hatmaker's Sign, The: A Story by Benjamin Franklin, 277, 296
Hattie and the Wild Waves, 133, 139
Hausherr, R., 316
Hautzig, Esther, 233, 240
Hawkes, Kevin, 18, 44, 83, 270, 342
Hawkins, S., 62
Haynes, C., 60
Hays, M., 243, 298, 365, 366
Healy, J. M., 9, 102
Heap, Sue, 106, 114
Hearn, M. P., 127
Hearne, Betsy, 53, 56, 67, 107, 109, 127, 146, 153, 157, 169, 246, 251, 255, 269
Heat, 259
Heath, S. B., 100
Heathcote, D., 286
Heckedy Peg, 75
Hellas, F., 53
Helldorfer, M. C., 351, 362
Heller, R., 193
Hello Amigos!, 352, 361
Hello Shoes, 104, 113
Helping Hands: How Monkeys Assist People Who Are Disabled, 308, 316
Hendershot, Judy, 321, 342
Henderson, D., 18, 96
Henderson, Kathy, 106, 114
Henkes, Kevin, 106, 114, 118–119, 139, 210, 218
Hennings, D., 262
Henny Penny, 135, 139, 176, 185, 194, 279, 297
Henry and Mudge, 61
Hepler, S., 225
Herculeah Jones (mystery series), 225
Hero Ain't Nothin' But a Sandwich, A, 311, 315
Hero and the Crown, The, 56, 68
Heroes, 354, 364
Hesse, Karen, 29, 32, 43–44, 49, 67, 202, 215, 218, 240, 305, 306, 310, 316, 352–353, 362, 363
Hewett, R., 266, 267, 314
Hey-How for Halloween, 159
Hickman, Jane, 208, 218, 225, 229, 240
"Hickory Dickory Dock," 148

Hickox, Rebecca, 359
Hide and Seek, 233, 244
Hide and Snake, 133
Hiebert, E. H., 10, 62
Higgins, D., 62
Highlights' Teacher Net, 153
Highwater, J., 65, 69
Hill, Elizabeth Starr, 351, 363
Hill, Eric, 101, 114
Hill, Kirkpatrick, 211, 218
Hill, S., 50, 83
Hillenbrand, W., 216
Hillerich, R., 258
Himler, R., 238, 243, 316
Hindley, Judy, 104, 114, 259, 269
Hines, Anna Grossnickle, 104, 106, 109, 110, 112, 114–115, 115
Hines-Stephens, S., 115
Hippo, 265, 266
Hirshfeld, G., 273
History Workshop, 235
Hnizdovsky, Jacques, 159, 166
Ho, Minfong, 233–234, 240
Hoban, L., 318
Hoban, Tana, 12, 18, 61, 109, 133
Hobbit, The, 69
Hoberman, Mary Ann, 155, 159, 164, 350, 363
Hoboes: Wandering in America, 1870–1940, 254, 272
Hoffman, J., 88
Hoffman, J. V., 10
Hoffman, Mary, 78, 87, 96, 354, 356, 363
Hogg, Gary, 214, 218
Hogrogian, Nancy, 186, 187, 197
Holder, Heidi, 186, 194
Holes, 30, 45, 83, 92, 97
Holland, Isabelle, 231, 240
Holland, K., 72, 76
Holman, C. H., 14, 23, 28, 30, 34, 35, 36
Holman, Felice, 49, 68
Holmes, B. C., 261
Holt, David, 282, 297
Hom, N., 366
Home: A Journey Through America, 4, 121–122, 125, 127, 140
Homecoming, 93, 97–98, 309, 319
Home for Spooky, A, 131, 141
Home Run, 124, 125, 138
Home to Medicine Mountain, 353, 365
Honest Abe, 61, 250, 269
Honey, I Love, and Other Love Poems, 126, 139, 146, 164

Honeycutt, Natalie, 59, 68
Honeywood, V. P., 217
Hooks, William H., 279, 297
Hooray for Diffendoofer Day!, 7, 36, 45
Hopkins, Lee Bennett, 6, 18, 146, 147, 152, 153, 159, 161, 162
Hopkinson, Deborah, 73, 96, 353, 363
Hop on Pop, 61
Horn Book, 257
Horton Hatches the Egg, 279
Horwitz, Elinor L., 136, 139
Hospital Book, The, 61, 90, 96
Hottest, Coldest, Highest, Deepest, 253, 269
House Is a House for Me, A, 159, 164
House of Boo, The, 150, 165
House of Wings, The, 37, 43
House That Jack Built, The, 186, 295
House with No Door, The: African Riddle-Poems, 158, 166
Houston, Gloria, 122, 139, 321, 339, 342
Howard, Ellen, 308, 316
Howard, N., 273
Howard, P., 113
Howe, James, 61, 96
Howe, James & Deborah, 24, 44, 61, 96, 179, 194, 287, 297
Howell, T., 318
How It Feels When a Parent Dies, 64, 68
How Many Days to America? A Thanksgiving Story, 232, 238
How Tall, How Short, How Far Away, 253, 266
How the Rabbit Got a Short Tail, 176
How the Rooster Got His Crown, 356, 365
How the Snake Got Its Rattles, 176
Hoyt-Goldsmith, Diane, 25, 44
Hu, Evaleen, 354, 363
Hu, Y., 270, 361
Hubbard, E., 196
Hubbell, Patricia, 152, 157, 158
Huck, C., 225
Hucko, B., 363
Hudson, Jan, 227, 240
Huffman, T., 318
"Hughbert and the Glue," 148
Hughes, A., 273
Hughes, Dean, 213, 218, 316
Hughes, K., 235
Hughes, Langston, 149, 164
Hughes, S., 320
Hughes, Ted, 161

Human Body, The, 258, 270
Hungerford, R., 72
Hungry Woman, The: Myths and Legends of the Aztecs, 191
Hunt, C. C., 225
Hunt, Irene, 205, 218, 310, 316
Hunter, Clementine, 355, 363
Hunter, M., 170
Hunter, Sarah Hoagland, 353, 363
Hurd, C., 18, 341
Hurd, Edith Thacher, 77, 96
Hurricanes, 254, 270
Hutchins, Pat, 127, 334, 338, 342
Hutchinson, W. M., 296
Hutton, W., 197
Hyde, Margaret O., 311, 316–317
Hyman, Trina Schart, 129, 140, 192, 328
Hynes, R., 365–366

I, Houdini: The Autobiography of a Self-Educated Hamster, 282, 296
I, Too, Sing America: Three Centuries of African American Poetry, 355, 361
I Am an American: A True Story of Japanese Internment, 354, 366
I Am Regina, 229, 240
I Am the Cat, 279, 298
I Am Writing a Poem About—A Game of Poetry, 153, 165
I Can Paint!, 133, 139
Iceberg Hermit, The, 227
I Dance in My Red Pajamas, 77, 96
If a Bus Could Talk, 365
If I Were In Charge of the World and Other Worries: Poems for Children and Their Parents, 97, 161, 166
If the Owl Calls Again: A Collection of Owl Poems, 159, 165
If You Give a Moose a Muffin, 102–103, 115
"If You're Happy and You Know It, Clap Your Hands," 158
...If You Traveled on the Underground Railroad, 236, 241
I Go With My Family to Grandma's, 270
Igus, Toyomi, 12, 18, 363
I Hadn't Meant To Tell You This, 310–311, 319
I Have a Friend, 332, 343
I Have Heard of a Land, 353, 366
I Know an Old Lady Who Swallowed a Fly (Rounds), 285, 298
I Know an Old Lady Who Swallowed a Fly (Westcott), 299

Iktomi and the Berries: A Plains Indian Story, 336, 342
I Like Weather, 161
I'll Protect You From the Jungle Beasts, 136, 138
Illustrated Thesaurus, 254
I Lost My Bear, 106, 114
Images in Language, Media, and Mind, 264
In Coal Country, 321, 342
In Daddy's Arms I Am Tall: African Americans Celebrating Fathers, 351, 366
Indian School, The, 230, 244
Ingham, R., 154
Insectlopedia, 159, 163
Insects, 259, 269
Inside Noah's Ark, 197
International Reading Association and the National Association for the Education of Young Children, 10
In the Haunted House, 120, 121, 138
In the Small, Small Pond, 112, 114
In the Tall, Tall Grass, 104, 133
In the Time of the Drums, 356, 366
In the Year of the Boar and Jackie Robinson, 226, 241
Into the Land of the Unicorns, 178, 193
Iqbal Masih and the Crusaders Against Child Slavery, 353, 364
I Read Signs, 12, 18
Isaacs, Anne, 140, 150, 164, 194
Isaacson, R., 53
Isadora, Rachel, 126, 136, 140
I Sailed with Columbus, 228, 243
I See the Moon, 205, 217
I See the Rhythm, 12, 18, 355, 363
Is It Rough? Is It Smooth? Is It Shiny?, 133
Island Boy, 230, 239
Island Light, 141
Island of the Blue Dolphins, 65, 68, 277, 297
I Spy (series), 112, 127, 133, 140
I Spy: An Alphabet in Art, 133, 140
I Spy School Days, 115
I Spy Treasure Hunt: A Picture Book of Riddles, 142
It Ain't Always Easy, 215, 240
I Took A Walk, 259, 268
Itse Selu, The Cherokee Harvest Festival, 348
It's Hard to Read a Map with a Beagle on Your Lap, 131, 141

Iverson, W. J., 26, 34, 36, 37, 79, 80
I Was Born About 10,000 Years Ago, 277, 297
I Went Walking, 101, 133, 142

Jack and the Beanstalk, 122, 168, 172, 176, 284–285
    Kellogg edition, 282, 297
    Ross edition, 186
Jack and the Bean Tree, 186, 194, 287, 297
Jack and the Giant: A Story Full of Beans, 57
Jackie Robinson, 353, 365
Jackson, N. R., 44
Jack Tales, The, 282, 296
Jacobs, Joseph, 169, 194
Jacque, D., 325
Jacques, Brian, 58
Jaffe, Nina, 169, 194, 356, 363
Jaggar, A., 103, 276
Jakobsen, Kathy, 287, 297
James and the Giant Peach, 277, 296
James Marshall Library, The (video), 65
Janeczko, Paul B., 146, 153, 154, 155, 164
Jataka Tales, 175
Jay, Betsy, 7, 18, 125, 140
Jazz of Our Street, The, 146, 166
Jefferson, Thomas, 269
Jenkins, C. B., 89
Jenkins, J., 273
Jenkins, Steve, 253, 269
Jeram, A., 297
Jericho, 208, 218
Jerusalem, Shining Still, 256, 269
Jesse Bear, What Will You Wear?, 113–114, 136, 139, 296
Jewell, T., 75, 84
Jim and the Beanstalk, 175, 186, 193
Jiménez, Francisco, 354, 363
Jim Ugly, 207, 218
Jip: His Story, 242
Joey Pigza Swallowed the Key, 7, 18
Johnny Cake, 176
Johnson, Adrian, 131, 140
Johnson, Angela, 150, 164
Johnson, D., 192
Johnson, J., 26
Johnson, L., 241
Johnson, L. S., 341
Johnson, Steve, 175
Johnson, Terry, 322, 326
Johnston, Julie, 208, 218

Jonas, Ann, 291, 297
Jones, Bill T., 356, 363
Jones, Charlotte Foltz, 339, 342
Jones, J. N., 219
Jones, M. T., 217
Jordan, Anne Devereaux, 203, 212, 222
Jorgensen, K., 235
Journal of James Edward Pease, a Civil War Union Soldier, The, 226, 242
Journal of Joshua Loper, The: A Black Cowboy, 226, 242
Journal of William Thomas Emerson, The, a Revolutionary War Patriot, 226, 239
Journey, 89, 96, 208, 219
Journey, The: Japanese Americans, Racism, and Renewal, 232, 240
Journey Home, 232, 243–244
Journey to the New World: The Diary of Remember Patience Whipple, 226, 241
Journey to Topaz, 232, 243
Joyce, W., 271
Joyful Noise: Poems for Two Voices, 154, 155, 159, 163
Jukes, Mavis, 218, 311, 317
Julie of the Wolves, 67
Jumanji, 28, 45, 182, 191, 196
Jump Ship to Freedom, 229, 239
Junebug, 206, 219
Jungle Book (film), 65
Just Another Ordinary Day, 8, 18, 132, 139
Just Juice, 306, 316
Just One Friend, 309, 316

Kamii, C., 102
Kane, H. B., 165
Karas, B. G., 361
Karas, G. B., 298
Karen, 308, 317
Karl, Jean, 257, 269
Karr, Kathleen, 215, 240
Katie's Trunk, 215, 243
Keams, Geri, 171, 356, 363
Keats, Ezra Jack, 239
Keehn, Sally M., 229, 240
Keith, E., 297
Keller, H., 343
Kelley, G., 165
Kelley, T., 268, 340
Kellogg, Steven, 54, 58, 68, 132, 137, 140, 277, 282, 297, 315, 328
Kelly, P. R., 85

Kelly's Creek, 309, 318
Kendall, Russ, 254, 269
Kennedy, Dorothy M., 154, 164, 186
Kennedy, X. J., 154, 164
Kennemer, P. K., 235
Kent, Jack, 186, 194
Kenyon, S., 235
Kerr, Judith, 215, 233, 240
Kesey, Ken, 27, 44
Key, Alexander, 178, 180, 194
Kidnapping Kevin Kowalski, 205, 216
Kids Make Music!, 273
Kiefer, B., 118, 121, 124, 125, 126,
    127, 132, 258
Kiesten, E., 349
Killilea, Marie, 308, 317
Kimmel, Eric A., 356, 363
King, Casey, 236, 240–241
King, E. W., 348
King Arthur, 176–177
King Bidgood's in the Bathtub, 30, 45,
    137, 325, 344
Kingfisher Animal Atlas, 262
*Kingfisher First Encyclopedia of
    Animals, The,* 254, 267
Kingfisher First Picture Atlas, The,
    254, 270
*Kingfisher Young People's
    Encyclopedia of the United
    States, The,* 254, 271
King of Dragons, The, 312, 315
King of the Playground, 279, 297
King's Chessboard, The, 12, 18
King's Commissioners, The, 335, 341
King-Smith, Dick, 30, 44, 49, 68, 178,
    194, 291, 297
Kinsey-Warnock, Natalie, 205, 218
Kip: His Story, 231
Kipling, Rudyard, 65
Kipnis, Lynn, 308–309, 317
Kita, B., 103
Kitchen, Bert, 126, 141, 249
Kitt, Tamara, 285, 286, 297
Klass, Sheila, 32–33, 44
Klein, Norma, 312, 317
Knight, Margy Burns, 214, 218–219,
    260, 269, 354, 355, 363
*Knock at a Star: A Child's
    Introduction to Poetry,* 154, 164
Knudson, R. R., 154, 164
Kohlberg, W., 102
Koller, Jackie French, 104, 115, 183, 194
Komaiko, L., 348
Konigsburg, E. L., 29, 44

Kool Ada, 32–33, 44
Korean Cinderella, The, 169, 193
Krahn, F., 298
Kraus, Robert, 82, 96, 140, 164
Krauss, Ruth, 126, 334, 342
Krénina, K., 165
Kristo, J. V., 79
Kroll, Virginia, 205, 219
Kropp, J. J., 60
Krudop, W. L., 43, 296
Krulik, N. E., 342
Krull, Kathleen, 353–354, 363
Krupp, E. C., 334, 342
Krupp, R. R., 342
Kuhl, P., 100
Kuklin, Susan, 309, 317, 353, 356,
    363, 364
Kulleseid, E. R., 100, 102, 103
Kunhardt, Edith, 250, 269
Kurusa, 12, 18
Kushner, Donn, 33, 44
Kuskin, Karla, 148, 149, 153, 155,
    157, 164, 165, 256, 269

Labbo, L., 88, 274
Lacapa, Kathleen & Michael, 317,
    354, 364
Lacey, L. E., 128
Lacome, J., 268
*Lacrosse: The National Game of the
    Iroquois,* 25, 44
Ladybird First Facts About Space,
    334, 340
Lakota Hoop Dancer, 355, 364
Lambert, D., 254, 270
Lamborn, F., 44
Laminack, Lester L., 205, 219
Land of Hope, 232, 242
Landrum, J., 306
Lang, C., 364
Langer, J., 74, 75, 77, 78, 79, 82, 85
Langer, J. A., 9
Langton, J., 180
Language Arts, 257
Largent, M., 77
Larrick, Nancy, 84, 145, 153, 155,
    156, 157, 158, 165
Lasky, Kathryn, 12, 18, 33, 44, 83,
    226, 228, 241, 252, 270, 335, 342
Last Safe House, The, 236, 240
*Latin American Tales: From the
    Pampas to the Pyramids of
    Mexico,* 282, 296

Latrobe, K. H., 235
Lattimore, D. N., 168, 194
Lauber, Patricia, 254, 257, 259, 262, 270
Laugh-eteria, 149, 163, 277, 296
Laughing Time: Collected Nonsense,
    285, 298
Lavender, 202, 218
Lavies, Bianca, 260, 270
Lear, Edward, 151, 155, 165
*Learning About Ancient Civilizations
    Through Art,* 273
Leavitt, J. Sohn, D., 264
Le Cain, Errol, 186
Lee, Dennis, 154
Lee, Dom, 19, 224, 364
Left Hand Bull, Jacqueline, 355, 364
Legend of Sleeping Bear, The, 126,
    141, 177, 196
Legend of the Bluebonnet, The, 336, 341
*Legend of the Lady Slipper: An
    Ojibwe Tale,* 356, 364
Legends in Music (recording), 285
Le Guin, Ursula, 182, 194
Lehman, B. A., 58
Lehr, S., 34, 35
Leighton, Maxine R., 215, 241
Lelooska, Chief, 355, 364–365
Lempke, Susan, 348
Lena, 319
L'Engle, Madeline, 18, 179, 180, 194,
    326, 342
Lenski, L., 197
Lenz, L., 145, 156
*Leonardo da Vinci: The Artist,
    Inventor, Scientist,* 250, 271
Leong, C. K., 282
Leon's Story, 6, 19
Lessac, F., 343
Lesser, Rika, 134, 140
Less Than Half, More Than Whole,
    317, 354, 364
Lester, Helen, 178, 194–195
Lester, Julius, 176, 177, 186, 195, 254,
    270, 276, 280, 282, 297
Let's Dance!, 356, 361
Let's Do a Poem!, 153
*Letters from a Slave Girl: The Story of
    Harriet Jacobs,* 231, 241, 339, 342
Letters from Rifka, 215, 240, 305, 316,
    352, 362
Let the Circle Be Unbroken, 234, 243
Letting Swift River Go, 321, 344
*Level Playing Field, A: Sports and
    Race,* 354, 363

Levine, Ellen, 236, 241
Levine, Gail C., 326, 342
Levinson, R., 270
Levitin, Sonia, 215, 241
Levstik, L., 258
Levy, Constance, 151, 165
Levy, Janice, 35, 44
Levy, M., 193
Lewis, C. S., 68, 81, 178, 195
Lewis, E. B., 166
Lewis, J. Patrick, 150, 151, 158, 165
Lewis Hayden and the War Against Slavery, 353, 366
Librarian Who Measured the Earth, The, 12, 18, 252, 270, 335, 342
Lickona, Thomas, 304
Liggett, T. C., 53
Light, 259
Light at Tern Rock, The, 73, 97
Light Princess, The, 178–179
Like Jake and me, 311, 317
Lima, C., 118
Lima, C. W., 53
Lima, J., 118
Lima, J. A., 53
Lincoln: A Photobiography, 252, 268
Lindgren, Astrid, 32, 44
Lindley, T., 141
Line in the Sand, A: The Alamo Diary of Lucinda Lawrence, 226, 239–240
Lines, 133
Lion, the Witch and the Wardrobe, The, 68, 195. *See also Chronicles of Narnia, The*
Lionni, Leo, 9–10, 18, 277
Lion's Whiskers, The: An Ethiopian Folktale, 171, 193
Lippert, Margaret H., 356, 365
Literature of Delight, The, 282
Little, Jean, 227, 241, 270, 303, 307, 308, 317
Little Bear, 61
Little Bill (series), 202
Little by Little: A Writer's Education, 270, 303, 317
Littlechild, George, 277, 297, 355, 364
Little Farm By the Sea, 114
Little Farm in the Ozarks, 230
Little Fish Lost, 102, 106, 109, 115
Little Heroes, 282, 297
Little House (series). *See* Wilder, Laura Ingalls
Little House in the Big Woods, 230, 244
Little House on Rocky Ridge, 230, 241

Little House on the Prairie, 244, 277, 299
(television show), 230
Little House Rocky Ridge Years (series), 230
Littlejohn, 342
Little Penguin's Tale, 8, 106, 115
Little Plum, 170, 197
Little Red Hen, The, 135, 139, 172, 174, 175, 176, 183
Little Red Riding Hood, 25–26, 58, 171, 173, 287
de Regniers & Gorey edition, 130
Hyman edition, 129, 140
Little Ships, The: The Heroic Rescue of Dunkirk in World War II, 278, 296
Little Tricker the Squirrel Meets Big Double the Bear, 27, 44
Little Weaver of Thai-Yen Village, The, 352, 366
Little Women, 67
Liu, L., 363
Living Books, 65
Livingston, Myra Cohn, 2, 148, 149, 150, 151, 153, 155, 159, 160, 161, 162, 177
Living Treasure: Savings Earth's Threatened Biodiversity, 253, 271
Livo, N. J., 185, 280, 282
Lobel, Anita, 9, 18–19
Lobel, Arnold, 61, 128, 154, 165, 166, 186, 195, 277
Locker, Thomas, 4, 121–122, 124, 138, 140, 261, 267
Loftus, D., 273
Lolo & Red-Legs, 353, 365
Lomas Garza, Carmen, 74, 96, 352, 355, 364
London, J., 261, 267
Long Way from Chicago, A: A Novel in Stories, 8, 19
Lon Po Po; A Red-riding Hood Story from China, 61, 130, 142
Look-Alikes Jr., 127, 141
Look Around: A Book About Shapes, 133, 139
Look at Physical Handicaps, A, 308, 316
Look What Happened to Frog: Storytelling in Education, 282
Lorbiecki, Marybeth, 234, 241
Lord, Betty Bao, 226, 241
Lost Star, 270
Lost Summer, 315
Lottery Rose, The, 205, 218, 310, 316

Louie, Ai-Ling, 169, 186, 195, 280, 297, 359
Louis, Daphne, 322, 326
Lovejoy, L., 267
Lowell, Susan, 75
Lowry, J., 365
Lowry, Lois, 183, 195, 233, 241, 339, 342
Luenn, Nancy, 6, 124, 140
Lukens, R., 4, 121, 149, 249, 251, 257
Lum, Kate, 131, 140
Lunch, 114
Lundin, A., 76
Lunge-Larsen, Lise, 356, 364
Lunn, Janet *(The Root Cellar)*, 182, 195, 326, 342
Lurie, Alison, 171, 195
Lutzeier, Elizabeth, 215, 241
Lyddie, 91, 92–94, 97, 231, 242
Lye, K., 270
Lyon, George Ella, 40–41, 44, 74, 96, 155, 159, 165
Lyons, Mary E., 231, 241, 339, 342, 353, 355, 363, 364

Maberly, Kate, 235
Macaulay, David, 257, 264, 270
MacBride, Roger Lea, 230, 241
MacDonald, George, 178, 195
MacDonald, Margaret Read, 282
Machines, 259, 269
Mackey, M., 58
MacLachlan, Patricia, 56, 68, 89, 96, 97, 208, 219, 307, 317
Macon, J. M., 83–84
Madaket Millie, 227, 244
Madison, A., 28, 31, 34
Maestro, Betty, 263, 270
Maestro, Giulio, 263, 270
Maestro Play, The, 273
Magic Bean Tree, The: A Legend from Argentina, 356, 366
Magic Flute, The, 136, 141
Magic School Bus, 65, 69
Magic School Bus, The: In the Time of the Dinosaurs, 255, 268
Magic School Bus at the Waterworks, The, 259, 268
Magic School Bus on the Ocean Floor, The, 255, 268
Magic Windows, 355, 364
Ma'ii and Cousin Horned Toad, 193, 336, 340
Make Like a Tree and Leave, 209, 217

Making Puppets Come Alive, 288
Maley, T., 163
Malloy, Philip, 201
Malmgren, D., 11
Malone, N. L., 297
Mama and Papa Have a Store, 353, 361
Mama Cat Has Three Kittens, 106, 114, 125, 139
Maniac Magee, 211, 221
Mann, Peggy, 311, 317
Manna, A., 84
Manna, A. L., 278
Manning, G., 58
Manning, M., 58
Mantell, P., 273
Many, J., 77
Many Lives of Benjamin Franklin, The, 339, 343
Many Moons, 279, 298
Many Troubles of Andy Russell, The, 214, 216
Marantz, 137
Marcellino, F., 192
Marchall, F., 366
Marcon, R., 100
Marcos, Subcomandante, 356, 364
Marcus, Leonard S., 138
Mars, 258, 271
Marschall, K., 267
Marsh, T. J., 106, 115
Martha Calling, 131, 140
Martha Graham, A Dancer's Life, 277, 297
Martin, Ann M., 202, 210, 217, 219
Martin, B., 273
Martin, Bill, Jr., 61, 281, 297, 342
Martin, J. B., 97
Martin, Jacqueline Briggs, 82, 127
Martin, Rafe, 169, 195, 336, 342, 359
Martinez, M., 77, 81, 110, 276, 278
Martinez, M. G., 289
Martin's Mice, 194
Martorell, A., 193
Marven of the Great North Woods, 33, 44, 83
Marvin, Isabel R., 226, 241
Marvin Redpost: Class President, 40, 45
Marzollo, Jean, 112, 115, 127, 133, 140, 142
Masoff, Joy, 253, 270
Mason, Anthony, 254, 270
Master Puppeteer, The, 91, 97
Math Curse, 9, 19

Mau, Christine, 280, 298
Max, 136, 140
Max's Breakfast, 101, 115
Max's Dragon Shirt, 106, 110, 115, 141
Max's First Word, 110, 115, 141
Mayer, Mercer, 65, 69, 109, 115
Maynard, B., 7, 19
Mazer, Norma Fox, 210, 219
McAuley, K., 256
McCaslin, N., 278, 285, 286, 287, 288
McClure, A., 54
McClure, A. A., 79
McCord, David, 149, 155, 157, 165
McCormick, C., 348, 349
McCracken, R. and M., 157
McCully, Emily Arnold, 96, 231, 241
McCutcheon, M., 235
McDermott, Gerald, 125, 140
McDonald, J., 219
McElhoe, Janice S., 205
McGovern, Ann, 155
McGuire, Paula, 309, 317
McKinley, Robin, 56, 68
McKissack, Patricia C., 179, 195
McKissack, Patricia C. & Frederick L., 236, 241
McLaughlin, Frank, 213, 219
McMahon, S., 85, 86
McMillan, Bruce, 61, 352, 364
McNaughton, Colin, 181
McPhail, David, 119, 140, 160
Me, Mop, and the Moondance Kid, 32, 44, 212, 219
Mead, Alice, 206, 219
Meade, Holly, 15, 60, 267
Me and My Name, 207, 219
Me and My Shadow, 341
Meanwhile–, 124, 127, 139
Meddaugh, Susan, 120, 131, 138, 140
Media Yearbook, 14
Medieval Feast, A, 61, 264, 266
Mee, C. L., Jr., 197
Meek, M., 4
Meinback, A., 328
Mel's Diner, 348
Meltzer, M., 248, 251
Merriam, Eve, 155, 159, 165
Merrill, Jean, 287, 297, 335, 339, 343
Merrily Comes Our Harvest In, 159
"Merry-Go-Round Song, The," 156
Mervar, K., 62
Me Too, 309, 315
Meyer, B., 11, 39

Miccinati, J., 285, 286
Mice Are Nice, 145, 155, 165
Michael Foreman's Mother Goose, 106, 114
Michelson, Richard, 352, 364
Micklethwait, Lucy, 133, 140, 273
Midnight Is a Place, 231, 238
Midwife's Apprentice, The, 235
Mieko and the Fifth Treasure, 233, 239
Miel, A., 349
Migdale, L., 44
Mikolaycak, C., 141
Miller, C. G., 97
Miller, D., 296
Miller, Jonathon, 258, 270
Miller, Mary Beth, 313, 315, 317
Miller, Mary Jane, 207, 219
Miller, S., 168
Miller, William, 250, 270
Miller-Lachmann, L., 53
Mill Girls, The: Lucy Larcon, Harriet Hanson Robinson, Sarah G. Bagley, 93, 97
Millman, Isaac, 307, 317
Milne, A. A., 136, 140, 179, 195, 276, 297
Milnes, Gerald, 175, 195
Milone, Karen, 147
Minarick, Else, 61
Mine for Keeps, 308, 317
Miner, J., 363
Mine's the Best, 61
Minnie and Moo Go Dancing, 277, 296
Minor, W., 196
Missing May, 208, 220
Mississippi Bridge, 234, 243
"Miss Mary Mack," 157, 164
Mistakes That Worked: 40 Familiar Inventions and How They Came to Be, 339, 342
Mist Over the Mountains: Appalachia and Its People, 253
Mitchel, J., 194
Mitchell, Barbara, 352, 364
Miyake, Yoshi, 86
Mochizuki, Ken, 12, 19, 224, 353, 354, 364
Mochizukuk, K., 242
Mockingbird, 113
Moe, J., 295
Moeri, Louise, 310, 317
Mole Music, 119, 140
Molly Whuppie, 172

Mom, the Wolf Man, and Me, 312, 317
Mommy, Buy Me a China Doll, 136, 142
Monkey Island, 211, 218
Monroe, C., 44
Monson, D., 58, 256
Monson, R. C., 10
Monster Book of ABC Sounds, The, 24, 45
Monster Garden, The, 36–37, 43, 183
Monster Soup and Other Spooky Poems, 49, 67
Monvel, Boutet de, 90
Moon and You, The, 334, 342
Moon Bear, 333, 340
Moon Bridge, The, 354, 366
Moonfleet, 81
Moon Jumpers, The, 136, 141
Moon Lake Angel, 311, 315
Moon of Two Dark Horses, 229, 240
Moon Over Tennessee: A Boy's Civil War Journal, 28
Moore, E., 297
Moore, Lillian, 161
Mop, Moondance, and the Nagasaki Knights, 212, 219
Mora, Pat, 351, 356, 364
More, More, More, Said the Baby: Three Love Stories, 106, 115
More Notes from a Different Drummer, 306
More Tales of Uncle Remus: Further Adventures of Brer Rabbit, His Friends, Enemies and Others, 195
Morgan, S., 270
Morin, P., 366
Morner, K., 24, 25, 31, 36, 37, 146, 148, 149, 150, 151
Morning Is a Little Child, 35
Moroney, L., 340
Morpurgo, Michael, 225, 233, 242, 339, 343
Morris, Juddi, 312
Morrison, Lillian, 156, 158, 165
Morrow, L., 60, 62, 81, 103, 106, 107, 110
Morrow, L. M., 276
Moser, Barry, 44, 344, 351, 364, 365
Moses Goes to a Concert, 307, 317
Moss, M., 348
Moss Pillows: Voyage to the Bunny Planet, 110, 115
Most Amazing Science Pop-Up Book, The, 255, 272

Mother Earth's Counting Book, 334, 341
Moulton, C., 235
Mountain Valor, 339, 342
Mouse, Clement C., 159
Mouse Count, 106, 115, 284
Mouse Paint, 133
Mr. and Mrs. Noah, 197
Mr. Grumpy's Outing, 287, 296
Mrs. Frisby and the Rats of NIMH, 277, 297
Mrs. Katz and Tush, 353, 365
Mud, 104, 115
Mud Pony, The: A Traditional Skidi Pawnee Tale, 336, 341
Mufaro's Beautiful Daughters, 133
Mullens, P., 268
Mullins, June, 306
Multiculturalism & the Arts, 356
Munowitz, Ken, 197
Munsch, Robert, 56, 68
Munsinger, L., 194–195, 343
Murphy, Jim, 226, 242
Music, Music for Everyone, 136, 142
Musical Instruments, 270, 273
Music of Dolphins, The, 32, 43, 305, 316
Music of What Happens, The: Poems That Tell Stories, 146, 155, 164
Muskrat Will Be Swimming, 365–366
Musthafa, B., 72, 84
Muth, J. J., 363
My Ballet Class, 136, 140
My Best Shoes, 348
My Brother Ant, 279
My Brother Sam Is Dead, 229, 239
My Brother Steven is Retarded, 309–310, 318–319
My Daddy Is a Cool Dude, 155
My Dad Lives in a Downtown Hotel, 311, 317
Myers, Christopher, 25, 44, 122, 125, 140
Myers, Walter Dean, 32, 44, 49, 68, 203, 207, 208, 209–210, 212, 219, 226, 236, 242, 261, 270, 311, 318, 352, 353, 364
My Five Senses, 259, 266
My Friend Jacob, 310, 315
My Friend Leslie, 308, 318
My Heart Is on the Ground: The Diary of Nannie Little Rose, a Sioux Girl, 226, 243
My Mane Catches the Wind: Poems About Horses, 162

My Name is America (series), 226
My Name is Georgia, 56, 69, 252, 271
My Name is Not Angelica, 225, 228–229, 242
My Nine Lives by Clio, 82, 97, 177
My Own Big Bed, 110, 114
My Picture Book of the Planets, 342
My Side of the Mountain, 211, 218
My Song Is Beautiful, 350
Mysteries of Harris Burdick, The, 191
My Two Feet, 247, 271

Nail Soup, 169
Namioka, Lensey, 204, 210, 219–220
Napoli, Donna Jo, 7, 19
Napping House, The, 3–4, 20, 122, 123, 133, 142, 281, 299, 333, 344
Narahashi, Keiko, 332, 343
Nash, G. B., 225
Nash, M. F., 77, 81
Nash, Ogden, 195
Natarella, M., 154
National Association for the Education of Young Children (NAEYC), 100, 101, 107
National Center for History in the Schools, 234
National Council of the Social Studies, 234
Native American Animal Stories, 356, 361
Natti, S., 216
Nature's Green Umbrella, 269
Nature's Tricksters: Animals and Plants That Aren't What They Seem, 267
Navajo: Visions and Voices Across the Mesa, 336, 340
Naylor, A., 84, 85, 276
Naylor, Phyllis Reynolds, 24, 44, 168, 195, 201, 210, 213, 220, 279, 297
Near the Window Tree, 153, 164
Nedeff, A. R., 75
Neuhaus, D., 318, 319
Neuman, S., 103
New Advocate, 257
New Dawn on Rocky Ridge, 230
New Kid on the Block, The, 97, 153, 161
Newsom, T., 243
New Year's Poems, 159
Nickle, J., 6, 19
Night/Day: A Book of Eye-Catching Opposites, 141
Night in the Country, 334, 343

Nightjohn, 231, 242
Night Journeys, 224, 238
Night Noises, 341
Night on Neighborhood Street, 350, 362
Nikola-Lisa, W., 350, 364
Nine O'Clock Lullaby, 334, 343
Nixon, Joan Lowry, 213, 220, 232, 242, 311, 318
Noah (Mee & Munowitz), 197
Noah and the Ark
  Baynes edition, 197
  dePaola edition, 197
Noah and the Ark and the Animals, 197
Noah and the Great Flood, 197
Noah and the Rainbow, 197
Noah's Ark
  Diamond edition, 197
  Fussennegger & Fuchshuber edition, 197
  Haley edition, 197
  Hogrogian edition, 197
  Ray edition, 197
Nobody's Dog, 131, 139
Nobody's Family Is Going to Change, 204, 218
Noddings, Nel, 304
Nodelman, P., 132
Nolan, D., 241
Nolen, Jerdine, 23–24, 44, 55, 73, 97, 195, 348, 364
No One Is Going to Nashville, 311, 317
No Place to Be: Voices of Homeless Children, 312, 314
No Pretty Pictures: A Child of War, 9, 18–19
Normandin, Christine, 355, 364–365
Norton, D., 26, 225
Norton, Mary, 50, 68
Norwegian Folk Tales, 295
Notes for Another Life, 309, 314
Notes from a Different Drummer, 306
Not for a Billion, Gazillion Dollars, 209, 217, 225, 239
Nothing But the Truth, 201
Not My Dog, 59, 68
Nowhere to Call Home, 59, 67
Now Is Your Time!, 270
Number the Stars, 233, 241, 339, 342
Numeroff, Laura, 102–103, 115, 131, 140

Obligado, Lillian, 161
O'Brien, A. S., 218–219, 269, 363
O'Brien, J., 342

O'Brien, Robert C., 277, 297
O'Callahan, Jay, 282, 297
Ocvirk, O., 118, 125, 132
Odean, K., 49
O'Dell, Scott, 65, 68, 225, 228–229, 230, 242, 277, 297
Of Pelicans and Pussycats: Poems and Limericks, 155
Oh, Freedom! Kids Talk About the Civil Rights Movement With the People Who Made It Happen, 236, 240–241
Oh, That's Ridiculous, 157
Ohanian, S., 53
Okie, Susan, 254, 256, 271
Ombligo de la Luna y Otros Poemas de Verano, Del, 163
Once on This River, 223, 229, 236, 244
Once Upon a Heroine, 49
On City Streets, 155
One at a Time, 155
One Day Two Dragons, 61
One-Eyed Jake, 338, 342
100 Inventions That Shaped World History, 338, 344
O'Neil, J. M., 108
O'Neill, Charlotte, 311, 318
Only One, 335, 342
On My Honor, 56, 67
On the Far Side of the Mountain, 211, 218
On the Frontier with Mr. Audubon, 251, 267
On the Long Trail Home, 230
Oodgeroo, 177, 195
Oops!, 181
Opie, I. & P., 175
Oppenheimer, Joan L., 205, 220
Orchard Book of Nursery Rhymes, The, 155
Originals, The: Animals That Time Forgot, 24, 45
Ornithology, 259
Orphan for Nebraska, An, 311, 319
Orphan Train (series), 58
Ortiz, Simon J., 354, 365
Osage, The, 244
Osband, G., 261, 270
Osborne, Linda Barrett, 236, 240–241
Osborne, Mary P., 339, 343
Osiecki, Lori, 18, 125, 140
Other Bells for Us to Ring, 215, 227, 239
Other Side, The: Shorter Poems, 150, 164

Other Way to Listen, The, 122, 138, 150, 154, 155, 163
Otiz, F., 361
Oubrerie, C., 141
Ouch! A Tale from Grimm, 171, 192
Our Family Our Friends Our World, 53
Outer Banks Mysteries & Seaside Stories, 177
Out of Control, 210, 219
Out of Nowhere, 221
Out of the Dust, 29, 43–44, 49, 67, 305, 316
Outward Dreams: Black Inventors and Their Inventions, 338, 342
Overheard in a Bubble Chamber and Other Science Poems, 156, 165
Owen, 118–119, 139
Owl Eyes, 86
Oxenberry, Helen, 298

Pablo's Tree, 351, 364
Padak, N., 350
Paddington (series), 136, 138
Paek, Min, 354, 365
Pahl, M., 10
Paint and Painting, 270, 273
Painters of the Caves, 262, 270
Palladini, D., 197
Pancake, The, 285
Panzer, Nora, 321, 343
Paper Bag Princess, The, 56, 68
Paper Crane, The, 137, 138
Pappas, C. C., 258
Parish, Peggy, 277
Park, Ruth, 326, 343
Parker, L., 317
Parker, R. A., 196, 296, 316
Parker, Steve, 61, 260, 270–271
Parks, Rosa, 339, 343
Park's Quest, 233, 242
Parnall, Peter, 122, 133, 138, 150, 159, 163, 165
Parsons, L., 156, 159
Passage to Freedom: The Sugihara Story, 12, 19, 224, 242, 353, 364
Pass the Poetry, Please!, 153
Pate, R., 219
Paterson, Katherine, 4, 5, 10, 19, 31, 35–36, 44, 68, 81, 90, 97, 125, 140, 203, 210, 220, 223, 231, 233, 242, 328
Patrick DesJarlait: Conversations with a Native American Artist, 349, 362
Paul, Anthony, 178, 195

Paul, K., 193
Paul Bunyan, 132, 140
Paulsen, Gary, 28–29, 44, 49, 56, 65, 68, 69, 208, 211–212, 213, 220, 231, 242, 339, 343, 348
Paye, Won-Ldy, 356, 365
Peabody, 136, 141
Peanut Butter and Jelly: A Play Rhyme, 155, 285, 286, 299
Pearce, Philippa, 33, 45, 181, 182, 195, 326, 343
Pearson, P. D., 26
Peck, B., 217, 238
Peck, P., 152, 154, 302, 303
Peck, Richard, 8, 19
Pedro's Journal, 228, 239
Pelham, David, 258, 270
"Pelican Chorus," 151
Pennington, D., 348
People Could Fly, The: American Black Folktales, 186, 194, 356, 362
People Shall Continue, The, 354, 365
People Who Make a Difference, 251, 267
Perez-Stable, M. A., 235
Perfect, K. A., 276
Perkins, D., 119
Perrault, Charles, 169, 170, 186, 191, 195, 298
Perrine, L., 146, 160
Person, D., 62
Pertzoff, A., 97
Peter and the Wolf, 136, 141, 273
Peterson, B., 321
Peterson, L. K., 52
Peter Spier's Rain, 141
Pete's a Pizza, 77, 78, 97
Pfeffer, Susan Beth, 213, 220
Pfeffer, W., 343
Philbrick, Rodman, 214, 220
Piaget, J., 60, 102, 104
"Pickety Fence, The," 157
Picture This: A First Introduction to Paintings, 20
Piece of String is a Wonderful Thing, A, 259, 269
Pieronek, F. T., 59
Piggies, 106, 115
Pigs, 125, 139
Pilger, M. A., 271
Pilger, Mary Ann, 254
Pilgrims of Plimoth, The, 125, 141
Pilkey, Dav, 189, 195
Pinballs, The, 310, 314

Pink and Say, 353, 365
Pinkerton: America's First Private Eye, 339, 344
Pinkney, A. D., 365
Pinkney, B., 297
Pinkney, Brian, 356, 365, 366
Pinkney, Gloria J., 352, 365
Pinkney, Jerry, 97, 186, 192, 195, 196, 243
Pinsent, P., 56
Piping Down the Valleys Wild, 155
Pippi Longstocking, 32, 44
Pirates: Robbers of the High Seas, 338, 341–342
Pitcher, E., 170
"Pitcher, The," 146–147
Pittman, Helena Clare, 335, 343
Pizza Puzzle, The, 213, 220
Place My Words Are Looking For, The: What Poets Say About and Through Their Work, 153, 164
Planets in Our Solar System, The, 259, 267
Planning the Impossible, 209, 218
Planting a Rainbow, 9, 18, 61, 255
Play, Learn & Grow, 53
Playing Beatie Bow, 326, 327, 343
Plotkin, Mark J., 122, 125, 139, 277, 296
Poem-Making: Ways to Begin Writing Poetry, 153, 165
Poems for Jewish Holidays, 155, 165
"Poem to Mud," 147, 166
Polacco, Patricia, 353, 365
Polar Express, The, 51, 69, 125, 141, 191
Politi, L., 348
Polkabats and Octopus Slacks: 14 Stories, 151, 163
Pollock, Penny, 169, 195, 359
Poole, Amy Lowry, 356, 365
"Poor Old Lady Who Swallowed a Fly, The," 157, 158, 160
Popp, K. W., 241
Porter, J. L., 314
Portraits of Women Artists for Children: Mary Cassatt, 273
Portraying Persons with Disabilities: An Annotated Bibliography of Fiction for Children and Teenagers, 306
Portraying Persons with Disabilities: An Annotated Bibliography of Nonfiction for Children and Teenagers, 306

Potential of Picturebooks, The, 132
Potluck, 348
Potter, Beatrix, 50, 68, 121, 138, 141
Powell, Randy, 212, 220
Prairies and Grasslands, 243
Prairie Visions: The Life and Times of Solomon Butcher, 264, 268
Pratt, D., 75, 84
Prelinger, E., 170
Prelutsky, Jack, 7, 19, 36, 45, 75, 97, 146, 151, 152–153, 154, 155, 161, 162, 165, 166, 277, 279, 298
Pressley, M., 107
Preus, Margi, 356, 364
Price, C., 343
Priceman, Marjorie, 82, 97
Primavera, Elise, 44, 55, 97, 195, 364
Princess and the Pea, The, 176, 279, 295
Pringle, Laurence, 253, 259, 271
Probst, R., 74, 75
Professor Noah's Spaceship, 197
Prokofiev, Sergei, 136, 141, 273
Provensen, Alice and Martin, 166, 250, 271
P.S. Longer Letter Later, 210, 217
Puppeteers of America, 288
Purcell-Gates, V., 102, 107, 276
Purple Mountain Majesties, 127, 142
Pursell, Margaret S., 308, 316
Purves, A., 58, 59, 256
Pushcart War, The, 287, 297

Quest for a King: Searching for the Real King Arthur, 264, 266
Quiet, 159, 165

Rabe, Bernice, 308, 318
Rachlin, A., 273
Rachlin, J., 50
Raczek, Linda Theresa, 124, 141, 292, 293, 298
Radiance Descending, 310, 316
Raffi, 65, 334, 343
Raffi Songs to Read, 334, 343
Rain, 127
Rainbow at Night, A, 355, 363
Rainbow-Colored Horse, The, 187
Rainbow Crow: A Lenape Tale, 336
Rainbows are Made: Poems, 161
Rain Talk, 161
Rainy's Powwow, 124, 141, 292–294, 298
Raisel's Riddle, 356, 366

Raising Dragons, 23–24, 44, 55, 73, 97, 111, 188, 195, 348, 364
Raising Sweetness, 279, 298
Raising Yoder's Barn, 353, 367
Ramage, S., 11
Ramona and Her Father, 204, 217
Ramona's World, 202, 217
Ramsey, P., 349, 350
Rand, Gloria, 131, 141
Rand, William B., 157, 285, 298
Random House Book of Poetry for Children The, 154, 165, 166
Rankin, Laura, 307, 313, 318
Raphael, T., 85, 86
Rappaport, Doreen, 234, 242
Rapunzel, 134, 171, 197
Rasinski, T., 350
Rattigan, J. K., 348
Rausch, R., 24, 25, 31, 36, 37, 146, 148, 149, 150, 151
Ray, D., 166, 317
Ray, D. K., 239
Ray, J., 197
Ray, Mary Lyn, 104, 115
RCA Victor, 285
Read-Aloud Handbook, 49
Reading Rainbow Guide to Children's Books, 53
Reading Teacher, 260
Real Christmas This Year, A, 310, 319
Real McCoy, The: The Life of an African-American Inventor, 261, 271
Rebounder, The, 213, 217
Recycle! A Handbook for Kids, 341
Red-Eyed Tree Frog, The, 249, 253–254, 268, 277, 296
Red Feather (series), 202
Red Leaf, Yellow Leaf, 133
Red Racer, The, 39, 45, 122, 124, 126
Red Riding Hood, 139. *See also Little Red Riding Hood*
Redwall (series), 58
Reed, A., 225
Reeder, Carolyn, 29, 31, 45, 59, 68, 343
Reese, D., 350
Reeve, Kirk, 353, 365
Regalo para Abuelita, Un: En Celebración del Dia de los Muertos, 6
Regular Rolling Noah, A, 159, 165
Reimer, K., 347
Reisberg, V., 196, 340
Relatives Came, The, 279, 298, 352, 365

Renfro, Nancy, 288
Return to Bitter Creek, 205, 221
Rhythm Road: Poems to Move To, 158, 165
Rice, G., 11, 39
Richard "Pancho" Gonzales: Tennis Champion, 354, 362
Richards, Laura, 151, 157, 166, 285, 298
Riches, J., 343
Riddle-Lightful: Oodles of little Riddle-Poems, 158, 165
Riddle of the Rosetta Stone, The, 92, 96
Ride, Sally, 254, 256, 271
Rietz, S. A., 185, 280, 282
Riggio, A., 362
Riley, Terry, 282, 296
Rinaldi, Ann, 226, 228, 229, 242–243
"Ring Around the Rosie," 149
Ringgold, Faith, 124–125, 141, 252, 271, 355, 358, 365
Riordan, James, 356, 365
River, The, 220
River Ran Wild, A: An Environmental History, 259, 261, 267
Robertson, Debra, 306
Robinet, Harriette Gillem, 354, 365
Robin Hood, 176, 177
Robinson, C., 243, 316, 318
Robinson Crusoe, 50, 67
Rochman, Hazel, 289, 348
Rocket in My Pocket, A: The Rhymes and Chants of Young Americans, 158, 166
Rock River, 7, 19
Rodowsky, Colby, 59, 68
Roe, B., 282
Rogers, J., 67
Rohmer, H., 196, 348
Rolling Harvey Down the Hill, 153, 155, 161, 279, 298
Roll of Thunder, Hear My Cry, 234, 243, 276, 298
Romeo and Juliet, 152
Roney, R. C., 281
Rooster Crows, 333, 343
Root, B., 139
Root, K. B., 96
Root Cellar, The, 182, 195, 326, 342
Rosa Parks: My Story, 339, 343
Rosen, B., 80
Rosen, Michael J., 131, 141, 276, 298
Rosenberg, Maxine, 308, 312, 318
Rosenberry, Vera, 40–41, 44

Rosenblat, Barbara, 235
Rosenblatt, L. M., 5, 77, 320
Roser, N., 88, 110, 278
Rosh, M., 273
Ross, R. R., 276, 285
Ross, Tony, 186, 217
Roth, Arthur, 227, 243
Roth, S., 19
Rothlein, L., 328
Rothman, R., 171
Roucher, N., 365
Rough-Face Girl, The, 169, 195, 336, 342, 359
Round and Round Again, 334, 335, 343–344
Rounds, Glen, 197, 254, 285, 298
Routman, R., 38
Rowan, J. P., 243
Rowling, J. K., 58, 68, 196
Roy, Ron, 309, 318
Ruby, Lois, 210, 220
Rudeen, Kenneth, 353, 365
Rudman, M. K., 304, 306
Rumelhart, D. E., 38
Rumplestiltskin, 134
Runner, The, 213, 221
Runner's Song, 213, 219
Runs With Horses, 230, 238
Rupp, Rebecca, 189, 196
Russell, D. L., 146, 202, 225, 251, 252
Ruth, George Herman, Jr., 125
Ryan White, My Own Story, 309, 319
Ryder, Joanne, 334, 343
Rylant, Cynthia, 61, 147, 155, 156, 166, 208, 220, 279, 298, 334, 343, 351, 352, 365
Rymill, Linda R., 104, 115

Sachar, Louis, 30, 40, 45, 83, 92, 97
Sachs, M., 220
Sage, M., 304
Salisbury, Graham, 233, 243
Salmon Summer, 352, 364
Salva, S., 360
Sam and the Lucky Money, 351, 361
Sammy Keyes and the Skeleton Man, 59, 69
Sanborn, L., 10, 50, 53
Sánchez, E. O., 361, 363
Sandburg, Carl, 150, 161
Sanderson, E., 348
Sanderson, R., 315
Sandin, J., 242, 295, 317
Sanford, J., 364

San Souci, Robert D., 45, 97, 169, 196, 279, 298, 359

Santiago, Chiori, 353, 365

Sarah, Plain and Tall, 56, 68

"Sarah Cynthia Sylvia Stour Would Not Take the Garbage Out," 151

Sarny: A Life Remembered, 231, 242

Sauer, Julia L., 45, 97, 182, 196

Saul, W., 267

Savageau, C., 365–366

Saver, Julia, 25

Savin, Margaret, 354, 366

Saving the Peregrine Falcon, 265, 266

Savitz, Harriet M., 308, 318

Sawyer, Ruth, 280

Saxby, M., 35, 36, 170, 171, 177

Say, Allen, 45, 252, 271

Say It!, 146, 166

Scala, M., 144

Scamell, Ragnhild, 333, 343

Scarry, Richard, 65, 69

Schertle, Alice, 148, 166, 247, 271, 279, 298

Schindelman, J., 193

Schindler, S. D., 194

Schlager, N., 60

Schlein, Miriam, 228, 243

Schmitt, Barbara, 88

School Mouse, The, 30, 44

Schroder, V., 144

Schroeder, A., 366

Schuett, S., 142

Schulz, L., 11

Schwarcz, C., 122

Schwarcz, J. H., 122

Schwartz, A., 171

Schwartz, D., 43

Science Experiments Index for Young People, 254, 271

Science Teacher, 259

Scieszka, Jon, 9, 13, 19, 175, 196

Scorpions, 49, 68, 203, 216, 219

Scott, J. A., 10

Scott, S., 164

Scott-Mitchell, C., 121

Seabrooke, Brenda, 189, 196

Sea Otter, 94, 97

Search for the Delicious, The, 335, 340

Search for the Shadowman, 213, 220

Season Songs, 161

Sebesta, S., 26, 34, 36, 37, 59, 79, 80, 154

Sebestyen, Ouida, 211, 221

Secret Garden, The, 28, 43, 50, 67

Secret Knowledge of Grown-Ups, The, 6, 20, 127, 142, 277, 299

Secret of Sarah Revere, The, 229, 243

Secrets of a Wildlife Watcher, 67

Sector 7, 127, 142

Seeger, Pete, 282, 287, 298

Seeing Things My Way, 307, 315

Sees Behind Trees, 239

Seixas, Judith S., 309, 318

Selden, G., 196

Seldon, Bernice, 93, 97

Selsam, Millicent E., 257

Sendak, Maurice, 14, 19, 27–28, 45, 50, 68, 90, 115, 121, 126, 141, 178

Sensenbaugh, R., 10

Serfozo, Mary, 133, 161

Service, Pamela F., 92, 97, 196

Settel, Joanne, 254, 271

Seuss, Dr., 7, 19, 36, 45, 61, 279, 298

Seven Brave Women, 56, 67, 251, 269

Sewall, Marcia, 125, 141, 244, 297, 354, 366

Shades of Gray, 31, 45, 339, 343

Shadows of Night: The Hidden World of the Little Brown Bat, 259, 263, 267

Shafer, P. J., 51

Shaik, F., 146, 166

Shaman's Apprentice, The, 122, 125, 139, 277, 296

Shanahan, P., 346, 348

Shanahan, T., 12, 258

Shannon, D., 195, 244, 342, 344

Shannon, Margaret, 168, 189, 196

Shape of Things, The, 268

Shapes, Shapes, Shapes, 133

Shapiro, William E., 254, 271

Sharp, Susan, 203

Shelby, S., 348

Shelter Folks, 205, 219

Shepard, E. H., 140, 195, 297

Sherrill, A., 58

Shiloh, 24, 44, 168, 195

Shlain, L., 178

Shoes, 247, 271–272

Shoes from Grandpa, 247, 268

Short, K., 11

Short, 72

Shulevitz, Uri, 82, 97, 121, 123–124, 141

Shulman, Jeffrey, 311, 318

Shy Charles, 110, 115, 141

Shyer, M. F., 318

Shyer, Marlene Fanta, 309

"Sick," 147

Siebert, Diane, 159, 166, 285, 298

Siegelson, Kim L., 356, 366

Sign of the Beaver, The, 68

Siks, G., 286

Silver Days, 215, 241

Silverman, Erica, 356, 366

Silver Rain Brown, 351, 362

Silverstein, Shel, 147, 151, 154, 161, 166, 277

Silvey, A., 30, 153

Simmons, Jane, 109, 115

Simon, C., 141

Simon, Seymour, 254, 258, 259, 271

Simont, Marc, 126, 140, 241, 298, 342

Simple Simon, 176

Simple Simon Says: Take One Magnifying Glass, 249, 267

Sims, B., 316

Singer, I. B., 197

Singer, Marilyn, 131, 141, 162, 334, 343

Sing Hey for Christmas, 159

Sister Anne's Hands, 234, 241

Six Swans, The, 178

Skurzynski, Gloria, 232, 243

Sky Dogs, 336, 344

Sky Songs, 161

Slack, C., 218

Slake's Limbo, 49, 68

Slaughter, J. P., 111

Slave Dancer, The, 276, 297

Slepian, Jan, 308, 318

Slote, Alfred, 213, 221

Small Poems, 149, 155, 156, 166

Small Poems Again, 166

Smart Dog, 180

Smidt, Inez, 233, 244

Smith, Doris Buchanan, 205, 221, 309, 318

Smith, F., 5, 53, 104, 179, 180

Smith, J. A., 67, 218

Smith, J. W., 195

Smith, K., 163

Smith, L. H., 118

Smith, Lane, 7, 19, 36, 45, 196

Smith, M., 102, 103

Smith, Roland, 94, 97

Smith, S., 282

Smith, William Jay, 157, 159, 162, 166, 285, 298

Smoky Night, 354, 361

Smolkin, L., 103

Snail Girl Brings Water: A Navajo Story, 171, 356, 363

Snapshots from the Wedding, 366
Snow, 82, 97, 123–124, 141
Snow, A., 24, 45
Snowballs, 128
Snowflake Bentley, 82, 97, 127
Snowman, The, 61, 133, 138
Snow White and the Seven Dwarfs, 56, 67, 175
Snyder, Diane, 37, 45
Snyder, Zilpha Keatley, 147, 166
Soap! Soap! Don't Forget the Soap! An Appalachian Folktale, 193
Soap Soup and Other Verses, 165
Sobol, Harriet L., 309–310, 318–319
Social Education, 260
Solbert, R., 297
"So Long as There's Weather," 285, 286
Solt, M. L., 52
Something Big Has Been Here, 151, 153, 155, 166
Something Special for Me, 136, 142
Somewhere in the Darkness, 207, 219
"Song of the Train," 149, 165
Song of the Trees, 234, 243
Sorrow's Kitchen: The Life and Folklore of Zora Neale Hurston, 353, 364
Soto, Gary, 282, 298, 354, 366
Souci, Sam, 76
Souhami, J., 195
Sounds All Around, 343
Spaceman, 306, 315
Spanfeller, J., 296
Spangler, S., 186
SPEAK!: Children's Illustrators Brag About Their Dogs, 131, 141
Speare, Elizabeth George, 68, 228
Spencer's Adventures (series), 214
Spender, Stephen, 136, 141
Spengler, K. J., 115
Spider Boy, 209, 216, 218
Spier, Peter, 127, 141
Spinelli, Eileen, 34, 45
Spinelli, Jerry, 209, 211, 221
Spirit of the Cedar People: More Stories and Painting of Chief Lelooska, 355, 365
Splash!, 291, 297
Splish Splash, 164
Sports Pages, 155
Sports! Sports! Sports!: A Poetry Collection, 6, 18
"Stagolee," 177
Stanchfield, J., 62
Stanley, Diane, 279, 298

Stanley, Jerry, 250, 271, 354, 366
Star, Little Star, 334, 341
Star Wars (movie series), 168, 178, 339
Staub, Leslie, 323
Stay Away from Simon!, 305, 315
Steadfast Tin Soldier, The, 178, 192
Steal Away, 231, 236, 238
Steele, M., 202
Steig, Jeane, 196
Steig, William, 77, 97, 182, 196
Stein, N. L., 38
Steiner, Joan, 127, 141
Stella and Roy Go Camping, 344
Stellaluna, 122, 138–139, 263, 267
Stepping on the Cracks, 233, 240
Steptoe, Javaka, 133, 351, 366
Sterlin, Jenny, 235
Sterman, Betsy & Samuel, 189, 196
Stevens, Janet, 186, 196, 279, 298
Stevens, Jan Romero, 280, 298, 322, 343
Stevens, K., 196
Stevenson, J., 166
Stevenson, Robert Louis, 343
Stevenson, Susie, 285
Stewart, Elizabeth J., 230
Stewig, J., 26, 31, 59, 127, 137, 253
Still as a Star: A Book of Nighttime Poems, 147
Stine, R. L., 57, 202, 221
Stinker from Space, 92, 97
Stinky Cheese Man and Other Fairly Stupid Tales, The, 13, 19
Stinson, O., 118
Stock, C., 348
Stodart, E., 255, 258
Stoddard, Sandol, 335, 343
Stone, K. G., 163
Stone Fox, 275, 297
Stone Soup, 127, 169, 184
Stonewords, 326, 327, 341
Stoodt, Barbara D., 86, 118, 248, 262, 288, 349, 357
Stoodt-Hill, B., 50, 58, 305
Stop, Look, and Write, 264
Stopping By the Woods on a Snowy Evening, 155
Stories and Songs for Little Children, 282, 298
Stories I Ain't Told Nobody Yet, 146, 163
Stories to Begin On, 148–149, 163
Story of Colors, The, 356, 364

Story of Ourselves, The: Teaching History Through Children's Literature, 235
Story Painter: The Life of Jacob Lawrence, 252, 268, 355, 362
Storyteller's Sourcebook, The: A Subject, Title and Motif Index to Folklore Collections for Children, 282
Storytelling with Puppets, 288
Storytelling World, 283
Stow, J., 365
Stranded at Plimoth Plantation, 228, 238, 256, 267
Stranger at the Window, 30, 43
Strangis, Joel, 353, 366
Straub, L., 341
Strecker, S., 278
Streets Are Free, The, 12, 18
"Streets of Laredo, The," 177
Strickland, D., 100, 102, 103, 106, 107, 276
Strider, 216, 217
Striking Out, 212, 221
Stringer, L., 115
Stroud, B., 366
Stroud, Betty, 352
Stuart, D., 271
Suba, S., 166
Subject Guide to Children's Books in Print, 53
Sugihara, Hiroki, 224
Sukiennik, Adelaide, 306
Sulzby, E., 100, 102, 104, 107
"Summer Sun," 147
Sunday Outing, The, 352, 365
Sunken Treasure, 257, 269
Sunsets of Miss Olivia Wiggins, The, 205, 219
Sutcliff, Rosemary, 224, 225
Sutherland, Zena, 155, 177, 251
Sutton, Roger, 257
Sutton, W. K., 53
Swamp Angel, 140, 194
  film, 177
Swann, Brian, 158, 166
Swanton, S., 58, 62, 179
Sweet Creek Holler, 33–34, 45, 354, 366
Sweetest Fig, The, 131, 141, 191
Sweetgrass, 227, 240
Sweet Whispers, Brother Rush, 310, 316
Swenson, May, 154, 164
Swiftly Tilting Plant, A, 326, 342
Swimming Lessons, 7, 18, 125, 140

Swimmy, 9–10, 18
Swine Divine, 277, 296
Szilagyi, M., 343

Tagholm, Sally, 126, 141
Tailybone, 282, 297
Talbot, Charlene, 311, 319
Tale of Peter Rabbit, The, 50, 68,
    121, 141
Tale of the Mandarin Ducks, 91, 97,
    125, 140
Tale of Willie Monroe, The, 366
*Tales of Uncle Remus: The Adventures
    of Brer Rabbit,* 186, 282, 297
Tales of Wonder and Magic, 356, 362
Talking Eggs, The, 76, 97
Talking to Faith Ringgold, 355,
    358, 365
Talking Walls, 260, 269, 355, 363
*Talking Walls: The Stories
    Continue,* 355
Talking with Artists, 138
*Talking with Tebe: Clementine Hunter,
    Memory Artist,* 355, 363
Tar Beach, 124, 141, 252, 271, 355, 365
Taste of Blackberries, A, 309, 318
Taste the Raindrops, 114
Tattercoats
    Greaves edition, 280, 297
    Jacobs & Tomes edition, 169, 194
Taxel, J., 204
Taylor, D., 235
Taylor, Mildred D., 97, 234, 243, 276,
    298, 354, 366
Teaching Kids to Care, 304
*Teaching Through Stories: Yours,
    Mine, and Theirs,* 282
Teale, W., 100, 107
Teale, W. H., 276, 289
Teammates, 352, 362
*Teammates: Michael Jordan, Scottie
    Pippen,* 352, 362
Team Picture, 213, 218, 316
Tedrow, T. L., 230, 243
Temple, Frances, 201, 212, 214, 221
*Tending the Fire: The Story of Maria
    Martinez,* 312
Ten Suns: A Chinese Legend, 356, 363
Terry, A., 154
Thacker, D., 78
Thanksgiving Poems, 159
Thanksgiving Visitor, The, 208, 217
*That Sweet Diamond: Baseball
    Poems,* 146, 164

There's a Little Bit of Me in Jamey,
    308, 314
There's Something in My Attic, 109, 115
Thinking About Colors, 273
Think of an Eel, 255, 256, 271
Third Grade Pet, 37, 43
Thirteen Going on Seven, 204, 220
Thirteen Moons on Turtle's Back,
    261, 267
This Land Is My Land, 277, 297,
    355, 364
This Land Is Your Land, 287, 297
This Old Man, 210, 220
"Thistles," 149
Thomas, J. L., 53, 122
Thomas, Joyce C., 353, 366
Thomas Jefferson, 251, 269
Thompson, K., 273
Thompson, S., 170, 175
Three Aesop Fox Fables, 186, 193–194
Three Billy Goats Gruff, The, 174, 176
    Asbjornsen & Brown edition,
        186, 192
    Galdone edition, 185, 186, 194
Three Cheers for Tacky, 178, 194–195
Three Javelinas, The, 75
Three Little Pigs, The, 135, 139, 174,
    282–283, 296
Three Names, 89, 90, 97
Three Stalks of Corn, 348
Three Wishes, The, 187
Three Young Pilgrims, 228, 240
Through Grandpa's Eyes, 307, 317
*Throw Your Tooth On the Roof: Tooth
    Traditions from Around the
    World,* 356, 361
Thumbelina, 192
Thunder from the Clear Sky, 354, 366
Thunder Rolling in the Mountains,
    230, 242
Thurber, James, 279, 298
Tiegreen, A., 217, 318
Tierney, R., 26
Tiger Who Lost His Stripes, 178, 195
Tillage, Leon Walter, 6, 19
Tilley, D., 165
Time for Bed, 334, 341
Time for Poetry
    Arbuthnot edition, 148, 163, 298
    Kuskin edition, 157
Titanic Crossing, 234, 244
To Be a Slave, 254, 270, 276, 297
Tobin, N., 266
Today is Saturday, 166

Together, 40–41, 44, 155
Tolkien, J. R. R., 69
Tomes, M., 96, 194, 269
Tomie dePaola's Book of Poems,
    155, 163
Tompkins, G. E., 127
Tom's Midnight Garden, 33, 45, 181,
    182, 195, 326, 343
Tom Thumb, 168
Tonight, by Sea, 201, 212, 214, 221
Toothpaste Millionaire, The, 335,
    339, 343
Top Cat, 125, 139
Tortilla Factory, The, 348
To Space & Back, 254, 256, 271
Totally Uncool, 35, 44
Toth, M., 87
*Touching the Distance: Native
    American Riddle-Poems,* 158, 166
Tough Boris, 338, 341
Toughboy and Sister, 211, 218
Towle, W., 261, 271
Townsend, J. R., 120, 121, 178
Tracker, 211–212, 220
Train, The, 159, 166
Train Song, 159, 166, 285, 298
Tran, Khanh Tuyet, 352, 366
Trapped in Tar, 265, 266
Trashy Town, 101, 116
Traveler in Time, A, 326, 343
"Traveler's Tale, A," 148
Treasure Hunt, 291, 296
Tree Trunk Traffic, 260, 270
Treiman, R., 107
Trelease, J., 49
Trial Valley, 279, 296
Trottier, Maxine, 352, 366
Trouble at the Mines, 234, 242
Trout Summer, 207, 217
Truck Song, 159, 166, 285, 298
Truesdell, S., 296
True Story of the 3 Little Pigs, The, 13,
    19, 175, 196
Truth About Castles, The, 264, 268
Truth About Santa Claus, The, 92, 96
Tseng, J. & M., 298
Tucker, Kathy, 338, 343
Tuck Everlasting, 61, 181–182, 192
Tullet, H., 141
Tune Beyond Us, A, 153
Tunnell, M., 234
Tunnell, Michael O., 9, 19, 277, 298
*Turkey Girl, The: A Zuni Cinderella
    Story,* 169, 195, 359

"Turkey Shot Out of the Oven, The," 151
Turkle, Brinton, 61
Turner, Ann, 215, 243
Turner, R., 273
Turtle Day, 334, 341
Turtle in July, 162
Turtle Time, 335, 343
Twain, Mark, 50, 69
Twelve Lizards Leaping, 280, 298
26 Fairmount Avenue, 251, 268
Twister, 259, 267
Two Pairs of Shoes, 348
Two Tickets to Freedom, 231, 239
Tyrannosaurus was a Beast: Dinosaur Poems, 152, 155, 162, 166

Uchida, Yoshika, 232, 243–244
Udry, Janice May, 136, 141
Ugly Duckling, The, 178, 192
"Umbrella Brigade, The," 157, 285, 298
Unbreakable Code, The, 353, 363
Uncle Nacho's Hat, 196, 348
Uncle Smoke Stories, 277
Understanding American History Through Children's Literature, 235
Under the Blood-Red Sun, 233, 243
Under the Moon, 334, 343
Under the Royal Palms: A Childhood in Cuba, 352, 361
Under the Sunday Tree, 154, 164
Untold Tales, 179, 193
Up in the Air, 155, 160
Urehara, C., 239
Using Literature to Teach Middle Grades About War, 235
Uttley, Alison, 326, 343

Valentine Poems, 159
Valley of the Shadow, The, 229, 240
Vampires Don't Wear Polka Dots, 214, 217
Van Allsburg, Chris, 28, 45, 51, 69, 125, 131, 141, 182, 191, 196
Vande Velde, Vivian, 8, 19, 180
Van Draanen, Wendelin, 59, 69
Van Frankenhuyzen, 126, 141
Van Gogh, 273
Van Laan, Nancy, 102, 106, 109, 115, 334, 336, 343, 356, 366
Van Raven, Pieter, 232, 244
Van Vliet, L., 22, 26
Van Wright, C., 270, 361

Veltze, L., 235
Velveteen Rabbit, The, 136, 142
Venti, Anthony Bacon, 227
Vertebrate Zoology, 259
Very Hungry Caterpillar, The, 101, 112, 113
    video, 65, 69
Vidal, Beatriz, 192, 356, 366
View from Saturday, The, 29, 44
Vigil, Angel, 277, 298
Viguers, R. H., 6
Village by the Sea, The, 29, 43
Viorst, Judith, 7, 9, 19, 78, 97, 161, 166, 295, 298
Visit from St. Nicholas and Santa Mouse, Too, A!, 159
Visit to William Blake's Inn, A: Poems for Innocent and Experienced Travelers, 155, 166
Vivas, J., 142
Vogt, M. E., 83–84
Voigt, Cynthia, 93, 97–98, 213, 221, 309, 310, 319
Volcano: The Eruption and Healing of Mount St. Helens, 257, 270
Vos, Ida, 233, 244
Voss, M., 102
Voyage on the Great Titanic: The Diary of Margaret Ann Brady, 226, 244
Vygotsky, L., 11, 84, 101

Wadham, T., 27
Wagon Wheels, 236–237, 238
Waiting for Anya, 225, 233, 242, 339, 343
Waiting for the Evening Star, 115
Waiting to Waltz: A Childhood, 147, 155, 156, 166
Waldo, B., 89
Walker, Sally M., 24, 45
Walker's Crossing, 201, 220
Walk on the Great Barrier Reef, A, 61, 265, 266
Wall, The, 233, 238
Wallace, Ian, 189, 196, 231, 244
Wallace, Karen, 6, 19, 255, 256, 271
Walmsley, S., 320, 324
Walmsley, S. A., 248
Walsh, Ellen Stoll, 106, 115, 133, 284
Walt Disney, 338, 341
Walter, Mildred Pitts, 234, 244
Walter, V. A., 235
Walter Wick's Optical Tricks, 9, 20, 142

"Waltzing Matilda," 177
War and Peace: Literature for Children and Young Adults, 235
Ward, Jennifer, 106, 115
Ward, L., 45, 196
Wargin, Kathy-Jo, 126, 141, 177, 196
Warne, F., 141
Warshaw, M., 96
Washday on Noah's Ark, 197
Washington, George, 177
Watching Desert Wildlife, 254, 266
Water, 106, 113, 277, 296
Water Horse, The, 49, 68
Water Sky, 12, 18
Watling, J., 43, 96, 361
Watsons Go to Birmingham—1963, The, 234, 239
Waugh, S., 225
Way Meat Loves Salt, The: A Cinderella Tale from the Jewish Tradition, 169, 194, 356, 363
Way Out in the Desert, 106, 115
Way Things Work, The, 257, 270
Weave of Words: An Armenian Tale, 45
Weaver, C., 10
Weaver, Will, 212, 221
Weinhaus, K. A., 164
Weiss, M. Jerry, 57
Welber, Robert, 159, 166
Welch, Roger, 277
Welcome Home, Jellybean, 309, 318
Welcome to the Ice House, 162
Weller, Frances Ward, 227, 244
Wells, Gordon, 4, 9, 103
Wells, H., 97
Wells, Rosemary, 101, 106, 109, 110, 115, 136, 141, 196, 352, 366
Wenzel, D., 196
We're Going on a Bear Hunt, 276, 298
Westcott, Nadine Bernard, 155, 285, 286, 295, 299, 343
Western Wind, 205
Weston, L., 328
West to a Land of Plenty: The Diary of Teresa Angelino Viscardi, 226, 242
Whales and Dolphins, 61, 260, 270–271
What Can You Do in the Rain?, 104, 110, 114–115
What Can You Do in the Snow?, 110, 115
What Can You Do in the Sun?, 106, 110, 115

What Can You Do in the Wind?, 110, 115

What! Cried Granny: An Almost Bedtime Story, 131–132, 140

What Do Illustrators Do?, 139

What Do You Do When Your Wheelchair Gets a Flat Tire? Questions and Answers about Disabilities, 308, 314

What Hearts, 207, 216

What Jamie Saw, 31, 43, 81

What Joe Saw, 112, 114

What Lives in a Shell?, 259, 272

What the Moon is Like, 334, 340

Whedbee, Charles Henry, 177

Wheelchair Champions: A History of Wheelchair Sports, 308, 318

Wheeling and Whirling-Around Book, The, 259, 269

Wheels on the Bus, The, 101, 115–116, 134, 142

"Wheels on the Bus Go Round and Round, The," 158

Wheelwright, S., 268

Whelan, Gloria, 230, 244

When Agnes Caws, 88, 96

"When Dinosaurs Ruled the Earth," 152, 164

When Hitler Stole Pink Rabbit, 215, 233, 240

When It Comes to Bugs, 155

When Mama Comes Home Tonight, 34, 45

When She Hollers, 310, 319

When the Sky Is Like Lace, 136, 139

When Will This Cruel War Be Over? The Civil War Diary of Emma Simpson, 226, 239

Where Are You Going Manyoni?, 348

Where in the World Is Carmen Sandiego?, 65, 69

Where's Buddy?, 309, 318

Where's Spot?, 101, 114

Where's Waldo, 133, 139

Where the Lilies Bloom, 279, 296

Where the Sidewalk Ends: The Poems and Drawings of Shel Silverstein, 147, 151, 161, 166

Where the Wild Things Are, 14, 19, 27–28, 45, 50, 68, 109, 115, 121, 126, 141

While I Sleep, 334, 341

While No One Was Watching, 7, 18

White, E. B., 7, 14, 19–20, 26, 33, 45, 53, 69, 78, 179, 181, 182, 196, 277, 299

White, Ellen Emerson, 226, 244

White, M. M., 297

White, Ruth, 33–34, 45, 205, 221, 304, 352, 354, 366

White, Ryan, 309, 319

Who Belongs Here?: An American Story, 214, 218–219, 260, 269, 354, 363

Who Came Down That Road?, 74, 96

Whoever You Are, 323, 341

Who Said Red?, 133

Whose Mouse Are You?, 82, 96, 145, 164

Who's Hiding Here?, 133

Who's in Rabbit's House?, 185, 192

Why Leopard Has Spots: Dan Stories from Liberia, 356, 365

Why Mosquitos Buzz in People's Ears: A West African Tale, 125, 138, 282, 295

Why Noah Chose the Dove, 197

Wick, Walter, 9, 12, 20, 112, 115, 127, 133, 140, 142

"Wide-Mouthed Frog, The," 282–283, 284

Widow's Broom, The, 191

Wielan, O. P., 58

Wiesner, David, 127, 142

Wigg, P., 118

Wigg, R., 118

Wilde, Sandra, 304

Wilder, Laura Ingalls, 53, 230, 244, 277, 299

Wildlife Rescue: The Work of Dr. Kathleen Ramsay, 259, 268

Wildsmith, B., 197

Wild Swans, The, 178

Wilensky, R., 38

Wilhelm, Jeffrey D., 290

Wilkinson, I. A., 10

Wilks, S., 8

Willard, Nancy, 155, 166

Williams, Barbara, 234, 244

Williams, G., 19–20, 45, 196, 244, 299

Williams, Karen Lynn, 310, 319

Williams, Laura E., 233, 244

Williams, Margery, 136, 142

Williams, Sue, 101, 133, 142

Williams, Vera B., 106, 115, 136, 142

William's Doll, 136, 142

William Shakespeare & the Globe, 248, 266

William Sidney Mount: Painter of Rural America, 273

Wilma Unlimited: How Wilma Rudolph Became the World's Fastest Woman, 353–354, 363

Wilson, L., 11

Wilson, P., 62, 258

Wilson, R. H., 256

Wilson, T. P., 244

Wimmer, Mike, 124, 125, 138, 166, 261, 267, 298

Winch, G., 35, 36, 170, 171, 177

Winkel, L., 53

Winnie-the-Pooh, 136, 140, 179, 195, 276, 297

Winter, Jeanette, 56, 69, 252, 271, 353, 366

Winter, Paula, 127

Winter of Magic's Return, 196

Winter of the Red Snow, The: The Revolutionary War Diary of Abigail Jane Stewart, 226, 240

Winthrop, Elizabeth, 182, 197, 247, 271

Wish on a Unicorn, 310, 316

Wisniewski, David, 6, 20, 127, 142, 277, 299

Witch of Blackbird Pond, The, 228

Withers, Carl, 158, 166

Wolff, A., 344

Wolff, Virginia E., 232, 244

Wolfson, B., 58

Woman Who Fell From the Sky, The: The Iroquois Story of Creation, 191

Women of the Lights, 96

Wonderful Alexander and the Catwings, 182, 194

Wonderful Wizard of Oz, The, 179, 192–193

Wong, P., 347

Won't Know Till I Get There, 209–210, 219

Wood, A. J., 142

Wood, Audrey, 39, 45, 106, 115, 122, 124, 126, 142

Wood, Audrey and Don, 3–4, 8, 11, 20, 30, 45, 75, 106, 115, 121, 122, 123, 133, 137, 142, 299, 325, 333, 344

Wood, M., 18

Wood, Michelle, 355, 363

Woodruff, M. C., 289

Woods, Ponds, and Fields, 259

Woodson, Jacqueline, 310, 319
Woolf, F., 20
Words about Pictures: The Narrative Art of Children's Picture Books, 132
Words of Stone, 210, 218
World in 1492, The, 223
Wormser, Richard, 254, 272, 339, 344
Worth, Valerie, 149, 155, 156, 166
Wreck of the Zephyr, The, 191
Wright, Orville, 341
Wright, Wilbur, 341
Wright Brothers, The: How They Invented the Airplane, 338, 341
Wringer, 209, 221
Wrinkle in Time, A, 18, 179, 180, 194, 326, 342
Writer's Guide to Everyday Life in Colonial America, The: From 1811–1901, 235
Writer's Guide to Everyday Life in Regency and Victorian England, The: From 1811–1901, 235
Writer's Guide to Everyday Life in Renaissance England, The: From 1485–1649, 235
Writer's Guide to Everyday Life in the Middle Ages, The: The British Isles from 500 to 1500, 235
Writer's Guide to Everyday Life in the 1800s, The, 235
Writer's Guide to Everyday Life in the Wild West, The: From 1840–1900, 235
Writing Books for Young People, 92
Wurster, S. R., 62
www.teachingk-8.com, 153

Wyeth, Sharon Dennis, 223, 229, 236, 244
Wyndham, L., 28, 31, 34
Wyse, L., 269

Xuan, Yongsheng, 356, 363

Yaakov, J., 53
Yaccarino, D., 116
Yaden, D., 103, 110
"Yak," 157
Yang the Youngest and His Terrible Ear, 204, 219
Yardley, J., 244
Yates, Elizabeth, 38
Year of the Perfect Christmas Tree, The: An Appalachian Story, 122, 125–126, 139, 321
Yeh-Shen: A Cinderella Story from China, 169, 186, 195, 280–281, 297, 359
Yellow Ball, 113
Yellow Butter Purple Jelly Red Jam Black Bread, 155
Yenawme, P., 133
Yenne, Bill, 338, 344
Yep, Laurence, 189, 197, 208, 221, 232, 244
Yezerski, T., 68
Yoko, 352, 366
Yokota, J., 350
Yolen, Jane, 24, 45, 74, 152, 154, 157, 159, 162, 166, 178, 197, 228, 235, 244, 256, 321, 336, 338, 344, 353, 367
Yorinks, Arthur, 254

Yoshi, 133
Yoshida, Toshi, 262
You Can't Catch Diabetes From a Friend, 308–309, 317
You Gotta Be the Book, 290
You Gotta Try This! Absolutely Irresistible Science, 254, 268
Young, D., 315
Young, Ed, 61, 120, 130, 142, 165, 170, 190, 195, 197, 297, 341
Young, J., 255, 272
Younger, B., 127, 142
You Read to Me, I'll Read to You, 161
Your Own Best Secret Place, 133
You Want Women to Vote, Lizzie Stanton?, 251, 269

Zarnowski, M., 250
Zeldis, Malcah, 61, 269
Zelinsky, Paul O., 101, 115–116, 134, 140, 142, 171, 194, 197, 217
Zeller, Paula Klevan, 311, 319
Zemach, Harve, 136, 142
Zemach, M., 142
Ziehler-Martin, Richard, 171, 356, 363
Zimet, S., 62
Zimmerman, A., 101, 116
Zinsser, William, 78, 248
Zoehfeld, Kathleen Wilder, 259, 272
Zolotow, Charlotte, 136, 142, 146, 166
Zora Hurston and the Chinaberry Tree, 250, 270

Credits